AGING AND MENTAL HEALTH

POSITIVE PSYCHOSOCIAL
AND BIOMEDICAL APPROACHES

FIFTH EDITION

ROBERT N. BUTLER, M.D.
Mount Sinai School of Medicine

MYRNA I. LEWIS, M.S.W.
Mount Sinai School of Medicine

TREY SUNDERLAND, M.D.
National Institute of Mental Health

ALLYN AND BACON
Boston   London   Toronto   Sydney   Tokyo   Singapore

Editor-in-Chief, Social Sciences: Karen Hanson
Series Editor, Social Work and Family Therapy: Judy Fifer
Editorial Assistant: Mary Visco
Marketing Manager: Susan E. Brown
Editorial-Production Administrator: Donna Simons
Editorial-Production Service: Omegatype Typography, Inc.
Composition and Prepress Buyer: Linda Cox
Manufacturing Buyer: David Suspanic
Cover Administrator: Jenny Hart
Electronic Composition: Omegatype Typography, Inc.

Copyright © 1998 by Allyn & Bacon
A Viacom Company
160 Gould Street
Needham Heights, MA 02194

Internet: www.abacon.com
America Online: Keyword: College Online

Previous editions copyright 1991 by Macmillan Publishing Company, 1986 by Merrill Publishing
Company, and 1982, 1977, 1973 by C. V. Mosby Company.

Library of Congress Cataloging-in-Publication Data
Butler, Robert N.
    Aging and mental health : positive psychosocial and biomedical
approaches / Robert N. Butler, Myrna I. Lewis, Trey Sunderland. —
5th ed.
        p.   cm.
    Includes bibliographical references and index.
    ISBN 0-205-19336-6
    1. Aged—Mental health.   2. Geriatric psychiatry.   3. Aged—Mental
health services—United States.   I. Lewis, Myrna I.
    II. Sunderland, Trey.   III. Title.
RC451.4.A5B87   1998
362.2'084'6—dc21   97-30861
                                                          CIP

Printed in the United States of America
10   9   8   7   6   5   4   3   02   01   00

CONTENTS

APPENDIXES   415

Foreword to the Fourth Edition

I have worked with the problems of those suffering from mental illnesses for many years, ever since I first became aware of their needs while campaigning with my husband for governor. What I have learned over these years of work and study is that mental illnesses are less understood than almost any other major health problem, and that most people who experience difficulties can be helped. Many suffer needlessly. The mystery, stigma, and misconceptions that surround mental illness prevent many people in need of psychiatric help from seeking treatment. This applies doubly to our older citizens, who experience not only the stigma of mental illness, but also the stigma of old age.

I first met Dr. Robert Butler when my husband was president, and I was honorary chairperson of the President's Commission on Mental Health. At the time, Dr. Butler was director of the National Institute on Aging and helped with the Commission's Task Force on Mental Health and Aging. We worked together again with the late Senator Claude Pepper on developing hearings on aging and mental health in Congress.

While working on the mental health commission I was shocked to find that not only is there a great need for mental health personnel for the elderly, but that there are relatively few doctors in our country trained in the special needs of our older citizens. In addition, older people continue to face the problems of insufficient access to mental health services under Medicare and of high incidences of Alzheimer's disease, depression, and suicide. The need to address such problems and make more progress in these areas will become increasingly important in the years ahead.

We are living longer and longer. The statistics are eye-opening: Today some 27.4 million Americans are over 65. The elderly over 75 are one of the fastest growing segments of the U.S. population, and within that segment the fastest growing group is the 100-year-old group. This "graying of America" is expected to continue so that by the year 2020, 20% of the population will be over 65. Demographics alone tell us that increasing demands are going to be placed on the health care system by the problems of the elderly. Also, just like others of us, the chronically mentally disabled, the mentally retarded, and the developmentally disabled are living into old age. They are going to need services, too.

One of my major concerns in the areas of mental illness and aging is the associated stigma. This is where I have spent the majority of my efforts, since this is the area in which I have always thought I might be able to help. I have had some good "bully pulpits." Since we left the White House, I have continued to have a forum at the Carter Center in Atlanta. Each year, we have a conference on a major mental health issue. My focus is still stigma, and in 1989 we combined my interest in the elderly and in mental health in a symposium entitled "Mental Illness and the Elderly: Double Stigma, Double Jeopardy."

The stereotypes of mentally ill people are absolutely misleading and create an atmosphere in which persons suffering from mental illness are hesitant to let anyone know about their problems, and therefore do not seek treatment. The sad part is that stereotypes of older citizens as unhappy, lonely, ill, frail, senile, unproductive, and disoriented cause people who are approaching retirement age to believe that this is going to happen to them and that their productive and enjoyable years are over.

Those of us in the fields of aging and mental health, both lay and professional, must work together to find ways to educate people and help eliminate the stigmas associated with being mentally ill and with being elderly. Robert Butler, Myrna Lewis, and Trey Sunderland have made significant contributions to this education, not only in helping us overcome the stigmas, but in writing a seminal book on mental health and aging that has already benefited many of those who deal with older people in emotional and other crises.

This fourth edition of *Aging and Mental Health* incorporates the progress that has been made in the field since the last edition in 1986. It includes advances in the fields of neurobiology and psychopharmacology, and changes in the theory and practice of psychotherapy. The book will appeal to a wide variety of professionals involved in the care of older people and will help them understand what keeps the old well, rather than merely what makes them ill. I hope that in addition to being read by those who work with the elderly, *Aging and Mental Health* will be read by older people in general.

Jimmy and I are convinced that our later years can be the best years of our lives. It takes some involvement. It takes some adjustment. It has already taken some adjustment in our own lives. But what is life if not adjustment—to different times, to changing circumstances, to shifting health habits, and to each other?

We are deeply indebted to Dr. Butler, Ms. Lewis, and Dr. Sunderland for their contributions in making life better for our older citizens and for us all.

Rosalynn Carter

PREFACE

The fifth edition of *Aging and Mental Health* constitutes a major revision of the entire book. This new edition uses the latest demographic and epidemiological data to create an all-encompassing portrait of older people in America today, their mental health care needs, and ways to respond to those needs. The book incorporates the newest information, often technical, concerning the dementias of old age, the neurobiology of depression, and geriatric psychopharmacology. The chapters concerning the dynamics of the family and the special issues that confront our multi-ethnic and multi-racial society are organized in a manner valuable to both the scholar and the practitioner. Family caregiving has been especially emphasized. The sections on psychiatric assessment, psychological testing, and individual treatment planning have been updated, and the full range of psychosocial and biological therapies are covered as well.

A number of important developments and trends since the last edition deserve mention, because they impact on the care and well-being of older persons. The failure of governmental health reforms proposed in 1994 has contributed to the growth of managed care. Without a doubt, managed care is having a profound and not always salutary influence on the delivery of mental health services beyond that occasioned by the introduction of either health insurance coverage for mental health services or the community mental health center movement. The failure of health care reform also underscores the need for a revitalized vision of long-term health care. Private long-term care insurance initiatives have advanced only modestly and are so costly that they are accessible to only a minority of Americans.

Tax resistance has been reinforced by ideological attacks on the "welfare state," with consequent reductions in Medicare, Medicaid, and various governmental services, as well as the transfer of welfare to the states, ending it as an entitlement. Under the new welfare law, states could decide to end Medicaid coverage of older legal immigrants presently residing in nursing homes.

The 1995 White House Conference on Aging called for the preservation of Medicare and Social Security, the Older Americans Act, and other programs devoted to serving older persons. To some degree, the delegates also called for intergenerational efforts to meet the needs of other age groups, particularly children. But although older Americans constitute an important constituency and although organizations that represent them, such as the American Association of Retired Persons and the National Council of Senior Citizens, have been effective up to a point, those organizations represent only a few of the many special interest groups in America and as such pale in comparison with other powerful groups.

Despite the fact that Medicare beneficiaries are older persons and the disabled, graduate medical education funds have gone primarily to support specialty medical training and relatively little to support fellowships in geriatrics. However, in 1996 the Health Care Financing Administration extended the full Medicare direct payment for geriatric psychiatry to a fifth year of residency.

Academic and clinical geriatrics have not developed significantly in the United States. There are only two academic departments of geriatrics among 140 allopathic and osteopathic medical schools. However, about 20 of the schools have major geriatrics programs. There are also now examinations for "certificates of added qualification" in geriatrics and geriatric psychiatry administered by the Boards of Internal Medicine, Family Medicine, and Psychiatry. It is hoped that medicine, along with nursing, social work, psychology, and other allied professions, will increasingly face the training and service challenge imposed by the growing number and proportion of older people.

Research in Alzheimer's disease has progressed. Particular attention is now being paid to the role of genetics in early onset cases and to amyloid deposits. Also, apolipoprotein E4 has been discovered to be a risk factor for developing Alzheimer's. However, there has been only modest progress in the realm of therapy. The Alzheimer's Association continues to play a critical role, contributing to advocacy, research, and services that offer caregivers relief from the burdens of caring for a family member with Alzheimer's.

The Open Society Institute, funded through the financier and philanthropist George Soros, created the Project on Death in America (PDIA), which is devoted to altering the experience and culture of dying. Issues regarding dying are major concerns that need to be addressed. Death and dying are inevitably entwined in the practices of mental health providers who work with older people, who deal with both the dying and survivors. Mental health providers confront a rising rate of depression and suicide among older persons, especially old men, in response to the realization of impending death. Physician-assisted suicide is a highly emotional national issue. In the Netherlands, physician-assisted suicide has been condoned even for such highly treatable conditions as depression. To many health care providers, the increasingly casual attitude toward physician-assisted suicide is a matter of great concern. Policy makers in the United States should pay close attention to the effects such legislation has had abroad.

HOW THIS BOOK IS ORGANIZED

Mental health care of the elderly involves members of many professions and service groups working collaboratively and collegially. These include physicians, social workers, nurses, and psychologists; nurses' aides and nursing assistants; homemaker/home health aides; physical, occupational, recreational, and speech therapists; and paraprofessionals of all kinds. Mental health practitioners ideally should have a broad-based set of skills so that they can provide optimal care to the elderly. For this reason, this book offers a wide range of knowledge and skills aimed at anyone involved with mental health care of the elderly, while targeting some chapters and parts of chapters toward specific practitioners.

Chapters 1 through 4 give an overview of the elderly sociologically, demographically, and epidemiologically (in terms of mental health issues), and provide a baseline of psychologically healthy old age against which to measure illness or problems. These chapters are designed for general use by all practitioners.

Chapter 5, "Common Psychiatric Disorders," Chapter 6, "Cognitive Disorders," and Chapter 13, "Drug and Other Somatic Therapies," have a dual purpose: (1) to give non-medical practitioners up-to-date medical and psychiatric information that will enhance their work and (2) to provide in-depth information for medical students and physicians interested in geriatric mental health care. These are the most technical and demanding chapters, particularly the drug chapter, but we hope we have presented the material clearly enough without depending on jargon, so that anyone can gain a practical sense of what is involved in these areas and can make use of such knowledge.

Chapter 7, "Special Concerns," is an eclectic chapter, drawing together a number of important themes in work with older persons—race and ethnic issues, crime, elder abuse, the special problems of older women, alcoholism, sensory problems, and sexuality.

Chapter 8, "General Treatment Principles," and Chapter 12, "Psychotherapy and Environmental Therapy," focus on the psychotherapy aspects of medical health care. It is here that we rely most heavily on our own clinical work and that of others in an ongoing effort to delineate a "psychotherapy of aging."

Chapter 9, "Diagnostic Evaluation," demonstrates more clearly than any other chapter the complexities of mental health care of the elderly—the need to consider as a whole the many aspects of each person's life in arriving at a diagnosis and treatment plan, and the need to enlist the skills of a wide variety of professional and service groups. This chapter leads inexorably to the understanding that no one profession can claim centrality; all are important at different times for different reasons and should be linked in a comprehensive package of evaluation and care.

Chapter 10, "How to Keep People at Home," and Chapter 11, "Proper Institutional Care," look at the continuum of mental health care now available, both in terms of the physical location in which care is given and the range of services that should be available at any stage of an older person's care. These chapters present the issues in the current national policy debate over long-term care—issues that should be understood by all mental health practitioners.

The appendixes have been carefully updated and expanded, and it is our intent that they will serve as convenient and useful references for a wealth of specific information related to mental health care of the elderly.

The Selected Readings at the end of each chapter represent literature particularly pertinent to each topic, both classic references as well as newer information. The endnotes provide additional reference sources.

Readers of the previous editions of this book often told us how much they enjoyed the photographs, which offered significant insights into the human condition in late life. However, those photographs were unavailable for this new edition of the text.

ACKNOWLEDGMENTS

We are exceptionally indebted to Mia Oberlink and Alexis Stern for their patience, dedication, excellent research, and editorial support in this major revision. Milagros Marrero, Morriseen Barmore, and Tomasina Wilson facilitated the work in an exemplary manner.

PART ONE

THE NATURE
AND PROBLEMS
OF OLD AGE

WHO ARE THE ELDERLY?

In this chapter we will acquaint you with a general profile of the United States' older population as well as detail some specifics about the more disadvantaged minorities. Successful intervention in meeting the mental health needs of older people depends on maintaining a basic awareness of the general facts of their lives while focusing attention on the unique social, economic, and familial context of each individual.

WHO ARE THE ELDERLY?

This is a century marked by great changes and achievements for the elderly. The most spectacular is a gain of some 25 years in average life expectancy—and the century is not yet over. This gain, found throughout the industrialized world, is nearly equal to the added years of life expectancy amassed during the preceding 5,000 years of human history from the Bronze Age (3000 B.C.) until today. In the United States, the average life expectancy has grown by 28 years since the year 1900. At the founding of the American Republic in 1776, the average life expectancy for men and women was 35. Today it is over over 75. This longevity revolution, attributed to a combination of better public sanitation and personal hygiene, improved nutrition, and general medical progress, provides the backdrop for the focus of our discussions on aging and mental health.

How do older people first come to the attention of mental health personnel? We will give a few typical examples of situations that are likely to propel older people into the hands of those who offer mental health services.

Mr. H is an 80-year-old white, middle-class male who retired two years ago. Since that time, his wife, family, and friends report that he has become increasingly depressed. His chief complaint is dizziness and chest discomfort, but upon lying down, all the symptoms disappear. He has seen approximately 20 physicians and has had dozens of examinations without any positive findings. After the psychiatrist diagnosed his problem as depression, he became angry and denied it. He maintained that if he was depressed it was because of the failure to find a reason for his symptoms—that the depression was not primary, but secondary. It was also apparent that Mr. H sustained some memory loss.

Is Mr. H suffering from depression, or does he have incipient Alzheimer's disease with accompanying depression, in part reactive to the dementia, but also possibly part of the dementia process per se? Should he return to his doctor for neuropsychological evaluation and Holter monitoring of blood pressure and other vital signs? Could circulatory disease be playing a part?

Mr. K is African American, age 66. He has come to a psychiatric hospital on his own, stating that he is depressed and has recently felt almost uncontrollable impulses to harm others. Occasionally he worries that he is being followed, that his phone may be tapped, or that his food has been tampered with. He appears in poor health and is underweight, although dressed neatly and appropriately. He lives with a 68-year-old widowed sister in two rented rooms; he was married and separated years ago and has no children. He has been employed regularly all his life in a variety of jobs, from service station attendant to cook in a hamburger shop. Two years ago he was forced to stop work because of ill health, but his sister is still employed as a housekeeper. Income is minimal. He responds to an African American female nursing assistant at the hospital with an outpouring of his feelings of anger and bewilderment but becomes strikingly passive and vague in the presence of both black and white male resident physicians.

Are Mr. K's psychiatric symptoms a result of his personality characteristics and early history? Or could a physical disease condition be affecting his personality? What part may be played by malnutrition? Is he underweight because he is either physically sick or psychologically unable to care for himself, or is it because he has almost no money for food from month to month? Is his depression an acute reaction to physical illness or a lifelong response to social conditions? Why does he speak to the nursing assistant but turn silent at the sight of doctors? Why does he seem to have so little retirement income?

Mrs. P, white, age 88, has become disoriented and wanders out on the streets at night. After neighbors called the police, a public health nurse was notified and made a home visit. Mrs. P's husband died 15 years previously, and she has been living alone in a home they purchased 50 years ago in the central part of the city. Her income is higher than that of most widows. The home is orderly but badly in need of repair. The heat has been turned off by the gas company. Mrs. P's hearing has deteriorated. She expresses a terror of intruders and has armed herself with a stick and a kitchen knife. She determinedly announces she will never leave her home.

Why is she living alone in a big house, and why has she allowed the home to deteriorate and the gas to be shut off? Is her disorientation caused by poor health, isolation resulting from hearing loss, or lack of a proper diet? Is her fear of intruders exaggerated or realistic in her neighborhood? What has she been doing with her money, since she appears to have very little food? Should she be moved forcibly to a nursing institution, or is there some way to help her remain at home?

70-year-old Mr. H is Asian American. He has contacted a private psychiatrist because he is feeling suicidal. He is well-off financially, lives with his wife, but feels increasingly upset and self-destructive. He retired as a college professor earlier in the year. His health is good but recently he has panicked because he feels his memory is failing.

Is Mr. H overreacting to a minor memory change? If so, why is this so upsetting to him? Or does he perhaps have an undiagnosed brain disease? Are suicidal thoughts rare for a man his age?

Mrs. F is a 79-year-old, Spanish-speaking woman who is progressively disoriented and confused. She becomes agitated at night and has been returned home by neighbors and police after being found confused, walking the streets. She has been incontinent of urine and feces but has no apparent neurological symptoms. Is she suffering from senile dementia of the Alzheimer type? If so, can she be cared for at home? Is the disease treatable?

Each of these older persons came to the attention of mental health personnel because of psychiatric symptoms. But evaluation of the symptoms requires an understanding of the person's entire life situation—physical status, personality, family history, racial and ethnic background, income, housing, social status, educational level. Realistic and appropriate treatment is greatly facilitated by a fairly sophisticated understanding of social, psychological, and medical phenomena. We shall therefore proceed with an overview of the social and environmental realities of older persons in order to provide a background for our later discussion of the more specific aspects of their mental health care.

WHAT AGE IS CONSIDERED "OLDER"?

Aging, of course, begins with conception.[1] The selection of age 65 for use as the demarcation between middle and old age is an arbitrary one, patterned after social legislation of the late nineteenth and early twentieth centuries. This definition of old age has been adhered to for social purposes— as a means of determining the point of retirement or the point of eligibility for various services available to older persons. But the age of 65 has more limited relevance in describing other aspects of functioning such as general health, mental capacity, psychological or physical endurance, or creativity. Gerontologists have attempted to deal with this unreliable concept of "oldness" after 65 by dividing old age into two groups: early old age, 65 to 74 years, and advanced old age, 75 and above. But the obvious point is that age is a convenient yet frequently inaccurate indicator of a person's physical and mental status and must not be relied on too heavily for evidence about human beings.

NUMBER OF OLDER PERSONS IN THE UNITED STATES

Total Older Population

In the United States in 1995 there were an estimated 33.5 million people age 65 and older—

about 13% of the population.[2] 18.8 million people were 65 to 74 years old, 11.1 million were 75 to 84, 3.6 million were 85 years old and older, and 1.3 million were at least 90 years of age.[3] The 75-plus and 85-plus age groups are the fastest growing age segments of the U.S. population. These statistics are of great social, economic, and medical importance because of the dramatic increase in the need for care in the 75-plus and, especially, in the 85-plus age groups. Over 40% of nursing home residents are age 85 and older, and 75% are at least age 75. In 1990, 24% of those age 85 and older lived in nursing homes.[4] The 85-plus population is expected to double in size between 1995 and 2030, and to be five times as large in 2050.[5]

The number of people age 100 and older is also growing. In 1980 there were approximately 15,000 centenarians in the United States. By 1995, the number of centenarians had grown to about 53,000. Eighty-three percent of centenarians were women, 17% were men; 85% were white, 13% were African American, 2% were other races.[6] In 1980, 80% of centenarians were widowed, 10% were married, 8% were never married, 2% were divorced or separated; 82% were American born, 18% were immigrants.[7] The Bureau of the Census estimates that there will be over 800,000 American centenarians by the year 2050.[8] In all nations—including the developing nations—there is an increase in the absolute numbers of older people because of major decreases in maternal, childhood, and infant mortality as well as in middle- and late-life mortality from heart disease and stroke. In the developed nations there is also a significant increase in the relative proportions of older versus younger persons.

The age composition of the United States is undergoing extraordinary change. In 1900 the average life expectancy was 47 years and only 4% of the population was 65 and older. The high rates of maternal, childhood, and infant mortality contributed to the low life expectancy. Social, economic, and health progress have made a vast difference. By 1991 the average life expectancy at birth was greater than 75.[9]

Between the years 2020 and 2030—when the post–World War II baby boom grows old—about 20%, or one of five, U.S. citizens could be over 65 according to current projections (Figures 1.1 and 1.2). It is important to note that so far in the twentieth century, all projections of the numbers of older people have turned out to be underestimations. This is partly because of the unprecedented drops in mortality in the middle and later years from heart disease and stroke, which have coincided with improvements in risk factors such as smoking, high blood pressure, and high blood cholesterol, as well as greater access to sophisticated medical services. A continuing 0.6% annual decline in deaths is projected by the Social Security Administration until the year 2070, for a total decline of 36% between 1996 and 2070.[10] In fact, breakthroughs in research on the prevention and treatment of cancer alone could lead to annual mortality reductions far in excess of current pre-

dictions. The other major factor in the underestimation is a drop in the birthrate, bringing it below zero population growth. In summary, with new medical discoveries, improved health care, and a persisting low birthrate, the population of older persons may increase dramatically. Researchers at the National Institute on Aging and the University of Southern California, Los Angeles, predict that by the year 2040 the number of Americans age 65 and over could reach 86.8 million and the number of elderly age 85 and over could reach 23.5 million.

This "demographic revolution" should be seen as a triumph of survivorship rather than as a cause for despair. What it means is that more and more people have the opportunity to live out a full life course.[11] This revolution or triumph will increase the median age of the population from 30 in 1980 and 34.3 in 1995, a record high, to a peak of 38.7 in 2035[12]—hardly an "aging" or "graying" soci-

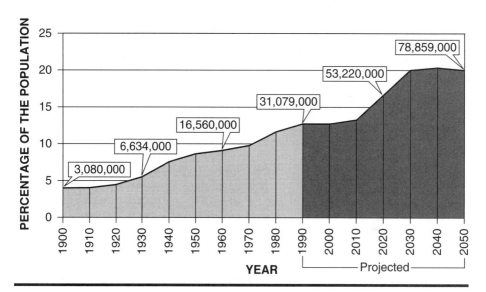

FIGURE 1.1   Percentage of U.S. population age 65 and older from 1900 to 1990, with projections for 2000 to 2050

Sources: Data for 1900 to 1990 from: U.S. Bureau of the Census (1996). *65+ in the United States. Current population reports, special studies,* Series P-23, No. 190. Washington, DC: U.S. Government Printing Office. Projections for 2000 to 2050 from: U.S. Bureau of the Census (1996). Population projections by age, sex, race and hispanic origin: 1995–2050. *Current population reports,* Series P-25, No. 1130. Washington, DC: U.S. Government Printing Office.

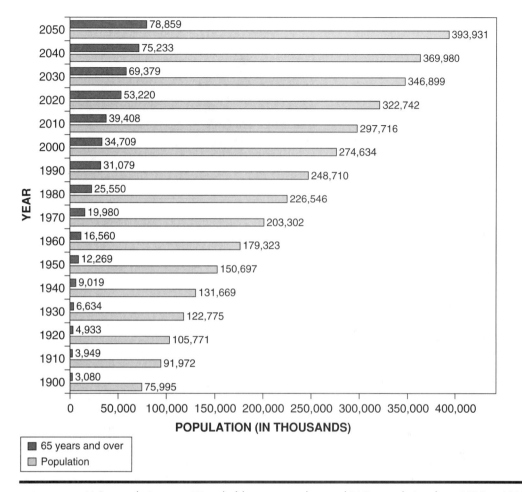

FIGURE 1.2   U.S. population age 65 and older compared to total U.S. population from 1900 to 1990, with projections for 2000 to 2050

Sources: Data for 1900 to 1990 from: U.S. Bureau of the Census (1996). 65+ *in the United States. Current population reports, special studies,* Series P-23, No. 190. Washington, DC: U.S. Government Printing Office. Projections for 2000 to 2050 from: U.S. Bureau of the Census (1996). Population projections by age, sex, race and hispanic origin: 1995–2050. *Current population reports,* Series P-25, No. 1130. Washington, DC: U.S. Government Printing Office.

ety but certainly one with a different blend of age groups and generations. The age distribution of the total population in 1995 compared to 2050 provides a clearer overall picture of our future society than either the percentage of persons over 65 or the median age (Figure 1.3).

A word should be said here about the considerable concern of policymakers and the public over what is known as the "dependency ratio"—

the income maintenance and health costs of the burgeoning older population. In truth, the proportional financial "burden" on the middle working generations has not changed much because there are also fewer children and youths for these people to support (Table 1.1). Figure 1.4 compares the actual and projected distribution of children and the elderly from 1900 to 2050. Needed, of course, is an analysis of the actual cost of care of those

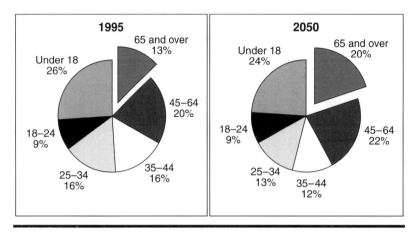

FIGURE 1.3   Age distribution of total population of the U.S. in 1995 compared to projections for the year 2050

Sources: Data for 1995 from: U.S. Bureau of the Census (February 14, 1996). *U.S. population estimates by age, sex, race, and hispanic origin: 1990–1995.* PPL-41. Washington, DC: Population Projections Branch, Population Division, U.S. Bureau of the Census. Projections for 2050 from: U.S. Bureau of the Census (1996). Population projections by age, sex, race and hispanic origin: 1995–2050. *Current population reports,* Series P-25, No. 1130. Washington, DC: U.S. Government Printing Office.

under 18 compared to that of those over 64. All sources of funding have to be considered. If one looks only at federal funding, older persons seem to receive more than young people, including children. On the other hand, the public education of children is supported primarily by local property taxes in order to reduce central governmental control of education.

Of the present older population, 8.6% were born somewhere other than in the United States. Many immigrated in their youth with the great migrations from Europe. Others came later from countries like Mexico and Cuba. Not all are citizens of the United States, not all speak English, and many still carry on the customs and cultural patterns of their mother countries in adapting to old age. This adds to the richness and uniqueness of the older population but makes the provision of services in later life more complicated.

Men versus Women

This is not only the century of increasing proportions of older people but also the century of in-

creasing proportions of older women. A marked difference exists between the life expectancies of men and women (Table 1.2). As of 1991 in the United States, women are expected to live 6.9 years longer from birth and 3.8 years longer from age 65. Older women numbered more than 19.8 million in 1995 compared to 13.7 million men. Women outlive men every place in the world where women no longer perform backbreaking physical labor and where adequate sanitation and a reduced maternal mortality rate are present.

In 1995 there were 104.8 females per 100 males in the total U.S. population. More boy babies were born than girl babies, and males continue to outnumber females until age 30. At this point a shift occurs in the opposite direction, becoming most pronounced in the older generations. The life expectancy of a baby boy born in the United States in 1991 is 72 years and that of a baby girl is 78.9 years, almost 7 years longer. In 1991, for people who were already 65 years old, life expectancy was 17.4 additional years, again with a differential between men (15.3 years) and women (19.1 years).

TABLE 1.1   "Dependency ratio": comparison of numbers of persons under 18 and over 65 (the "dependents") to the middle generations (the "workers")

YEAR	NUMBER OF PERSONS UNDER AGE 18 PER 100 PERSONS AGE 18 TO 64	NUMBER OF PERSONS AGE 65+ PER 100 PERSONS AGE 18 TO 64	TOTAL NUMBER OF "DEPENDENTS" PER 100 "WORKERS"
Estimates			
1900	72.6	7.3	79.9
1910	65.7	7.5	73.2
1920	64.0	8.0	72.0
1930	58.6	9.1	67.7
1940	48.8	10.9	59.7
1950	51.1	13.4	64.5
1960	65.3	16.9	82.2
1970	61.1	17.6	78.7
1980	46.2	18.7	64.9
1990	41.7	20.3	62.0
Projections			
1995	42.8	20.9	63.7
2000	41.8	20.5	52.4
2010	39.0	21.2	60.2
2020	40.4	27.7	68.2
2030	43.0	35.7	78.7
2040	43.1	36.6	79.7
2050	43.9	36.0	79.9

Source: U.S. Bureau of the Census. (Feb. 1996.) Population projections of the United States by age, sex, race, and hispanic origin: 1995 to 2050. *Current population reports,* P25-1130. Washington, DC: U.S. Government Printing Office, p. 9.

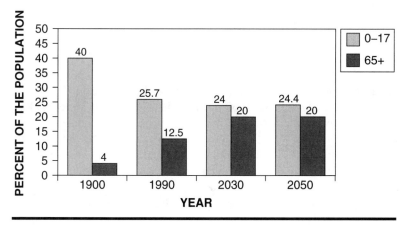

FIGURE 1.4   Actual and projected distribution of children and elderly in the population: 1900–2050

Adapted from: U.S. Bureau of the Census (1996). Population projections of the United States, by age, sex, race, and hispanic origin: 1995–2050. *Current population reports,* P25-1130. Washington DC: U.S. Government Printing Office, p. 10.

TABLE 1.2 Life expectancy at birth and age 65 by race and sex: 1900–1991

YEAR	ALL RACES[1]			WHITE			BLACK		
	BOTH SEXES	MALE	FEMALE	BOTH SEXES	MALE	FEMALE	BOTH SEXES	MALE	FEMALE
At birth									
1900[2,3]	47.3	46.3	48.3	47.6	46.6	48.7	33.0[4]	32.5[4]	33.5[4]
1950[3]	68.2	65.6	71.1	69.1	66.5	72.2	60.7	58.9	62.7
1960[3]	69.7	66.6	73.1	70.6	67.4	74.1	63.2	60.7	65.9
1970	70.8	67.1	74.7	71.7	68.0	75.6	64.1	60.0	68.3
1980	73.7	70.0	77.4	74.4	70.7	78.1	68.1	63.8	72.5
1985	74.7	71.1	78.2	75.3	71.8	78.7	69.3	65.0	73.4
1990	75.4	71.8	78.8	76.1	72.7	79.4	69.1	64.5	73.6
1991	75.5	72.0	78.9	76.3	72.9	79.6	69.3	64.6	73.8
At 65 years									
1990–1902[2,3]	11.9	11.5	12.2	*	11.5	12.2	*	10.4	11.4
1950[3]	13.9	12.8	15.0	*	12.8	15.1	13.9	12.9	14.9
1960[3]	14.3	12.8	15.8	14.4	12.9	15.9	13.9	12.7	15.1
1970	15.2	13.1	17.0	15.2	13.1	17.1	14.2	12.5	15.7
1980	16.4	14.1	18.3	16.5	14.2	18.4	15.1	13.0	16.8
1985	16.7	14.5	18.5	16.8	14.5	18.7	15.2	13.0	16.9
1990	17.2	15.1	18.9	17.3	15.2	19.1	15.4	13.2	17.2
1991	17.4	15.3	19.1	17.5	15.4	19.2	15.5	13.4	17.2

Source: National Center for Health Statistics (April, 1995). *Trends in the health of older Americans: United States, 1994.* Series 3: *Analytical and epidemiological studies* No. 30. DHHS Publication No. (PHS)95–1414. Hyattsville, MD: U.S. Dept. of Health and Human Services.

[1]Data includes races other than white and black.

[2]Death registration area only. The death registration area increased from 10 states and the District of Columbia in 1900 to the coterminous United States in 1933.

[3]Includes deaths of nonresidents of the United States.

[4]Figure is for "all other" population.

In the United States women outlive men because of the higher male mortality from arteriosclerotic heart disease, lung cancer and emphysema (associated with tobacco intake), industrial accidents and toxicity, motor vehicle and other accidents, suicide, cirrhosis of the liver (associated with alcoholism), and so forth. These account for perhaps three-quarters of the sex differential in mortality—the other one-quarter is still unclear.[13] Life-style, life stress, hormonal differences, genetic differences in immune resistance, and other possible differences between the sexes must be further studied.[14] Fears that American women will lose their capacity for long life as they move into the labor force (the proportion of women in the labor force increased from 28% in 1950 to 58% in 1990; most were married women) have so far been unsubstantiated. For example, an eight-year study of 352 housewives, 387 working women, and 580 men involved in the Framingham Heart Study found that working women did not have a significantly higher incidence of coronary heart disease (CHD) than did housewives (7.8% versus 5.4%), and, in fact, those women working the longest period of time, for example, single women, had the lowest rate of CHD. (A factor here could be that relatively healthy women are the most likely to join the labor force, leaving less healthy women at home.) However, clerical workers with children who were married to men in blue-collar jobs had a higher risk of CHD. This suggests either that clerical work is a particularly stressful occupation, especially when combined with the demands of raising a family, or that women with personalities prone to develop stress diseases select clerical work when they become employed. Elderly women outnumber elderly men three to two. In 1995, for every 100 women age 65–69, there were only 83 men in that same age group. The ratio continues to widen with age, with only 39 men per 100 women in the 85-plus category.

African Americans[15] versus Whites

The survival pattern for the white U.S. population has always been more favorable than that of non-white populations.[15] In 1950, life expectancy at birth for whites was 8.4 years longer than that for blacks. In 1983 and 1984 the difference narrowed to 5.6 years. Unfortunately, due to higher death rates from killings, accidents, and diseases such as AIDS and tuberculosis, as well as a higher infant mortality rate, in 1991 the difference in life expectancy between blacks and whites grew to 7 years. For black men, the difference was 11.7 years (76.3 years for whites of both sexes, 64.6 years for black men). However, differences in life expectancy from age 65 are smaller. In 1991, at age 65, black men could expect to live 13.4 more years, compared to 15.4 more years for white men. Black women age 65 could expect to live 17.2 years, 2 years less than white women.[17]

The number of black older persons has risen from 1.2 million in 1960 to 2.7 million in 1995. Black older persons constituted slightly over 8% of the total black population of almost 34 million in 1995. Their lower life expectancy results, we can safely assume, from the generally lower socioeconomic status accorded to blacks in the United States.

Although they comprise almost 13% of the total population, blacks make up only 8% of the older age group. The effects of institutionalized

racism fall most heavily on black men—their life expectancy in 1991 of 64.6 years was 8.3 years less than that of white men, who could expect to live 72.9 years. White and black women had life expectancies of 79.6 and 73.8 respectively, with a 5.8 year difference between them (see Table 1.2).

Black older women outlive black men to an increasing degree, as do their white counterparts. The ratio of older black men per 100 black women has decreased from 83 in 1960 to 63 in 1995, and black females made up 62% of the total black population in 1995.

The Impact of Socioeconomic Class on Survivorship

One's class definitely affects one's life expectancy. Demographic data show conclusively that an increasing life expectancy follows in the wake of increasing income and status. Professional and white-collar workers have lower mortality than blue-collar workers. In fact, the impact of social class may be even greater than is currently evident. Mortality studies are usually done by demographers and epidemiologists rather than by economists, and thus most studies fail to take note of wealth beyond yearly income. Yet such wealth enormously affects the capacity to maintain health (through greater opportunities for rest, good nutrition, recreation, emotional security, and status) and to treat illness (through greater access to the finest acute and chronic care).

MARITAL STATUS

In looking at the marital situation of older people, one fact becomes strikingly clear. Most older men are married (77% in 1994); most older women are widows (47%; See Table 1.3). One finds over five times as many widows as widowers. This imbalance of women versus men, resulting from a combination of the greater female life expectancy and the fact that most women are younger than their husbands to begin with, represents one of the most striking consequences of old age in its present form. Older men, if they survive, have greater

TABLE 1.3   Distribution of older persons by marital status, 1900 and 1994

| | 1994 | | 1900 | |
STATUS	MEN	WOMEN	MEN	WOMEN
Married	77.2	42.8	67.3	34.3
Widowed	13.1	46.4	26.5	59.5
Other				
Divorced	5.0	6.0	0.5	0.3
Never married	4.7	4.3	5.8	6.0

Source: U.S. Bureau of the Census (1994). Marital Status and Living Arrangements: March 1994. *Current population reports,* P20-484. Washington DC: U.S. Government Printing Office.

options with regard to the opposite sex than women do. Chances are their wives are younger and will outlive them. But if not, a man can quite easily find a second wife. The odds are with him. There are many women from whom to choose. It is socially acceptable for a man to find a partner in either his own age group or any of the younger age groups. An older woman, however, may be looked on with suspicion if she marries or even simply dates someone much younger, although this attitude is slowly changing. In 1990, about 71,000 persons age 65 and over married in the United States. Of these 25,000 were women; 46,000 were men.

The 1987 Commonwealth Fund Commission on Elderly People Living Alone provided a close-up of the realities that older people living alone face. They experience double the poverty, tend to be persons 75 and older, are largely women, and are at higher risk of hospitalization and institutionalization. Many are overwhelmed by the situation in which they find themselves, and present government policies do not adequately address the structural problems they confront.

A larger number of older African Americans than whites do not live with their spouses. This has been attributed to the greater economic pressures on families, including unemployment and public welfare laws that have encouraged black men to leave home early in life. The shorter life expectancy of black men also is an important factor, leaving a black married woman widowed much earlier than a white married woman.

HOUSING STATUS

With Whom Do Older Persons Live?

One of the still prevalent myths about older people is that large numbers of them live in institutions: chronic disease hospitals, homes for the aged, nursing homes, mental institutions, foster homes, and so on. If one asks any group of ordinary citizens—or for that matter a group of medical, nursing, or social work students—what percentage of older people live in such settings, the answers will range all the way up to 50%. The reality is that at any one time only 5% of all older people are in such institutions.[18] This is, of course, a substantial number of people and rightly deserves serious attention. But it is important to remember that in 1994, 95% lived in the community, either by themselves (30%), with spouses (55%), with children or other relatives (12%), or with nonrelatives (2%). Again the situation differs with regard to men and women. Men, because of their shorter life expectancy, usually live with a spouse or other family members. But only slightly more than half of women do so. Women are over twice as likely to live alone or with nonrelatives. In 1994, 7.2 million older women lived alone compared with 2 million older men.[19]

In reference to the older African American population, another widely held idea bears another look. It has been frequently stated that older African Americans are more likely to live in extended families than are older whites. Yet in 1995, 31% of black people age 65 and older lived entirely alone. In addition, black men are more likely to live alone than white men (see Figure 1.5). It is true that older black persons are more likely than older white persons to be living with relatives other than their spouses: 24% of older blacks, as compared to 11% of older whites, lived with relatives. We can surmise that this is a result of economic necessity or convenience, which solidified in a cultural style of living earlier in the life cycle. Data contrasting men and women show that 63% of all older black men live with their wives but, again because of longer life expectancy, only 28% of older black women live with their husbands.[20]

Geographical Distribution

Up to the present, older people lived most frequently in central parts of cities and in rural locations. But in 1980, for the first time, a greater number of older persons lived in the suburbs (10.1 million) than in central cities (8.1 million). The Midwest and upper New England rural areas have concentrations of older people because many of the young have left the farms. Older people have the lowest migration rates of all age groups; those older persons who do migrate tend to be the most affluent. Florida has the highest proportion of elderly, with 19% of its population comprised of older residents in 1993. Over one quarter of the older people in the United States live in three states: California, New York, and Florida. Over half of the nation's aged live in nine states, adding Pennsylvania, Texas, Illinois, Ohio, New Jersey, and Michigan. In 33 states older people comprise at least 14% of the total population (see Figure 1.6). New York, California, and Florida each have more than 2 million older residents, while Illinois, Ohio, Texas, Pennsylvania, Michigan, and New Jersey each have more than 1 million older persons. The highest growth in percentage since 1980 is in Alaska, Arizona, Florida, Hawaii,

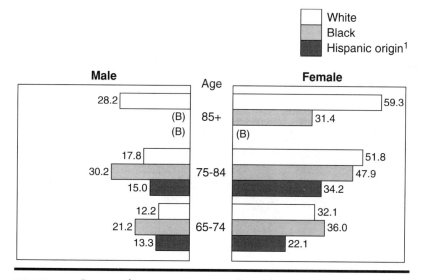

FIGURE 1.5   Percent of persons 65 years and over living alone by age, sex, race, and hispanic origin: 1993 (Civilian noninstitutional population)

Source: U.S. Bureau of the Census (1996). 65+ in the United States. *Current population reports, special studies,* Series P-23, No. 190. Washington, DC: U.S. Government Printing Office.

B Base is less than 75,000.

[1]Hispanic origin may be of any race.

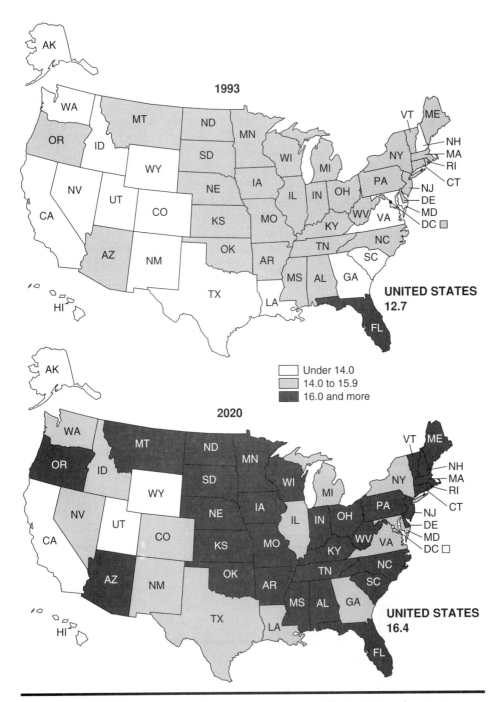

FIGURE 1.6   Percent of total state population aged 65 and older in 1993 and projections for 2020

Source: U.S. Bureau of the Census (1996). 65+ in the United States. *Current population reports, special studies,* Series P-23, No. 190. Washington, DC: U.S. Government Printing Office.

Nevada, and New Mexico—with the exception of Alaska, these states have warm climates and low industrialization, which older people find appealing.[21]

Older African Americans show a somewhat different geographic distribution than older people as a whole. Over half still reside in the South, many in rural areas. But because large numbers moved to urban areas in the rural-to-urban migrations of the early 1900s, older African Americans are now also concentrated in central cities, primarily in those areas with the worst housing. Indeed, four of five older African Americans live in metropolitan areas. Many are trapped there under the dual influence of economic hardship and a continuing racism that tends to preserve the suburban areas for whites. One must add, however, that the suburbs often welcome only whites with adequate finances and acceptable credentials. Public housing and housing for older persons, the mentally ill, or white drug or alcohol abusers are fought with the same vehemence as black or integrated housing. Older African Americans increasingly share the inner city with younger African Americans and those older whites who cannot afford to leave. Recently, however, a growing number of African Americans have migrated back to the South.

Standards of Housing

It has been estimated that 10% of older persons in the United States live in inadequate housing. This is largely a result of outright poverty or marginal income. In 1994, 78% of the 20.8 million older householders owned their own homes. However, one third of these homes were purchased in early adulthood at least 30 years before, and many have become substandard.[22] The cost of maintenance, utilities (especially fuel), and property taxes has increased so that upkeep and needed improvements have become impossible for many older people on fixed incomes. The remaining one-quarter of older persons are renters, and many of these live either alone or with relatives or friends, in retirement villages, tenements, retirement hotels, low- and middle-class government-subsidized housing, or housing sponsored by unions, churches, and benevolent associations. Some older people live in public housing, which is often seen by them as a highly desirable resource in view of the wretched alternatives available.

INCOME

Extent of Poverty

Poverty, like substandard housing, is typically associated with old age. People who were poor all their lives can expect to become poorer in old age. But they are joined by a multitude of people who become poor only after becoming old (Figure 1.7). About 11.7% (almost 3.7 million) of older people were below the official poverty level in 1994.[23] The unrealistically low annual income levels of $7,108 for a single person and $8,967 for a couple, were used to demarcate that poverty level. In our opinion this is a gross underestimation of poverty. Over 26% of older people were "near poor," or had incomes of under 150% of the official poverty level in 1994. We believe this figure, based on Leon Keyserling's Deprivation Index[24], is a more realistic estimate of poverty.[25]

Of the older poor, 78% are white.[26] There are clearly many more poor whites in actual numbers than poor blacks. However, a greater proportion of the African American older persons are poor (27% of older blacks as opposed to 10% of older whites) and their poverty is more profound. Hispanic American, Native American, and certain Asian and Pacific Island American older persons are also especially disadvantaged, as are women of all ethnic and racial groups, especially women over age 85.

Older persons receive a little more than half the income of younger persons. In 1994, the median income of families headed by an older person was $18,095 as compared with $37,247 for families with heads under 65. The median income of an older person living alone or with nonrelatives in 1994 was $14,080 for men ($270 a week), and $10,572 for women ($203 a week). The median annual income for people of all ages living

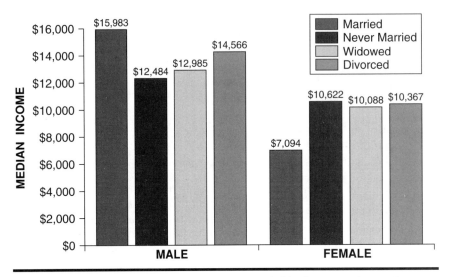

FIGURE 1.7   Median income of persons age 65 and older by sex and marital status: 1994

Source: U.S. Bureau of the Census (1994), *Current population survey,* unpublished data.

alone was $24,082 ($463 a week) for men, and $20,353 ($391 a week) for women.[27]

Without Social Security the economic picture for older people would be even more bleak. The average monthly Social Security payment to the retired worker in 1994 was $697; to the worker's wife or husband, $359; and to the worker's children, $309.[28] Almost half of older workers retire before age 65 and therefore receive "reduced benefits." Some do so out of choice, but others are forced to because of poor health or unemployment. In March 1996, over 2.1 million older people received Supplementary Security Income (SSI) benefits averaging about $263 per month.[29] However, only about 50–60% of those eligible for SSI actually receive it; many are not aware of its existence while others are reluctant to accept "welfare" because of pride or embarrassment.

Most income must go for food, shelter, and medical expenses—the essentials of existence. The lack of money has supported the myth that the aged can live on less because they do not need as much for clothing, transportation, entertainment, recreation, or education as the young. The truth is simply that older persons may not be able to af-

ford these items, which for young people are considered necessary for mental health, social status, avoidance of isolation, and personal growth.

Middle and Upper Incomes

There are, of course, middle- and upper-class older persons. Not all the old are poor. But, as we have seen, the rich "merry widow" is rare. In 1995 there were 21.4 million households headed by persons over age 65. Of these, approximately 45% had incomes in excess of $20,000 per year; 12% had incomes in excess of $50,000; and 2.7% had incomes in excess of $100,000 annually.[30]

Sources of Income

Older people earn 18% of their aggregate income from continuing employment, 18% from assets, 42% from Social Security, 19% from pensions, and 3% from other sources.[31] It is commonly believed that older persons are adequately provided for by Social Security and Medicare, but these programs have not met their needs. Many unskilled jobs, held primarily by minorities and women, were not covered by Social Security until recently. Even now, some employees (for example, many domestic workers) are not covered. Medicare, too, needs improvements. Only 45% of the health expenses of older persons are met; the rest must be paid for out of their incomes. Hearing aids, glasses, dental care, podiatry, various drugstore supplies, and, most importantly, long-term care are not covered under Medicare.

EMPLOYMENT

Employment should ideally be a matter of choice after age 65. Indeed older people do earn 18% of their income. But their ability to work is hampered by two major factors: the Social Security ceiling on earnings (which says in effect that, up to age 70, an older person is allowed only a small amount of earnings, since if more is earned, the Social Security check is reduced) and age discrimination in employment, including bias against hiring older people. (Fortunately, mandatory retirement has virtually ended in the United States as a result of the 1986 amendment to the Age Discrimination in Employment Act.) In addition, educational and technological obsolescence and the possible physical limitations of older persons combine to squeeze them out of the job market. Most of their work is concentrated in three low-earning categories: agricultural work, part-time work, and self-employment. Since 1900 the number of older men in the labor force has dropped from two-thirds to less than one-sixth (16%). The percentage of older women workers is about 8.8%.

Older African American men do not participate in the labor force as much as whites and, when they do, they earn less, do harder physical work, and are in poorer health. The proportion of older black and white women who work is about the same, but black women, like black men, earn less, usually doing domestic and service work. Retirement by choice is less of an option because African Americans' retirement benefits are often meager, in line with their previous low earnings. Indeed there may be no benefits at all. When they can no longer work, many older African Ameri-

cans are simply mustered out of the labor market. They frequently must turn to SSI as the only income source available. Thus SSI programs have a disproportionate number of older blacks on their rolls, compared to whites, and it is important to understand why.

PHYSICAL AND MENTAL HEALTH

It is obvious that old people get sick more frequently than the young. Yet most move about on their own legs, and only 5.4% are confined to institutions for physical or emotional care. Most have chronic health problems of one kind or another that require more frequent visits to the doctor and more hospital stays, although the average length of stay has gone down to 8.6 days from 14 days some years ago, driven by new Medicare regulations. More periods of illness at home that result in more physical and emotional disability are experienced as well. The 1986 National Health Interview Survey Supplement on Functional Limitations found that about one-quarter (23%) of the 65-and-over population living in the community had difficulty with one or more of the seven personal care activities (activities of daily living or ADLs) inventoried, and about the same proportion (28%) had difficulty with at least one of the six home management activities (instrumental activities of daily living or IADLs). The Annual per capita expenditure for the health care of older persons in 1987 was $5,360, over four times greater than expenditures on the average person under 65 years old ($1,286). The average annual health care expenditure for those age 85 and older was $9,178. These are the latest available figures. Since 1987, health care costs have risen considerably.[32]

The mental health needs of older persons are substantial (see Chapters 5 and 6 regarding the extent of mental illness in this population). Emotional and mental illnesses escalate over the course of the life cycle. Depression in particular rises with age, and suicide attains its peak in white men in their eighties. The suicide curves of white women and black men and women rise in the middle years and then decline. Depression and hypochondriasis commonly accompany the many physical ailments of old age, which range from cardiovascular disease to arthritis and hearing loss.

EDUCATION

Although still well below that of the younger population, the educational level of the elderly has been steadily increasing. The percentage of older people who had completed high school rose from 28% in 1970 to 60% in 1993; almost 12% had a bachelor's degree or more. However, education levels vary considerably by race. In 1993, 16% of whites age 65 to 74, and 29% of whites age 75 and older never attended high school; for blacks it was approximately 38% and 61% respectively. In 1993, 63% of older whites completed high school, compared to 33% of older blacks, and 26% of older Hispanics. Only about 6% of older blacks attained a bachelor's degree or more, compared to almost 13% of older whites. Fifty-eight percent of Hispanics age 65 to 74, and 71% of Hispanics age 75 and older never attended high school.[33]

One-third of today's 17 to 21 million illiterate adults are aged 60 and over. The present elderly population has a much higher proportion of foreign-born persons who have a higher illiteracy rate and lower educational attainment than the native population.

POLITICAL POTENTIAL

The political strength of older persons is growing and is already proving to be a major force in political life. Eight states have 40% of the country's electoral votes: New York, Pennsylvania, Ohio, Illinois, Texas, California, Michigan, and Florida; all have a greater concentration of elderly residents than the national average. Over 75% of older people are registered to vote, and two-thirds vote regularly—many more than in any other age group. Older people are organizing themselves for political action and influence. Some fear a growing restlessness and militancy among the elderly

for "senior power." But evidence strongly indicates that the elderly are concerned about the welfare of all the generations. Along with the political strength of the elderly have come a new sense of self-respect and a respect from others that is not dependent on solicitude but rather on a sober recognition of the elderly's ability to have an impact on public issues.

NATIONAL AND ETHNIC IDENTIFICATION

As a consequence of the civil rights movement and the "war on poverty" of the 1960s, federal legislation focused on various racial and ethnic groups in the United States with the aim of offsetting previous and ongoing discrimination. It has been important and necessary to those who have been especially disadvantaged in our society. As we moved into the 1990s, U.S. society became even more extraordinarily diverse, multicultural, multiethnic, and multiracial with major increases in the Asian and Hispanic populations. It is important for the mental health provider or specialist to fully recognize this diversity.

Throughout the earlier parts of this chapter we presented data on the African American elderly. The following discussion includes the elderly of the other most prominent minority populations. (See Chapter 7 for mental health issues of minority elderly.)

HISPANIC OR LATINO OLDER PERSONS

Not enough is known about our second largest minority, the Hispanic population, which in fact may be the largest racial/ethnic group in the United States by the year 2000.[34] A great difficulty in talking about the so-called Hispanic American population is in simply defining that population. The various names used to describe parts or all of the group are in themselves confusing, for example, Hispanics, Chicanos, Boricuas, Mexican Americans, Latinos, Puerto Ricans, Spanish Americans, Razas, Latin Americans, "persons of Spanish origin," and "persons with Spanish surnames." Researchers and demographers have used various measures such as Spanish surname, Spanish-speaking, birthplace of the individual or of the individual's parents, Spanish-origin (self-identification of descent), and race (Indian, white [Spanish], black, or mestizo [mixture of Indian and Spanish]) to try to clarify populations under study, but no single method of "naming" has yet been generally successful. Race and class bias are built into most descriptions. We shall use "Hispanic," a term that seems more widely recognizable to the U.S. public.

The United States Hispanic population totaled almost 27 million in 1995, comprising more than 10% of the total population.[35] By the year 2000, their numbers will reach over 31 million, or over 11% of the total population.[36] Currently 5.6% of the Hispanic population is age 65 and older. Among Hispanic subgroups in the United States in 1990, Mexicans numbered 13.5 million, Puerto Ricans 2.7 million, Central and South Americans 2.3 million, Cubans 1 million, and persons from other nations numbered 2.9 million.

More than half of all Hispanics live in California or Texas. New York has 10% of the Hispanic population of the United States and Florida 7%. Illinois, Arizona, New Jersey, New Mexico, and Colorado also have sizable Hispanic populations.[37] The population of almost 27 million does not include over 3.6 million Spanish-speaking persons in Puerto Rico and the unknown number of Spanish-speaking illegal aliens now living in the United States. The 1986 Immigration Reform Act made it possible for "undocumented" and "illegal" aliens who had lived in the United States prior to January 1, 1982, to request U.S. citizenship. Nonetheless, there are still a considerable number of aliens, particularly political refugees, from Central America, specifically Honduras, Nicaragua, and El Salvador. It is difficult to estimate their number.

In addition to a lower life expectancy than that of whites, as well as poverty, poor housing, and lack of medical care and education, older Hispanics face the turmoil of drastic changes in their traditional life-styles. The young are breaking rapidly with their past, the extended family is shrinking into the nuclear family, and the aged tend to be cut adrift from their rich culture and tradition. A sense of personal privacy and pride make it difficult for older persons to ask for and accept financial or medical aid. The government's Supplementary Security Income (SSI) is not popular and often is unused. Furthermore, Spanish-speaking older persons face a language barrier and are too frequently expected to adapt to English with no instruction, rather than receiving the courtesy of translations or Spanish-speaking and Spanish-oriented services. In spite of all these problems, the number of Hispanic elderly is expected to rise dramatically, from 5.5% of the total Hispanic population in 1995 to about six and a half times larger in 2030, and over ten times larger by 2050.

NATIVE AMERICAN (AMERICAN INDIAN, ESKIMO, AND ALEUT) OLDER PERSONS

Of the 2.2 million American Indian, Eskimo, and Aleut (AIEA)[38] persons in 1995, approximately 96% were American Indians and 4% were Eskimo and Aleuts. The proportion of older persons among the Native American population has grown twice as fast as that of the African American or white elderly population, increasing by 65% between 1980 and 1990. In 1995, there were 141,000 Native Americans age 65 and older, about 6% of the total Native American population.[39] Almost half live in rural areas, a far greater proportion than any other major minority group. Approximately one-fourth of Native American elderly live on reservations or in Alaskan native villages. The majority of Native Americans are concentrated in the Southwest: Oklahoma, California, Arizona, New Mexico and Texas. Most of the remainder reside in states along the Canadian border.[40] According to the Indian Health Service, the average life expectancy at birth for Native Americans increased from only 51 years in 1940 to 71.5 years in 1987–89—still, however, over three years less than that of the general population of the United States in the same period.[41]

Native Americans are among the poorest people in the United States. In 1989, the median income for Native Americans age 60 and over was $7,109, while the median income for non-Hispanic whites age 60 and over was $11,581. Although approximately the same percentage of older Native Americans and older whites remain in the workforce, nearly twice as many older Native Americans are unemployed and actively seeking work. Older Native Americans report almost twice the level of work disability (almost 37%) as any other major minority group. Malnutrition is a constant problem. Overall, one-third of Native American elderly live below the official poverty level.[42] The traditional kinship support of the family is not feasible when the family itself has no resources. Older persons are left impoverished—particularly if their children leave to live and work elsewhere.

The medical care provided by the U.S. Public Health Service is considered less than adequate to care for the Native American population. It is said that service is provided predominately for those who manage to make it to a hospital alive, although in recent years the Public Health Service has established an outreach program. Nonetheless, older persons, along with the poor, the young, and the very sick, are at considerable risk in terms of survival on the desperate trek to the nearest medical facility.

Through all this, growing numbers of Native Americans do manage to survive to old age, imbued with a fierce sense of reverence for their land. To older Indians, Eskimos, and Aleuts the physical aspect of land is an essential element in their identity and sense of belonging—this in spite of the deprivation they experience in tenaciously holding on to that land.

Because of their physical remoteness, the Eskimo and Aleut populations in Alaska are seldom noted in discussions of American older persons. The Aleuts have a greater life expectancy than the Eskimos, perhaps because the latter live in the more demanding environments of northern Alaska and Greenland. The perilousness of the environment is demonstrated in the fact that accidents are the leading cause of death for older Alaskan natives.

ASIAN AMERICAN AND PACIFIC ISLAND AMERICAN OLDER PERSONS

In 1995, as a combined minority group, the nearly 9.3 million Asian and Pacific Islanders in the United States (primarily Chinese, Filipino, and Japanese) made up about 3.6% of the total United States population, over three times the percentage in 1980.[43] About 95% of Asian and Pacific Islanders are Asian and 5% are Pacific Islanders (mostly Hawaiian). Currently, the Chinese are the largest Asian American minority group, surpassing the Japanese, who had been the largest group since 1910.

In 1995 approximately 617,000 (6.6%) of the Asian and Pacific Islander population were age 65 and older; 36,000 (.03%) were age 85 and older.[44] Only about 7% live in rural areas. Almost two-thirds are concentrated in just two states—California and Hawaii.

Of the remainder, most live in the New York/New Jersey metropolitan area, in Illinois, or in Washington State. The ratio of women to men is somewhat lower than for the general population, reflecting pre–World War II immigration laws that prohibited women and children from accompanying men to the United States. However, only among Indonesian and Tongan (in Polynesia) older Asian and Pacific Islanders are women still in the minority. Recent Asian and Pacific Islander immigrants include many well-educated professionals; however, more Asian and Pacific Islander elderly lack formal education than do whites. Compared with the total United States population, older Asians and Pacific Islanders have the greatest proportion of those with a bachelor's degree or more, at 13% compared to 11%. Ironically, they also have the highest percentage of those with less than a ninth grade education, at 39% compared to 26%. Asians and Pacific Islanders are more likely to remain in the labor force after age 65 than whites, at 16% compared to 12%. They are also less likely to be unemployed, however this varies among nationalities.[45]

Groups within the Asian and Pacific Islander population in the United States differ significantly in language, customs, social class structure, and levels of assimilation. Of the 134,000 Chinese age 65 and older in 1990 (8% of the total Chinese American population), 98% live in cities. Nationally, 15% of older Chinese Americans had incomes below the official poverty rate in 1990. Although a larger proportion of Chinese Americans hold professional or managerial positions as compared to whites, the majority hold menial jobs.[46]

As a group, fewer older Asian and Pacific Island Americans are in poverty than the general older population. This may be, in part, because of an emphasis on familial responsibility in caring for older relatives. However, some groups of older Asian and Pacific Islanders, including Hmong (a minority group from Laos), Cambodian, Laotian, Korean, Vietnamese and Samoans, suffer from a much higher rate of poverty than the general population, as high as 47% in the case of Hmong older people.[47]

Traditional patterns of kinship and community have been damaged by the experiences of immigration and forced disruption of normal family life. Many of the older people speak little English, and can neither read nor write English or their native language, thus increasing their difficulties in an alien culture.

In 1990, 106,000 Japanese Americans, or 12.5% of the total Japanese American population were age 65 or older. Japanese Americans appear to have been able to provide their older persons with greater family support and economic security, since they were not so severely restricted from bringing their families with them when immigrating. Yet 5% of these older Japanese are poor, especially in areas outside California and Hawaii. Older Japanese men usually speak at least minimal English, but older women tend to speak only Japanese. Health surveys have found that many of these older people are physically healthy and long-lived.

Filipino Americans are the second largest Asian and Pacific Islander subgroup, with a population of over 1.4 million, yet they have only the third largest number of older people, with 104,000, or 7.4% of their population. In the 1980 Census, older Filipino men still outnumbered women, comprising 67% of the older population.[48] Most of these men were laborers recruited to work in California and Hawaii from 1910 to the 1930's. After the Tydings-McDuffie Act of 1934, Filipino immigration was restricted to only 50 people per year. Many more Filipinos were recruited during World War II, but a larger influx began after restrictions were relaxed in 1965. Many of these immigrants were older family members of Filipino American health care workers.[49] By the 1990 Census women made up 52% of the older Filipino population of the United States, but there are still a large number of single older Filipino men. Many older Filipinos are highly educated, with 16% having obtained a bachelor's degree or more, although 40% never attended high school.[50]

RURAL AND SEMIRURAL OLDER PERSONS

Although 25% of older persons lived in rural areas by 1990, only 1% actually lived on farms. The remaining 24% resided in small towns of less than 2500 people.[51] Since the 1970s, a larger proportion of elderly compared to the rest of the population have moved from urban to nonurban areas, especially areas with mild climates. Other elderly already in nonurban areas are "aging in place" where they have always lived. The benefits of rural and especially semirural life are many: fresh air and sunshine, opportunity to play and work out-of-doors, a leisurely life-style, lack of congestion, and friends and neighbors of long acquaintance. But there are also unfavorable features: transportation for older people can be especially difficult because of poor roads, lack of public transport, and the need to maintain private cars or rely on someone else. Medical facilities are often inadequate, since most health care and medical services are urban-based. Many communities are without a doctor or nurse. Income levels are low; few rural and semirural people are covered by private pension plans. Social Security, employment, savings, and welfare are the usual income sources, but Social Security benefits are lower because agricultural workers and the self-employed have only recently been covered. There is a shrinking tax base and an increasing scarcity of services and loss of family members caused by the migration of young people to cities in search of work. Semirural older persons are often left with rising property and sales taxes to maintain communities and services. A disproportionate share of the nonurban elderly live in substandard and dilapidated housing. A shortage of paid jobs hampers older people in their attempts to supplement income, and present federal programs do little to help—although nearly 40% of all older people live in nonurban areas, most federal programs primarily address the needs of urban older persons. Some progress has been made in provision of more community services.[52]

SELECTED READINGS

Aaron, H. J., Bosworth, B. P., & Butless, G. (1989). *Can America grow old? Paying for Social Security.* Washington, DC: The Brookings Institution.

American Association of Retired Persons, and Administration on Aging. (1995). *A profile of older Americans: 1995.* Washington, DC: Author.

Angel, J. L., & Hogan, D. P. (1991). The demography of minority aging populations. In The Gerontological Association of America, *Minority elders: Longevity, economics, and health, building a public policy base.* Washington, DC: The Gerontological Society of America, pp. 1–13.

Applewhite, S. R. (Ed.). (1988). *Hispanic elderly in transition: Theory, research, policy and practice.* Westport, CT: Greenwood Press.

Browne, C., & Broderick, A. (1994, May). Asian and Pacific Island Elders: Issues for social work practice and education. *Social Work, 39*(3), 252–259.

Butler, R. N. (1975). *Why survive? Being old in America.* New York: Harper & Row.

Butler, R. N. (1983, July-August). A generation at risk. When the baby boomers reach Golden Pond. *Across the Board,* 37–45.

Castex, G. M. (1994, May). Providing services to Hispanic/Latino populations: Profiles in diversity. *Social Work, 39*(3), 288–296.

Cheung, M. (1989, Sept.). Elderly Chinese living in the United States: Assimilation or adjustment? *Social Work,* 457–461.

Commonwealth Fund Commission on Elderly People Living Alone. (1987). *Old, alone, and poor.* New York: Commonwealth Fund Communications Office.

Commonwealth Fund Commission on Elderly People Living Alone. (1987). *Medicare's poor.* New York: Commonwealth Fund Communications Office.

Commonwealth Fund Commission on Elderly People Living Alone. (1989). *Poverty and poor health among elderly Hispanic Americans.* New York: Commonwealth Fund Communications Office.

Coward, R. T., & Lee, G. R. (Eds.). (1985). *The elderly in rural society: Every fourth elder.* New York: Springer.

Daniels, N. (1988). *Am I my parents' keeper? An essay on justice between the young and old.* New York: Oxford University Press.

Faulkner, A., Heisel, M. A., Holbrook, W., & Geismar, S. (1982). *When I was comin' up: An oral history of aged blacks.* Hamden, CT: Archon Books.

Gelfand, D. E. (1994). *Aging and ethnicity: Knowledge and services.* New York: Springer.

Gelfand, D. E., & Barresi, C. M. (1987). *Ethnic dimensions of aging.* New York: Springer.

Grad, Susan. (1996). *Income of the population 55 or older, 1994.* Washington, DC: U.S. Department of Health and Human Services, Social Security Administration, U.S. Government Printing Office.

Institute of Medicine. (1993). *Forecasting survival, health, and disability: Workshop summary.* Washington, DC: National Academy Press.

Jackson, J. S. (Ed.). (1988). *The Black American elderly: Research on physical and psychosocial health.* New York: Springer.

Jackson, J. S. (1995). African-American aged. In Maddox, G. L. (Ed.), *The encyclopedia of aging* (pp. 30–32). New York: Springer.

John, R., & Baldridge, D. (1996). *The National Indian Council on Aging report: Health and long-term care for Indian elders.* Washington, DC: National Indian Policy Center.

Kitagawa, E. M., & Hauser, P. M. (1973). *Differential mortality in the United States: A study in socio-economic epidemiology.* Cambridge, MA: Harvard University Press.

Kramer, B. J. (1995). Native-American aged. In Maddox, G. L. (Ed.), *The encyclopedia of aging* (pp. 671–673). New York: Springer.

Krout, J. A. (1986). *The aged in rural America.* Westport, CT: Greenwood Press.

LaVeist, T. A. (1995). Data sources for aging research on racial and ethnic groups. *Gerontologist, 35,* 328–339.

Manson, S. M., & Callaway, D. G. (1988). Health and aging among American Indians: Issues and challenges for the biobehavioral sciences. In Manson, S. M., & Dinges, N. G. (Eds.), *Behavioral health issues among American Indians and Alaska natives.* Denver, CO: University of Colorado Health Sciences Center.

Manton, K. G., Singer, B. H., & Suzman, R. M. (1993). *Forecasting the health of elderly populations.* New York: Springer-Verlag.

Markides, K. S. (1989). Consequences of gender differentials in life expectancy for Black and Hispanic Americans. *International Journal of Aging and Human Development, 29*(2), 95–102.

Markides, K. S., & Rudkin L. (1996). Racial and ethnic diversity. In Birren, J. E. (Ed.), *Encyclopedia of gerontology* (vol. 2, pp. 371–376). San Diego, CA.: Academic Press.

National Center for Health Statistics. (1993). Health data on older Americans: United States, 1992. *Vital and Health Statistics,* Series 3, No. 30. DHHS Publication No. (PHS)93–1411. Hyattsville, MD: U.S. Department of Health and Human Services.

National Center for Health Statistics. (1995). Advance report of final marriage statistics, 1989 and 1990. *Monthly Vital Statistics Report, 43*(12), suppl. DHHS Publication No.(PHS)95–1120. Hyattsville, MD: U.S. Department of Health and Human Services.

National Center for Health Statistics. (1995). Trends in the health of older Americans: United States, 1994. *Vital and Health Statistics,* Series 3, No. 30. DHHS Publication No.(PHS)95–1414. Hyattsville, MD: U.S. Department of Health and Human Services.

Olson, L. K. (Ed.). (1994). *The graying of the world: Who will care for the frail elderly?* Binghamton, NY: The Haworth Press.

Shanas, E., & Streib, G. F. (1965). *Social structure and the family: Generational relations.* Englewood Cliffs, NJ: Prentice-Hall.

Sotomayor, M. (1995). Hispanic elderly. In Maddox, G. L. (Ed.) *The encyclopedia of aging* (pp. 458–459). New York: Springer.

U.S. Bureau of the Census. (1994). Educational attainment in the United States: March 1993 and 1992. *Current Population Reports, Population Characteristics,* Series P-20, no. 276, Washington, DC: U.S. Government Printing Office.

U.S. Bureau of the Census. (February 14, 1996). *U.S. population estimates by age, sex, race, and hispanic origin: 1990–1995.* PPL-41. Washington, DC: Population Projections Branch, Population Division, U.S. Bureau of the Census.

U.S. Bureau of the Census. (1996). 65+ in the United States. *Current Population Reports, Special Studies,* Series P-23, No. 190. Washington, DC: U.S. Government Printing Office.

U.S. Bureau of the Census. (1996). Marital status and living arrangements: March 1994. *Current Population Reports,* Series P-20, No. 484. Washington, DC: U.S. Government Printing Office.

U.S. Bureau of the Census. (1996). Population projections by age, sex, race and hispanic origin: 1995–2050. *Current Population Reports,* Series P-25, No. 1130. Washington, DC: U.S. Government Printing Office.

U.S. Department of Health and Human Services, Social Security Administration. (1996). *Income of the population 55 or older.* Washington, DC: U.S. Government Printing Office.

Waldron, I. (1985). What do we know about causes of sex differences in mortality? A review of the literature. *Population Bulletin of the United States,* no. 18.

Wykle, M., & Kaskel, B. (1991). Increasing the longevity of minority older adults through improved health status. In The Gerontological Society of America, *Minority elders: Longevity, economics and health, building a public policy base.* Washington, DC: The Gerontological Society of America.

Yeo, G., & Hikoyeda, N. (1995). Asian and Pacific Islander American elders. In Maddox, G. L. (Ed.), *The encyclopedia of aging* (pp. 80–82). New York: Springer.

Young, J. J., & Gu, N. (1995). *Demographic and socioeconomic characteristics of elderly Asian and Pacific Island Americans.* Seattle, WA: National Asian Pacific Center on Aging.

ENDNOTES

1. Strictly speaking, aging begins before conception. A female is born with all her ova (eggs) and they age as she ages. There are no new eggs. Because of this, there is an increased incidence of Down syndrome, causing mental retardation, in children born to older women.

2. Each day, 5,700 Americans turn 65 and 4,280 age 65 and older die. Thus, the "turnover rate," or daily gain in the 65+ population, is 1,420 (based on 1992 statistics).

3. U.S. Bureau of the Census. (February 14, 1996). *U.S. Population estimates by age, sex, race, and hispanic origin: 1990–1995.* PPL-41. Washington, DC: Population Projections Branch, Population Division, U.S. Bureau of the Census.

4. U.S. Bureau of the Census. (1996). 65+ in the United States. *Current population reports, special studies,* Series P-23, No. 190. Washington, DC: U.S. Government Printing Office.

5. U.S. Bureau of the Census. (1996). Population projections by age, sex, race and hispanic origin: 1995–2050. *Current Population Reports,* Series P-25, No. 1130. Washington, DC: U.S. Government Printing Office.

6. U.S. Bureau of the Census. (February 14, 1996). *U.S. population estimates by age, sex, race, and hispanic origin: 1990–1995.* PPL-41. Washington, DC: U.S. Bureau of the Census.

7. U.S. Bureau of the Census. (1987). America's centenarians (data from the 1980 census). *Current Population Reports,* Series P-23, No. 153. Washington, DC: U.S. Government Printing Office.

8. U.S. Bureau of the Census (1996). Population projections by age, sex, race, and hispanic origin: 1995–2050. *Current Population Reports,* Series P-25, no. 1130. Washington, DC: U.S. Government Printing Office.

9. The sharp increase in survival has had many profound social consequences; for example, when marriage was made a sacrament in the 9th century A.D., the prospect of marriage lasting into the couple's forties was small. The concepts of retirement and late-life leisure were rudimentary at best.

10. O.A.S.D.I. *1996 annual report of the board of trustees,* Baltimore, MD: Author.

11. The twentieth century has seen increased life expectancy but not increased natural or maximal life span. It is most important to distinguish between "life expectancy," the actuarial projection of probable years of life from a base year, such as birth or age 65, and "life span," the inherent, maximal length of life of a species.

12. U.S. Bureau of the Census. (1996). Population projections of the United States by age, sex, race, and Hispanic origin: 1995 to 2050. *Current Population Reports,* Series P-25, no. 1130. Washington, DC: U.S. Government Printing Office.

13. Waldron, I. (1986). What do we know about causes of sex differences in mortality? A review of the literature. *Population Bulletin of the United Nations,* No. 18-1985.

14. See Haynes, S. G., & Feinlieb, M. *Women, work and coronary heart disease: Prospective findings from the Framingham Heart Study,* paper presented at the 86th Annual Meeting of the American Psychological Association, Toronto, Canada, August 1978. For a summary on women and heart disease, see Brody, J. E. (1989, February 2). Personal health, *The New York Times,* B7. Also, see Eaker, E. D., Chesebro, J. H., Sacks, F. M., et al. (1993). Cardiovascular disease in women. *Circulation, 88,* 1999–2009.

15. Many people of African descent in the United States prefer to be called *African American.* We have decided to use this term wherever possible. However, the term *black* is used by the U.S. Bureau of the Census and other major data collecting agencies, in part because figures used include people from the Caribbean, Latin America, Africa, and many people who are not U.S. citizens and, therefore, would not consider themselves African American. Therefore we have used the term *black* in reference to any such data.

16. This is with the exception of Asian Americans of all ages, particularly Japanese and Chinese, who generally fared better than did whites in the mortality statistics. Asian Americans had the highest levels of income and education and the lowest death rates, while African Americans had the lowest income and educational levels and the highest death rates. The death rates for blacks as well as for American Indian and Alaskan natives have been particularly high in the younger and middle age groups. Deaths among black infants are more than twice as high as those among white infants. The death rate for blacks age 22 to 44 is significantly higher than that for whites of the same age, with violent causes of death—accidents and homicides—especially high.

17. National Center for Health Statistics. (1995, April). Trends in the health of older Americans, United States, 1994. Series 3. *Analytical and Epidemio-*

logical Studies, no. 30. DHHS Publication No. (PHS) 95-1414. Hyattsville, MD: U.S. Department of Health and Human Services.

18. Although only 5% of older people are in institutions at any one time, estimates are that up to 40% of all older persons will receive nursing home care at some point in their lives.

19. U.S. Bureau of the Census. (1996). Marital status and living arrangements: March 1994. *Current Population Reports,* Series P-20, no. 484. Washington, DC: U.S. Government Printing Office.

20 *Ibid.*

21. U.S. Bureau of the Census. (1996). 65+ in the United States. *Current Population Reports, Special Studies,* Series P-23, no. 190. Washington, DC: U.S. Government Printing Office.

22. American Association of Retired Persons (AARP). (1995). A Profile of Older Americans. Washington DC: Author.

23. The poverty index was adopted by a federal interagency committee in 1969. The index is based on the Agriculture Department's 1961 Economy Food Plan and reflects the different consumption requirements of families based on their size and composition, sex and age of the family head, and farm or nonfarm residence. For example, studies determined that families of three or more persons spend about a third of their income on food. As a result, the poverty level of these families was set at about three times the cost of the Economy Food Plan. "Income" refers only to money income and does not reflect nonmoney transfers such as food stamps, health benefits, and subsidized housing.

24. Butler, R. N. (1975). *Why survive? Being old in America.* New York: Harper & Row, p. 28.

25. Poverty statistics from U.S. Bureau of the Census. (1995, March). *Current Population Survey,* March Supplement. Washington, DC: U.S. Bureau of the Census.

26. A little-known example of poverty among whites is that found among the Jewish elderly. In Los Angeles alone a study found 8,000 older Jewish poor on public assistance and another 10,000 eligible who had not applied. See also the account of elderly Jews in Venice, California, by anthropologist B. Myerhoff. (1979). *Number our days.* New York: E. P. Dutton.

27. U.S. Bureau of the Census. (1995, March). *Current Population Survey,* March Supplement. Washington, DC: U.S. Bureau of the Census.

28. U.S. Department of Health and Human Services, Social Security Administration. (1995). Annual statistical supplement, 1995, to the social security bulletin.

29. U.S. Department of Health and Human Services, Social Security Administration. (1996, March). Summary Data, Social Security Record.

30. U.S. Bureau of the Census (1995, March). *Current Population Survey,* March Supplement. Washington, DC: U.S. Bureau of the Census.

31. U.S. Department of Health and Human Services, Social Security Administration. (1996). *Income of the population 55 or older.* Washington DC: U.S. Government Printing Office.

32. National Center for Health Statistics. (1993). Health data on older Americans: United States, 1992. *Vital and Health Statistics,* Series 3, No. 30. DHHS Publication No.(PHS)93–1411. Hyattsville, MD: U.S. Dept. of Health and Human Services.

33. U.S. Bureau of the Census. (1994). Educational attainment in the United States: March 1993 and 1992. *Current Population Reports, Population Characteristics,* Series P20, no. 476. Washington, DC: U.S. Government Printing Office.

34. See Castex, G. M. (1994, May). Providing services to Hispanic/Latino populations: Profiles in diversity. *Social Work, 37*(3), 288–296.
    The U.S. Bureau of the Census directly measured the "Spanish origin" (the Census Bureau term) population in the 1980 Census and the "Hispanic Origin" population in the 1990 Census, in contrast to the past when the Bureau took limited samplings of the group, using different identifiers (language, surname, national origin) in different states. Partly because of fear and distrust, some, and perhaps many, members of the Hispanic community have avoided the census taker. Thus there is probably an undercount, affecting federal funding to assist Hispanic Americans in need.

35. U.S. Bureau of the Census. (February 14, 1996). *U.S. population estimates by age, sex, race, and hispanic origin: 1990–1995.* PPL-41. Washington, DC: Population Projections Branch, Population Division, U.S. Bureau of the Census.

36. U.S. Bureau of the Census. (1996). Population projections by age, sex, race and hispanic origin: 1995–2050. *Current Population Reports,* Series P-25, No. 1130. Washington, DC: U.S. Government Printing Office.

37. U.S. Bureau of the Census. (1991). Resident population distribution for the United States, regions, and states, by race and hispanic origin: 1990. *Press release* CB91-100. Washington DC: U.S. Bureau of the Census.

38. The U.S. Bureau of the Census uses this term. Criteria include at least one-fourth Indian ancestry and registration on a recognized and approved tribal roll.

39. U.S. Bureau of the Census. (February 14, 1996). *U.S. population estimates by age, sex, race, and hispanic origin: 1990–1995.* PPL-41. Washington, DC: Population Projections Branch, Population Division, U.S. Bureau of the Census.

40. Kramer, B.J. (1995). Native-American aged. In Maddox, G. L. (Ed.), *The encyclopedia of aging* (pp. 671–673). New York: Springer.

41. John, R., & Baldridge, D. (1996). *The National Indian Council on Aging report: Health and long-term care for Indian elders.* Washington, DC: National Indian Policy Center.

42. *Ibid.*

43. U.S. Bureau of the Census. (February 14, 1996). *U.S. population estimates by age, sex, race, and hispanic origin: 1990–1995.* PPL-41. Washington, DC: Population Projections Branch, Population Division, U.S. Bureau of the Census.

44. *Ibid.*

45. Young J. J., & Gu, N. (1995). *Demographic and socio-economic characteristics of elderly Asian and Pacific Island Americans.* Seattle, WA: National Asian Pacific Center on Aging.

46. *Ibid.*

47. *Ibid.*

48. *Ibid.*

49. Yeo, G., & Hikoyeda, N. (1995). Asian and Pacific Islander American elders. In Maddox, G. L. (Ed.), *The encyclopedia of aging* (pp. 80–82). New York: Springer.

50. Young, J. J., & Gu, N. (1995). *Demographic and socio-economic characteristics of elderly Asian and Pacific Island Americans.* Seattle, WA: National Asian Pacific Center on Aging.

51. U.S. Bureau of the Census. (1990). *Social and economic characteristics, United States summary,* CP-2-1. Washington, DC: U.S. Government Printing Office.

52. Coward, R. T. & Lee, G. R. (Eds.). (1985). *The elderly in rural society: Every fourth elder.* New York: Springer Publishing Co.

CHAPTER 2

OLDER PEOPLE AND THEIR FAMILIES

Understanding the family life of older people is central to understanding the mental health issues of later life. The family—both the immediate and extended family—is the arena in which the majority of us develop our sense of others and ourselves. It is a critical force that shapes our feelings and thoughts about the very meaning and value of life, and it is a vital piece of our environment that either promotes or obstructs our mental health. In old age the quality of family life can be pivotal in determining what resources one has to draw on in times of trouble. And when that quality is good, family life can provide a unique blend of warmth and personal satisfaction that can transform the later years into a rich and gratifying stage of life. But can this be true in the United States, where the prevailing view is that the elderly are isolated and rejected by their families? We will spend a good part of this chapter refuting that negative view of family life. It is certainly true that old age itself is not highly valued by many people in the United States. A number of factors have had a negative influence on U.S. attitudes toward old age:

1. A history of mass immigration, still ongoing, mostly consisting of the young leaving the elderly behind in Europe and Asia
2. A nation founded on principles of individualism, independence, and autonomy
3. The development of technologies that demand rapid change and specialized skills
4. A general devaluation of tradition
5. Increased mobility of the population within a large continental space
6. Medical advances that have relegated most deaths to later life, producing a tendency to associate death with old age

All of these have made it difficult to embrace old age itself as a valued and contributory phase of life. But can a culture so institutionalize its negativism against old age that ties of affection and loyalty between elderly parents and their adult children are discarded? Probably not. The tenacity of kinship bonds throughout history—in spite of wars, conquest, slavery, immigration, political ideology, and cultural change—should lead one to doubt easy assumptions concerning the demise of parent–child relationships. And indeed, as we shall see in the following discussion, kinship ties have survived in the United States. Only the impact of major addictions to drugs and alcohol or the stress of mental illness, too frequently compounded by poverty, have been shown to threaten natural family relationships and loyalties, leaving older parents threatened, abused, or abandoned by their adult or adolescent children.

From the standpoint of mental health it has been established that young human beings can never function or grow in a healthy manner without reasonably warm, emotional, and interactive bonds with adults who care about them. This drive for emotional sustenance does not disappear as people reach adulthood. (A small but important piece of evidence is the common complaint of many elderly that they are not physically touched and hugged enough.) The strength of the impulse toward human closeness is all the more impressive in a country like the United States, which has not yet learned to appreciate old age itself as a valuable stage of life. In fact, survival in a productivity-focused society may make kinship support between the generations *more* necessary and meaningful, as human beings are buffeted by constant challenges, competition, and reexaminations of their worth in the outside world.

Some believe that kinship relationships may become more intense in the future because of changes in mortality and fertility patterns. Most people now survive into old age, and therefore relationships have a long time to build. In addition, because of a lower birthrate, there may be more time and inclination to invest in the adult relationships across generational lines.[1]

Serious historical studies of the U.S. family and aging have been undertaken only since 1960.[2] Before that, historians showed little interest in the family, and those studying the family showed little interest in history. By 1978 two major historical studies had been completed—*Growing Old in America,* by David H. Fischer, and *Old Age in a New Land,* by W. Andrew Achenbaum—as well as a number of articles on the history of old age. All of these have broadened our understanding of aging and the contemporary family in its historical context. However, attention now needs to be paid to the great variety of family styles, as well as racial and ethnic variations within the United States and cross-national comparisons with other countries.

FAMILY LIFE CYCLE[3]

Lowered birthrates and increased longevity have greatly lengthened the time people have in which to build their family life. A family may span three to five living generations, encompassed by a past reaching farther back than one can trace and a future stretching beyond the lives of any present family members. Each person experiences his or her individual life cycle from birth to death while at the same time participating as an integral part of a family with a collective life cycle of its own. Four-fifths of all older people have living children. (Half of these have only one or two, and half have three or more children.) But even for those who are childless, it is rare to find an older person who truly has no "family," even if it means only distant relatives. The closeness of kin in terms of blood relationships and the number of kin give no clear indication of the amount of meaningful contacts. But they do indicate the *kin potential,* implying usually an emotional tie, whether positive or negative. A person cannot easily "divorce" his blood relatives, since his or her own identity is intricately bound up with those to whom he or she is physically related. (For example, adopted children seem inevitably to yearn at various points in their lives for knowledge of their kin and may actively search for them even though their lives may be otherwise satisfactory.) A feeling of kin relatedness is probably an essential element in orienting oneself in time and space as a significant human being.

The number of people who are considered "family" by an older person may change markedly throughout a lifetime. Some older people have grown up with brothers and sisters but never married and therefore have no immediate family of children and grandchildren. Others may have expanded from a small childhood family unit to produce a large number of sons, daughters, grandchildren, and great-grandchildren with their assorted in-laws. Some older people relate closely to distant kin, and others even adopt as kin people to whom they are not related at all. One should never be deceived by statements from older people claiming they have broken off contact with a family member (for example, not speaking to a brother or sister for 30 years). Such relationships usually have as much emotional content as more directly active ones—or even more—as demonstrated by the concerted expenditure of effort to deny emotional involvement. Holding the memory of someone "in hate" can require more emotional energy than holding them "in love" or "in friendship."

The development and changing use of birth control has greatly altered the "traditional" kin family. People over 70 years of age are likely to have larger numbers of brothers and sisters (and nephews and nieces) and smaller numbers of children than the middle generation (over 50), which has fewer siblings and more offspring because of the post–World War II baby boom. The baby boom children themselves, ages 33 to 51 in 1997, will be somewhat more like their grandparents, with more siblings and fewer children of their own, than their parents.

People who are now 35 years of age or younger are the first generation to truly feel the birth-control–produced, generational "kin squeeze": Many have few or no brothers and sisters, and most will have no more than one and at the most two children. (The average number of children per mother has decreased from 3.9 in 1900 to 1.8 today.) Yet this generation is likely to have parents, grandparents, and even great-grandparents in their immediate family. For the first time, the average married couple has more parents than children.[4] The kin family is shrinking increasingly within each generation (not only will there be fewer brothers and sisters, but also fewer nephews and nieces and fewer aunts and uncles), but it is stretching out for the first time in human history over four and even five generations. This means

multiple sets of grandparents. It is fascinating to speculate on the consequences of large numbers of people from different generations interacting with one another. For one thing, it means that the greater part of one's life will be spent relating to other family members as fellow adults. China has gone furthest as a government in institutionalizing the generational "kin squeeze." If its one child policy succeeds, the 21st century will bring *only* vertical relationships in China: Except for husbands and wives, who will share the same generation, individuals will grow up with no siblings, cousins, aunts, or uncles.[5]

There is great potential for family life under the new demographic conditions. Hagestad comments, "Current patterns of longevity create new opportunities for long-lasting, complex relationships and emerging roles for the able elderly. They represent a major family and societal resource."[6]

Gutmann extends this idea as an imperative to society:

> Instead of thinking of the aged as hopeless recipients of services over which they have little control, they can begin to study the ways in which postparental potentials can be transformed—into resources and capacities—not only for elders, but for us all.[7]

The concept of the family itself is changing— the great "classical family of western nostalgia," as Stanford University sociologist William J. Goode once called it, does not exist and probably never existed to any great degree. The so-called extended family of early America often consisted of conglomerations of nuclear family members, unmarried siblings of the nuclear couple, lodgers, hired hands, slaves, indentured servants, apprentices, and a relatively small number of older kin who managed to survive the infections, ailments, and accidents that made life so generally short and brutal. Whether older people fared any better in these households than they do today is still a matter of debate, as is the romantic urban view that the early American rural existence was a gentler way of life for older folks. Table 2.1 details the contemporary family of America.

TABLE 2.1   Family living and working arrangements

Living Arrangements

HOUSEHOLD TYPE	% OF ALL HOUSEHOLDS
Family Households	
Married couples with children under 18	25.8
Married couples without children under 18	29.0
Female householder (no spouse present) with own children under 18	7.9
Female householder (no spouse present) without own children under 18	4.9
Male householder (no spouse present) with own children under 18	1.4
Male householder (no spouse present) without own children under 18	1.6
Nonfamily Households	
Male householder, living alone	9.7
Female householder, living alone	14.6
Other nonfamily households	5.2

Working Arrangements

WORKING ARRANGEMENT TYPE	% OF ALL MARRIED COUPLES
Married couple, husband and wife in labor force	55.00
Married couple, only husband in labor force	21.95
Married couple, only wife in labor force	5.80
Married couple, neither in labor force	17.25

Source: U.S. Bureau of the Census, (1994, March). Household and Family Characteristics. *Current Population Reports,* Series P-20, no. 483.

Imagine the families of the next decades! Families will come in increasingly varied forms—single-parent families, two-paycheck couples, the blended families of divorce, and generational and intergenerational communes, to name a few. Another new pattern is the return of an adult child to the family nest after a personal setback or a need to conserve financial resources. (See Table 2.2 for definitions of families.) Betty Friedan, a founder of the latest wave of U.S. feminism who has also become interested in aging issues, has coined the phrase "the extended family of choice." This is a new definition of "family" and an additional option for those who prefer literally to choose those whom they identify as their family, whether they are related by blood and law or not. Such choice is based primarily on affection and mutual interests.

Less than 4% of American families meet the traditional concept of husband-breadwinner, housewife, and two dependent children. Some of the likely consequences of the variety in family structure will be more effective child-care as well as day-care programs for older persons who cannot be left alone and more opportunities for families to work at home, with spouses sharing in the care of the children and infirm older parents. New problems may arise. For example, it is not clear whether the less traditional family forms, such as the "extended family of choice," or communal groups will be able or willing to handle crises of illness and disability among older members.

TABLE 2.2   Definitions of families and other family-like arrangements

General definition of family   Those who consider themselves economically and emotionally related to each other by blood (consanguinity) or by marriage (conjugality).

Nuclear family   A married pair (conjugal) with dependent children and an independent household, bound to outside kin by voluntary ties of affection or duty.

Extended family   All of those related to one another by blood or marriage.

Modified and extended family   Separate households for all but very old or sick, with a complex, viable, supportive pattern of family relationships with kin. The nuclear family is part of the extended kin family. The latter is a highly integrated network of social relations and mutual assistance—vertical over generations and bilateral to other kin.

Household   A number of persons who share a residence, exchange services, and give emotional support to each other.

Social network   Those individuals with whom one interacts during the course of one's daily life.

Support system   A group of individuals who join together to give support and assistance to each other, sometimes for a specific purpose.

However, anecdotal reports suggest that such support depends on the quality of the relationships, much the same as in more traditional families.

A whole new possibility of kin networks for the old (as well as the opposite possibility of loss of kin contact) is appearing with rising divorce and remarriage rates. While 50% of all new marriages are projected to end eventually in divorce, 80% of those who divorce remarry, bringing a whole clan of step-relatives along to add to their partner's potential kin network. Two or more divorces bring even more kin potential. The popular image of step-families is usually something similar to the feud between the Hatfields and the McCoys, with each side of the family staking out its emotional territory. The reality is that many amicable and lifelong alliances form among family members who become related through first, second, or more marriages even though the marriages themselves may or may not succeed. This is especially true of women family members (mothers and daughters-in-law, sisters-in-law, nieces-in-law), who are more likely to maintain contacts with each other after divorce than male family members. Some attribute this to women's "kin-keeping" tendencies; others see it as wom-

en's shared involvement with the children in a family as mothers, grandmothers, and aunts. For the paternal grandmother, "a daughter-in-law is no longer a son's wife [due to divorce], but she is still the mother of her grandchildren."[8]

DO AMERICAN FAMILIES "ABANDON" THEIR OLDER MEMBERS?

Research Evidence

Urbanization and industrialization have led to theories about changes and/or breakdown in family structure. The nuclear family consisting of mother, father, and several children has been postulated as the most functional family unit in industrialized societies; it requires mobility, compactness, and an emotional self-sufficiency that can be built in and carried along. Older people and other extended family members are seen as failing to fit into this streamlined picture. The popular public image is that the nuclear family has closed its ranks and its heart, determined to manage on its own, while older parents and grandparents are left to fend for themselves. This may sound plausible, but it has not happened in the United States and is not likely to.

In fact, in one of the few cross-national studies of attitudes toward the elderly, a comparison of three generations of women in Japan and the United States found the following:

It is worth noting that in Japan which is noted for her cultural tradition of "respect for the elderly," and where in fact elders are paid high regard in many aspects of social life, the attitudes toward aging and old people seem to be more negative than in the United States regardless of generation.[9]

The emerging picture of family life in the United States, as clarified by research, is one of separate households for all but the very old or sick, while at the same time maintaining a complex pattern of family relationships that are viable and supportive. As an early observer, Sussman called this the "modified and extended" family system in which the nuclear family is not isolated but is part of "an extended kin-family system, highly integrated within a network of social relationships and mutual assistance that operates along bilateral kin lines and vertically over several generations."[10]

Even earlier, Litwak defined the modified extended family in relation to what he called the "classical extended" and nuclear types:

[It] differs from the "classical extended" family in that it does not demand geographical propinquity, occupational involvement, or nepotism, nor does it have an hierarchical authority structure. On the other hand, it differs from the isolated nuclear family structure in that it does provide significant continuing aid to the nuclear family.[11]

Aid to older persons takes the form of economic help, household services, living arrangements with families when this is imperative, and affection and companionship. Brothers, sisters, children, grandchildren, aunts, uncles—even nephews, nieces, and cousins—may be involved in the flow of mutual aid. When families do not offer help to their older members, a whole range of personal, social, and economic forces are usually at work rather than a simple attitude of neglect and abandonment.

Many studies over the years have verified the continuing existence of strong family ties in the United States and elsewhere. A 1959 World Health Organization report stated:

Wherever careful studies have been carried out in the industrialized countries, the lasting devotion of children for their parents has been amply demonstrated. The great majority of old people are in regular contact with their children, relatives, or friends. . . . Where distance permits, the generations continue to shoulder their traditional obligations, of the elders toward their children, and the children to the aged.[12]

Townsend, in England in 1965, found that the families of institutionalized aged showed "much more evidence of genuine affection and loyalty than the reverse. . . ."[13]

Studies indicate that the majority of older people choose independent living quarters with a spouse or alone as long as this is possible and then expect to move in with family members when their health or financial situation deteriorates. Approximately three out of every ten older people in the United States currently live alone. Most of these are single, widowed, or divorced, and a large proportion are women. Many have children but prefer to live apart from them. A greater proportion of the very old (over 80) live with family members because of declining capacities. Unmarried people in frail health may live with siblings or friends.

In commenting on intergenerational ties, Shanas observed in 1980:

While the proportion of old people who live with their children has decreased over the last 20 years, the proportion living close to children has increased substantially. In 1975, the proportion of old people living in the same household with one of their children was 18 percent. [By 1985 this proportion had declined to 13%.] Thirty-four percent of all persons over 65 with children, however, live apart from children, but within 10 minutes distance from at least one of them. As a result, in 1975, half of all people with children (52 percent) lived either in the same household with a child, or next door, down the street, or a few blocks away. Old people who live alone are commonly considered a particularly vulnerable group among the elderly. Yet, among those old people who have children and who live alone, half are within 10 minutes distance of a child.[14]

A number of more recent studies continue to confirm the existence of active and viable family supports.[15] In New York City, Mary Mayer, Director of Research for the Department of Aging, reported in 1989 that:

> Eighty percent of the City's elderly have children and two-thirds of this group have at least one child who lives very nearby. Almost a third have a child a few hours away. Moreover, almost all elderly who have children (95 percent) are in at least weekly telephone contact with them and nearly two-thirds receive weekly visits from children.
>
> Additionally, most elderly (92 percent) say they have someone to care for them should they need help for a few days. However, if the days grow into weeks, significantly fewer (85 percent) will have someone to assist them. Not surprisingly, those living alone or without children tend to be less likely to have assistance.[16]

Shanas believes that the "myth of alienation" or the notion of families abandoning their elderly has been created and perpetuated by two groups: *professional workers* in the field of aging, who tend to see those older persons who do not have sufficient family supports, and *childless old people,* who constitute one-fifth of all older people and are likely to believe that the aged are neglected by their children. For most elderly, however, Shanas sees the family as a "safe harbor" where the elderly have a role in old age and a haven in time of need.

Evidence has begun accumulating that ethnic and racial minorities such as African Americans, Hispanic Americans, and Asian Americans make even heavier use of extended kin and friendship networks because of generally more limited economic resources and also because of ongoing cultural traditions.[17]

There is, of course, no doubt that elder neglect and abuse exist in some families, as will be discussed in Chapter 7. The "battered older person" syndrome is the most shocking form of such abuse; verbal disparagement and cruelty are more common.

Living independently from relatives can be demonstrated to be a sign of medical and economic advances rather than family neglect. Markson reports a striking decline in past years in the proportion of those elders over age 75 who are living with relatives. This is partly due to greater longevity, resulting in more married persons who are still living with their spouses. But another factor is the greater tendency of older women to live alone, probably as a result of an increased economic capacity to do so.[18]

"Filial" Economic Responsibility

Filial responsibility includes more than just law and custom, since it refers also to personal attitudes of responsibility toward parents: the ethical and emotional responses of adult children toward their mothers and fathers.[19] Historically, grown children were held totally accountable for the care of their parents under medieval church law; it was not until the Elizabethan Poor Law that the concept of community assistance was introduced. However, families were expected to do everything they could before receiving outside help. During the early part of the twentieth century, filial responsibility versus a wider societal responsibility began to be tested to a greater degree. There were greater numbers of older people, sometimes two generations of them in one family, and the preindustrial, agricultural society was disappearing. In its place came industrialization, separating wages from the ownership of the means of production. Older people no longer had the power of ownership of land, tools, and animals or the sustenance of the agricultural community; therefore they became more vulnerable economically as they aged. Their children were forced to take on more responsibility for them or look to the larger society, especially government, for assistance.

Social Security, beginning in 1935 in the United States, provided basic economic maintenance for increasing numbers of older people. Instead of individual families supporting their own older members, Social Security was predicated on the concept of intergenerational support whereby the entire middle- and younger-aged generations in the labor force support the older generation. Financial insurance for health care under Medicare and the state-federal program of welfare assistance for health care, namely Medicaid, began in 1965, supplanting earlier federal-state and local health-care financing programs for the aged. Supplementary Security Income in 1972 brought the poor aged, who had been receiving "welfare" income transfers under Old-Age Assistance, under the umbrella of the Social Security Administration.

The results of these programs are obvious. For example, a survey of 17,000 U.S. households (the Survey of Income and Program Participation [SIPP]), conducted by the Bureau of the Census in 1985 (the most recent data available), examined the number of persons who were regularly making cash payments for the support of persons not living with them in their households. (Noncash transfers such as food, clothing, or services to individuals were not included.) Of about 2.9 million adults who received financial help from someone outside their households, about one-third were older parents of adult children. (Remember that there were altogether about 29 million persons aged 65 or over.) The average support payment was $1,484 annually. This study demonstrates that financial cash support is now relatively uncommon, and when it does exist, it is usually modest. As would be expected, persons with higher incomes ($45,000 or over) were much more likely (three times more likely) to be supporting their parents financially than persons with incomes under $15,000.[20]

Older persons, age 65 or older, constitute about 7% of all adults who provide cash help to others, and 94% of these elderly are supporting other adults. In fact, old people often support other old people. About one-half of all financially dependent persons in nursing homes who received cash help from others received that help from persons—usually a noninstitutionalized spouse—who were themselves 65 years of age or over. The

other half received help from their adult children. The average amount of cash help for nursing home care was $2,886 annually.[21]

The SIPP study did not examine a major form of help in U.S. family support networks: the noncash goods and personal services given by the old to the young and by the young to the old. Examples are the caregiving (known to be substantial) of young children by older grandmothers and the caregiving of the elderly by family members, usually wives of elderly men and daughters and daughters-in-law. A major methodological problem has been both a reluctance as well as a very real difficulty in quantifying such care (classified generally as "housework") and then placing a monetary value on it. Such a methodology began to be developed by the National Center of Health Statistics, under the leadership of Dorothy Rice, for the purpose of determining costs of illness.[22] Morgan also attempted a measurement and valuation of time spent in various forms of inter-family and intra-family transfers of help, based on a 1980 Panel Study of Income Dynamics at the Survey Research Center, University of Michigan at Ann Arbor. His data indicated that affluent families are more likely to send money to needy elderly relatives, while less affluent, larger families are more likely to invite the elderly to share their home as their way of helping.[23]

Morgan's work suggests a number of other interesting points:

1. Measurements of family or individual well-being ideally must include some estimation of the value of time spent or received in the form of housework, child care, and elder care in order to accurately reflect available resources. The value of such time should be seen as part of the total real income of the family or individual, together with labor income, other taxable and nontaxable income, and cash and noncash transfer payments such as Social Security, pensions, food stamps, and so forth.

2. Overall, in family life, women are the major providers of time, while men and children are the beneficiaries; however, with time contributions to the elderly, although the providers are still likely to be women, the beneficiaries are also likely to be women, albeit elderly women. The reason lies in the fact that women outlive men.

3. Contributions of time to others often come at a real cost to the provider of that time, namely a loss of leisure, an increase in stress, a decline in health, and so on. Caregiver exhaustion and burnout can result.

4. After considering both time and money transfers between and among family members, it is clear that there is still real sharing in our society. "The growth of public transfer systems has not supplanted all of the old private altruism or extended family responsibilities." In fact, according to Morgan, "We have not 'socialized' the responsibility for dependent members of society as far as we might think; families remain responsible for most of the burden."[24]

A major new role for families is that of intermediaries and advocates for the elderly as they negotiate their way through state, federal, and local bureaucracies. However, although the Social Security Administration and other governmental agencies are necessarily providing financial support and services for older persons, some financial policies still reflect the earlier traditions of total filial or family responsibility. The "responsible relative" clause in many state welfare programs is the most obvious example. Although seldom enforced, more than half of the states still have laws that could be used to require children to provide financial help to needy parents. Such requirements, if enforced, would result in many families having to deny other family members' needs, including children, in order to finance an older person's care. Family savings could easily be completely used up in a single bout of illness, endangering the family's future. Much painful pauperization of spouses of older persons has already been brought about by the "spend-down" requirement to gain Medicaid coverage for nursing homes and home care. (See Chapters 10 and 11.)

Family responsibility laws are questionable from a civil liberties perspective because of the potential for arbitrary and capricious enforcement. But more practically, with two generations of elderly, the young-old and the old-old, present in more and more families, the younger generations simply cannot afford to be financially "responsible" relatives to all, especially when even one long-term or catastrophic illness can deplete most families' financial resources. The remaining financial burdens of care, mostly for long-term care of the elderly, should be removed from families so that they can attend to the many other emotional and personal needs of older people. Ongoing efforts to provide public or public/private financing for long-term institutional and home care is expected to eventually succeed.

One of the fears of public policymakers is that liberalization of federal benefits such as Medicare home care might lead to an abandonment of older persons by families already providing support. Thus there would be a "raid on the federal treasury" or a "woodwork effect," with families seemingly coming "out of the woodwork" to claim services and supports, withdrawing their own usual supports in the meantime. However, experiences of other nations that offer such assistance do not confirm this fear.

In Denmark, older persons are completely independent financially from their children because of the comprehensive welfare structure; yet they maintain a high degree of interaction and mutuality with their families in every other respect. Old people are not dependent on the politics of potentially emotion-laden family largess for necessary services. Instead, the interaction with family members is voluntary, based on mutual interest and emotional interdependence. In Norway, another country with no financial family-responsibility laws, even for long-term care, the continued involvement of family members, particularly women, is so obvious that it has been called "the hidden welfare state,"—a complex, family-run system of provision of an array of services and supports.[25]

Cherlin is optimistic about family relations that do not include financial responsibilities. He suggests the hypothesis that "the relations between the elderly and their adult children tend to be more emotionally satisfying—closer, warmer, more loving, and more affectionate—when neither generation is economically dependent on the other."[26] He believes this condition is more possible in the present than in our nation's past. In colonial America, the elderly controlled most of society's resources, and the relations between the generations were "correct but cold," as the middle-aged and young contended with financial dependency and the power and authority of the old.[27]

Sussman postulates that providing "back up supports," especially economic and health care assistance to care-giving kin and other caregivers, could serve to strengthen family and friendship support to the elderly, particularly among potential caregivers who are not yet giving care. These latter might move into the home-care or service-provider role if given financial assistance and supports to do so.[28]

Are Older People "Dumped" into Institutions?

The image of Americans "dumping" their elderly into nursing homes is another of the myths that confuse the realities of life in old age. (Remember that only 5% of those over the age of 65 are in nursing homes or other institutions.) There are, of course, some families who abandon their responsibilities to older family members by placing them prematurely and precipitously in institutions. More commonly, isolated older people without families may be institutionalized when they become ill or feeble, simply because there is no other place for them to go. For example, in New York City, 7% of the elderly have no living children or siblings. Friends and neighbors may provide supports to some, but these elderly are essentially without immediate family support.[29]

Most people who have families move in with their relatives when they can no longer live independently. Institutional care is reserved as the last recourse after everything else has been tried. Families will often go through unbelievable hardship before deciding on placement. The following is a letter we received from a son seeking help for his mother:

> My 84-year-old mother lives with me in my four-room apartment. Her senility has become worse and she is totally confused, unable to sit still, care for herself, or even remain continent. Three years ago I had to quit my job in order to stay home with her, as she used to wander the streets and get lost. I live on my savings; I am unmarried. I am 52 years old, still unemployed and have passed up two good jobs. I am at my wit's end. What should I do? I love the poor woman. But I cannot enjoy life at all. What is the best thing for her? And me?

Ideally, families should have a whole range of services to assist them in keeping the older person at home, including economic aid (see Chapter 10 on home care). But when the burden becomes too great, institutional care may be necessary and appropriate—and such care should be reliable, therapeutic, and reasonably priced. (Chapter 11 discusses institutional care in greater detail.)

OLDER PEOPLE AS PARENTS

Parent–child interactions in late life have focused primarily on how adult children meet the needs of their older parents (filial responsibility and filial maturity). It is curious that we have shown so little attention to the ways in which elderly parents relate to and meet the needs of their adult children. This no doubt reflects the lagging societal appreciation of the contribution of the elderly. Older parents are parents until either their own death or that of their children; many now live to see their own children grow old. One-fourth of women who were age 60 in 1980 still had living mothers.[30]

What role do these older parents play? One view is that they become "emeritus parents," with older women, especially, managing and monitoring extended families.[31] Hagestad calls such women the "ministers of the interior."[32] The female pattern of greater emphasis on interpersonal intimacy and "kin-building" would seem logically related to a major yet unacknowledged role in providing supports to younger generations. And if Gutmann is correct that men move toward greater interpersonal sensitivity and interaction in old age, they may be playing such a role as well.

Hagestad comments on how little is known about parenting over time and muses about whether "parenting styles" are stable throughout life or are subject to individual or predictable changes.[33]

GRANDPARENTHOOD, GREAT-GRANDPARENTHOOD, AND GREAT-GREAT-GRANDPARENTHOOD

Longer lives have increased the likelihood of families with three, four, or even five generations. Increased survivorship is a result of fewer women dying in childbirth, fewer children dying of childhood disease, fewer infants dying in utero or at birth, and fewer older people dying of infections. Modern medicine and improved public health measures can be thanked for these life-giving contributions. Almost one-half of all persons 65 and over with living children are members of four-generation families. A sizable number of persons over 65 years of age have one or two living parents. About one out of ten older people has a child over 65. In fact, aging parents may have their aging children living with them, rather than vice versa. It is not uncommon to see parents in their eighties caring for aging and ailing children in their sixties.

Reliable nationwide figures for the number of older people with living children and grandchildren (and those older persons with living parents) are not available. These questions have not been included in any known U.S. census survey or other large representative sampling. Such important data are necessary to evaluate the amount of potential family support an older person has available. In a national survey by Shanas, nearly three-fourths of those studied who were 80 and above were great-grandparents, as were one-fourth of those 65 to 66. These figures are increasing, with the continual improvement in life expectancy and a decreasing fertility rate.[34]

All in all, an estimated three-fourths of adults will live to be grandparents.[35] Of the four-fifths of persons over 65 with living children, 94% are grandparents (three generations) and 46% are great-grandparents (four generations). A proportion are also great-great-grandparents (five generations). One 1986 survey estimates that overall there are 49 million U.S. grandparents, great-grandparents, and great-great-grandparents.[36] (See Table 2.3 for ages of grandparents and grand-children.) The following reveals how the chances of being a grandparent have increased dramatically:

> Studies show that in 1920 only four out of five children at the age of 10 were apt to have one living grandparent whereas 50 years later 19 out of 20 were apt to. In 1920 the chance of a 10-year-old child having at least two grandparents alive was two in five. In 1970 it was three in four. The chance of a 10-year-old having at least three living grandparents has risen from one in ten to three in eight. The chance of having all four has gone from one in 90 to one in 14. (These figures pertain to white children.)[37]

The duration of grandparenthood is growing. Many will be grandparents for 30, 40, or more years, eventually adding great-grandparenthood and, possibly, great-great-grandparenthood to the repertoire of family roles. Some have suggested that there may already be more great-grandparents currently alive than there were grandparents at the turn of the century. In contrast to the growing duration of grandparenthood, grandparents have fewer grandchildren today (an average of three

TABLE 2.3 Modern grandparents

AGES OF GRANDPARENTS		WITH GRANDCHILDREN AGES	
35–44 years	6.4%	Under 1 year	22%
45–49	10.1	1–2	27
50–54	10.8	3–5	42
55–64	34.9	6–11	47
65+	37.8	12–15	30
		16–21	28
		Adults	20

Source: Meredith Corporation, 1987.

grandchildren) compared to 1900 (an average of 12 to 15 grandchildren). Grandparenthood, like many of the other aspects of late life, has received only meager research attention, primarily in the form of small pilot studies, which may or may not be generalizable to grandparents as a whole. But they do add intriguing pieces of clarifying information about a function so familiar to us.

Early psychoanalytic interpretations of grandparenthood were rather grim and villainous, reflecting patriarchal values. Ferenczi pictured the grandfather as either an imposing, authoritarian old man who frightened and challenged his grandchild or a helpless, feeble person who invited the grandchild's disparagement because he was weak and near death.[38] Ferenczi conceded that boy children may learn about death for the first time through contacts with grandfathers, but he viewed this essentially in an Oedipal context as an opportunity to learn a new way of getting rid of father.

Grandmothers likewise received stern treatment historically from scholars and practitioners (for example, Abraham, 1955). A zealous social worker defending children from the evils of grandmothers wrote an article in 1942 titled "Grandma Made Johnny Delinquent," in which the author argued that grandparents "interfering with the raising of a child" should be removed from the home. LaBarre, Jessner, and Ussery (1960) wrote in the same vein in their paper, "The Significance of Grandmothers in the Psychopathology of Children."[39]

In 1958, Rappaport warned of the possible "detrimental effect" of grandparents living in the home of their children. Such a living arrangement "infantilized the parents and created feelings of omnipotence in the grandchild if the grandparent is also weak. In addition, grotesque and bizarre character traits are apt to develop [in grandchildren] because of grandparental identification."[40]

Others were more positive. Haber wrote,

> Regarding grandparents, it is obvious that the grandparent can serve as a modulating function of significance in view of both their presence and concern and real position of objectivity and experience. They can fulfill and be fulfilled. The goal of

thoughtful involvement containing an appropriate degree of emotion by oldsters with their younger relative should be studied and encouraged.[41]

Contemporary evidence shows that grandparents, somewhat less than 10%, function as surrogate parents, and many of these have been lifesavers rather than evildoers in the lives of grandchildren.

Benedek identified the grandparent role as one available universally to most older people:

> Grandparenthood is a new lease on life because grandparents—grandmothers more intensely than grandfathers—relive the memories of the early phase of their own parenthood in observing the growth and development of their grandchildren. Grandparenthood is, however, parenthood one step removed. Relieved from the immediate stresses of motherhood and the responsibilities of fatherhood, grandparents appear to enjoy their grandchildren more than they enjoyed their own children. Their instinctual wish to survive being gratified, they project the hope of the fulfillment of their narcissistic self-image to their grandchildren. Since they do not have the responsibility for raising the child toward that unconscious goal, their love is not as burdened by doubts and anxieties as it was when their own children were young.[42]

Neugarten and Weinstein (1964) differentiated types of grandparents in their study of 70 middle-class, older couples: the formal grandparent, the "compassionate" or fun-seeker grandparent, the surrogate parent, the reservoir of family wisdom, and the distant figure who arrives only on holidays and family occasions. They found the fun-seeker and the distant figure most common of the types. It was noted that not all older people wanted the grandparent role or expressed satisfaction with it. Some felt exploited by their children (as babysitters, etc.); others expressed negative attitudes toward their own children through their grandchildren. Some joined forces with the young in secret struggles against the middle generation.

Kahana and Kahana (1970) studied grandparenthood from the grandchild's perspective (white, middle-class sample). The feelings of grandchildren depend on the amount of contact, grandparents' behavior toward them, parents' relationships with grandparents, and the child's perceptions of older people in general and grandparents in particular. Children's responses to grandparents change as the youngsters develop; very young children react to gifts, favors, and open affection, whereas slightly older ones prefer sharing activities and having mutual fun.

Some suggest that grandparents tend to feel closest to grandchildren when the children are between the ages of 3 and 12. But grandchildren also value and need their grandparents during adolescence, when rebellions against parents are common and emotional confusion is rampant. Grandparents can be a stable, accepting port in the storm, acting as counselors and confidants. Biological continuity, emotional self-fulfillment, vicarious accomplishment, teaching, and helping in various ways were some of the meaningful roles in grandparentage.

Grandparenthood now occurs in middle age as well as old age. The new longevity may produce uncertainty. The possible roles a grandparent can play are becoming more open to individual interpretation: "In a society where grandparents range from twenty-five years old to centenarians, and where grandchildren run the spectrum from infants to retirees, we should not be surprised to find that cultural images of grandparenthood harbor both variety and uncertainty."[43]

When grandparents have power and responsibility (as in the role of surrogate parents), they are likely to be more formal and perhaps authoritarian. But when removed from responsibility, they tend to be indulgent, enjoying the grandchildren but not feeling burdened. (Even the travel industry has begun to focus on doting grandparents. Organizations like Grandtravel, a division of the Ticket Counter, 6900 Wisconsin Ave., Chevy Chase, Maryland 20815 (301) 986-0790, and Vistatours' Grandparents and Grandchildren's Tours (a division of Frontier Tours) (702) 882-2100, 1923 N. Carson, Carson City, Nevada 89701, arrange special tours for grandparents and their grandchildren.) Some volunteer to be surrogate grandparents to other people's children, as in the Foster Grandparent Program. Youthful grand-

parents may avoid any element of the traditional grandparent role, preferring to be called by their first names and functioning as friends. The image of the white-haired, elderly grandpa and grandma may eventually have to be reserved for great-grandparents.

The "safety-valve" or indirect stabilizing function of grandparents is an intriguing one. Hagestad suggests that one must look beyond the *actual* contribution of the elderly to the young and examine the *potential* contributions that could be drawn on in case of illness, divorce, inflation, desertion, and other crises and emergencies. This potential may never be used, but because it is there, the younger generation may be less restrained in their life choices and feel a greater sense of personal security.[44]

Grandparenthood undoubtedly also has an impact on the mental health of grandparents themselves. The grandparent role has potential for continuing delight as well as for ongoing bitterness; for satisfaction as well as disappointment. Kivnick has attempted to formulate a model to measure the emotional impact of grandparenthood on individual grandparents as well as to suggest "self-help" mechanisms that might make the grandparent role more fulfilling.[45]

There is a growing need to look at the impact of rising divorce rates and single parent families on grandparents' roles. (Marital breakup and remarriage are not new phenomena in the United States. What is new is that these now occur largely because of divorce whereas in the past they were caused by high death rates, particularly high maternal mortality.) Nearly 28% of the nation's 67 million children under 18 years of age lived with only one of their parents in 1994. Thirty-seven percent of these children lived with a divorced parent, 18% with a separated parent, 36% with a parent who had never been married, 4% with a widowed parent, and 4% with a parent whose spouse was absent for reasons other than marital divorce.[46] About 72% of children lived with two parents: Of this group, 82% lived with both biological parents, 15% with their biological mother and stepfather, and 1% with their biological father and stepmother.[47]

There is evidence that divorce, and probably single parenthood as well, tend to intensify grandparent–grandchild relationships on the maternal side (since most children live with their mothers, and these mothers tend to remain close to their own mothers). Conversely, there is often a weakening of relations on the paternal side, unless the children's father makes successful efforts to remain positively involved, thereby increasing the likelihood that his parents' role as grandparents is welcomed by the children's mother.[48] It is clear that the quality of the grandparents' relationships with their divorcing children and in-laws is critical since it is the adult children, particularly those who have custody of the grandchildren, who act as the mediators between grandparents and grandchildren. Matthews and Sprey expand on this point, namely that to understand the impact of divorce on the grandparent role, one must understand the dynamics of the extended family relationships with each other. For example, the position of grandparents is strengthened if they control resources that are important to the parents of their grandchildren, such as a family business or property. If this is not the case, their position is less secure and they must rely on the goodwill of the middle generation in maintaining contacts with grandchildren.[49]

Since the 1970s, all states have passed laws providing some kind of protection for grandparents' rights to interact with grandchildren after divorce. In most states, grandparents can petition courts for visitation rights in case of divorce, separation, or widowhood of the adult children. The court then determines if it is in the best interest of the child to allow the grandparents to visit. The state of Illinois has gone furthest, allowing that same right of petition to grandparents when the child's parents are still married and are refusing contact with grandparents. Some states encourage mediation or family therapy to work out grandchildren contacts that are mutually agreeable to all. Groups have formed to represent grandparents.

Divorce of adult children may also pose a threat to grandparents' retirement plans specifically or to the financial or emotional well-being

of the elderly generally. Family disruption of all kinds may place grandparents, especially grandmothers, in the position of rescuers. For example, the drug epidemic of crack in the Harlem community of New York City has brought many middle-aged and older grandmothers into active mothering roles for grandchildren.

OLDER MARRIED COUPLES

The "postparental" period (after the children have grown up and gone) of life for older couples has been extended because of greater longevity, generally earlier marriage, and fewer children. In 1890 the last child married an average of two years *after* the death of one of the parents; in 1950 the last child married 13 to 14 years *before* the death of one parent.[50] Most parents have completed childrearing by their late forties and early fifties, leaving them an average of 13 years alone together, or one-third of their entire married life. In 1994, 55.1% of the nation's 28.5 million persons 65 years and over were married and living with their spouses. However, the pattern of men and women is quite different. Both sexes are highly likely to marry when young. But men are more likely than women to be married throughout life. In 1994, 81% of men aged 55 to 64 were married, as were 80% of men aged 65 to 74 and 72% of men 75 and older. In striking contrast, while 69% of women aged 55 to 64 were married, only 54% of those aged 65 to 74 and 28% of those aged 75 and older were married. Most of this is due to longer life expectancy for women and thus an increased chance of widowhood.[51]

Care during illness, household management, and emotional gratification are three expectations found in older marriages. The older couple married for many years will find they have a different marriage in old age than they had in middle or early life. Each of them has been changing and experiencing life individually as well as together. They may have grown more different or more alike. Conflicts between them can intensify or dissipate as they age, with more tolerance or, on the other hand, more rigidity in their expectations of each other. Some researchers have maintained that there is a degree of deterioration in up to one-third of older marital relationships.[52] But that also means that two-thirds are doing well.

Studies of marriage in old age, particularly marital satisfaction, have been criticized on both conceptual and methodological grounds. Data have been largely cross-sectional; but longitudinal studies are enormously expensive and time-consuming.[53] Further, it is difficult to assess an adult in his or her total environment because the circumstances are much more complicated than those of a child. Many more people, life experiences, accidental happenings, stresses, losses, and accomplishments are involved, and prediction of eventual individual outcome is precarious. It requires an innocent and hopeful faith to promise in marital vows to love and honor someone "until death do us part," for in 20, 30, or 40 years the partner one married may have become quite a different human being. Men who married "sweet young things" may not accept the fact that women age just as they themselves do. Women who doted on their roles as wives and mothers may rebel at the thought of being nursemaid to an ailing and aging husband. Of course there are people who expect and accept change with dignity and constructive response, having reached maturity with relatively few personality handicaps that would impede adaptability. Environmental influences, physical and mental health, and the historical period of time in which one is living are other variables affecting marriages over a long span of time.

Divorce in old age received little attention in gerontological literature until recently, probably because late-life divorce was relatively uncommon. In the past, divorce was more easily risked in youth or middle age when resources and options were greater. Children and grandchildren served as a strong bond between marital partners. Couples who reached old age together usually adapted to each other in a way that each found supportive or at least more acceptable than the uncertain world of divorce and the disapproval of society.[54]

In 1990, about 32,000 people aged 65 and older divorced in the U.S.[55] Those 65 and older

account for about 1% of all divorces in the United States in a year (remembering that the elderly are 13% of the population), and only about 6% of all persons age 65 and over are divorced. Even during the overall rapid increase of divorce during the 1970s and 1980s, late-life divorce showed little change. But the situation may begin to shift. In the future, divorce may become more common as women enter old age with greater economic resources of their own, making them less economically dependent on their husbands.[56]

Most older marriages are broken by death rather than divorce. In 1994, 33% of those over 65 were widowed, while only 6% were divorced.[57] African American and Hispanic elderly are more likely to be widowed, divorced, or separated, reflecting both a lower life expectancy and greater economic pressures. Older people can become intensely dependent on each other for intimacy, personal services, and mutual support. A major psychological blow then occurs when one partner dies. As we have said before, factors of the immediate environment are very closely related to the older person's behavior and attitudes, with significant persons being the most important of these factors. Thus, in general, divorce is more likely to occur before old age, if it is to occur at all, and older married couples seem to perceive threats to themselves emanating from outside the marital relationship as more significant than those from within. It might be said that marriage becomes a more valued human relationship by the very fact of powerful outside forces and eventual death. When so many other losses are occurring naturally, marriage may be one of the more familiar and comfortable patterns remaining.

Older marriages, although less likely to dissolve, may have problems that carry over from the past or develop as a result of current stress.

Mr. and Mrs. H had been married 40 years. They had arrived at serious disagreements and mistrust early in the marriage but had stayed together because of the children. They reached a state of truce in which there was as little contact between them as possible. Mr. H obtained employment that required him to travel about 80% of the time. For 30 years he devoted his energy and interest to his work and to impermanent, extramarital relationships. After retirement at 65, he returned to their loveless home.

He became depressed and thought often of death. Finally he developed numerous hypochondriacal symptoms, which occupied his time and energy in much the same manner as had his former job. He and Mrs. H continue to live together, each obviously unwilling to leave the other.

A common difficulty in older marriages is the disequilibrium caused by the physical or emotional illness of either spouse. Major chronic changes occurring with dementia, for example, can drastically alter the marital relationship. One partner may become the caretaker or nursemaid of the other, often with little help from elsewhere. Illnesses can drain the physical, emotional, and financial capacities of the caretaker spouse. Anger and depression may occur, and it is not unusual to find the formerly well spouse developing physical or psychiatric symptoms of his or her own.

Patterns of dominance may shift in old age, with the female assuming a more active and responsible role than formerly.[58] Many of today's older persons were brought up in a male-dominant, female-subordinate culture. But with shorter life expectancies for men and their practice of marrying women younger than themselves, they are usually older than their mates and consequently less capable physically. As early as 1960 Gold, in studying age and sex patterns of familial dominance in 24 preliterate societies, found a shift to female dominance in later life in 14 of these. She stated, "Although old women did not gain the upper hand in all societies studied, aging in no instance led to the husband's gaining in authority."[59] She suggested that husbands may be willing to accept female domination as the price of security as they age. Women, having been deprived of equal cultural status all their lives, may greatly enjoy the opportunity to exert their influence. Unfortunately their taste of greater autonomy and independence is frequently mitigated by the need to provide nursing services to husbands who become dependent and infirm more quickly. When their husbands die, women's hard-won role of greater influence and control over their lives depends on a number of factors such as health, economic circumstances, and living conditions. In the future, mutuality and greater equality (for example, in sex roles and age of marriage) throughout life may produce less extreme patterns and carry over to a more consistently mutual relationship in old age.

There seems to be some interdependence between the life spans of husband and wife. In addition, a comprehensive study of 16 industrial countries' death rates back to the 1940s concludes that married people live longer than unmarried people.[60] This may be a result of selection (healthy people may select other healthy people as partners, while frailer men and women may not marry) or to the marital environment itself, which is posited as encouraging a moderate, temperate life. Suicide rates are also lower for married men and higher for divorced. Further studies will attempt to clarify why marriage is beneficial and nonmarriage, whether single or divorced, is hazardous, especially for men. In old age the mutual aid and support in a marriage may become the crucial factor in the health of each partner, just as depression and loss of support after the death of a spouse can contribute to the deterioration of the surviving partner's health, particularly for males.

For many older men, the maintenance of closeness with a spouse is the center of existence up to the very end of life. As we have seen, this is less true for women, for whom remarriage after widowhood or divorce is less likely. However, remarriage, after death or divorce of a spouse, does occur with some frequency. In 1990 some 71,000 older persons married in the United States—about 25,000 women and 46,000 men 65 years of age and over. Older males are more likely to remarry than older females for two reasons: They have a larger pool of partners from which to choose (since women outlive men), and they have a long cultural history of marrying younger women as well as their own age peers. However, although there are May–December marriages in which an older man marries a much younger woman, marriages between people of approximately the same age are more usual.

Children from an earlier marriage may or may not welcome the new union. Their negative attitudes may be voiced strongly, particularly if they believe a parent is being taken advantage of, is acting foolishly, or is endangering their inheritance; on the other hand, children may actively encourage parents to find new lives for themselves through remarriage. McKain, in an early study, found that success of late-life marriage is related to the following factors: the children encouraged the marriage, the couple knew each other a number of years before marriage, there was sufficient income, the couple pooled financial resources, and both were reasonably satisfied with their lives.[61] Common sense would lead one to believe these factors still hold true.

It is interesting to note that very few people marry for the first time in old age. The entire pool of never-marrieds is very small. For example, in 1994, some 94% of women and 92% of men in the 45–54 age group had been married at some point in their lives.[62] After age 75, only 4% of men and 5% of women had never been married.

IN-LAWS

Sooner or later almost everyone becomes an in-law. Each person who marries receives an average of six members of the spouse's family as in-laws. In the public mind, "in-law" means "trouble," especially if it happens to be a mother-in-law closely involved with her son's or daughter's life. When a mother-in-law "problem" exists, it partly stems from the cultural encouragement of competition among women from the time they are small girls for the attention of men. Added to this are the stresses facing the older woman because of her longer life span and low social status. Overinvolvement with children is another possible factor. But the entire problem is very likely exaggerated, since numbers of people manage to get along reasonably and often superbly well with in-laws, including mothers-in-law. In-laws can be supportive as well as trouble-making. Personality factors are probably as critical as social roles in determining the quality of in-law relationships.

SIBLINGS

The siblings of older persons, particularly those older persons who are widowed or living alone, play a relatively invisible, but frequently vital role in maintaining a sense of family, connectedness, and well-being. There is little written on this subject in the field of gerontology, leading one to speculate on why such an obvious and often life-sustaining and life-enhancing set of relationships has been overlooked. Since female siblings assume the major role in tending and preserving these relationships, has their role been overlooked as insignificant or taken for granted, as has been the case in much of our recent history with housework, caregiving to children and the elderly, and other traditionally female-designated activities? Rosenthal's study of *kinkeeping* (defined as the person in an extended family who fosters family interactions and rituals) found that female siblings were most likely to play this role, usually during their 50s and 60s. The role was most likely to be assumed by a sister sibling after the illness or death of the clan mother. Thus, female siblings often play a critical role in keeping male siblings connected to the family and in providing them with supports when needed.[63]

Cicirelli comments on a number of important points surrounding sibling-ship:

1. Sibling relationships last longer than most other relationships, beginning at birth and continuing until the death of a sibling.

2. The sibling relationship can apply to step-siblings, half-siblings, and adoptive siblings, as well as biological siblings.

3. The uniqueness of sibling relationships includes not only their long duration, but also their typically egalitarian nature, their common cultural and, often, common genetic heritage, and, frequently, their common early experiences from childhood.

4. Even most of the advanced elderly currently have at least one living sibling. A 1975 national survey found eight out of ten old people had living siblings (75-year-olds came from families with an average of five children). Those who were unmarried had closer bonds with their siblings and many lived in the same house.[64]

5. Sibling contact tends to renew itself in late middle age (perhaps connected with more leisure time and with intimations of mortality) and then gradually declines with age as siblings become more infirm and contact becomes more difficult. But even then, most continue to write, talk on the phone, visit when possible, or send messages through kin.

6. Sister siblings are the closest affectionately, and brother siblings are least close.

7. Brother and sister siblings tend to become closer as they grow older.

8. Sisters do most of the tending of sibling and other family relationships. Some suggest that one reason women invest more time and energy in kinkeeping may be enlightened self-interest, namely the realization that most of them will outlive their husbands and require supports from others. (It is not uncommon for five-generation families to have three generations of widows.) But it is also clear that human relationships have a higher priority for females, whether culturally or biologically derived, from childhood on.

9. Rivalry between siblings tends to decline with age, although some rivalries manage to persist to the bitter end or reappear under stress. The more common pattern, however, is for siblings to mellow or to work actively to repair their relationships.

10. Some of the strength of the sibling bond arises from the joint sibling experience of loss of parents through death and the desire to maintain a sense of the childhood family.[65]

Rising divorce rates and similar family restructurings may make sibling relationships even more meaningful as a source of emotional support and stability in the future. On the other hand, an increase in one-child families will lessen the possibility of having a sibling. The impact of these demographic changes on what has long been a major, but seldom fully acknowledged support in old age deserves further study.

FRIENDSHIP

Friends are considered "family" by many older persons, adding to the extended support system that protects an older person in times of illness or other need. The definition of friendship differs by age, sex, class, race, and ethnicity, but most elderly appear to choose friends near their own age, based largely on shared interests, experiences, and concerns. Such friendships contribute as much or more to the physical and emotional well-being of older persons as contacts with family members.[66]

Kinship and friendship often overlap. A relative may be defined foremost as a friend rather than a relative. Friends may be considered "part of the family" and may be referred to with titles like "aunt" or "uncle." Neighbors represent a special category of friend-potential and can be important for both socializing and day-to-day help. They may be especially helpful in emergencies and sudden illness because of their close proximity.

There is general agreement that female friendships are more likely to be intimate and emotionally self-disclosing, while males are more superficial—reflecting the larger social roles of males as more emotionally reserved and even repressed. Men are more likely to turn to their spouse for emotional intimacy, thus making them exceptionally vulnerable to loss of a spouse in old age. Research is beginning to indicate that one reason for greater female longevity may be women's skills in seeking and maintaining friendships. "Network analysis" has been an effective research technique in uncovering and clarifying friendship patterns and their meaning in old age.[67]

OLDER "ISOLATES" VERSUS "DESOLATES"

Isolates, as we are defining it here, refer to individuals who have minimal or no contact with other human beings. Some people become isolated in old age because of life circumstances and would choose to live differently if they could.

Others isolate themselves by choice, often fol-lowing a lifelong pattern of existence as "loners." Townsend distinguishes between "isolates" and "desolates":

Those who are secluded from family and society, as objectively assessed on the basis of defined criteria, are the isolates. Those who have been recently de-prived by death, illness or migration of someone they love—such as a husband or wife or child—are the desolates. A major conclusion of the present analysis is that though the two are connected, the underlying reason for loneliness in old age is deso-lation rather than isolation."68

The emotional meaning of isolation depends on whether it is a habitual life-style or whether it has come about or been exacerbated by emotional loss.

Shanas made much the same point when she commented that isolation is not synonymous with loneliness, nor is it a direct causative factor in mental illness.[69] Some older people have lived alone so long they have lost the notion of what loneliness means. Shanas found that the loneliest and most isolated people appear to be those wid-owed persons who have no children and live alone. On the other hand, isolation and loneliness of people are not necessarily relieved by closeness of children or frequent contact with them. In this case, isolation is a state of mind rather than actual social alienation.

Attempting to explain the fact that a greater number of single or widowed people over 65 are admitted to mental hospitals, as compared to mar-ried people, Shanas believed the blame cannot be placed on social isolation. Instead, she postulated that serious illnesses can devastate the person who is alone because there is no one to care for him or her; thus continuation in the community becomes impossible, whereas this would not be the case for someone with family or friends. Lowenthal, in tracing the connection between social isolation and mental illness in old age, found:

Lifelong extreme isolation (or alienation) is not nec-essarily conducive to the development of the kinds of mental disorder that bring persons to the psychi-

atric ward in their old age; lifelong marginal social adjustment may be conducive to the development of such disorder; late-developing isolation is appar-ently linked with mental disorder but it is of no greater significance among those with psychogenic disorders than among those with organic disorders, and may be more of a consequence than a cause of mental illness in the elderly; finally, physical illness may be the critical antecedent to both the isolation and the mental illness.70

The choice to be a loner must be respected. As we have seen, people who isolate themselves are not all frail, dependent, lonely persons. We must be able to differentiate this group from those older people who truly want and need assistance in making changes in their lives. Above all, both lon-ers and those isolated unwillingly by circum-stance should have the help they require in order to maintain the kind of life most satisfactory to them.

INHERITANCE AND THE FAMILY

The issue of who gets the inheritance, if there is any, is a sensitive one for many families, and the manner in which this is handled is a good indica-tor of family problem solving. Some older people make their wills early and in secret. Others fully inform each child. For many people, making a will is such a painful process that it is put off and they die intestate (without a will). Children who are used to sharing with each other and who have re-solved their major conflicts with parents may be able to settle an estate amicably with no ill will. But for others this is precisely the time for angry, hurt, and disappointed feelings to come to the fore, and a royal battle ensues.

The making of a will can be therapeutic for several reasons. The older person, by his or her own action, takes the potential for conflict out of the hands of the children. The estate will be han-dled according to the parent's own wishes. The disposing of the burden of possessions through a will can free older people and simplify their lives; many give things away even before they die. The will tells a great deal about the relations of the legator to his or her legatees (children, charitable interests, etc.). The nature of wills varies according to the stage of life of the testator. For example, if one has young children, trusts may be set up. Selection of executors and trustees is important: The executor is appointed to execute the will; the trustees are persons or agents, such as a bank, holding legal title to property in order to administer it for a beneficiary.

In some states a person may make an oral or nuncupative will; in others a holographic will—one written in the testator's own handwriting and unwitnessed—is acceptable. Older people may need to know that there are two main classes of property: real and personal. The former refers to such immovable objects as land, houses, and trees. The latter includes all other kinds of property (called legacy). If no will has been made, the property descends to lawful heirs, as legally prescribed, or to the state. Property passes into the hands of the executor who sells it and divides the proceeds among the next of kin. If a will has been made and the person dies, the will must be probated, or proved to be authentic. The executor brings the will before the court (probate or surrogate's court), and any possible heir is given the opportunity to object to the probate of the will.

It is likely that the future will bring changes in laws of inheritance, since many question the right of ownership in fee simple—that is, absolute ownership—in a complex society providing many goods and services funded through public revenues.

The use of *prenuptial agreements* is a time-honored method, in most states, of allaying the fears of children when their parents remarry in old age. Such agreements also protect older people themselves by keeping their resources intact and unavailable to anyone but designated persons. Wealthy people are inclined to use prenuptial agreements even in earlier marriages to protect family estates. With people now living longer, with more late-life marriages, and with more inherited wealth, prenuptial agreements are increasingly common. Legal consultation is necessary. The agreement customarily describes what will

not be available to the opposite spouse. Trusts can be alternatives to prenuptial agreements.

FAMILY INVOLVEMENT IN MENTAL HEALTH CARE OF OLDER PERSONS

Family Caregiving

Twelve and a half percent of elderly people live with their children or other family members—6% of all older men and 17% of older women live with children or other family members. Such arrangements generally occur when the older person has become too infirm mentally or physically or too impoverished to live alone. Since most people move in with their relatives at an advanced age, the average length of their stay is not a long one because of death or serious illness requiring hospital or nursing care. But the actual length of caregiving for any one individual can range from days to years. In most instances the pattern is one of an older mother moving in with her daughter and family. The manner in which these two women relate is often the key to success or failure of the living arrangement. Many families manage the inevitable problems of caregiving and joint households quite well. Others experience mild to severe physical and/or emotional stress and financial hardship, which can turn family caregiving into a major challenge. Genuine affection combined with a sense of ethical responsibility motivates a high proportion of children to voluntarily assist their elderly parents. Others carry out what they perceive to be their "duty," in spite of conflicting emotional feelings. Care for an aged parent can, in fact, be one way of overcoming emotional ambivalence, resolving guilt, and even building a new relatedness. Family caregiving will be discussed further in Chapter 10.

Family Therapy

By now it should be clear that most older people are *not* alienated from their families; therefore one must go further and assume that any problems, crises, and changes affecting an older person also affect his or her family. The newly form-ing field of family therapy, begun in the 1950s, has recognized that the problems of older people have impact on the entire kinship network. How do adult siblings work out a division of labor in caring for older parents? How does the entire family network handle change in its oldest mem-bers? Even the youngest family members will be reacting emotionally to events in the lives of their grandmother and grandfather. It is through these experiences that they learn firsthand about late life, and many of their attitudes toward older persons and their own eventual aging will be modeled after the situations and attitudes in the family circle. Family therapy involving everyone from young to old can be a way of helping to un-derstand what is happening to the older person, clarify feelings, review and deal with old con-flicts (which may be surprisingly undiluted by the passage of time), and mobilize everyone in the care and concern for the older member. (See Chapter 12 for discussion of family therapy and counseling.)

"Filial Maturity"

Blenkner has used the term "filial maturity" to de-scribe a middle-aged developmental stage beyond the usual Freudian framework.[71] (The latter en-compasses development from birth through early adulthood, with little theoretical consideration given to middle and late life.) Adults in their for-ties and fifties experience a "filial crisis" when it becomes evident that their parents are aging and the offspring will be called on to provide the sup-port and comfort that older parents need. This may contrast with childhood visions of parents as pow-erful and nurturing individuals who assist and support their offspring, rather than vice versa. In view of the vicissitudes of early parent–child re-lationships, there is often unfinished developmen-tal work to be done in freeing middle-aged adults from hostile, ambivalent, or immature parental ties that impede a healthy relationship. Maturity for the middle-aged child "involves being *de-pended on* and therefore being dependable insofar

as his parent is concerned," with full recognition of the parent as an individual with his or her own rights, needs, limitations, and life history. "It is often necessary to assist the child to complete his unfinished emancipation from the parent *in order that he may then be more free to help his par-ent.*"[72] Neurotic guilt toward parents must be dif-ferentiated from the real guilt of failure to assume filial responsibility. Neurotic guilt can lead to doing too much for parents and interfering with their independence and autonomy. A failure to ad-dress real guilt may result in the adult child doing too little for a parent. Silverstone and Hyman have emphasized the importance of determining the "right" amount of help by looking at problems re-alistically and by becoming aware of the feelings underlying the relationship between older parent and the adult child.[73]

Much past psychiatric and social work litera-ture has treated the interactions between older people and their children in a negative, patroniz-ing fashion. The term "role-reversal" has been a favored concept because it fits so comfortably with the negative stereotypes depicting the aged as dependent or regressed; the child supposedly be-comes the parent to his or her own parents as they slip from self-sufficient adulthood to a state of childish dependency. But surely a more mislead-ing interpretation of the realities of old age could not be imagined.[74] This is true even in the face of advanced dementia. Spark and Brody comment: "The behavior of a brain-damaged regressed old person may appear child-like but he is not a child. Half a century [or more] of adulthood cannot be wiped out."[75] The complexities of caring for an older person are far different than those of caring for an infant or a child, requiring specialized skills. But most importantly, the older person remains an adult, and every effort should be made to view and treat him or her as such. The presence of physical or mental impairment does not alter that reality. And remembering this simple fact can have pro-found effects on caregivers, care receivers, and the process of care-giving itself.

Adult children may also need help in differ-entiating what can't be done from what can be done. For example, the aging and eventual decline of a parent will inevitably occur and cannot be avoided, but much can be done to protect and even improve functioning and quality of life at every stage, even up to the very point of death.

Some of the more practical matters of helping the elderly can be easily learned.[76] Indeed, several rehabilitation centers and hospitals now teach families how to perform required therapies and other services. Classes for adult children can provide knowledge about aging and the illnesses frequently occurring in old age, as well as offering a

means of coping and an opportunity for sharing concerns with others. Visiting nurses and home health specialists perform a teaching function within the family (see Chapter 10). It is clear that many older people can remain at home if their problems are detected early and prompt psychiatric, social, medical, and economic resources are made available. When given adequate support, families often provide the unique blend of affection and personal services that is so essential to mental health and comfort in old age.

SELECTED READINGS

Abraham, K. (1955). Some remarks on the role of grandparents in the psychology of neuroses. In Abraham, H. (Ed.), *Selected papers: Clinical papers and essays in psychoanalysis* (vol. 2). New York: Basic Books.

Achenbaum, W. A. (1979). *Old age in the new land.* Baltimore: Johns Hopkins Press.

Adelman, R., & Butler, R. N. (1989). Elder abuse and neglect. In Kaplan, H. I., & Sadock, B. J. (Eds.), *Comprehensive textbook of psychiatry V* (Chap. 46.7a). Baltimore, MD: Williams & Wilkins.

Bass, S. A., & Caro, R. G. (1996, Spring). The economic value of grandparent assistance. *Generations, 20*(1), 29–33.

Bengtson, V. L., & Achenbaum, W. A. (1993). *The changing contract across generations.* Hawthorne, NY: Aldine de Gruyter.

Bengtson, V. L., & Hartootyan, R. (Eds.). (1994). *Intergenerational linkages: Hidden connections in American society.* New York: Springer.

Bengston, V. L., & Robertson, J. F. (Eds.). (1985). *Grandparenthood.* Beverly Hills, CA: Sage.

Bengtson, V. L., Rosenthal, C. J., & Burton, L. M. (1995). Paradoxes of families and aging at the turn of the century. In Binstock, R. H., & George, L. (Eds.), *Handbook of aging and the social sciences,* 4th ed. San Diego, CA: Academic Press.

Bengtson, V. L., Schaie, K. W., & Burton, L. M. (Eds.). (1995). *Adult intergenerational relations: Effects of societal change.* New York: Springer.

Bergeman, C. S., Plomin, R., Pedersen, N. L., Mc-Clearn, G. E., & Nesselroade, J. R. (1990, May).

Genetic and environmental influences on social support: The Swedish adoption/twin study of aging. *Journal of Gerontology, 45*(3), 101–106.

Blenkner, M. (1965). Social work and family relationships in later life with some thoughts on filial maturity. In Shanas, E. & Streib, G. F. (Eds.), *Social Structure and the family: Generational relations* (pp.46–59). Englewood Cliffs, NJ: Prentice Hall.

Blieszner, R., & Bedford, V. H. (Eds.). (1995). *Handbook of aging and the family.* Westport, CT: Greenwood.

Brody, E. (1990). *Women in the middle: Their parent-care years.* New York: Springer.

Bumagin, V. E., & Hirn, K. E. (1990). *Helping the aging family: A guide for professionals.* Glenview, IL: Scott, Foresman.

Cain, B. S. (1988, November). Divorce among elderly women: A growing social phenomenon. *Social Case Work: The Journal of Contemporary Social Work,* 563–568.

Cantor, M. H. (1993). *Growing older in New York City in the 1990's: A study of changing lifestyles, quality of life, and quality of care,* vol. 2. New York: New York Center for Policy on Aging, New York Community Trust.

Cicirelli, V. G. (1987). Siblings. In Maddox, G. L. (Ed.), *The encyclopedia of aging* (pp. 608–609). New York: Springer.

Cicirelli, V. G. (1992). Siblings as caregivers in middle and old age. In Dwyer, J. E., & Coward, R. T. (Eds.), *Gender, families, and elder care* (pp. 84–101). Newbury Park, CA: Sage Publications.

Cicirelli, V. G. (1994). Sibling relationships in cross-cultural perspective. *Journal of Marriage and the Family,* col. 56, 7–20.x

Cicirelli, V. G. (1995). Siblings. In Maddox, G. L. (Ed.), *The encyclopedia of aging* (pp. 857–859). New York: Springer.

Commonwealth Fund Commission on Elderly People Living Alone. (1987). *Old, alone, and poor.* New York: Commonwealth Fund Communications Office.

Cutler, N. E., & Devlin, S. J. (1996, Spring). A framework for understanding financial responsibilities among generations. *Generations, 20*(1), pp. 24–28.

Finley, N. J., Roberts, M. D., & Banaham, B. F. (1988). Motivators and inhibitors of attitudes of filial obligation towards aging parents. *The Gerontologist, 28,* 73–78.

Fischer, D. H. (1978). *Growing old in America.* Expanded edition. New York: Oxford University Press.

Giarrusso, R., Silverstein, M., & Bengtson, V. L. (1996, Spring). Family complexity and the grandparent role. *Generations, 20*(1), 17–23.

Gibson, R. C. (1986). Outlook for the black family. In Pifer, A. & Bronte, L. (Eds.), *Our aging society* (pp. 181–97). New York: W. W. Norton.

Gold, D. (1987). *Siblings in old age: Their relationships and roles* (monograph). Chicago: Center for Applied Gerontology.

Gutmann, D. (1987). *Reclaimed powers: Toward a new psychology of men and women in later life.* New York: Basic Books.

Gutmann, D. (1985) The parental imperative revisited: Towards a developmental psychology of adulthood and later life. In Menchem, J. A. (Ed.), *Contributions to human development.* Basel: Karger.

Hagestad, G. (1985). Continuity and connectedness. In Bengtson, V. L. & Robertson, J. F. (Eds.), *Grandparenthood* (pp. 31–48). Beverly Hills: CA: Sage.

Hagestad, G. (1986). The family: Women and grandparents as kin-keepers. In Pifer, A. & Bronte, L. (Eds.), *Our aging society* (pp. 141–160). New York: W. W. Norton.

Hamon, R. R., & Blieszner, R. (1990, May). Filial responsibility—expectations among adult child-older parents pairs. *The Journal of Gerontology, 45*(3), 110–112.

Hardgrave, T. D., & Anderson, W. T. (1992). *Finishing well: Aging and reparation in the intergenerational family.* New York: Brunner/Mazel.

Hu, Y., & Goldman, N. (1990, May). Mortality differences by marital status: An international comparison. *Demography, 27*(2), 233–250.

Jarvik, L., & Small, G. (1988). *Parentcare: A commonsense guide for adult children.* New York: Crown Publishing.

Kingson, E. R., Hirshorn, B. A., & Cornman, J. M. (1986). *The ties that bind: The interdependence of generations.* Washington, DC: Seven Locks Press.

Morris, V. (1996). *How to care for aging parents.* New York: Workman Publishing.

Parsons, T. & Bales, R. (1955). *Family, socialization and interaction process.* New York: Free Press of Glencoe.

Pillemer, K. A., & Wolf, R. S. (Eds.). (1986). *Elder abuse. Conflict in the family.* Dover, MA: Auburn House.

Pruchno, R. A., & Johnson, K. W. (1996, Spring). Research on grandparenting: Review of current studies and future needs. *Generations, 20*(1), 65–70.

Robertson, J. F. (1995). Grandparenting in an era of rapid change. In Blieszner, R., & Bedford, V. H. (Eds.), *Handbook of aging and the family.* Westport, CT: Greenwood Press.

Rossi, A. S., & Rossi, P. H. (1990). *Of human bonding: Parent–child relations across the life course.* New York: Aldine de Gruyter.

Schiff, H. S. (1996). *How did I become my parent's parent?* New York: Viking.

Schorr, A. L. (1960). *Filial responsibility in the modern American family.* Washington, DC: U.S. Department of Health, Education, and Welfare, Social Security Administration, U.S. Government Printing Office.

Shanas, E. (1980, February). Older people and their families: The new pioneers. *Journal of Marriage and the Family,* 9–15.

Shanas, E., & Streib, G. F. (1965). *Social structure of the family: Generational relations.* Englewood Cliffs, NJ: Prentice-Hall.

Townsend, P. (1957). *The family life of old people.* London: Routledge and Kegan Paul.

Troll, L. (Ed.). (1987). *Family issues in current gerontology.* New York: Springer.

Troll, L. E., & Bengtson, V. L. (1992). The oldest old in families: An intergenerational perspective. *Generations, 17,* 39–44.

U.S. Bureau of the Census. (1992). 65+ in America. *Current population reports, special studies,* Series P-23, No. 190. Washington, DC: U.S. Government Printing Office.

ENDNOTES

1. Hagestad, G. (1986). The family: Women and grandparents as kin-keepers. In Pifer, A., & Bronte, L. (Eds.), *Our aging society* (pp. 141–160). New York: W. W. Norton.
2. Elder, G. H. (1980, October). *History and the family.* Burgess Award Lecture, National Council on Family Relations, Portland, OR.
3. Models of the developmental processes of families are as important as models of individual personality development. Sociology, anthropology, psychiatry, and social work all have valuable experience in this area, which they do not often share with each other. Margaret Mead has said, "We've never adequately differentiated between a household, a biological nuclear family and whatever else people think the family really is. . . . We have no way of dealing with people who are members of a biological family but who aren't living within the nuclear family."
4. Preston, S. H. (1984, December). Children and the elderly. *U.S. Scientific American, 44–49.*
5. Hagestad, *The family,* p. 146.
6. Hagestad, G. (1987). Able elderly in the family context: Changes, chances and challenges. *The Gerontologist, 27*(4), 421.
7. Gutmann, D. L. (1985). The parental imperative revisited: Towards a developmental psychology of adulthood and later life. In Manchem, J. A. (Ed.), *Contributions to human development* (Vol. 14, pp. 31–60). Basel: Karger.
8. Johnsen, L. J., & Barer, B. M. (1987). Marital instability and the changing kinship networks of grandparents. *The Gerontologist, 27*(3), 334.
9. Maeda, D., Brody, E., Campbell, R., Okuyama, S., & Okuyama, N. (1985). *Attitudes of three generations of Japanese women toward aging and old people,* a paper presented at the XIII International Congress of Gerontology, 1985, New York.
10. Sussman, M. B. (1965). Relationships of adult children with their parents in the United States. In Shanas, E., & Streib, G. F. (Eds.), *Social structure and the family: Generational relationships.* Englewood Cliffs, NJ: Prentice-Hall.
11. Litwak, E. (1960). Extended kin relations in industrial democratic societies: Occupational mobility and extended family cohesion. *American Sociological Review, 25,* 9–21. See also Litwak, E. (1960). Geographic mobility and extended family cohesion. *American Sociological Review, 25,* 385–394.
12. World Health Organization. (1959). *Mental health problems of the aging and the aged,* Technical Report Series No. 171, Geneva: World Health Organization.
13. Townsend, P. (1965). The effects of family structure on the likelihood of admission to an institution in old age: The application of a general theory. In Shanas, E., & Streib, G. (Eds.), *Social structure and the family* (pp. 163–88). Englewood Cliffs, NJ: Prentice-Hall.
14. Shanas, E. (1980). Older people and their families: The new pioneers. *Journal of Marriage and the Family, 42*(l), 12. This three-decade-old study focuses on those four out of five noninstitutionalized older persons with living children.
15. For example, Kivett, V. R., & Atkinson, M. P. (1984). Filial expectations, associations, and helping as a function of number of children among older rural-transitional parents. *Journal of Gerontology, 39,* 499–503; Bengtson, V. L., Rosenthal, C. J., & Burton, L. M. (1995). Paradoxes of families and aging at the turn of the century. In Binstock, R. H., & George, L. (Eds.), *Handbook of aging and the social sciences.* San Diego, CA: Academic Press; Blieszner, R., & Bedford, V. H. (Eds.). (1995). *Handbook of aging and the family.* Westport, CT: Greenwood; Finley, N. J., Roberts, M. D., & Banaham, B. F. (1988). Motivators and inhibitors of attitudes of filial obligation towards aging parents. *The Gerontologist, 28,* 73–78. Rossi, A. S., & Rossi, P. H. (1990). *Of human bonding: Parent–child relations across the life course.* New York: Aldine de Gruyter.
16. Mayer, M. J. (1989). *The New York City elderly: A changing population.* Presented at Visions for the Future, a conference of the Council of Senior Centers and Services of New York City, Fordham University, June 15, 1989, pp. 6–7.
17. McAdoo, H. P. (1982). Levels of stress and family support in black families. In McCubbin, H., Cauble, A. E., & Patterson, J. (Eds.), *Family stress, coping and social supports.* Springfield, IL: Charles C. Thomas; Jackson, J. J. (1980); Gelfand, D. E. (1994). *Aging and ethnicity: Knowledge and services.* New York: Springer; Lockery, S. A. (1991, Fall/Winter). Family and social supports: Caregiving among racial and ethnic minority elders. *Generations, 15*(4), 58–62; Luckey, I. (1994, February). African American elders: The support network of generational kin. *Families in society:*

The journal of contemporary human services, 75(2), 82–89.

18. Markson, E. (1995). Marital status. In Maddox, G. L. (Ed.), *The encyclopedia of aging* (pp. 602–604). New York: Springer.

19. The classic work on the subject is that of Schorr, A. L. (1960). *Filial responsibility in the modern American family.* Washington, DC: U.S. Department of Health, Education, and Welfare, Social Security Administration, U.S. Government Printing Office.

20. U.S. Bureau of the Census. (1988). Who's helping out? Support networks among American families. *Current Population Reports,* Series P-70, No. 13. Washington, DC: U.S. Government Printing Office.

21. *Ibid.*

22. Lewis, M. I. *Economic perspectives in calculating the costs of women family members providing home elder care.* Unpublished paper, Mount Sinai School of Medicine, New York, 1990.

23. Morgan, J. N. (1984). The role of time in the measurements of transfers and economic well-being. In Moon, M. (Ed.), *Economic transfers in the United States* (pp. 199–238). Chicago: University of Chicago Press.

24. *Ibid.,* pp. 206, 214.

25. Waerness, K. (1978). The invisible welfare state: Women's work at home. *Acta Sociologica,* Supplement 1978, 193–207.

26. Cherlin, A. (1983). A sense of history: Recent research on aging and the family. In Riley, M. W., Hess, B. B., & Bond, K. B. (Eds.), *Aging in society: Selected reviews of recent research* (p. 8). Hillsdale, NJ: Lawrence Erlbaum Associates.

27. *Ibid.*

28. Sussman, M. B. (1985). The family life of old people. In Binstock, R. H., & Shanas, E. (Eds.), *Handbook of aging and the social sciences,* 2nd ed. (pp. 415–445). New York: Van Nostrand Reinhold.

29. Mayer, M. J. *The New York City elderly: A changing population.* Presented at Visions for the Future, a conference of the Council of Senior Centers and Services of New York City, Fordham University, June 15, 1989, pp. 6–7.

30. Winsborough, H. H. (1980). A demographic approach to the life cycle. In Back, K. W. (Ed.), *Life course: Integrative theories and exemplary populations.* (pp. 65–76). Boulder, CO: Westview Press.

31. Gutmann, The parental imperative revisited.

32. Hagestad, G., Able elderly in the family context.

33. Hagestad, G. O. (1984). The continuous bond: A dynamic multigenerational perspective on parent–child relations. In Perlmutter, M. (Ed.), *Minnesota Symposium on Child Psychology* (vol. 17, pp. 129–58). Hillsdale, NJ: Lawrence Erlbaum Associates.

34. Shanas, E. (1978). *A national survey of the aged.* Final report to the Administration on Aging. Washington, DC: U.S. Department of Health, Education, and Welfare.

35. Pruchno, R. A., & Johnson, K. W. (Spring, 1996). Research on grandparenting: Review of current studies and future needs. *Generations,* 65–70.

36. From a 1986 sampling by the Valley Forge Survey Co. for Meredith Corporation, the publisher of *Grandparents Magazine.*

37. *Metropolitan Life Statistical Bulletin, 52,* 8–10, 1972.

38. Ferenczi, S. (1926). The "grandfather complex." In Rickman, J. (Comp.), *Theory and technique of psychoanalysis* (pp. 323–324). London: Hogarth Press.

39. Presented at 1958 annual meeting, University of North Carolina School of Medicine, Chapel Hill.

40. Rappaport, E. A. (1958). The grandparent syndrome. *Psychoanalytic Quarterly, 27,* 518–538.

41. Haber, M. (1965). The importance of grandparents in family life. *Family Process, 4,* 228–240.

42. Benedek, T. (1970). Parenthood during the life cycle. In Anthony E. J. (Ed.), *Parenthood* (p. 201). Boston: Little, Brown.

43. Hagestad, *The family,* p. 148.

44. *Ibid.,* p. 152.

45. Kivnick, H. Q. (1982). Grandparenthood: An overview of meaning and mental health. *The Gerontologist, 22*(1), 59–66.

46. U.S. Bureau of the Census. (1994, March). Marital status and living arrangements. *Current Population Reports,* Series P-20, No. 484. Washington DC: U.S. Government Printing Office.

47. U.S. Bureau of the Census. (1992, October). Marriage, Divorce and Remarriage in the 1990's. *Current Population Reports,* Series P-20, no. 180.

48. Hagestad, G. O., Sanger, M. A., & Stierman, K. L. (1984). Parent-child relations in adulthood: The impact of divorce in middle age. In Cohen, R., Weissman, S., & Cohler, B. (Eds.), *Parenthood: Psychodynamic perspectives* (pp. 247–62). New York: Guildford Press; Fisher, E. O. (Ed.). (1982). *Impact of divorce on the extended family.* Binghamton, NY: The Haworth Press.

49. Matthews, S. H., & Sprey, J. (1984). The impact of divorce on grandparenthood: An exploratory study. *The Gerontologist, 24*(1), 41–47.

50. Glick, P. C. (1957). *American families.* New York: John Wiley.

51. U.S. Bureau of the Census. (1994, March). Marital status and living arrangements. *Current Population Reports,* Series P-20, No. 484. Washington DC: U.S. Government Printing Office.

52. Yarrow, M. R., Blank, P., Quinn, O. W., Youmans, E. G., & Stein, J. (1963). Social psychological characteristics of old age. In Birren, J. E., Butler, R. N., Greenhouse, S. W., Sokoloff, L., & Yarrow, M. R. (Eds.), *Human aging: A biological and behavioral study.* Pub. No. (PHS) 986. Washington, DC: U.S. Government Printing Office (reprinted as Pub. No. [HSM] 71–9051 1971, 1974). See also Pineo, P. C. (1968). Disenchantment in the later years of marriages. In Neugarten, B. L. (Ed.), *Middle age and aging* (pp. 258–262). Chicago: University of Chicago Press.

53. Markides, K. S. (1995). Marital satisfaction. In Maddox, G. L. (Ed.), *The encyclopedia of aging.* (pp. 601–602). New York: Springer.

54. It is noteworthy that in the NIMH study of healthy older men, there were many criticisms and complaints about wives, yet only one man reported even considering separation from his spouse, and none believed that either his marriage or his choice of a spouse was a mistake. Whether this is a tribute to the success of these marriages or an indication that such an indictment of a large segment of their lives was too painful to face is an interesting question. Generally, however, these men appeared to "tell it like it was," or at least close to like it was, about their marriages.

55. National Center for Health Statistics. (1995). Advance report of final divorce statistics, 1989 and 1990. *Monthly Vital Statistics Report, 43*(8), supplement. Hyattsville, MD: Author.

56. Cain, B. S. (1988, November). Divorce among elderly women: A growing social phenomenon. *Social Case Work: The Journal of Contemporary Social Work,* 563–568; Ulenberg, P., & Meyers, M. P. (1981). Divorce among the elderly. *The Gerontologist, 21*(3), 276–281.

57. U.S. Bureau of the Census. (1994, March). Marital status and living arrangements. *Current Population Reports,* Series P-20, No. 484. Washington DC: U.S. Government Printing Office.

58. Gutmann, D. (1987). *Reclaimed powers: Toward a new, psychology of men and women in later life.* New York: Basic Books.

59. Gold, S. (1960, Spring). Cross-cultural comparisons of role change with aging. *Student Journal of Human Development,* 11a.

60. Hu, Y., & Goldman, N. (1990, May). Mortality differences by marital status: An international comparison. *Demography, 27*(2), 233–250.

61. McKain, W. C. (1969). *Retirement marriage.* Storrs, CT: University of Connecticut, p. 168.

62. U.S. Bureau of the Census. (1994, March). Marital status and living arrangements. *Current Population Reports,* Series P-20, No. 484. Washington DC: U.S. Government Printing Office.

63. Rosenthal, C. (1985, November). Kinkeeping in the familial division of labor. *Journal of Marriage and the Family,* 965–974.

64. Shanas, E. (1979). Social myth as hypothesis: The care of the family relations of old people. *The Gerontologist, 19*(1), 3–9. Also see U.S. Bureau of the Census. (1979). Marital status and living arrangements, March 1978. *Current Population Reports,* Series P-20, No. 338, Washington, DC: U.S. Government Printing Office.

65. Cicirelli, V. G. (1987). Siblings. In Maddox, G. L. (Ed.), *The encyclopedia of aging* (pp. 608–609). New York: Springer; Cicirelli, V. G. (1985). The role of siblings as family caregivers. In Sauer, W. J., & Coward, R. T. (Eds.), *Social support networks and the care of the elderly* (pp. 93–107). New York: Springer; and Cicirelli, V. G. (1985). Sibling relationships throughout the life cycle. In L'Abate, L. (Ed.), *The handbook of family psychology and therapy* (vol. 1, pp. 177–214). Homewood, IL: Dorsey Press.

66. Chappell, N. L. (1983). Informal support networks among the elderly. *Research on Aging, 5,* 77–99.

67. Cohen, C. I., & Rajkowski, H. (1982). What's in a friend? Substantive and theoretical issues. *The Gerontologist, 22,* 261–266.

68. Townsend, P. (1968). The emergence of the four-generation family in industrial society. In Neugarten, B. L. (Ed.), *Middle age and aging: A reader in social psychology* (pp. 255–257). Chicago: University of Chicago Press.

69. Shanas, E. (1964). The older person at home—a potential isolate or participant. Reprinted from National Institute of Mental Health. In *Research utilization in aging: An exploration,* proceedings of a conference sponsored by Community Research and Services Branch, April 30–May 3, 1963. Washington, DC: U.S. Government Printing Office.

70. Lowenthal, M. F. (1968). Social isolation and mental illness in old age. In Neugarten, B. L. (Ed.), *Middle age and aging: A reader in social psychology* (p. 234). Chicago: University of Chicago Press.

71. For an excellent summary on family relationships in old age, see Blenkner, M. (1965). Social work

and family relationships in later life with some thoughts on filial maturity. In Shanas, E., & Streib, G. F. (Eds.), *Social structure and the family: Generational relations* (pp. 46–59). Englewood Cliffs, NJ: Prentice-Hall.

72. *Ibid.*, p. 50.

73. Silverstone, B., & Hyman, H. K. (1976). *You and your aging parent.* New York: Pantheon Books.

74. See series of five articles on the issue of "role reversal," presented at a symposium: Role reversal: Is it a valid concept? 41st Annual Scientific Meeting of the Gerontological Society of America, in San Francisco, November 18–22, 1988. Reprinted in *Journal of Gerontological Social Work, 15*(½), 1–38, 1990.

75. Spark, G., & Brody, E. (1972). The aged as family members. In Sager, C., & Kaplan, H. (Eds.), *Progress in group and family therapy* (p. 717). New York: Brunner Mozel.

76. Useful books for the families of older persons are Shelley, F. D. (1988). *When your parents grow old.* New York: Harper & Row; Jarvik, L., & Small, G. (1988). *Parentcare: A commonsense guide for adult children.* New York: Crown Publishing; and Morris, V. (1996) *How to care for aging parents.* New York: Workman Publishing.

HEALTHY, SUCCESSFUL OLD AGE

Old age can be an emotionally healthy and satisfying time of life with a minimum of physical and mental impairment. But what are the optimal conditions that make this possible? This chapter has been designed as an overview of healthy old age and some of its important components.

Mr. S, a 76-year-old retired businessman, is spontaneous, talkative, and in touch with reality. He has varied emotional response appropriate to the situation and no sign of psychomotor retardation. When interviewed, he spoke in a frank and integrated manner about his achievements. Although some general forgetfulness is noted on his history, there is no sign of a marked intellectual decline, and no memory impairments were found on the mental status examination.

Mr. S was born on a farm in central Europe, the oldest of ten children. He was already employed at age 9 and left home at age 13. He describes his parents as having some problems, and he states that he felt closer to his mother but attained a greater understanding of his father as years went by. At age 23 he married and emigrated to the United States. His marriage is viewed by him as an excellent one, and his wife is in good health. Mr. S has experienced a modest decrease in sexual desire and continues sex relations on a less frequent basis. His relation-

ship with children and grandchildren is satisfying, with moderate interaction. He remembers that his children's adolescent rebellions gave him a chance to look anew at his own early years.

Mr. S had made plans for his older years and continues to plan optimistically for the future. He feels concerned about death and hopes he will have a sudden death or die in his sleep. He feels some interest in religion but denies any marked change since youth. He has made out a will and has arranged for a burial site.

In viewing his aging condition, Mr. S shows a reasonable recognition of his capacities and limitations, with no obvious denial. He appears to have accepted his physical changes. He is no longer very active but takes walks and moves about the house and yard with regularity. He shows no history of lifelong psychopathology, and there is no evidence of new psychopathology as he ages. There is no psychological isolation, and it is deemed unlikely that he will have a functional breakdown in the future.

Mr. S is an example of an older person who has adapted to old age with minimal stress and a high level of morale. With old age, just as with any other age, one can learn much about pathological conditions by understanding healthy developmental processes. Unfortunately, until recently, healthy older people have rarely been the subjects of research investigation or theoretical constructs. The study of "normal" development, seldom explored beyond early adult years, must now expand to include older persons. The psychology of human development will then reach a new dimension, encompassing the entire life span.

NEGATIVE STEREOTYPE OF OLD AGE

Although many Americans still find difficulty in thinking of old age as a time of potential health and growth, an increasing number of older persons are able to lead healthy and vigorous lives. There has been some steady improvement in their lot in recent years. But those who are widowed, live alone, belong to minorities, or are very old are still vulnerable to a wide array of stresses and struggles in late life. And these vulnerable elderly continue to fuel national stereotypes of old age as a time of decrepitude and decline.

In a larger sense, Western civilization itself produces a negative view of aging. The Western concept of the life cycle is decidedly different from that of the Far East, since they derive from two opposing views of what "self" means and what life is all about. Eastern philosophy places the individual's self, life, and death *within* the process of the human experience. The personal experience blends with the universal. Life and death are familiar and intertwined. Death is characteristically seen as a welcome relief from suffering or, as in Japanese ancestor worship, a step upward in social mobility to join the revered ancestors.[1] In Buddhism, death is merely a passage to another reincarnation unless the person achieves an enlightenment that releases him or her from the eternal cycle.

In the West, death is considered to be *outside* of the process of the human experience. To be a self (a person) one must be alive, in control, and aware of what is happening. The greater and more narcissistic Western emphasis on individuality and control makes death an outrage, a tremendous affront to humans rather than the logical and necessary process of old life making way for new.

The opposite cultural views of East and West evolved to support two very different ways of life, each with its own merits; but the Western predilection for "progress," conquest over nature, and personal self-realization has produced difficult problems for older persons and for those preparing for old age. This is particularly so when the national spirit of the United States and the spirit of this period in time have emphasized and expanded the notion of measuring human worth in terms of individual productivity and power. Older people are led to see themselves as "beginning to fail" as they age, a phrase that refers as much to self-worth as it does to physical strength. Religion has been the traditional solace by promising another world wherein the self again springs to life, never to be further threatened by loss of its own integrity. Thus the consummate dream of immortality for Westerners is fulfilled by religion, yet the integration of the aging experience into their life process remains incomplete. To make matters more complicated, increasing secularization produces a frightening void around the subject of death itself, which frequently is met by avoiding and denying the thought of one's own decline and death and by forming self-protective prejudices against the old.

Medicine and the behavioral sciences have mirrored societal attitudes by presenting old age as a grim litany of physical and emotional ills. Until 1960 most of the medical, psychological, psychiatric, and social work literature on the aged was based on experience with the sick and the institutionalized, even though only 5% of older people were confined to institutions. Decline of the individual was the key concept. Fortunately, research studies that have concentrated on the healthy aged give indications of positive potential for the entire age group.

WHAT IS A HEALTHY OLD AGE?

In thinking about health, one is led to the understanding that, in addition to the general lack of interest in older persons, science and medicine have historically been more concerned with treating "what went wrong" than with clarifying the complex, interwoven elements necessary to produce and support health. Typical of this is the treating of coronary attacks after the fact rather than prescribing a preventive program of diet, exercise, protection from stress, and absence of smoking. Most of the major diseases of older people can be cited as examples of this same phenomenon. The tedious and less dramatic process of prevention requires an understanding of what supports or what interferes with healthy development throughout the course of the life cycle.

The World Health Organization in 1946 first defined health as "a state of complete physical, mental, and social well-being and not merely the absence of disease or infirmity." This, of course, represents an ideal with many possible interpretations. But the broad elements of health—physical, emotional, and social—are the framework in which one can begin to analyze what is going well in addition to what is going wrong. The attempt must be made to locate those conditions that enable humans to thrive, not merely survive.

Old age does involve unique developmental work. Childhood might be defined as a period of gathering and enlarging strength and experience, whereas a major developmental task in old age is to clarify, deepen, and find use for what one has already attained in a lifetime of learning and adapting. Older people must teach themselves to conserve their strength and resources when necessary and to adjust in the best sense to those changes and losses that occur as part of the aging experience. The ability of the older person to adapt and thrive is contingent on physical health, personality, earlier life experiences, and on the societal supports he or she receives: adequate finances, shelter, medical care, social roles, recreation, and the like. An important point to emphasize is that, as is true for children, adolescents, and the middle-aged, it is imperative that older people continue to develop and change in a flexible manner if health is to be promoted and maintained. Failure of adaptation at any age or under any circumstance can result in physical or emotional illness. Optimal growth and adaptation can occur

throughout the life cycle when the individual's strengths and potentials are recognized, reinforced, and encouraged by the environment in which he or she lives.

Popular ideas of human development need revision to encompass the experience of older persons. They should not have to view themselves as "failing" or "finished" because one or another element of life is changing or declining. For example, a loss in physical health or the loss of a loved one is indeed a serious blow, but the potential for continuing adjustment and growth needs therefore to be even more carefully exploited than under less critical circumstances. In our too quick assumption that old age is a relentless downhill course, we ignore the potential of older persons for strength as well as for a richer emotional, spiritual, and even intellectual and social life than may be possible for the young. Youth must concentrate on the piece-by-piece accumulation of personality and experience. Old age, in its best sense, can mean enjoyment of something closer to the finished product—a far more mature, complex human being.

BECOMING "OLD"

To attempt to clarify and disentangle what "old" means, we must emphasize that the concern here is not with those characteristics of old people that are the result of preexistent personality factors. The kind of personality one carries into old age is a crucial factor in how one will respond to the experience of being older; personality traits produce individual ways of being old. However, we wish to deal with the more general characteristics of old age and the changes that are fairly common to the aging population as a whole in the United States.

Physical Changes

Some of the outward alterations experienced by older persons are graying of hair, loss of hair and teeth, elongation of ears and nose, losses of subcutaneous fat, particularly around the face, wrinkling of skin, fading of eyesight and hearing, postural changes, and a progressive structural decline that may result in a shortened trunk with comparatively long arms and legs. Not all of these changes happen to everyone—nor at the same rate. A person can be a "young" 90-year-old, in a physical sense, or an "old" 60-year-old. Little is known about the onset and progress of many of these changes, since they were long thought to be simply the inescapable and universal consequences of growing old. But recent research has revealed that some, or perhaps many, are results of disease states that occur with greater frequency in late life and may be treatable—either by slowing the course of the disease or by preventing it entirely. Atherosclerosis and osteoporosis are cases in point. The rate of heart disease in the United States has already shown some decline. Even cancer may someday be conquered, although not many years ago someone dying of cancer was said to be dying of "old age." Other reasons for bodily changes have been identified as results of unusual amounts of exposure to some pathogenic element—too much sun (causing skin wrinkles), cigarette smoke, and air pollution, to name a few. Genetic traits can be responsible for changes like graying hair and loss of hair. Yet in the best of all future worlds, with acute and chronic disease states identified and eliminated, undesirable genetic traits nullified, and pathogenic environmental conditions removed, a process called aging will still occur. The potential for life can be lengthened and enhanced, but the mysterious flow of human existence from birth through death will prevail. As many older people realize more calmly than the young, aging and death must be accepted as part of human experience.

The overall physical health of the body plays a critical role in determining the energies and adaptive capacities available to older people. They experience a good deal more acute and chronic disease than the younger population. Specific physical disabilities and diseases, such as cardiovascular and locomotor afflictions, are particularly debilitating, especially when they affect the integrative systems of the body—the endocrine, vascular, and central nervous systems. Severe or even mild organic brain disease can interfere markedly

with functioning. Perceptual losses of eyesight and hearing can deplete energy and cause social isolation. However, although more than four out of five older persons have one or more chronic health problems, 95% are able to live in the community. Their conditions are mild enough to enable 80% or so of older persons to get around with no outside assistance. If significant breakthroughs occur in research and treatment of diseases of the aged (heart disease, cancer, arthritis, arteriosclerosis, and acute and chronic brain syndromes), one can envision a very different kind of old age. Assuming adequate environmental supports, including proper nutrition, old age could become a time of lengthy good health with a more gentle and predictable decline. Older persons would not have to battle the ravages of disease, and a fuller measure of their physical strength could be available for other uses. Already today one can see the possibilities in those older people who are disease-free. They can cope more vigorously with the emotional and social changes specific to their age group and in so doing have the opportunity for a successful and satisfying later life.

Emotional Changes

Older people are often stereotyped as slow thinkers, forgetful, rigid, mean-tempered, irritable, dependent, and querulous. Certainly they do suffer from anxiety, grief, depression, and paranoid states that may be experienced at any age. But one must separate out the personality traits demonstrated in earlier life, realistic responses to actual loss of friends and loved ones, personal reactions to the idea of one's own aging and death, and the predictable emotional responses of human beings at any age to physical illness or social loss. The emotional aspects of aging are more fully discussed in Chapter 4.

Intellectual Changes

The effects of aging on intellectual functioning have been studied since the post–World War I era. The earliest assumptions were that intelligence declined progressively with age. The Army Alpha Test of World War I on officers and recruits 18 to 60 years of age and older seemed to confirm the idea of intellectual decline, since lower and lower test scores were found as age increased. In 1932 Miles and Miles reported much the same results with 823 subjects ranging from age 5 to 94.[2] Intelligence scores were shown to increase until age 18 and then begin a long decline. Jones and Conrad in 1933 produced similar general results with 1,191 subjects age 10 to 60, including children, parents, and grandparents.[3] In 1955 Wechsler (the Wechsler Adult Intelligence Scale [WAIS]) developed an IQ test adjusted for each age group, which artificially gave older people a boost in their otherwise declining raw test scores.

All the above studies were cross-sectional, with each subject interviewed once. This methodology produced inherent biases favoring the better educated young and reflecting historical and environmental differences between the generations. On the other hand, longitudinal studies on the same individual over a period of time were also being done, making it possible to measure actual intelligence changes over the life cycle while avoiding the pitfalls of cross-sectional research.[4] In the 1920s both Bayley and Bradway conducted longitudinal studies, still continuing today, in which they have tested and retested persons (now in later life), beginning with childhood.[5] They found IQ scores increasing until the twenties and then eventually leveling off, remaining unchanged until late in life. There was no overall decline with age. The work of Owens and others corroborated these findings.[6]

Lorge, meanwhile, tested the assumption that one aspect of intelligence—speed of reaction— may indeed decrease with age.[7] (Reaction time studies, such as those by Birren, demonstrate a loss in speed of response in the central nervous system with age.) He concluded that, generally speaking, if older persons were given enough time on tests, they functioned as accurately as younger persons. The health factor in later life has also been evaluated for its effect on intelligence and other psychometric tests. Even minimal poor health can adversely affect test scores.[8] Jarvik and others found a drop in intellectual measures in the period just before death.[9]

The distinction between "crystallized" intelligence and "fluid" intelligence, introduced by Horn and Cattell, has been a useful one.[10] Crystallized intelligence is a result of experience and tends to increase throughout life in healthy, active people. Meanwhile, fluid intelligence is determined biologically and is thought to be more subject to decline with aging.

Eisdorfer and others found that the overarousal of the autonomic nervous system during stress affected the verbal learning abilities of older people.[11] Therefore, by giving an adrenergic blocking agent to one group and a placebo to another they found fewer errors as well as lower pre-fatty acid levels (a reflection of stress).

In general, with good physical and mental health, adequate educational levels, and intellectual stimulation, it appears that there is not as great a decline in intellectual abilities with age as previously thought, especially in the 60 and 70 year age group.[12] Some abilities, such as judgment, accuracy, and general knowledge, may, in fact, increase. However, if one lives long enough there are decrements in important abilities of intelligence that are not yet readily accounted for by disease.[13] There appear to be losses in brain cells, for example, and brain cells, unlike other cells in the body, do not continue to replace themselves throughout life. Nonetheless, the significance of the cell loss, since there is a redundancy of cells, is not established. There are also changes in the nerve cell (neuron) itself, especially the dendrites, which participate in neurotransmission.[14]

Studies of intellectual function and memory decline among the aged have shown that when older persons were presented with real problems, they scored much better than when they were tested with trivial or artificial problems. Sternberg and Wagner (1986) have studied practical intelligence in the performance of real-life situations. In addition, studies of aerobically trained individuals suggest that exercise is associated with improved cognitive function.

The Seattle Longitudinal Study (Schaie) found wide individual differences in intellectual changes over time, with a large number of elderly persons showing little decline, even in their eighties. Schaie has postulated a number of factors that characterize such elderly: (1) they have no cardiovascular disease; (2) they are not poor—rather, they are at least average economically; (3) they have an active involvement in life; and (4) they describe themselves as having already been flexible in attitudes and behavior in mid-life.[15]

Social Changes

It is in the social realm of an older person's life that the most clearly age-specific patterns can presently be seen. The nature of families and societies in the course of the life cycle decrees certain conditions that can be described as "natural" for older people. They find themselves the eldest group in the population with two, three, or even four generations below them. Many have grown children and grandchildren with whom they are involved. Grandparentage becomes a new social role. The older husband and wife each face prospects of widowhood and membership in a peer group with a large proportion of widowed contemporaries. There are increasing numbers of women compared to men as they age. Many older persons are less involved than previously in work and income-related activities and thus have more time available for their own use.

Beyond these certain basic social conditions, older people experience wide variations from culture to culture. The old may be venerated or scorned, treated overly sentimentally or rejected, protected or abandoned. At times they are arbitrarily respected for great wisdom and counsel while at other times, paradoxically, they are seen as burdens that waste their society's strength and resources. Cross-cultural studies in the psychology of later life give insights concerning universal features of aging and offer opportunities for borrowing new social and cultural arrangements from each other.

The older person's relative position in any society tends to be favorably influenced by several institutional factors:

1. Ownership of property and control over the opportunities of the young
2. Command of strategic knowledge and skills
3. Strong religious and sacred traditions
4. Strong kinship and extended family bonds
5. A less product-oriented society
6. High mutual dependence and reciprocity among society members

In the United States, a split and contradictory set of roles exists for older men, since some of them remain active in government, political parties, religious affairs, and business life. They may have strong executive and administrative responsibilities. In the United States Supreme Court, 85% of all service has been supplied by men over 65. Such opportunities exist for relatively few older men, however, and this generation of older women, because of their major roles as homemakers, have far fewer positions of public power and status.

The feelings of social loss among the aged can be tremendous. Retirement and Social Security regulations put them out of the work force when many would prefer employment. Income becomes drastically reduced, in many cases to outright poverty. Thirty percent live alone and 55% live with a spouse. Children and grandchildren who live miles away may have few face-to-face contacts. It must be added, however, that outright neglect or isolation from families is *not* the norm, except when geographical distances are a factor in creating isolation. Even though they may live in separate households, which both generations may prefer, many families are deeply supportive of their older members.

Old age, then, is a multiply-determined experience that depends on an intricate balance of physical, emotional, and social forces, any one of which can upset or involve the others. An older person who is socially lonely may not eat well and therefore may develop physical symptoms of malnourishment, which in turn cloud intellectual functioning. Hearing loss can lead to a suspiciousness that irritates people and causes them to shun the person's company, leaving that person isolated. A widower, grieving the loss of his wife, may develop psychosomatic symptoms and lose his job.

We already have the knowledge and skills available to alleviate much of the suffering in old age. We know that people need to be fed and sheltered decently, they must have medical and psychiatric care, they need loving and supportive personal contacts, and, finally, they require meaningful social roles. Health is not really an elusive concept, but it does require that we make commitments *as* human beings *to* human beings, and these commitments require much energy and many resources.

HISTORICAL FACTORS IN ADAPTATION

People are shaped not only by their own personal history, family environment, and inherent personality characteristics, but also by the larger world around them. So in understanding the aged it is useful to consider those factors in local, national, and world history that may have influenced them as they grew from infancy to old age.[16]

The present 65-plus population was born around the time when Herbert Spencer's social Darwinism or "survival of the fittest" was the popular social theory. Huge fortunes were amassed by families with names like Gould, Morgan, Rockefeller, and Carnegie, while poorly paid immigrant workers provided labor. The Protestant ethic, inspired by Calvin's philosophy of success through hard work and self-sacrifice, was the dominant religious influence. The labor movement, women's suffrage, and child labor laws were evolving as protection against exploitation. Thus the nation had reached a crossroads between accepting the notion of survival of the strongest and attempting to protect everyone, including the weak.

This raw dichotomy was the earliest societal experience of the now-older population. Many of

them still feel the tug of these forces in their personal lives and insist on being independent in the face of real personal limitations. They may berate themselves for not being allowed or able to work. They may accept their difficult economic and social conditions as evidence that they are not among the elite or "fittest." The massive depression of the 1930s served to propel scores of such "rugged individualists" into reluctant acceptance of governmental intervention in their lives, but many saw such intervention as evidence of personal failure rather than overwhelming social forces. They have contended with the tumultuous concept of progress through industrialization and automation and with the technological notion of human obsolescence. All this has served to increase their sense of uncertainty about their own value if their productive capacities wane.

POPULAR MYTHS ABOUT AGING

It is a myth that chronological age determines how "old" one is. A more apt measure of actual age might be that old maxim "You're as old as you feel." Young 80-year-olds can look very different from old 80-year-olds. It is well established that large disparities often exist between physiological, psychological, chronological, and social ages. People age at such different rates that physiological indicators show a greater range from the mean in old age than in any other age group, and people may become more diverse rather than similar as they age.[17] Of course certain diseases have a leveling effect, which causes a look-alike appearance from person to person. Massive organic brain damage and the major illnesses can so damage body and brain that their victims may react and behave very much like each other. Poverty and illiteracy also tend to obscure individual uniqueness and variation.

Another widespread myth surrounding aging is the conviction that all old people are "senile." *Senility,* although not an actual medical term, is still often used by doctors and lay people alike to explain the behavior and condition of older people. Many of the reactive emotional responses of older people, such as depression, grief, and anxiety, are labeled senile and thus considered chronic, untreatable states. Senility is an especially convenient tag put on older women by doctors who do not wish to spend the time and effort necessary to diagnose and treat their complaints. The popular medical school term for older people is "crocks"; thus attitudes are formed that affect future practice. To be sure, brain damage from multi-infarct dementia and Alzheimer's disease is a realistic problem, probably causing 50% or more of cases of mental disorder in old age. But even with brain disease there can be overlays of depression, anxiety, and psychosomatic disorders that are responsive to medical and psychotherapeutic intervention.

A third myth, the *tranquility myth,* presents a strange and contradictory position, considering the general situation of older persons. This myth sets forth the sugar-coated "Grandma-baking-goodies" vision of old age as a time of idyllic serenity and tranquility when older persons enjoy the fruits of their labors. A combination of wishful thinking about their own future old age and denial of the realities that presently exist is evident in the younger generation's image of happy-go-lucky older people.

Mrs. G and her husband retired with an estate of a quarter of a million dollars. He had been a successful doctor in a Midwestern city. Dr. G was 69 when he chose to retire and his wife was four years younger. Only two years later he was dead. Their son, age 44, died of a coronary a year afterward. Mrs. G paid many of the expenses of her son's terminal illness and also helped her daughter-in-law meet the college expenses of her grandchildren. Ten years later, at 77 years of age, Mrs. G, the respected and wealthy physician's wife, was herself impoverished and enfeebled. Her money had run out.

We cite this example to illustrate how people who may have entered old age in the most favorable circumstances can nonetheless be subject to major and continuing emotional and financial crises.

There is also the *myth of unproductivity* associated with old age. It is assumed that older people can no longer produce in a job or be active socially and creatively. They are presumed to be disengaged from life, declining and disinterested. But in the absence of disease and social adversity, this does not happen. Older people tend to remain actively concerned about their personal and community relationships. Many are still employed. Numbers of others do "bootleg work" to avoid reporting their earnings, because of Social Security income ceilings.

The *myth of resistance to change* is as suspect as all the others. It is true that adult character structure is remarkably stable, but ability to change depends more on previous and lifelong personality traits than on anything inherent in old age. Often when conservatism occurs, it derives not from aging but from socioeconomic pressures. An example might be the decision of older people to vote against school loans because of the increase those loans would mean in their personal property taxes.

NEW INTERPRETATIONS OF AGING FROM RESEARCH

In attempting to gain a more realistic picture of aging, a few midcentury investigators, responding to the paucity of information in this area, began studying healthy older people. Community-resident and socially autonomous older people were examined from a wide range of research perspectives in studies beginning in the late 1950s and early 1960s. The Busse et al. (1985) and National Institute of Mental Health (NIMH) studies (Birren et al., 1963) were responsible for some of the first work, and Shock (1984) studied some 600 men longitudinally every 18 months. The NIMH undertook collaborative studies involving separate academic disciplines and medical specialties over a period of 11 years. The NIMH findings were surprisingly optimistic and in general reinforced the hypothesis that much of what has been called aging is really disease.

Decreased cerebral (brain) blood flow and oxygen consumption were found to be probable results of arteriosclerosis rather than an inevitable companion of aging. Healthy older men with an average age of 71 presented cerebral physiological and intellectual functions that compared favorably with those in a younger control group with an average age of 21. Some evidence of slowing in speed and response was found, but this correlated with environmental deprivation and depression as well as with physical decline.

Older persons were found to have the same psychiatric disorders as the young with similar genesis and structure. Adaptation and survival appeared to be associated with the individual's self-image and sense of ongoing usefulness as well as continuing good physical health. Current environmental satisfaction and support were found to be critical to psychological stability. Individuals who were "self-starters" and could structure and carry out new contacts, activities, and involvements were found to have the least disease and the longest survival rates. The interrelating between sound health and adaptability was validated by the sensitivity of psychometric test results to even

minimal disease. In general the healthy aged were characterized by flexibility, resourcefulness, and optimism, whereas manifestations of mental illness were attributed to medical illness, personality factors, and sociocultural effects rather than the aging process.

See Table 3.1 for illustrative longitudinal studies involving older people. Such studies are important to our understanding of human change over time.

PSYCHOSOCIAL THEORIES OF AGING

G. Stanley Hall was a pioneer, writing the first major American book on the psychology of old age in 1922. Since then, a variety of theories have evolved concerning the psychology of aging. The controversial "disengagement theory" in gerontology evolved from the Kansas City aging studies conducted by the University of Chicago Committee on Human Development in the late 1950s.[18] This theory postulated that older people

TABLE 3.1   Illustrative longitudinal studies involving normal older people

STUDY	YEAR BEGAN	SEX STUDIED
Berkeley/Oakland Human Development Studies (National Institute of Child and Human Development/National Institute on Aging)	1928/1932	Male and female
Adaptation to Life (Harvard Medical School)	1937	Male
Thousand Aviators (U.S. Navy)	1940	Male
Framingham Study (National Heart Lung and Blood Institute and National Eye Institute)	1950	Male and female
Duke University I and II (National Institute on Aging—supported)	1955	Male and female
National Institute of Mental Health of the National Institutes of Health	1955	Male
Baltimore Longitudinal Study (National Institute on Aging—intramural)	1958	Male and female
Langley-Porter/University of California, San Francisco (National Institute of Child and Human Development/National Institute on Aging)	1958	Male and female
Veterans Administration Normative Study	1958	Male
Gothenburg, Sweden Studies (A. Svanborg)	1971	Male and female

and society mutually withdraw from each other as part of normal aging, and that this withdrawal is characterized by psychological well-being on the part of the older person. Later the disengagement theory was modified by Havighurst et al. in a series of papers beginning in 1963, using the original Kansas City data.[19] Disengagement was redefined by them as simply a process rather than a theory of optimum aging and as only one of many possible patterns of aging. Of 88 subjects studied, all but 18 fell into the following psychological groups: (1) the integrated, who were high on most positive personality variables; (2) the "defended" group, aggressive and full of energy; (3) the passive-dependent group; and (4) the unintegrated group, low on almost all personality measures. These four categories were common to both men and women. There were two further groups of men: One group was characterized as introspective, timid, stable, and high on super-ego control but lacking in internalization of institutional values. The other group was fearful of failure and of becoming dependent on others. One group of women had feelings of inferiority and self-doubt and was overcontrolled and dissatisfied. Another group of women similarly was self-doubting but very aggressive and competitive.

Reichard et al. interviewed 87 men, 55 to 84 years of age, in California.[20] They found 64 of these subjects fit into five groups. Three of these groups were accepting of aging: (1) the mature, philosophical men, (2) the rocking chair men who seemed glad to have time to relax, and (3) the armored men who tried to keep active at all costs and used this as a defense against old age and death. The fourth group was labeled aggressive and seemed to blame others for its disappointments and frustrations. Those in the fifth group were intrapunitive (Reichard's term for self-punitive), depressed, and gloomy. Of the 87 men, 23 did not fit neatly into any of these categories.

Carp's study of residents in a home for the aging in Texas produced evidence that in a positive environment older people generally moved toward activity and informal social contacts, rather than disengagement.[21] She raised the possibility that so-called "age-related behavior" such as disengagement may be the result of the environmental conditions that so often accompany old age. Carp also observed that rigidity was not intrinsic to the aging personality. Rigid behavior could be brought on by difficult social or physical situations; but once the difficulties were alleviated, the rigidity disappeared.

Rosow (*The Social Integration of the Aged,* 1967) showed that older people who live among other older people make more friends than those who live among the young, refuting a conclusion of the disengagement theory. His sample included 1,200 older people living in three kinds of housing—one with a mix of ages, one with a number of older people, that is, "age concentrated," and one almost totally aged, that is, "age dense." Hochschild (*The Unexpected Community,* 1973) also found in her intensive study of 43 older people residing in a small apartment building that "age dense" housing arrangements expand the potential circle of friends for older people. An "exchange" theory pertaining to imbalances in social exchange and their relationship to rewards and power has been posited as an explanation for the disengaging behavior seen in some older persons.[22] Martin and Dowd, in particular, have advanced the notion that the more one values rewards, the more one loses power.[23]

Havighurst and colleagues from Holland, Italy, Germany, and the United States conducted a cross-national study of steelworkers and retired teachers in order to test and expand on the findings of the Kansas City studies.[24]

Out of all of this has come the current and prevailing view that activity rather than disengagement produces the most agreeable psychological climate for older people.[25] The "activity theory" maintains that older people should remain active as long as they possibly can. When certain activities and associations must be given up (for example, employment), substitutes should be found. The older person's personality is a key element in shaping reactions to biological and social changes—an active rather than a passive role is important for mental health and satisfaction.

Lowenthal and associates studied 216 adults at four points in their lives, beginning with high school seniors and ending with men and women about to retire.[26] They compared life-styles, adaptation, and attitudes and examined concepts such as intimacy, mutuality, and time orientation. They identified ways in which adults cope with changes and compared the socialization and response to stress and change in women versus men. Differences between the sexes were more significant than between the old and the young. The authors found that the old were no more rigid psychologically than the young and that an individual's point of view, values, and outlook depended on how well one had managed to adapt to one's particular life stage.

Neugarten and Gutmann advanced the interesting conclusion that men and women begin to reverse roles in terms of authority within the family structure somewhere in their mid-fifties.[27] Their study found men becoming more nurturing and women more aggressive and assertive. (Jung described this as the emergence of animus or the masculine component in women, and anima or the feminine component in men.)

David Gutmann's work based upon studies of several cultures, the Druze in Israel, middle-class white Americans in Kansas City, the Navajo Indians, and the Mayan Indians, found universal themes suggesting that, with aging, women characteristically become more assertive as men become more nurturant. His book *Reclaimed Powers* (1987) concludes that potentials that had been denied to men and women earlier in life are available to them in later life since they are freed from what he calls the "parental emergency."[28]

In spite of the work already done, the study of the effects of age and other elements on personality development in later life is just beginning. The more obvious problems at this point are the measurement of generational differences and the lack of adequate norms against which to measure behavior. There is growing attention to what has been called "life-span developmental psychology"—the attempt to study development as a lifelong process.[29]

Alvar Svanborg's longitudinal studies of aging involved 70-year-olds in Gothenburg, Sweden. The subjects fall into one of three representative groups: (1) born in 1901–1902; (2) born in 1906–1907; and (3) born in 1911–1912. By 1988, the groups had been followed through ages 85, 79, and 72, respectively. An intervention program was added to the third cohort in order to further examine relationships between vitality and the state of health, as well as life-style or ecology. Direct evidence of age cohort differences was observed concerning longevity, cognitive function, disability, and certain medical disorders. Memory was not changed significantly at ages 70 and 75 in the healthy elderly. Perceptual speed apparently started to decline in early life. Most importantly, each successive cohort appeared healthier than the preceding one.[30]

The Framingham study, from which the coronary heart disease profile was derived, convened in 1950. Now, as the children of the original sample are under study, Framingham has become a major, multigenerational research program. It focuses upon a variety of late-life disease outcomes, including dementia and cataracts.[31]

The University of Southern California Andrus Gerontology Center longitudinal study of three-generation families in 1971 followed 2,044 individuals, including grandparents, parents, and grandchildren, representing 328 families. In 1985, the study leaders contacted the surviving 1,300 participants again to compare 1970 and 1985 results. They concluded that there was somewhat less of a perceived generation gap in 1985, compared to 1970. This trend continues in ongoing triannual surveys (1988, 1991, 1994).[32]

SOME SPECIAL CHARACTERISTICS OF OLDER PEOPLE

A number of characteristics that we have seen quite frequently in older people are connected with the unique sense of having lived a long time and having accepted the concept of life as a cycle from birth through death.

Desire to Leave a Legacy

Human beings have a need to leave something of themselves behind when they die. This legacy may be children and grandchildren, work or art, personal possessions, memories in the minds of others, even bodies or body parts for use in medical training and research. Motivations for the tendency toward legacy are generally a combination of not wanting to be forgotten, of wanting to give of one's self magnanimously to those who survive, of wishing to remain in control in some way even after death (for example, through wills), and of desiring to tidy up responsibly before death. Legacy provides a sense of continuity, giving the older person a feeling of being able to participate even after death.

The "Elder" Function

Closely connected with legacy, the "elder" function refers to the natural propensity of the old to share with the young the accumulated knowledge and experience they have collected. If unhampered and indeed encouraged, this "elder" function takes the form of counseling, guiding, and sponsoring those who are younger. It is tied to the development of an interconnectedness between the generations. It is important to a sense of self-esteem to be acknowledged by the young as an elder, to have one's life experience seen as interesting and valuable; on the other hand, it can be devastating to be shrugged off by seemingly uninterested younger people as old-fashioned and irrelevant. Not all older people, however, have a nurturant feeling toward the young. Some, because of their life experience, look on the young with envy and distrust.

Mental health personnel can learn much about how to help older people by respecting and benefiting from what the elderly have to teach. This occurs through listening to them with an open mind, reading the writings of older people, viewing their arts, hearing their music, and in general absorbing the culture created by them.

Attachment to Familiar Objects

In the very old, an increasing emotional investment in the things surrounding their daily lives—home, pets, familiar objects, heirlooms, keepsakes, photo albums, scrapbooks, old letters—may be noticed. Such objects provide a sense of continuity, aid the memory, and provide comfort, security, and satisfaction. Fear of loss of possessions at death is a frequent preoccupation. Older people generally feel better if they can decide in an orderly manner how their belongings will be distributed and cared for. Younger family members or friends should take such concerns seriously, offering their help rather than denying that the older person will someday die. Possessions may have to be painfully given up before death as a result of moves from a house to an apartment, an institution, and so on. Some institutions are now recognizing the value of encouraging people to bring some of their own familiar possessions with them.

Change in the Sense of Time

There may be a resolution of fears about time running out, with an end to time panics and to boredom, and the development of a more appropriate valuation of time. While the middle-aged begin to be concerned with the number of years they have left to live, older persons tend to experience a sense of immediacy, of here and now, of living in the moment. This could be called a sense of "presentness" or "elementality." The elemental things of life—children, friendship, nature, human touching (physical and emotional), color, shape—assume greater significance as people sort out the more important from the less important. Old age can be a time of emotional and sensory awareness and enjoyment.

Sense of the Life Cycle

Older people experience something that younger people cannot: a personal sense of the entire life cycle. We discuss this further in Chapter 8. There may be a greater interest in philosophy and religion, in enduring art or literature. For example, in Japan it is common for old men to begin to write poetry, thus giving another expression of life and its meaning. A sense of historical perspective and a capacity to summarize and comment upon one's time, as well as one's life, sometimes develop.

Creativity, Curiosity, and Surprise

Creativity does not necessarily decline with age. Many persons recognized as creative have continued their work far into old age—Cervantes, Voltaire, Goethe, Tolstoy, Picasso, Martha Graham, Georgia O'Keefe, and Marguerite Yourcenar—to name a few. It is of course easy to recognize persons of achievement who continue to be productive in late life. But less well known is the fact that *most* older people remain productive and active in the absence of disease and social problems. Many become creative for the first time in old age, and the list does not begin and end with Grandma Moses. Factors that impede or support creativity and activity must be studied.

Curiosity and an ability to be surprised are other qualities that have a strikingly adaptive quality. Such qualities are especially attractive to younger people, who take heart and hope in them for their own old age. This type of enthusiasm probably reflects lifelong personality traits and serves the individual well in old age.

Sense of Consummation or Fulfillment in Life

A feeling of satisfaction with one's life is more common than recognized but not as common as possible. It is a quality of "serenity" and "wisdom," which derives from resolution of personal conflicts, reviewing one's life and finding it acceptable and gratifying, and viewing death with equanimity. One's life does not have to be a "success" in the general sense of that word in order to result in serenity. The latter can come from a feeling of having done one's best, from having met challenge and difficulty, and sometimes from simply having survived against terrible odds.

MIDDLE AGE AND THE TRANSITION TO OLD AGE

An understanding of old age requires consideration of the transition from the middle years. Neugarten and Lowenthal have contributed much to the study of mid-life. Middle age is usually regarded as the period from age 40 to 65, during which most people are engaged in providing the livelihood for a family and finishing the rearing of children. The middle-aged are the people in command in society in terms of power, influence, norms, and decisions. They make up roughly 25% of the population and carry much responsibility for the old and the young.

Two themes that predominate in mid-life are the growing awareness of personal aging (eventual death) and the changes in life patterns that occur as the middle-aged person's children grow up, parents grow old, and new roles are assumed personally and socially. People become aware of a different sense of time; they begin to think about how long they have left to live rather than about how long they have lived. Men are aware of the possibility of their own imminent death, whereas women, who have a longer life expectancy and often are married to an older spouse, worry first about the death of the husband and later about their own aging and demise. They may consciously or unconsciously prepare for widowhood. Many women become concerned about outliving their financial resources and a good number of them actually do. (See case of Mrs. G. on page 61.)

A personal sense of death can no longer be easily denied and avoided. The death of parents leaves the middle-aged next in line. Friends and peers begin to die; unmistakable physical changes occur; one's own children reach adulthood. But the perception of death may be a matter-of-fact acceptance rather than negative fears and worries. It can lead to greater respect for and attention to one's physical health; Neugarten (1968) has called this "body monitoring": the activities undertaken to keep the body in physical condition and to care for any physical illnesses or chronic conditions that have developed. It also leads to a reassessment of one's life, a stocktaking in terms of marriage, career, personal relationships, values, and other commitments made earlier in youth, According to Neugarten, an increased "interiority" takes place. Career changes and divorces are not infrequent, and sometimes the whole way of life may be changed. Mid-life has been compared to a second adolescence—one in which people reassess, change, and strike out in new directions.

Other such periods may occur after retirement or after widowhood, when again one sees reevaluation, with new identities and directions emerging. A conception of personal death may become consciously realized. At first this can be frightening and painful, but if favorably resolved, a mature resignation frees the person from fear. (Some, of course, must maintain a denial of death because of vulnerabilities that do not allow for direct confrontation with the end of life.) Mid-life and eventually old age can then be enjoyed but with a full or at least partial awareness of the eventuality of death. Appreciations of some of the elemental things that people tend to value more highly as they age—human love and affection, insight, pleasures of the senses, nature, children, pets—are probably a result of the restructuring and reformulation of concepts of time, self, and death.

Studies thus far seem to indicate that the majority of people adjust and adapt remarkably well to the demands and problems of middle life. But difficulties do occur and are sometimes called "mid-life crises." Middle-aged people may panic and attempt to recapture youth by adopting inappropriately young dress, manners, and behavior. They may envy the young and feel inferior to them or, on the other hand, hate and disparage them. There can be an overexaggeration of body monitoring, which becomes hypochondriacal. There can be such a fear of change that people will remain in pressured or boring jobs and marriages or will leap into almost identical situations if they do decide to take action. There may be preoccupations with age and appearance and self-consciousness about how to act and relate. Depression and alcoholism tend to increase. Although the "empty nest" (when children have left home) and the menopause do not ordinarily cause serious problems for women (and indeed may bring a sense of freedom and spontaneity), both of these may become overemphasized as potential problem areas. Sexual promiscuity in order to prove youth and attractiveness may develop, as well as increased religiosity that has a hollow and desperate ring to it. Men may be haunted by a need to "succeed." All of these represent unresolved fears of aging and attempts to deny it by trying to turn back the clock. One can see fixation, rigidity, fatalism, pessimism, or overexpansiveness.

Middle age can be and is for most people the prime of life. But it can be complicated by periods of genuine crises, ranging from the superficial and reversible to the profound and more pathological. The middle-aged person who truly wants to be young again is rare, but most would like to preserve the good health and energy of youth. In its best sense mid-life can become a time of increasing sensitivity, self-awareness, use of capacities and skills to the fullest, and separation of that which is valuable from the less valuable in order to use time wisely and enjoyably. It can in this sense become a healthy preparation for the transition to old age.[33]

THE CHANGING AWARENESS OF OLD AGE

A large aged population is a new phenomenon, with older people no longer considered a rarity. Older people have become more highly visible since the nineteenth century as greater life expectancy and various social and economic conditions have unfolded the life cycle, making its stages stand out in bolder relief. At the beginning of the twentieth century, only 1 in 25 Americans was over 65; in 1995, 1 in 8 was at least 65. Each day there are over 1,000 more older Americans; each year nearly 400,000 more. By the year 2030, older people could make up one-fifth of the total population. As their numbers grow, older people have slowly begun to be of interest to U.S. sociologists and psychologists, although the medical and psychotherapeutic professions, which come most closely in contact with older people, still have not made an active enough commitment to their special concerns and problems. Politicians have begun to grasp the value of supporting programs to benefit older persons since they have become a major political constituency. Older people have begun to show a growing self-awareness and sophisticated use of public opinion and public policy. Their financial power is impressive, with people over 50 now controlling 50% of discretionary income in the United States. These facts, combined with their increasing good health and survival rates, may at last bring older people hope for a vital participation in a better future for themselves and all of us.

SELECTED READINGS

Atchley, R. C. (1991). *The social forces in later life.* Belmont, CA: Wadsworth Publishing.

Atchley, R. C. (1994). *The social forces and aging: An introduction to social gerontology.* Belmont, CA: Wadsworth Publishing.

Bates, P. B., & Brim, O. G., Jr. (Eds.). (1984) *Life span development and behavior.* Orlando, FL: Academic Press.

Bengtson, V. L., Reedy, M. N., & Gordon, C. (1985). Aging and self-conceptions: Personality pressures and social contexts. In Birren, J. E., & Schaie, K. W. (Eds.), *Handbook of the psychology of aging,* 2nd ed. (pp. 544–593). New York: Van Nostrand Reinhold.

Bengtson, V. L., & Robertson, J. F. (1985). *Grandparenthood.* Beverly Hills, CA: Sage.

Bengtson, V. L., Silverstein, M., & Giarrusso, R. (1995). Longitudinal study of generations. In Maddox, G. L. (Ed.), *The encyclopedia of aging* (pp. 582–584). New York: Springer.

Binstock, R., & George, L. K. (Eds.). (1990). *Handbook of aging and the social sciences,* 3rd ed. San Diego, CA: Academic Press.

Birren, J. E., & Bengtson, V. L. (Eds.). (1988). *Emergent theories of aging.* New York: Springer.

Birren, J. E., Butler, R. N., Greenhouse, S. W., Sokoloff, L., & Yarrow, M. R. (Eds.). (1963). *Human aging: A biological and behavioral study.* Pub. no. (PHS) 986. Washington DC: U.S. Government Printing Office. (Reprinted as Pub. no. (HSM) 71–9051, 1971, 1974).

Birren, J. E., & Shaie, K. W. (Eds.). (1991). *Handbook of the psychology of aging,* 3rd ed. San Diego: Academic Press.

Bond, L. A., Cutler, S. J., & Grams, A. E. (Eds.). (1995). *Promoting successful aging.* Thousand Oaks, CA: Sage.

Buhler, C. (1968). The general structure of the human life. In Buhler, C., & Massarik, F. (Eds.), *The course of human life: A study of goals in the human perspective.* New York: Springer.

Busse, E. W., & Maddox, G. L. (1985). *The Duke Longitudinal Studies of Normal Aging 1955–1980: An overview of history, designs, and findings.* New York: Springer.

Butler, R. N. (1989). Productive aging. In Bengtson, V. L., & Shaie, K. W. *The course of later life.* New York: Springer.

Butler, R. N. (1989). Psychosocial aspects of aging. In Kaplan, H. I., & Saddock, B. J. (Eds.), *The Comprehensive textbook of psychiatry,* 5th ed. (pp. 2014–2019). Baltimore: Williams & Wilkins.

Butler, R. N., Oberlink, M. R., & Schechter, M. (1989). *Promise of productive aging.* New York: Springer.

Costa, P. T., Jr., & McCrae, R. P. (1989). Personality continuity and the changes of adult life. In Storandt, M., & Vanden Bos, G. R. (Eds.), *The adult years: Continuity and change* (pp. 45–77). Washington, DC: American Psychological Association.

Field, D. (Guest Ed.). (1991). Special issue: Personality and aging. *Journal of Gerontology: Psychological Sciences, 46*(6).

Granick, S., & Patterson, R. (1971). *Human aging II: An eleven-year follow-up biobehavioral study.* Washington, DC: National Institute of Mental Health, Pub. no. (HSM) 71–9037.

Granick, D. (1987). *Reclaimed powers: Toward a new psychology of men and women in later life.* New York: Basic Books.

Hall, G. S. (1922). *Senescence: The last half of life.* New York: D. Appleton.

Lowenthal, M. F., & Chiriboga, D. (1972). Transition to the empty nest: Crisis, challenge, or relief? *Archives of General Psychiatry, 26,* 8–15.

McCrae, R. R., & Costa, P. T., Jr. (1984). *Emerging lives, enduring dispositions: Personality in adulthood.* Boston: Little, Brown.

Myerhoff, B. G. (1979). *Number our days.* New York: E. P. Dutton.

Neugarten, B. L. (Ed.). (1968). *Middle age and aging.* Chicago, IL: University of Chicago Press.

Palmore, E. (1970). *Normal aging: Reports from the Duke Longitudinal Study, 1955–1969.* Durham, NC: Duke University Press.

Palmore, E., Busse, E. W., Maddox, G. L., Nowlin, J. B., & Siegler, I. C. (1985) *Normal aging III.* Durham, NC: Duke University Press.

Perlmutter, M., Adams, C., Berry, J., et. al. (1987). Aging and memory. In Shaie, K. W., & Eisdorfer, C. (Eds.). *Annual Review of Gerontology and Geriatrics, 8* (pp. 57–92). New York: Springer.

Pressey, S. L., & Kuhlen, R. G. (1957). *Psychological development through the life cycle.* New York: Harper & Row.

Riley, M. W. (Ed.). (1979). *Aging from birth to death.* Boulder, CO: Westview Press.

Rosow, I. (1975). *Socialization to old age.* Berkeley, CA: University of California Press.

Rowe, J. W., & Kahn, R. L. (1987). Human aging: Usual and successful. *Science, 237,* 143–149.

Schaie, K. W. (1983). *Longitudinal studies of adult psychological development.* New York: Guilford Press.

Schaie, K. W. (1994) The course of adult intellectual development. *American Psychologist, 49,* 304–313.

Schaie, K. W. (1995). *Intellectual development in adulthood: The Seattle Longitudinal Study.* New York: Cambridge University Press.

Schaie, K. W., Campbell, R. T., Meredith, W. M., & Rawlings, S. C. (Eds.). (1988). *Methodological issues in aging research.* New York: Springer.

Shock, N. W., Greulich, R. C., Andres, R., Arenberg, D., Costa, P. T., Jr., Lakatta, E. G., & Tobin, J. D. (1984). *Normal human aging: The Baltimore Longitudinal Study of Aging.* NIH Publication No. 84–2450. Bethesda, MD: National Institutes of Health.

Thomae, H. (1976). *Patterns of aging: Findings from the Bonn Longitudinal Study of Aging.* Basel, Switzerland: S. Karger.

World Health Organization. (1946). Constitution of the World Health Organization. *Public Health Report, 61,* 1268–1277.

ENDNOTES

1. There appears to be a relative absence of fear of death. For a discussion of psychological attitudes toward death among older Japanese-Americans, see Osako, M. (1980). Aging, social isolation and kinship ties among Japanese-Americans. In *Project Report to the Administration on Aging.* (pp. 116–120). Washington, DC: The Administration on Aging.

2. Miles, C. C., & Miles, W. R. (1932). The correlation of intelligence scores and chronological age from early to late maturity. *American Journal of Psychology 44,* 44–78.

3. Jones, H. E., & Conrad, H. S. (1933). The growth and decline of intelligence. A study of a homogeneous group between the ages of ten and sixty. *Genetic Psychological Monograph 13,* 223–298.

4. Longitudinal research presents methodological problems of its own, as described by Greenhouse and Morrison (1963) and Schaie (1965, 1983). When a sample is studied over a span of time, differentiating intrinsic changes from those caused by environment becomes difficult, and it is impossible to rule out the bias of survivorship itself. See Greenhouse, S. W., & Morrison, D. F. (1963). Statistical methodology. In Birren, J. E., Butler, R. N., Greenhouse, S. W., Sokoloff, L., & Yarrow, M. R. (Eds.), *Human aging: A biological and behavioral study,* Pub No. (PHS) 986, Washington, DC: U.S. Government Printing Office (reprinted as Pub. No. [HSM] 71–9051, 1971, 1974); Schaie, K. W. (1965). A general model for the study of developmental problems. *Psychological Bulletin* 64:92–107. Baltes, P. B. (1968). Longitudinal and cross-sectional sequences in the study of age and generation effects. *Human Development 11,* 145–171, and Schaie, K. W. (1993). *Longitudinal studies of adult psychological development.* New York: Guilford Press.

5. Bayley, N., & Oden, M. H. A. B. (1955). The maintenance of intellectual ability in gifted adults. *Journal of Gerontology 10,* 91–107.

6. Owens, W. A. (1966). Age and mental abilities: A second adult follow-up. *Journal of Educational Psychology 57,* 316–25.

7. Lorge, I. (1936). The influence of the test upon the nature of mental decline as a function of age. *Journal of Educational Psychology 32,* 100–110.

8. Botwinick, J., & Birren, J. E. (1963). Mental abilities and psychomotor responses in healthy aged men. In Birren, J. E., Butler, R. N., Greenhouse, S. W., Sokoloff, L., & Yarrow, M. R. (Eds.), *Human aging: A biological and behavioral study,* Pub. No. (PHS) 986, Washington, DC: U.S. Government Printing Office (reprinted as Pub. No [HSM] 71–9051, 1971, 1974).

9. Jarvik, L. F., Eisdorfer, C., & Blum, J. E. (Eds.). (1975). *Intellectual functioning in adults.* New York: Springer Verlag.

10. Horn, J. L., & Cattell, R. B. (1966). *Age differences in primary mental ability factors. Journal of Gerontology 21,* 210–220; Craik, F. J., & Tehub, S. (Eds.). (1982). *Aging and cognitive processes.* New York: Plenum.

11. Eisdorfer, C. (1972). Autonomic changes in aging. In Gaitz, C. M. (Ed.), *Aging and the brain.* New York: Plenum Publishing.

12. Birren, J. E., & Schaie, K. W. (1985). *Handbook of the psychology of aging.* 3rd ed. New York: Van-Nostrand Reinhold; Ivnik, R. J., Malec, J. F., Smith, G. E., et al. (1992). Mayo's older Americans normative studies: WAIS-R norms for ages 59–97. *Clinical Neuropsychologist 6,* pp. 1–30.

13. Horn, J. L., & Donaldson, G. (1976). On the myth of intellectual decline in adulthood. *American Psychologist 31*(10), 701–719; Perlmutter, M., Adams, C., Berry, J., et al. Aging and memory. In Schaie, K. W., & Eisdorfer, C. (Eds.), *Annual review of Gerontology and Geriatrics* (Vol. 8, pp. 57–92). New York: Springer; Schaie, K. W. (1995). *Intellectual development in adulthood: The Seattle Longitudinal Study.* New York: Cambridge University Press; Schaie, K. W. (1994a). The course of adult

intellectual development. *American Psychologist, 49,* 304–313.

14. Scheibel, M. E., Lindsay, R. D., Tomiya, V. & Scheibel, A. B. (1975). Progressive dendritic changes in aging human cortex. *Experimental Neurology 47,* 392–403.

15. Schaie, K. W. (1995). Longitudinal Research (pp. 575–576) & Intelligence (pp. 513–514). In Maddox, G. L. (Ed.), *The encyclopedia of aging.* New York: Springer.

16. For an overview of the experience of today's older persons, it is useful to read Barbara Tuchman's *The proud tower* and Frederick Lewis Allen's *The big change.*

17. See the National Institute of Mental Health's *Human Aging* studies (Birren et al.) and the work of Heron and Chown (1967).

18. Cummings, E., & Henry, W. E. (1961). *Growing old: The process of disengagement.* New York: Basic Books.

19. Havighurst, R. J., Neugarten, B. L., & Tobin, S. S. (1968). Disengagement and patterns of aging. In Neugarten, B. L. (Ed.), *Middle age and aging.* Chicago: University of Chicago Press.

20. Reichard, S., Livson, F., & Peterson, P. G. (1962). *Aging and personality.* New York: John Wiley & Sons.

21. Carp, F. M. (1966). *A future for the aged: Victoria Plaza and its residents.* Austin: University of Texas Press.

22. Homans, G. (1961). *Social behavior: Its elementary forms.* New York: Harcourt Brace and World; and Blau, P. (1964). *Exchange and power in social life.* New York: John Wiley and Sons.

23. Martin, J. D. (1971). Power, dependence and the complaints of the elderly. A social exchange perspective. *Aging and Human Development 2,* 108–112; and Dowd, J. J. (1975). Aging as exchange: A preface to theory. *Journal of Gerontology, 30,* 584–594.

24. Havighurst, R. J. (1963). Successful aging. In Williams, R. H., Tibbitts, C., & Donahue, W. (Eds.), *Processes of aging.* New York: Atherton Press.

25. For discussions of the disengagement theory see Carp, F. M. (1968). Some components of disengagement. *Journal of Gerontology, 23,* 383–386; Hochschild, A. R. (1975). Disengagement theory: A critique and proposal. *American Sociology Review 40,* 553–569; Tallmer, M., & Kutner, B. (1970). Disengagement and morale. *The Gerontologist, 110,* 317–320; and Orbach, H. L. (1973). Disengagement—activity controversy: Underlying theoretical models of aging. *The Gerontologist, 13,* 72.

26. Lowenthal, M. F., et al. (1975). *Four stages of life: A comparative study of women and men facing transitions.* San Francisco: Jossey-Bass.

27. Neugarten, B., & Gutmann, D. (1968). Age-sex roles and personality in middle age: A thematic apperception study. In Neugarten, B. L. (Ed.), *Middle age and aging.* Chicago: University of Chicago Press.

28. Gutmann, D. (1987). *Reclaimed powers: Toward a new psychology of men and women in later life.* New York: Basic Books.

29. There have been four important books on life-span developmental psychology, all generated by West Virginia University and published in New York by Academic Press: Goulet, L. R., & Baltes, P. (Eds.), *The theory and status of lifespan research,* 1979; Nesselroade, J., & Reese, H. W. (Eds.), *Methodological issues,* 1973; Baltes, P. B., & Schaie, K. W. (Eds.), *Life-span developmental psychology: Personality and socialization,* 1973; and Datan, N., & Ginsberg, L. H. (Eds.), *Life-span developmental psychology: Normative life crises,* 1975.

30. Svanborg, A. (1977). Seventy-year-old people in Gothenburg. A population study in an industrialized Swedish city. II. General presentation of social and medical conditions. *Acta Medica Scandinavica,* Suppl. *611,* 5–37.

31. Kannel, W. B. (1987). Rethinking the good life: Forty years at Framingham. In Bernstein, E. (Ed.), *The Encyclopedia Britannica Medical and Health Annual.* Chicago: Encyclopedia Britannica, pp. 24–39.

32. Bengston, V. L., Silverstein, M., & Giarrusso, R. (1995). Longitudinal Study of generations. In Maddox, G. L. (Ed.), *The encyclopedia of aging* (2nd ed., pp. 582–584.) New York: Springer.

33. There have been two books of considerable theoretical interest about middle age, although limited only to men: Levinson, D. J., Darrow, C. M., Klein, E. B., Levinson, M. H., & McKee, B. (1978). *The seasons of a man's life.* New York: Alfred A. Knopf; and Vaillant, G. E. (1977). *Adaptation to life.* Boston: Little, Brown. There is also Rubin's book on middle-aged women: Rubin, L. S. (1979). *Women of a certain age: The midlife search for self.* New York: Harper & Row. This is an in-depth study of the psychological identity of 160 women. Rubin concludes that issues around the stages of life are not intraspsychic per se but rather directly connected with social events and trends. The future should bring increasing research attention to the middle-life period of men and women.

COMMON EMOTIONAL PROBLEMS

Older persons experience the same emotions as those of people of every age, but as with each age, there is a uniqueness in the character of such emotions. Both the uniqueness and the similarities bear examination if one is to clarify the distinctive nature of old age.

Loss is one of the predominant themes in characterizing the common emotional problems of older people. Losses in every aspect of late life compel many older persons to expend enormous amounts of physical and emotional energy in grieving and resolving grief, adapting to the changes that result from loss, and recovering from the stresses inherent in these processes. The psychological treatment goal is obtaining insight and restitution possibilities within the limits of the life situation and individual personality. Older people can be confronted by multiple losses, which may occur simultaneously: death of marital partner, older friends, colleagues, relatives; decline of physical health and coming to personal terms with death; loss of status, prestige, and participation in society; and, for large numbers of the older population, additional burdens of marginal living standards. Inevitable losses that can accompany aging may be aggravated by cultural devaluation and neglect. In the complex of factors affecting subjective experience, overt behavior, and level of adaptation of the older persons, any or all of the following may be significant.

Environmental or Extrinsic Factors
Personal losses or gains
- Marital partners; other loved and significant figures (friends, children)

Social forces (losses or gains)
- Status changes, prestige changes: in social groups other than family and as paterfamilias
- Socioeconomic adversities: income drop, inflation
- Unwanted retirement: arbitrary retirement policies
- Cultural devaluation of older persons: sense of uselessness, therapeutic pessimism, forced isolation, forced segregation

Intrinsic Factors
Nature of personality
- character structure (defensive and integrative mechanisms), life history, survival characteristics

Physical diseases
- disease of any organ system
- perceptual decrements
- sexual losses

- disease of integrative systems (hormonal, vascular, and central nervous systems)
- brain damage
- arteriosclerosis, senile dementia, etc.
- physical limitations (such as arthritis)

Age-specific changes (largely obscure and mysterious, but inexorable with the passage of time)
- losses of speed of processes and response
- involutionary processes
- others (heredity, survival qualities)
- changes in body size and appearance ("slipping" and "shrinkage")

Experience of bodily dissolution and approaching death (subjective passage of time)

Older people often are handicapped by their own bodies, which respond to challenge with less energy and strength than were formerly available, particularly if major illnesses have taken their toll. Emotionally, a rapid succession of losses can leave individuals with accumulated layers of unresolved grief along with fatigue and a sense of emptiness. There may be little societal support for grief and mourning as the rituals of religion and custom are increasingly questioned and discarded.

It is an odd distortion of reality when older persons are popularly depicted as weak, unassuming, gently tranquil people who passively wait out their last days. Becoming old, being old, and dying are active physical and emotional processes that test the mettle of each person. Reluctance to accord older people appropriate recognition for their strengths and capacities indicates a failure to understand what is required in being old. We have lost our naiveté about the carefree nature of childhood as we have developed our understanding of the difficult and frightening developmental work each child must do to grow up. But simplistic illusions about old age continue, with little conceptualization of the normative stages one must pass through in later life.[1] Certain dramatic events (for example, widowhood) have been more widely studied than others, but there is as yet no cohesive, reliable body of information against which to measure adjustment patterns.

COMMON EMOTIONAL REACTIONS AS EXPRESSED IN OLD AGE

Grief (Mourning)

Grief as a result of loss is a predominate factor in aging. Loss of the marital partner or other significant and loved people can be profound, particularly since it becomes more difficult in later life to find substitutes for such losses. This is illustrated in the tender and grief-stricken reference to his mother's death by St. Augustine in his *Confessions:*

> I pressed her eyes closed, and a huge wave of sorrow flooded my heart and flowed outward in tears. . . . What, then, was it which caused grievous pain within me, if not the fresh wound arising from the sudden breaking of a very sweet and cherished habit of living together? Since I was thus bereft of such great comfort from her, my soul was wounded and it was as if life which had been made one from hers and mine was torn to shreds. . . . It was a relief to weep in Thy sight about her and for her, about myself and for myself.[2]

Older persons in the United States today do not receive necessary cultural support for grief and mourning. Learning how to mourn productively and restoratively requires models in ritual and custom as well as in personal experiences with others who mourn. Lack of such support can prolong depression and leave grief unresolved. Patterns of mourning for the dead are in disarray as many time-honored customs become discarded (wearing black clothing, abstaining from social events for a period of time) and others are practiced piecemeal (religious rituals, the rallying around of friends and family). Still other patterns are recent and psychologically suspect innovations (funeral directors or morticians who "console" the family, the use of sedatives to calm nerves and deaden the feelings). Gorer remarks that, up to 1900, every society in the world had definite rules for mourners to follow.[3] This is no longer true. Our culture seems reluctant to acknowledge the pain of death and to bear the agony of experiencing it through to acceptance. Some churches and many individuals deny the existence of death, preferring to speak of it as "merely sleep" or "the beginning of life hereafter." This may reassure individuals but it does not help them resolve the pain of separation and the need to find new attachments.

In the United States people receive some support in the period of initial shock, from the time of the death to burial. But after the church services are over, the undertaker disappears with a sizable portion of the mourner's money and relatives and friends go home, taking away their casserole dishes and other gestures of help and support. But for the mourner the intense period of mourning is just beginning, and it must usually be experienced alone. Onlookers may try to divert the mourner's attention to other things. Crying may be considered indulgent and possibly harmful rather than a psychological necessity. Gorer compares our present attitudes toward death and mourning with the prudish attitudes toward sex in the past: death has become an obscenity—one should not discuss it in public, the feelings are "bad," and any indulgence in mourning must be done in secret.

Gorer goes on to point out the maladaptive behavior that results. Exaggerated depression, aimless busyness, deification of the dead person, or callous denial of others' grief as well as one's own may occur. People may become excessively preoccupied with death or violence. Since death is an unavoidable crisis inherent in the human life cycle, it is peculiar that a society can so determinedly avoid the provisions of cultural custom and ritual that could make it easier to bear.

The primary adaptive purpose of grief and mourning is to accept the reality of the loss and to begin to find ways of filling up the emptiness caused by the loss through movement toward a new style of life and new people.

Mary and Zelda were two maiden sisters who had lived together for over 45 years when Zelda suddenly died of a heart attack. Mary was devastated. Initially, friends and distant relatives who lived nearby offered both consolation and practical support in day-to-day living. But after several weeks of *grieving, it was clear that Mary, who had been functioning quite independently prior to Zelda's death, could no longer manage alone. Without giving up her apartment, she was admitted to a rehabilitation facility, despite the fact that she had no physical impairment. After several weeks there, she was transferred to a low supervision nursing home where she eventually met Helen, another woman in her 60s, who was in good health but had nowhere to live and few friends in the area. Mary and Helen struck up an immediate friendship and soon moved into Mary's apartment where they now live happily and frequently entertain other friends.*

Parkes, in his studies of London widows, describes the futile search for the lost love object in which the mourner is torn between the desire to recover or resurrect the dead person and the knowledge that this is irrational.[4] Studies indicate that some widowed people have hallucinations and delusions of contact with the lost spouse. These may last for years and are more likely to occur in individuals who had been happily married. The most common hallucination reported was feeling the dead spouse's presence; others thought they saw, heard, were touched by or spoken to by the spouse.

A cultural adaptation regarding grief is found in the practice of ancestor worship in Shintoism and Buddhism, where the mourner believes the presence of a departed loved one remains (to be fed, prayed to, etc.) yet in a new spirit form that does not allow direct physical contact. Thus both the reality of death and the wishful recovery of the person are provided for, in a religious belief that gives structure to the grief process.

A typical grief reaction has an almost predictable pattern of onset, regardless of age—numbness and inability to accept the loss, followed by the shock of reality as it begins to penetrate. There are physical feelings of emptiness in the pit of the stomach, weak knees, perhaps a feeling of suffocation, shortness of breath, and a tendency to deep sighing. Emotionally the person experiences great distress. As mentioned earlier, there may be a sense of unreality, including delusions and obsessive preoccupations with the image of the lost person and acting as though the deceased were still present. Generally feelings of guilt are present as well as anger and irritability, even toward friends and relatives. There is usually a disorganization of normal patterns of response, with the bereaved person wandering about aimlessly, unable to work or take social initiative. Anxiety and longing alternate with depression and despair. Insomnia, digestive disturbances, and anorexia are common. Acute grief ordinarily lasts a month or two and then begins to lessen; on the average, grief may be largely over in six to twelve months, although further loss, stress, or some reminder can reactivate it.

Exaggerated grief reactions may occur:

A 66-year-old woman was as angry and depressed over the loss of her husband 16 months after his death as she was in the immediate weeks. She had passed through the "markers" of a year—the anniversary of their marriage, Thanksgiving, Christmas, Valentine's Day, Easter, and summer vacation reminiscence. But she could not shake her oppressive depression. She was furious at her brother-in-law, who she felt would find ways to cheat her of her inheritance. She chastised her two sons for their neglect. It was only through open exploration of her anger, first with the help of her emotionally sophisticated clergyman and then with a psychiatrist, that her depression began to lift.

"Morbid" grief reactions are distortions or prolongations of typical grief. Such reactions may take the form of delay, in which the grief is delayed for days, months, or even years, and in its extreme form is generally bound up with conscious or unconscious antagonism or ambivalence toward the deceased. Inhibited grief, according to Parkes, produces minimal mourning but other symptoms develop, such as somatic illnesses, overactivity, or disturbed social interaction. Chronic grief, yet another of the morbid grief reactions, is the prolongation and intensification of normal grief over an extended or limited period of time; psychotherapy and/or medication may be indicated.

We have observed a not infrequent form of grief reaction that we call "enshrinement," in which the survivor attempts to keep things just as they were before the death of a loved one occurred. The dead person's possessions and even entire rooms may be kept intact as shrines to the person's memory. The survivor may surround himself or herself with photographs and memorabilia connected with the lost person and make regular and conscious attempts to evoke memories of the deceased. There may be frequent references to the dead person in conversation with others, as well as a deliberate avoidance of new contacts that might replace the role of the one who died. Much of this is a result of survival guilt and a misplaced fear of infidelity if one were to take an active role in getting life moving again. It can also be symptomatic of a silent and internal adult temper tantrum—a stubborn refusal to accept death.

Anticipatory grief is the process of mourning in advance, before an actual loss is sustained. This form of mourning can occur during long illnesses; for example, a wife caring for a sick husband may go through a grief reaction and may have reached some degree of acceptance before death occurs. Such grief is seen as a protective device that prepares the bereaved for the loss, but it can lead to problems if it causes loved ones to disengage themselves prematurely, leaving the dying person isolated and alone.

Interrelationships between grief and vulnerability to both physical and emotional illness have been the subject of a number of investigations. Bereavement over a loss is hypothesized to be the single most crucial factor in predicting decline or breakdown in functioning on a physical or emotional level. Research data on large numbers of surviving spouses have in fact revealed marked increases in mortality of the spouses, especially the male survivors, in the first three months of bereavement.[5] In addition, losses of health, money, possessions, employment, or social status or changes in appearance seem to be possible factors in precipitating decline or lowering resistance.

Guilt

While old age can be a time of proud reflection and happy reminiscence, it can also evoke difficult memories and a resurgence of past conflicts and regrets. Guilt feelings may play a significant role as the older person reviews life, attempting to consolidate a meaningful judgment as to the manner in which life has been lived and to prepare for death and cope with any fears of death. The sins of omission and commission for which an individual blames himself weigh even more heavily in the light of approaching death and dissolution. If expiation and atonement are to occur, they must occur now; time for procrastination begins to run out. Individuals who have held grudges for a lifetime may decide to resolve their differences. Some may undertake a variety of reparations for the past. Others become more religiously active, in the hope of gaining forgiveness. Such feelings should be dealt with seriously and not simply treated with facile reassurance. For many the resolution of guilt feelings is an essential part of final acceptance of their lives as worthwhile.

Other forms of guilt are the "death survival guilt" from outliving others, especially if chance occurrences like accidental death or homicide appear to have a role in the earlier demise of the spouse or loved one.[6] Those who survive often carry the burden of guilt and unresolved conflicts for decades, supporting the observation in Thomas Mann's *The Magic Mountain* that "a man's dying is more the survivor's affair than his own."

Loneliness

In infancy, being alone is a condition that provokes terror, anger, and disconsolation. A baby's early cries communicate the primitive drive for physical survival. But very early a new element is introduced. As the child alternately experiences the gratifying warmth and comfort of his family and the aloneness of his crib, he learns a new fear, the fear of not being able to get back to people—of being left alone. Thus there appear to be two elements in the early sense of loneliness: *aloneness,* or the fear for physical survival in a threatening, uncertain world, and *loneliness,* the fear of emotional isolation, of being locked inside oneself and unable to obtain the warmth and comfort that one has learned is available from others if one can gain it. Growth and a refinement occur as children

move outside of themselves and their isolation, not only toward other people but also toward an absorption in play, learning, work, and other creative efforts. That moment is significant when the child first learns to escape his own aloneness or consciousness of himself and becomes totally involved in a task—a moment described as an escape from loneliness, which is not dependent on the presence of another person. (Paul Tillich describes this as a distinction between loneliness and solitude.)

The developmental etiology of loneliness is significant in regard to older people, not in a simplistic sense of comparing them to children but in attempting to comprehend the special character of loneliness in old age. The primitive fears concerning physical survival and emotional isolation recede as human beings grow to adulthood and learn to provide successfully for their own physical sustenance and achieve emotional satisfactions through family, friends, and work. But with old age, the combination of harsh external forces and a diminishing self-mastery revives once again the latent threats. The old adage that we are born alone and we die alone reflects the experience that each of us encounters in the course of the life cycle. But, unlike the usual experience of children, the older person does not suffer so much from a fear of being unable to relate as from the reality of having no one to relate to. With the death of loved ones, there is a diminishing circle of significant people who are not readily replaceable. Former compensations of work may be gone. Children and grandchildren, if they exist, may live far away. The all too limited outlets of religious activities, hobbies, television, pets, and a few acquaintances, which form the daily existence of so many older persons, are not enough to satisfy emotional needs.

The American dream of self-reliance and independence can further isolate the older person within himself. At a time when increased human contact could be supportive, older people hold on to cultural notions that living alone and "doing for oneself" must be maintained. Familiarity with and determination to continue such patterns can make communal living in hospitals, nursing homes, or group homes difficult in sheerly social terms. It has been observed that older people in more group-oriented societies, such as the rural kibbutzim in Israel, can enjoy the companionship and involvement inherent in a close living situation with others without the same loss of self-esteem and sense of dependency felt by "rugged individualists." Cultures that advocate societal and group responsibility for the individual are perhaps more in sympathy with the natural needs of older people.

Depression

Depressive reactions increase in degree and frequency with old age as a corollary to the increased loss of much that is emotionally valued by the older person. Unresolved grief, guilt, loneliness, and anger are expressed in mild to severe depressions with symptomatology including insomnia, despair, lethargy, anorexia, loss of interest, and somatic complaints.

Sadness is a normal part of life and an emotion experienced frequently by the elderly. But it should not be the predominant emotion at this or any other time of life. When sadness progresses to depression with increased symptoms of tearfulness, appetite disturbances, decreased energy, decreased concentration, and increased somatic complaints, a diagnosis of major depression and psychiatric consultation should be considered[7] (see Chapters 5 and 9 for further descriptions). Interestingly, some studies have shown that the incidence of major depression may actually go down slightly with age,[8] suggesting a successful coping strategy within most elderly. Some have suggested that this strategy involves maintaining close confiding relationships well into old age.[9]

Anxiety

The sense of free-floating anxiety can intensify in older people as illness and imminent death undermine illusions of invulnerability built up as protection during a lifetime. (A very powerful anxiety is the fear of becoming a pauper.) In addition, new modes of adaptation become necessary, creating additional anxieties in the face of constant change. Notice is seldom taken of the amount of new learning an older person must undergo to adapt to the accelerating changes in body, feelings, and environment. As with any new learning, anxiety develops in proportion to the task at hand, the resources available to master it, and the chances for and consequences of failure.

Anxiety manifests itself in many forms: rigid thinking to protectively exclude external stimuli (a person may "hear" only what he wants to hear), fear of being alone, and suspiciousness to the point of paranoid states. It may also become somatized into physical illness. Frequently anxiety and its expressions are incorrectly diagnosed as "early dementia" and wrongly considered untreatable.

One type of anxiety derives from life history such as observations of older people when they themselves were children. For example, the fear that they will have the diseases of old age that as children they observed in their grandparents or in other older people is one possible ingredient in the denial or projection seen in the aged.

A 70-year-old retired chemist who had been born when his mother was 40 years old had seen her develop severe Parkinsonism and become increasingly helpless when he was 20 years old. He carried this image with him all his life, but after he retired, it became obsessional. He gradually convinced himself and his doctors that he did have the disease. If he did, it was clinically negligible.

Sense of Impotence and Helplessness

A significant reaction of older men, particularly those white men who as a group can be postulated to have once held the major power and influence in American society, is a sense of their present impotence and helplessness. The highest suicide rates occur among older white men in their eighties. The older African American man and all women, be they African American, white, or other races, are affected by loss of esteem and cultural status as they age but do not experience quite the same degree of loss of power and privilege. In fact, an interesting reversal can occur for older women within the traditional marital relationship. As their husbands decline, wives may assume more of the initiative, taking over financial management, nursing care, and household repairs; they may therefore experience more control and influence than at any previous point in their lives.

Older people may "learn" to be helpless if family, friends, and health professionals too quickly attempt to compensate for the physiological or emotional losses that may occur with age. The result is not only an acceleration of the older person's helplessness, but also the possibility of greater susceptibility to disease and disability.[10]

As a reaction to a sense of helplessness, some older persons may flaunt their positions of status and financial worth over their children and use inheritance as a way of manipulating them. King Lear was a prime example of this when he required his three daughters to publicly declare their love for him in order to collect their inheritance.[11]

Rage

Another of the emotional manifestations of old age is a sense of rage at the seemingly uncontrollable forces that confront older persons, as well as the frequent indignities and neglect of the society that once valued their productive capacities. The description of some older people as cantankerous, ornery, irritable, or querulous would be more realistically interpreted if one became sensitive to the degree of outrage older people feel, consciously or unconsciously, at viewing their situation. (Interestingly, grouchiness and pugnacity have been related to a longer life expectancy in one study.) Much of the rage is an appropriate response to inhumane treatment. Some older people, of course, rage against the inevitable nature of aging and death, at least at some point in their coming to terms with these forces, but this too would seem to be a legitimate reaction. Dylan Thomas's words, "Do not go gently into that good night," express the desire of many to be alive to the end and to die with a sense of worth and pur-

pose, if not righteous indignation at being obliged to leave life.

EMOTIONAL REACTIONS TO AGE-RELATED LIFE CRISES

Certain life crises occur in old age regardless of socioeconomic and cultural circumstances, as part of the current aging experience in the United States.

Widowhood

The loss of a spouse represents a major psychological issue. The mourning process itself occurs at the same time as the need to make practical though emotion-laden decisions about where to live, what to do about the family home and possessions, how to dispose of the spouse's personal effects, what kind of contact to maintain with the spouse's relatives, what to do about new social roles, and, in some cases, whether or not even to go on living. Although research data are not available on the progress of couples (or of individuals, for that matter) through the entire life span, one can observe the interdependence that results from years of living together. The interdependence or mutual support of *some* older couples can become symbiotic to the extent that the remaining member may die shortly after the death of the other, even though he or she has been seemingly healthy. In other cases, severe depression may occur. Studies by Helsing et al.[12] and Mellstrom et al.[13] found that increased morbidity and mortality following the death of the spouse are greater in the male than the female, possibly as a result of women's better social networks. Women are more likely to share intimate feelings, including grief, as compared to men, whose conversations and relationships among fellow men are focused more upon activities such as business and sports. However, as evidence of the resilience of most individuals, McCrae and Costa found in a ten-year follow-up of a national sample of respondents age 25 to 74 that, although those who were widowed had less income and were more likely to have been hospitalized at some point, they were no different from those who were married in terms of psychological health.[14]

There are other complications of widowhood as well. The widowed and their children may be ambivalent about the more involved roles that many grown children feel compelled to accept in relation to the remaining parent. Friends and associates tend to socially ostracize the widowed individual for varieties of reasons: pain over the reminder of the loss of a friend; anxieties and denial of their own aging; awkwardness in knowing how to comfort a grieving person; and uneasiness about accepting a single man or woman into a cultural pattern of couples. Thus widows and widowers may be forced to seek out each other's companionship or fall back on their own resources. Programs such as the widow-to-widow program, begun by Silverman in 1964, can be immensely valuable in facilitating adjustment.[15]

Marital Problems[16]

Couples who enter old age together find new situations awaiting them. There is a greater amount of close contact and free time for each other. With retirement, the older man spends most of his day at home for the first time in his adult life. Those women who spent their lives as housewives may complain of husbands being underfoot all day with nothing to do as the wives continue their accustomed routines of housework. Some men actively pursue new interests but many encounter difficulties in finding a meaningful substitute for work. Women who retire from the outside work force may experience similar adjustment problems. As one or the other becomes ill and requires nursing care, the healthy spouse is torn between the desire to provide such care for the sick person and a need to have a life of his or her own outside the sickroom.[17] These decisions and the increased physical burden in caring for a loved one can in themselves lead to psychiatric morbidity,[18] although this point is debated in the literature.[19]

Typically, because of a shorter life expectancy and a tendency to be older than his wife at the time of marriage, it is the husband who becomes ill, often chronically so, and the wife who nurses him until his death. If the illness is a long and draining one, the wife can be expected to feel some bitterness and sense of exploitation. This becomes a more serious problem when the wife denies her feelings and insists on the pretense that her husband is no burden. The husband, sensing his wife's frustrations, may react with hurt and anger, and a troubled marital relationship ensues wherein both need guidance and reassurance.

Discrepant rates of change, narcissism, fear of death, and the relationship to the children are among critical variables that are pertinent to marital problems in late life and require study.

A daughter of a 78-year-old patient wrote concerning the present relationship of her parents: "I might note here that when I was growing up, my father objected to even the words 'darned' or 'damned.' He now swears freely and will mutter 'Jesus Christ' under his breath the minute he hears mother call. He seems to feel that both her present philosophical outlook and her physical inabilities could be improved if she 'had the guts.' He bitterly resents her balkings and her standard 'I can't answer.' His answer to her frequent plea 'love me' is 'give me something to love'. . . . He is crushed by her condition. She is crushed by his cruelty and intolerance."

At times, underlying disease states may be misread by a spouse as emotional moods.

The wife of a 75-year-old patient bitterly complained of her husband's glum, depressed nature. He denied being as depressed as she insisted. He had the typical "ironed-out" facial expression of Parkinsonism, although no other manifestations of this disorder were present. A medical examination revealed that he did indeed have Parkinsonism.

Mental health personnel must be alert for danger signals between couples, collaborating when necessary with other family members and friends to protect both parties.

John B has for 40 years been a kindly and devoted husband. Since the onset of his cognitive difficulties, however, he has had a marked personality change. In addition to being increasingly withdrawn and depressed, he has also become irritable and, at times, physically abusive. The wife denies to the physician that the intermittent physical outbursts are a problem. In private, however, the daughter reports that on at least three occasions the mother has had unexplained bruises on her shoulders and arms, which she claims were the result of "accidental falls." The daughter also reports that her father, previously a pious and quiet man, is now frequently heard shouting expletives at the slightest provocation in the home and that the mother is actually quite frightened for her safety, but is too embarrassed to discuss the issue openly.

Sexual Problems

Sex relations, although tending to be diminished in frequency, are practiced by many older people; however, problems can arise physically and emotionally in relationship to aging and illness. Surgery requiring a colostomy, for example, can seriously deter sexual expression for esthetic and physical reasons. Physiological changes in females (for example, untreated atrophic vaginitis) and prostatic problems in males are some of the possible organic impediments to sexual intercourse. Other impediments may be psychological or even ethical, as evidenced by a follow-up report on the case of John B.

Within weeks of receiving treatment for his depression and agitation, John B was calmer and his wife was greatly relieved. Six months later, however, she returned with another dilemma. Despite becoming increasingly impaired cognitively, Mr. B frequently approached Mrs. B sexually. While she still very much enjoyed the encounters and occasionally initiated them herself, she always felt guilty that she was "taking advantage of him" or "giving in to animal instincts" rather than controlling herself. The

anxiety was building to the point where she found herself frequently "putting him off" and thereby avoiding sexual relations altogether.

Older people, like the young, tend to react with anxiety and depression over threats to potency and sexual fulfillment. In addition, new fears can present themselves. One of the more common worries is fear of the effects of sexual exertion on the heart or circulatory system. Studies indicate that much of this fear is unwarranted. Other problems result from spending a long life together: One partner may begin to find the other less and less sexually attractive as they age or be simply bored by the routine of the same partner over a period of years. A widow has an especially difficult situation, since chances for remarriage are so slight. Older people are inclined to follow the strict sexual customs of their youth—no sex outside of marriage—and are therefore forced into celibacy regardless of personal inclination. (We discuss sexual issues more fully in Chapter 7.)

Iatrogenicity (a physician's induction of pathological reactions) is pertinent to the discussion of sexual problems. By means that range from the injunction to "take it easy," said to the active man now suffering from a cardiac disorder, to the failure to prepare the patient who is about to have a prostatectomy or orchidectomy, to the induction of impotence as an unwanted consequence of prescribed medications, the physician may unwittingly contribute both to sexual dysfunction and to the depression that often accompanies it in older people. Practical advice about the physiology and psychology of sexuality in aging can be very valuable to older patients.[20]

Retirement

Everyone reacts to retirement, but not everyone goes through a "retirement crisis." Retirement does not mean the same thing for everybody. Although some view it as the end of their worthwhile life and think that anything beyond is downhill, others see retirement as a relief from hard work, a chance to rest, a period of enjoyment and relaxation. Still others believe that it marks the completion of their commitment to society and the beginning of their active commitment to themselves and all the things they have been waiting and wanting to do. It is not unusual to see second and even third careers occurring in late life, creative ventures beginning, and whole new personalities emerging as people discover and rediscover themselves. The emotional quality of retirement depends on the individual personality, income, health, social circumstances, and sense of worth.

Women enjoy a mixed blessing in relation to retirement. Many of the current generation of older women have never worked outside the home and therefore are not as subject as men to the psychological difficulties many individuals find with retirement. The traditional housewife's job identity is threatened in mid-life as her children leave home, but as she adjusts to caring for only herself and her husband, she has a definite pattern of work—at least until her husband dies. Even in her widowhood a woman continues to have the routines of homemaking available to her. For those women who do work outside the home, many carry the dual role of homemaker and employed worker, thus ameliorating the impact of retirement.

For men, retirement is a concern that can affect the very essence of their lives. A large number of men derive an almost singleminded identity from their work (some even becoming "workaholics"—addicted to work). Many develop no diversified interests outside their employment and are caught up in a narrow definition of who they are and what they are worth as people. Work and life become so interconnected that the loss of a job can eliminate the reason for living.

Dr. P, a 72-year-old retired surgeon, has been increasingly restless and irritable over the last six months. He retired as a cardiovascular surgeon five years ago but kept a busy consulting practice until earlier this year. His wife had wanted to travel more, and he had agreed to end his career, only to become disgruntled around the house. He was also described as "being less fun" when they traveled together on vacation with the family. When interviewed, he freely admitted that he missed his exalted position as one of the preeminent surgeons in the community. He stated that he especially missed the sense of being needed.

Men should be encouraged to take a more active part in all aspects of life—with more involvement in the care of children and home, a sharing of responsibility for financial support with the wife, more leisure time throughout life for rest and study, and active involvement in cultural and social activities. A call for male as well as female liberation is in order if men are to escape the crushing burden of overidentification with work and problems of stress, coronary disease, retirement shock, and shortened life expectancy that are associated with it.

The syndrome of the restless and depressed retired person is common indeed, but the abolition of mandatory retirement and the establishment of pre- and postretirement programs have begun to address this situation. Both common sense and research indicate that people adjust better if they can choose when and how to retire. Eventually a redefinition of work itself may bring a more satisfying retirement picture. Work, leisure, and study could be alternated throughout the life cycle instead of being parceled out according to age group.

The phenomena of both overpreparation and underpreparation for retirement can be observed. The overly prepared are those who anxiously begin to plan ahead in early middle age, with elaborate attentions to the details of their future life. Such overachievers are usually indicating that they are unhappy or insecure in their present life and are trying desperately for something better in the future. On the other extreme are those who do not even conceive of, let alone prepare for, retirement and who are sadly surprised when it catches them unaware. The most successful retirees are those who take reasonable precautions for their old age but enjoy living in the present rather than expecting some future "golden age."

Financial Worries

There is considerable financial distress among older persons, as we have emphasized earlier. Poverty and the fear of poverty do of course influence mental health. Moreover, continuing public discussion of the integrity and unfunded liability of Social Security and Medicare, as well as public and private pension systems other than Social Security, add to the worries of older people. Economic projections into the future have emphasized the declining number of workers to contribute to the support of older people. Frequently, the fact that there is also a declining number of young people for the working generation to support is not emphasized. (See Chapter 1, Table 1.1, "Dependency Ratio.")

Sensory Loss

Hearing loss is approximately seven times more prevalent for people age 65 to 74 than for people under 45 years old.[21] According to most estimates some degree of hearing loss is experienced by approximately 30% of people aged 65 to 75, and 50% of people aged 75 and older.[22] This high prevalence in the elderly is very important because hearing loss can reduce reality testing and lead to marked suspiciousness and even paranoia. The finding that this deficit is generally underreported suggests that clinicians should be vigilant in looking for evidence of hearing loss in their patients even before the problem becomes overtly symptomatic.[23]

Hearing loss causes greater social isolation than blindness, perhaps because verbal communication is so vital to human interaction. Onlookers may mistake the hard-of-hearing as mentally abnormal or "senile." There is little social sympathy—older people who are deaf are often excluded from activities and become less and less well oriented. The loud or badly articulated speech associated with hearing loss can have a negative effect on others, and the hard-of-hearing are given less consideration than the elderly blind, probably because their handicap is not so obvious to the onlooker. As a result, it is a common clinical observation that hearing loss is associated with depression.[24]

Although most old people need glasses, poor vision is not as widespread as is usually thought. While about one in eight older people are severely visually impaired,[25] many have fair to adequate visual acuity to age 90 and even beyond. Often one eye may continue to function, even if the other does not. Older persons find the possibility of cataracts, glaucoma, and other disorders frightening because of the isolating and immobilizing effects. Visual loss can cause decreasing mobility, poor orientation, and frightening visual impressions that resemble hallucinations. Reading, television, and other visual pastimes are reduced or eliminated. Social and travel plans are often restricted to accommodate visual limitations. Furthermore, older people feel more vulnerable to danger and crime when handicapped by sensory loss.

Smell also declines with age and up to 30% of people who are over 80 years have difficulty identifying common substances by smell.[26] Taste also may be affected, since taste sensations are often dependent on the ability to smell; in addition, taste buds decrease in number with age. However, recent and highly sophisticated studies of taste acuity of healthy community residents have found that, basically, the gustatory system functions reasonably well across the age span.[27] Taking advantage of the National Institute on Aging's Baltimore Longitudinal Study, Weiffenbach et al. saw the automatic decline in taste acuity over time as modest (10%). Environmental factors such as tobacco and medications are more influential in such decreases than is age. For example, 30% of those on medication experience some loss of taste.

There is also a falloff of tactile response as both perception and motor expression decline in reaction to stimuli. However, the slowing of speed and response, which at first appears to be a characteristic of old age, was found in the NIMH studies to be also related to environmental deprivation and depression.

Disease and Disability

Contrary to persistent popular belief, old age is not always accompanied by illness and sadness.

However, the chronic and acute illnesses and diseases in old age do provide the fulcrum determining the physical functioning and energy levels that are available to older people. Just as loss and grief define the critical emotional variable for the old, so illness presents the prime physical variable. The Roman adage *mens sana in corpore sano* ("a sound mind in a sound body") recognizes the interrelationships between the two. To provide a perspective on the most prominent of the chronic diseases and impairments, elderly women have higher rates than men for arthritis, diabetes, hypertension, back pain, and visual impairment. Men have higher rates of asthma, chronic arthritis, hernia, peptic ulcer, and hearing impairments. Psychometric tests, especially those sensitive to concurrent levels of depression, have proved to be unusually sensitive to even minimal disease. Physical illness frequently generates both appropriate and distorted emotional reactions, since it represents so much that is inherently frightening to human beings.

When physical illness is chronic, the incidence of psychiatric disorder increases significantly.

Mary B is a 75-year-old former school teacher with a history of chronic and painful arthritis. She retired from her position as a music instructor ten years ago, but continued her private lessons until recently. She felt she had to give up her remaining pupils because of increasing pain in her hands due to arthritis and her inability to tolerate the significant side effects of the treatment regimen. She is married and has a very supportive family locally, but was noted to display signs of increasing irritability and social withdrawal over the last few months. She sometimes keeps busy with housework and various activities with the family, but keeps to herself most of the time. Remarkably, she rarely listens to music in her home, previously a passionate hobby.

Clearly, Mrs. B was adjusting to her medical plight. To have lost her beloved teaching due to arthritis was obviously a devastating blow. She had further reason to be frustrated by the lack of tolerance to the medication side effects (often a major problem with arthritis sufferers). Her emotional reaction was a global one of disappointment. Consultation and therapy might be directed at helping her adjust to her impediments and exploring whether she could obtain continued enjoyment from music and the coaching of students in some way that would be both possible and satisfying for her.

Hospitalization and Surgery

Heart and circulatory diseases, digestive conditions, and disturbances of the nervous system are the primary causes of hospitalization after age 65. Hospitalization is drastic and dramatic proof that something is wrong or may be wrong. Fears become heightened and, since so many older persons now die in hospitals and nursing homes rather than at home, such institutions come to be viewed as places to die as well as places to regain health. There is still far too little attention paid to the emotional feelings of sick people, and this is especially the case with the aged. The emphasis on treating physical disease, the often cold and cheerless environment of hospitals, the generally efficient but overworked and impersonal medical staff, and visiting regulations that are either too lax or too rigid combine to make the older person feel isolated, unprotected, lonely, and bored. There is often little to do except watch television, a problematic pastime that becomes even more limited if hearing or sight is impaired. Occupational and recreational therapies are usually minimal. Removal from the home environment (with consequent deprivation of adequate contact with family and friends, lack of responsibility, and restriction of mental and somatic activity) encourages anxiety, irritability, disorientation, and eventual regression.

Insufficient thought has been given to the side effects of various surgical procedures. A classic example is the "black patch" syndrome, which some years ago puzzled the medical profession. Following bilateral cataract surgery when patches were placed over both eyes, certain older people became delirious and disoriented. It was observed that the syndrome did not occur when one eye was operated on at a time, leaving the sight in the other available to the patient. Finally, the conclusion was correctly drawn that the black patch reaction was simply the result of loss of contact with people and environment. Therefore, operating on one eye at a time and providing additional sensory stimuli will allow patients to maintain orientation. It seems logical that other undesirable side effects of surgery might be alleviated through just such careful thinking through of the problems.

Several organizations assist persons undergoing particular kinds of surgery. The Reach to Recovery program of the American Cancer Society is a rehabilitation program for women who have had breast surgery. The United Ostomy Association offers information and counseling to those who have had colostomies and ileostomies.[28]

Fears, Body Image Anxiety, and Chronic Pain

Since there are so many potential problems, medical and otherwise, for the elderly, it is understandable why fears may increase. Whereas the fears in the young and middle-aged are often of the accidental or avoidable tragedies of life (i.e., motor vehicle accidents, flying, lightening), the fears of the elderly often relate to threats that may not be avoidable (i.e., cancer, memory loss, financial ruin, death). Elderly people can become consumed with fears. Currently, "Alzheimer-phobia" is one such powerful fear, causing elderly and not-so-elderly patients to frequent their doctors' offices in unprecedented numbers just to get a "memory check-up."

The fear of injury in older persons is well-founded. In 1993, almost 28,000 elderly deaths were the result of accidents.[29] Approximately 800,000 older Americans are disabled by injury for at least one day a year. Burns and scalds are three times more likely to occur among older persons. Falls account for three out of four accidents in the elderly and 60 to 90% of home-related deaths. Between 15 and 50% of those who need to go to a hospital due to a fall die within a year.[30]

Although fall-related deaths increase with age, most falls do not lead to death. However, considerable morbidity results from falls. Approximately 25% of hospital admissions and 50% of nursing home admissions of the elderly are directly related to falling.

Latent fear and anxiety about death surface with illness and suffering. Feelings of helplessness and vulnerability buried deep within the individual may be resurrected in the face of implacable illness and the aging process. Hope for cures from medicines, luck, or a supreme being may diminish. Older people's sense of pride in their own body's reliability can be shaken when they experience greater susceptibility to communicable diseases, air pollution, dampness, cold weather, and exertion. Moreover, aging and disease threaten people's sense of who they are—their identities—as their bodies change "in front of their eyes." People report feelings of shock and disbelief at their mirror image, in reaction both to aging (Is that old person really me?) and to illness, which even more rapidly changes the size, shape, and appearance of the body. The line between symptom and fear often blurs as the duration and severity of chronic illness grows.

Eighty-six percent of older persons have some kind of chronic health problem requiring more visits to the doctor, added stays in the hospital, special diets, exercises, drugs, rehabilitative therapy, or additional provisions for daily life at home. With 81% of older people ambulatory, and to a substantial degree responsible for their own self-care, it is apparent that body monitoring—the need to concern oneself with the care of one's body and its functions in a more concerted way than before—is a compelling preoccupation. Bodily processes that formerly took care of themselves or required minimal attention begin to demand more and more time as people age. Some older people welcome the relief from other anxieties, which occurs as they absorb themselves in their own care. But others are annoyed, wearied, or bored by the routines imposed on them by ill health and the decline of their bodies. The composer Stravinsky, in his eighties, wrote of his irritation at having to spend so much time on his body when he wanted to write music. One can assume that his complaint is echoed by many who wish to continue active, interesting lives.

While pain is not found only in the elderly, it is certainly more common with age. Acute illnesses such as myocardial infarction and cerebrovascular accidents are now recognized as being associated with subsequent depression and anxiety, and the need for psychiatric assessment is well documented.[31] What is perhaps less well known is the degree to which depression and the other psychiatric syndromes are also associated with chronic pain.

The periodic aches and pains of rheumatism, the throbbing relentless pains of arthritis, the sharp distress of angina pectoris—these are examples of pain in some of its shapes and forms. Older persons deal with pain according to their life-style, personality, and cultural background, as well as the nature and extent of the pain. Individual pain thresholds vary from person to person and vary also in intensity at different times in the same individual. For many persons, the use of drugs offers the most consistent relief, yet drugs often produce side effects that can be particularly devitalizing or disorienting to older people—dizziness, loss of appetite, weakness, nausea, or dulling of consciousness. Drug use for pain requires careful monitoring for the best balance between freedom from pain and freedom from the side effects of the pain medication (see Chapter 13).

Dying and Death (See Chapter 12)

Preparation for death involves a condition unknown in past or present experience, for one cannot truly imagine one's own nonexistence. Yet, strangely, although fear of death is part of human experience, older people tend to fear it less than the young do and often are more concerned about the death of those they love than about their own. Many can accept personal death with equanimity. In terminal illness it may even be welcomed as a release from pain and struggle. Reactions to death are closely related to a resolution of life's experiences and problems as well as a sense of one's contributions to others. Profound religious and

philosophical convictions facilitate acceptance. The process of working through one's feelings about death begins with a growing personal awareness of the eventual end of life and the implications of this for one's remaining time alive. For some people the process begins early; for others the physical signs of aging occur before awareness is allowed to surface. Some few attempt to deny death to the very end. A resolution of feelings about death may be responsible for those elusive qualities, seen in various old people, known as "wisdom" and "serenity." The German philosopher Feurbach has written that "anticipation of death is seen as the instrument of being—of authentic existence." There are of course varying degrees and levels of acceptance; perhaps the most satisfying is that described by another philosopher, Spinoza: "The adult who sees death as completion of a pattern and who has spent life unfettered by fears, living richly and productively, can integrate and accept the thought that life will stop."

Few older persons today have the opportunity to die at home as their parents and grandparents did. More than 50% of all deaths take place in hospitals, and many in nursing homes. The process of dying is made more difficult by this shift from home to institutions, where the emphasis is on physical rather than emotional concerns. Short and inflexible visiting hours and lack of accommodations for intimate family contact encourage families and friends to withdraw from dying persons, in anticipatory grief (working out feelings of grief as though the person were already dead). Thus the aged person, who may have resolved many of his own difficult feelings about death itself, is left without human comfort and warmth as death approaches. Older people often remark that their greatest fear is of "dying alone."

There is an increasing interest in the subject of death and dying, as evidenced by a growing body of research and literature. One of the best-known reports is the Kübler-Ross book on the stages of dying, in which she suggests five more or less distinct stages or levels of experience during the actual course of dying. The first stage is *denial of death,* in which the person simply refuses to believe the evidence of his or her own approaching demise. In the second stage, denial is replaced by *anger and rage* at the injustice and unfairness of life's ending. Third, the person moves into a *bargaining stage* during which he or she tries to make a deal with God or fate in return for life (promises of being a better person, showing more concern for others, etc.). When this is seen to be futile, the person moves into a period of *depression* and preparatory grief over the loss of life and loved ones. Finally, in the last stages, a level of *acceptance* is reached—a quiet expectation of death and a lessening of interest in the outer world, including loved ones. In our experience and that of many others working with dying persons, these stages seldom occur as neatly and orderly as described here. Therefore, keeping the various stages in mind can be very useful in understanding the dying, as long as one does not depend on them too rigidly.

COMMON ADAPTIVE TECHNIQUES

Defense Mechanisms

Older persons have throughout their lifetimes acquired individual and characteristic methods of handling anxiety, aggressive impulses, resentments, and frustration. Such methods, known as *defense mechanisms,* are internal, automatic, unconscious processes whereby the personality protects itself by attempting to provide psychological stability in the midst of conflicting or overwhelming needs and stresses that are part of human existence. As people mature, new defenses may be added and old ones discarded; but others persist throughout life, taking on different tones and colorations at different stages in the life cycle. Emphasis here will be on the defense mechanisms that most often appear in old age and on nuances that are characteristic of older people.

Denial.   The denial of old age and death found in the young person's attitude of "This won't happen to me" may also occur in old age in the form of "This isn't happening to me." In one of its ex-

treme forms, denial can manifest itself in a "Peter Pan" syndrome, with the older person pretending to be young and refusing to deal with the realities of aging. There may be a self-attribution of strength—claiming that one is still capable of everything. Not all denial is pathological. It is, in fact, a necessary and useful component for maintaining a sense of stability and equilibrium. But the usefulness of denial is eroded when it begins to seriously interfere with the developmental work of any particular age. In old age, an individual who denies that he or she is sick and refuses to take medicine or see a doctor demonstrates an example of denial that no longer accomplishes a life-protective purpose.

Denial, like other defenses, often responds to psychotherapy:

Chief complaint: *"I can't catch my breath." This is the case of a man who was always in a hurry and had eventually to stop to catch his breath.*

A 68-year-old, highly intelligent and intellectual sociologist developed a severe cough on his return from an extended and exciting journey abroad. An X-ray shadow increased the medical suspicion of malignancy. Without prior discussion and preparation, the patient was inadvertently but directly told this by a secretary arranging his admission for surgery. The operation revealed a lung abscess and the patient responded well physically both to the operative procedure and in the recovery period, with one exception: he could not catch his breath. His internist suggested an extended vacation, and later tranquilizers, and offered reassurance. After some months the doctor strongly recommended psychotherapy, as he realized the patient was becoming increasingly agitated and depressed without adequate medical explanation. The patient was extremely tense and restless. He appeared somewhat slovenly. His pants hung loose from his suspenders and his fly was partly open. In short, he gave the impression of having some organic mental disorder but he spoke clearly and well. Despite his obvious gloom, he managed some humor and clarity in giving his present and past history.

His situation was socially and personally favorable. He had a good relationship with a devoted wife. He had many good friends and professional colleagues. He was well regarded professionally. He was under no pressure to retire, and consultancies were open to him. He had a wide range of interests in addition to his professional field. His relationships with his brothers and sisters were good. With the exception of the chief complaint, his physical status was excellent. He believed his physician's report that there was no major organic disease; in other words, he was not suffering from a fear that he was being misled. But despite all of this, he was tense and depressed. Recurrent dreams included one in which "a paper was due" and another in which he was "behind in an exam." He had never taken out any life insurance. He had made no conscious admission to himself that he might age. He had made nothing of birthdays. Nor did he have a very clear concept of the natural evolution of the life cycle. He did not have any sense of stages and development of middle and later life. He had an enormous capacity for work and had kept busy all his life as though unaware of the passage of time. He had never been bored. He had great capacity for self-discipline and was not given to marked expression of either grief or anger but only to a narrow spectrum of affects, including fearfulness and pleasure. He was a kind of Peter Pan, and he and his wife eventually concluded in the course of his psychotherapeutic work that he, and in some measure she, had imagined themselves as remaining in their twenties instead of being in their late sixties. As he reviewed his life and the realities of aging and death, he became freer in his expression of more negative affect. His depression and tension improved and he remained well in a follow-up of some six months. He was no longer short of breath.

Projection.   Some older persons attempt to allay anxieties by projecting feelings outward onto someone else. They may appear suspicious and fearful, with characteristic complaints of merchants cheating them, doctors ignoring them, their children neglecting them. They often become concerned about physical safety on the streets. Much of what is termed projection may indeed be legitimate complaints and fears about situations that exist, either potentially or in actuality, and one runs the risk of denying reality by labeling them projection. But actual projection itself does occur, signifying internal stress (people with hearing

losses are prime victims) and can reach paranoid proportions unless the stress is alleviated.

Fixation.   Fixation is most often associated with old age as a carryover defense from earlier life, implying that the fixation point occurred somewhere in childhood. But if one views old age as having developmental work of its own, fixation is a useful concept in describing the older person who may reach a particular level of development and be unable to go further. An example might be the person who has adapted well to living alone, without a spouse, but cannot accept in an insightful manner the need for outside help as physical strength wanes. Such a person may unconsciously want to stop the action and refuse to accept a new change.

Regression.[32]   Regression, or a return to an earlier level of adaptation, is an overused and catchall explanation for much behavior in old age. Familiar descriptions of older people as "childlike," "childish," or "in second childhood" imply a slide back to earlier developmental stages with no cognizance of a lifetime of experience that unalterably separates them from their childhood patterns of coping. A pejorative connotation is given, with the notion that older people lose their "adultness" under stress of illness and age and begin to act like children. Regression implies a disruptive, deteriorative, nonadaptive retreat in which the personality is not up to facing the stress it must overcome; the weakness is internal. But in old age much of the stress is from external sources that strain the resources of even the most healthy personalities. The use of the concept of regression to describe the attempts of older people to adapt in such situations is similar to the popular use of the term "paranoid" to describe the reactions of certain minority groups to racial discrimination. What appears to be pathological may indeed be the typical and even necessary patterns of response to stressful circumstances.

Displacement.   The function of displacement is to disguise the real source of anxiety or discomfort for a person by placing it on some other object or circumstance. For example, a person whose body is drastically undergoing change may displace the cause of his or her emotional distress by declaring that the world is going to ruin or that things are not the way they were when he or she was young.

Counterphobia. Counterphobia is the compelling and sometimes risky tendency to look danger in the face in an attempt to convince oneself that it can be overcome.[33] An older man with dizzy spells may insist on climbing a ladder to fix his own roof. Another, with a history of visual blackouts, may demand that he drive the family car just as before. A woman with heart trouble ignores her racing pulse as she continues to carry tubs of laundry from her basement. In each case the individual ignores a realistic appraisal of limitations and relies upon sheer force of will to undo the danger.

Idealization.   One type of defense is the idealization of the lost object, be it person, place, lifestyle, or status. A person may, for instance, idolize a deceased mate, glorifying the past and the good old days. The purpose is often to make one's life seem meaningful and not wasted, but the result is more often to alienate those people who remain.

Jim H is a 79-year-old retired plumber of good means with a large extended family. He is in excellent physical health and has no immediate complaints himself, but is brought in for consultation by his daughters and second wife of 21 years because of his increasing irritability over the last three months. They complain that no matter what the wife does, he finds fault with her. Their recent vacation was ruined when he insisted on driving to an old family campground and staying there despite poor weather. Furthermore, he has been sexually much less attentive lately and has been criticizing how "old" his wife looks. The daughters also report that their father has been "different" lately; he has spent an inordinate amount of time reminiscing with them about their childhoods, something he rarely did until recently. They worry that he is lost in the "good

old days" and paying less attention to his grandchildren and other family duties.

On further evaluation and review with Mr. H, it became clear that he was indeed quite critical of his "new" wife. Although he has been married to her for over two decades, his children had all been raised by his first wife before her sudden death 25 years ago. As it turned out, the 50th wedding anniversary with his first wife was rapidly approaching, and he stated that no one except him seemed to be aware of that fact. Over the next several weeks, he was able to talk more openly about the pain he still felt about the sudden and unexpected loss of his first wife and the hollowness he initially felt after her death. Eventually, he was able to share these feelings with his current wife. As she had done some 25 years before, when they first met and fell in love, she consoled and comforted him through his memories of the grief. Later, in a quiet ceremony, the family as a whole did mark the 50th anniversary with a memorial dinner. Once reassured of his current wife's continuing love for him, he was able to stop comparing the idealized image of his first wife with her. His criticism of her stopped, and they went on to celebrate their own silver anniversary several years later.

Rigidity.   There is little evidence that older people become more rigid in personality as they age. Rather, when rigidity is seen, it is a defense against a general sense of threat or actual crises.

OTHER DEFENSIVE BEHAVIOR

While not necessarily considered classic defense mechanisms, the following types of defensive behavior are commonly employed by older people.

Psychosomatic Complaints

Although actual data on the incidence and prevalence of psychosomatic disorder is hard to come by, there is little disagreement that exaggerated physical complaints do occur in the elderly and that they can be defensive in nature. It is rare, for instance, that a typical psychosomatic disorder has its beginnings in old age, with the exception perhaps of systemic hypertension, but psychological components of such traditional diseases of the elderly as rheumatoid arthritis and coronary artery disease are common. More common somatization reactions or episodes of hypochondriasis are also frequent in the elderly and include symptoms of back pain, stomach distress, trouble breathing, or bowel irregularities. These symptoms often herald underlying anxieties, depression, or other strongly felt emotions that are difficult to express more directly.

Selective Attention

The dulling of memory and the propensity to remember distant past events with greater clarity than events of the recent past have generally been attributed to atherosclerotic and senile brain changes in old age. However, it appears that such memory characteristics can at times have a psychological base, in that the older person may be turning away from or tuning out the painfulness of the present to dwell on a more satisfying past. The adaptive value of "forgetfulness" in dealing with vast amounts of information has also been emphasized. It may be a mechanism for sorting out the relevant from the irrelevant.

A process of "exclusion of stimuli" has been observed in older people, by which they block off the sensorium that they feel unprepared to deal with.[34] This is more often observed in people with hearing problems who, at times, seem to hear what they want to hear. This may be the only way an older person can control the amount of input impinging upon him. At the same time, however, older people have been shown to use "escapist fantasy" less often than younger subjects, suggesting that avoidance of painful stimuli is not always the motivating factor.

Exploitation of Age and Disability

Older people can use changes occurring in their lives to obtain secondary gains—that is, benefits which in and of themselves may be satisfying or desired. An example is shown by older persons who insist they must remain in a hospital or other care facility, even though they no longer need medical care, because they enjoy the extra attention

and sense of importance accruing from the illness. Or an individual with a proclivity to control others may use illness or impending death to manipulate those around him. Examples are the tyrant on the sick bed who terrorizes family and friends through guilt, and the invalid who commandeers personal services from everyone through appearing totally helpless and passive. Exploitation of age and disability can also result in freedom from social expectation, with the older person not feeling bound by the social amenities and established patterns. In this sense, the defensive behavior may allow the person to try on a new identity or a new way of relating. Behavior that in youth might have been considered unacceptable or even bizarre can be viewed in old age as pleasantly idiosyncratic, or at least harmless.

An interesting form of age exploitation is what we have called the "old man" or "old woman" act. This is the older person who, even when physically and mentally sound, puts on an act of being a tottering, frail, helpless "old" person. This phenomenon can occur as early as the fifties but may be used by older people at any age to avoid responsibility toward themselves and others and to evoke sympathy. Sometimes the older person uses this act very selectively on those who are most gullible, while appearing quite sound and capable to others.

Restitution, Replacement, or Compensatory Behavior

Numerous activities may be adopted to make up for a loss. These may include practical measures such as memory pads and reminders of all kinds to compensate for poor memory. Or they can take the form of finding new persons to replace lost ones. Attempted restitution is frequently seen, in which a person tries to give back or get back that which has been lost or taken away.

Use of Activity or Busyness

General busyness, known as "working off the blues," is a defense against depression, anxiety, and other conditions that are painful or unacceptable. It involves concentrating on activity of some kind, whether productive or nonproductive, with the purpose of warding off the unwanted feelings.

Use of Groups

In part thanks to the "support group" approaches that have been developed over recent years, many individuals have survived experiences such as widowhood, chronic illness, and chronic stress much better than before. The reduction of isolation has been considerable and the adaptive techniques of strong social networks have been extremely valuable. One possible drawback, however, is that group identification, particularly if immediately following a crisis or during a continuing stress, may partially suppress an individual's expression of painful emotions. Thus a balance between group support and opportunities for individual expression appears necessary for the continuing maturation and adaptation of the older person.

Humor as an Adaptive Technique

Most people would agree that a joke, even a bad joke, can provide a welcome relief in a tense or otherwise difficult situation. Positive thinking and joking are characteristic of youth, but it is unclear how prevalent they are among the elderly. McCrae found that these defense mechanisms appeared less frequently as coping skills in his sample of older versus younger or middle-aged populations. Perhaps the development of humor should be considered a goal of both psychological maturity and, when a psychotherapeutic relationship exists, of psychotherapy itself.

Norman Cousins writes about the healing power of humor from his own experience as a patient:[35]

> Any medical student can give you a horrendous catalogue of all the terrible things that happen to the body under the impact of negative emotions: fear, hate, rage, exasperations, frustration. You learn about constriction of the blood vessels, increase in blood pressure, excess flow of hydrochloric acid, adrenal depletion, indigestion, headaches. But we

haven't yet sufficiently recognized that the body does not operate only on one wave length. It doesn't respond just to the negative emotions, it also responds to the positive emotions. It's impossible to have one without having the other. But the salutary effect is not as well understood.

The Changing Adaptive Value of Psychopathology

Related to adaptation is the changing adaptiveness found with psychopathology, which will be discussed in Chapter 9. Paranoid personality structures appear to become even less adaptive with age as the few persons in the paranoid's circle die, isolation grows, and crises occur. On the other hand, the schizoid personality structure may insulate against loss. The obsessional and compulsive personality whose fussbudget behavior may have impaired effectiveness earlier in life may adjust well to the void left by retirement or losses, through meticulous and ritualistic activities.

Insight as an Adaptive Technique

Insight, or understanding of one's motivations and behavior, is the most widely used and successful adaptation found in healthy older people. Successful adjustments to real-life conditions are not optimally possible if feelings and behavior are unconsciously motivated and therefore not subject to conscious control. Similarly, it can prove nonadaptive to be unaware of the natural course of life: what to expect, what can be changed, and what cannot. Thus insight requires not only an inner sense of oneself and motivations but also an inner knowledge of the human life cycle—a realization of life and how it changes. The older individual who has a steady comprehension of the life process from birth to death is thereby assisted in his or her efforts to decide what to oppose and what to accept, when to struggle and when to acquiesce, and, ultimately, to understand the limits of what is possible. An example is what coauthor Myrna Lewis calls "responsible dependency." This concept implies the realistic evaluation of when one begins to require help from others and an ability to accept that help with dignity and co-operativeness, rather than denying the need or abusing the opportunity to be dependent. Insight includes the willingness and ability to substitute available satisfactions for losses incurred.

Exercising rational control over one's life is a mature, effective concomitant of insight. The conscious suppression of problems ("sufficient unto the day is the evil thereof"), the mastery of feelings, the unanxious anticipation of events, seeking pleasures and avoiding pain, and sublimation of unacceptable feelings by more acceptable ones are illustrative. Moreover, deliberate altruism, the personal and social concern for others, is a sophisticated and enlightened form of self-interest.

THE LIFE REVIEW

The tendency of older persons toward self-reflection and reminiscence used to be thought of as indicating a loss of recent memory and therefore a sign of aging. However, in 1961 coauthor Robert Butler first postulated that reminiscence in the aged was part of a normal life review process brought about by realization of approaching dissolution and death.[36] It is characterized by the progressive return to consciousness of past experiences and particularly the resurgence of unresolved conflicts that can be looked at again and reintegrated. If the reintegration is successful, it can give new significance and meaning to one's life and prepare one for death by mitigating fear and anxiety.[37]

This is a process that is believed to occur universally in all persons in the final years of their lives, although they may not be totally aware of it and may in part defend themselves from realizing its presence. It is spontaneous, unselective, and seen in other age groups as well (adolescence, middle age); but the intensity and emphasis on putting one's life in order are most striking in old age. In late life, people have a particularly vivid imagination and memory for the past and can recall with sudden and remarkable clarity early life events. There is renewed ability to free associate and bring up material from the unconscious. Individuals realize that their own personal myth of in-vulnerability and immortality can no longer be maintained. All of this results in reassessment of life, which brings depression, acceptance, or satisfaction.[38] The life review is not synonymous with reminiscence, although it includes this activity; it is one level or type of reminiscence.

The life review can occur in a mild form through mild nostalgia, mild regret, a tendency to reminisce, story-telling, and the like. Often the person will give his life story to anyone who will listen. At other times it is conducted in silent monologue without witnesses. It is in many ways similar to the psychotherapeutic situation in which a person is reviewing his or her life in order to understand present circumstances.

As part of the life review one may experience a sense of regret that is increasingly painful. In severe forms it can yield anxiety, guilt, despair, and depression. And in extreme cases, if a person is unable to resolve problems or accept them, terror, panic, and suicide can result. The most tragic life review is that in which a person decides life was a total waste.

Some of the positive results of reviewing one's life can be a righting of old wrongs, making up with enemies, coming to acceptance of mortal life, a sense of serenity, pride in accomplishment, and a feeling of having done one's best. It gives people an opportunity to decide what to do with the time left to them and work out emotional and material legacies. People become ready but are in no hurry to die. Possibly the qualities of serenity, philosophical development, and wisdom observable in some older people reflect a state of resolution of their life conflicts. A lively capacity to live in the present is usually experienced, including the direct enjoyment of elemental pleasures such as nature, children, forms, colors, warmth, love, and humor. One may become more capable of mutuality with a comfortable acceptance of the life cycle, the universe, and the generations. Creative works may result, such as memoirs, art, and music. People may put together family albums and scrapbooks and study their genealogies.

One of the greatest difficulties for younger persons (including mental health personnel) is to listen thoughtfully to the reminiscences of older people. (See Chapter 12 for a discussion on life review therapy.) We have been taught that this nostalgia represents living in the past and a preoccupation with self and that it is generally boring, meaningless, and time-consuming. Yet as a natural healing process it represents one of the underlying human capacities on which all psychotherapy depends. The life review should be recognized as a necessary and healthy process in daily life as well as a useful tool in the mental health care of older people.

SELECTED READINGS

Ariès, P. (1982). *The hour of our death.* New York: Vintage Books.

Bartoshuk, L. M., Rifkin, B., Marks, L. E., & Bars, P. (1986). Taste and aging. *Journal of Gerontology, 41,* 51–57.

Birren J. E., Butler, R. N., Greenhouse, S. W., Sokoloff, L., & Yarrow, M. R. (1963). Summary and interpretations. In Birren, J. E., Butler, R. N., Greenhouse, S. W., Sokoloff, L., & Yarrow, M. R. (Eds.), *Human aging: A biological and behavioral study,* pub. no. (PHS) 986. Washington, DC: U.S. Government Printing Office (reprinted as pub. no. [HSM] 71–9051, 1971, 1974).

Blieszner, R., & Hilkevitch Bedford, V. (Eds.). (1995). *Handbook of aging and the family.* Westport, CT: Greenwood Press.

Butler, R. N. (1963). The life review: An interpretation of reminiscence in the aged. *Psychiatry, 26,* 65–76.

Butler, R. N., & Lewis, M. I. (1995). Late-life depression: When and how to intervene. *Geriatrics, 50*(8), 44–55.

Butler, R. N., & Lewis, M. I. (1995). *Love and sex after sixty.* New York: Ballantine.

Castillo, C. S., Schultz, S. K., & Robinson, R. G. (1995, August). Clinical correlates of early-onset and late-onset poststroke general anxiety. *American Journal of Psychiatry, 152*(6), 1174–1179.

Chappell, N. L., & Badger, M. (1989). Social isolation and well-being. *The Journal of Gerontology, 44*(5), S169–S176.

Coffey, C. E., & Cummings, J. L., with Lovell, M. L., & Pearlson, G. D. (Eds.). (1994). *Textbook of geriatric neuropsychiatry.* Washington, DC: American Psychiatric Press.

Conway, P. (1988, November). Losses and grief in old age. *Social Casework,* 541–549.

Coombs, R. H. (1991). Marital status and personal well-being: A literature review. *Family Relations, 40,* 97–102.

Coroni-Huntley, J., Brock, D. B., Ostfeld, A. M., Taylor, J. O., & Wallace, R. B. (Eds.). (1986). *Established populations for epidemiologic studies of the elderly.* Resource data book, NIH Publication no. 86–2443. Washington, DC: National Institute on Aging.

Fasey, C. N. (1990, March/April). Grief in old age: A review of the literature. *International Journal of Geriatric Psychiatry, 5*(2), 67–76.

Flint, A. J. (1994). Epidemiology and comorbidity of anxiety disorders in the elderly. *American Journal of Psychiatry, 151,* 640–649.

Glaser, B. G., & Strauss, A. C. (1965). *Awareness of dying.* Chicago: Aldine.

Goldman, N., Korenman, S., & Weinstein, R. (1994). Marital status and health among the elderly. *Office of Population Research Working Paper,* no. 94–3. Princeton, NJ: Princeton University, Office of Population Research.

Gorer, G. (1965). *Death, grief, and mourning.* New York: Doubleday.

Helsing, K. J., Szklo, M., & Comstock, G. W. (1981, August). Factors associated with mortality after widowhood. *American Journal of Public Health, 71,* 802–809.

Hollingshead, A. B., & Redlich, F. (1958). Social class and mental illness. New York: John Wiley & Sons.

Lindemann, E. (1965). Symptomatology and management of acute grief. In Parad, H. J. (Ed.), *Crisis intervention: Selected readings* (pp. 7–21). New York: Family Service Association of America.

Lopata, H. Z. (1995). Feminist perspectives on social gerontology. In Blieszner, R. & Hilkevitch Bedford, V. (Eds.), *Handbook of aging and the family* (pp. 114–131). Westport, CT: Greenwood Press.

Lopata, H. Z. (1996). *Current widowhood: Myths and realities.* Newbury Park, CA: Sage Publications.

Martin-Matthews, A. (1991). *Widowhood in later life.* Toronto, Canada: Butterworths/Harcourt Brace.

McCrae, R. R., & Costa, P. T., Jr. (1988). Psychological resilience among widowed men and women: A 10-year follow-up of a national sample. *Journal of Social Issues, 44*(3), 129–142.

Mellstrom, D., Nilsson, A., Oden, A., Rundgren, A., & Svanborg, A. (1982). Mortality among the widowed in Sweden. *Scandinavian Journal of Social Medicine, 10*, 33–41.

National Advisory Mental Health Council. (1993, October). Health care reform for Americans with severe mental illness: Report of the National Advisory Mental Health Council. *American Journal of Psychiatry, 150*(10), 1447–1465.

O'Bryant, S. L., & Hansson, R. O. (1995) Widowhood. In Blieszner, R., & Hilkevitch Bedford, V. (Eds.), *Handbook of aging and the family* (pp. 440–458). Westport, CT: Greenwood Press.

Pellman, J. (1992) Widowhood and elderly women: Exploring its relationship to community integration, hassles, stress, social support and social support seeking. *International Journal of Aging and Human Development, 35*(4), 253–264.

Perlin, S., & Butler, R. N. (1963). Psychiatric aspects of adaptation to the aging experience. In Birren, J. E., Butler, R. N., Greenhouse, S. W., Sokoloff, L., & Yarrow, M. R. *Human aging: A biological and behavioral study,* pub. no. (PHS) 986. Washington, DC: U.S. Government Printing Office. (Reprinted as pub. no. [HSM] 71–9051, 1971, 1974).

Stroebe, M. S., Stroebe, W., & Hansson, R. O. (Eds.). (1993). *Handbook of bereavement.* New York: Cambridge University Press.

Tolstoy, L. (1886). *The death of Ivan Ilych.*

Umberson, D., Wortman, C., & Kessler, R. (1992). Widowhood and depression: Explaining long-term gender differences in vulnerability. *Journal of Health and Social Behavior, 33*(1), 10–24.

Valliant, G. E. (1986). An empirical validated hierarchy of defense mechanisms. *Archives of General Psychiatry, 42,* 597–601.

Weinberg, J. (1956). Personal and social adjustment. In Anderson, J. E. (Ed.), *Psychological aspects of aging.* Washington, DC: American Psychological Association.

Weisman, A. D., & Kastenbaum, R. (1968) The psychological autopsy: A study of the terminal phase of life. *Community Mental Health Journal.* Monograph no. 4. New York: Behavioral Publications.

Wolinsky, F., & Johnson, R. (1992). Widowhood, health status, and the use of health services by older adults: A cross sectional and prospective approach. *Journal of Gerontology,* S8–S16.

ENDNOTES

1. *Senescence* is a term that has been used to describe the developmental stages of later life. It is an analogue to pubescence and adolescence; no similar term has been formulated for middle age.

2. Pusey, E. B. (trans.). (1949) *The confessions of St. Augustine* (book IX). New York: Modern Library.

3. Gorer, G. (1965). *Death, grief and mourning.* New York: Doubleday Anchor.

4. Parkes, C. M. (1970). Seeking and finding a lost object. *Social Science and Medicine, 4,* 187–201; Parkes, C. M., & Weiss, R. S. (1983). *Recovery from bereavement.* New York: Basic Books.

5. Mellstrom, D., Nilsson, A., Oden, A., Rundren, A., & Svanborg, A. (1982). Mortality among the widowed in Sweden. *Scandinavian Journal of Social Medicine, 10, 33*–41.

6. Chodoff especially has emphasized "survival guilt" as a result of concentration camp experiences. We have observed this also in older people who have outlived their peers and spouses, although, of course, many take pride in survival as well. See Chodoff, P. C. (1963). Late effects of the concentration camp syndrome. *Archives of General Psychiatry, 9,* 323–333.

7. Butler, R. N., & Lewis, M. I. (1995). Late-life depression: When and how to intervene. *Geriatrics, 50*(8), 44–55.

8. Blazer, D., Hughes, D. C., & George, L. K. (1987). The epidemiology of depression in an elderly community population. *Gerontologist, 27,* 281–287.

9. Murphy, E. (1982). Social origins of depression in old age. *British Journal of Psychiatry, 141,* 135–142.

10. Rats subjected to Jay Weiss's "yoke" electric shock paradigm dramatically demonstrate the relationship between learned helplessness and disease. See Sklar, L. S., & Anisman, H. (1979). Stress and coping factors influence tumor growth. *Science, 205,* 512–515; Visintainer, M. A., Volpicelli, J. R., & Seligman, M. E. (1982). Tumor rejection in rats after inescapable or escapable shock. *Science, 216,* 437–439.

11. Hess, N. (1987). King Lear and some anxieties of old age. *British Journal of Medical Psychology, 60,* 209–215.

12. Helsing, K. J., Szklo, M., & Comstock, G. W. (1981). Factors associated with mortality after widowhood. *American Journal of Public Health, 7,* 802–809.

13. Mellstrom et al., *Mortality among the widowed,* 33–41.

14. McCrae, R. R., & Costa, P. T. (1988). Psychological resilience among widowed men and women: A

10-year follow-up of a national sample. *Journal of Social Issues, 44*(3), 129–142.

15. Silverman, P. (1985). *Widow to widow.* New York: Springer.

16. Very little data are available on old-age marital relationships. There have been few studies of husband and wife through the life span. Therefore, we must largely theorize from clinical experience.

17. Morycz, R. K. (1985). Caregiving strain and the desire to institutionalize family members with Alzheimer's disease. *Research on Aging, 7,* 329–361.

18. Goldman, L. S., & Luchins, D. J. (1984). Depression in the spouses of demented patients. *American Journal of Psychiatry, 141,* 1467–1468; Cohen, D., & Eisdorfer, C. (1988). Depression in family members caring for a relative with Alzheimer's disease. *Journal of the American Geriatrics Society, 36,* 885–889.

19. Eagles, J. M., Beattie, J. A. G., Blackwood, G. W., Restall, D. B., & Ashcroft, G. W. (1987). The mental health of elderly couples: I. The effects of a cognitively impaired spouse. *British Journal of Psychiatry, 150,* 299–303; Eagles, J. M., Craig, A., Rawlinson, F., Restall, D. B., Beattie, J. A. G., & Besson, J. A. O. (1987). The psychological well-being of supporters of the demented elderly. *British Journal of Psychiatry, 150,* 293–298.

20. Butler, R. N., & Lewis, M. I. (1993). *Love and sex after sixty.* New York: Ballantine.

21. Corso, J. F. (1995). Hearing. In Maddox, G. L. (Ed.), *The encyclopedia of aging.* (pp. 449–452). New York: Springer.

22. Weinstein, B. E. (1994, August). Age-related hearing loss: How to screen for it, and when to intervene. *Geriatrics, 49*(8), 40–45.

23. Older people usually first notice hearing loss in the high-frequency range. This includes the consonants. To get a sense of what many older people miss, write a sentence and remove the *f*'s, *s*'s, and *th*'s.

24. Eastwood, M. R., Corbin, S. L, Reed, M., Nobbs, H., & Kedward, H. B. (1985). Acquired hearing loss and psychiatric illness: An estimate of prevalence and co-morbidity in a geriatric setting. *British Journal of Psychiatry, 147,* 552–556.

25. American Foundation for the Blind. (1996). *Fact sheet: Facts about aging and vision.* Available from: American Foundation for the Blind, 11 Penn Plaza, Suite 300, New York, N.Y. 10001. (800)232-5463.

26. Doty, R. L., Shaman, P., Applebaum, S. Z., Giberson, R., Siksorski, L., & Rosenberg, L. (1984). Smell identification ability: Changes with age. *Science, 226,* 1441–1443.

27. Thus, Shakespeare was wrong, at least about taste, when in *As You Like It* he described old age as "sans teeth, sans eyes, sans taste, sans everything."

28. Central office—36 Executive Park Ste., Irvine, CA. 92714, with 580 local chapters.

29. National Center for Health Statistics. (1996). Advance Report of Final Mortality Statistics, 1993. *Monthly Vital Statistics Report, 44*(7), supplement. Hyattsville, MD: National Center for Health Statistics.

30. Tideiksaar, R. (1989). *Falling in old age: Its prevention and treatment.* New York: Springer.

31. Robinson, R. G., Stan, L. B., & Price, T. R. (1984). A two-year longitudinal study of mood disorder following stroke: Prevalence and duration at six months follow-up. *British Journal of Psychiatry, 14,* 256–262; Carney, R. M., Rich, M. W., Tevelde, A., Saini, J., Clark, K., & Jaffe, A. S. (1987). Major depressive disorder in coronary artery disease. *American Journal of Cardiology, 60,* 1273–1275; Castillo, C. S., Schultz, S. K., & Robinson, R. G. (1995, August). Clinical correlates of early-onset and late-onset poststroke generalized anxiety. *American Journal of Psychiatry, 152*(8), 1174–1179.

32. Originally a neurological rather than a psychological concept, constructed by English neurologist Hughlings Jackson.

33. See the original contribution of Frenichel, O. (1939). The counterphobic attitude. *International Journal of Psychoanalysis, 20,* 263.

34. Weinberg, J. (1956). Personal and social adjustment. In Anderson, J. E. (Ed.), *Psychological aspects of aging* (pp. 17–20). Washington, DC: American Psychological Association.

35. Cousins, N. (1979). *Anatomy of an illness as perceived by the patient.* New York: W. W. Norton.

36. Butler, R. N. (1961). Reawakening interest. *Nursing Homes, 10,* 8–19; and Butler, R. N. (1963). The life review: An interpretation of reminiscence in the aged. *Psychiatry, 26,* 65–76.

37. In *The Experience of Old Age: Stress, Coping, and Survival* (New York: Basic Books, 1983), authors M. Lieberman and S. Tobin confirm that reminiscence is crucial to the emotional livelihood of an older person, helping to resolve past conflicts and enabling the development of a coherent life history.

38. Coleman, P. G. (1974). Measuring reminiscence characteristics from conversation and adaptive features of old age. *International Journal of Aging and Human Development, 5,* 281–294.

CHAPTER 5

COMMON PSYCHIATRIC DISORDERS

With the publication of the *Diagnostic and Statistical Manual,* 4th Edition (DSM-IV), there has been a significant change in the approach taken with psychiatric conditions in the elderly. No longer are there distinctions made between the "organic" and "functional" disorders, as with previous editions. In fact, the term "organic mental disorder" has been eliminated entirely because of the implication that the other conditions were without an underlying organic component. Instead, the psychiatric disorders are viewed independently with attention to the current foundation of clinical research information. The diagnostic nomenclature thus reflects the separation of clinical syndromes by their defining features. This does not suggest that all subjects with the same syndrome are alike or that syndromal boundaries are mutually exclusive. Rather, these diagnostic categories are meant to be useful to communicate important characteristics of a diagnostic category, however heterogeneous that category might be. The categories are also meant to allow a foundation for further clinical research to advance the understanding of that syndrome. For the elderly, this common ground is essential as the field of geriatric psychiatry expands and considers crucial clinical research questions.

The extent of psychiatric disorders in the elderly is considerable. It has been estimated by the American Psychiatric Association that 15 to 25% of the elderly suffer from symptoms of mental illness.[1] While depression is considered the most common mental disorder, afflicting up to 20% of people 65 years and older, many other conditions are found in this age group, including anxiety, alcoholism, drug abuse, schizophrenia, and personality disorders. In addition, psychiatric symptoms are known to be prevalent in older patients suffering from conditions such as Alzheimer's disease and other chronic illnesses.

In general medical settings, it is estimated that up to 10% of acute care geriatric patients have a depressive illness and as many as 30% have clinically significant depressive symptoms,[2] but only a small minority ever receive psychiatric treatment. This is an unfortunate oversight, because the depressive syndromes of the elderly are often responsive to treatment when diagnosed properly.[3] Even in nursing homes, where more than 50% of the elderly residents are thought to be suffering from one or more psychiatric syndromes, fewer than 5% receive mental health services either through a trained specialist or an interested general practitioner.[4]

For some elderly, a psychiatric disorder may have been part of their lives for many decades. Illnesses such as bipolar disorder and schizophrenia generally manifest themselves in early adulthood and are known to have chronic courses which can certainly extend into later life. Major depressive disorder, dysthymic disorder (a milder form of depression), and delusional disorder can all have much later onsets so that an older person might be stricken for the first time after the age of 65 years. Whether these late onset syndromes are biologically distinct from the younger onset illnesses is not yet known. What is too often assumed, however, is that the psychiatric syndromes arising in later life are secondary to the problems of aging itself and thus diagnosis and treatment are often not pursued. On the other hand, while many health problems do increase in the elderly, these changes do not always give rise to psychiatric disorders and cannot be used as a blanket explanation for emotional difficulties. As with any younger patient, the new onset of a psychiatric disorder in an older patient must be evaluated and, when appropriate, treated actively.

MOOD DISORDERS IN THE ELDERLY

Perhaps the most widely diagnosed psychiatric conditions in the elderly, the mood disorders actually are made up of several distinct but overlapping entities:

1. Major Depressive Disorder
2. Bipolar Disorder
3. Dysthymic Disorder

While bipolar disorders are possibly better known, perhaps because of the often flamboyant presentations of bipolar patients, the depressive disorders are far more common. Psychotic features (gross impairment of reality testing) may be present but are not a necessary prerequisite in either condition. A psychological stress may set off the first episode of bipolar or unipolar depressive disorders, but recurrent episodes can occur apparently without a precipitating factor. For many other people, stressful events are *not* a necessary condition for the development of a mood disorder.

Major Depressive Disorder

When introducing the topic of depression, it is important to define terms. *Major depression* is a syndrome with well-defined features as described in DSM-IV.[5] The essential feature of a major depressive episode is the existence of depressed mood or a marked loss of interest or pleasure for at least two consecutive weeks. Associated symptoms include sleep disturbance, appetite and weight changes, decreased concentration, feelings of fatigue or loss of energy, psychomotor disturbances, and recurrent thoughts of death. By definition, the syndrome of depressive disorder involves a significant impairment in normal daily functioning. In order to reach criteria for a major depressive disorder, an individual must manifest at least one of the essential features and five or more of the nine symptoms listed in Table 5.1.

TABLE 5.1   Diagnostic features of a major depressive episode as listed in the American Psychiatric Association's DSM-IV manual

MAJOR DEPRESSIVE DISORDER: DIAGNOSTIC CRITERIA

Essential Features (1 of 2 required):
1. Depressed mood
2. Loss of interest or pleasure
Associated Symptoms (5 of 9 required):
1. Depressed mood for most of the day
2. Marked reduction in interest in daily activities
3. 5% weight loss or significant change in appetite (increase or decrease)
4. Almost daily insomnia or hypersomnia
5. Almost daily physical agitation or retardation
6. Almost daily decreased energy or fatigue
7. Almost daily feelings of worthlessness or feelings of guilt
8. Almost daily decreased concentration or decreased decisiveness
9. Frequent thoughts of death or suicide

Depression is the most common of the emotional disorders found in older people and can occur at any time in life. Depression varies all the way from transient "blues," which everyone experiences, to the extremes of psychotic withdrawal or suicide. Although epidemiologic estimates vary from study to study, the current data suggest that rates for major depression are actually lower (approximately 2%) in the elderly compared to younger adults (3–5%).[6] When using more inclusive criteria for major depressive disorder, this figure increases to approximately 6% for the elderly. Other surveys using structured interviews have reported depression prevalence rates of 19 to 31% in the elderly. In outpatient settings, significant depressive symptoms have been seen in 7 to 25% of patients surveyed.[7] These discrepancies across studies over the last twenty years regarding the rates of depression in the elderly are perplexing but may in part be explained by the higher incidence of atypical symptoms, including increased socioeconomic problems, concurrent medical illnesses, and changing epidemiologic and diagnostic techniques.[8]

Depression in the elderly is frequently considered to be much different from that seen in younger adults. This misconception is understandable since there are so many medical and psychosocial variables that change with age. Indeed, many of the medical conditions that occur with more frequency in the elderly, such as stroke, heart disease, and arthritis, can precipitate or be associated with major depression. The differential diagnosis of depression is often confounded by concurrent medical conditions, especially those which impair cognitive functioning (e.g., Alzheimer's disease or vascular dementia) and lead to diagnostic and therapeutic dilemmas (see Chapter 9 for further discussion of diagnostic evaluation). Nonetheless, the signs and symptoms of major depression in the elderly may not be as different as previously believed.

Mr. W, a 69-year-old businessman, has been severely depressed for eighteen months. He has a previous history of major depression which had generally responded to tricyclic antidepressant medications. Since the death of his wife last year, he has been in a profound depression with symptoms of tearfulness, insomnia, early morning awakening, weight loss, hopelessness, and suicidal preoccupations. Several antidepressants have been tried on an outpatient basis with only partial success, and he has recently suffered a serious downturn which has required him to temporarily take a leave of absence from his part-time job. He was admitted to the hospital when he developed the belief that his internal organs were "shutting down and rotting away," thus preventing him from eating any food. During a course of 10 unilateral (one side of the head) electroconvulsive therapy (ECT) treatments, he began to show gradual improvement and was discharged from the hospital three weeks later.

To address the question of symptom differences across age amongst depressed patients, Blazer and colleagues compared middle-aged and older inpatients.[9] Somewhat surprisingly, these two groups were remarkably similar. While the older group was more likely to suffer weight loss and symptoms of constipation and less likely to have suicidal thoughts, the two groups of patients with depression were otherwise comparable across a host of symptom profiles, family histories, and treatment responses. When studying less depressed groups of outpatients, differences between the middle-aged and those who were older did emerge[10]; the older patients reported increased physical symptoms, such as abdominal complaints, sleep disturbances, lethargy, and constipation, as well as increased thoughts of death and feelings of depression. The response to medications does not necessarily differ according to age, however, and will be discussed in Chapter 13.

When comparing groups of elderly and younger depressed subjects, Alexopoulos and colleagues[11] reported that while objective clinical ratings of depression were similar across age groups, the older subjects experienced generally lower levels of self-rated depression, anger and psychotic thoughts. Similarly, Lyness and colleagues find a general underreporting of depressive symptoms in the older subjects.[12] Since the objective measures of depression were not significantly different between the two groups, it can only be assumed that older subjects tend to underreport the severity of their symptoms. This subjective–objective dichotomy should be seriously considered when evaluating an older depressed subject, especially during an initial evaluation.

Bipolar Disorders (Manic-Depressive Illness)

Bipolar disorders are characterized as severe mood swings from depression to elation or the full or partial development of one or more manic episodes alone with a persistent elevated, expansive, or irritable mood (see the glossary at the end of this chapter for descriptions of the individual diagnostic terms). Bipolar disorders typically occur before age 30 and are apparently found equally commonly in men and women. They can persist into old age, but the typical lifelong course is not yet clearly understood.

There are two major bipolar disorders: *bipolar disorder* itself, in which there are one or more manic episodes associated with one or more major depressive episodes; and *cyclothymia,* in which there is a history of several hypomanic episodes (similar to but less severe than manic episodes) and numerous depressive episodes. A third bipolar disorder, called *bipolar disorder NOS* ("not otherwise specified") replaces the older classification of "atypical bipolar disorder" and includes what is sometimes referred to as "bipolar II"—patients who have hypomanic but not manic episodes along with major depressive episodes.

Because bipolar disorder is by definition a recurrent illness, episodes occurring in later life are generally not first attacks.[13] However, there is a slow but steady incidence of first admissions for mania in both men and women with increasing age.[14] When bipolar illness does develop for the first time in later decades, concurrent medical disorders, especially those involving the central nervous system, should be investigated.[15] The lifetime risk of death from bipolar illness is estimated to be approximately 1 to 3%.[16] It is believed that bipolar disorder is a familial illness and numerous family histories attest to this fact, but the genetics of the illness are far from being fully explained.

Mrs. Q, an 83-year-old widow, has had episodes of mania and hypomania for over 60 years. Currently, she lives with her devoted sister who helps her with her medication (lithium) and accompanies her to doctor visits at a local psychiatric clinic. Over the last several decades of widowhood, she has had more doctors take care of her than episodes of mania, and her sister carefully documents all treatment to facilitate the transition from doctor to doctor. Currently, she is well-maintained on a low dose of lithium, but she remembers the days long before the advent of lithium. During that era, she required large doses of anti-psychotic drugs and hospitalization to control her manic episodes. Before the drugs were introduced, she was forced to undergo a series of long-since abandoned psychiatric "cures" including cold wet packs, sleep therapy, and isolation, just to name a few, until her bipolar episodes subsided spontaneously. She leads a quiet life now with only occasional episodes of hyper-irritability and insomnia which are successfully treated with brief increases in her lithium level and low doses of a sedating anti-psychotic drug (i.e., chlorpromazine). She is still in full control of her faculties and can regale any interested listener with a complete history of psychiatry as it developed into the modern era of psychopharmacologic management.

Dysthymic Disorder

While considered a milder form of depression, *dysthymic disorder* can nonetheless pose a significant and chronic problem for elderly patients. Symptoms of dysthymic disorder include low self-esteem, poor concentration, difficulty with decision-making, over-eating or poor appetite, low energy, insomnia or hypersomnia (too much sleep), and feelings of hopelessness. These symptoms are generally less acute than those found in major depression, but they can interfere with day-to-day experiences and last at least two years by definition. Sadness, which can of course be a normal mood experience, is also a frequent problem in the elderly. While sadness is not formally considered a diagnostic entity in the DSM-IV, its symptoms can include frequent tearfulness, social isolation, decreased ability to take action, anhedonia (the inability to experience pleasure), and increased physical complaints. All too frequently, these symptoms are simply labeled as part of the aging process. In fact, when sadness encroaches on one's mood more often than a "normal" amount (different for each individual), then it too can be considered a pathologic symptom worthy of some therapeutic intervention.

Not all sadness and depression is reason for an older person to see a psychiatrist. While this fact may seem obvious, it is important to remember that sadness and occasional periods of depression can be a very normal reaction to the changes which come with aging. Stressors such as bereavement, retirement followed by declining socioeconomic status, and deteriorating physical health can be powerful influences on overall mood and self-esteem.[17] For most individuals, these stresses lead to some difficult times and understandable temporary changes in mood. For other older individuals, including those with a previous history of depression, these same stresses may precipitate a major depressive episode. Other more pervasive but perhaps less acute factors, such as alcohol consumption, slowly increasing physical disabilities, problems with sexual dysfunction, and personality disorders, can also play a role in the development of depression in the elderly (see Sunderland et al., 1988[18] and Chapter 7). It is, therefore, the job of the clinician to help families recognize when the depressive reaction goes beyond "normal" and would perhaps benefit from some therapeutic intervention.

The underlying cause of mood disorders in the elderly is no better understood than that in younger adults. Theories of neurotransmitter abnormalities in both the norepinepherine and serotonin system have been proposed for years,[19] and there have been suggestions of "dysregulation" of these systems,[20] but convincing biochemical and neuropathologic evidence is, for the most part, still lacking. However, the fact that these patients generally respond therapeutically to psychiatric medications certainly favors a specific biologic cause, as yet undetermined, of these conditions. Perhaps the most exciting lead in this direction is the longstanding recognition of a genetic or familial factor in the mood disorders. With the rapid evolution and expanding availability of powerful molecular biology techniques, the initial finding of an abnormality in chromosome 11 in certain families with a high prevalence for bipolar disorder[21] has been followed by a series of contrasting studies, which leaves the field quite confusing.[22] The early excitement regarding the genetic "mapping" of mood disorders for purposes of diagnostic evaluation and potential earlier therapeutic intervention has not yet been realized. In the meantime, the coexistence of depression with other medical illnesses in the elderly such as dementia of the Alzheimer type and strokes provides us with a potential human model for depression.[23] These conditions have known neuropathologic changes and may well provide clues into the pathophysiology (underlying physical causes) of depression as well as a human model for the testing of new psychopharmacologic agents.

OTHER MOOD DISORDERS IN THE ELDERLY

Medical and Psychiatric Comorbidity (Coexistent Illness) in the Elderly

Clinicians are often asked to differentiate between medical and mental health problems in the elderly. Depression is a well-recognized concomitant of many chronic medical illnesses, and the medical difficulties can certainly enter into the differential diagnosis of any elderly patient with depressive symptoms.[24] In fact, depression can occasionally be the presenting symptom for some medical conditions. With the elderly, these diagnostic criteria are sometimes confused with intercurrent medical illnesses which may interfere with a clinician's evaluation of these symptoms.

While it is obviously important not to overinterpret expected mood symptoms which are entirely related to physical ailments, the careful clinician must also be sensitive to the possibly exaggerated physical complaints with routine medical conditions. Much like a pediatrician would be attentive to a slowed weight gain in an otherwise normal, growing child as a possible sign of depression, a geriatrician should be aware of accelerated weight loss in a cancer patient as a possible sign of superimposed depression. In fact, it is estimated that 20 to 25% of individuals with certain medical conditions (i.e., cancer, cerebrovascular accidents, diabetes and myocardial infarction) will at some point develop a major depressive episode (see Table 5.2).[25]

The comorbidity of Alzheimer's disease and depression is of particular interest because of the overlapping symptoms and overlapping biology.[26] In one study of 37 depressed demented patients, for instance, the autopsy revealed evidence of degeneration in both the locus coeruleus and substantia nigra.[27] These findings are consistent with the catecholamine hypothesis of affective disorders. Similarly, Zweig and colleagues have shown a relationship between major depression and degeneration of the locus coeruleus and the dorsal raphe nuclei (serotonergic) in Alzheimer's disease.[28]

Late Onset Depression.   The concept of "late onset" depression has received a great deal of attention recently. Whether the initial development of depression after the age of 60 represents a distinct biologic subtype of depression remains controversial.[29] One important issue raised by this controversy is the existence of concurrent medical illness, especially cardiovascular disease, in the elderly with depression.[30] One type of "late-onset" depression that is particularly interesting includes depressed subjects who first present with mild cognitive impairments. While the initial diagnosis is not clearly Alzheimer's disease (AD), it has been reported that up to 47% of these patients go on to develop progressive dementia within three years.[31] Other studies have reported somewhat lower rates of conversion to dementia,[32] but they all show a greater rate of AD compared with controls. Although it is still preliminary, there is also some suggestion that these older depressives are more likely to have APO E4

TABLE 5.2   Medical conditions commonly associated with depression in the elderly

CONDITION
Coronary artery disease
Hypertension, myocardial infarction, coronary artery bypass surgery, congestive heart failure
Neurologic disorders
Cerebrovascular accidents, Alzheimer's disease, Parkinson's disease, amyotrophic lateral sclerosis, multiple sclerosis, Binswanger's disease
Metabolic disturbances
Diabetes mellitus, hypothyroidism or hyperthyroidism, hypercortisolism, hyperparathyroidism, Addison's disease, autoimmune thyroiditis
Cancer
Pancreatic, breast, lung, colonic, and ovarian carcinoma; lymphoma, and undetected cerebral metastasis
Other conditions
Chronic obstructive pulmonary disease, rheumatoid arthritis, chronic pain, sexual dysfunction, renal dialysis, chronic constipation

Source: Sunderland, T., Lawlor, B. A., Molchan, S. E., & Martinez, R. A. (1988). Depressive syndromes in the elderly: Special concerns. *Psychopharmacology Bulletin* 24:567. Reprinted by permission.

alleles,[33] a known associative marker for AD (see Chapter 13 for more details). This finding is intriguing and does lend evidence to the speculation that "late-onset" depression is a biologically distinct classification. Careful prospective follow-up with large groups of late-onset depressives is now required to address this important clinical research question more directly.

Mrs. D had a history of nervousness all her life. When she experienced her menopause at age 55, she suffered a series of depressive symptoms of tiredness, irritability, forgetfulness, and frequent crying. Her physician prescribed replacement hormones which alleviated her symptoms quickly. Ten years later, at the age of 65, the symptoms of sadness, forgetfulness, and irritability returned, but this time, they did not respond to replacement hormone therapy. Subsequent antidepressant trials with amitriptyline and doxepin created acute confusional states before being discontinued. Trazodone, however, in low doses reduced the depressive symptoms for several years. Then, at age 69, Mrs. D returned for follow-up care with a history of gradual worsening of her cognitive state. On formal examination, she had bilateral slowing on her EEG, enlarged ventricles on CT scan, and neuropsychological testing indicating marked deterioration. A presumptive diagnosis of Alzheimer's disease was made at that time.

Suicide in Old Age.   Whatever the underlying epidemiology of depression, it is clear that depression is a significant factor for the elderly, because suicide rates are higher in the elderly than in any other age group.[34] In fact, suicide remains one of the 10 leading causes of death in the United States. The highest rate of suicide occurs in white men in their eighties. Older persons, representing 13% of the population, accounted for roughly 20% of reported suicides—about 6,000—in 1995.[35] Furthermore, the percentage of people who have attempted suicide previously goes down tremendously with age (51% in the young versus 20% in those over 60 years of age).[36]

In general, older depressives are much more likely to commit suicides than younger depressives. Women are more likely to attempt suicide than men, but men are more likely to succeed when they make an attempt. The peak rate of suicide for white women occurs in middle age. However, throughout the world, suicide rates have been increasing for women, especially older women. Rates for nonwhite men and women are lower, with a peak for black men in the years 25 to 34.[37] Table 5.3 shows suicides per 100,000 population by age and sex.[38] The increased suicide rate with age is found in all countries which keep reliable statistics.

Older people use all the usual methods of killing themselves: drugs, guns, hanging, and jumping off high places. In the United States firearms and explosives are at the top of the list. Suicide may also be accomplished "subintentionally," by the slower means of not eating, not taking medicines, drinking too much, delaying treatment, and taking risks physically. This long-term process of suicidal erosion is of course not part of suicide statistics, since suicide is seen as a single act. More common in the elderly is a process of slow deterioration ("chronic suicide") where the will to live is lessened and important recurrent needs of the individual are neglected either consciously or unconsciously in a self-destructive manner. Most laws regarding commitment require specific evidence of a current and active danger to oneself or to others (rightfully

TABLE 5.3   Suicides per 100,000 population by age and sex, United States: 1995

AGE	TOTAL	MALE	FEMALE
15–24	13.3	22.5	3.7
25–34	15.4	25.6	5.2
35–44	15.2	24.1	6.5
45–54	14.6	22.8	6.7
55–64	13.3	22.0	5.3
65–74	15.8	28.7	5.4
75–84	20.7	44.8	5.5
85+	21.6	63.1	5.5
Total	11.9	19.8	4.4

Source: Unpublished data, National Center for Health Statistics, 1997.

protecting the civil liberties of people). Therefore such long, drawn-out self-destructive behavior often presents a touchy legal problem: is intervention warranted or not?

A 72-year-old man lived by himself in a small apartment in a large inner city. He was in failing health due to chronic asthma but refused to live with his son and family in the country where the air was cleaner because he did not want to be a "burden." Without clear medical precipitant, he began to slowly lose weight. He also stopped taking care of himself in the usual manner. Having previously been a fastidious man, he was now disheveled. His apartment was no longer hygienic. Despite many protestations from his family, he continued to lose weight and died alone in his apartment during a long cold winter. He was of sound mind throughout this period leading to his death.

Mary B, a 66-year-old executive, was found dead of a lethal injection two weeks after learning that she had been diagnosed with early Alzheimer's disease. She had played competitive tennis one week before the diagnosis and was active socially before her death, which was ruled a suicide by police.

Police in Blaine, Minnesota, reported that an 85-year-old man, depressed over a painful illness, arranged for his own funeral, then drove to the mortuary and shot himself in his car. Police said he telephoned the Wexler Funeral Home Sunday and inquired about the cost of cremation, telling an employee he would be over later. He wrote a note to his wife. Authorities found him dead in his car with a $300 check made out to the funeral home.

Attitudes toward Suicide. In German, *suicide* (*Selbstmord*) means "self-murder." This etymology tells something of the motives of hatred of self or others that are present in many suicides. Freud in 1925 said that perhaps no one could find the psychic energy to kill himself unless in the first place he was thereby killing at the same time someone with whom he had identified himself. Menninger in 1938 has written that the suicide

victim wishes to die, to kill, and to be killed. Indeed, suicide is three times more common than homicide. Perhaps it is emotionally less threatening to consider killing oneself than others.

Self-control is an important motivational element in suicide. Seneca said, "Against all the injuries of life, I have the refuge of death"; and Nietzsche stated, "The thought of suicide gets one successfully through many a bad night." Death itself is certain but its timing and its character are not. One can defy and control death by virtue of initiating the act of one's own death. Control also extends beyond the grave—survivors are deeply affected and a grim, unmistakable legacy of guilt, shame, and regret may be left for them to bear.

A rational or *philosophical* decision to kill oneself is undoubtedly more common in old age as people perceive themselves to be failing. Older men, especially, may decide to kill themselves rather than leave their widows penniless from the cost of a long illness. Married couples may commit double suicide or a combination of mercy killing of one and suicide of the other.

Documents left by the married couples yield a typical picture of an aging man and woman, one or both suffering from grave illness, which is never absent from their thoughts. A deeply devoted pair, childless, in modest circumstances and with few interests and friends, they are deeply absorbed in their own small world. Prolonged insomnia speeds the decisive act. "We are at the end of our rope" is a phrase which repeatedly occurs. Here is a typical situation. A 56-year-old ex-miner, with impaired vision and an injured leg, underwent an operation for cancer of the bowel. The operation was not successful and he was confined to his bed with frequent, violent attacks of pain. His wife was disabled by Parkinson's disease and had been partly paralyzed for 15 years.[39]

A sacrificial romantic quality can be present in the double suicide pacts of lovers, old or young, as noted below:

In death pacts between lovers we meet the age-old belief, found in myth and history, that two people who die together are united forever beyond the grave. This belief is also encountered in the German Romantic Period. In Japan it is known as shinju. It is but a step from such a belief towards symbolization of the grave as a bridal bed.[40]

Mental health personnel should take suicide threats of older persons seriously. Persons attempting suicide are more likely to fail if below age 35 and to succeed if over 50. It is most rare for an attempt by anyone over 65 to fail. Men are more successful than women. (For indicators of suicide risk, see Chapter 9.) It has been suggested in the research literature that a "lenient" or generally accepting attitude toward suicide or assisted suicide is in itself a risk factor for suicide. While elderly subjects polled showed a lower overall rate of leniency toward suicide compared with younger adults, there was an association between a lenient response and risk factors for suicide (i.e., alcoholism, depression, hopelessness and recent losses).[41] This suggests that clinicians should inquire about individuals' attitudes towards suicide and perhaps use that information, if "lenient" attitudes are discovered, as an avenue for exploration of possible underlying risk factors for suicidal behavior.

Reducing the frequency of depression and providing for its effective treatment when present are the major ways of reducing suicide in old age. One must be especially alert with people whose depressions seem to have lifted. They may be gathering enough energy to commit the suicide they had contemplated earlier. When there is evidence of suicidal preoccupations, one must schedule extra time and additional sessions. It is important to openly discuss the subject rather than, ostrichlike, hope it will go away. Ongoing studies of Conwell and associates have supported the observation that the majority of elderly suicides occur in first episode depressions of mild-to-moderate severity.[42] The obvious suggestion of this work is that appropriate but aggressive intervention with pharmacologic and behavioral treatment might well be effective in preventing suicide among the elderly subjects. This tells us that outreach services are imperative to reach depressed people who may have withdrawn and become isolated. If suicide is seen as a reasonable alternative (i.e., "leniency" in attitude) and the underlying factors associated with suicidal behavior are present (i.e., depression, hopelessness, recent stressors, etc.), then the clinical situation should be viewed as a psychiatric emergency and treated aggressively. Perhaps the French novelist and essayist, Albert Camus, was correct when he saw suicide as submission and stated, "there is only one truly serious philosophical problem and that is suicide."[43]

SCHIZOPHRENIA AND PARANOID DISORDERS

It is generally believed that *schizophrenia* is a disorder of youth. In fact, until the introduction of DSM IIIR in 1987, one of the criteria for the diagnosis of schizophrenia was the onset of illness prior to age 45. With the advent of DSM-IV in 1994, there is no age specification, and there is an acceptance of later onset schizophrenia, especially in women. In the elderly, schizophrenia is more likely to include paranoid delusions and hallucinations while negative or disorganized symptoms are less common. The overall lifetime prevalence of schizophrenia is still estimated to be 0.5 to 1% of the population, with first degree relatives having about ten times greater risk of developing the illness than the overall population.[44]

By definition, schizophrenia is a severe psychiatric disorder marked by disturbances of thinking, mood, and behavior. Thought disorder is the primary feature of the illness and characteristic features include hallucinations, delusions, and poor reality testing. Typically, the disturbance has been going on continuously for at least six months and is associated with a decline in work productivity, social relationships, and self-care. In the active phase of schizophrenia, there must be at least one month with two of the following symptoms:

- Delusions
- Hallucinations
- Disorganized speech

- Grossly disorganized or catatonic behavior
- Negative symptoms

Many older people have developed types of schizophrenia in earlier years and carried them into old age.[45] These persons are often called "chronic schizophrenics." One sees persons with schizophrenia who have been hospitalized as long as 50 or 60 years; many never received treatment and were simply "stored" out of sight in hospitals, beyond the mainstream of medicine and psychiatry. Originally, it was assumed that all early-onset chronic schizophrenics suffered a uniformly downhill course over time. Recent longitudinal studies have called that assumption into question, as it appears that chronic schizophrenia may well have a more variable outcome, with some patients remaining quite stable over time. The following is an example of a chronic schizophrenic patient hospitalized for 40 years:

Mr. M is 67 years of age. The diagnosis in his case was schizophrenic reaction, chronic undifferentiated type, of moderate severity, with onset at approximately 21 years of age. He was also diagnosed as showing a moderate depressive reaction for the past two years. Mr. M was first hospitalized about 40 years ago and in the last six months has been moved to a foster care home where he now lives with a long-despised brother. He has only minimal impairment of his recent memory and his level of intellectual functioning has not declined. His impairments of judgment and abstraction are interpreted as psychogenic and not organic. Psychiatric symptoms include hypochondriacal ideas, suspiciousness, depressive trend, illusions, obsessions, compulsions, phobias, nightmares, sexual maladaptation (he claims he never had sexual intercourse), and psychosomatic symptoms. There is a history of auditory hallucinations.

Over the last six months, Mr. M has become increasingly nervous and depressed. Although he sees himself as trapped in a home with a despised brother and deserted by the death of sisters, he holds out the hope that he "may find the answer" to a better life for himself. His defense is to continue to be future-oriented. In addition to his personality characteristics it seems clear that there was little basic understanding of the environmental stresses

on Mr. M at the time of his breakdown and little treatment given, beyond minimal care. But 40 years later he is still hoping for a cure and a better future. One could say either that he is denying reality or that in spite of everything he has refused to give up.

While American researchers have generally limited their study of schizophrenia to younger subjects, European investigators have recognized the existence of late-onset schizophrenia.[46] Paraphrenia was first introduced by Kraepelin near the turn of the century[47] and furthered by Sir Martin Roth[48] and others.[49] More recent study of late-onset schizophrenia in several American research centers has revealed that these patients are mostly women, have a high prevalence of visual or auditory impairment, are less likely to demonstrate a marked thought disorder, and have a predominance of paranoid symptoms.[50]

Mrs. Q is a 75-year-old former professional dancer who lives alone in her large home in New England. She has been widowed for 15 years but has managed quite well on her husband's pension and modest income from a rental property. Her daughter, who lives in the same city and visits her frequently, has become increasingly concerned about the mental state of her mother over the last few months. While there has never before been any need for psychiatric help, she arranged for a psychiatric consultation in the home. During the visit, it became immediately clear that Mrs. Q has been cloistered in her home for quite some time. There are multiple locks on all the entrances to the house, all the shades are drawn, and the pictures hanging on the wall are each covered with aluminum foil. Mrs Q is convinced that the neighbors are involved in a plot to overthrow the government and that they are spying on her. The aluminum foil is "strategically placed" to avoid microwave monitoring of her activities in the home. Mrs. Q is calm when she describes these beliefs and is knowledgeable about the current affairs in her community as reported in the daily news. She speaks coherently and articulately. For instance, she rationally explains away the lack of alarm in the world around her by pointing out that the news media is being manipulated by the anarchists. Before bidding goodbye to the psychiatrist, who she thought was a member of the underground resistance movement, she offers advice on how to better fortify the defenses in his part of town.

Clinical Presentation of Schizophrenia

Clinically, the schizophrenic disorders are still subdivided into five types in the DSM-IV manual: catatonic, disorganized, paranoid, undifferentiated, and residual. These differentiations are made primarily based on the clinical picture and are not yet known to have tremendous prognostic or treatment validity. As with all major disorders, however, it is important to carefully differentiate schizophrenia from other diagnoses, especially organic mental disorders in elderly subjects. It is not uncommon, for instance, for Alzheimer's disease or drug intoxication to first present with symptoms identical to those found in schizophrenia.[51] Other risk factors for the onset of late-life schizophrenia include premorbid (pre-existing) personality abnormalities, physical illness, social stresses, and possible genetic factors.[52]

Delusional (Paranoid) Disorder is defined as the persistence of pseudo-logical delusions that are not due to other medical or organic causes. The age of onset is generally much later than in schizophrenia, and it is not uncommon for the first symptom to appear after the age of 65. Behavioral symptoms can be associated with a delusional disorder but are not usually prominent. Premorbid personality factors have often been associated with the onset of late-life paranoid disorder.[53] Perhaps more crucial is the association between various forms of motor and sensory impairment, particularly hearing loss, and the development of paranoid ideation or thought processes.[54] The subtypes of delusional disorders include: (1) Erotomanic, (2) Grandiose, (3) Somatic, (4) Persecutory, (5) Jealous, and (6) Unspecified. Little is known about the familial pattern of the delusional disorders in the elderly. While the prevalence for the overall population is estimated to be low (about 3%), it is generally accepted that these conditions are found more commonly in the elderly with "mild schizophrenic symptoms" being found in as many as 6.7% of the noninstitutionalized elderly.[55]

Biology of Schizophrenia and the Delusional Disorders

The search for a single gene to explain the biology of schizophrenia has been frustrated by the difficulties in defining a single phenotype (clinical presentation) for the syndrome. Furthermore, there has been a discouraging series of non-replicated genetic findings in the scientific literature.[56] While many researchers continue to search for a single gene, the general consensus is that the illness probably involves a complex inheritance pattern with polygenic factors. This genetic heterogeneity would help explain the wide variability in clinical presentations in this patient population and the fact that three different chromosomes (6, 8, and 22) have now been linked to the illness.[57] Although there are still no specific genes which have been directly associated with schizophrenia, several of the known genes for the brain dopamine receptor subtypes have been excluded by linkage analysis.[58]

Other biological markers have previously been investigated in the older schizophrenics and in delusional disorders. For example, studies of CT scans have revealed that late-onset schizophrenics have significantly larger ventricle-to-brain ratios (i.e., greater cortical atrophy) than age-matched controls, much like early-onset schizophrenics.[59] Findings in these radiologic studies have been supported by a 6% overall decrease in brain size seen at autopsy compared to elderly depressives; the most striking area of relative decrease is in the temporal lobes.[60] Comparison of cerebrospinal fluid (CSF) metabolites between Alzheimer and schizophrenic patients revealed a relative decrease in the schizophrenics for the dopamine metabolite, homovanillic acid (HVA), and the serotonin metabolite, 5-hydroxyindoleacetic acid (5-HIAA); there was no relationship in the schizophrenic group with either age or cognitive function and the levels of these metabolites.[61] In postmortem studies, relationships in schizophrenics have been found between CSF concentrations of HVA and the norepinephrine metabolite, 3-methoxy-4-hydroxyphenylglycol (MHPG) with antemortem measures of depressed mood.[62] An association was also found in this study between brain dopamine and MHPG content in the nucleus accumbens and antemortem cognitive functioning. Finally, autopsy studies have also revealed selective decreases in the B-form of the monoamine oxidase enzyme in selected brain areas of older schizophrenics with primarily negative symptoms.[63] Other biologic variables include the significant over-representation of women among the late-onset schizophrenics and the increased likelihood of developing tardive dyskinesia.[64] Nonetheless, the combined power of all these results has not yet led to a clear picture of the biology of the schizophrenic illnesses.

Psychosocial Factors and Prognosis

Social isolation and increasing loneliness is thought to play a role in late-onset schizophrenia. Most studies have revealed the older schizophrenic patients to have more often been unmarried, have fewer surviving children, live alone, and belong to a lower socioeconomic class than nonschizophrenics.[65] As noted previously, sensorimotor impairment, particularly hearing impairments and mild cognitive decline are frequently associated with the late-onset schizophrenias and paranoid delusions.

The clinical course and prognosis of late-onset schizophrenia is usually noted to be chronic and poor.[66] Many patients, often due to their general lack of social supports, are relegated to institutional living. On the other hand, many, and perhaps most, people with paranoid disorders go through life outside hospitals. They may be relatively harmless to others but are unable to experience intimacy and full psychological growth. They are seen as cranks, eccentrics, hard to get along with, touchy, angry. They are avoided, and what few human and other attachments they may have in life increasingly disappear with advancing age. Following is an example of the growing late-life isolation of a person suffering from a paranoid disorder.

Dr. J, a 72-year-old man, was diagnosed as having paranoid personality with obsessive features, chronic, severe, and of lifelong duration. His second diagnosis was depressive reaction, moderate, and of two or three years' duration. He compensated well in a suitable, supportive, and structured environment. He was a dentist in semiretirement who was irritable, suspicious, depressed, and anxious. He was extremely intelligent and integrated very well during interviews. He was paranoid, belligerent, and self-centered; yet it was remarkable how he could put aside his belligerence and tell of his delusions. He was in semiretirement because of a failing practice and not of his own choice. He applied for room in an old age home because he felt he was at the end of his rope. He saw his situation as resulting from the imperfections of the world and other people but at other times described his life adjustment as poor and said he hated himself.

He was born in Poland, came to the United States at 20, was unusually attached to his mother, and had "nothing in common" with his siblings. His father died when Dr. J was 12. He rebelled against education and did not enter dental school until he was 32. He married at 37 against his own desires, out of fear of an implied breach of promise suit, and was divorced 4 years later. He never considered remarriage. Marriage was his first and only sexual experience. He practiced dentistry in a poor neighborhood and had no close personal relationships. He distrusted others and thought that only his alertness saved him from being exploited by them. As Dr. J grew older, his isolation became more complete and he developed an angry depression through which he despised himself and the world. He seemed unable to experience pleasure.

As Dr. J illustrates, such a person may paradoxically get along in the community by being isolated. No one bothers with him and he bothers no one. But eventually a problem will emerge in which the person no longer can care for himself and must obtain help in some way. This is frequently the paranoid person's path to the mental hospital or, as in Dr. J's case, to an old age home.

Sometimes the paranoid symptoms may be very discrete or circumscribed. An older woman in her late seventies may seem free of major psychopathological symptoms, but at nighttime she thinks that the neighbor above is purposely taking a cane and pounding on the ceiling or that fumes are being sent out from the radiator in the bathroom. However, study may uncover the fact that this is a discrete, circumscribed delusion related to fears, say, of being alone at night or lacking visual orientation in the dark. Such symptoms are, characteristically, isolated and may not influence everyday activities.

A shared psychotic disorder (formerly known as *folie à deux*) is a mental disorder in which two persons who are intimately associated with each other develop the same delusions. One person is dominant. The submissive partner may be more shaky in his or her beliefs and when separated from the stronger personality may give up the delusional system. It is more frequent among people with similar backgrounds, such as siblings, parents, and children, but it can develop among unrelated (nonconsanguineous) persons, including husband and wife. Misperception may attain paranoid proportions.

The frightened voice of a woman begged me (R.N.B.) on the phone to see her and her mother because (and she lowered her voice) "mother wants to move again." Otherwise "they" will get her.

At the appointed hour a woman of 42 and of faded attractiveness arrives, with a frail, sharp-faced woman of 70. In the office they insist on my seeing them together, not separately. They describe the harassment they have received from two men living below. They mention the possibility that some wires are used to listen to them, perhaps in connection with their TV set or toaster. The older woman reveals excellent intellectual functioning, but she states that a man in the apartment above is shooting rays at her body, including "indecent places." He wants to kill her and she is powerless. He brings pains to her hands and knees, scorches parts of her body, and "stuns my consciousness." She refuses to see doctors, considers medications "harmful," and denies any illnesses (despite the obvious malnutrition, manifestation of probable hypovitaminosis, arthritic changes, and a Meniere-like syndrome). She also insists that she has aged very little. Her unmarried daughter, deeply conflicted, nearly "be-

lieves" there are men responsible. Such quasi folies à deux are not rare.

The older paranoid person can be dangerous. Paranoid rage and murderousness do occur.

A slight, 89-year-old man who needed a cane to walk killed his daughter, a librarian, with a hatchet. "I wanted to see her die before I do," he said. The body of the daughter, 57, was found in her bed with deep wounds in her head and body. Her father, who notified police by telephone that he had slain his daughter, was booked on a murder charge. "The devil prompted me to do this," he told police.

However, such extreme behavior is the exception. In general, the following rule of thumb can be followed in evaluating paranoid disorders: "Show me one truly paranoid person and I will show you ten who are truly persecuted." Much of what appears to be paranoid behavior is a reaction to extraordinary and unbearable stress—physical, emotional and environmental. Studies are now investigating the relative importance of selective psychosocial stresses on these late-onset conditions. See Chapter 13 for a discussion of the drug treatment of late-onset schizophrenia and the delusional disorders.

ANXIETY DISORDERS

While anxiety itself is part of everyday life, commonly associated with many physical illnesses, and may affect up to 10% of the population over age 65 at any one time,[67] the actual prevalence of specific anxiety disorders is reported to be reduced in the older populations.[68] A. J. Flint conducted a meta analysis of literature from 1970 through 1994 to explore the epidemiology of anxiety disorders and common comorbidities in older persons. Flint found that the prevalence rates of all anxiety disorders, phobic disorders, and generalized anxiety disorders in the elderly varied. Rates for panic disorders and obsessive compulsive disorders were more consistent. Anxiety disorders are less common in older persons than younger persons, but as many as 18.6% of those over age 65 suffer from them.[69] Still, anxiety disorders remain one of the most common psychiatric conditions in the elderly.[70] This group of psychiatric conditions includes *panic disorder* with or without *agoraphobia, social phobia, simple phobia,* and *generalized anxiety disorder.* Each of these conditions is distinguished by the precipitant, the time course, and accompanying behaviors of the predominant anxiety.[71] With the anxiety disorders, anxiety is experienced directly by a person rather than controlled unconsciously by conversion, denial, or other psychological defense mechanisms. Although the overall condition may be less common in the elderly, these disorders can nonetheless appear for the first time in old age or represent an increase in a previous history of anxiety. They may take the form of a nameless dread and sense of threat when no obvious danger is present, or they may be an exaggerated response to real trouble and danger. Also, like people of all ages, older people may be struggling to curb unconscious and unacceptable impulses, aggressive or sexual. Finally, anxiety symptoms may portend some oncoming physical disease or condition that is beginning to unfold. While not considered identical illnesses, there is a great deal of clinical, epidemiologic, biologic, and treatment response overlap between panic disorder and major depression.[72]

Mrs. C is a 69-year-old retired secretary who had 25 years of work experience after raising her family of three boys and one girl. She lost one boy in battle during the Vietnam war. She has a history of mild claustrophobia throughout her life, but the only time she required psychiatric treatment was after the death of her son when she received antianxiety agents to help her sleep for several weeks only. She is now widowed for five years and living on a modest pension. Mrs. C has a broad social support system and appeared to be doing quite well when suddenly she developed an intense fear of tunnels. At one point, she actually stopped her car in the middle of a tunnel and ran out, leaving her car to tie up traffic for hours. She stated that she "panicked" in the tunnel while experiencing an intense shortness of breath, a rapid heart beat, and a strong sense of dying. Her ability to get out and about town was severely impaired when Mrs. C's fear was extended to

include bridges as well as tunnels. Mrs. C's daughter soon took her to see a local psychiatrist. After several months of weekly sessions and a course of low-dose imipramine, Mrs. C was able to drive again without experiencing panic attacks near bridges or tunnels. She now recognized that these attacks were associated with thoughts of her husband and son, and she was beginning to review in therapy the intense sadness those losses had caused her.

Understanding the biology of the anxiety disorders has been difficult, in part because of the diagnostic uncertainties reflected by the rapidly changing nomenclatures. Nonetheless, great technical strides have been made in recent years with animal, pharmacologic, and brain mapping studies.[73] Theories have emerged with conflicting data to support the central role of the noradrenergic and serotonergic neurotransmitter systems in anxiety and obsessive compulsive disorders, but definitive conclusions as to the exact mechanisms of the disorders are currently far from reached.

Obsessive Compulsive Disorder is also classified as an anxiety disorder because of the distress caused by the recurrent obsessions and compulsions. When these intrusive thoughts and impulses are resisted, for instance, the individual suffers a marked increase in inner tension which can lead to significant disruption in the normal work or personal life. Common examples of these obsessions include thoughts of contamination, sexuality, violence, or danger. While compulsions do not always accompany obsessions, they frequently include idiosyncratic rituals of washing, touching, pacing, and checking which can appear unusual and be time-consuming and distressing. As with most anxiety disorders, the incidence of obsessive compulsive disorder is thought to decrease with age.[74] Interestingly, the incidence of anxiety as a comorbid condition with depression is no less frequent in older depressives than younger depressives.[75]

SOMATOFORM DISORDERS

The somatoform disorders exhibit physical symptoms that suggest a physical disorder, but on examination they appear to be psychologically rather than physically caused. These disorders include *conversion disorder,* an example of which is the person who cannot move an arm or leg although there is no physical reason for the impairment. Only the special senses or the voluntary nervous system are involved. The mechanism for causing this is unconscious, thus keeping the underlying conflict hidden ("primary gain") as opposed to the conscious manipulations of the malingerer who is well aware of the subterfuge. The autonomic nervous system is not usually involved in the conversion disorders and thus provides diagnostic differentiation from the psychophysiological (psychosomatic) disorders. In older people with this tendency, symptoms or illnesses may be exaggerated, and in this way a "secondary gain" is achieved in the form of extra attention and help and the avoidance of a noxious stimulus.

Hypochondriasis, another somatoform disorder, is an overconcern with one's physical and emotional health, accompanied by various bodily complaints for which there is no physical basis. However, this does not mean that the complaints are "imaginary." They have an emotional basis that requires treatment. Hypochondriasis is commonly associated with depressive feelings, but it may stand alone. It has many meanings, one of which may be a symbolization of the older person's sense of defectiveness and deterioration (see self-drawings, Chapter 9, p. 252). It may be a means of communication and interaction with others—family members, doctors, nurses, social workers. It can be used to displace anxiety from areas of greater concern. It can include identification with a deceased loved one who had similar symptoms. And it can serve as punishment for guilt, as an inhibition of impulses, and as an aid in the desire to control others.

There is much overlap between depression and hypochondriasis. Most depressive individuals show some hypochondriacal preoccupations, and hypochondriasis has a gloomy and depressive mood associated with it. But whereas a basically depressed person will withdraw and not seek help,

the hypochondriac sees his or her problems as physical and goes frequently to the doctor, thus at least relieving the isolation. Even if the symptom cannot be eliminated, a service is being provided. Patients with hypochondriasis should be listened to and accepted. Of course, special difficulties arise if hypochondriasis is connected with a real organic condition. Then, diagnosis and treatment may be difficult. Because of the steep rise in organic conditions found in the elderly, great care must be taken before ascribing any consistent complaint arising in the elderly as hypochondriacal.[76] A case of a brain tumor first presenting as anxiety attacks in a 69-year-old woman with no previous history of such attacks is a powerful reminder of the importance of careful differential diagnosis in the elderly.[77]

Psychotherapy can be helpful, as demonstrated in the following case example:

Mr. B visited to ask our help for a pruritic scalp condition on his essentially bald head; he "incidentally" told us of the recent death of his wife. He could not get himself to say Kaddish, the mourner's prayer in his Jewish faith. The scalp condition was similar in shape to the rim of a skull cap, worn by men in the synogogue. After his already infected lesions were treated medically, short-term psychotherapy focused on his wife and the question of saying Kaddish. Months later, he reported having said the prayer and having a "clear" scalp. (He also reported newly growing hair!)

DISSOCIATIVE DISORDERS

Dissociative disorders are seen when the integration of an older person's consciousness, identity, memory or perception of the environment is suddenly and temporarily altered, resulting in fugue states, stupor, amnesia, and confusion. Sleep walking or night wandering is sometimes included in this category when there is no physical basis for such behavior. Psychotic features may also be present. Little epidemiologic information is available to estimate how common these conditions are in the elderly relative to younger adults.

SEXUAL AND GENDER IDENTITY DISORDERS

We discuss some of these disorders in Chapter 6, but sexual exhibitionism is a specific paraphilia that is often associated in the public's mind with older men and will be dealt with here. Simply put, sexual exhibitionism in older people is overestimated and overstated. Most studies have shown that such sexual pathology is related to young adulthood. Sensationalism in court cases concerning children who have been "molested" by older people has been misleading in many instances. The sexual element may have been less significant than the loneliness of the older person, who may have no children or grandchildren. Some older men have fantasies of rejuvenation in contact with young children,[78] rather than any direct sexual preoccupation. By all means, children must be protected from any exploitation that may occur. But the older person needs sympathetic understanding rather than punishment, and efforts should be made to provide that which is lacking in their lives. In some cases, total misinterpretation occurs. We have known of older people who were supposedly molesting younger children and have been arrested for exhibitionism; actually they were confused, needed to urinate, and found the most convenient spot. Where the charge is warranted, then indeed, the act is strictly punishable under the law and should be pursued. In today's environment, however, with its frequent accusations and fears of abuse, the presumption of innocence must be protected, especially with those who are easily confused.

PERSONALITY DISORDERS

There are ten recognized personality disorders in DSM-IV,[79] and they are designated as encoding patterns of inner experience and behavior that are markedly different from the expectations of the person's surrounding culture. Personality traits become personality disorders only when they are so inflexible and maladaptive that they cause serious problems for an individual. Personality disorders are coded separately from the other disorders in the DSM-IV classification, in part to avoid overlooking them. In this broad group of disorders we see defects in personality development that are of lifelong nature. There is little sense of anxiety or distress associated with them. Maladaptive patterns of behavior are deeply ingrained and may actually become less evident with increasing age.

Certain personality disorders serve different adaptive functions, depending on the stage in the life cycle. This phenomenon, the changing adaptive nature of psychopathology, was observed in the early NIMH studies by Perlin and Butler. For example, a so-called schizotypal personality may function somewhat better in old age. Such an individual tends to be insulated against the experiences of life and therefore may feel relatively more comfortable with some of the loneliness and difficulties of old age. On the other hand, he or she may become even more of a recluse with almost no human contact. The person with a paranoid personality has perhaps the most problems in later life, as the individual loses what few friends and relationships he or she has and becomes increasingly isolated.[80] The inadequate, dependent person may welcome and enjoy the opportunity for greater dependence in old age and the freedom from work responsibilities. Obsessive compulsiveness can become useful in scrupulous caretaking of oneself and in keeping busy with many details; in fact, this type of individual can create a whole life for himself by "taking care" of things—possessions, spouse, grandchildren, bodily ailments, and personal finances.

Mr. H has been retired for three years. His obsessions and compulsions are useful mechanisms in filling the vacuum of a forced retirement. "My home is always in order," says Mr. H, as he putters around the house, arranging everything according to strict schedule in a careful, meticulous manner. He is thrifty and even hoarding of his possessions, not to mention his feelings.

He takes care of his health with religious fervor and follows the doctor's orders precisely. He has arranged for two grave sites (one in St. Louis and one in Florida) so he can be well taken care of in case he dies, whether at home or on vacation. He has checked actuarial tables to predict his death at age 88, leaving no stone unturned.

From a therapeutic perspective, it is important to realize the possible adaptive qualities of personalities. A dependent personality can be fostered by the therapist to help activate an individual psychologically. Persons with obsessions may be encouraged to make constructive use of ritual. The therapist can help a person with a histrionic personality keep alive their dramatic qualities and, at times, their childlike expectations. The antisocial criminal activities of an antisocial personality are rare in late life. Violent crimes are seldom committed, although embezzlement and other less violent crimes do occur. Old "sociopaths" do fade away, it seems. Thus geriatric delinquency is not a problem to rouse one's keen interest.

HOW IMPORTANT IS DIAGNOSTIC CLASSIFICATION?

Throughout this chapter, we have emphasized the importance of the diagnostic nomenclature. Still, we must acknowledge the primitive status of our scientific understanding in this area. Unlike many of the organic brain disorders (see Chapter 6), we do not have known lesions and specific pathologic verification available to us at autopsy for these conditions. At present, most of the psychiatric disorders in the elderly are therefore defined operationally, based on clinical symptoms and, quite often, retrospectively, after response to drug treatment (see Chapter 13). Therefore, we must be cautious in our assumptions that each of these disorders is a homogeneous entity with its own biology. Most likely, many of these conditions will be interrelated genetically and biochemically (i.e., panic disorder and major depression) with much overlap in both young and older groups. Research studies with experimental diagnostic approaches such as genetic markers, brain imaging tests (i.e., PET, functional MRI, and SPECT scans), pharmacologic challenge tests, and peripheral cell markers may eventually be helpful in differentiat-

ing these conditions as well as distinguishing the effects of aging on the expression of psychiatric disorders. (See Chapter 9 for further discussion of diagnostic approaches.)

DIAGNOSTIC NOMENCLATURE

We are including abbreviated outlines of the American Psychiatric Association's *Diagnostic and Statistical Manual of Mental Disorders* (DSM-IV) in the following glossary.[81] Earlier versions of this nomenclature left much to be desired in diagnosing conditions of older persons, particularly in the case of acute and chronic brain disorders. Fortunately, the 1980 DSM-III and 1987 DSM-IIIR represent some improvements in the classification of the mental disorders of older persons. The DSM-IV features much more specific diagnostic criteria, an expanded description of disorders, and a multilevel or multiaxial approach to evaluation that takes into consideration the following five axes:

1. Clinical Syndromes
2. Developmental and Personality Disorders
3. Physical Disorders and Conditions
4. Severity of Psychosocial Stressors
5. Global Assessment of Functioning

Assessment of the older person's functioning is critical. For example, an older person who is diagnosed as having severe brain damage (by sophisticated psychiatric examination and psychological test scores) may function quite well in a supportive milieu. Another person may have minimal brain damage but have no economic, personal, and social supports and thus have more trouble functioning—not because of any inherently serious mental condition, but because he or she has no environmental supports. Thus, diagnosis and treatment, as well as prevention, must go beyond the traditional psychiatric diagnostic evaluation in the elderly to include the *context* in which symptoms develop and the assets and resources of the individual.

We might add here that the use of insurance forms requiring a therapist to state the diagnosis of a patient creates a sticky, ethical problem. The patient's interest may be compromised if a diagnosis is given that can be later used irresponsibly. We have no assurances about the confidentiality of insurance records; and they do get lost, misplaced, and confused with other patients' records. On the other hand, a vague, general diagnosis can make the whole matter of insurance information irrelevant, especially when data are collected from these sources on the "mental illness" of policyholders. Nonetheless, many practitioners choose to protect their patients as much as possible. Diagnoses such as schizophrenia or personality disorder may be downplayed. The nomenclature more commonly used includes such designations as anxiety, depression, and other terms that are less revealing.

Glossary of Psychiatric Nomenclature as Applied to the Elderly

Mania.   Most people think of mania as a high-flying period of joyous mood unbridled by normal restraints. In fact, the essential feature of mania is a distinct period of abnormal and persistently elevated, expansive, or irritable mood that is sufficient to cause disruption in work or social settings. Associated symptoms of mania include grandiosity, racing thoughts, distractibility, decreased need for sleep, increased physical agitation and activity, persistent talkativeness, and excessive involvement in pleasurable but potentially harmful activities. The important clarification is that mania is not always associated with an elated or elevated mood. In fact, an "irritable" mania is fairly common in the elderly and has led to the use of the terms of "dysphoric mania" or "mixed manic state" to describe the contrasting moods found in manic patients. *Hypomania* is essentially a milder form of the above without the marked impairments in occupational and social functioning that often lead to hospitalization for manic subjects. In addition, hypomania is never associated with the delusions that can sometimes accompany mania. For the elderly, it is especially important to realize that manic symptoms may change with age

and course of illness. It is not uncommon for a typical elderly manic patient to be quite different from a younger patient, that is, showing agitation rather than euphoria.

Anxiety.   As with depression, the discussion of anxiety requires a careful definition of terms. Symptoms of anxiety can range from a simple nervousness before an important event to a sense of having a heart seizure during a panic attack. These symptoms each represent anxiety but reflect the tremendous range included under one classification. One of the common behaviors associated with anxiety is avoidance, so it is not surprising that *phobias* are the most prevalent of the anxiety disorders, especially in the older age groups. These phobias represent a persistent fear of a certain stimuli (i.e., shopping, snakes, closed spaces, etc.). Approaching those stimuli is generally associated with an anticipatory anxiety response including increased heart rate, feeling sweaty, a sense of panic, and difficulty breathing. *Panic attacks* are more distinct, with intense periods of fear and discomfort. The associated symptoms are more severe than those mentioned for phobia and may include a sense of choking, chest pain, dizziness, shortness of breath, nausea, trembling, and a fear of dying or going crazy. These attacks often come out of the blue and are usually followed by a period of persistent fear of a return of the symptoms. *Obsessions* and *compulsions* can also be symptoms of anxiety. Obsessions are intrusive and senseless thoughts or impulses which are persistent and irrepressible. (Compulsions are repetitive behaviors performed in response to an obsession, and designed to neutralize some dreaded event or situation, for example, repeatedly checking the gas stove in the kitchen, continuously checking to see that the doors are locked, or repetitive washing of the hands.) Any attempt to change the regular routine of a compulsion is generally met with increasing tension and anxiety. *Fear* is differentiated from anxiety by the degree of awareness of the fact that one is afraid. In the elderly, when fear of death and loss is quite real, the associated anxiety or nervousness is often internalized and unconscious. The source of nervousness may not always be so obvious as in a simple phobia or an obsessive-compulsive ritual, and the anxiety may be focused on physical symptoms or the fear of having a disease (hypochondriasis) rather than the more common manifestations (rapid heart beat, shortness of breath, increased sweating, etc.).

Psychosis.   This term involves major distortions in reality testing. It does not apply to minor impairments in reality testing or perception. For example, a depressed woman who believes that her life is "over" because her husband has died is not necessarily psychotic, but a woman who feels she must kill herself to join her dead husband in the afterlife may be delusionally depressed. *Psychosis* is a general term which can describe many different behaviors. Hallucinations are perhaps the best known of the psychotic symptoms and can be defined as a sensory perception of sights, sounds, and so forth that are not actually present. These perceptions seem very real to the individual. Hallucinations can take the form of any of the five senses, but most commonly they are auditory (sounds) or visual (sights). With the decreasing hearing capacities of increasing age, auditory hallucinations are particularly common in the elderly. Hallucinations should be distinguished from *illusions,* where the incoming stimuli are misinterpreted or misperceived by the individual. *Delusions* are false personal beliefs firmly held despite the external reality and the repeated attempts by others to show evidence and obvious proof to the contrary. Delusions are often subdivided by their content for more specific psychiatric classification (i.e., persecutory, grandiose, somatic, bizarre, ideas of reference, nihilistic, and jealous). It is important to differentiate mental delusions from religious beliefs or strong personal convictions, although they may look very similar to someone who is not familiar with an individual's cultural environment.

Paranoid ideation (thought processes) involves suspiciousness or the sense of being treated unfairly. Typical examples of paranoia are thoughts of continued harassment or persecution by an outside, often malicious, source. Paranoia may also be associated with isolation from others and a sense of being easily slighted by others. Paranoid individuals are ofter quick to react with anger and may question, without obvious reason, the fidelity of a spouse or loyalty of friends. Excessive paranoid ideation can develop into the more firmly held paranoid delusions. When a person's behavior is so disturbed that individual hallucinations, delusions, or paranoid ideation do not show themselves, the general term *psychotic* may be appropriate. A wildly manic patient with incoherent speech or a delirious alcoholic in acute withdrawal from alcohol may both be psychotic despite obviously different underlying causes of their behavior.

Agitation and *psychomotor retardation* are bodily manifestations of underlying problems. Excessive physical movements that are generally repetitive, nonproductive, and associated with inner tension are described as *agitation.* This symptom can be relatively mild, as demonstrated in the lower leg restlessness (i.e., mild akasthisia) sometimes caused by neuroleptic medications (major tranquilizers or anti-psychotic drugs), or quite severe and requiring physical restraints, as seen in patients with acute alcohol withdrawal (i.e., delirium tremens). Associated behaviors can include shouting, complaining, throwing objects, pacing, and sleep-wake cycle disturbances. The source of the agitation is often unknown to the patient and can reflect mental disturbances ranging from anxiety to severe depression to psychosis. *Psychomotor retardation* is the generalized and visible slowing of physical responsiveness, including self-initiated movements, speech, and even facial reactions. While such motor retardation is often associated with depression, it can also be secondary to physical problems (i.e., Parkinsonism or stroke), drug intoxication or withdrawal, and other organic conditions (i.e., Alzheimer's disease).

Grief Reactions.   While mourning can be a natural part of life at any age, it is particularly important in the elderly. Issues of death and dying are often central to an older person's life and learning to deal with these challenges can be a major concern. Acute grief reactions can frequently mimic a full depression syndrome, at least temporarily. Symptoms of grief include sleep disturbance, appetite disturbance, thoughts of death, increased guilt feelings, impairment in daily functioning, and a sense of worthlessness. The reactions can occur immediately after the loss of the loved one or several months later; the duration of "normal" grief reaction symptoms are quite variable from person to person and can differ in each cultural group. Generally, if grief reactions are severely interfering with normal day-to-day functioning or persist beyond six months, then the reaction may be considered abnormal and professional attention may be warranted. Careful differentiation and eventual treatment is important because there is a marked increase in both psychiatric morbidity and overall mortality associated with prolonged or pathologic grief reactions (see Chapter 14 for a more detailed discussion).

The elderly are also susceptible to other losses, such as physical and mental impairments, which can in turn be associated with grief reactions. Symptoms of chronic complaining, tearfulness, feelings of self-pity, and irritability are not uncommon in these cases. Conversely, psychosomatic complaints and intense worries about memory loss (i.e., "Alzheimer's Phobia") are increasingly common symptoms for those elderly unable to express their grief in other ways.

SELECTED READINGS

Alexopoulos, G. S., Young, R. C., Meyers, B. S., Abrams, R. C., & Shamoian, C. A. (1988). Late-onset depression. *Psychiatric Clinics of North America, 11,* 109–115.

American Psychiatric Association (1987). *Diagnostic and statistical manual of mental disorders,* Revised 3rd Edition. Washington, DC: American Psychiatric Association.

American Psychiatric Association (1994). *DSM-IV diagnostic and statistical manual of mental disorders,* Fourth Edition. Washington, DC, American Psychiatric Association.

Arean, P. A., Perri, M. G., Nezu, A. M., et. al. (1993). Comparative effectiveness of social problem-solving therapy and reminiscence therapy as treatments for depression in older adults. *Journal of Consulting and Clinical Psychiatry, 61,* 1003–1010.

Baldwin, R. C. (1994). Is there a distinct subtype of major depression in the elderly? *Journal of Psychopharmacology, 8*(3), 177–184.

Baughman, O. L. (1989). Diagnosis and management of anxiety in the older patient: The role of azapirones. *Advances in Therapy, 6*(6), 269–286.

Berkman, L. F., Berkman, C. S., Kasl, S., Freeman, D. H., Leo, L., Ostfeld, A. M., Cornoni-Huntley, J., & Brody, J. A. (1986). Depressive symptoms in relation to physical health and functioning in the elderly. *American Journal of Epidemiology, 124,* 372–388.

Blazer, D., Bachar, J. R., & Hughes, D. C. (1987). Major depression with melancholia: A comparison of middle-aged and elderly adults. *Journal of the American Geriatrics Society, 35,* 927–932.

Blazer, D., George, L., & Landerman, R. (1986). The phenomenology of late life depression. In Bebbington, P. E. & Jacoby, R. (Eds.), *Psychiatric disorders in the elderly.* (pp. 143–152). London: Mental Health Foundation.

Blazer, D., George, L. K., & Hughes, D. (1988). Schizophrenic symptoms in an elderly community population. In Brody, J. A., Maddox, G. L. (Eds.), *Epidemiology and aging: An international perspective* (pp. 134–149). New York: Springer.

Blazer, D., Hughes, D. C., & George, L. K. (1987). The epidemiology of depression in an elderly community population. *Gerontologist, 27,* 281–287.

Bohm, C., Robinson, D. S., Gammans, R. E., Shrotriya, R. C., Alms, D. R., Leroy, A., & Placchi, M. (1990). Buspirone therapy in anxious elderly patients: A controlled clinical trial. *Journal of Clinical Psychopharmacology, 10,* 47S–51S.

Borson, S., Barnes, R. A., Kukull, W. A., Okimoto, J. T., Veith, R. C., Inui, T. S., Carter, W., & Raskind, M. A. (1986). Symptomatic depression in elderly medical outpatients. I. Prevalence, demography, and health service utilization. *Journal of the American Geriatrics Society, 34,* 341–347.

Breslau, L. & Haug, M. (Eds.). (1983). *Depression and aging: Causes, care and consequences,* New York: Springer.

Bridge, T. P., Kleinman, J. E., Soldo, B. J., & Karoum, F. (1987). Central catecholamines, cognitive impairment, and affective state in elderly schizophrenics and controls. *Biological Psychiatry, 22,* 139–147.

Bridge, T. P., & Wyatt, R. J. (1980). Paraphrenia: Paranoid states of late life: I. European research. *Journal of the American Geriatrics Society, 27,* 193–200.

Brown, R., Colter, N., Corsellis, J. A. N., Crow, T. J., Frith, C. D, Jagoe, R., Johnstone, E. C., & Marsh, L. (1986). Postmortem evidence of structural brain changes in schizophrenia. *Archives of General Psychiatry, 43,* 36–42.

Burns, B. J., Wagner, D. R., Taube, J. E., Magaziner, J., Pernutt, T. & Landerman, L. R. (1993). Mental health service use by the elderly in nursing homes. *American Journal of Public Health, 83,* 331–337.

Caligiuri, M. P., Lohr, J. B., Panton, D., & Harris, J. (1993). Extrapyramidal motor abnormalities associated with late-life psychosis. *Schizophrenia Bulletin 19*(4), 747–754.

Carney, S. S., Rich, C. L., Burke, P. A., & Fowler, R. C. (1994). Suicide over 60: the San Diego Study. *Journal of the American Geriatrics Society, 42,* 174–180.

Chen, W. J., Faraone, S. V. & Tsuang, M. T. (1992). Linkage studies of schizophrenia: a simulation study of statistical power. *Genetic Epidemiology, 9,* 123–139.

Christenson, R., & Blazer, D. (1984). Epidemiology of persecutory ideation in an elderly population in the community. *American Journal of Psychiatry, 141,* 1088–1091.

Clayton, P. J. (1981). The epidemiology of bipolar affective disorder. *Comprehensive Psychiatry, 22,* 31–43.

Conwell, Y. (1994). Suicide in elderly patients. In Schneider, L. S., Reynolds, C. F., Lebowitz, B. D., & Friedhoff, A. J. (Eds.) *Diagnosis and treatment of depression in late life* (pp. 397–418). Washington, DC: American Psychiatric Press.

Conwell, Y., Olsen, K., & Caine, E. D. (1990). Completed suicide at age 50 and over. *Journal of the American Geriatrics Society, 38,* 640–644.

Copeland, J. R. M., Davidson, I. A., Dewey, M. E., et al. (1992). Alzheimer's disease, other dementias, depression and pseudodementia: prevalence, incidence and three-year outcome in Liverpool. *British Journal of Psychiatry, 161,* 230–239.

Costa, P. T., McCrae, R. R., & Norris, A. H. (1981). Personal adjustment to aging: Longitudinal prediction from neuroticism and extroversion. *Journal of Gerontology, 36,* 78–85.

Craig, T. J., & Bregman, Z. (1988). Late onset schizophrenia-like illness. *Journal of the American Geriatrics Society, 36,* 104–107.

De Leo, D., Carollo, G., & Buono, M. D. (1995). Lower suicide rates associated with a tele-help/tele-check service for the elderly at home. *American Journal of Psychiatry, 152,* 632–634.

Denmark, J. S. (1985). A study of 250 patients referred to a department of psychiatry for the deaf. *British Journal of Psychiatry, 146,* 282–286.

Duberstein, P. R., Conwell, Y., Cox, C., Podgorski, C. A., Glazer, R. S., & Caine, E. D. (1995). Attitudes toward self-determined death: A survey of primary care physicians. *Journal of the American Geriatrics Society, 43,* 395–400.

Eagles, J. M., & Whalley, L. J. (1985). Ageing and affective disorders: The age of first onset of affective disorders in Scotland, 1969–1978. *British Journal of Psychiatry, 147,* 180–187.

Eastwood, M. R., Corbin, S. L., Reed, M., Nobbs, H., & Kedward, H. B. (1985). Acquired hearing loss and psychiatric illness: An estimate of prevalence and co-morbidity in a geriatric setting. *British Journal of Psychiatry, 147,* 552–556.

Egeland, J. A., Gerhard, D. S., Pauls, D. L., Sussex, J. M., Kidd, K. K., Allen, C. R., Hostetter, A. M., & Housman, D. E. (1987). Bipolar affective disorders linked to DNA markers on chromosome 11. *Nature, 325,* 783–787.

Finch, E. L. J., Ramsay, R. & Katona, C. L. E. Depression and physical illness in the elderly. *Clinics in Geriatric Medicine, 8,* 275–287.

Freimer N. B., Reus, V. I., Escamilla, M. A., McInnes,L. A., Spesny, M., Leon, P., Service, S. K., Smith, L. B., Silva, S., Rohas, E., Gallegos, A., Meza, L., Fournier, E., Bahorloo, S., Blankenship, K., Tyler, D. J., Batki, S., Vinogradov, S., Weissenback, J., Barondes, S. H., & Sandkuijl, L. A. (1996). Genetic mapping using haplotype, association and linkage methods suggests a locus for severe bipolar disorder (BPI) at 18q22-q23. *Nature Genetics, 12,* 436–441.

George, L. K., Blazer, D. G., Winfield-Laird, I., Leaf, P. J., & Fischbach, R. L. (1988). Psychiatric disorders and mental health service use in later life: Evidence from the epidemiologic catchment area program. In Brody, J. A., Maddox, G. L. (Eds.), *Epidemiology and aging: An interna-*

tional perspective (pp. 189–219). New York: Springer.

Gershanik, O. S. (1994). Drug-induced Parkinsonism in the aged: Recognition and prevention. *Drugs and Aging, 5*(2), 127–132.

Ghadirian, A. M., Gauthier, S., & Bertrand, S. (1986). Anxiety attacks in a patient with a right temporal lobe meningioma. *Journal of Clinical Psychiatry, 47,* 270–271.

Glesia, G. L., & Ban, A. N. (1970). Psychosis and other manifestations of levodopa therapy. *Archives of Neurology, 23,* 193–200.

Greenwald, B. S., & Kramer-Ginsberg, E. (1988). Age at onset in geriatric depression: Relationship to clinical variables. *Journal of Affective Disorders, 15,* 61–68.

Gurland, B. J. (1994). The range of quality of life: Relevance to the treatment of depression in elderly patients. In Schneider, L. S., Reynolds, C. F., Lebowitz, B. D., & Friedhoff, A. J. (Eds.), *Diagnoses and treatment of depression in late life* (pp. 61–80). Washington, DC: American Psychiatric Press.

Gurland, B. J., Dean, L., Cross, P., & Golden, R. (1980). The epidemiology of depression and dementia in the elderly: The use of multiple indicators of these conditions. In Cole, J. O., & Barrett, J. E. (Eds.), *Psychopathology of the aged* (pp. 37–62). New York: Raven Press.

Hanninen, T., Hallikainen, M., Koivisto, K., Helkala, E. L., Reinikainen, K. J., Soininen, H., Mykkanen, L., Laakso, M., Pyorala, K., & Riekkinen, P. J. (1995). A follow-up study of age-associated memory impairment: Neuropsychological predictors of dementia. *Journal of the American Geriatrics Society, 43,* 1007–1015.

Hendrie, H. C., Callahan, C. M., Levitt, E. E., Hui, S. L., Musick, B., Austrom, M. G., Nurnberger, J. I. Jr., & Tierney, W. M. (1995). Prevalence rates of major depressive disorders: The effects of varying the diagnostic criteria in an older primary care population. *American Journal of Geriatrics Psychiatry, 3,* 119–131.

Holden, N. L. (1987). Late paraphrenia or the paraphrenias? A descriptive study with a 10-year follow-up. *British Journal of Psychiatry, 150,* 635–639.

Hunter, R. C. A., & Cleghorn, R. A. (1982). Psychosomatic disorders in the elderly. *Canadian Journal of Psychiatry, 27,* 362–365.

Jamison, K. R. (1979). Manic-depressive illness in the elderly. In Kaplan, O. J. (Ed.), *Psychopathology of aging* (pp. 79–95). New York: Academic Press.

Jenike, M. A. (1989). *Geriatric psychiatry and psychopharmacology: A clinical approach.* Boca Raton, FL: CRC Press.

Jeste, D. V., Harris, M. J., Pearlson, G. D., Rabins, P., Lesser, I., Miller, B., Coles, C., & Yassa, B. (1988). Late-onset schizophrenia: Studying clinical validity. *Psychiatric Clinics of North America, 11,* 1–13.

Jeste, D. V., Lacro, J. P., Gilbert, P. L., Kline, J., & Kline, N. (1993). Treatment of late-life schizophrenia with neuroleptics. *Schizophrenia Bulletin 18*(4), 817–830.

Kalish, S. C., Bohn, R. L., Mogun, H., Glynn, R. J., Gurwitz, J. H., & Avorn, J. (1995). Antipsychotic prescribing patterns and the treatment of extrapyramidal symptoms in older people. *Journal of the American Geriatrics Society, 43,* 967–973.

Katon, W. & Schulberg, H. C. (1992). Epidemiology of depression in primary care. Special section: Developing guidelines for treating depressive disorder in the primary care setting. *General Hospital Psychiatry, 14,* 237–247.

Katz, I. R., & Alexopoulos, G. S. (1996, Fall). Consensus update conference: Diagnosis and treatment of late-life depression, proceedings of the Geriatric Psychiatry Alliance—January 20, 1996. *The American Journal of Geriatric Psychiatry, 4*(4), supplement 1.

Kay, D. W. K. (1963). Late paraphrenia and its bearing on the etiology of schizophrenia. *Acta Psychiatrica Scandinavica, 39,* 159–169, 1963.

Kay, D. W. K., & Roth, M. (1961). Environmental and hereditary factors in the schizophrenias of old age ("late paraphrenia") and their bearing on the general problem of causation in schizophrenia. *Journal of Mental Science, 107,* 649–686.

Kendler, K. S., & Diehl, S. R. (1993). The genetics of schizophrenia: A current, genetic-epidemiologic perspective. *Schizophrenia Bulletin, 19,* 261–285.

Kendler, K. S., & Walsh, D. (1995). Gender and schizophrenia: Results of an epidemiologically based family study. *British Journal of Psychiatry, 167,* 184–192.

Klerman, G. L., Lavori, P. W., Rice, J., Reich, T., Endicott, J., Andreasen, N. C., Keller, M. B., & Hirschfield, R. M. A. (1985). Birth-cohort trends in rates of major depressive disorder among relatives of patients with affective disorder. *Archives of General Psychiatry, 42,* 689–693.

Kraepelin, E. (1900). Psychiatrie. In *Ein Lehrbuch fur Studierende und Artzte* (pp. 1909–1915). Leipzig: Barth.

Kral, V. A., & Emory, O. B. (1989). Long-term follow-up of depressive pseudodementia of the aged. *Canadian Journal of Psychiatry, 34,* 445–446.

Krishnan K. R. R., Tupler, L. A., Richie, J. C., McDonald, W. M., Knight, D. L., Nemeroff, C. B., & Carroll, B. J. (1996). Apolipoprotein E-4 frequency in geriatric depression. *Biological Psychiatry, 40,* 69–71.

Lebowitz, B. D., Martinez, R. A., Niederehe, G., Pearson, J. L., et al. (1995). Treatment of depression in late-life. *Psychopharmacology, 31*(1), 185–202.

Lipsey, J. R., Robinson, R. G., Pearlson, G. D., Rao, K., & Price, T. R. (1984). Nortriptyline treatment of post-stroke depression: A double-blind study. *Lancet, I,* 297–300.

Lyness, J. M., Cox, C., Curry, J., Conwell, Y., King, D. A., & Caine, E. D. (1995). Older age and the underreporting of depressive symptoms. *Journal of the American Geriatrics Society, 43,* 216–221.

Manton, K. G., Blazer, D. G., & Woodbury, M. A. (1987). Suicide in middle age and later life: Sex and race specific life table and cohort analyses. *Journal of Gerontology, 42,* 219–227.

Markovitz, P. J. (1993). Treatment of anxiety in the elderly. *Journal of Clinical Psychiatry, 54*(Suppl. 5), 64–68.

Murphy, E., & Brown, G. W. (1980). Life events, psychiatric disturbance and physical illness. *British Journal of Psychiatry, 136,* 326–338.

Naguib, M., McGuffin, P., Levy, R., Festenstein, H., & Alonso, A. (1987). Genetic markers in late paraphrenia: A study of HLA antigens. *British Journal of Psychiatry, 150,* 124–127.

National Institutes of Health Consensus Development Conference. (1991, November 4–5). Diagnosis and treatment of depression in late life. Reprinted from: *NIH Consensus Development Conference Consensus Statement,* vol. 9, no. 3. Bethesda, MD: NIH.

National Institutes of Health, Office of the Medical Applications of Research. (1992). Consensus Development Panel on Late Life: Diagnosis and treatment of depression in late life. *Journal of the American Medical Association (JAMA), 268,* 1010–1024.

Norquist, G., Wells, K. B., Rogers, W. H., Davis, L. M., Kahn, K., & Brook, R. (1995). Quality of care for depressed elderly patients hospitalized in the speciality units of general medical wards. *Archives of General Psychiatry, 52,* 695–701.

Owen, F., Crow, T. J., Frith, C. D., Johnson, J. A., Johnstone, E. C., Lofthouse, R., Owens, D. G. C., & Poulter, M. (1987). Selective decreases in MAO-B activity in post-mortem brains from schizophrenic patients with type II syndrome. *British Journal of Psychiatry, 151,* 514–519.

Parnetti, L., Gottfries, J., Karlsson, I., Langstrom, G., Gottfries, C.-G., & Svennerholm, L. (1987). Monoamines and their metabolites in cerebrospinal fluid of patients with senile dementia of Alzheimer type using high performance liquid chromatography and gas chromatography-mass spectrometry. *Acta Psychiatrica Scandinavica, 75,* 542–548.

Pauls, D. L., Ott, O., Paul, S. M., Allen, C. R., Fann, C. S. J., Carulli, J. P., Falls. K. M., Southillier, C. A., Gravius, T. C., Keith, T. P., Egeland, J. A., & Ginns, E. I. (1995). Linkage analyses of chromosome 18 markers do not identify a major susceptibility locus for bipolar affective disorder in the older order Amish. *American Journal of Human Genetics, 57,* 636–643.

Pearlson, G., & Rabins, P. (1988). The late-onset psychoses: Possible risk factors. *Psychiatric Clinics of North America, 11,* 15–32.

Pekkarinen, P., Terwilliger, J. Bredbacka, P., Lonnqvist, J. & Peltonen, L. (1995). Evidence of a predisposing locus to bipolar disorder on Xq24-q27.1 in an extended Finnish pedigree. *Genome Research, 5,* 105–115.

Pickar, D. (1995). Prospects for pharmacotherapy of schizophrenia. *Lancet, 345,* 557–562.

Post, M. (1966). *Persistent persecutory states of the elderly.* Oxford: Pergamon Press.

Post, R. M., Ballenger, J. C., & Goodwin, F. K. (1984). Cerebrospinal fluid studies of neurotransmitter function in manic and depressive illness. In Post, R. M., & Ballenger, J. C. (Eds.), *Neurobiology of Mood Disorders* (pp. 685–717). Baltimore: Williams and Wilkins.

Rabins, P., Pearlson, G., Jayaram, G., Steele, C., & Tune, L. (1987). Increased ventricle-to-brain ratio in late-onset schizophrenia. *American Journal of Psychiatry, 144,* 1216–1218.

Rabins, P. V., Harvis, K., & Koven, S. (1985). High fatality rates of late-life depression associated with cardiovascular disease. *Journal of Affective Disorders, 9,* 165–167.

Reding, M., Haycox, J., Blass, J. (1985). Depression in patients referred to a dementia clinic: A three-year prospective study. *Archives of Neurology, 42,* 894–896.

Retterstol, N. (1968). Paranoid psychoses: The stability of nosological categories illustrated by a personal follow-up investigation. *British Journal of Psychiatry, 114,* 553–562.

Rich, C. L., Young, D., & Fowler, R. C. (1986). San Diego suicide study. *Archives of General Psychiatry 43*, 577–582.

Richelson, E. (1994). The pharmacology of antidepressants at the synapse: Focus on newer compounds. *Journal of Clinical Psychiatry, 55*(9, Suppl. A), 34–39.

Robinson, R. G., Lipsey, J. R., Bolla-Wilson, K., Bolduc, P. L., Pearlson, G. D., Rao, K., & Price, T. R. (1985). Mood disorders in left-handed stroke patients. *American Journal of Psychiatry, 142,* 1424–1429.

Robinson, R. G., Starr, L. B., Kubos, K. L., & Price, T. R. (1983). A two-year longitudinal study of post-stroke mood disorders: Findings during the initial evaluation. *Stroke, 14,* 736–741.

Rodin, G., & Voshart, K. (1986). Depression in the medically ill: An overview. *American Journal of Psychiatry, 143,* 696–705.

Roose, S. P., Glassman, A. H., Attia, E., & Woodring, R. (1994). Comparative efficacy of selective serotonin reuptake inhibitors and tricyclics in the treatment of melancholia. *American Journal of Psychiatry, 151,* 1735–1739.

Roth, M. (1955). The natural history of mental disorders in old age. *Journal of Mental Science, 101,* 281–295.

Roth, M. (1987). Late paraphrenia: Phenomenology and etiological factors and their bearing upon problems of the schizophrenia family of disorders. In Miller, N. E., & Cohen, G. D. (Eds.), *Schizophrenia, paranoia and schizophreniform disorders in later life* (pp. 217–234). New York: Guilford Press.

Rovner, B. W., German, P S., L. J., et al. (1991). Depression and mortality in nursing homes. *Journal of the American Medical Association, 265,* 993–996.

Ruegg, R. G., Zisook, S., Swerdlow, N. R. (1988). Depression in the aged: An overview. *Psychiatric Clinics of North America, 11,* 83–99.

Schildkrant, J. J. (1965). The catecholamine hypothesis of affective disorders: A review of supporting evidence. *American Journal of Psychiatry, 122,* 509–522.

Schneider, L. S., Reynolds, C. F., Lebowitz, B., & Friedhoff, A. (Eds.). (1994). *Diagnosis and treatment of depression in late life: Results of the NIH consensus development conference.* Washington, DC: American Psychiatric Press.

Seidlitz, L., Duberstein, P. R., Cox, C., & Conwell, Y. (1995). Attitudes of older people toward suicide and assisted suicide: An analysis of Gallop poll findings. *Journal of the American Geriatrics Society, 43,* 993–998.

Sheikh, J. I. (1996). Anxiety disorders. In Sadavoy, J., Lazarus, L. W., Jarvik, L. F. & Grossberg, G. T. (Eds.), *Comprehensive Review of Geriatric Psychiatry II,* Second Edition (pp. 615–636). Washington, DC: American Psychiatric Press.

Shulman, K., Post, F. (1980). Bipolar affective disorder in old age. *British Journal of Psychiatry, 136,* 26–32.

Siever, L. J., & Davis, K. L. (1985). Overview: toward a dysregulation hypothesis of depression. *American Journal of Psychiatry, 142,* 1017–1031.

Stern, T. A., & Tesar, G. E. (1988). Anxiety and the cardiovascular system. *Mount Sinai Journal of Medicine, 55,* 230–239.

Straub, R. E., MacLean, C. J., O'Neill, A. O., Burke, J., Murphy, B., Duke, F., Shinkwin, R., Webb, B. T., Zhang, J., Walsh, D. & Kendler, K. S. (1995). A potential vulnerability locus for schizophrenia on chromosome 6p24–22: Evidence for genetic heterogeneity. *Nature Genetics, 11,* 287–293.

Sunderland, T., Cohen, R. M., Molchan, S., Lawlor, B. A., Mellow, A. M., Newhouse, P. A., Tariot, P. N., Mueller, E. A., & Murphy, D. L. (1994). High-dose selegiline in treatment-resistant older depressive patients. *Archives of General Psychiatry, 51,* 607–615.

Sunderland, T., Lawlor, B. A., Molchan, S. E., & Martinez, R. A. (1988). Depressive syndromes in the elderly: Special concerns. *Psychopharmacology Bulletin, 24,* 567–576.

Sunderland, T., Little, J., Cantillon, M., Bahro, M., & Molchan, S. (1994). Pharmacologic treatment of depression in elderly neuropsychiatric patients. In Langer, S. Z., Brunello, N., Racagni, G., & Mendlewicz, J. (Eds.), *Critical issues in the treatment of affective disorders* (pp. 52–57). Basel, Switzerland: S. Karger AG, Int. Acad. Biomed. Drug Res., Vol. 9.

Sunderland, T., Molchan, S. E., & Zubenko, G. S. (1995). Biological markers in Alzheimer's disease. In Bloom, F. E. & Kupfer, D. J. (Eds.), *Psychopharmacology: The fourth generation of progress* (pp. 1389–1399). New York: Raven Press.

Tran-Johnson, T. K., Krull, A. J., & Jeste, D. V. (1992). Late life schizophrenia and its treatment: Pharmacologic issues in older schizophrenic patients. *Clinics of Geriatric Medicine, 8*(2), 401–410.

Veith, R. C., Raskind, M. A. (1988). The neurobiology of aging: Does it predispose to depression? *Neurobiology of Aging, 9,* 101–117.

Watt, J. A. G. (1985). The relationship of paranoid state to schizophrenia. *American Journal of Psychiatry, 142,* 1456–1458.

Weissman, M. M., & Myers, J. K. (1978). Affective disorders in a U.S. urban community. *Archives of General Psychiatry, 35,* 1304–1311.

Wells, K. B., & Burnam, M. A. (1991). Caring for depression in America: Lessons from early findings of the medical outcomes study. *Psychiatric Medicine, 9,* 503–519.

Woods, R. T., & Britton, P. G. (1985). *Clinical psychology with the elderly.* Rockville, MD: Aspen Publications.

Yassa, R., Nair, V., & Schwartz, G. (1986). Early versus late onset psychosis and tardive dyskinesia. *Biological Psychiatry, 21,* 1291–1297.

Zisook, S., Shuchter, S. R., Sledge, P. A., et. al. (1994). The spectrum of depressive phenomena after spousal bereavememt. *Journal of Clinical Psychiatry, 55,* 29–36.

Zubenko, G. S., Moossy, J., & Kopp, U. (1990). Neurochemical correlates of major depression in primary dementia. *Archives of Neurology, 47,* 209–214.

ENDNOTES

1. American Psychiatric Association. (1994). *DSM-IV diagnostic and statistical manual of mental disorders,* Fourth Edition. Washington, DC: American Psychiatric Association.

2. Finch, E. L. J., Ramsay, R., & Katona, C. L. E. (1992). Depression and physical illness in the elderly. *Clinics of Geriatric Medicine, 8,* 275–287.

3. Katon, W., & Schulberg, H. C. (1992). Epidemiology of depression in primary care. Special section: developing guidelines for treating depressive disorder in the primary care setting. *General Hospital Psychiatry, 14,* 237–247.

4. Burns, B. J., Wagner, D. R., Taube, J. E., Magaziner, J., Pernutt, T., & Landerman, L. R. (1993). Mental health service use by the elderly in nursing homes. *American Journal of Public Health, 83,* 331–337.

5. American Psychiatric Association. (1994). *DSM-IV diagnostic and statistical manual of mental disorders,* Fourth Edition. Washington, DC: American Psychiatric Association.

6. Lyness, J. M., Cox, C., Curry, J., Conwell, Y., King, D. A., & Caine, E. D. (1995). Older age and the underreporting of depressive symptoms. *Journal of the American Geriatrics Society, 43,* 216–221; Hendrie, H. C., Callahan, C. M., Levitt, E. E., Hui, S. L., Musick, B., Austrom, M. G., Nurnberger, J. I. Jr., & Tierney, W. M. (1995). Prevalence rates of major depressive disorders: The effects of varying the diagnostic criteria in an older primary care population. *American Journal of Geriatric Psychiatry, 3,* 119–131; Klerman, G. L., Lavori, P. W., Rice, J., Reich, T., Endicott, J., Andreasen, N. C., Keller, M. B., & Hirschfield, R. M. A. (1985). Birth-cohort trends in rates of major depressive disorder among relatives of patients with affective disorder. *Archives of General Psychiatry 42,* 689–693; and Blazer, D., Hughes, D.C., & George, L. K. (1987). The epidemiology of depression in an elderly community population. *Gerontologist, 27,* 281–287.

7. Hendrie, H. C., Callahan, C. M., Levitt, E. E., Hui, S. L., Musick, B., Austrom, M. G., Nurnberger, J. I. Jr., & Tierney, W. M. (1995). Prevalence rates of major depressive disorders: The effects of varying the diagnostic criteria in an older primary care population. *American Journal of Geriatric Psychiatry, 3,* 119–131.

8. Lebowitz, B. D., Martinez, R. A., Niederehe, G., Pearson, J. L., et al. (1995). Treatment of depression in late-life. *Psychopharmacology, 31*(1), 185–202; Baldwin, R. C. (1994). Is there a distinct subtype of major depression in the elderly? *Journal of Psychopharmacology, 8*(3), 177–184; Ruegg, R. G., Zisook, S., & Swerdlow, N. R. (1988). Depression in the aged: An overview. *Psychiatric Clinics of North America, 11,* 83–99.

9. Blazer, D., Bachar, J. R., & Hughes, D. C. (1987). Major depression with melancholia: A comparison of middle-aged and elderly adults. *Journal of the American Geriatrics Society, 35,* 927–932.

10. Blazer, D., George, L., & Landerman, R. (1986). The phenomenology of late life depression. In Bebbington, P. E., & Jacoby, R. (Eds.), *Psychiatric disorders in the elderly.* London: Mental Health Foundation; Blazer, D., Bachar, J. R., & Hughes, D. C. (1987). Major depression with melancholia: A comparison of middle-aged and elderly adults. *Journal of the American Geriatrics Society, 35,* 927–932.

11. Alexopoulos, G. S., Meyers, B. S., Young, R. C., Chester, J., Feder, M., & Einhorn, A. (1995). Anx-

iety in geriatric depression: Effects of age and cognitive impairment. *American Journal of Geriatric Psychiatry, 3,* 108–118.

12. Lyness, J. M., Cox, C., Curry, J., Conwell, Y., King, D. A., & Caine, E. D. (1995). Older age and the underreporting of depressive symptoms. *Journal of the American Geriatrics Society, 43,* 216–221.

13. Jamison, K. R. (1979). Manic-depressive illness in the elderly. In Kaplan, O. J. (Ed.), *Psychopathology of aging.* New York: Academic Press, pp. 79–95.

14. Eagles, J. M., & Whalley, L. J. (1985). Ageing and affective disorders: The age of first onset of affective disorders in Scotland, 1969–1978. *British Journal of Psychiatry, 147,* 180–187.

15. Shulman, K., & Post, F. (1980). Bipolar affective disorder in old age. *British Journal of Psychiatry, 136,* 26–32.

16. Clayton, P. J. (1981). The epidemiology of bipolar affective disorder. *Comprehensive Psychiatry, 22,* 31–43; and Weissman, M. M., & Myers, J. K. (1978). Affective disorders in a U.S. urban community. *Archives of General Psychiatry 35,* 1304–1311.

17. Lebowitz, B. D., Martinez, R. A., Niederehe, G., Pearson, J. L., et al. (1995). Treatment of depression in late-life. *Psychopharmacology, 31*(1), 185–202; Murphy, E., & Brown, G. W. (1980). Life events, psychiatric disturbance and physical illness. *British Journal of Psychiatry, 136,* 326–338; and Woods, R. T., & Britton, P. G. (1985). *Clinical psychology with the elderly.* Rockville, MD: Aspen Publications.

18. Sunderland, T., Lawlor, B. A., Molchan, S. E., & Martinez, R. A. (1988). Depressive syndromes in the elderly: Special concerns. *Psychopharmacology Bulletin, 24,* 567–576.

19. Schildkrant, J. J. (1965). The catecholamine hypothesis of affective disorders: A review of supporting evidence. *American Journal of Psychiatry, 122,* 509–522; Post, R. M., Ballenger, J. C., & Goodwin, F. K. (1984). Cerebrospinal fluid studies of neurotransmitter function in manic and depressive illness. In Post, R. M., & Ballenger, J. C. (Eds.), *Neurobiology of mood disorders* (pp. 685–717). Baltimore: Williams and Wilkins; and Veith, R. C., & Raskind, M. A. (1988). The neurobiology of aging: Does it predispose to depression? *Neurobiology of Aging, 9,* 101–117.

20. Siever, L. J., & Davis, K. L. (1985). Overview: toward a dysregulation hypothesis of depression. *American Journal of Psychiatry, 142,* 1017–1031.

21. Egeland, J. A., Gerhard, D. S., Pauls, D. L., Sussex, J. M., Kidd, K. K., Allen, C. R., Hostetter, A. M., & Housman, D. E. (1987). Bipolar affective

disorders linked to DNA markers on chromosome 11. *Nature, 325,* 783–787.

22. Freimer N. B., Reus, V. I., Escamilla, M. A., McInnes,L. A., Spesny, M., Leon, P., Service, S. K., Smith, L. B., Silva, S., Rohas, E., Gallegos, A., Meza, L., Fournier, E., Bahorloo, S., Blankenship, K., Tyler, D. J., Batki, S., Vinogradov, S., Weissenback, J., Barondes, S. H., & Sandkuijl, L. A. (1996). Genetic mapping using haplotype, association and linkage methods suggests a locus for severe bipolar disorder (BPI) at 18q22–q23. *Nature Genetics, 12,* 436–441; Pauls, D. L., Ott, O., Paul, S. M., Allen, C. R., Fann, C. S. J., Carulli, J. P., Falls. K. M., Southillier, C. A., Gravius, T. C., Keith, T. P., Egeland, J. A., & Ginns, E. I. (1995). Linkage analyses of chromosome 18 markers do not identify a major susceptibility locus for bipolar affective disorder in the older order Amish. *American Journal of Human Genetics, 57,* 636–643; and Pekkarinen, P., Terwilliger, J. Bredbacka, P., Lonnqvist, J., & Peltonen, L. (1995). Evidence of a predisposing locus to bipolar disorder on Xq24–q27.1 in an extended Finnish pedigree. *Genome Research, 5,* 105–115.

23. Robinson, R. G., Starr, L. B., Kubos, K. L., & Price, T. R. (1983). A two-year longitudinal study of post-stroke mood disorders: Findings during the initial evaluation. *Stroke, 14,* 736–741; Robinson, R. G., Lipsey, J. R., Bolla-Wilson, K., Bolduc, P. L., Pearlson, G. D., Rao, K., & Price, T. R. (1985). Mood disorders in left-handed stroke patients. *American Journal of Psychiatry, 142,* 1424–1429; Reding, M., Haycox, J., & Blass, J. (1985) Depression in patients referred to a dementia clinic: A three-year prospective study. *Archives of Neurology, 42,* 894–896; and Lipsey, J. R., Robinson, R. G., Pearlson, G. D., Rao, K., & Price, T. R. (1984). Nortriptyline treatment of post-stroke depression: A double-blind study. *Lancet 1,* 297–300.

24. Baldwin, R. C. (1994). Is there a distinct subtype of major depression in the elderly? *Journal of Psychopharmacology, 8*(3), 177–184; Rodin, G., & Voshart, K. (1986). Depression in the medically ill: An over-view. *American Journal of Psychiatry, 143,* 696–705; Berkman, L. F., Berkman, C. S., Kasl, S., Freeman, D. H., Leo, L., Ostfeld, A. M., Cornoni-Huntley, J., & Brody, J. A. (1986). Depressive symptoms in relation to physical health and functioning in the elderly. *American Journal of Epidemiology, 124,* 372–388; and Sunderland, T., Lawlor, B. A., Molchan, S. E., & Martinez, R. A. (1988). Depressive syndromes in the elderly: Spe-

cial concerns. *Psychopharmacology Bulletin, 24,* 567–576.

25. American Psychiatric Association. (1994). *DSM-IV Diagnostic and Statistical Manual of Mental Disorders,* Fourth Edition. Washington, DC: American Psychiatric Association.
26. Sunderland, T., Molchan, S. E., & Zubenko, G. S. (1995). Biological markers in Alzheimer's disease. In Bloom, F. E., & Kupfer, D. J. (Eds.), *Psychopharmacology: The fourth generation of progress.* New York: Raven Press, pp. 1389–1399.
27. Zubenko, G. S., Moossy J., & Kopp, U. (1990). Neurochemical correlates of major depression in primary dementia. *Archives of Neurology, 47,* 209–214.
28. Zweig, R. M., Ross, C. A., Hedreen, J. C., Steele, C., Cardillo, J. E., Whitehouse, P. J., Folstein, M. F., & Price, D. L. (1988). The neuropathology of aminergic nuclei in Alzheimer's disease. *Annals of Neurology, 24,* 233–242.
29. Alexopoulos, G. S., Young, R. C., Meyers, B. S., Abrams, R. C., & Shamoian, C. A. (1988). Late-onset depression. *Psychiatric Clinics of North America, 11,* 109–115; and Greenwald, B. S., & Kramer-Ginsberg, E. (1988). Age at onset in geriatric depression: Relationship to clinical variables. *Journal of Affective Disorders, 15,* 61–68.
30. Rabins, P. V., Harvis, K., & Koven, S. (1985). High fatality rates of late-life depression associated with cardiovascular disease. *Journal of Affective Disorders, 9,* 165–167.
31. Baldwin, R. C. (1994). Is there a distinct subtype of major depression in the elderly? *Journal of Psychopharmacology, 8*(3), 177–184; Reding, M., Haycox, J., & Blass, J. (1985). Depression in patients referred to a dementia clinic: A three-year prospective study. *Archives of Neurology, 42,* 894–896.
32. Baldwin, R. C. (1994). Is there a distinct subtype of major depression in the elderly? *Journal of Psychopharmacology, 8*(3), 177–184; Kral, V. A., & Emory, O. B. (1989). Long-term follow-up of depressive pseudodementia of the aged. *Canadian Journal of Psychiatry, 34,* 445–446; and Copeland, J. R. M., Davidson, I. A., Dewey, M. E., et al. (1992). Alzheimer's disease, other dementias, depression and pseudodementia: prevalence, incidence and three-year outcome in Liverpool. *British Journal of Psychiatry, 161,* 230–239.
33. Krishnan K. R. R., Tupler, L. A., Richie, J. C., McDonald, W. M., Knight, D. L., Nemeroff, C. B. & Carroll, B. J. (1996). Apolipoprotein E-4 frequency in geriatric depression. *Biological Psychiatry, 40,* 69–71.

34. Carney, S. S., Rich, C. L., Burke, P. A., & Fowler, R. C. (1994). Suicide over 60: the San Diego Study. *Journal of the American Geriatrics Society, 42,* 174–180; Rich, C. L., Young, D., & Fowler, R. C. (1986). San Diego suicide study. *Archives of General Psychiatry, 43,* 577–582; and Manton, K. G., Blazer, D. G., & Woodbury, M. A. (1987). Suicide in middle age and later life: Sex and race specific life table and cohort analyses. *Journal of Gerontology, 42,* 219–227.
35. The actual rate of suicide is underreported because of shame and guilt. Some religious groups such as Catholics and Orthodox Jews have denied burial rites to persons who committed suicide. It is also underestimated because of deception to protect life insurance benefits.
36. Carney, S. S., Rich, C. L., Burke, P. A., & Fowler, R. C. (1994). Suicide over 60: the San Diego Study. *Journal of American Geriatrics Society, 42,* 174–180.
37. Conwell, Y., Olsen, K., & Caine, E. D. (1990). Completed suicide at age 50 and over. *Journal of the American Geriatric Society, 38,* 640–644.
38. For national suicide rates, see U.S. Bureau of the Census (1987). *Statistical abstract of the United States: 1988,* 108th edition. Washington, DC: U.S. Government Printing Office; and Rich, C. L., Young, D., & Fowler, R. C. (1986). San Diego suicide study. *Archives of General Psychiatry, 43,* 577–582.
39. From Cohen, J. (1964). Forms of suicide and their significance, *Triangle, 6,* 280–286.
40. *Ibid.*
41. Seidlitz, L., Duberstein, P. R., Cox, C., & Conwell, Y. (1995). Attitudes of older people toward suicide and assisted suicide: An analysis of Gallop poll findings. *Journal of the American Geriatrics Society, 43,* 993–998.
42. Lyness, J. M., Cox, C., Curry, J., Conwell, Y., King, D. A., & Caine, E. D. (1995). Older age and the underreporting of depressive symptoms. *Journal of the American Geriatrics Society, 43,* 216–221; Conwell, Y., Olsen, K., & Caine, E. D. (1990). Completed suicide at age 50 and over. *Journal of the American Geriatrics Society, 38,* 640–644.
43. Camus, A. (1959). *The myth of Sisyphus.* New York: Vintage Books.
44. Tran-Johnson, T. K., Krull, A. J., Jeste, D. V. (1992). Late life schizophrenia and its treatment: Pharmacologic issues in older schizophrenic patients. *Clinics in Geriatric Medicine, 8*(2), 401–410.
45. For an investigation of changes over time in the manifestations of schizophrenia, including the the-

ory that schizophrenic illness "burns out" as one ages, see Lawton, M. P. (1972). Schizophrenia 45 years later. *Journal of the Genetic Psychology, 121,* 133–143.

46. Bridge, T. P., & Wyatt, R. J. (1980). Paraphrenia: Paranoid states of late life: I. European research. *Journal of the American Geriatrics Society, 27,* 193–200.

47. Kraepelin, E. (1900). Psychiatrie. In *Ein Lehrbuch fur Studierende und Artzte* (pp. 1909–1915). Leipzig: Barth.

48. Roth, M. (1955). The natural history of mental disorders in old age. *Journal of Mental Science, 101,* 281–295.

49. Bridge, & Wyatt, R. I., (1980).

50. Tran-Johnson, T. K., Krull, A. J., & Jeste, D. V. (1992). Late life schizophrenia and its treatment: Pharmacologic issues in older schizophrenic patients. *Clinics in Geriatric Medicine, 8*(2), 401–410; Eastwood, M. R., Corbin, S. L., Reed, M., Nobbs, H., & Kedward, H. B. (1985). Acquired hearing loss and psychiatric illness: An estimate of prevalence and co-morbidity in a geriatric setting. *British Journal of Psychiatry, 147,* 552–556; Jeste, D. V., Harris, M. J., Pearlson, G. D., Rabins, P., Lesser, I., Miller, B., Coles, C., & Yassa, B. (1988). Late-onset schizophrenia: Studying clinical validity. *Psychiatric Clinics of North America, 11,* 1–13; and Pearlson, G., & Rabins, P. (1988). The late-onset psychoses: Possible risk factors. *Psychiatric Clinics of North America, 11,* 15–32.

51. Christenson, R., & Blazer, D. (1984). Epidemiology of persecutory ideation in an elderly population in the community. *American Journal of Psychiatry, 141,* 1088–1091.

52. Pearlson, G., Rabins, P. (1988). The late-onset psychoses: Possible risk factors. *Psychiatric Clinics of North America, 11,* 15–32.

53. Kay, D. W. K., & Roth, M. (1961). Environmental and hereditary factors in the schizophrenias of old age ("late paraphrenia") and their bearing on the general problem of causation in schizophrenia. *Journal of Mental Science, 107,* 649–686; Post, M. (1966). *Persistent persecutory states of the elderly.* Oxford: Pergamon Press; and Retterstol, N. (1968). Paranoid psychoses: The stability of nosological categories illustrated by a personal follow-up investigation. *British Journal of Psychiatry, 114,* 553–562.

54. Caligiuri, M. P., Lohr, J. B., Panton, D., & Harris, J. (1993). Extrapyramidal motor abnormalities associated with late-life psychosis. *Schizophrenia Bulletin, 19*(4), 747–754; Denmark, J. S. (1985). A

study of 250 patients referred to a department of psychiatry for the deaf. *British Journal of Psychiatry, 146,* 282–286; Eastwood, et al. (1985); Post (1966); and Watt, J. A. G. (1985). The relationship of paranoid state to schizophrenia. *American Journal of Psychiatry, 142,* 1456–1458.

55. Blazer, D., George, L. K., & Hughes, D. (1988). Schizophrenic symptoms in an elderly community population. In Brody, J. A., & Maddox, G. L. (Eds.), *Epidemiology and aging: An international perspective* (pp. 134–149). New York: Springer.

56. Kendler, K. S., & Walsh, D. (1995). Gender and schizophrenia: results of an epidemiologically based family study. *British Journal of Psychiatry, 167,* 184–192; Chen, W. J., Faraone, S. V., & Tsuang, M. T. (1992). Linkage studies of schizophrenia: A simulation study of statistical power. *Genetic Epidemiology, 9,* 123–139; Kendler, K. S., & Diehl, S. R. (1993). The genetics of schizophrenia: A current, genetic-epidemiologic perspective. *Schizophrenia Bulletin, 19,* 261–285.

57. Straub, R. E., MacLean, C. J., O'Neill, A. O., Burke, J., Murphy, B., Duke, F., Shinkwin, R., Webb, B. T., Zhang, J., Walsh, D., & Kendler, K. S. (1995). A potential vulnerability locus for schizophrenia on chromosome 6p24-22: evidence for genetic heterogeneity. *Nature Genetics, 11,* 287–293; Pulver, A. E., et al. (1994). Follow-up of a report of a potential linkage for schizophrenia on chromosome 22q12–q13.1: Part 2. *American Journal of Medical Genetics, 54,* 44–50.

58. Su, Y. et al. (1993). Exclusion of linkage between schizophrenia and the D2 dopamine receptor gene region of chromosome 11q in 112 Irish multiplex families. *Archives of General Psychiatry, 50,* 205–211.

59. Rabins, P., Pearlson, G., Jayaram, G., Steele, C., & Tune, L. (1987). Increased ventricle-to-brain ratio in late-onset schizophrenia. *American Journal of Psychiatry, 144,* 1216–1218.

60. Brown, R., Colter, N., Corsellis, J. A. N., Crow, T. J., Frith, C. D, Jagoe, R., Johnstone, E. C., & Marsh, L. (1986) Postmortem evidence of structural brain changes in schizophrenia. *Archives of General Psychiatry, 43,* 36–42.

61. Parnetti, L., Gottfries, J., Karlsson, I., Langstrom, G., Gottfries, C.-G., & Svennerholm, L. (1987). Monoamines and their metabolites in cerebrospinal fluid of patients with senile dementia of Alzheimer type using high performance liquid chromatography and gas chromatography-mass spectrometry. *Acta Psychiatrica Scandinavica, 75,* 542–548.

62. Bridge, T. P., Kleinman, J. E., Soldo, B. J., & Karoum, F. (1987). Central catecholamines, cognitive impairment, and affective state in elderly schizophrenics and controls. *Biological Psychiatry, 22,* 139–147.

63. Owen, F., Crow, T. J., Frith, C. D., Johnson, J. A., Johnstone, E. C., Lofthouse, R., Owens, D. G. C., & Poulter, M. (1987). Selective decreases in MAO-B activity in post-mortem brains from schizophrenic patients with type II syndrome. *British Journal of Psychiatry, 151,* 514–519.

64. Pearlson & Rabins (1988); Roth (1955); Roth (1987); and Yassa, R., Nair, V., & Schwartz, G. (1986). Early versus late onset psychosis and tardive dyskinesia. *Biological Psychiatry, 21,* 1291–1297.

65. Jeste, D. V., Harris, M. J., Pearlson, G. D., Rabins, P., Lesser, I., Miller, B., Coles, C., & Yassa, B. (1988). Late-onset schizophrenia: Studying clinical validity. *Psychiatric Clinics of North America, 11,* 1–13.

66. Post (1966); and Jeste, et. al. (1988).

67. Markovitz, P. J. (1993). Treatment of anxiety in the elderly. *Journal of Clinical Psychiatry, 54* (Suppl.5), 64–68.

68. Stern, T. A., & Tesar, G. E. (1988). Anxiety and the cardiovascular system. *Mount Sinai Journal of Medicine, 55,* 230–239; and George, L. K., Blazer, D. G., Winfield-Laird, I., Leaf, P. J., & Fischbach, R. L. (1988). Psychiatric disorders and mental health service use in later life: Evidence from the epidemiologic catchment area program. In Brody, J. A., & Maddox, G. L. (Eds.). *Epidemiology and aging: An international perspective* (pp. 189–219). New York: Springer.

69. Flint, A. J. (1994, May). Epidemiology and Co-morbidity of Anxiety Disorders in the Elderly. *American Journal of Psychiatry, 151*(5), pp. 640–649.

70. Sheikh, J. I. (1996). Anxiety Disorders. In Sadavoy, J., Lazarus, L. W., Jarvik, L. F., & Grossberg, G. T. (Eds.), *Comprehensive review of geriatric psychiatry II,* Second Edition (pp. 615–636). Washington, DC: American Psychiatric Press.

71. The landmark National Comorbidity Survey, conducted from 1990 to 1992, found that 3.5% of adults had panic disorder at some time in their lives. Unfortunately, this survey of 8,000 Americans covered ages 15 to 54 only. [Kessler, R. C., et. al. (1994, January). Lifetime and 12-month prevalence of DSM-III-R psychiatric disorders in the United States. *Archives of General Psychiatry, 51,*

8–19.] Another major survey, the National Institute of Mental Health's Epidemiologic Catchment Area Study, for which 20,000 adults of all ages were interviewed in the 1980s, found that fewer than one percent of people age 65 and older had panic disorder in their lives. [Robins, L. N., Regier, D. A. (Eds.) (1991). *Psychiatric disorders in America: The epidemiologic catchment area study.* New York: The Free Press.] This low figure is due in part to the fact that the disorder usually occurs in young adulthood, and to the relatively strict definition of panic disorder, which requires the incidence of at least three intense attacks in any three-week period and at least one occurring with no obvious phobic stimulus. As many as 10% of Americans, however, have had panic attacks at some time in their lives.

72. Stern, T. A., & Tesar, G. E. (1988). Anxiety and the cardiovascular system. *Mount Sinai Journal of Medicine, 55,* 230–239.

73. Salzman, C., Schneider, L. S., & Alexopoulos, G. S. (1995). Pharmacological treatment of depression in late life. In Bloom, F. E., & Kupfer, D. J. (Eds.). *Psychopharmacology: The fourth generation of progress* (pp. 1471–1477). New York: Raven Press; Sunderland, T., Lawlor, B. A., Martinez, R. A., & Molchan, S. E. (1991). Anxiety in the elderly: Neurobiological and clinical interface. In Salzman, C., & Lebowitz, B. (Eds.), *Anxiety in the elderly: Treatment and research* (pp. 105–129). New York: Springer.

74. George, L. K., Blazer, D. G., Winfield-Laird, I., Leaf, P. J., & Fischbach, R. L. (1988). Psychiatric disorders and mental health service use in later life: Evidence from the epidemiologic catchment area program. In Brody, J. A., & Maddox, G. L. (Eds.). *Epidemiology and aging: An international perspective* (pp. 189–219). New York: Springer.

75. Alexopoulos, G. S., Meyers, B. S., Young, R. C., Chester, J., Feder, M., & Einhorn, A. (1995). Anxiety in geriatric depression: Effects of age and cognitive impairment. *American Journal of Geriartics Psychiatry, 3,* 108–118.

76. Gershanik, O. S. (1994). Drug-induced Parkinsonism in the aged: Recognition and prevention. *Drugs Aging, 5*(2), 127–132; Hunter, R. C. A., & Cleghorn, R. A. (1982). Psychosomatic disorders in the elderly. *Canadian Journal of Psychiatry, 27,* 362–365.

77. Ghadirian, A. M., Gauthier, S., & Bertrand, S. (1986). Anxiety attacks in a patient with a right temporal lobe meningioma. *Journal of Clinical Psychiatry, 47,* 270–271.

78. This idea is of a standard Biblical conception. The elderly King David, for example, was advised to "lay" with young girls.

79. American Psychiatric Association. (1994). *DSM-IV diagnostic and statistical manual of mental disorders.* Fourth Edition. Washington, DC: American Psychiatric Association.

80. Occasionally a *folie à deux* (as defined earlier on page 106) may result, involving the older person and someone close to him or her. One kind of "eccentricity" is observed when a mother and daughter, two brothers, or two sisters become recluses, living in a house that ages as they do—or, more precisely, deteriorates. It is usually the health department that becomes alerted for purposes of cleanup or eviction. Electricity may be off, plumbing and toilets may not function, there may have been small fires, human feces may be found on the bathroom floor, cat litter may be evident, window screens may be rusting, the house may need painting and repairs, the garden may be overgrown.

81. Notes on the history and evolution of the DSM's are included in Chapter 6, p. 152, note 3.

CHAPTER 6

COGNITIVE DISORDERS

Once neglected by American medicine, the dementias and other cognitive disorders are now one of the most intensely studied syndromes in all of medicine. Perhaps because of the epidemiologic imperative, researchers and clinicians alike are turning their attention to the cognitive disorders of the elderly, and the pace of scientific advance is frenetic. While no cures are yet available, the first FDA-approved medication for the specific treatment of Alzheimer's disease is now available, and many more pharmacotherapies are in the "pipeline" of drug development. The field is moving ahead furiously, with both clinical and basic science advances shedding light on a previously quiescent corner of medicine and psychiatry.

DELIRIUM, DEMENTIA, AND OTHER COGNITIVE DISORDERS

It is estimated that up to five million Americans suffer from some form of cognitive decline.[1] The most common causes of cognitive impairment are dementia and delirium with specific amnestic syndromes and other cognitive disorders far less prevalent (see Table 6.1). While each of these conditions can present with memory failure, they often manifest themselves with different presentations and usually reflect divergent underlying pathologies. As a result, recognizing and understanding the differences between these cognitive conditions is vitally important in the clinical classification and care of patients.

Delirium is characterized by a potentially reversible alteration in one's state of consciousness accompanied by a change in cognition. Although most diagnosticians associate delirium with a typically rapid (over hours) change in consciousness, this is not always the case. In the elderly, chronic medication side effects may slowly (over days) lead to a subacute delirium sometimes referred to as a confusional state. Behavioral disturbances are commonly associated with delirium as well, but they generally recede when the underlying metabolic disturbance is reversed.

Dementia, on the other hand, is generally a slowly progressive and irreversible condition best characterized by multiple cognitive impairments

TABLE 6.1 Four classes of cognitive disorders outlined in the American Psychiatric Association's Diagnostic and Statistical Manual, IVth edition[2]

1. Dementia
2. Delirium
3. Amnestic Disorder
4. Cognitive Disorder Not Otherwise Specified

including memory difficulties. The underlying organic pathology with dementia is presumably localized or widespread permanent brain damage. In contrast to delirium, the etiology of dementia is not readily detectable, and the diagnosis is therefore commonly one of exclusion after an extensive evaluation.

Amnestic disorders are quite rare and are defined as isolated memory conditions without other cognitive impairments. Patients may have selective or broad new learning deficits or free recall difficulties in the absence of changes in consciousness or progressive dementia. In other words, amnestic disorders are not diagnosed in conjunction with delirium or dementia. However, there may be broad behavioral and vocational complications associated with the memory deficits, as the amnestic disorder may be quite disruptive of normal functioning.

Dementia, delirium, and amnestic syndromes can occur at any age in the life cycle, but they are far more common at both ends of the age spectrum and are most prevalent in the elderly. The course of illness depends on the underlying cause and may be quite variable, even within the same diagnostic category. While "acuteness" was in the past associated with "reversibility," and "chronic" was synonymous with "irreversibility," such pairing of concepts has not been demonstrated to be clinically accurate.

The prognosis of specific memory disorders is largely dependent on the underlying etiology. For instance, intoxication and withdrawal reactions are usually directly related to the offending agents and are generally of limited duration if properly managed. On the other hand, any disorder causing structural damage in the brain itself (i.e., vascular dementia) is likely to cause permanent impairment. But even when damage is permanent, many of the emotional and physical symptoms can be treated, resulting in support and actual improvement of functioning.

Psychological or behavioral changes frequently accompany the organic mental syndromes in the older person. These changes may include the onset of paranoia, decreased control over sexual or aggressive impulses, shifts in personality traits, or other emotional disturbances such as increased irritability, mood lability, social withdrawl, apathy, and overt depression. It is often difficult to determine whether these changes are caused by direct damage to the brain or by the person's emotional reaction to cognitive and other psychological changes secondary to the brain disorder. A course of treatment, both physical and psychological, often helps to clarify the diagnosis, although diagnostic "fine tuning" in this area may be impossible with our present state of knowledge (see Chapter 13 for more details).

CHANGES IN NOMENCLATURE

In the ever-evolving world of diagnostic nomenclature, perhaps the best approach to the complex subject of organic mental disorders would be a brief historical review of the classification systems. Before the twentieth century, the organic brain disorders of late life were grouped together in a category known as *organic senile dementia*. But at the turn of the century, neuropathologists examining the brain in autopsies began separating arteriosclerotic conditions from senile dementia, and both of these from neurosyphilis. Kraepelin, in emphasizing clinical description and symptomatology, described five signs of an organic brain disorder: (1) simple dementia, (2) delirium, (3) paranoid states, (4) depressed and agitated types, and (5) presbyophrenic types; but these subdivisions did not differentiate between the mental conditions themselves and the affective reactions to, and in connection with, such mental changes. In the 1950s, Roth devised a more sophisticated classification by dividing all the disorders of old age into (1) affective psychoses, (2) senile psychoses, (3) arteriosclerotic psychoses, (4) delirious states, and (5) late paraphrenia.[2] The American Psychiatric Association's *Diagnostic and Statistical Manual of Mental Disorders* (DSM) and its revisions constructed new diagnostic terminology.[3] DSM-I (1952) presented the acute and chronic brain disorders, with qualifying psychotic, neurotic, and behavioral reactions; DSM-II (1968) reversed the emphasis by describing psychotic and nonpsychotic disorders, with a single introductory remark distinguishing acute from chronic conditions. DSM-III (1980) did not divide the "organic mental disorders" into psychotic/nonpsychotic or acute/chronic forms. Instead, the DSM-III classification contained seven descriptive organic brain syndromes[4] and used the concepts of acuteness and chronicity to refer to mode of onset and duration of a disorder rather than reversibility or irreversibility of the disorder.

DSM-IIIR (1987) continued the important differentiation between a syndrome (cause unknown) and disorder (cause is known and an associated medical diagnosis is listed). Six major categories of organic mental syndromes and disorders remained, including (1) delirium and dementia, (2) amnestic syndrome and organic hallucinosis, (3) organic delusional syndrome, (4) organic personality syndrome, (5) intoxication and withdrawal and (6) organic mental syndrome not otherwise specified.

DSM-IV (1994) has come a long way in clarifying the nomenclature. The term "organic mental disorder" (formerly the title of this chapter) is no longer used because it incorrectly implied that the other mental disorders (i.e., mood disorders and schizophrenia) did not have a biologic basis. Rather, DSM-IV establishes four major classes of cognitive disorders (see Table 6.1) and then subdivides them according to underlying etiology. For instance, dementia is broadly defined as a syndrome with multiple cognitive deficits including an impairment in memory; dementia of the Alzheimer type and vascular dementia are therefore considered specific members of this class.

This classification system is meant to help clarify the confusion surrounding the multiple terms used historically to describe demented subjects. Reviewing any older textbook or medical charts, it would be easy to be quickly mired in terms such as "chronic brain syndrome," "organic brain syndrome," "senility," "presenile dementia," or even the more recent "primary degenerative dementia." Many of these terms were used to describe what we now know as dementia of the Alzheimer type, the most prevalent form of dementia in the elderly. For years, the more general terms were used interchangeably without reference to clear diagnostic classifications. In an odd turnabout over recent years, the specific diagnosis of dementia of the Alzheimer type has become much more prominent as researchers, clinicians, and the public turned their attention to the tragedies associated with this illness. As a result, the diagnosis of Alzheimer's disease is often employed more generally even when the underlying cause of the dementia is unknown or, worse yet, directly related to some other cause of dementia such as cerebrovascular disease. According to the DSM-IV classification, the general term should simply be "dementia" with specific diagnosis of dementia of the Alzheimer type as the most common subclassification.

DELIRIUM

Delirium is a fluctuating clinical state characterized by disturbances of attention, cognition, arousal, mood, and self-awareness. Delirium usually develops over a short period of time, but it can develop more insidiously, particularly when superimposed on a preexistent chronic intellectual impairment. However, since "acute brain syndrome" has been a traditional term for delirium, some clarification is warranted. "Acute" carries with it the notion of rapid onset, dramatic symptoms, and short duration—none of which is reliably present in the delirium of older people. Delirium may evolve slowly, especially if it results from systemic illness or metabolic imbalance. The term "reversible" is perhaps a more useful description; reversibility of the clinical course, even if not the cause of the brain pathology, remains the one consistent characteristic, especially if the diagnosis and treatment are applied promptly and accurately. Left untreated, however, most patients with delirium have a poor prognosis, including premature death, prolonged hospitalization, and extended symptom duration.

TABLE 6.2   Different classifications of delirium in the elderly*

1. Delirium due to general medical conditions
2. Delirium due to substance abuse
3. Delirium due to substance withdrawal
4. Delirium due to multiple etiologies
5. Delirium not otherwise specified

*See International Classification of Diseases, 10th Revision, Clinical Modification (ICD-10-CM) in the appendix for a listing of specific conditions and their associated codes.

Delirium in its more subtle forms remains a frequently undiagnosed illness. In hospitalized medical patients, it is estimated that up to 30% of the elderly show evidence of delirium. Given that the elderly may already be receiving multiple medications or have underlying cognitive changes, they are particularly prone to delirium, especially considering the added stress of hospitalization.[5]

Symptoms of Delirium

Two of the most prominent signs of delirium are the impairments in attention and disorientation. Evidence of distracted, slowed, and disorganized thinking is usually obvious, and cognitive status should be monitored carefully.[6] There is generally a fluctuating level of awareness, which may vary from mild confusion all the way to stupor or active delirium. Hallucinations may be present, particularly of the visual rather than auditory type. The person typically is disoriented or mistaking one person for another; other intellectual functions can also be impaired. Speech may be incoherent and confusion regarding day-to-day procedures or individual roles is common. Remote as well as recent memory is markedly impaired. Behaviorally, restlessness, a dazed expression, or aggressiveness may be present, and the person can appear frightened either by the disorientation or as a result of the vivid visual hallucinations. Delusions of persecution may be present. A predominant feature of delirium is disturbance of the sleep-wake cycle. Anxiety and lack of cooperativeness are other symptoms. Disturbances tend to fluctuate unpredictably in the course of a day, but the impairments are often most severe at night. There may be occasional lucid intervals. (See Table 6.3.)

While neurologic signs are inconsistent, the EEG often reveals a generalized slowing of background activity or an increase in fast activity. Signs of heightened autonomic activity (i.e., tachycardia, sweating, flushed face, dilated pupils, and elevated blood pressure) are frequent, depending on the underlying etiology of the delirium. If an infection is the suspected cause of delirium, then an examination of the cerebrospinal fluid is required to determine the underlying infectious agent. Drug screens may be helpful if the suspected cause is an exogenously administered agent.

Causes of Delirium

There are a myriad of possible causes of delirium. Most organic causes of delirium can be classified

TABLE 6.3   Contrasting clinical presentations of delirium and dementia

DELIRIUM	DEMENTIA
Rapid onset	Usually insidious onset
Marked attentional disturbance	Memory systems impaired
Confusion prominent	Consciousness intact
Fluctuating clinical course	Slower, progressive course
Agitation & behavioral symptoms	Subtle behavioral symptoms
Potentially reversible	Usually irreversible

as *metabolic, structural,* or *infectious* disturbances. For the proper diagnosis, obtaining a detailed history from an observer (family, friend, acquaintance) is essential, since the patient is unlikely to be able to supply it. Onset of the illness should be documented, with an account of preexistent disorders. Exposure to toxic substances should be carefully checked. Some of the most common causes include acute strokes or transient ischemic attacks, drug intoxication or withdrawal, exacerbations of a underlying medical illness, and postoperative stress. It should be noted, however, that nonorganic ("functional") causes of delirium such as psychotic depression, mania, and schizophrenia must also be considered. These functional causes of delirium are usually preceded by a history of psychiatric disturbances. (See Chapter 9 for a staged approach to the diagnosis of these conditions and a comprehensive tabulation of causes.)

Course of Illness and Treatment of Delirium

Delirium has a relatively brief duration, usually less than a week. One consequence of failure to identify and treat delirium is death from the underlying and undiagnosed cause; another is that the disorder may shift to a more stable dementia, and the older person then becomes a chronic patient, often in a long-term institutional care facility or nursing home. Currently, even with proper diagnosis and treatment, a high immediate death rate during delirium is common (an estimated 40% die, either from exhaustion or from accompanying physical illness); but of those who survive the immediate crisis, a fast recovery and discharge from the hospital are also common. The person who survives the crisis has a good chance of returning to the community. It appears that much delirium can result in complete recovery, although little follow-up work has been done on older recovered patients to determine whether their health is maintained. Other causes of delirium are only partially reversible, especially when there is an underlying chronic disorder.

The specific treatment for delirium is always dictated by the proper identification of the underlying etiology. When the diagnosis is rapidly established and managed appropriately, many of the symptoms of delirium are reversible, especially with respect to the infections, drug withdrawal, or iatrogenic causes. Nonetheless, several general principles for the treatment of delirious patients apply. First, under the guidance of a physician or trained nurse, a *carefully-controlled environment* should be maintained to ensure a physically secure surrounding as much as possible. The physical restlessness, disorientation, or hallucinations of a delirious patient can lead to agitated wandering and precipitate a needless fall, seriously exacerbating the already complicated situation. A good rule of thumb is to *simplify the environment* to moderate the stimuli as much as possible. The use of bed rails when available, reduced noise levels, soft lighting, night lights, limited visiting hours, and consistent caregivers are all helpful suggestions. Second, *brief but continued reassurances* can be important to the patient, especially in the brief periods of near-lucidity that punctuate the fluctuating course of the disorder. The acute medical setting can be very upsetting, even to the intellectually intact patient, so frequent explanations to patient and family are essential when dealing with a delirious patient. Third, the *nutritional and fluid status* of the patient should be rigorously observed. Because delirious patients often ignore their own needs and have often failed to do so for several days, metabolic imbalances may further complicate the clinical picture, even if they are not directly involved in the underlying pathology. With the superimposed agitation and confusion, it is easy to overlook the basics, but they are particularly important in the elderly delirious patient. Finally, while drugs are often the underlying cause of delirium and should generally be avoided if at all possible some behaviors, such as physical agitation, hallucinations, severe anxiety, or profound insomnia, do require pharmacologic intervention. When psychiatric medications are contemplated, those with the least anticholinergic properties are recommended. As always in the elderly, the lowest possible dose should be employed for the shortest possible time. Doses of haloperidol as low as 0.25 mg/day can be of help in managing delirium in the elderly (see Chapter 13 for general guidelines regarding the use of psychiatric medications).

DEMENTIA

General Observations

It is estimated that between 2 and 5% of the population over the age of 65 has some form of dementia. The incidence of dementia is strongly associated with age, so the estimates go up markedly as the age group gets older. For instance, as many as 10% of 75-year-olds may have evidence of dementia and the figure goes to 20% for those over 85.[7] Dementia of the Alzheimer type is by far the most common, but the diagnosis is uncertain clinically and remains one of exclusion. Other causes, though less frequent, are plentiful (see Table 6.4) and must be considered carefully in any initial diagnostic evaluation, especially since some of the causes are associated with potentially meaningful treatments.

Symptoms of Dementia

The hallmark of any dementia is the abnormality of short and long-term memory. There can also be associated changes in judgment, intellectual abilities, activities of daily living, and in some cases,

personality. The onset and course of dementia depends on the underlying cause and varies considerably from one cause to the next. Whereas dementia is usually considered to be irreversible, it is important to point out that as used in the DSM-IV, "dementia" is a descriptive term which is based on a series of clinical symptoms (see Table 6.5). A specific dementia may be irreversible and progressive, stable, or partly reversible depending on the cause and resultant treatment.

Memory.   Memory changes are one of the most obvious and noticeable symptoms of dementia, since memory so intimately affects interpersonal relationships with family and friends. Everyone has seen the older person whose memory for past events is clear although he or she is unable to remember who came to visit today or what happened in the news yesterday. Dementia represents a more profound and pervasive loss of memory. It is a common notion that recent memory is more vulnerable to the deteriorative process in the brain, with memories from the past remaining intact longer. This conjures up a picture of a brain filing system for memory storage, which protects its contents proportionate to the time elapsed since filing. Studies of the brain have not confirmed any such occurrence, nor are there reliable tests for remote memory that enable us to judge how accurate past reminiscences are. A more

TABLE 6.4   Selected causes of non-Alzheimer dementia

STRUCTURAL	METABOLIC	INFECTIOUS
Vascular dementia	Hypothyroidism	Tuberculosis
Parkinson's disease	Hypercalcemia	Creutzfeldt-Jacob
Lewy Body dementia	Chronic ETOH	Viral encephalitis
Pick's disease	Nutritional deficits	Neurosyphilis
Head trauma	Pernicious anemia	HIV-related dementia
Cerebellar degeneration	Folic acid deficiency	Gerstmann-Straussler
Korsakoff's dementia	Hepatic encephalopathy	
Brain tumor	Uremic encephalopathy	
Huntington's chorea	Bromide intoxication	
PSP, ALS, NPH	Respiratory encephalopathy	

TABLE 6.5 Five common signs in dementia

1. **Impairment of memory.** This is an essential feature of dementia and may involve the initial registration of stimuli in the mind, the retention of the memory that was registered or the ability to recall the memory voluntarily.
2. **Multiple disturbances of cognition.** Dementia involves more than just memory problems. Other cognitive functions impaired may include comprehension, language skills, calculation, general fund of information and the ability to learn.
3. **Impairment of executive function.** Comprehension and the ability to think abstractly and formulate decisions and actions must be checked. Inappropriate choices may be defended vehemently, and memory problems in general may be denied entirely.
4. **Disorientation.** Orientation for time, place, and person depend on the capacities for attention, perception and memory. Time is often the first sphere to be impaired, place is next, and the identities of others and of oneself are usually the last sphere to be affected.
5. **Behavioral changes.** Excessive emotional responses, blunting of feeling and response, and shallowness and inappropriate affect can be demonstrated. Emotional symptoms may be prominent throughout or variable during the course of the illness.

relevant explanation for recent memory loss is the postulation that brain damage interferes with registration of incoming stimuli and affects the ability for retention and recall. In this event, an experience that ordinarily would become a memory registers either inaccurately or not at all.

Attentional Deficits

I feel very often that Henry is simply not receiving new knowledge, that he does not retain the facts and experiences he does receive, that he is not registering visual experience. . . . On a recent trip he tried to follow the instructions of tour guides ("on your left you see . . . ,") but would look straight ahead or turn to the left long after the scene had passed.

An added factor in memory loss is the possibility of emotional influence on recall capacities. Older people may need to deny, to disremember, or to distort that which is overwhelming or too painful to face; depression and preoccupation with problems may not be noticed yet can interfere with learning and memory.

Anxiety and Denial

Judge G has been experiencing slow, progressive, organic changes but is only slightly aware of them.

He cannot face up to the degree and the implications of what is happening to him. He seems to live in a state of constant fear, inadequate to even small demands on him, forgetting everything, missing trains, and becoming confused about schedules or well-rehearsed plans. I am never sure whether the confirmation of his fears that he will do everything badly is a true mental disability or a self-fulfilling prophecy.

In some cases, the deficits are not obvious, and the clinician must think carefully whether the changes are age-related or due to an underlying dementia.

Normal versus Pathological Memory Changes

Mrs. J, a hearty, good-natured woman of 83, compensated for her waning memory in a variety of ways. She made lists of things to remember, she tied letters to be mailed to the doorknob so she would see them when she went out, and she attached her wallet and keys onto her belt or slip strap. She asked friends to call and remind her of appointments, and she made deliberate efforts to read and talk about the daily newspapers "to keep my brain active."

Is this early Alzheimer's disease or simply a normal variant of aging?

Age-Related Cognitive Decline

V. A. Kral first introduced the term *benign senescent forgetfulness* to describe the "inability of the subject to recall relatively unimportant data and parts of an experience (e.g., a name, a place, or a date). . . ." Since then, this concept has undergone numerous metamorphoses, including "age-associated memory impairment"[8] and most recently "age-related memory decline." The disorder appears to occur equally in males and females and may represent the "normal" decline of physiologic aging. However, whether there is a relationship between this form of memory impairment and eventual dementia is not yet determined. Only time and careful documentation of the progression of memory difficulties will help establish a clinical diagnosis of dementia and distinguish it from the normal memory loss associated with aging.

Disorientation is a more easily and accurately tested symptom. Disorientation about time (the day, the hour, the year) is the first major confusion to occur as a result of dementia. Loss of sense of place (where am I, what is this place, what country am I in?) is likely to follow and, last, the person loses the ability to recognize other people and eventually cannot remember who he or she is. One sees this in individuals who do not recognize themselves in the mirror, do not know their own names or the names of loved ones, and so on.

Disorientation

Six months later, Henry is now disoriented as to date and time. He is frequently confused in new surroundings . . . Last week he shocked several women when he wandered into the ladies' bathroom by mistake in the local shopping mall. He is also having increasing difficulties assisting his wife at the grocery store. Instead of dividing the shopping list in two and going down the aisles separately, he now requests simply to push the cart and accompany his wife while she manages the shopping on her own. When they happen upon friends in the store, Henry smiles politely but rarely initiates a conversation.

People react to threats to their intellectual capacities in highly individualized ways, and this is most true in the beginning phases of decline. A conspicuous feature is often the presence of a successful social facade in which everything looks normal until one begins to examine responses more carefully. Friends and relatives gradually notice small differences in physical, mental, and emotional functioning.

Other areas of higher cortical function are also impaired in dementia including *language, judgment, motor function,* and *attention*. It is worthy of note that the language disorder (*aphasia*) of dementia often differs depending on the underlying pathology. For instance, in vascular dementia, the aphasia most commonly occurs when the stroke involves known speech centers of the brain such as Broca's area. Patients with Alzheimer's disease, on the other hand, rarely display discrete aphasias without evidence of other intellectual impairments. Whereas language difficulties and geographic disorientation may be readily apparent to family and friends early in the course of illness, *errors in judgment* are often more difficult to discern.

Errors in Judgment

Ray C, a 62-year-old engineer, has experienced increasing difficulties at work with the complexities of the turbine engines for which he is responsible. He writes himself complete lists of the details and procedures of his daily routines but tells no one of his difficulties despite the inherent dangers of the job. In addition, Ray has recently been called by his local stock broker. Over the next few months, without any discussions with his wife or family, he drastically changed his formerly conservative investment strategy and traded risky securities, ultimately losing a large portion of his life savings before his increasing dementia was finally diagnosed and his financial matters were taken over by his wife.

While this clinical example may represent a sad extreme of the judgment errors displayed by patients with dementia, it is not all that uncommon.

Behavioral changes can occur at any time during the course of dementia. While drastic alterations in the person's underlying personality are relatively rare, there can be the behavioral manifestations including agitation, anxiety, depression, irritability, sleep disorder, and apathy. These changes can occur suddenly or develop gradually depending on the underlying pathology. In fact, it has been estimated that up to 50% of dementia patients suffer from depression at some point in their illness. Paranoid delusions and hallucinations can also be present. Some researchers report up to 70% of patients with dementia develop symptoms of psychosis within seven years of getting the diagnosis.[9] In some cases, the behavioral symptoms can actually precede the medical diagnosis of dementia.

Depression as Presenting Symptom

Lee M, a 70-year-old housewife, had growing problems in managing her home and has become more withdrawn socially. She would neglect to adequately stock the house with normal amounts of food and spent much of the day sitting alone. Her husband has taken on many of the responsibilities and is worried that his wife is depressed. After a visit to a local psychiatrist, she was started on a trial of antidepressant medication. The first medicine, a highly anticholinergic antidepressant, caused Lee to become severely agitated and confused, so it was discontinued. A subsequent medication indeed helped with the symptoms of social withdrawal and apathy. She was noted to be more active and appeared more alert, but she still had some mild memory difficulties. Over the next few months, Lee's memory difficulties and time disorientation became increasingly obvious and a clinical diagnosis of progressive dementia was soon established.

Physiological correlates of dementia are entirely dependent on the underlying cause of the illness. In the dementia associated with Parkinson's disease, for instance, patients often display various extrapyramidal motor symptoms (signs and symptoms of neurological disturbances) characteristic of the illness, in addition to the intellectual impairments. With vascular dementia, there may be focal neurologic symptoms (in one particular limb or muscle group) consistent with the areas of cerebral damage. Dementia of the Alzheimer's

type, on the other hand, may be diagnosed without evidence of any concurrent physiologic or motor abnormality. As the illness progresses, however, there may be associated sleep disorders, physical restlessness, incontinence, and even seizures on occasion. It is worth noting that opthalmologic problems are often suspected in the mild-to-moderately affected dementia patient because of increasing visuospatial difficulties related to the improper interpretation of visual stimuli by the brain.

Visuospatial Abnormalities

Mr. B is a 62-year-old truck driver who initially complained of trouble reading his maps while on long routes. He recently had become lost several times on a cross-country trip he had made repeatedly without difficulty over the last 10 years. When questioned, he also admitted to having increasing problems reading the morning paper. He said he just could not focus as well as in the past and that his glasses were 10 to 15 years old. On exam, however, his doctor noted that his visual acuity was unchanged. Mr. B later admitted that he was having trouble keeping a proper tally of receipts on the long trips; the "figures just never seemed to come out right anymore."

While it is always wise to investigate physical complaints, especially those with potential treatments, such as hearing and vision problems, these complaints can sometimes be seen as evidence of more generalized cognitive difficulties. For obvious reasons, it is often more acceptable for the patient to recognize a physical problem such as increased visual impairments than to admit to increasing intellectual difficulties and the possibility of an incipient dementia.

Progression of Dementia

Eventually, a leveling effect takes place as impairment increases, and in the final stages—"end-stage dementia"—the effect is one of "look alike" or sameness in response as vital basic capacities drop away. People may become completely mute or inattentive. There is also less immediate individuality of reaction when damage is sudden and massive (as with cerebrovascular accidents) rather than gradual.

When there is a clear progression in the illness over time, the general diagnosis of dementia becomes more apparent. Even so, the exact diagnosis frequently is not known until autopsy verification of the neuropathologic changes which distinguish one dementia from another.

Dementia of the Alzheimer Type

When Alois Alzheimer first described the case of a 51-year-old woman, the incidence of progressive dementia was rare at any age. Over the past century, there has been an astounding change in numbers of patients with the illness that now bears Alzheimer's name. It is currently estimated that 2.5 to 4 million individuals in the United States suffer from Alzheimer's disease. While the name used to describe this illness has frequently changed (i.e., senility, organic brain disease, presenile dementia, primary degenerative dementia, probable Alzheimer's disease and dementia of the Alzheimer type), the disease progression has remained consistent, and the total numbers of people afflicted has climbed steadily as the older population has increased and diagnostic accuracy has improved.

What is perhaps even more disturbing is that given the rapidly aging population in this country combined with the fact that our risk of getting dementia increases by approximately 1% with each year after the age of 65, there may be as many as seven to nine million victims of Alzheimer's disease by the year 2025. (At current costs and routine expenditures for the care of such patients, that would mean an estimated increase in annual expenses in this country from $100 billion to approximately $200 billion over the next several decades.) The disorder occurs more frequently in women that men, probably because of their longer life expectancy. And while accurate figures are not available for all parts of the world, it does appear that the incidence of dementia is similar throughout.

Diagnosis of Dementia of the Alzheimer Type. Since dementia of the Alzheimer type is a diagnosis of exclusion, there are no specific, clinically-acceptable diagnostic markers as of yet. Rather, the clinical diagnosis still relies on satisfying the inclusion criteria of the syndrome and falling outside the diagnostic categories of any other major illness related to cognitive impairment. In practice, dementia of the Alzheimer type makes up the vast majority of dementia cases and even represents the clinical diagnosis in 70% of cases presenting with memory disorder.[10] Even without reliable physiologic or radiologic tools, the clinical tools of medical evaluation and cognitive testing provide clinicians with an enviable rate of 80 to 90% accuracy in making a diagnosis that is later verified by autopsy criteria (see Table 6.6).[11]

Brain Pathology. More than ninety years after the original report of neurofibrillary tangles and senile plaques, such changes remain the characteristic neuropathologic findings of Alzheimer's disease. While clinical diagnostic criteria are becoming increasingly sophisticated, definitive diagnosis always awaits either autopsy or biopsy verification. The plaques and tangles are best visualized with special silver staining techniques and are found throughout the neocortex, especially in the hippocampus, frontal, parietal, and temporal lobes. The plaques are usually composed of a ß-amyloid core surrounded by a collection of dendritic processes, glial cells, and other degenerating cell parts. The neurofibrillary tangles are made up of highly insoluble paired helical filaments and microtubule-associated proteins.[12] Current research is focusing on how the large amyloid precursor protein (APP) is metabolized to create abnormal collections of the smaller ß-amyloid protein and whether the ß-amyloid itself is neurotrophic (promoting growth of brain cells) at low, physiologic concentrations or neurotoxic (causing destruction of brain cells) at higher concentrations. One outgrowth of this research has been an intensive search for measurable levels of ß-amyloid in peripheral tissues such as cerebrospinal fluid (CSF). First characterized by Seubert and

TABLE 6.6   Pathologic diagnoses given to patients diagnosed as having dementia antemortem

PATHOLOGIC DIAGNOSIS	TOTAL	(%)
Alzheimer's disease (AD)	88	45%
AD plus other	29	15%
AD plus cerebrovascular disease	25	13%
Other causes:	23	12%
Lewy Body dementia	13	7%
Cerebrovascular disease	9	5%
AD plus Parkinson's disease	8	4%
Parkinson's disease	1	0%
TOTALS	196	100%

Source: Modified from Victoroff, J., Mack, W. J., Lyness, S. A., and Chui, H. C. (1995, Oct.) Multicenter clinicopathological correlation in dementia. *American Journal of Psychiatry, 152*(10): 1476–1484. Copyright 1995, the American Psychiatric Association. Reprinted by permission.

colleagues,[13] ß-amyloid, specifically the ß-amyloid-42 that is found to predominate the extracellular amyloid plaques in Alzheimer brains, has now been documented to be reduced in the CSF of Alzheimer patients versus controls.[14] Previously, others had shown that the soluble APP, the precursor to ß-amyloid, was also reduced in the CSF of Alzheimer patients.[15] This finding suggests a reduced central clearance of ß-amyloid-42, which may in time support the suggestion that ß-amyloid-42 is preferentially deposited in the brains of subjects with Alzheimer's disease, leading to neuronal toxicity and the brain pathology associated with plaques.

Another known pathologic hallmark of Alzheimer's disease is the presence of abnormal *tau* (a structural protein important in brain cells) in neurofibrillary tangles in the brain. While tau is a constitutive microtubule protein found in a normal human brain, it is hyperphosphorylated in Alzheimer brains to generate the abnormal paired helical filaments (PHF) that make up neurofibrillary tangles.[16] This so-called *PHF-tau* is known to be hyperphosphorylated at several serine-threonine sites compared to the normal tau molecule, and CSF measures of tau have been shown to be elevated in Alzheimer CSF compared to controls.[17] Interestingly, the phosphorylation of tau

has also been connected to the biologic effects of the ß-amyloid precursor protein, at least in the laboratory, suggesting these two mechanisms of neurotoxicity may be related in the clinical disease.[18] In the meantime, both CSF assays are being developed for potential commercial applications as diagnostic measures in the evaluation of dementia patients.

Genetics of Dementia of the Alzheimer Type.
As research groups around the world focus on the etiology and genetics of AD, it is now generally accepted that the inheritance pattern for this disease or family of diseases is complex. Four different chromosomes, each with multiple loci, have been identified that confer inherited susceptibility to dementia of the Alzheimer type. For instance, multiple mutations in the gene for ß-amyloid precursor protein (APP) on chromosome 21 were initially found in a small number of the families with autosomal dominant, early-onset illness. A larger percentage of the early-onset, autosomal dominant families were found to have an inherited abnormality at the AD3 locus of chromosome 14. Subsequent research has revealed two specific gene mutations (S182 and STM2) on chromosomes 4 and 1, respectively, and these genes have now been renamed SP1 and

SP2 to simplify the nomenclature. Finally, the E4 allele of the apolipoprotein E gene (Chromosome 14) has been shown to be associated with a large proportion of late-onset, sporadic cases of Alzheimers's disease.[19]

It has long been suggested that AD is a multifaceted syndrome, and the discovery of four different genetic loci may further support this speculation. At the very least, the inheritance pattern is complicated and may instead represent a myriad of illnesses or susceptibility markers for disease if properly stimulated by as of yet unknown environmental factors. Until the direct connection between inherited abnormal genes and pathophysiology is made, however, the search continues. In the meantime, clinicians will soon have to deal with the question of genetic testing in suspected AD patients or family members at risk for developing the illness. Since the risk conferred by each marker and the time course associated with that factor is currently unknown, genetic counseling is difficult. Prospective studies with at-risk groups are needed to study the time course and likelihood of disease development as well as the interaction of various risk factors; these studies are now ongoing.

Pathology of Dementia of the Alzheimer Type.
The three characteristic pathologic changes in the brains of subjects with AD are *cell loss, extracellular amyloid plaques* and *neurofibrillary tangles.* While each of these findings can be seen in normal brain tissue, it is the extent of devastation in AD brains that leads to the diagnosis and, in turn, the clinical symptoms associated with the illness. As a result, the pathologic criteria for the diagnosis of AD are age-adjusted such that a small number of plaques and tangles are diagnostic for a 45-year-old whereas many more amyloid plaques per high power field are necessary to establish the diagnosis in persons over the age of 75.[20]

The amount of cell loss in the brains of AD patients is quite significant. Up to 40% of brain mass is lost by the time of death in end-stage AD, making the pathologic diagnosis straightforward in a typical case. The cell loss is most often characterized by the decrease in cholinergic cells and their

constituent markers such as the enzyme choline acetyl transferase.[21] Specifically, the nucleus basalis of Meynert (a small cholinergic nucleus in the basal forebrain) is usually devastated by the illness.[22] However, it should be pointed out that many other neurotransmitters (e.g., serotonin, norepinephrine and dopamine) and peptides (e.g., somatostatin) are also effected by the pathology of AD.[23] The cholinergic system may be the first, but it is certainly not the only system affected by the neuronal destruction.

On a cellular level, the ß-amyloid protein has been targeted as the most likely source of toxicity in AD, and much research has focused on the biologic function of this peptide and possible mechanism(s) of its neuronal toxicity.[24] Similarly, the function of tau, a basic building block of microtubules, has been intensively examined as it is abnormally phosphorylated in AD brains, leading to the neurofibrillary tangles characteristic of the illness.

Apolipoprotein E is known primarily for its importance in cholesterol transport in the body, but it has also been found to be associated with AD. One of the alleles, APO E4 is found more often in AD patients, while APO E2 may actually confer some protection against the illness. The fact that APO E4 binds strongly to ß-amyloid is now being investigated as a possible link to the pathophysiology of the illness.[25] Clinically, APO E4 has been found to be associated with parietal hypometabolism in cerebral glucose utilization on positron emission tomography (PET) scans both in relatives of AD patients and cognitively normal subjects who are homozygous for the E4 allele.[26] Individuals with mild cognitive impairments who do not meet criteria for dementia are also more likely to have the E4 alleles and subsequently go on to develop AD.[27]

Another suspect in the search for a pathophysiologic explanation of AD is the neuroimmune system. While few would argue a primary role for the neuroimmune system, there is growing evidence of an inflammatory response in AD which may exacerbate the process. Specifically, there are activated microglia and complement proteins in the brains of AD subjects over controls. Furthermore, there is an inverse relationship between treatment with anti-inflammatory therapies and the incidence of AD in various retrospective studies.[28] Perhaps the initiation of an inflammatory response following ß-amyloid-induced neuronal toxicity leads to a prolonged "bystander lysis" cascade and further neuronal destruction.[29]

Many other hypotheses relating to the pathophysiology of AD have been proffered in the past. Some of these theories include aluminum toxicity, slow viruses, accelerated aging and environmental toxins, but none have yet gathered the scientific weight of the aforementioned group of ß-amyloid, hyperphosphorylated tau and the secondary inflammatory response. While many researchers still assume some environmental co-conspirators in the development of AD, none have yet been convincingly elucidated, and exploratory research continues.

Subtypes of Alzheimer's Disease.   As of yet, there are no specific biologic markers by which we can separate Alzheimer's disease into subtypes. Previous attempts to distinguish subgroupings of Alzheimer's patients by age of onset, family history, or clinical symptoms have generally failed to reveal pathologically or biologically distinct entities. Such efforts continue, however, in search of a subtype in the hopes of finding a group of dementia patients more responsive to the available treatments. One recent clinical subclassification involves the presence or absence of behavioral symptoms such as depression.[30]

Lee M, the 70-year-old housewife previously misdiagnosed as having depression, was now appropriately recognized as suffering from "probable Alzheimer's disease." Her husband took over more and more of her household chores as the intellectual deficits increased. In addition, she was less inclined to socialize when friends visited and rarely accompanied her husband on his outings to town. She appeared less interested in her usual activities at home and showed few signs of pleasure, even when her grandchildren visited. During most days, she sat alone on the porch and stared aimlessly at passing

cars. After several months of this behavior, her husband again took her to a local psychiatrist for evaluation. This time, a diagnosis of dementia with secondary depression was made, and several clinical steps were taken to help alleviate her symptoms. First, a structured set of outside-the-home activities was established including regular visits to a local senior citizen facility which specialized in treating elders with cognitive difficulties. Second, a list of simple "chores" was posted for Mrs. M to carry out during the day (e.g. make bed, get paper in the morning, help feed the cat, etc.). These chores were adjusted according to her level of functioning and were maintained with the occasional help of her husband. Third, the local psychiatrist prescribed a low dose of an antidepressant with few anticholinergic side effects. While this combined regimen did not alter the slow progression of Mrs. D's memory impairments, she was more active and clearly took more enjoyment in her surroundings over the next several months.

Clinical Symptoms.   The symptoms of dementia of the Alzheimer's type are much as described earlier for dementia generally (p. 129). It is rare for a family or physician to miss the clinical presentation of Alzheimer's disease once it has reached the moderate stage where daily functions are definitely impaired. In the very early stages patients themselves are often able to "cover up" and even deny their problems without too much difficulty. In fact, the older person may pass from normal old age, with its "age-related memory loss," to dementia with no abrupt changes. (This "slippery slope" explanation is in no way meant to link the onset of dementia with the process of normal aging. Instead, the normal memory changes of aging may sometimes act as camouflage for the prodromal pathological symptoms of Alzheimer's disease, thereby obscuring the diagnosis initially.) Friends, coworkers, and relatives may notice gradual, small differences in physical, emotional, and mental functioning. If the diagnosis is not obvious, it is best to document the deficits with clinical, medical, and neuropsychological testing, if available, so that on follow-up any deterioration can be detected and quantified.

This insidious but progressive deterioration over time is characteristic of Alzheimer's disease. Perhaps as a result of the considerable publicity given to Alzheimer's disease over the last decade, it is not uncommon for cognitively intact older individuals to complain bitterly of Alzheimer-like symptoms, often with much associated anxiety and fear. While some degree of age-related memory impairment probably does exist in a certain percentage of those individuals and should be properly assessed, "Alzheimer phobia" has become an increasing diagnostic problem for many physicians and memory clinics evaluating large groups of patients. In the absence of reliable diagnostic markers, the only course of action with such individuals is careful clinical follow-up with neuropsychologic testing when appropriate.

Course of Illness.   People do not die of Alzheimer's disease *per se*. (Note: There is a move within the medical profession to list AD in the death certificate so that future generations will have documentation of the illness. Still, it is rarely the actual cause of death.) Rather, they eventually succumb to other natural causes or to illnesses associated with the decreasing self-care and self-awareness characteristic of late-stage Alzheimer's disease. Thus, they die *with* Alzheimer's disease. The life expectancy of Alzheimer patients depends on two major factors. First, how early is the diagnosis established? With the increased attention surrounding Alzheimer's disease, many more individuals are coming to medical attention sooner than they would have a decade ago; thus, the diagnosis is being made earlier in the course of the illness. Second, the duration of illness in the later stages is very much dependent on the type of medical supervision provided. Because there is usually a lack of self-awareness and proper personal hygiene in these patients, infections are common. Vigilant supervision and treatment of urinary tract infections, skin lesions, poor nutritional intake, and aspiration pneumonias can make a large difference in survival. With earlier diagnosis and careful attention to medical treatment, the life expectancy can be much longer than the four to eight years cited in many textbooks. Definite life expectancies are not known, but a more likely estimate is from 8 to 18 years.[31] How long it takes to progress from one stage of Alzheimer's disease to another (i.e., mild to moderate to severe) is currently under study at multiple research centers.

Treatment of Alzheimer's Disease.   When reviewing treatments for dementia of the Alzheimer type, one must consider two separate approaches: research and clinical. While there are some overlaps between the two approaches, there are many differences. Physicians and consumers must be very careful to distinguish between the two, especially as the underlying population is cognitively impaired and therefore vulnerable from the perspective of informed consent.

Research treatments are advancing at a rapid pace. No longer are the treatment options only involving the cholinergic replacement hypothesis. Although currently the only FDA-approved medication for AD is tacrine (Cognex), a cholinesterase inhibitor that augments the naturally occurring acetylcholine that remains in the brains of AD patients, many other medications are now being tested in research clinics around the country. In fact, there are presently over 20 medications in various stages of FDA-approved review, compared to only a handful a few years ago. These research medications range from tacrine-like, which may have fewer side effects, to nicotine-like drugs, specific muscarinic agonists, metabolic enhancers, and agents designed to impede the build-up of ß-amyloid in the brains of AD patients. As this research progresses, several groups are continuing to attempt overlapping treatments to search for synergistic combinations of these individual agents.[32] Furthermore, other therapeutic tactics are being investigated, most notably the anti-inflammatory approach where drugs are being used in an attempt to slow the body's immune response to the neuronal destruction presumably initiated by ß-amyloid toxicity.[33] To stop the neuronal toxicity before it crosses the clinical threshold, agents are also being developed to retard the buildup of ß-amyloid in the brain. This line of therapeutic drug development has been greatly aided by the introduction of a mouse model expressing excessive amyloid precursor protein[34] that opens the way for potential prophylactic drug treatment trials in the future.

The current clinical treatment of Alzheimer's patients is primarily supportive in nature. In the absence of a therapeutic agent that has real promise concerning the slowing or reversal of the cognitive impairments of the illness, the clinician is forced to treat the secondary symptoms. The treatment of associated medical illnesses has already been discussed and can make a difference in the extension of life expectancy. As for the possible "reversibility" of some dementia symptoms, actual treatment is the only reliable way to judge the reversibility of symptoms. We also wish to emphasize that advanced dementia is not necessarily the fixed condition it first appears to be. Orientation, for example, may be improved by providing direct instruction and supplying orientation aids such as lights, signs, colors, and sounds as well as clocks and calendars. Chronicity is often used as an excuse for not doing anything when there may be many treatment techniques that could comfort, support, and even greatly increase the functioning of brain-damaged individuals.

Since behavioral symptoms such as agitation, depression, sleep disorder, paranoia, and apathy are common, pharmacologic treatment with the neuroleptics, antidepressants, benzodiazepines, and other medications can prove of great value. As with all elderly subjects, and especially with Alzheimer patients who appear to be even more sensitive to the anticholinergic effects of these medications, caution must be observed to use these drugs at the lowest dose and for the shortest duration possible.

As for nonpharmacologic interventions, much can be done for the patient by suitably adjusting the environment. Structuring of a medically and socially prosthetic milieu, whether at home or in an institution, is important. Simplification, order, the balancing of care and self-care, moderation of excessive stimuli, the provision of recreational and occupational therapy, and the utilization of objects, personnel, and techniques to preserve orientation are among general procedures of value. Music therapy is a desirable approach because it does not require as much discrete intellectual attention as does drama or reading therapy. Home care services oriented toward patients with AD or other dementias can be excellent when available.

Supportive individual and/or group psychotherapy for the patient and his or her family is often advisable. Psychotherapy is most effective when heavily oriented toward affect, the experiencing of warmth, and enhanced self-esteem. Smiles, hugs, hand-holding, and a warm, supportive manner are communications to which even the most severely demented person may respond. Much repetition and little "new material" distinguish the psychotherapeutic process in treating dementia.

Cognitive therapy approaches have also been attempted with demented individuals in the early stages of their illness with some success.[35] Sensitivity to the level of mental and emotional functioning is crucial. We learned of one older man who refused to be bathed unless he was wearing his cap. A sensitive nurse learned that he was remembering from his past a caution by his mother that he would catch a cold if his head was wet. The nurse wisely let the man wear his cap in the bathtub—a form of security that comforted him in the often frightening world of mental confusion.

Family education and involvement are of great help to the older person with Alzheimer's disease or other dementias. Studies of spouses and other caregivers of AD victims have revealed that the level of depression in the nonaffected family member is also higher than would be expected in the general population. Support groups for these family members have demonstrated that increased awareness and guidance can be of great benefit both to the family members and the care of the dementia patient.

The Alzheimer's Association, founded in 1979 and based in Chicago, is a national federation of chapters from cities and towns across the country. Its goals include (1) public and professional education on dementia, (2) the building of family support groups for families with one or more members suffering from dementia, and (3) the fostering of research on dementia. The local chapters are an immense resource to those families with a loved one suffering from dementia. Chapters in areas throughout the country can be located by calling (800) 272-3900.

Vascular Dementia

Formerly called "multiinfarct dementia," *vascular dementia* is a chronic disorder that often shows an uneven and erratic downward progression, as compared to the more steady decline seen in dementia of the Alzheimer type. The disorder is associated with damage to the cerebral blood vessels through arteriosclerosis (a term that includes both *arteriosclerosis*—a hardening of the vessel wall, and *atherosclerosis*—a narrowing and closing of the vessel itself), but the exact relationship between dementia and cerebrovascular disease is difficult to assess.[36] As a result, the clinical differentiation between vascular dementia and dementia of the Alzheimer type is frequently difficult, especially as each condition is relatively common and can occur independently in the same patient.

Vascular dementia is found in middle and later life because it is a progressive disease that may remain asymptomatic until that point. Age of onset is generally between 50 and 70 years, and it is usually associated with concurrent hypertension. Although less common than Alzheimer's dementia, vascular dementia can account for up to 20% of unselected dementia cases in autopsy surveys.[37] Vascular dementia can be characterized as showing progressive cognitive decline, often with step-wise deterioration associated with new vascular incidents. The intellectual and behavioral functions affected are related to the specific areas of the brain involved in the vascular accidents. Previous attempts to separate Alzheimer's disease and vascular dementia have led to a list of 13 criteria developed by Hachinski and colleagues.[38] Follow-up clinicopathologic study has suggested that eight of the original criteria for the "Ischemic

Score" are valid (see Table 6.7). The presence of four or more of these factors is highly suggestive of vascular dementia.

Brain Pathology. The brain typically shows areas of softening with complete deterioration of cerebral tissue over a circumscribed, limited area. The damaged area may be anemic or hemorrhagic, resulting from the inadequate blood supply caused by blocked vessels. Multiple pockets of brain degeneration or "lacunes" of varying size may be visualized throughout the brain by MRI, with lesions often appearing in both grey and white matter structures, including nuclei and other subcortical areas. While individual lacunes have been described at autopsy in patients without any known cognitive impairment during life, it is believed that the accumulated effect of multiple cortical and subcortical infarcts leads to the clinical presentation of vascular dementia.

Clinical Symptoms. Early symptoms are dizziness, headaches, decreased physical and mental vigor, and vague physical complaints. Onset can be gradual or sudden, with over 50% of cases occurring acutely in the form of a sudden attack of confusion or delirium. Cases with slower onset can look much like senile dementia. There is usually a gradual intellectual loss, and impairment of memory tends to be spotty rather than complete. A person may be unable to remember anything one minute and regain total capacity the next. There may be a certain loss of insight and judgment, again in a spotty sense. Subtypes of the

TABLE 6.7   Summary of Hachinski's Ischemia criteria

1. Abrupt onset
2. Step-wise deterioration
3. Somatic complaints
4. Emotional incontinence
5. History of presence of hypertension
6. History of cerebrovascular accidents
7. Focal neurologic symptoms
8. Focal neurologic signs

illness include dementia with delirium, depression, or uncomplicated. The course is up and down rather than progressively downhill. (Note the "lucid interval" in forensic psychiatry; see Chapter 9.) The person may hallucinate and become delirious, indicating the insufficiency of cerebral circulation. Focal neurological abnormalities are often present, along with *dysarthria* (speech disturbance) and an abnormal gait with short steps. The limbs may be spastic and the reflexes brisk.

Causes of Vascular Dementia.   The causes of arteriosclerosis are still unclear, although many explanations have been offered. Lipid dysfunction, heredity, diet (especially cholesterol), smoking, environmental pollution, lack of exercise, and other elements have been held contributory. Hypertension still appears to be the most common risk factor for the development of vascular dementia, and as such, men are reported to develop this condition more than women.[39] The type of vascular dementia can be classified according to the location of the predominant lesions (i.e., basal ganglia, subcortical white matter, or cortical grey matter) and size of the vessels involved in the damaged area (i.e., small, medium, or large arteries).

Course of Illness and Treatment in Vascular Dementia.   With dementia due to cerebrovascular disease there is great diversity from person to person, even within the same person at different times, although the onset is often abrupt. An acute cerebrovascular accident causing confusion or clouding of the mental state can lead quickly to a fatal outcome or may produce an organic condition lasting as long as 10 to 15 years. The average survival of those admitted to a mental hospital has been estimated in the past to be three to four years. Vascular dementia is also common amongst those with severe vascular disease. Many die soon after the onset of the dementia symptoms, but those who survive may experience a subsidence of the problem, with varying amounts of intellectual impairment.

Early treatment of hypertension and vascular disease may prevent further progression. However, if new attacks follow, each does additional damage in a classic stepwise temporal pattern. Often the person's physical condition is worse than that seen in dementia of the Alzheimer type because of the neurological or cardiac problem; many are bedridden, at least during acute stages. Death, when it occurs, is usually from cerebrovascular accidents, arteriosclerotic heart disease, or pneumonia.

In treatment there is a greater need for special medical care because of the critical physical involvement in vascular dementia.[40] If and when remission occurs, the person is at greater risk for significant depression that can in some cases respond to pharmacologic treatment.[41] In addition, these patients can often benefit from psychotherapy, physical therapy, recreation, and all the usual therapeutic supports and services. Physical capacities are often a greater problem than intellectual capacities, although intellectual damage can be profound after massive or repeated cardiac attacks or strokes.

Binswanger's disease, another variant of cerebrovascular disease, is a slowly progressing dementia and subcortical demyelination, apparently resulting from arteriosclerosis of small arteries supplying the white matter. Generally, it occurs in persons between the ages of 50 and 65, and evidence of focal cerebral disease is always present. Diagnosis is impossible until autopsy.

Parkinson's Dementia

The exact prevalence of dementia in Parkinson's patients is not known, but estimates vary from 20% to 60%.[42] The dementia is more likely found in older subjects with more advanced motor disease. The cognitive impairments of Parkinson's disease have previously been characterized as evidence of "subcortical dementia" to denote the primary involvement of subcortical brain areas without the significant number of grey matter plaques and tangles usually associated with Alzheimer's disease.[43] The clinical changes most often observed include forgetfulness, a slowing of thought processes, altered personality, and an impaired ability to manipulate acquired knowledge.[44] While the overt motor findings of Parkinson's patients can often clearly differentiate them from the other dementias, the neuropsychological pattern is more confusing.[45] Concurrent medication, especially those with anticholinergic potency, can also pose a threat to clinical differentiation as patients with idiopathic (unknown cause) Parkinson's and Alzheimer's disease have both been shown to be especially sensitive to drug-induced confusion.[46] Furthermore, recent evidence has suggested a great deal of biochemical and neuropathologic overlap between the two conditions, which may help explain the clinical similarities often noted.[47]

The pathophysiology of Parkinson's dementia is unknown, but bilateral atrophy in frontal and temporal lobes is reported along with the characteristic pigmentation loss in the basal ganglia. There are also neurofibrillary changes in the cerebral cortex and brain stem similar to those seen in dementia of the Alzheimer type. While environmental factors may account for some of the Parkinson's syndrome, dementia is more commonly seen in Parkinson's patients without known exposure to exotic toxins. One toxin, MPTP, has been implicated in the neurodegenerative process of Parkinson's disease. Discovered during a series of studies with addicts who had mysteriously developed severe Parkinsonism while still quite young, MPTP has now provided an important animal and human model for the study of this condition and is already generating potential therapeutic candidates such as the neurotrophic gangliosides.[48]

Another line of research has focused on the Parkinsonism-dementia complex of Guam that is particularly common among the Chamorro population of the Mariana islands.[49] Parkinson's disease occurs in males two or three times more frequently than in females and accounts for some 7% of deaths among adult Chamorros. Recent investigation has revealed that the extensive brain damage in these patients may be related to the seed of the neurotoxic plant, Cycus Circinalis, which was a traditional source of food and medi-

cine for the Chamorro people before World War II.[50] The pathologic findings in this condition are similar to those found in dementia of the Alzheimer type; however, senile plaques are not generally present.

Korsakoff's Syndrome

Korsakoff's syndrome is a neurologic disorder distinguished by a profound short term memory failure. Distinct from the acute thiamine deficiency characteristic of the Wernicke-Korsakoff syndrome, the Korsakoff syndrome can develop despite an adequate nutritional intake and is associated with a chronic dementia that is resistant to treatment.[51] The primary offending agent in this syndrome is, of course, alcohol, but the principal presenting symptom is a dense amnesia for recent events. Other areas of cognition, including judgment and the ability to carry out previously learned skills, are generally much less affected by the progressive illness. This pattern of intellectual change and history of marked alcohol abuse usually allows for straightforward clinical differentiation from other major dementia syndromes.

Neuropathologically, Korsakoff's syndrome is associated with small lesions in the brain area surrounding the collections of ventricular fluids. While these changes are quite different from those found in Alzheimer, stroke, and Parkinson's dementia patients, there are some similarities suggested by reports of abnormalities of neurotransmitter metabolites in the cerebrospinal fluid of Korsakoff patients.[52] Progression of the dementia is usually halted by the cessation of drinking, but restorative therapy is currently limited to experimental studies with the various agents designed to augment endogenous neurotransmitter function.[53]

Pick's Disease

Pick's disease is a less common disorder but is clinically very similar to Alzheimer's and differentiation may be impossible until autopsy reveals the distinctive pathologic brain condition. There is usually an earlier onset (in the fourth decade), although it may occur also after age 65. General behavior is most often a lack of initiative rather than the overactivity frequently seen with the Alzheimer patient. Symptomatology includes early selective impairment of mental functioning with the memory reasonably intact except for new material. Focal signs begin to appear at a later stage (aphasia, apraxia, etc.), and eventually, the person sinks into a vegetative existence before death. The Kluver-Bucy syndrome, characterized by emotional blunting, visual agnosias, hypersexuality, and hyperorality (e.g., sucking and smacking of lips with associated food foraging) may be found early in the course of Pick's disease. The cause is unknown, but genetic factors appear relevant. The prognosis is always fatal, with survival from 2 to 15 years. The course of Pick's disease is steadily progressive, and treatment of secondary symptoms is all that can be done presently. Pathologically, the brain shows distinctive "Pick bodies" with a clear-cut and circumscribed rather than global atrophy, concentrating on the anterior portions of the frontal and temporal lobes of the brain.

Normal Pressure Hydrocephalus

Normal pressure hydrocephalus is an uncommon but treatable dementia. First described by Hakim and Adams in the 1960s, it is marked by three major symptoms—dementia, gait difficulty or apraxia, and incontinence of urine.[54] It is associated with gradual enlargement of ventricles while cerebrospinal fluid pressure remains normal. The cause is thought to be an obstruction to the absorption of spinal fluid, and the syndrome may follow a subarachnoid hemorrhage, meningitis, or previous head trauma. There is no evidence of cortical atrophy or of air over the surface of the brain when tested by a computer-assisted tomography of the head. For years, treatment consisted of shunting the cerebrospinal fluid from the ventricular space to the peritoneal space, the atrium of the heart, or the pleural cavity.[55] These surgical techniques are still in practice and retrospective studies indicate that up to 75% of patients improve at some point after the operation.[56] How-

ever, the differential diagnostic criteria for normal pressure hydrocephalus, specific surgical indications, and prognostic indicators for a successful surgical outcome remain unproved and have led some to reexamine the clinical criteria for the surgical therapeutic approach.[57]

Huntington's Disease (HD)

Huntington's disease is a hereditary disease (a single autosomal dominant gene on the short arm of chromosome 4) that usually begins in middle age but can occur in children and octogenarians. It progresses inexorably to death some 10 to 20 years following inception. Early clumsiness becomes the incessant, uncontrollable, twisting, choreiform movements associated with progressive dementia and behavioral problems.[58] The cognitive impairments of Huntington's disease are characterized by a loss of finely detailed memories as well as decreased skills in organizing and sequencing higher cortical functions and are usually distinguishable from the abnormalities seen in dementia of the Alzheimer type. Interestingly, the average performances on generalized intelligence testing does not show profound change in the early stages of Huntington's disease.[59] Biochemically, increases in dopamine activity and brain levels of various neuropeptides have been reported compared to normal controls and other psychiatric populations.[60] Neuropathologically, Huntington's disease is associated with a loss of small neurons in the striatum (a motor control center) of the brain as well as severe atrophy ("shrinkage") and gliosis (scar tissue in the brain) resulting in ventricular enlargement in the area of the caudate (another motor control center). There have been occasional reports of the coexistence of Alzheimer's disease and Huntington's disease in individual patients, but this phenomenon is considered very rare.[61]

While genetic techniques may allow us to diagnose Huntington's disease long before the clinical symptoms become apparent, even before birth, there currently is no therapeutic agent available that has proven effective in the treatment of the underlying cause of this disorder. Because of the profound psychological impact of early diagnostic markers, it is recommended that genetic counseling be performed at centers with experience with Huntington's disease patients and their families.

Creutzfeldt-Jakob Disease (CJD)

Creutzfeldt-Jakob disease is a rare progressive neurological and dementing disorder (also called *spongiform encephalopathy*) caused by "slow viruses" or prions. It is estimated that 200 Americans die annually of CJD; internationally, there is one death from CJD per million people annually. The syndrome commonly begins in the fifth or sixth decade of life. The dementia and general decline associated with CJD is usually more rapidly progressive than that of Alzheimer's disease, and death may occur within 9 to 12 months. Myoclonus, seizures, motor findings, and gross EEG abnormalities frequently develop along with a rapidly progressive dementia. Behavioral syndromes, including anxiety, mood changes, sleep disorder, fatigue and difficulty concentrating, can precede the onset of dementia. Diagnosis is usually made on the basis of the rapid clinical course but is only confirmed by pathologic findings at biopsy or autopsy.

Dementia Associated with Down Syndrome

Down syndrome is the most prevalent cause of mental retardation, accounting for 10 to 20% of all patients. Because of the increased mortality associated with Down Syndrome and other forms of mental retardation, the percentage of older retarded persons is low compared to the population at large. While diagnostic differentiation between dementia of the Alzheimer's type and the dementia of Down syndrome would never present a clinical dilemma, the clinical overlap between these two syndromes includes the occurrence of seizures or electroencephalographic changes, focal neurologic signs, and personality changes in many but not all Down syndrome patients over the age of 30 years. Anatomically, there are also pathologic similarities between the plaques and neu-rofibrillary tangles of Alzheimer's disease and Down syndrome documented for over 50 years.[62] Researchers have also demonstrated a decrease in cholinergic cells in the nucleus basalis of Meynert like that associated with Alzheimer's disease.[63] The fact that chromosome 21 is duplicated in 96% of cases with Down syndrome and is also the site of amyloid precursor protein mutations in at least some of the familial Alzheimer's disease (FAD) pedigrees makes this line of comparative research particularly interesting.[64]

POSSIBLE REVERSIBLE CAUSES OF COGNITIVE IMPAIRMENT

Because reversibility may be possible in both dementia and delirium, we have organized a list of some of the most prevalent reversible causes of these two mental impairments. (See Chapter 9 for a more comprehensive list of reversible disorders leading to delirium and dementia or both.)

Pseudodementia

The dementia associated with depression, especially depression in the elderly, is perhaps the most important of all the reversible dementias. Since antidepressant medications are currently available for this condition (see Chapter 13 for details), careful diagnostic differentiation and pharmacologic treatment is essential; yet, surveys of general dementia clinics consistently reveal a large percentage of depressed patients misdiagnosed as demented. Part of this diagnostic dilemma can be explained by the high degree of clinical overlap between these two conditions. Twenty to 50% of Alzheimer patients will, at some point in the illness, demonstrate symptoms of depression, such as social withdrawal, guilt feelings, somatic complaints, crying, weight loss, and insomnia.

Hypoxia

Congestive heart failure refers to decompensation resulting from the heart's declining capacity to pump blood. Thus oxygen, sugar, and necessary nutrients are undersupplied to the brain; a conservatively estimated 13% of acute myocardial infarctions come to medical attention primarily as confusional states. Acute myocardial infarctions can also be associated with reversible deliriums as well as postoperative coronary bypass patients. These patients are frequently found to be disoriented or delirious by the staffs of intensive care units but differ significantly from demented patients in that the course of their delirium is normally short-lived and responsive to acute treatment. Pulmonary disease such as Chronic Obstructive Pulmonary Disease (COPD) can also lead to a chronic reduction of oxygen supply to the brain and result in mental deterioration.

Malnutrition and Anemia

A large proportion of the older population of the United States is undernourished, although this is vehemently denied by some medical and lay people. Older people develop reversible brain syndromes associated with avitaminosis, pellagra,[65] and metabolic disorders. Malnourishment in older persons has both social and economic associations. Poverty forces many to go hungry, while social isolation and depression from living alone can result in persons' simply not eating regularly or well enough to maintain proper nutrition. Older people may have problems in getting to stores for shopping, especially when physical infirmities are present. Appetites may decline as a result of depression, anxiety, or illness, and the loss of teeth can interfere with eating solid foods. Therefore, even middle-class and upper-class older persons may be surprisingly malnourished.

Infection

Infection may not provoke the same level of effective bodily protection as in the young (fever, increase in blood white cell count, etc.). With infection comes fatigue and sometimes dehydration, which leave the individual vulnerable to mental confusion. Of particular concern is the acute worsening of demented patients with an oc-

cult (undetected) infection, such as that found with a silent urinary tract infection. While the underlying dementia cannot be reversed even with adequate medical attention, the precipitous decline can often be averted or reversed if the infection is treated.

Drugs and Other Toxic Substances

One of the major clues that Alzheimer's disease was related to the cholinergic system came from drug studies. When the cholinergic blocking agent scopolamine was administered to young volunteers, for instance, a temporary memory impairment was created.[66] More recently, it has been learned that older subjects in general and Alzheimer patients in particular are even more sensitive to the effects of this anticholinergic agent.[67] This discovery takes on clinical significance in light of the fact that many of the therapeutic drugs such as the antidepressant medications have marked anticholinergic properties and potentially strong antimemory effects, suggesting extreme caution when prescribing these drugs in the elderly.

With increasing use of drugs of all kinds in the medical and psychiatric management of older people, drug reactions are a significant cause of reversible disorders.[68] Attempted suicide through use of drugs or toxic materials is another factor. In addition to the above mentioned difficulties with antidepressants, barbiturates, tranquilizers, bromides, thiocyanates, gases, and hormones are not unmixed blessings; for example, both reversible and irreversible organic brain disorders can occur with use of the cortisone series. Tranquilizers may cause damage if prescribed too long; steroids can affect mood, with manic or depressive manifestations. Older people who are undernourished or who have markedly reduced kidney function or arteriosclerosis may show greater negative response to even small amounts of drugs. The pathologic brain conditions resulting from medications ordered by doctors are termed "iatrogenic" disorders, meaning they have resulted paradoxically from medical treatment itself and not from any usual physical dysfunction. Diuretics (such as the thiazides) may lead to dehydration and mental confusion. Levodopa (antiparkinsonian) and indomethacin (antiarthritic) may cause psychotic behavior.

Older people may also have exaggerated drug reactions that do not reach acute confusional proportions; examples are agitation from barbiturates or depression from tranquilizers. Such reactions can increase if the person is not clear about the side effects of various drugs and adds his or her own fears to the clinical picture. Thus tranquilized persons may become extremely depressed if they fear loss of physical powers and are not aware that this is a transitory reaction to a medication. Doctors and medical personnel owe each person an exact description of what to expect from drugs, so unnecessary emotional complications can be avoided.

Head Trauma

For people over age 65, 72% of all deaths from falls and 30% of all pedestrian fatalities are a result of head trauma. Older people are more subject than younger ones to brain injuries in any type of accident, even minor ones. Nonfatal head injuries may leave the older person severely disabled (for example, by the subdural hematomas that occur after falls resulting from weakness, lack of coordination, or alcoholism). Tumor growths (neoplasms) and brain surgery are other traumas that can impair brain functioning. Head trauma can result in delirium followed by an irreversible disorder; for example, a head injury may lead to concussion or coma, traumatic delirium, and then Korsakoff's syndrome with confabulation and fabrication.

Alcohol

Alcoholism is more common in old age than is generally recognized. Alcohol, as a central nervous system depressant, impairs intellectual functioning. Intoxication at any age results in a reversible brain syndrome. Chronic alcoholism can lead to more serious permanent cognitive

changes as described in the section on Korsakoff's syndrome (see page 141). More commonly, alcohol contributes to the clinical picture of dementia by exacerbating an underlying chronic brain syndrome or exaggerating the memory-impairing effects of other medications. Therefore, a thorough history regarding alcohol use is essential when diagnosing any elderly subject with complaints of memory problems.

Other Causes

Diabetic acidosis, liver failure, dehydration, uremia, emphysema, hypothyroidism (myxedema), brain tumors, general surgery, blindfolding during eye surgery, drastic environmental changes, and bereavements are some of the other common causes of reversible delirium or other acute exacerbations of an underlying dementia. Another cause is hypercalcemia caused by metastatic carcinoma of lung or breast, primary hyperparathyroidism, multiple myeloma, or Paget's disease. Nonketotic hyperosmolarity syndrome, in which hyperglycemia and confusion occur without any ketosis, is not an uncommon cause of reversible brain syndrome.[69] Older persons show much the same reactions as younger people to exhaustion, vitamin deficiencies, and general disease—but they are likely to be more vulnerable. In general, studies have reported that elderly patients with any underlying brain damage are more prone to the transient and reversible cognitive disorders caused by concurrent medical, social, or environmental perturbations.[70]

SUMMARY

While dementia of the Alzheimer type is by far the most common form of progressive cognitive decline, it still accounts for only 60% of the autopsy-verified cases of dementia. Many other syndromes must be considered when first evaluating a patient with progressive memory decline. Furthermore, the clinical presentations of Alzheimer and non-Alzheimer patients are sufficiently variable that great care should be taken when diagnosing and treating such patients. As more reliable diagnostic markers, including genetic tests, become available, and the pathologic mechanisms are better elucidated for each of the dementias, rapid progress should follow in the development of therapeutic and prophylactic interventions. In the meantime, many of the associated behavioral symptoms are treatable conditions and should be aggressively managed to preserve the individual's level of functioning for as long as possible (see Chapter 13 for specific medication recommendations).

A glossary of neurological deficits[71] commonly found in demented patients, especially those with vascular dementia, would include the following:

acalculia   Loss of a previously possessed facility with arithmetic calculation.

agnosia   Inability to recognize objects presented by way of one or more sensory modalities that cannot be explained by a defect in elementary sensation or a reduced level of consciousness or alertness.

agraphia   Loss of a previously possessed facility for writing.

anosognosia   The apparent unawareness of or failure to recognize one's own functional defect, for example, hemiplegia, hemianopia.

aphasia   Loss of a previously possessed facility of language comprehension or production that cannot be explained by sensory or motor defects or diffuse cerebral dysfunction.

anomic or *amnestic aphasia*   Loss of the ability to name objects.

Broca's aphasia   Loss of the ability to produce spoken and (usually) written language with comprehension retained.

Wernicke's aphasia   Loss of the ability to comprehend language, coupled with the production of inappropriate language.

apraxia   Loss of a previously possessed ability to perform skilled motor acts that cannot be explained by weakness, abnormal muscle tone, or elementary incoordination.

constructional apraxia   An acquired difficulty in drawing two-dimensional objects or forms or in producing or copying three-dimensional arrangements of forms or shapes.

confabulation   Fabrication of stories in response to questions about situations or events that are not recalled.

dysarthria   Difficulty in speech production as a result of incoordination of speech apparatus.

perseveration   Tendency to emit the same verbal or motor response again and again to varied stimuli.

SELECTED READINGS

Adolfsson, R., Gottfries, C. G., Oreland, L., et al. (1978). Reduced levels of catecholamines in brain and increased activity of MAO in platelets in Alzheimer's Disease. In Katzman, R., Terry, R. D., & Bick, K. L. (Eds), *Aging,* (vol. 17, pp. 447–481). New York: Raven Press.

Adolfsson, R., Gottfries, C. G., Ross, B. E., & Winblad, B. (1979). Changes in the brain catecholamins of patients with dementia of the Alzheimer type. *British Journal of Psychiatry, 135,* 216–223.

Aisen, P. S., & Davis, K. L. (1994). Inflammatory mechanisms in Alzheimer's disease: Implications for therapy. *American Journal of Psychiatry, 151,* 1105–1113.

Albert, M. L. (1978). Subcortical dementia. In Katzman, R., Terry, R. D., & Bick, K. L. (Eds.), *Alzheimer's disease: Senile dementia and related disorders* (pp. 173–180). New York: Raven Press.

American Psychiatric Association. (1994). *DSM-IV diagnostic and statistical manual of mental disorders.* Fourth Edition. Washington, DC: American Psychiatric Association.

Anderson, M. (1986). Normal pressure hydrocephalus. *British Medical Journal, 293,* 837–838.

Arai, H., Terjima, M., Miura, M., Higuchi, S., Muramatsu, T., Seiki, H., Takase, S., Clark, C. M., Lee, V. M. Y., Trojanowski, J. Q., & Sasaki, H. (1995). Tau in cerebrospinal fluid: A potential diagnostic marker in Alzheimer's disease. *Annals of Neurology, 38,* 649–652.

Barclay, L. L., Zemcov, A., Blass, J. P., & Sansone, J. (1985). Survival in Alzheimer's disease and vascular dementias. *Neurology, 35,* 834–840.

Bierer, L. M., Haroutunian, V., Gabriel, S., Knott, P. J., Carlin, L. S., Purohit, D. P., Perl, D. P., Schmeidler, J., Kanof, P., & Davis, K. L. (1995). Neurochemical correlates of dementia severity in Alzheimer's disease: Relative importance of the cholinergic deficits. *Journal of Neurochemistry, 64,* 749–760.

Braekhus, A., Laake, K., & Engedal, K. (1995). A low, "normal" score on the mini-mental state examination predicts development of dementia after three years. *Journal of the American Geriatrics Society, 43,* 656–661.

Breitner, J. C. S., Gau, B. A., Welsh, K. A., Plassman, B. L., McDonald, W. M., Helms, M. J., & Anthony, J. C. (1994). Inverse association of anti-inflammatory treatments and Alzheimer's disease: Initial results of a co-twin control study. *Neurology, 44,* 227–232.

Brown, P., Cathala, F., Sadowsky, D., & Gajdusek, D. C. (1979). Creutzfeldt-Jakob disease in France: II. Clinical characteristics of 124 consecutive verified cases during the decade 1968–1977. *Annals of Neurology, 6,* 430–437.

Cabelos, R., Nordberg, A., Caamano, J., Franco-Maside, A., Fernandez-Novoa, L., Gomez, M. J., Alvarex, X. A., Takeda, M., Prous, J., Nishimura, T., & Winblad, B. (1994). Molecular strategies for the first generations of antidementia drugs (I). Tacrine and related compounds. *Drugs of Today, 30*(4), 295–337.

Caine, E. D., Hunt, R. D., Weingartner, H., & Ebert, M. H. (1978). Huntington's dementia. *Archives of General Psychiatry, 35,* 377–384.

Caine, E. D., & Shoulson, I. (1983). Psychiatric syndromes in Huntington's disease. *American Journal of Psychiatry, 140,* 728–733.

Casanova, M. F., Walker, L. C., Whitehouse, P. J., & Price, D. L. (1985). Abnormalities of the nucleus basalis in Down's syndrome. *Annals of Neurology, 18,* 310–313.

Chapman, J., Bachar, O., Korczyn, A. D., Wertman, E., & Michaelson, D. M. (1988). Antibodies to cholinergic neurons in Alzheimer's disease. *Journal of Neurochemistry, 51,* 479–485.

Chan-Palay, V., & Asan, E. (1989). Alterations in catecholamine neurons of the locus coeruleus in senile dementia of the Alzheimer type and in Parkinson's disease with and without dementia and depression. *The Journal of Comparative Neurology, 287,* 373–392.

Chen, Y. C., Stern, Y., Sano, M., & Mayeux, R. (1991). Cumulative risks of developing extrapyramidal signs, psychosis, or myoclonus in the course of Alzheimer's disease. *Archives of Neurology, 48,* 1141–1143.

Chui, H. C., Mortimer, J. A., Slager, U., Zarow, C., Bondareff, W., & Webster, D. D. (1986). Pathologic correlates of dementia in Parkinson's disease. *Archives of Neurology, 43,* 991–995.

Collins, M. A. (1982). A possible neurochemical mechanism for brain and nerve damage associated with chronic alcoholism. *Trends in Pharmacological Sciences, 3,* 373–375.

Coleman, L. M., Fowler, L. L., & Williams, M. E. (1995). Use of unproven therapies by people with Alzheimer's disease. *Journal of the American Geriatrics Society, 43,* 747–750.

Corder, E. H., Saunders, A. M., Strittmatter, W. J., Schmechel, D. E., Gaskell, P. C., Small, G. W., Roses, A. D., Haines, J. L., & Pericak-Vance, M. A. (1993). Gene dose of apolipoprotein Etype 4 allele and the risk of Alzheimer's disease in late onset families. *Science, 261,* 921–923.

Crook, T. H., & Larrabee, G. J. (1988). Age associated memory impairment: diagnostic criteria and treatment strategies. *Psychopharmacology Bulletin, 24,* 509–514.

Cummings, J., Benson, D. F., & LoVerme, S. (1980). Reversible dementia. *Journal of the American Medical Association, 243,* 2434–2439.

Cummings, J. L., & Benson, F. (1984). Subcortical dementia: Review of an emerging concept. *Archives of Neurology, 41,* 874–879.

Dalton, A. J., & Crapper-McLachlan, D. R. (1986). Clinical expression of Alzheimer's disease in Down's syndrome. *Psychiatric Clinics of North America, 9,* 659–670.

Davies, P., & Mahoney, A. J. (1976). Selective loss of central cholinergic neurons in Alzheimer's disease. *Lancet, 2,* 1403–1405.

DeSmet, Y., Ruberg, M., Serdaru, M., Dubois, B., Lhermitte, F., & Agid, Y. (1982). Confusion, dementia and anticholinergics in Parkinson's disease. *Journal of Neurology, Neurosurgery and Psychiatry, 45,* 1161–1164.

Dikmen, S., Reitan, R. M., & Temkin, N. R. (1983). Neuropsychological recovery in head injury. *Archives of Neurology, 40,* 333–338.

Drachman, D. A., & Leavitt, J. (1974). Human memory and the cholinergic system. *Archives of Neurology, 30,* 113–121.

Dubois, B., Danze, F., Pillor, B., Cusimano, G., Lhermitte, F., & Agid, Y. (1987). Cholinergic-dependent cognitive deficits in Parkinson's disease. *Annals of Neurology, 22,* 26–30.

Eisdorfer, C., & Cohen, D. (1981). Management of the patient and family coping with dementing illness. *The Journal of Family Practice, 12*(5), 831–837.

Farlow, M., Ghetti, B., Benson, M. D., Farrow, J. S., VanNostrand, W. E., & Wagner, S. L. (1992). Low cerebrospinal-fluid concentrations of soluble amyloid ß-protein precursor in hereditary Alzheimer's disease. *Lancet, 340,* 453–454.

Feinberg, T., & Goodman, B. (1984). Affective illness, dementia, and pseudodementia. *Journal of Clinical Psychiatry, 45,* 99–103.

Forstl, H., Levy, R., Burns, A., Luthert, P., & Cairns, N. (1994). Disproportionate loss of noradrenergic and cholinergic neurons as cause of depression in Alzheimer's disease: a hypothesis. *Pharmacopsychiatry, 27,* 11–15.

Games, D., Adams, D., Alessandrini, R., Barbour, R., Berthelette, P., Blackwell, C., Carr, T., Clemens, J., Donaldson, T., Gillespie, F., Guido, T., Hagopian, S., Johnson-Wood, EK., Khan, K., Lee, M., Leibowitz, P., Lieberburg, I., Little, S., Masliah, EE., McConlogue, L., Montoya-Zavala, M., Mucke, L., Paganini, L., Penniman, E., Power, M., Schenk, D., Seubert, P., Snyder, B., Soriano, F., Tan, Hua., Vitale, J., Wadsworth, S., Wolozin, B., & Zhao, J. (1995). Development of neuropathology similar to Alzheimer's disease in transgenic mice overexpressing the 717V-F ß-amyloid precursor protein. *Nature, 373,* 523–528.

Geldmacher, D. S., & Whitehouse, P. J. (1996). Evaluation of dementia. *The New England Journal of Medicine, 335*(5), 330–336.

Goldstein, K. (1942). *Aftereffects of brain injuries in war and their evaluation and treatment.* New York: Grune & Stratton.

Glenner, G. G., & Wong, C. W. (1984). Alzheimer's disease: Initial report of the purification and characterization of a novel cerebrovascular amyloid protein. *Biochemical and Biophysical Research Communications, 120,* 885–890.

Greenberg, S. M., Koo, E. H., Selkoe, D. J., Qiu, W. Q., & Kosik, K. S. (1994). Secreted ß-amyloid precursor protein stimulates mitogen-activated protien kinase and enhances tau phosphorylation. *Proceedings of the National Academy of Sciences of the United States of America, 91,* 7104–7108.

Gusella, J. F., Wexler, N. S., Conneally, P. M., Naylor, S. L., Anderson, M. A., Tanzi, R. E., Watkins, P. C., Ottina, K., Wallace, M. R., Sakaguchi, A. Y., Young, A. B., Shoulson, I., Bonilla, E., & Martin, J. B. (1983). A polymorphic DNA marker genetically linked to Huntington's disease. *Nature, 306,* 234–238.

Hachinski, V. C., Iliff, L. D., Phil, M., Zilhka, E., Du Boulay, G. H., McAllister, V. L., Marshall, J., Russell, R. W. R., & Symon, L. (1975). Cerebral blood flow in dementia. *Archives of Neurology, 32,* 632–637.

Hardy, J. A., Mann, D. M. A., Wester, P., & Winblad, B. (1986). An integrative hypothesis concerning the pathogenesis and progression of Alzheimer's disease. *Neurobiology of Aging, 7,* 489–502.

Heston, L., Mastri, A., Anderson, E., White, J. (1981). Dementia of the Alzheimer type: Clinical genetics, natural history, and associated conditions. *Archives of General Psychiatry, 38,* 1085–1090.

Heyman, A., Wilkinson, W., Hurwitz, B., Schmechel, D., Sigmon, A. H., Weinberg, T., Helms, M. J., & Swift, M. (1983). Alzheimer's disease: Genetic aspects and associated clinical disorders. *Annals of Neurology, 14,* 507–515.

Jacobs, D. M., Sano, M., Dooneief, G., Marder, K., Bell, K. L., & Stern, Y. (1995). Neuropsychological detection and characterization of preclinical Alzheimer's disease. *Neurology, 45,* 957–962.

Jarvik, L. F., & Winograd, C. H. (Eds.), (1988). *Treatments for the Alzheimer patient: the long haul.* New York: Springer.

Jellinger, K. (1976). Neuropathological aspects of dementias resulting from abnormal blood and cerebrospinal fluid dynamics. *Acta Neurologica Belgica, 76,* 83–102.

Judd, B. W., Meyer, J. S., Rogers, R. L., Gandhi, S., Tanahashi, N., Mortel, K. F., & Tawaklna, T. (1986). Cognitive performance correlates with cerebrovascular impairments in multi-infarct dementia. *Journal of the American Geriatrics Society, 34,* 355–360.

Kosik, K. S., Joachim, C. L., & Selkoe, D. J. (1986). Microtubule-associated protein tau is a major antigenic component of paired helical filaments in Alzheimer disease. *Proceedings of the National Academy of Sciences of the United States of America, 83,* 4044–4048.

Leverenz, J., & Sumi, S. M. (1986). Parkinson's disease in patients with Alzheimer's disease. *Archives of Neurology, 43,* 662–664.

Levy, R., & Howard, R. (Eds.). (1995). *Developments of dementia and functional disorders in the elderly.* Stroud, Petersfield, and Hampshire, UK: Wrightson Biomedical.

Lieberman, A., Dziatolowski, M., Kuppersmith, M., Serby, M., Goodgold, A., Korein, J., & Goldstein,

M. (1979). Dementia in Parkinson's disease. *Annals of Neurology, 6,* 355–359.

Lipowski, Z. J. (1983). Transient cognitive disorders (delirium, acute confusional states) in the elderly. *American Journal of Psychiatry* 140, 1426–1436.

Lipsey, J. R., Robinson, R. G., Pearlson, G. D., Rao, K., Price, T. R. (1984). Nortriptyline treatment of post-stroke depression: A double-blind study. *Lancet I,* 297–300.

Liston, E. H., & La Rue, A. (1983). Clinical differentiation of primary degenerative and multi-infarct dementia: A critical review of the evidence. Part II: Pathological studies. *Biological Psychiatry, 18,* 1467–1484.

Manuelidis, E. E., de Figueiredo, J. M., Kim, J. H., Fritch, W. W., & Manuelidis, L. (1988). Transmission studies from blood of Alzheimer disease patients and healthy relatives. *Proceedings of the National Academy of Sciences of the United States of America, 85,* 4898–4901.

Marin, D. B., & Davis, K. L. (1995). Experimental therapeutics. In Bloom, F. E., & Kupfer, D. J. (Eds.), *Psychopharmacology: The fourth generation of progress* (pp. 1417–1426). New York: Raven Press.

Mas, J.-L., Bousser, M.-G., Lacombe, C., & Agar, N. (1985). Hyperlipidemic dementia. *Neurology, 35,* 1385–1387.

Masur, D. M., Sliwinski, M., Lipton, R. B., Blau, A. D., & Crystal, H. A. (1994). Neuropsychological prediction of dementia in the absence of dementia in healthy elderly persons. *Neurology, 44,* 1427–1432.

Matsuo, E. S., Shin, R. W., Billingsley, M. L., deVoorde, A. V., O'Connor, M., Trojanowski, J. Q., & Lee, V. M. Y. (1994). Biopsy-derived adult human brain tau is phosphorylated at many of the same sites as Alzheimer's disease paired helical filament tau. *Neuron, 13,* 989–1002.

McEntee, W. J., Mair, R. G., & Langlais, P. J. (1984). Neurochemical pathology in Korsakoff's psychosis: Implications for other cognitive disorders. *Neurology, 34,* 648–652.

McGeer, P. L., & Rogers, J. (1992). Medical hypothesis: antiinflammatory agents as a therapeutic approach to Alzheimer's disease. *Neurology, 42,* 447–449.

Mohs, R. C. (1995). Neuropsychological assessment of patients with Alzheimer's disease. In Bloom, F. E., & Kupfer, D. J. (Eds.), *Psychopharmacology: The fourth generation of progress* (pp. 1377–1388). New York: Raven Press.

Molchan, S. E., Hill, J. L., Martinez, R. A., Lawlor, B. A., Mellow, A. M., Rubinow, D. R., Bissette,

G., Nemeroff, C. B., & Sunderland, T. (1993). CSF Somatostatin in Alzheimer's disease and major depression: Relationship to hypothalamic-pituitary-adrenal axis and clinical measures. *Psychoneuroendocrinology, 18,* 509–519.

Molchan, S. E., Martinez, R. A., Hill, J. L., Weingartner, H. J., Thompson, K., Vitiello, B., & Sunderland, T. (1992). Increased cognitive sensitivity to scopolamine with age and a perspective on the scopolamine model. *Brain Research Reviews, 17,* 215–226.

Mortimer, J. A., Christensen, K. J., & Webster, D. D. (1985). Parkinsonian dementia. In Frederiks, J. A. M. (Ed.), *Handbook of clinical neurology. Vol. 2. Neurobehavioral disorders* (pp. 371–384). Amsterdam: Elsevier Science Publishers.

Mortimer, J. A., French, L. R., Hutton, J. T., & Schuman, L. M. (1985). Head injury as a risk factor for Alzheimer's disease. *Neurology, 35,* 264–267.

Motter, R., Vigo-Pelfrey, C., Kholodenko, D., Barbour, Johnson-Wood, K. Galasko, D., Chang, L., Miller, B., Clarke, C., Green, R., Olson, P. Southwick P., Wolfert, R., Munroe, B., Lieberburg, I., Seubert, P., & Schenk, D. (1995). Reduction of amyloid beta peptide[42] in the CSF of Alzheimer's patients. *Annals of Neurology, 38,* 643–648.

Mulrow, C. D., Feussner, J. R., Williams, B. C., & Vokaty, K. A. (1987). The value of clinical findings in the detection of normal pressure hydrocephalus. *Journal of Gerontology, 42,* 277–279.

Nemeroff, C. B., Youngblood, W. W., Manberg, P. J., Prange, A. J., & Kizer, J. S. (1983). Regional brain concentrations of neuropeptides in Huntington's chorea and schizophrenia. *Science, 221,* 972–975.

Nitsch, R. M., Slack, B. E., Wurtman, R. J., & Growdon, J. H. (1992). Release of Alzheimer amyloid precursor derivatives stimulated by activation of muscarinic acetylcholine receptors. *Science, 258,* 304–307.

Nordberg, A. (1993). Effect of long-term treatment with tacrine (THA) in Alzheimer's disease as visualized by PET. *Acta Neurologica Scandinavica Supplementum, 149,* 62–65.

Oakley, F., Sunderland, T., Hill, J. L., Phillips, S. L., Makehon, R., & Ebner, J. (1991). The daily activities questionnaire: A functional assessment for people with Alzheimer's disease. *Physical & Occupational Therapy in Geriatrics, 10*(2), 67–81.

O'Donnell, V. M., Pitts, W. M., & Fann, W. E. (1986). Noradrenergic and cholinergic agents in Korsakoff's syndrome. *Clinical Neuropharmacology, 9,* 65–70.

Palmer, A. M., Wilcock, G. K., Esiri, M. M., Francis, P. T., & Bowen, D. M. (1987). Monoaminergic innervation of the frontal and temporal lobes in Alzheimer's disease. *Brain Research, 401,* 231–238.

Petersen, R. C., Mokri, B., & Laws, E. R. (1985). Surgical treatment of idiopathic hydrocephalus in elderly patients. *Neurology, 35,* 307–311.

Petersen, R. C., Smith, G. E., Ivnik, R. J., Tangalos, E. G., Schaid, D. J., Thibodeau, S. N., Kokmen, E., Waring, S. C., & Kurland, L. T. (1995). Apolipoprotein E status as a predictor of the development of Alzheimer's disease in memory-impaired individual. *Journal of the American Medical Association, 273,* 1274–1278.

Post, S. J. (1995). *The moral challenge of Alzheimer disease.* Baltimore, MD: Johns Hopkins University Press.

Reding, M. J., Orto, L. A., Winter, S. W., Fortuna, I. M., Di Ponte, P., & McDowell, F. H. (1986). Antidepressant therapy after stroke. *Archives of Neurology, 43,* 763–765.

Reiman, E. M., Caselli, R. J., Lang, S. Y., Chen, K., Bandy, D., Minoshima, S., Thibodeau, S. N., & Osborne, D. (1996). Preclinical evidence of Alzheimer's disease in persons homozygous for the E4 allele for apolopoprotein E. *New England Journal of Medicine, 334,* 752–758.

Reyes, M. G., & Gibbons, S. (1985). Dementia of the Alzheimer's type and Huntington's disease. *Neurology, 35,* 273–277.

Rosen, W. G., Terry, R. D., Fuld, P. A., Katzman, R., & Peck, A. (1980). Pathological verification of ischemic score in differentiation of dementias. *Annals of Neurology, 7,* 486–488.

Sahakian, B. J., & Coull, J. T. (1993). Tetrahydroaminoacridine (THA) in Alzheimer's disease: An assessment of attentional and mnemonic function using CANTAB. *Acta Neurologica Scandinavica, Supplementum 149,* 29–35.

Salmon, D. P., Thal, L. J., Butters, N., & Heindel, W. C. (1990). Longitudinal evaluation of dementia of the Alzheimer type: A comparison of three standardized mental status examinations. *Neurology, 40,* 1225–1230.

Schaie, K. W. (1996). Normal cognitive development in adulthood. In Fillit, H., & Butler, R. N. *Cognitive decline: Strategies for prevention* (pp. 9–21). London: Greenwich Medical Media Limited.

Schlageter, N. L., Carson, R. E., & Rapoport, S. I. (1987). Examination of blood-brain barrier permeability in dementia of the Alzheimer type with [68Ga]EDTA and positron emission tomography. *Journal of Cerebral Blood Flow and Metabolism, 7,* 1–8.

Schneider, J. S., Pope, A., Simpson, K., Taggart, J., Smith, M. G., & DiStefano, L. (1992). Recovery from experimental Parkinsonism in primates with Gm1 ganglioside treatment. *Science, 256,* 843–846.

Schweber, M. (1985). A possible unitary genetic hypothesis for Alzheimer's disease and Down Syndrome. *Annals of the New York Academy of Sciences, 450,* 213–238.

Seubert, P., Vigo-Pelfrey, C., Esch, F., Lee, M., Dovey, H., Davis, D., Sinha, S., Schlossmacher, M., Whaley, J., Swindlehurst, C., McCormack, R., Wolfert, R., Selkoe, D., Leiberburg, I., & Schenk, D. (1992). Isolation and quantification of soluble Alzheimer's ß-peptide from biological fluids. *Nature, 359,* 325–327.

Sherrington, R., Rogaev, E. I., Liang, Y., Rogaeva, E. A., Levesque, G., Ikeda, M., Chi, H., Li, G., Holman, K., Tsuda, T., Mar, L., Foncin, J. F., Bruni, A. C., Montesi, M. P., Sorbi, S., Tainero, I., Pinessi, L., Nee, L., Chumakov, I., Pollen, D., Brookes, A., Sanseau, P., Polinsky, R. J., Wasco, W., DaSilva, H. A. R., Haines, J. L., Pericak-Vance, M. A., Tanzi, R. E., Roses, A. D., Fraser, P. E., Rommens, J. M., & St. George-Hyslop, P. H. (1995). Cloning of gene bearing missense mutations in early-onset familial Alzheimer's disease. *Nature, 375,* 754–760.

Small, G. W., Mazziotta, J. C., Collinis, M. T., Baxter, L. R., Phelps, M. E., Mandekern, M. A., Kaplan, A., La Rue, A., Adamson, C. F., Chang, L., Guze, B. H., Corder, E. H., Saunders, A. M., Haines, J. L., Pericak-Vance, M. A., & Poses, A. D. (1995). Apolipoprotein E type 4 allele and cerebral glucose metabolism in relatives at risk of familial Alzheimer disease. *Journal of the American Medical Association, 273,* 942–947.

Spencer, P. S., Nunn, P. B., Hugon, J., Ludolph, A. C., Ross, S. M., Roy, D. N., & Robertson, R. C. (1987). Guam amyotrophic lateral sclerosis—Parkinsonism—dementia linked to a plant excitant neurotoxin. *Science, 237,* 517–522.

St. George-Hyslop, P. H., Tanzi, R. E., Polinsky, R. J., Neve, R. L., Pollen, D., Drachman, D., Growdon, J., Cupples, L. A., Nee, L., Myers, R. H., O'Sullivan, D., Watkins, P. C., Amos, J. A., Deutsch, C. K., Bodfish, J. W., Kinsbourne, M., Feldman, R. G., Bruni, A., Amaducci, L., Foncin, J.-F., & Gusella,

J. F. (1987). Absence of duplication of chromosome 21 genes in familial and sporadic Alzheimer's disease. *Science, 238,* 664–666.

Stern, M. B., Gur, R. C., Saykin, A. J., & Hurtig, H. I. (1986). Dementia of Parkinson's disease and Alzheimer's disease: Is there a difference. *Journal of the American Geriatrics Society, 34,* 475–478.

Stern, Y., Gurland, B., Tatemichi, T. K., Tang, M. X., Wilder, D., & Mayeux, R. (1994). Influence of education and occupation on the incidence of Alzheimer's disease. *Journal of the American Medical Association, 271,* 1004–1010.

Strittmatter, W. J., Saunders, A. M., Schmechel, D., Pericak-Vance, M., Enghild, J., Salvesen, G. S., & Roses, A. D. (1993). Apolipoprotein E: high-avidity binding to ß-amyloid and increased frequency of type 4 allele in late-onset familial Alzheimer disease. *Proceedings of the National Academy of Sciences of the United States of America, 90,* 1977–1981.

Sunderland, T., Esposito, G., Molchan, S. E., Coppola, R., Jones, D. W., Gorey, J., Little, EJ. T., Bahro, M., & Weinberger, D. R. (1995). Differential cholinergic regulation in Alzheimer's patients compared to controls following chronic blockade with scopolamine: A SPECT study. *Psychopharmacology, 121,* 231–241.

Sunderland, T., Molchan, S., Lawlor, B., Martinez, R., Mellow, A., Martinson, H., Putnam, EK., & LaLonde, F. (1992). A strategy of "combination chemotherapy" in Alzheimer's disease: Rationale and preliminary results with physostigmine plus deprenyl. *International Psychogeriatrics, 4,* 291–309.

Sunderland, T., Molchan, S. E., & Zubenko, G. S. (1995). Biological markers in Alzheimer's disease. In Bloom, F. E., & Kupfer, D. J. (Eds.), *Psychopharmacology: The fourth generation of progress* (pp. 1389–1399). New York: Raven Press.

Sunderland, T., Tariot, P. N., Cohen, R. M., Weingartner, H., Mueller, E. A., & Murphy, D. L. (1987). Anticholinergic sensitivity in patients with dementia of the Alzheimer type and age-matched controls: A dose-response study. *Archives of General Psychiatry, 44,* 418–426.

Tanzi, R. E. (1995). A promising animal model of Alzheimer's disease. *New England Journal of Medicine, 332*(22), 1512–1513.

Teri, L., McCurry, S. M., Edland, S. D., Kukull, W. A., & Larson, E. B. (1995). Cognitive decline in Alzheimer's disease: A longitudinal investigation of risk factors for accelerated decline. *Gerontology: Medical Sciences 1,* M49–M55.

Thal, L. (1988). Dementia: Characteristics of a referral population and factors associated with progression. *Neurology, 38,* 1083–1090.

Thompson, T. L., Filley, C. M., Mitchell, W. D., Culig, K. M., LoVerde, M., & Byyny, R. L. (1990). Lack of efficacy of hydergine in patients with Alzheimer's disease. *New England Journal of Medicine, 323*(7), 445–448.

Van Nostrand, W. E., Wagner, S. L., Shankle, W. R., Farrow, J. S., Dick, M., Rozemuller, J. M., Kuiper, M. A., Wolters, E. C., Zimmerman, J., Cotman, C. W., & Cunningham, D. D. (1992). Decreased levels of soluble amyloid ß-protein precursor in cerebrospinal fluid of live Alzheimer disease patients. *Proceedings of the National Academy of Sciences of the United States of America, 89,* 2551–2555.

Victoroff, J., Mack, W. J., Lyness, S. A. & Chui, H. C. (1995). Multicenter clinicopathological correlations in dementia. *American Journal of Psychiatry, 152,* 1476–1484.

Vigo-Pelfrey, C., Seubert, P., Barbour, R., Blomquist, C., , Lee, M., Lee, D., Coria, F., Chang, L., Miller, B., Lieberburg, I., & Schenk, D. (1995). Elevation in microtubule-associated protein tau in the cerebrospinal fluid of patients with Alzheimer's disease. *Neurology, 45,* 788–792.

Whitehouse, P. J., Price, D. L., Struble, R. G., Clark, A. W., Coyle, J. T., DeLong, M. R. (1982). Alzheimer's disease and senile dementia: loss of neurons in the basal forebrain. *Science 215,* 1237–1239.

Yankner, B. A., & Mesulam, M. M. (1991). ß-amyloid and the pathogenesis of Alzheimer's disease. *New England Journal of Medicine, 325*(26), 1849–1857.

Zubenko, G. S., Moossy, J., & Kopp, U. (1990). Neurochemical correlates of major depression in primary dementia. *Archives of Neurology, 47,* 209–214.

Zubenko, G. S., Moossy, J., Martinez, J., Rao, G., Classen, D., Rosen, J., & Kopp, U. (1991). Neuropathologic and neurochemical correlates of psychosis in primary dementia. *Archives of Neurology, 48,* 619–624.

Zweig, R. M., Ross, C. A., Hedreen, J. C., Steele, C., Cardillo, J. E., Whitehouse, P. J., Folstein, M. F., & Price, D. L. (1988). The neuropathology of aminergic nuclei in Alzheimer's disease. *Annals of Neurology, 24,* 233–242.

ENDNOTES_____

1. Mohs, R. C. (1995). Neuropsychological assessment of patients with Alzheimer's disease. In Bloom, F. E., & Kupfer, D. J. (Eds.), *Psychopharmacology: The fourth generation of progress* (pp. 1377–1388). New York: Raven Press.

2. Paraphrenia is a diagnosis used by some investigators to apply to paranoid-hallucinative disturbances in late life. Others deny the existence of the late-life schizophrenia implied in this description.

3. We will include here a few words on the evolution of the DSMs since the changes in the five editions have been confusing to many. The American Psychiatric Association adopted an official classification of mental disorders for the United States in 1952, called the Diagnostic and Statistical Manual of Mental Disorders (DSM-I, 1952). The primary concern for this classification was to facilitate communication. The DSM-I represented a series of compromises with a conglomeration of different conceptual approaches to the area of psychopathology. Psychiatry next became concerned with differences in nomenclature across national boundaries. The second edition of the DSM (DSM-II, 1968) was formed in conjunction with the World Health Organization, and the result was intended to form the basis for international communication. Because the two editions of the DSM were designed primarily for communication purposes, their scientific quality left much to be desired. Studies concluded that the reliability of these systems was mediocre. In DSM-III (1980) the emphasis was put on enhancing the scientific value of the new classification, studying it through field trials at approximately 125 different institutions in the United States. Categories within the DSM-III are accompanied by detailed descriptions with explicit diagnostic rules. The DSM-III R was issued in order to incorporate data from new studies that revealed inconsistencies with some diagnostic criteria of DSM-III. DSM-IV was released in 1994 to further clarify the diagnostic nomenclature for clinical diagnoses based on an empirical foundation and to facilitate the communication between clinicians and researchers.

4. The organic brain syndromes are (1) delirium, (2) dementia, (3) amnestic syndrome, (4) organic hallucinosis, (5) organic personality syndrome, (6) organic delusional syndrome, (7) organic affective syndrome.

5. Lipowski, Z. J. (1983). Transient cognitive disorders (delirium, acute confusional states) in the elderly. *American Journal of Psychiatry, 140,* 1426–1436.

6. Christensen, K. J., Bettin, K. M., Jilk, K. M, Weldon, D. T., & Mach, J. R. (1996). Neuropsychological test for monitoring delirium severity in elderly patients. *American Journal of Geriatric Psychiatry, 4,* 69–76.

7. Sunderland, T., Molchan, S. E., & Zubenko, G. S. (1995). Biological markers in Alzheimer's disease. In Bloom, F. E., & Kupfer, D. J. (Eds.), *Psychopharmacology: The fourth generation of progress* (pp. 1389–1399). New York: Raven Press.

8. Crook, T. H., & Larrabee, G. J. (1988). Age associated memory impairment: Diagnostic criteria and treatment strategies. *Psychopharmacology Bulletin, 24,* 509–514.

9. Chen, Y. C., Stern, Y., Sano, M., & Mayeux, R. (1991). Cumulative risks of developing extrapyramidal signs, psychosis, or myoclonus in the course of Alzheimer's disease. *Archives of Neurology, 48,* 1141–1143.

10. Thal, L. (1988). Dementia: characteristics of a referral population and factors associated with progression. *Neurology, 38,* 1083–1090.

11. Victoroff, J., Mack, W. J., Lyness, S. A., & Chui, H. C. (1995). Multicenter clinicopathological correlations in dementia. *American Journal of Psychiatry, 152,* 1476–1484.

12. Kosik, K. S., Joachim, C. L., & Selkoe, D. J. (1986). Microtubule-associated protein tau is a major antigenic component of paired helical filaments in Alzheimer disease. *Proceedings of the National Academy of Sciences of the United States of America, 83,* 4044–4048.

13. Seubert, P., Vigo-Pelfrey, C., Esch, F., Lee, M., Dovey, H., Davis, D., Sinha, S., Schlossmacher, M., Whaley, J., Swindlehurst, C., McCormack, R., Wolfert, R., Selkoe, D., Leiberburg, I., & Schenk, D. (1992). Isolation and quantification of soluble Alzheimer's ß-peptide from biological fluids. *Nature, 359,* 325–327.

14. Motter, R., Vigo-Pelfrey, C., Kholodenko, D., Barbour, Johnson-Wood, K., Galasko, D., Chang, L., Miller, B., Clarke, C., Green, R., Olson, P., Southwick P., Wolfert, R., Munroe, B., Lieberburg, I., Seubert, P., & Schenk, D. (1995). Reduction of amyloid beta peptide[42] in the CSF of Alzheimer's patients. *Annals of Neurology, 38,* 643–648.

15. Van Nostrand, W. E., Wagner, S. L., Shankle, W. R., Farrow, J. S., Dick, M., Rozemuller, J. M.,

Kuiper, M. A., Wolters, E. C., Zimmerman, J., Cotman, C. W., & Cunningham, D. D. (1992). Decreased levels of soluble amyloid ß-protein precursor in cerebrospinal fluid of live Alzheimer disease patients. *Proceedings of the National Academy of Sciences of the United States of America, 89,* 2551–2555.

16. Matsuo, E. S., Shin, R. W., Billingsley, M. L., deVoorde, A. V., O'Connor, M., Trojanowski, J. Q., & Lee, V. M. Y. (1994). Biopsy-derived adult human brain tau is phosphorylated at many of the same sites as Alzheimer's disease paired helical filament tau. *Neuron, 13,* 989–1002.

17. Motter, R., Vigo-Pelfrey, C., Kholodenko, D., Barbour, Johnson-Wood, K. Galasko, D., Chang, L., Miller, B., Clarke, C., Green, R., Olson, P. Southwick P., Wolfert, R., Munroe, B., Lieberburg, I., Seubert, P., & Schenk, D. (1995). Reduction of amyloid beta peptide42 in the CSF of Alzheimer's patients. *Annals of Neurology, 38,* 643–648; Vigo-Pelfrey, C., Seubert, P., Barbour, R., Blomquist, C., Lee, M., Lee, D., Coria, F., Chang, L., Miller, B., Lieberburg, I., & Schenk, D. (1995). Elevation in microtubule-associated protein tau in the cerebrospinal fluid of patients with Alzheimer's disease. *Neurology, 45,* 788–792.

18. Greenberg, S. M., Koo, E. H., Selkoe, D. J., Qiu, W. Q., & Kosik, K. S. (1994). Secreted ß-amyloid precursor protein stimulates mitogen-activated protien kinase and enhances tau phosphorylation. *Proceedings of the National Academy of Sciences of the United States of America, 91,* 7104–7108.

19. Sherrington, R., Rogaev, E. I., Liang, Y., Rogaeva, E. A., Levesque, G., Ikeda, M., Chi, H., Li, G., Holman, K., Tsuda, T., Mar, L., Foncin, J. F., Bruni, A. C., Montesi, M. P., Sorbi, S., Tainero, I., Pinessi, L., Nee, L., Chumakov, I., Pollen, D., Brookes, A., Sanseau, P., Polinsky, R. J., Wasco, W., DaSilva, H. A. R., Haines, J. L., Pericak-Vance, M. A., Tanzi, R. E., Roses, A. D., Fraser, P. E., Rommens, J. M., & St. George-Hyslop, P. H. (1995). Cloning of a gene bearing missense mutations in early-onset familial Alzheimer's disease. *Nature, 375,* 754–760.

20. Mirra S. S., Heyman, A., McKeel, D., Sumi, S. M., Crain, B. J., Brownlee, L. M., Vogel, F. S., Hushes, J. P., van Belle, G., Berg, L. and participating CERAD neuropathologists (1991). The consortium to establish a registry for Alzheimer's Disease (CERAD). Part II. Standardization of the neuropathologic assessment of Alzheimer's disease. *Neurology, 41,* 479–486; McKhann, G., Drachman, D., Folstein, M., Datzman, R., Price, D., & Stadlan, E. M. (1984). Clinical diagnosis of Alzheimer's disease: report of the NINCDS-ADRDA Word Group under the auspices of the Department of Health and Human Services Task Force on Alzheimer's Disease. *Neurology, 34,* 86–101.

21. Davies, P., & Mahoney, A. J. (1976). Selective loss of central cholinergic neurons in Alzheimer's disease. *Lancet, 2,* 1403–1405.

22. Whitehouse, P. J., Price, D. L., Struble, R. G., Clark, A. W., Coyle, J. T., & DeLong, M. R. (1982). Alzheimer's disease and senile dementia: loss of neurons in the basal forebrain. *Science, 215,* 1237–1239.

23. Chan-Palay, V., & Asan, E. (1989). Alterations in catecholamine neurons of the locus coeruleus in senile dementia of the Alzheimer type and in Parkinson's disease with and without dementia and depression. *The Journal of Comparative Neurology, 287,* 373–392; Palmer, A. M., Wilcock, G. K., Esiri, M. M., Francis, P. T., & Bowen, D. M. (1987). Monoaminergic innervation of the frontal and temporal lobes in Alzheimer's disease. *Brain Research, 401,* 231–238; Zubenko, G. S., Moossy, J., Martinez, J., Rao, G., Classen, D., Rosen, J., & Kopp, U. (1991). Neuropathologic and neurochemical correlates of psychosis in primary dementia. *Archives of Neurology, 48,* 619–624; Zweig, R. M., Ross, C. A., Hedreen, J. C., Steele, C., Cardillo, J. E., Whitehouse, P. J., Folstein, M. F., & Price, D. L. (1988). The neuropathology of aminergic nuclei in Alzheimer's disease. *Annuals of Neurology, 24,* 233–242.

24. Yankner, B. A., & Mesulam, M. M. (1991). ß-amyloid and the pathogenesis of Alzheimer's disease. *New England Journal of Medicine, 325*(26), 1849–1857; Tanzi, R. E. (1995). A promising animal model of Alzheimer's disease. *New England Journal of Medicine, 332*(22), 1512–1513; Greenberg, S. M., Koo, E. H., Selkoe, D. J., Qiu, W. Q., Kosik, K. S. (1994). Secreted ß-amyloid precursor protein stimulates mitogen-activated protien kinase and enhances tau phosphorylation. *Proceedings of the National Academy of Sciences of the United States of America, 91,* 7104–7108.

25. Strittmatter, W. J., Saunders, A. M., Schmechel, D., Pericak-Vance, M., Enghild, J., Salvesen, G. S., Roses, A. D. (1993). Apolipoprotein E: high-avidity binding to ß-amyloid and increased frequency of type 4 allele in late-onset familial Alzheimer disease. *Proceedings of the National Academy of Sciences of the United States of America, 90,* 1977–1981; Corder, E. H., Saunders, A. M.,

•Strittmatter, W. J., Schmechel, D. E., Gaskell, P. C., Small, G. W., Roses, A. D., Haines, J. L., & Pericak-Vance, M. A. (1993). Gene dose of apolipoprotein Etype 4 allele and the risk of Alzheimer's disease in late onset families. *Science, 261,* 921–923; Petersen, R. C., Smith, G. E., Ivnik, R. J., Tangalos, E. G., Schaid, D. J., Thibodeau, S. N., Kokmen, E., Waring, S. C., & Kurland, L. T. (1995). Apolipoprotein E status as a predictor of the development of Alzheimer's disease in memory-impaired individual. *Journal of the American Medical Association, 273,* 1274–1278.

26. Reiman, E. M., Caselli, R. J., Lang, S. Y., Chen, K., Bandy, D., Minoshima, S., Thibodeau, S. N., & Osborne, D. (1996). Preclinical evidence of Alzheimer's disease in persons homozygous for the E4 allele for apolopoprotein E. *New England Journal of Medicine, 334,* 752–758; Small, G. W., Mazziotta, J. C., Collins, M. T., Baxter, L. R., Phelps, M. E., Mandelkern, M. A., Kaplan, A., LaRue, A., Adamson, C. F., Chang, L., Guze, B. H., Corder, E. H., Saunders, A. M., Haines, J. L., Pericak-Vance, M. A., & Roses, A. D. (1995). Apolipoprotein E type 4 allele and cerebral glucose metabolism in relatives at risk for familial Alzheimer disease. *Journal of the American Medical Association, 273,* 942–947.

27. Petersen, R. C., Smith, G. E., Ivnik, R. J., Tangalos, E. G., Schaid, D. J., Thibodeau, S. N., Kokmen, E., Waring, S. C., & Kurland, L. T. (1995). Apolipoprotein E status as a predictor of the development of Alzheimer's disease in memory-impaired individuals. *Journal of the American Medical Association, 273,* 1274–1278.

28. Breitner, J. C. S., Gau, B. A., Welsh, K. A., Plassman, B. L., McDonald, W. M., Helms, M. J., & Anthony, J. C. (1994). Inverse association of antiinflammatory treatments and Alzheimer's disease: Initial results of a co-twin control study. *Neurology, 44,* 227–232; McGeer, P. L., & Rogers, J. (1992). Medical hypothesis: Antiinflammatory agents as a therapeutic approach to Alzheimer's disease. *Neurology, 42,* 447–449.

29. McGeer, P. L., & Rogers, J. (1992). Medical hypothesis: Antiinflammatory agents as a therapeutic approach to Alzheimer's disease. *Neurology, 42,* 447–449.

30. Feinberg, T., & Goodman, B. (1984). Affective illness, dementia, and pseudodementia. *Journal of Clinical Psychiatry, 45,* 99–103.

31. Barclay, L. L., Zemcov, A., Blass, J. P., & Sansone, J. (1985). Survival in Alzheimer's disease and vascular dementias. *Neurology, 35,* 834–840.

32. Sunderland, T., Molchan, S., Lawlor, B., Martinez, R., Mellow, A., Martinson, H., Putnam, EK., & LaLonde, F. (1992). A strategy of "combination chemotherapy" in Alzheimer's disease: Rationale and preliminary results with physostigmine plus deprenyl. *International Psychogeriatrics, 4,* 291–309; Marin, D. B., & Davis, K. L. (1995). Experimental therapeutics. In Bloom, F. E., & Kupfer, D. J. (Eds.), *Psychopharmacology: The fourth generation of progress* (pp. 1417–1426). New York: Raven Press.

33. McGeer, P. L., & Rogers, J. (1992). Medical hypothesis: Antiinflammatory agents as a therapeutic approach to Alzheimer's disease. *Neurology 42,* 447–449; Aisen, P. S., & Davis, K. L. (1994). Inflammatory mechanisms in Alzheimer's disease: Implications for therapy. *American Journal of Psychiatry, 151,* 1105–1113.

34. Games, D., Adams, D., Alessandrini, R., Barbour, R., Berthelette, P., Blackwell, C., Carr, ET., Clemens, J., Donaldson, T., Gillespie, F., Guido, T., Hagopian, S., Johnson-Wood, EK., Khan, K., Lee, M., Leibowitz, P., Lieberburg, I., Little, S., Masliah, EE., McConlogue, L., Montoya-Zavala, M., Mucke, L., Paganini, L., Penniman, E., Power, M., Schenk, D., Seubert, P., Snyder, B., Soriano, F., Tan, Hua., Vitale, J., Wadsworth, S., Wolozin, B., & Zhao, J. (1995). Development of neuropathology similar to Alzheimer's disease in transgenic mice overexpressing the 717V-F ß-amyloid precursor protein. *Nature, 373,* 523–528; Teri, L., McCurry, S. M., Edland, S. D., Kukull, W. A., & Larson, E. B. (1995). Cognitive decline in Alzheimer's disease: A longitudinal investigation of risk factors for accelerated decline. *Geraotoloty: Medical Sciences, 1,* M49–M55.

35. Teri, L., McCurry, S. M., Edland, S. D., Kukull, W. A., & Larson, E. B. (1995). Cognitive decline in Alzheimer's disease: a longitudinal investigation of risk factors for accelerated decline. *Geraotoloty: Medical Sciences, 1,* M49–M55.

36. Liston, E. H., & La Rue, A. (1983). Clinical differentiation of primary degenerative and multi-infarct dementia: A critical review of the evidence. Part II: Pathological studies. *Biological Psychiatry, 18,* 1467–1484.

37. Judd, B. W., Meyer, J. S., Rogers, R. L., Gandhi, S., Tanahashi, N., Mortel, K. F., & Tawaklna, T. (1986). Cognitive performance correlates with cerebrovascular impairments in multi-infarct dementia. *Journal of the American Geriatrics Society, 34,* 355–360; Jellinger, K. (1976). Neuropathological aspects of dementias resulting from abnormal

blood and cerebrospinal fluid dynamics. *Acta Neurologica Belgica, 76,* 83–102.

38. Hachinski, V. C., Iliff, L. D., Phil, M., Zilhka, E., Du Boulay, G. H., McAllister, V. L., Marshall, J., Russell, R. W. R., & Symon, L. (1975). Cerebral blood flow in dementia. *Archives of Neurology, 32,* 632–637.

39. Judd, B. W., Meyer, J. S., Rogers, R. L., Gandhi, S., Tanahashi, N., Mortel, K. F., & Tawaklna, T. (1986). Cognitive performance correlates with cerebrovascular impairments in multi-infarct dementia. *Journal of the American Geriatrics Society, 34,* 355–360.

40. In an occasional case, surgical treatment (endarterectomy or angioplasty) is indicated in instances
of occlusive disease of the extracranial cerebrovascular supply, particularly in early and incomplete obstructions.

41. Reding, M. J., Orto, L. A., Winter, S. W., Fortuna, I. M., Di Ponte, P., & McDowell, F. H. (1986). Antidepressant therapy after stroke. *Archives of Neurology, 43,* 763–765; and Lipsey, J. R., Robinson, R. G., Pearlson, G. D., Rao, K., & Price, T. R. (1984). Nortriptyline treatment of post-stroke depression: A double-blind study. *Lancet, 1,* 297–300.

42. Lieberman, A., Dziatolowski, M., Kuppersmith, M., Serby, M., Goodgold, A., Korein, J., & Goldstein, M. (1979). Dementia in Parkinson's disease. *Annals of Neurology, 6,* 355–359; Mortimer, J. A., Christensen, K. J., & Webster, D. D. (1985). Parkinsonian dementia. In Frederiks, J. A. M. (Ed.), *Handbook of clinical neurology. Vol. 2. Neurobehavioral disorders* (pp. 371– 384). Amsterdam: Elsevier Science Publishers.

43. Albert, M. L. (1978). Subcortical dementia. In Katzman, R., Terry, R. D., & Bick, K. L. (Eds.), *Alzheimer's disease: Senile dementia and related disorders* (pp. 173–180). New York: Raven Press.

44. Cummings, J. L., & Benson, F. (1984). Subcortical dementia: Review of an emerging concept. *Archives of Neurology, 41,* 874–879.

45. Stern, M. B., Gur, R. C., Saykin, A. J., & Hurtig, H. I. (1986). Dementia of Parkinson's disease and Alzheimer's disease: Is there a difference? *Journal of the American Geriatrics Society, 34,* 475–478.

46. DeSmet, Y., Ruberg, M., Serdaru, M., Dubois, B., Lhermitte, F., & Agid, Y. (1982). Confusion, dementia and anticholinergics in Parkinson's disease. *Journal of Neurology, Neurosurgery and Psychiatry, 45,* 1161–1164; Sunderland, T., Tariot, P. N., Cohen, R. M., Weingartner, H., Mueller, E. A., &

Murphy, D. L. (1987). Anticholinergic sensitivity in patients with dementia of the Alzheimer type and age-matched controls: A dose-response study. *Archives of General Psychiatry, 44,* 418–426.

47. Chui, H. C., Mortimer, J. A., Slager, U., Zarow, C., Bondareff, W., & Webster, D. D. (1986). Pathologic correlates of dementia in Parkinson's disease. *Archives of Neurology, 43,* 991–995; and Leverenz, J., & Sumi, S. M. (1986). Parkinson's disease in patients with Alzheimer's disease. *Archives of Neurology, 43,* 662–664.

48. Schneider, J. S., Pope, A., Simpson, K., Taggart, J., Smith, M. G., & DiStefano, L. (1992). Recovery from experimental Parkinsonism in primates with Gm1 ganglioside treatment. *Science, 256,* 843–846.

49. Hirano, A., Kurland, L. T., Krooth, R. S., & Lassell, S. (1961). Parkinsonism-dementia complex on Guam, II. Pathological features, *Brain, 84,* 662–679.

50. Spencer, P. S., Nunn, P. B., Hugon, J., Ludolph, A. C., Ross, S. M., Roy, D. N., & Robertson, R. C. (1987). Guam amyotrophic lateral sclerosis—Parkinsonism—dementia linked to a plant excitant neurotoxin. *Science, 237,* 517–522.

51. O'Donnell, V. M., Pitts, W. M., & Fann, W. E. (1986). Noradrenergic and cholinergic agents in Korsakoff's syndrome. *Clinical Neuropharmacology, 9,* 65–70.

52. McEntee, W. J., Mair, R. G., & Langlais, P. J. (1984). Neurochemical pathology in Korsakoff's psychosis: Implications for other cognitive disorders. *Neurology, 34,* 648–652.

53. O'Donnell, et. al. (1986).

54. Hakim, S., & Adams, R. D. (1965). The special clinical problem of symptomatic hydrocephalus with normal cerebrospinal fluid pressure: Observations on cerebrospinal fluid hydrodynamics. *Journal of the Neurological Sciences, 2,* 307–327.

55. Adams, R. D., Fisher, C. M., Hakim, S., Ojemann, R. G., & Sweet, W. H. (1965). Symptomatic occult hydrocephalus with "normal" cerebrospinal fluid pressure: a treatable syndrome. *New England Journal of Medicine, 273,* 117–126.

56. Petersen, R. C., Mokri, B., & Laws, E. R. (1985). Surgical treatment of idiopathic hydrocephalus in elderly patients. *Neurology, 35,* 307–311.

57. Anderson, M. (1986). Normal pressure hydrocephalus. *British Medical Journal, 293,* 837–838; Mulrow, C. D., Feussner, J. R., Williams, B. C., & Vokaty, K. A. (1987). The value of clinical findings in the detection of normal pressure hydrocephalus. *Journal of Gerontology, 42,* 277–279.

58. Caine, E. D., & Shoulson, I. (1983). Psychiatric syndromes in Huntington's disease. *American Journal of Psychiatry, 140,* 728–733.

59. Caine, E. D., Hunt, R. D., Weingartner, H., & Ebert, M. H. (1978). Huntington's dementia. *Archives of General Psychiatry, 35,* 377–384.

60. Nemeroff, C. B., Youngblood, W. W., Manberg, P. J., Prange, A. J., & Kizer, J. S. (1983). Regional brain concentrations of neuropeptides in Huntington's chorea and schizophrenia. *Science, 221,* 972–975.

61. Reyes, M. G., & Gibbons, S. (1985). Dementia of the Alzheimer's type and Huntington's disease. *Neurology, 35,* 273–277.

62. Dalton, A. J., & Crapper-McLachlan, D. R. (1986). Clinical expression of Alzheimer's disease in Down's syndrome. *Psychiatric Clinics of North America, 9,* 659–670.

63. Casanova, M. F., Walker, L. C., Whitehouse, P. J., & Price, D. L. (1985). Abnormalities of the nucleus basalis in Down's syndrome. *Annals of Neurology, 18,* 310–313.

64. St. George-Hyslop, et al. (1987).

65. Pellagra is a disease characterized by mental, neurological, cutaneous, mucous membrane, and gastrointestinal symptoms. It is caused by a severe deficiency of niacin (nicotinic acid) or its amide (niacinamide) along with their amino acid precursor, tryptophan. As late as 1945, H. A. Meyersburg reported cases of brain syndrome from pellagra in older people in his work (See Meyersburg, H. A. [1945]. Senile psychosis and pellagra: A report of two cases, *New England Journal of Medicine, 233,* 173–176).

66. Drachman, D. A., & Leavitt, J. (1974). Human memory and the cholinergic system. *Archives of Neurology, 30,* 113–121.

67. Sunderland, T., Tariot, P. N., Cohen, R. M., Weingartner, H., Mueller, E. A., & Murphy, D. L. (1987). Anticholinergic sensitivity in patients with dementia of the Alzheimer type and age-matched controls: A dose-response study. *Archives of General Psychiatry, 44,* 418–426.

68. Lipowski, Z. J. (1983). Transient cognitive disorders (delirium, acute confusional states) in the elderly. *American Journal Psychiatry, 140,* 1426–1436.

69. Cummings, J., Benson, D. F., & LoVerme, S. (1980). Reversible dementia. *Journal of the American Medical Association, 243,* 2434–2439.

70. Lipowski, et al. (1983).

71. Modified from American Psychiatric Association (1988). *A psychiatric glossary,* Sixth edition. Washington, DC: American Psychiatric Association.

CHAPTER 7

SPECIAL CONCERNS: RACE AND ETHNICITY, OLDER WOMEN AND GENDER ISSUES, CRIME, ALCOHOLISM, DEAFNESS, BLINDNESS, AND SEXUALITY

How do race and ethnicity affect the lives of older people? Are older women at greater risk in old age because they are female? Do alcoholics live long enough to become old? Are there "geriatric criminals"? Are older people interested in and capable of sexuality? In this chapter we consider some of the important human issues that are part of old age.

THE IMPACT OF RACE AND ETHNICITY ON MENTAL HEALTH CARE[1]

Older people are a multiracial and multicultural group. Many are immigrants from other countries. Others, namely older African Americans, had ancestors who were brought to the United States by force. In 1995 more than 4.8 million, or almost 15% of the older population, were members of a minority group. Minority groups are generally defined as those who have suffered subordination and discrimination as a result of race or ethnicity, especially African Americans, Hispanics, Native Americans, and Asian and Pacific Island Americans. Other ethnic groups have also been or are still subject to prejudice—Poles, Greeks, Arabs,

and Jews, among others. Of the 33.5 million people aged 65 and older in 1995, 89.6% were white; 8.1% were black; 4.5% of Hispanic origin (this category is not exclusive, that is the Census Bureau has included people of Hispanic origin in other groups as well, especially the white and black groups); 1.8% Asian and Pacific Islanders; and 0.4% American Indian, Eskimo, and Aleut.[2] By 2050, 33% of the older population is likely to be non-white or Hispanic.[3]

A nation as diverse as the United States would greatly benefit from transcultural studies of the older persons within its own borders. Different cultural and ethnic groups have different conceptions of the life cycle and different attitudes toward use of formal as well as family help; each has been treated somewhat differently by the majority culture. Research on the minority elderly has become active since the 1960s, with most attention focused on African Americans and, to a lesser extent, Hispanics, particularly Southwest Mexican Americans. Since the 1980s, other minority groups have begun to receive attention as well. National ethnic organizations began forming in the 1970s, stimulated by the absence of focus on minority elderly in the initial planning phase of the 1971 White House Conference on Aging. The National Caucus and Center on the Black Aged was begun and funded in 1972 by the Administration on Aging. This was followed by the National Indian Council on Aging in 1976, the Asociacion Nacional Por Personas Mayores in 1975, the National Hispanic Council on Aging in 1978, and the National Pacific/Asian Resource Center on Aging in 1979. All of these organizations received support from the Administration on Aging and have been active in advocacy, promotion of research and training in minority aging, and creation of public and professional awareness of ethnic and minority aging. Each national group held its own mini Conference at the 1981 White House Conference on Aging. Individual states have been slower to develop their own state-level responses to minority aging, although such development is likely to occur in the future. Certain religious groups, such as Jews and Mormons, have formal associations and provide an array of special services to their own and other elderly.

Two major and distinctly separate issues are evident regarding minority older people. First are the unique cultural elements found in each minority group. These have bearing on the lives of the group's older members. Second are the effects on older persons of living as minority members in a majority culture. We would like to touch on both of these issues, even though most available research centers around vital statistics and the social and economic effects of various racial and ethnic groups' experience as minorities rather than the cultural life of individual groups. Much more needs to be done to recognize the varied and distinctive lifestyles within and between the various cultural groups in the United States. Jackson has called such studies *ethnogerontology,* namely "the study of the causes and the consequences of race, national origin, and culture on individual and population aging."[4] In the strictest sense, all Americans are ethnics. Our present focus on the more disadvantaged ethnic minorities is understand-

able. However, it is expected that study will broaden to include European and other ethnic groups as well, particularly Germans, Scandinavians, English, Polish, Irish, and Italians. Ethnic variety should be preserved, protected, and used as an important consideration in physical and mental health diagnosis and treatment.

In Chapter 1 we presented some of the general facts and figures of minority old age in America. This chapter deals with the direct and indirect effects of race and ethnicity on the mental health needs and care of older people.

Mental Health Care for Minority Elderly

In comparison with the overall population, older persons are underserved by the mental health system, with minority elderly the most severely underserved. Indifference and neglect, as well as overt and covert racial prejudice and discrimination, are operating to produce this unenviable inequity.

African American Elderly

A current debate surrounding African American aging is whether elderly blacks face a "double jeopardy," namely a wider disparity between blacks and whites than existed earlier, due to the combined effects of age and race. Two major factors have influenced scholars to question the validity of this debate. The first is the fact that income disparity between blacks and whites is actually less in old age than earlier, and the second is that in very late old age some studies have shown that blacks have a longer life expectancy than whites. However, both of these issues are complex, uncertain, and controversial. Retirement income tends to represent a dramatic drop for many whites, with less of a drop for blacks, reflecting earlier income disparities. Also wealth, as represented by income and resources outside of pensions and governmental subsidies, is higher for whites but is not counted in income figures. As for longer life expectancy, the so-called advantage of blacks, if true, seems a direct result of a disadvantage of greater mortality earlier in life, leaving the strongest to survive into old age.

Two of the most obvious effects of discrimination have been the overrepresentation of African American elderly on Supplemental Security Income and their shorter life expectancies at birth. Whites often have Social Security and private pensions, while many jobs open to blacks were never covered or only relatively recently have been covered by Social Security. And since blacks, especially men, are more likely to die at a younger age, they may never become eligible for retirement benefits even if they have accumulated them.

Outpatient Mental Health Care. It is a widely acknowledged fact that most mental health professionals, products of white middle-class America, are unable to bridge the cultural chasm between themselves and poverty-stricken black people in the context of mental health work. Diagnosis and treatment are based on traditional psychiatric concepts of mental health and mental disorder. These in turn hinge on white middle-class norms and values. Effective mental health workers must be able not only to identify with the culture of their clients, but also to distinguish between the effects of societal pathology and individual psychopathology.

In a classic analysis of black–white relations, psychoanalyst Franz Fanon wrote that any study of the psychology of a black person must include (1) a psychoanalytic interpretation of the actual life experience of the black man and woman and (2) a psychoanalytic interpretation of the Negro myth as it has been formulated by whites.[5] Grier and Cobbs made similar points.[6] A body of theory and treatment techniques designed especially for the African American population has been slow in emerging. Dr. William A. Reid emphasizes that too many mental health workers arbitrarily assign individual responsibility for misfortune rather than considering social factors.[7]

Outpatient mental health care for the African American aged has been inadequate in general. Hospital emergency rooms give minimal attention to psychiatric problems, particularly if a minority patient is both old and poor. Day hospitals and day-care center accommodations are rare. These services receive little priority in municipal and county hospital budgets, and private sponsorship is difficult to obtain.

Institutional Care. The African American family has been the subject of wide speculation, but until relatively recently, only minimal rigorous study. Two extreme views have persisted. The first is the idealistic position that most older blacks are cared for by loving, extended family networks. The second and opposite view is that poverty-stricken black elderly have been abandoned as a result of the disorganization and disintegration of the family. The reality falls somewhere in between, with families doing their best as long as they can, depending on their circumstances. Cultural institutions, such as African American churches, continue to be stabilizing forces and resources in the mental health care of the elderly, providing many older persons with social participation, prestige, and power.

A long-held view is that the African American community does not readily seek admission of its older people for institutional care. Some studies suggest that in black families the older person is more respected and considered less of a burden than in white families. Some have postulated that a wider range of behavior is tolerated in minority communities. But others believe that the tendency to avoid or delay institutionalization represents a basic distrust of institutions because of previous life experiences. What is readily apparent to all is the lack of institutional facilities for the older African American. Families simply have few places to turn to for institutional help with their elderly.

Many African American elderly simply cannot afford nursing home care, a particular problem in states with weak Medicaid provisions. African American-owned facilities having difficulty in meeting health, fire, and building standards may be closed rather than given assistance and encouragement.

The integration of public psychiatric hospitals has occurred relatively recently in most cases. St.

Elizabeth's Hospital in Washington, DC, one of the well-known hospitals in the nation, was segregated until 1955; the hospitals in North Carolina were segregated until 1966. Segregated black hospitals were underfinanced and consequently in worse condition than the already inadequate white hospitals. With integration and the sharing of facilities, blacks fared somewhat better than before in terms of physical accommodations, but it is doubtful that their medical or psychiatric treatment has improved, since custodial care rather than active treatment is still customary.

Lifelong attitudes and conditioning often persist in old age, even after mental impairment occurs. In one integrated hospital, an aged white woman with strong racial prejudices managed, in spite of brain damage and incoherence, consistently to call African American staff members, including her psychiatrist, "niggers." One can occasionally see older African American patients waiting on white patients by performing personal services, while the whites give orders. There may be rebellion among older African Americans; in one case an elderly African American man spent his last years giving verbal vent to his murderous feelings toward whites. His anger had been stored up for a lifetime, released only when his demented mental state caused him to lose both caution and control. Older African Americans may share a belief that African American health professionals are inferior. It is not unusual in an integrated institution for them to prefer white health care personnel. Conversely, other African American elderly feel more comfortable if their care is given by persons of their own race.

The specific psychological and cultural implications of African American old age are a growing subject of investigation. There are differences between rural and urban dwellers, Northerners and Southerners, upper- and middle-income citizens versus those with lower incomes, as well as the various age groups and professions. For example, the concept of retirement may be meaningless for those black elderly who are ineligible for adequate pensions and cannot afford to stop work. Thus "retirement crisis" does not apply to people who are in a "survival crisis." On the other hand, those who receive some form of stable pension, however small, may find old age more secure than an earlier life of sporadic, low-paying jobs in the labor market.[8] The task of future research is to capture the differences as well as the similarities within minority groups themselves.

Hispanic (or Latino) Elderly

Racial discrimination has had many of the same social and economic effects on the Hispanic elderly as on the African American elderly. Both groups are disproportionately poor and poorly served by mental health systems. The reasons for this underutilization of services by the Hispanic population is a complex combination of the following factors: discrimination, linguistic and cultural differences, lack of outreach, discriminatory policies of health agencies, discrimination due to immigration status, and factors due to class and level of education.

Hispanics are a very heterogeneous group, with origins in 26 nations, according to federal definition. The largest groups are of Mexican origin and ancestry in the southwest, Puerto Ricans in New York City and Cubans in Florida. Other growing populations come from the Dominican Republic, Columbia, Ecuador, El Salvador, and other Central and South American countries.

Hispanics are not culturally or linguistically heterogeneous. Although the majority of Hispanics are Roman Catholic, there are a growing number of Protestants and many Hispanics of other faiths, including traditional indigenous cultures. There are also differences in customs and beliefs between and within regions. Inability to speak English is a common difficulty among Hispanics; however, many Hispanics speak English only, and many do not speak Spanish as a first language, or at all. Other languages spoken by Hispanics are other European languages, such as Portuguese, Native American languages, such as Quechua, Mayan, Aymara and Guarani, and Creole languages, such as Garifuna, spoken in coastal Honduras.[9]

The accuracy and scope of health statistics are extremely inadequate with regard to the Hispanic population in the United States. The Hispanic population seems to have an average life expectancy near that of the non-Hispanic white population, despite a weaker socio-economic profile. This may be due to extreme inaccuracies in reporting on death certificates, thought to be greater than for African Americans. A major factor may be selective immigration (recent research indicates that immigrants from any group are healthier than non-immigrants), and the long life expectancy of economically advantaged groups, such as Cuban Americans. Similarly, older Hispanics have low rates of heart disease and major cancers. The reasons for this are also uncertain. Older Hispanics, however do have death rates of double the non-Hispanic white population from diabetes, chronic liver disease and cirrhosis, and high rates of mortality for these diseases. In addition, older Hispanics need more help with activities of daily living (ADLs) and instrumental activities of daily living (IADLs) than non-Hispanic whites.[10]

A 1988 Commonwealth Commission national survey of the three largest groups of elderly Hispanics—Mexican Americans, Puerto Ricans, and Cubans—found the following:

- Four in ten Hispanic elderly do not speak English.
- Three out of four have an eighth-grade education or less, twice the proportion of all elderly.
- Nearly one-third live with children, siblings, or others; many are unable to afford living alone.
- The poverty rate of elderly Hispanics is nearly twice that of all elderly (22% compared to 12%). The average Hispanic older person lives on less than $104 per week.
- Many are not eligible for Social Security or private pensions. Seventy-seven percent receive Social Security, compared to 92% of all elderly, and 19% receive private pensions, compared to 45% of all elderly.
- The Hispanic elderly are more dependent on Supplemental Security Income (SSI) and Med-

icaid. However, 55% of those elderly Hispanics who are eligible for SSI do not receive it. Of those eligible, 26% were not aware of SSI or their eligibility.
- They have greater physical handicaps and a greater need for long-term care services than do elderly people in general.
- They rely heavily on their families for long-term and other care.
- Elderly Mexican Americans have the highest rate of poverty among Hispanic subgroups, while elderly Puerto Ricans report the worst health status.
- The majority of elderly Mexican Americans were born in the United States (58%) while 98% of both Cuban and Puerto Rican elderly were born in Cuba or Puerto Rico.[11]

Torres-Gil has outlined the special challenge the elderly Hispanics present, now and in future years.[12]

Native American Elderly

The 116,153 Native Americans age 65 or older in 1990 represents the smallest elderly minority group in the United States. Native Americans have the youngest median age of the principal minority groups in the U.S.—16.8 years—and the smallest percentage of adults living to age 65—only 5.4%.[13]

As members of approximately 500 nations, tribes, bands, or Alaskan native villages, Native Americans are extremely diverse culturally and linguistically. Native Americans are the most rural of the major minority populations. However, partly as the result of government policy encouraging resettlement and as an attempt to escape poverty on the reservations, Native Americans have become increasingly urban. While 59% of all Native Americans, including elders, live in urban areas, 22% live on the 314 reservations and land trusts.[14] The increasing urbanization of Native Americans can not only create a sense of alienation for elders, but puts them out of reach of the Indian Health Service and tribal services. On the other hand, integration with the larger community has its advantages.

28.5% of Native Americans age 60 and older lived with incomes below the official poverty level in 1990, compared to only 9.8% of non-Hispanic whites aged 60 and older. 58.5% of Native Americans age 60 or older lived with incomes of only twice the poverty level or less, compared to 31.6% of older whites. 38% of rural Native Americans age 65 and older lived in poverty. In addition, 30% of Native American elders in rural areas had no vehicle available, 31% had no telephone, and 24% spoke English poorly.[15]

Health research about Native American older people is highly inadequate. However, a landmark study by National Indian Council on Aging (1981) found that at age 45 reservation-dwelling Native Americans had the health characteristics of the average American at age 65, and urban-dwelling Native Americans had these characteristics at age 55. Lowered age eligibility for services is now available through Title VI of the Older Americans Act, but only on reservations.

Native American older people have less heart disease and cancer than the general population, because they do not live long enough on average to develop them. However, they do have the poorest five-year survival rate for cancer of the major minority groups. They also have high death rates for pneumonia and influenza, diabetes mellitus, accidents, chronic liver disease, cirrhosis and other alcohol related deaths, and septicemia.[16] They also suffer from high rates of gallbladder disease and hypertension.

Although the Indian Health Service has made great progress in treating infectious and acute disease, a 1996 National Indian Council on Aging report criticized it for not attending to the health needs of older Native Americans. The Indian Health Service does not recruit geriatricians, provide geriatric training, or provide long-term care of any kind. Despite recent statements of a commitment to improve services for older people, little progress has been made, and the Indian Health Service continues to contend that it is not mandated to provide long-term care. Some tribes, par-

ticularly those with gaming or gambling revenue, have been able to sponsor long-term care facilities, but these facilities are inadequate, and no other federal agency has assumed responsibility. The few Native American nursing homes in existence are operating at full capacity.

It is important for providers of geriatric care for Native Americans to be culturally sensitive. For example, in the two nursing homes of the Navajo Nation, the largest reservation-based Native American nation, the majority of residents speak the Navajo language and eat traditional food. Respect is paid to Navajo cultural practices, such as bathing in sweat baths, sleeping on sheepskins or mattresses stacked on the floor, religious practices, visitation of clan members, and practices regarding death, such as not speaking about the dead.[17]

Ho has attempted to delineate shared characteristics of Native Americans as well as to acknowledge the tremendous tribal diversity.[18] Strong extended family ties and multiple household systems provide an interdependent family framework. In order to survive, the elderly have had to adopt skills related to the dominant white culture while trying to preserve their own rich traditions. All of this has taken place in the midst of fast-paced social change and the often insensitive attempts on the part of federal and state governments to identify and meet their needs.

Asian American and Pacific Island American Older Persons

Asian and Pacific Island Americans are an extremely diverse group, often with little in common due to vast differences in language, class, culture, religion and history. The largest groups of Asian Americans are Chinese (with 134,000 people age 65 and older in 1990), Filipino (with 104,000 older people), and Japanese (with 106,000 older people). Other Asian American populations are Korean, Asian Indian, Vietnamese, Cambodian, Laotian, Hmong (a tribal minority from Laos), Thai, Pakistani, and Indonesian. Only 5% of the total Asian Pacific Island American Population are Pacific Island American. The majority of Pacific

Island Americans are Hawaiian and Samoan. Others are Tongan or other Polynesian, Micronesian (includes Guam), and Melanesian (from Fiji).[19]

Although many generalizations are made about them, there are vast differences in the social and economic status of different Asian and Pacific Island Americans. Older Asian and Pacific Island Americans are more likely to be in the labor force than the general population and less likely to be unemployed, but the figures differ greatly among groups. The poverty rates for older Japanese, Filipino, and Asian Indian Americans are among the lowest in the United States, but the poverty rates for Southeast Asian older people (Hmong, Cambodian, Laotian, and Vietnamese) are among the highest—as high as 47% in the case of Hmong elders. Compared with other ethnic groups in the United States, older Asian and Pacific Island Americans have both the highest proportion of their people with less than a ninth grade education and the highest proportion of those with a bachelor's degree or more, and these statistics vary greatly among nationalities. Asian and Pacific Island Americans have almost equal numbers of older people who are native born, naturalized, or not U.S. citizens. A higher percentage (58%) of older Asian and Pacific Island Americans have limited English proficiency than all other major ethnic groups.[20]

Health statistics about Asian and Pacific Island Americans are problematic, and are often weighted towards the more healthy Asian groups. Chinese and Japanese have longer life expectancies then white Americans, but some subgroups, such as Southeast Asian immigrants and Native Hawaiians generally have poorer health. Asian and Pacific Island Americans in general have high rates of tuberculosis, hepatitis, anemia, hypertension, multiinfarct dementia, and osteoporosis.

Studies suggest that Asian Americans have higher rates of mental health problems than whites in the United States. The suicide rate for older Chinese American women, for example, is ten time that for older white women. This problem is compounded by low rates of mental health service use by older Asian Pacific Island Americans, possibly due to a distrust of government, belief in non-Western models of medicine, and barriers such as class, language, lack of sensitivity among providers to cultural differences, and prejudice, such as a still pervasive belief in the stereotype of the "problem-free" Asian.[21]

Service providers should be sensitive to different cultural and religious beliefs, such as filial respect, among many Asian and Pacific Island Americans, and efforts should be made, in many cases, to incorporate family, kinship groups, or other cultural organizations into care. Specific historical backgrounds should also be considered. There may be attitudinal differences between refugees (including those who may suffer from depression or Post-Traumatic Stress Disorder, those who were colonized, such as Native Hawaiians, or Japanese who were interned during World War II and who may distrust government services), and those who emigrated by choice. The degree to which the individual is assimilated into the new culture and whether he or she is an immigrant are also important factors to take into account.[22]

The traditional role of family supports has been weakened by immigration patterns. Chinese men were prohibited through the Chinese Exclusion Act of 1882 from bringing their wives and children with them, and they were forbidden to intermarry in America.[23]

Others chose to come alone as young men, hoping to make money quickly and then return to live in China. War and the subsequent Communist takeover prohibited their return. As a result, in most areas with Chinese American populations there have been large groups of single males without families.

American immigration policies changed after 1970, making it possible for the immigration of Chinese family groups. A new group of older Chinese are beginning to emerge as a result of the liberalization of immigration laws that permitted the reunion of long-separated families, including parents and other older relatives of U.S. citizens. This group appears to have a larger proportion of older women than men. Added to these are the increasing numbers of persons who were born in the United States and are now growing older, again a higher proportion of whom are women. Older Chinese Americans tend to prefer to live in ethnic communities rather than with their children in outlying areas. Many elderly are quite isolated from American culture. Younger Chinese Americans are much more acculturated and many have intermarried outside the Chinese community.

Early immigration of Filipinos produced an imbalance of males similar to that of the Chinese. Some came to the United States as farm laborers; others came because they were awarded U.S. citizenship as veterans of the U.S. armed forces after World War II. Most had no families here, and many lost contact with their relatives in the Philippines. A more recent wave of immigration came in the early 1970s because of political problems in the Philippines. This wave doubled the size of the Filipino population in California alone and many of these later immigrants arrived in families. In recent years, a number of elderly persons also have immigrated to the United States to join children, many of whom came as health care workers, who were already here.

Early Japanese immigration policies in the United States were not so devastating and dehumanizing as those of other Asians. Women and children were allowed to accompany men, and this has had a profound effect on the lives of present-day older persons. Family structure is much more stable and supportive. Japanese older people were able to weather the World War II internment in relocation centers with the loss of jobs and their roles in U.S. society primarily because their children carried on for them. Many of the children have become highly educated and successful while retaining patterns of loyalty to their parents.[24]

The widespread belief that respect for older persons is culturally stronger in Asian societies needs to be reevaluated from the viewpoint of economic and social class as well as immigration effects. Tradition, of course, has a powerful effect on shaping an individual's attitudes, but economic and social circumstances either support or undermine such traditions. For example, the American-

ization of younger Asian Americans has partially eroded the traditional role of, and respect for, the elderly.

What Can Be Done to Improve Mental Health Care for Minority-Group Older Persons?

1. Income maintenance, especially for the minority elderly who are more likely to experience poverty, is a prime requirement for improving the mental health and the mental health care of older members of minority groups. Supplemental Security Income should be raised to provide an adequate standard of living, ideally to some level above rather than below the poverty line. Efforts must be made to resolve the inequities in Social Security that arise from lower life expectancies in certain ethnic groups. Pension plans should become portable from one place of employment to another. Hiring and wage discrimination in the labor market, based on age or ethnicity, must be continuously monitored and addressed.

2. Minority professionals and older minority elderly themselves should be in key decision-making and advisory positions in any actions affecting older minority persons as a group.

3. Mental health staffs should reflect the racial and ethnic composition they serve. Training in the mental health field should be widely available for minority-group members.

4. Nonminority personnel should have special training and, ideally, supervisory monitoring by minority-group or ethnically sensitive professionals if they work with minority clientele.

5. Research from the minority perspective should be funded and encouraged. Problems pertinent to the minority aged need emphasis. The quality of minority aging research must be improved.[25]

6. More alternative methods of care must be made available—home-care services, nursing homes and homes for the aged, psychiatric hospitalization outside of state hospitals, day care, and day hospitals. Techniques of individual and group psychotherapy relevant to minority needs should be developed. Meals-on-Wheels could supply ethnic foods, and food stamps should be usable in ethnic groceries. Recreation and leisure therapy should be aimed at cultural interests. Information systems, service workers, legal assistance, and psychiatric therapy should all be provided on a bilingual basis for older persons who do not speak English.

The On Lok Senior Health Service in San Francisco began in 1972 as a rather rare example of the provision of ethnic-related services. On Lok is a day treatment center for frail older persons in San Francisco's Chinatown/North Beach area and serves those who would otherwise be placed in nursing homes or intermediate care facilities. Participants are of Chinese, Filipino, Hispanic, Italian, and other European ethnic backgrounds and often do not speak English. They receive medical evaluation; primary physician care; medical services such as podiatry, dentistry, optometry, and audiology; occupational, physical, and reality therapy; diet counseling; recreation; transportation; home-care services; "meals-on-wheels"; day health care services; sheltered/supervised apartments; brief nursing home care; and hospital placement when needed. Staff members at On Lok must be able to speak at least one of the languages spoken by participants, in addition to English. Programs are geared to the ethnic cultures; for example, Chinese as well as American food is served.[26]

Federal legislation passed in 1986 authorized national demonstration projects by nonprofit organizations nationwide for the replication of the On Lok model. By 1996 there were 27 such replications called Programs for All-Inclusive Care for the Elderly (PACE). The programs operate under dual capitation payments (Medicare and Medicaid) and are designed to keep members out of costly nursing homes.

Numbers of therapists and theorists are beginning to devise specific forms and styles of psychotherapy to reach the minority elderly. Ho's work (1987) is an example of important efforts to address mental health care of the four major ethnic groups (African Americans, Native Americans, Hispanics, and Asian Pacific Island Americans) from a cultural context. He uses a family systems approach, with the objective of supplementing already-existing family therapy theories by (1) identifying a "culturally relevant theoretical framework"; (2) providing an overview of the political, social, and economic problems that each minority family faces, along with the unique culturally derived strengths and weaknesses such families carry; (3) clarifying the cultural values and changing family patterns of each ethnic group; and (4) providing specific mental health practitioner guidelines on work with ethnic families, including single-parent families.[27] Ho recognizes the dangers of cultural stereotypes inherent in this approach; nonetheless he believes that such stereotyping can be mitigated by individuating each family within the context of a larger understanding of the possible impact of culture and ethnicity.

An example of his perspective can be found in a description of work with Hispanic families: "Many Hispanic Americans are gradually acculturated to the middle-class mainstream society, but a vast majority of them are still struggling with basic survival needs. . . . These families need more than feeling good about themselves and other family members; they need the basic necessities to survive. Hence the role of a therapist extends beyond the psychologically oriented healer role [and] . . . may consist of roles as cultural broker, mediator, educator and advocate."[28]

Boyd-Franklin has focused on therapy with the African American family, bringing together past and current research and cultural knowledge on the subject.[29] A major purpose is to provide mental health therapists with the clinical tools necessary to work effectively with black families. The author stresses that the issue of racism and, for many black families, poverty, must be part of the treatment process and that a multisystems approach is generally preferable.

Kim and Kim (1989) have made beginning attempts to develop a curriculum for training mental health professionals for work with Asian American elderly.[30] Die and Seelback have focused on elderly Vietnamese.[31] Ho provides insights into therapy with Native Americans.[32]

OLDER WOMEN AND GENDER ISSUES

In the United States, 17 million women were age 65 years or older in 1995. This constitutes 7.6% of the total population, 14.8% of all women, and 59.3% of the older population.[33] Sexism and ageism are the twin prejudices directed against them. Many have experienced sex discrimination all their lives, but age discrimination begins only after they have lost their youth and accelerates as they age. The end result is a greater rate of poverty and social unacceptability than for men, combined ironically with a longer life span. The cultural denigration of the older woman is taught to children at an early age through fairy tales that depict old hags, evil crones, scary old witches, and nasty biddies of all kinds. Negative mother-in-law stories abound. Doctors and medical students often call the very oldest female patients "crocks." Unmarried aunts may be scorned as "old maids." Even grandma can become a family nuisance as she outlives grandpa and experiences and expresses the emotional and physical facts of aging. Thus the message comes across that a woman is valuable for bearing and rearing children and perhaps to nurse her husband in his dotage and often through his terminal illness, but after that it is clearly useless and even burdensome to have her around. The mistreatment of older women is a national shame that has yet to be fully challenged even by older women themselves.

Low Visibility of the Older Woman

Except for unusual events, such as the passage of the Social Security Act in 1935, one of the tendencies of the U.S. social and political system is to attempt to resolve social problems piecemeal and intermittently. The most stubborn problems tend to persist under this approach. The economic and social conditions of the poor, now mostly women and children, and a number of our ethnic and racial minorities, are periodically "discov-ered" with great alarm and then allowed to sink back into oblivion and neglect. Older women living alone seldom even receive the benefit of occasional public scrutiny. It is assumed that they have shared equally with men in the progress made since 1935 in establishing nominal economic security in old age. We shall be examining that assumption in the following pages.

Profile of the Older Woman

What is the life of an *average* older woman like? In many cases it means being widowed and living alone, on a low or poverty-level income, often in substandard housing, with inadequate medical care and little chance of employment to supplement resources.

Income.   A small proportion of older women are well-off financially, and some few have inherited enormous wealth. At the other end of the spectrum are those women who have been poor all their lives and can expect even greater poverty in old age. But in between these two groups is a multitude of women who have lived comfortably throughout their lives and first experience poverty after they are old and widowed: They are the newly poor. Poverty is not reserved for women alone, since older men, too, are often in dire financial condition. Yet whenever poverty is found, it is generally more profound and of greater consequence for women.

According to the official poverty index in 1992, 71.3% of all of the older poor were women, most of them widows living alone. Of women aged 75 and older, 41.7% had incomes below or only slightly above the poverty level. Only 22% of women received income from private pensions in 1992, with an average benefit of $5,432 a year, compared to 49% of men, who received an average benefit of $10,131 per year.[34]

Due to less pay for equal work compared to men, discontinuous outside work experience (often due to care-giving for children and older persons), and built-in inequities in the Social Security system, women still receive less in Social

Security benefits than do men. In 1994, the average monthly Social Security benefit was $601 for women, compared to $785 for men. Social Security benefits for women workers in general averaged 77% of the amount for men. African American women received an average of only $476 monthly in Social Security benefits in 1994.[35]

One of several common paths to poverty in old age is to become a displaced homemaker in midlife. Displaced homemakers are women—10.5 million over the age of 65 in 1990—who have lost their primary source of income due to separation, divorce, or widowhood.[36] Compounding their precarious financial state, in 1989, 12% of such women (2.8 million) between the ages of 45 and 64 had no health insurance.[37]

In the current generation, even women with sufficient income may encounter problems; many of them have not learned to handle money on their own behalf. This generation of women has been encouraged to turn its money over to others to manage—to bank representatives, guardians, lawyers, adult children—and those women who do take care of their own finances are often untrained and ill-prepared to make sound decisions. Even women who are well above average in income, job level, education, and years of experience may know little about investments or how to increase capital. Money management for older women tends to be a passive activity in which they prefer the false security of savings, cash, and annuities over a sounder investment program that requires an understanding of economics and finance. Courses in finance designed especially for women are fortunately beginning to reverse this trend.

Employment. Over 1.5 million, or 8.5%, of women 65 years of age or older are employed, often out of necessity.[38] Although there has been a decrease in work among men age 55 and older, older women's work involvement has remained steady or has slightly increased. Many never worked outside their homes until their children left home. Others who were employed all their

lives usually earned much less than men of comparable talent, training, and initiative. Women workers of all ages earned 75 cents for every dollar earned by men in 1995.[39] All of this has resulted in lower Social Security and private retirement benefits and, combined with a longer life span for women, produces lower income that must be stretched over a greater number of years.

Employers are reluctant to hire older women because of stereotyped attitudes that they are not adaptable to today's jobs and technology; older women are seen as cantankerous, unattractive, overly emotional, and unreliable because of health problems. Yet corporate studies indicate that they make exceptionally good employees, with lower turnover, less absenteeism and equal productivity compared to younger women. Further, a majority of companies report that health insurance costs for older women workers are no greater than those for younger women workers.[40]

Social Security poses a peculiar problem regarding equity for women. It was devised in 1935 with the traditional family in mind, namely a working husband and an economically dependent housewife. However, today two-thirds of women are in the paid work force and only 20% are full-time homemakers. As more women have moved into the workplace, Social Security benefits continue to favor the wife at home. For example, two-earner couples often end up with lower benefits than one-earner couples with the wife at home. The concept of "marital earnings sharing" has been proposed as a solution to this inequity. This would mean that every couple would split their combined earnings in half, with each receiving equal Social Security credit. However, this would immediately require modification and supplementation in order to prevent loss of benefits for certain categories of recipients. Another solution, to give housewives Social Security credits for their unpaid work, has not yet produced a viable method of placing a value on such services and is considered more unworkable than the marital-earnings-sharing plan.

In other areas, such as the disability protection of Social Security, it is the housewife who is disadvantaged. If she is a disabled widow, she faces a stricter disability standard than a disabled employed woman and will receive the lowest Social Security benefit of any recipient group, with an average payment even lower than the maximum Supplementary Security Income (SSI) benefit for the very poor who are unqualified for Social Security. If she becomes disabled or dies while her husband is still alive, the loss of her unpaid but very real services is not covered by Social Security at all.

Social Security also penalizes women who take time out from employment for care-giving of children, the elderly, and the disabled in their families. Women average 11.5 years out of the work force compared to 1.3 years for men. These lost years are factored as zeros into the wage record for Social Security of 35 required years of work and have a large effect in reducing benefit levels. Alternative solutions proposed for this problem are (1) to simply leave out the "zero" years for caregivers and base the benefit on the remaining years, or (2) to provide Social Security credits for care-giving.

Divorced women must have been married ten years in order to receive their ex-husband's Social Security. Yet most divorces occur before 10 years of marriage, and such women are left without benefits if they themselves are not in the work force. Even if they do qualify for benefits as divorced wives, the spousal benefit is so low that women will be in poverty if they have no other source of income.

It is important to continue to amend Social Security to meet the needs of modern older women. Currently Social Security's weaknesses and incongruities are most noticeable in cases of two-earner families, care-giving, divorce, early retirement, and long life, all of which affect women disproportionately. In 1994 Social Security was the only source of income for 22% of unmarried older women, compared to 19% of unmarried older men.[41]

Social Security has proven to be the most effective of all antipoverty programs for the aged, compared to cash welfare programs, tax programs, and others. Approximately 50% of retirees would be below the poverty level if it were not for Social Security.[42] Its next challenge is to target the poverty of older women living alone.

Marriage. The average American woman born today can anticipate about 10 years of widowhood. Of the 18 million older women, 46.9% are widows and an additional 6% are divorced. Approximately 4.3% of older women have never been married.[43] Thus almost 60% of older women are on their own, an interesting fact when one remembers that they, more than any younger group, were raised from childhood to consider themselves dependent on men.

Why so many widows? Women outlive men their own age and also tend to marry men who are an average of about 2.5 years older than themselves. The difference in life expectancy from birth has been occurring from the turn of the century, if not before. Males born in 1920 could expect to live 53.6 years and females a year longer, but by 1991 a 6.9 year spread was evident, with a life expectancy at birth of 72 for men and 78.9 for women.[44]

Older men have a tremendous advantage over older women when it comes to marriage. Because they tend to marry younger women who will outlive them, they are much less likely to be widowed. More than that, they can count on a fairly healthy spouse to nurse them as they age. Should the wife die prematurely, they have usually plentiful options for remarriage. At ages 65 through 69 when men number 4.5 million, the over 5.4 million women already outnumber men by almost one million and the odds improve as men get older.[45] In remarrying, men can bypass their own age group altogether and marry women from 65 all the way down to girls in their twenties or teens. One can readily see what is happening to older women in all of this; their chances for remarriage are small, and only about 27,000 remarried in 1990. To exacerbate the situation, it is still less socially acceptable for older women than for older men to date or marry persons much younger than themselves.

Motherhood. Many contemporary older women are childless. The cohort (generation) of women born between 1905 and 1909, now in their late 80s, is a low-fertility cohort, since these women produced fewer children than any recorded group of American women before or after. At the height of its childbearing years, this group was confronted with the worst economic depression in U.S. history, with 25%—one of every four workers—unemployed. Many couples felt they could not support a large or even moderately sized family. About 20% of the women had no children, another 22% had only one, and another 20% two. The long-term result is that about 25% currently have no living children. (Nearly 30% of African American women in this age group are childless.) They are, however, likely to have brothers and sisters (and therefore nieces and nephews), because their own mothers had large families. Thus there may be extended family support for some of the childless.

Interestingly, the women born between 1925 and 1930, now in their 70s, were the high-fertility, post–World War II cohort. Only about 10% never had a child, and the "ideal" was four children. While many will face divorce or will become widowed because of the male–female differential life expectancy, most will have children.

Living Arrangements. In 1994, 9.3 million elderly lived alone and, of these, 78% or 7.2 million were women. Currently, 40% of all older women live alone, 41% live with husbands, 17% with relatives, and 2% with nonrelatives.[46] Many women have never lived alone until old age.

Physical Health. Major differences exist between the health condition of men and women in later life:

- Men have higher death rates than do women at all ages.
- In old age, women have more numerous, but less life-threatening health problems; older men's illnesses are less numerous, but more serious.

- Hospitalization rates are higher for older men (reflecting the more serious nature of their illnesses); women use more outpatient care and medications (reflecting a pattern of more frequent, but also milder, illnesses).

In summary, older women have higher rates of illness than men, but lower death rates. Verbrugge postulates five possible reasons for these differences:

1. Biological risk factors due to genetic and reproductive differences between men and women
2. Acquired risk factors, due to different social and environmental circumstances between men and women
3. Illness behavior: gender differences in response to illness
4. Health reporting: gender differences in talking about and reporting illness
5. Past history of illness behavior that has an impact on new health responses.[47]

Medicare insurance, with its strength in the area of hospital coverage and its weakness in home care and nursing home care, better fits the profiles of older men's illness than older women's. Women make up 75 to 80% of nursing home residents, yet Medicare makes very little contribution toward nursing home costs. Many women are forced to spend their resources down to the poverty level in order to be eligible for highly variable state-funded Medicaid help with such costs. The same can be said for home care. In addition, Medicare does not cover routine physical examinations, drugs, hearing aids, and eyeglasses, all of which are of importance to women because of the chronicity and multiplicity of their health problems. One view of reforms is to strengthen and adjust Medicare to better meet women's needs, but many others believe that only a comprehensive national health insurance program will provide the insurance coverage needed by older women.

Mental Health. Both older men and older women are heavily stereotyped in psychological theory as "old" people. As a further problem, sex differences are by and large invisible in theories about aging, and the old are viewed as gender-neutral. For example, psychoanalytic theory, with its view of very different psychosexual stages for boys and girls, does not carry this analysis into old age. Much of what is described as old age (with the exception of Jungian theory, see Chapter 12) is simply a description of the adaptation of the elderly to the stages in late life, such as retirement, widowhood or widowerhood, decline of health, and confrontation with death.

Gutmann's field studies challenge the gender-neutrality view of old age. He postulates that each sex has repressed a portion of its psychological potential early in childhood—males tend to repress nurturing characteristics while females repress assertive capacities. This allows children to survive and thrive in cultures that reward males for competitiveness and females for cooperativeness. However, in later life, each sex begins to reclaim its lost birthright, with males allowing their more nurturing qualities to develop and females their assertiveness. Gutmann's studies have suggested that this occurs in many different cultures and, perhaps, universally.[48]

Common sense, it would seem, should lead to examination of the gender-neutral view of the psychology of late life. Whether by nature (genetics) or nurture (the environment in which we grow up), women and men have differences which, in turn, produce differences in adjustment to the common stages and occurrences of later life.

Education and Research Efforts on Older Women

The major textbooks on geriatric medicine pay scant attention to the medical implications of females living longer than males. Nor do they attach much import to the question of whether women age differently than men, even at the same ages. The "unisex" quality of current geriatric medical literature represents a lag in recognizing the clinical implications of the differences between males and females.

Clinical and basic research efforts have long been biased against women in general and older women in particular. In a 1990 study by the U.S. General Accounting Office, the National Institutes of Health—the major research institutes in the United States—failed to implement their own 1987 policy requiring researchers to include women in federally funded studies. This failure extended also to preliminary research studies on animals, especially rats. Females, both human and animal, were routinely excluded from many studies because of the view that their hormonal cycles cause complications for researchers. In addition, they might become pregnant, further complicating research efforts. But as U.S. Representative Olympia Snow has wryly observed, "women have been bearing children for quite some time now, and are likely to continue doing so in the future. Medical research, rather than ignoring that fact as an inconvenience, should work to accommodate it."[49] It might be emphasized that older women have neither menstrual cycles nor pregnancies, yet the rate of inclusion of women in studies does not rise with age, strengthening the view that bias rather than sound judgment is operating.

One of the most important studies of aging, the Baltimore Longitudinal Study of Aging, examined men for over 20 years, before beginning to include women in 1978. The National Institute of Mental Health's landmark work on healthy aging, published in 1963, involved only men.[50] Certain processes common to all women as they age remain mysterious; for example, there is no agreement yet on the basic physiology of the menopausal hot flash. On a more urgent level, the breast cancer death rates in the United States have not significantly improved. Breast cancer mortality has remained about the same since 1950, with only a modest decline of 4.7% between 1989 and 1992.[51] In response to criticism regarding research on women's problems and the use of women as research subjects, the National Institutes of Health created an Office of Research on Women's Health to coordinate and accelerate women's health studies. A major nationwide study, the Women's Health Initiative, is now underway, focusing on a variety of health conditions experienced by women after the menopause.

Certain health conditions can be singled out as immediate targets for major new or expanded research efforts because of their impact on so many older women and because of current controversy surrounding treatment—Alzheimer's disease, breast cancer, uterine cancer, hypertension, stroke, osteoporosis (brittle bones), diabetes, arthritis, and urinary incontinence are some of the most apparent. Nearly half of the over 500,000 people who die of heart attacks in the United States each year are women. Further research around the use of estrogens, hysterectomies, and mastectomies is indicated. As already mentioned, the menopause and post-menopausal period require greater understanding. Occupational health hazards for women, both in the home and in the outside workplace, warrant further examination. Better understanding and prevention of hypothermia (dangerously low body temperature) and heat stroke are important, especially for the frail elderly.

What's Good about Being an Older Woman?

We have detailed some of the difficulties of older women. But there is more. Many older women have learned much about the mechanisms of sex and age discrimination and have a great deal to teach the young. Their experiences give us guidelines for combating prejudice and supporting older women in their efforts to find a satisfying life.

In terms of personal expression, older women today have both realized accomplishments and unexplored potential. In addition to their increasingly good records of health and longevity, they do not have to struggle with the conflicts between mothering and careers, which, even with a resolution of child care issues, often trouble younger women. They are in the interesting position of being the only adult females who are truly free of the demands of child responsibility (unless they are responsible for their grandchildren or other children) and, in many cases, marital responsibil-

ity. The idea of dependency on a male is deeply ingrained in white and in many minority cultures, but many older women do not conform to this stereotype, and, indeed, live independent and satisfying lives.

Older women who demonstrate successful aging give younger women confidence in the knowledge that a rich life can await them as they age. A considerable number of older women have forged unique positions for themselves in terms of identity, personal achievement, and even financial and political power. They need to be given greater visibility. Within the extended family, women are often the oldest and most influential members, frequently serving as the kin-keepers who provide contact and cohesion for others (Chapter 2).

Politically, the older woman is in an advantageous position that is likely to improve. With a voting strength of over 18 million, almost 75% of whom are registered voters and most of whom vote regularly,[52] they represent a major and fast-growing constituency that already could elect their own congresspersons in those states where they reside in high proportions. They have the available time and energy to lobby, campaign, and promote candidates, since over 90% are not employed. There is reason to suppose that women as candidates for the presidency and as additional appointees to the Supreme Court will come from this age group, since older people historically have often filled these positions.

In spite of widespread poverty for many women, there are tremendous sums of money in the hands of widows and female heirs. More women might be encouraged to take on their own financial management instead of entrusting it to male husband-surrogates. Women of wealth could exert much greater influence in economic, social, and other spheres than they now do. As an example, they could provide resources for solving the problems faced by women in later life.

Advocacy groups specifically for older women are beginning to form. The Older Women's League (OWL) was begun in 1978 by Tish Sommers and Laurie Shields and became a national organization in 1980. By 1996, OWL had 11,000 members and 62 chartered chapters in 30 states. Tish Sommers had earlier organized programs for "displaced homemakers," a phrase she coined for women who become displaced and economically vulnerable in mid-life through divorce, separation, or widowhood.

CRIMES AGAINST THE ELDERLY

According to crime statistics, the actual incidence of crime against persons over age 65 is lower than the incidence against other age groups. National crime surveys show that except for personal larceny such as purse-snatching and picking pockets, older persons have the lowest victimization rates of any age group in all types of crime.[53] However, the quality of the data must be questioned. Much crime against the elderly goes unreported. The elderly may be too feeble or too fearful to contact authorities. They may fear retaliation from their attackers, especially if the perpetrator lives in their neighborhood or, more frightening, is a member of their own household and family. Moreover, many older people live in fear—especially in cities—and often stay indoors to an unnatural degree, triple-locking their doors and thereby protecting themselves from crime by virtual self-imprisonment in their own homes. Thus, what appears to be a lower incidence of crime against the elderly compared to other age groups may be largely due to older people's extraordinary measures to protect themselves and to their reluctance to report crime when it occurs.

The District of Columbia Report to the 1971 White House Conference on Aging, subtitled "Metropolitan Police Contact with the Elderly,"[54] is among the few documents of even relatively recent date that show the degree to which crimes are committed against older persons. Project Assist co-director Phyllis Brostoff pointed to

> a large group of old people (over 60) . . . a depressed underclass . . . who are particularly vulnerable to crime, easy victims of street robbery, unable to move out of high-crime neighborhoods . . . and likely to have no other community resource to turn to other than the police if trouble occurs. . . .

Police reports often do not indicate the age of victims. However, the incidence of crime recorded against older persons indicates that crimes occur primarily where large numbers of older people are concentrated. Public housing complexes are a prime target. Bus and subway stops, basement laundry rooms in apartment buildings, dark halls, back doors, elevators, and short-cuts (paths and passageways hidden from view) can all be dangerous places for older people. Mailboxes in unguarded apartment vestibules are the province of thieves who know when Social Security and welfare checks arrive. Food stamps are a frequently stolen item. The disabilities of old age—deafness, slowness, blindness, spotty memory—make older people especially vulnerable.

In the Project Assist report, about 90% of crimes against older persons were robberies and 8% were assaults. Most robberies take place on the streets rather than at home. The methods used are purse-snatching, intimidation, and strong-arming. The amount of money stolen is often small, and little is ever recovered. Stolen checks and food stamps are recoverable, but the delay can mean having no food or rent money when it is needed. Many of the very poorest aged have no phone on which to notify police of crime. Crimes committed by relatives or landlords against older people rarely are prosecuted because they are not taken seriously.

Naturally, the primary responsibility of the police is law enforcement, and their focus is on prevention of crime and apprehension of criminals. When older people present social problems, the police are often the first neighborhood public service personnel who are called on for help. Many are uneasy, unwilling, or unable to provide social services, but will arrange for referral of social problems to appropriate agencies, especially if they have a responsive agency they can easily call. Social agencies serving the elderly could work more closely with the police than they now do. The police can be excellent sources of information about the location of older people who are isolated or vulnerable, including those with chronic brain syndromes who wander from home, older alcoholics who collapse on the street or become obstreperous, elder abuse victims, and acute brain syndrome victims who require emergency care.

A safe environment (versus one of fear and genuine danger) is crucial to the mental health of older people. In addition to referral mechanisms for a variety of social services, many steps could be taken to better protect older people from crime. Escort services could be arranged by volunteer groups; dead-bolt locks could be provided for the older person's residence. The federal government now arranges to send checks directly to banks free of charge for those persons who would prefer this, thus reducing the theft of checks. Special low-cost checking account service might encourage people not to carry cash but to establish credit and to pay by check whenever possible. If it were generally known that older people no longer dealt in cash, the incentive for criminal attack would be markedly reduced. Vertical policing throughout all the floors in high-rise buildings should be done by police on the beat or by volunteers. Police could perform security audits of buildings to spot crime hazards. Tenants themselves could guard mailrooms at the beginning of each month to protect against check thefts. An older woman might carry an old empty purse or an older man a wallet with a few dollars as decoys to give up under attack. Elderly people also need protection against fraud and deceit (for example, medical quackery, religious exploitation, and consumer fraud) that prey on their vulnerabilities.

Elder Abuse

Butler described the "battered old person syndrome"[55] (known in England as "granny-bashing" or "gran-slamming"), now more commonly called "elder abuse." Battering and abuse take place within the home or family circle, perpetrated by relatives or acquaintances or home-service workers, or in institutions where the elderly reside. Elder abuse is a problem that has existed throughout the history of family and institutional life, but it has only recently been defined as a social problem and is still rather poorly understood. Research

on elder abuse first began in the 1970s and focused national attention on the issue.

A growing literature has been accumulating since research began.[56] Pillemer and Finkelhor's random sample survey of 2,000 older Bostonians (1988) remains the only community based study on elder abuse. The study found that 3.2% of those surveyed had experienced some form of abuse or neglect since they had reached age 65.[57] National estimates of the prevalence of elder abuse range from 4% to 10%, but are unreliable. In response to 1992 amendments to the Older Americans Act, the Administration on Aging commissioned the formation of the National Center on Elder Abuse, which is conducting the first national elder abuse incidence study, scheduled for completion in the summer of 1997.[58]

The Definition of Elder Abuse has fluctuated over the past 20 years. However, five basic types of elder abuse are:

1. *Physical abuse:* The infliction of physical pain or injury (e.g., slap, cut, burn)
2. *Psychological abuse:* The infliction of mental anguish (e.g., name calling, intimidation, threats)
3. *Financial abuse:* The illegal or improper exploitation and/or use of resources
4. *Active neglect:* Refusal or failure to fulfill a caretaking obligation, *including* a conscious and intentional attempt to inflict physical or emotional stress on the elder (e.g., deliberate abandonment or deliberate denial of food or health-related services)
5. *Passive neglect:* Refusal or failure to fulfill a caretaking obligation, *excluding* a conscious and intentional attempt to inflict physical or emotional distress on the elder (e.g., non-provision of food or services because of inadequate knowledge or own infirmity)[59]

In a 1988 overview on elder abuse for the House and Senate Committees on Aging, the following points were emphasized:

1. There is no reliable evidence that the incidence of elder abuse is rising. Such abuse has

always existed. What is new is our recent national interest and focus on the issue.

2. According to several well-done studies, as many as a million elderly people have been victims of abuse at some point. However, this is substantially lower than the frequently quoted statistic that 4% of the elderly are abused each year, although the difficulty of case detection is acknowledged. A national incidence and prevalence study of elder abuse should be done to obtain a more reliable picture of the nature and extent of abuse.

3. Abuse of the elderly is a serious matter, involving physical as well as psychological and behavioral damage.

4. Abuse by a spouse is the most prevalent form of abuse, followed by abuse from an adult child.

5. Much abuse appears to be related to chronic psychological and/or physical conditions on the part of caregivers, such as developmental disabilities, mental illness, and alcoholism. Caregiver stress is less of a factor in elder abuse than deviance and the resultant dependency, often financial as well as emotional, of family abusers on their victims.

6. Mandatory elder abuse reporting laws may at times do more harm than good, especially when they are not coupled with a program of services. Such laws, which typically require physicians and other health providers to report suspected cases of elder abuse, remove decision making from the hands of the elderly and lead in many cases to institutionalization. Few states offer adequate services to explore remedies for the situation in the older person's own home. On the other hand, health care personnel may be the only link the older person has with the outside world, and mandatory reporting is an attempt to capitalize on this link.

7. A program of comprehensive and coordinated services to victims and their families is the best solution to elder abuse. Some examples are home-care services, consciousness-raising and support groups for both victims and abusers, greater police involvement and response to family violence involving the elderly, with possible use of arrest as a deterrent, direct help to abusers for their own personal problems, and a system of referral of elders and their families to community services such as case managers and elder abuse programs.[60]

Pillemer also points out the need for more well-constructed research, especially on the risk factors for elder abuse and on the effectiveness of various kinds of services in response to these risk factors. Breckman and Adelman (1988) have constructed a list of risk factors. The presence of one or more of these factors indicates increased risk for mistreatment.

- *Family member psychopathology:* Presence of mental illness, mental retardation, dementia, or drug or alcohol abuse
- *Transgenerational violence:* Family history of violence
- *Dependency:* Patient or family member dependent on the other for housing, finances, emotional support, or care-giving
- *Isolation:* Patient does not have the opportunities to relate with people or pursue activities and interests in a manner he or she chooses
- *Stress:* Recent occurrence of stressful life events such as loss of a job, moving, or death of a significant other
- *Living arrangements:* Patient and family member live together[61]

Crime Committed by the Elderly

Older people commit very little crime; they have the lowest arrest rates in every category of crime, and most arrests involve minor offenses, often alcohol-related.[62] The older man or woman who is convicted of a major crime such as homicide usually warrants front page news coverage as a curiosity.

However, many older people are in prisons for crimes committed earlier in life and the proportion of older prisoners is growing. This mirrors the growing number of elderly in the general population as well as longer sentencing that has decreased the possibility of parole.

A national survey conducted by Edith E. Flynn, of Northwestern University, found that the percentage of inmates age 55 and older has doubled in the last ten years, to 6% of the total inmate population of 1.2 million.[63] Specially designated prisons for the elderly have been forecast as the wave of the future in U.S. corrections. Already a few states such as North and South Carolina and Florida have begun to create such facilities. But most of the nation's current elderly prisoners still serve their time in the general prison population. The majority are male, reflecting a generation in which serious crime was predominately a male activity. Often called "Old Joes," these men place special demands on the prison system because of health-care problems and special needs typical of the elderly. The cost of incarcerating older prisoners has been estimated at up to three times the costs for younger inmates. State prisons are especially hard hit financially since inmates are not eligible for the usual federal benefits that include Medicare, veteran's benefits, or Social Security. Most states find that taxpayers balk at the thought of providing expensive medical procedures like heart bypass surgery and CAT scans as well as recreational and social programs suitable for the elderly. Meanwhile, even basic chronic disease and disability care is placing a strain on state prison budgets.

Some have suggested that age itself is a rehabilitator and that many older prisoners could be released, especially those serving long sentences for crimes committed many years ago. Prisons report that violent behavior tends to drop precipitously with age. Studies on the relationship between crime and age indicate that efforts at prevention directed at young offenders are more effective than the continued incarceration of the old. But others argue that releasing an elderly inmate, especially after a long incarceration, is itself a form of cruel and unusual punishment, depriving that person of familiar routines, physical security and guaranteed health care. Especially with frail elderly parolees, major social, financial, and health supports would be needed to assist them in adjusting to the outside world.

ALCOHOLISM[64]

Estimates of the number of older Americans who are problem drinkers vary widely. One source says that the prevalence of alcohol abuse in older people ranges from 2 to 5% for men and about 1% for women—lower figures than for younger age groups. Another source, however, says that 10% of the elderly have drinking problems, the same as the population as a whole. Still others say that 10% is a low estimate. There are a number of reasons for these wide-ranging estimates. For example, problem drinking is often a hidden condition in later life because most older problem drinkers are retired and can retreat to their homes while drinking. Standard measures for the diagnosis of alcoholism may not apply as well to older people as they do to younger age groups. Furthermore, physicians may be reluctant to make a diagnosis of alcoholism in their older patients because they believe it is too late in their patients' lives to do anything about it. Whatever the case, a number of sources say that alcoholism in the elderly will become more widespread in the next half century when the number of older people increases substantially with the aging of the baby boomers. It is estimated that between a third and a half of older people with an alcohol problem developed the problem late in life, perhaps due to the stresses so common in late life, such as illness, loss of a loved one, depression, and so on.

Response to alcohol changes with age. After drinking alcohol, older people have higher blood alcohol levels than younger people and become more prone to its toxic effects. Family members, even health professionals, may attribute memory loss, unsteady gait, confusion, disorientation, falls, and hostility to old age, when they are really a function of alcohol. In addition, the addiction to alcohol may not be recognized by the older alcoholic and his or her family if drinking has continued steadily but quietly over the years. When physical illness strikes, the alcohol may interact adversely with medication, confusing the clinical picture. Addiction may also become apparent when the older person is placed in an institutional setting like a hospital, where alcohol is not available. The older person then goes into withdrawal; if unrecognized, severe symptoms may follow.

The National Council on Alcoholism has issued a set of criteria to diagnose the "disease" of alcoholism.[65] Alcoholism is defined as a condition resulting from excessive ingestion of or idiosyncratic reaction to alcohol. A *problem drinker* is one who drinks enough to cause problems for him- or herself and society.[66] Acute alcoholism is a state of acute intoxication with temporary and reversible mental and bodily effects. *Dipsomania* refers to periodic or "binge" drinking. *Chronic alcoholism* is the fact and consequence of habitual use.

The major criteria that constitute alcoholism include the following:

1. Drinking a fifth of whiskey a day, or its equivalent in wine or beer, for a 180-pound person[67]
2. Alcoholic "blackouts"
3. Withdrawal syndrome—gross tremor, hallucinosis, convulsions, or delirium tremens (DTs)
4. Blood alcohol level above 150 mg/100 ml without seeming intoxicated
5. Continued drinking despite medical advice or family or job problems clearly caused by drinking

Minor criteria include such signs as gulping drinks, frequent car accidents, surreptitious drinking, repeated "going on the wagon," and drinking to relieve anger, fatigue, or depression.

Thus major criteria are symptoms that represent conclusive evidence of physiological or psychological dependence, while minor ones are symptoms usually associated with, but not specific to, alcoholism. (For diagnostic clues for the clinical presentation of alcoholism in old age, see Table 7.1.)

Alcoholism is a leading health problem in the United States.[68] Most deaths directly caused by alcoholism are a result of cirrhosis of the liver. A substantial portion of highway and home acci-

TABLE 7.1 Diagnostic clues for the clinical presentation of alcoholism in old age

1. Insomnia
2. Impotence
3. Problems with control of gout
4. Rapid onset of confusional state
5. Uncontrollable hypertension
6. Unexplained falls/bruises
7. Excessive sleepiness
8. Flushed face
9. Bloated appearance

dents are the result of drinking. It is estimated that alcoholism shortens life expectancy by 10 to 12 years. It may cause heart disease of several kinds and can damage the brain. It may lead to chronic impotence in men by damaging the central nervous system and upsetting hormonal balance. (Transient impotence from excessive drinking may also occur but is reversible.)

Alcohol is a central nervous system depressant substitute that adds to impairments that may already exist as a result of various forms of dementia. It is not, as many believe, a stimulant except as it indirectly inhibits cortical control (higher intellectual functions are associated with the cerebral cortex) and thereby releases emotional reactions. With inhibition of cortical control and impairment of intellectual functions comes failure in judgment, which adds to existing impairments resulting from cerebral atherosclerosis and senile brain disease. Alcohol can affect muscular coordination and bodily equilibrium, causing falls and accidents, including fire setting.

Opinions abound as to what causes alcoholism. Some believe it is genetically determined; others see it as a learned adaptation to psychological stresses. It may be secondary to depression, for example, or it may be an inability to tolerate frustration. Still others view alcoholism as a reflection of social conditions, such as poverty, or an outgrowth of the encouragement of drinking by various cultures.

Studies at the National Institute on Aging have shown that alcohol more severely impairs older subjects (55 to 80 years) than younger (20 to 54 years) on a number of important behavioral measures, including reaction time and delayed recognition (memory). Aging does not significantly influence alcohol metabolism but does impair physiological tolerance to alcohol. The older subjects not only were more severely impaired immediately after drinking but also recovered significantly more slowly.

Chronic alcoholism usually involves poor nutrition primarily caused by vitamin and protein deficiencies and liver dysfunction. In addition to a general deterioration of the personality, one may see delirium tremens followed by Korsakoff's psychosis.[69] Confabulations or fabrications of memory and inability to retain new information (retention defect) are the latter's most striking symptoms. Short-term memory loss (amnesia) and disorientation are present.

Wernicke's encephalopathy may also occur with chronic alcoholism. It is characterized by mental changes such as delirium, apathy, and/or Korsakoff's syndrome, ataxia, and eye signs (for example, motor palsies and nystagmus). Thiamine deficiency is the major cause, and prompt intravenous administration may be lifesaving.

The alcoholic amnestic syndrome (a loss of memory for events occurring during a drinking session, probably caused by bilateral damage to the hippocampal and limbic systems of the brain) has led some to postulate an "alcoholic dementia"—with mental and personal deterioration. However, the latter clear up on cessation of drinking and the provision of care. Only the amnestic syndrome remains. Therefore, the evidence for a dementia associated with alcoholic damage of the central nervous system is not very convincing.

Alcoholism in old age is of two types in terms of duration: early onset and late-life onset (although there is current debate about whether the latter is significant in terms of actual numbers of persons involved). Early onset alcoholism used to result in death of middle-aged persons, but because of antibiotics, better nutritional care, and hospital management, many alcoholics now live to grow old. Late-life onset alcoholism may ap-

pear as a self-medicating mechanism in reaction to grief, depression, loneliness, boredom, or pain. A grief-stricken widow who drinks to lessen her sorrow is an example of this. A more familiar pattern is a lifelong habit of controlled drinking that becomes more pronounced and uncontrolled as life stresses increase.

One sees a high proportion of alcoholism among older patients, mostly men, in veterans' hospitals and domiciliaries. It has been suggested that war experiences and exposure to the cultural drinking patterns of the armed services play a causative role, not to mention the special discount liquor stores run by the military in the United States and around the world.

One also sees many older men and women among the homeless derelicts who sleep on sidewalks, doorsteps, park benches, subway trains, and train stations.[70] However, the stereotype of the "Bowery bum" applies to only about 5% of alcoholics in the United States. The Salvation Army and other religious groups provide free care, food, and lodging. Dorothy Day's exemplary work in her Bowery mission concentrated on the homeless alcoholic. Canter and Koretzky emphasize the importance of a comprehensive after-care program, including halfway houses and counseling, for all older alcoholics and especially the homeless.[71]

Alcoholism in nursing homes and homes for the aging is another problem. Family members may bring alcohol to the patient directly or in a disguised bottle. (Old Listerine bottles are favorites for this use. Cough syrups containing alcohol are also common, innocuous-looking disguises.) In some nursing homes, older alcoholics are able to bribe staff members to get them drinks. Alcoholics Anonymous has become involved in some nursing homes with good results.

Treatment of chronic alcoholism usually consists of detoxification or "drying out," supplemented by vitamins, meals, rest, and medical care. There can be many associated physical problems. A full physical examination should be done, checking for such conditions as diabetes, pancreatitis, tuberculosis, peripheral neuropathy, and subdural hematomas. A mental status examination is indicated (ideally after two or three weeks abstinence) if cognitive problems are apparent.

Many alcoholics who are poor or isolated from their families come to medical attention through police. The middle- or upper-income alcoholic is often hospitalized under a disguised diagnosis, for example, malnutrition or gastritis, in order to avoid the stigma of alcoholism.[72]

Disulfiram (Antabuse) is a drug used to maintain sobriety while a person undergoes supportive or psychotherapeutic treatment. If taken as prescribed on a regular basis, it produces highly unpleasant symptoms whenever a person drinks, including pounding of the heart, nausea, vomiting, and shortness of breath (the result of acetaldehyde production). Side effects in the usual dose range of 0.25 gm daily include fatigue, reduced libido, and reduced potency. Toxic psychoses can occur at higher doses. In a patient over 60 it is of utmost importance to evaluate his or her cardiovascular status, since myocardial and coronary diseases are definite contraindications. Diabetes mellitus, cerebral damage, kidney disease, hypothyroidism, and hepatic cirrhosis or insufficiency all require extreme caution because of possible accidental reactions. Disulfiram may also affect the metabolism of other drugs. It should either be administered by a responsible family member or by a local emergency room, rather than self-administered by the patient.

Tranquilizers and sedatives mixed with alcohol can be life threatening. Many doctors believe that such drugs should only be given on an inpatient basis when alcohol is involved.

Alcoholics Anonymous (AA) has an impressive record of helping alcoholics achieve sobriety.[73] This organization, founded in 1935 by two men—one a stockbroker, the other a practicing surgeon—today has nearly 1.8 million members in over 89,000 groups around the world. Based on the simple proposition that recovered alcoholics can collectively reach out and help a fellow sufferer, AA has been called "an ever-expanding chain reaction of liberation."[74] AA also has a program for spouses and other relatives of alcoholics

(Al Anon) and one for teenagers whose parents drink (Alateen). Because of the magnitude of drinking problems among older people, it would be useful to have AA programs set up especially for them—perhaps called Ala-elder. Their adult children and their grandchildren should also be involved where possible, since families tend to be more negative and unsupportive to the older person who drinks heavily.

The Hanley-Hazelden Center in West Palm Beach, Florida, is one of the nation's few treatment centers that has a special unit for elderly alcoholics. The Hazelden method is based on the idea that alcoholism is a disease and that abstinence is the only cure. Individual and group therapy is facilitated by a multidisciplary team including a clergyman, a psychologist, a physician, and a chemical dependency counselor.

Nursing homes and other institutions should develop treatment programs. Group therapy (alone or with supportive psychotherapy and family counseling), is another useful approach. Recreation therapy and pastoral counseling may be helpful. Labor-management programs to treat problem drinking among employees have been successful because of the powerful added incentive of avoiding the loss of one's job. In general, however, alcoholism is extremely difficult to control. Determination and patience on the part of both the alcoholic and doctor, therapist, or other health practitioner are crucial. It may be necessary to start over again and again; the treatment of alcoholism is usually long-term or lifelong. Family and other social supports are immensely important.

For other referrals to treatment centers contact the National Council on Alcoholism and Drug Dependence, Inc. National Headquarters, 12 W. 21st St., 8th Floor, New York, NY, 10010, or call (800)NCA-CALL.

HEARING IMPAIRMENT[75]

Perceptual impairments, especially hearing loss, are of great import to older people. As the third most commonly reported chronic condition among older adults, hearing loss is more common than vision loss, although both increase with age. Over thirty percent of persons 65 years and older reported having hearing impairments. Hearing impairments rise gradually with age and then increase sharply over the age of 60. About 23% of individuals age 65 to 74 (30% of men and 17.5% of women) reported some problem in hearing, as did 32.7% of those age 75 to 84 (39.9% of men and 28.2% of women). This is compared to 48.4% of those 85 years and older (58.3% of men and 44.3% of women) with self-reported hearing loss.[76] About 13% of those 65 years and over and living in the community reported deafness in one or both ears. This was over 3 million of a total of 26 million elderly. Eight percent, or about 2 million, elderly reported using hearing aids. In earlier studies, the National Health Examination Survey of 1961–1962 studied pure tone audiometric measurements at six different frequencies in persons 18 to 79 years of age. Nearly 30% of persons age 65 to 74 and almost half of those age 75 to 79 showed hearing loss for speech alone, as compared to 10% in the general population. In the older age group 450,000 people were profoundly deaf and totally isolated from any sound. The National Health and Nutrition Examination Survey (HANES I) of 1971, which also included audiometric testing, found slightly lower percentages of hearing loss. However, in the 1977 Health Interview Survey, hearing impairment in those age 65 and over was again in the 30% range.[77] These surveys provide general estimates of the prevalence of hearing loss. In all, about 35% of those over 65 have hearing problems. (None of the studies addresses the type or cause of hearing loss.)

Hearing loss is more common among older men than older women; contrary to general belief, the Framingham study suggests that it is unlikely that a greater rate of exposure to noise in the workplace for males is the reason for male preponderance in hearing loss;[78] yet the actual cause or causes for the difference have not been found. Interestingly, intensive hearing loss is more common among older women than among older men, for reasons yet unclear.

In the late years one may experience nerve as well as conduction deafness. Conduction deafness is caused by middle or external ear pathologic conditions (sound waves are blocked before they reach the inner ear), whereas nerve deafness results from interruption of the auditory nerve pathway. Nerve deafness is much more serious since it implies damage to the nerve that carries impulses to the brain or damage to the brain itself.

Another source of hearing impairment involves the cochlea, a spiral tube of the inner ear, which resembles a small shell. The cochlea contains about 20,000 hair cells at birth. These gradually die off and cannot be replaced. Loss of these ganglion cells is called *presbycusis* and is believed to be associated with the aging of the body and/or brain. Presbycusis is the most common auditory disorder.[79] The central nervous system also is very important in hearing loss because it is the analyzing mechanism for sounds. Older people may be able to hear sounds but not understand them. Immigrants who have learned a second language appear to have special difficulty with their second language in this respect as they age.

Diseases like Meniere's syndrome may be characterized by hearing loss and are often treatable. It is also important not to overlook simple impacted wax (cerumen) in the ear as a cause of reduced hearing, although wax secretion probably diminishes with age. Infections, diabetes, cancer, chronic cardiovascular disease, and many other conditions can also cause ear problems; thus referral to the ear-nose-and-throat specialist is always indicated. Special measures may be necessary to differentiate hearing loss from cognitive impairment in older persons who are severely disabled by conditions such as stroke.

Medicines can have a cumulative effect leading to hearing loss. Extensive use of aspirin, antibiotics such as the aminoglycosides, certain common diuretics, anti-tumor agents, and other medications have a known ototoxicity (literally meaning "ear poisoning"), as do some drugs whose effects on hearing remain unknown. Many of the 38% of the older population who have arthritis consume large enough quantities of aspirin to affect their hearing. The increases in hypertension and heart failure with age signify a heightened probability of diuretic use and thus the danger of hearing loss. The possible effects on hearing must be taken into consideration when prescribing any drugs in large quantities or over a long term.

The hearing impairment occurring during aging is noted first in the higher sound frequencies and begins to be observed after age 50. This does not in itself interfere with normal speech, but the person may miss the songs of birds, a distant telephone ring, or the ticking of a watch. A person with no hearing defect can hear a whispered message at 20 feet in a reasonably quiet room. When a whisper cannot be heard at three feet, the person already has a moderate hearing loss and probably has difficulty with ordinary conversation. This is especially true if the speaker talks rapidly or there is background noise. If a conversational voice cannot be heard one foot away, the person has severe hearing loss. Obviously the loss is profound if the person cannot hear a loud shout with the mouth to the ear. Generally, it is easier for older people to hear hard consonants than soft ones, and there are often problems involving consonants such as *p* as in *pay, s* as in *sam, th* as in *then, t* as in *to, k* as in *keep, h* as in *house, sh* as in *shoe,* or *ch* as in *church.* Older persons simply may not hear any of these sounds or hear only some of them.

Noise pollution is increasingly a factor in hearing loss. The decibel level of the environment can become great enough to permanently damage the tiny hairs in the inner ear. (The decibel, named after Alexander Graham Bell, is the smallest difference in loudness the human ear can detect.) For example, violinists tend to develop slight deafness in the left ear. Many experts predict and are beginning to find hearing loss in young people who listen to loud music at high decibel levels. The increasing noise of city life portends hearing problems for the population in general. Studies of the Mabaans of Sudan, a tribe so isolated that they do not even use drums, show very clearly how lack of noise protects hearing, for they live with a background noise of 40 decibels and experience very little hearing damage. Hospitals themselves have a high decibel level in spite of their "Quiet, please" signs. Following are examples of noises and their decibel levels:

Normal breathing	10 decibels
Leaves rustling in the breeze	20 decibels
Whisper	30 decibels
Quiet restaurant	50 decibels
Normal speech	60 decibels
Busy traffic	70 decibels
Niagara Falls	90 decibels
Subway	100 decibels
Pneumatic riveter	130 decibels
Jet takeoff (discomfort)	140 decibels

The phenomenon of increased reaction time associated with decreased auditory acuity in the presence of depression warrants investigation,[80] as well as the association of mild hearing losses in the aged with diminished performance on verbal tests of intellectual ability.[81]

A comprehensive evaluation of hearing loss is essential. It is estimated that the majority of older persons wait 5 to 10 years after the beginning of their hearing loss to seek medical evaluation and treatment.[82] Careful early diagnosis is critical in salvaging what otherwise might be lost and in restoring as much function as is recoverable.

Hearing loss in older patients in mental hospitals and nursing homes is likely to be neglected. The attitude may be that it hardly matters. Yet institutions should ideally be places where verbal communication is both necessary and rewarding to patients. The results of careful diagnosis and treatment can be favorable even in a large population of institutionalized patients.

Most of the elderly with hearing problems first consult their primary care physician. He or she will refer the patient for an audiologic evaluation. Once a diagnosis has been established and the extent of hearing loss is known, audiologic rehabilitation may be called for. This includes (1) hearing aid fitting and orientation when appropriate; (2) personal and family counseling regarding strategies for aging with hearing loss; (3) speech reading instruction (teaching the person to watch face, body, and situation cues to understand another person better); and (4) referral to self-help groups.

A variety of devices may be helpful; for example, Assistive Listening Devices (ALDs) are remote microphones that bring sound from the source directly to a person's ears. One example is an infrared listening device for the television, which will eliminate room noise interference and allow for greater volume control. ALDs are also available for speech, telephones, and theatrical events. The two million older Americans who use hearing aids may choose from over one thousand different available models. Generally the stereophonic or binaural aids, which bring sound to both ears, are better than monaural aids, which bring sound to only one ear. Digitally programmable hearing aids are now available, which are effective but extremely costly ($1,500 to $3,000). Hearing aids, long associated with a dismal record of usefulness and even outright fraud, are now regulated under the Medical Devices Amendments to the Food, Drug, and Cosmetic Act and may be sold only to people who have had a medical evaluation of their hearing loss unless the examination is specifically waived by the purchaser. The evaluation must have taken place within six months of the purchase of the hearing aid. It must be remembered that not all hearing loss can be improved with a hearing aid. Cochlear implants may be recommended for certain types of hearing loss.

Hard-of-hearing individuals may also take courses in lip-reading at schools such as the Institute of Lifetime Learning of the American Association of Retired Persons—National Retired Teachers Association. The American Speech-Language-Hearing Association (ASHA), 10801 Rockville Pike, Rockville, MD 20852, can answer questions about hearing loss in the elderly and hearing aids, and provide a list of certified audiologists and speech-language pathologists in each state. Self-Help for Hard-of-Hearing People (SHHH), 7910 Woodmont Ave., Suite 1200, Bethesda, MD 20814, is a national organization that provides educational programs, self-help programs, publications, and gives referrals to local chapters.[83]

Depression and paranoid ideation are the most common severe emotional consequences of hearing loss:

> When a person becomes deaf through disease . . . not knowing what his fellow men are saying he becomes doubtful of auditory memories and images; he misinterprets auditory sense impressions which have been distorted by disease, and incorporates tinnitus caused by such disease into his world of inner phantasy. He projects his inner feelings of inferiority caused by his deafness onto his environment and develops ideas of reference. Systematization soon follows, with active delusions of persecution. If the personality is sufficiently unstable a psychotic illness results.[84]

In Chapter 5 we discuss the relationship between hearing loss and depression. Hard-of-hearing individuals are often mistakenly thought to be retarded or mentally ill. The dramatic story of Ludwig von Beethoven notwithstanding, the hearing impaired receive less interest and empathy than the visually impaired and are more subject to depression, demoralization, and even at times psychotic symptomatology. Hearing defects create irritation in others because they interfere so markedly with communication. The loud, badly articulated speech of the hard-of-hearing person and the need to shout and speak slowly make simple conversations frustrating. Wearing a hearing aid can result in a person feeling self-conscious and stereotyped as handicapped. Those with hearing problems may find themselves isolated in a crowd or at a large dinner party because the background noise exacerbates the hearing loss. Many persons with hearing problems worry about the embarrassment that might follow from missing or misunderstanding a comment in the conversation. Much of this is a reaction to the tendency of others to be impatient and insensitive to a person with a deficit.

Those with hearing deficits can often benefit from individual and group therapy and self-help groups. A sense of active help and the elimination of isolation are key components in the care of those with perceptual deficits. Therapy should initially be directed at expressing the underlying anger, grief, and sadness about having a sensory deficit in the first place, but should soon be focused on how the individual can improvise and move on to other accomplishments. Learning from and supporting others with similar deficits can be a major restorative.

A major unresolved problem with hearing loss is the lack of adequate third-party insurance reimbursement. This is a critical reason why so many elderly delay going for help with a hearing problem. Hearing aids range in price from $500 to $3,000 or more for a digital hearing aid. Medicare will reimburse for audiologic services to diagnose and evaluate hearing loss for medical or surgical treatment. However, it will *not* pay for hearing aid evaluation or consultation, nor will it pay for the hearing aid itself or any other assistive listening device. Medicaid coverage for hearing aids varies from state to state. A few private health plans provide some coverage for hearing aids, but such plans are relatively rare.

VISUAL IMPAIRMENT[85]

Vision loss is among the most frequently reported disabilities affecting older people. An estimated 4.1 million older Americans are blind or severely visually impaired. *Visual impairment* is defined as decreased visual ability that impacts on daily activities. *Severe visual impairment* is defined as the inability to read newspaper print, even with corrective lenses.[86] Five percent of people aged 65 to 74 are unable to read newsprint. The percentages are higher for older age groups: 16% at age 75 to 84 and 27% at age 85 and older are unable to read newsprint. Nearly one-half of nursing home residents aged 65 and older report some problem with vision.[87]

The four most common causes of visual impairment in people over 65 years are macular degeneration, cataracts (lens opacities), glaucoma, and diabetic retinopathy. *Macular degeneration* affects a vital part of the retina and leads to a loss of central vision, leaving peripheral vision intact. *Glaucoma* involves increased tension within and hardening of the eyeball as a result of increased

fluid. There are two basic types: acute congestive (narrow angle) and chronic (wide angle). The latter is the most common form of the disease. *Diabetic retinopathy* is a deterioration of the retina caused by chronic diabetes. Nearly half of the legally blind population is 65 years of age or older. (In legal blindness, central visual acuity does not exceed 20/200 in either eye with corrective lenses, or the visual field is less than an angle of 20 degrees.)

Much vision loss is avoidable either through prevention or treatment of the disability, especially cataracts and glaucoma. Glaucoma screening tests, for example, are an age-specific preventive health care measure recommended for persons over 40 years of age. Damage may be done to the optic nerve, with loss of vision, if glaucoma is not detected quickly enough.

Nonmedical members of mental health teams should learn the common physical symptoms of eye problems in order to avoid placing a psychiatric label on a physical process and also to increase empathy and understanding. For instance, if a person reports colored halos around lights, this could be one of the classic prodromal symptoms of glaucoma and not an illusion caused by psychological processes. Such knowledge can result in quicker referral for diagnosis and treatment.

Nearly 95% of elderly use glasses. About 50% of the oldest old, including those who wear glasses, describe some difficulty visually. Deterioration of close vision is common with aging. Nearly all older people who wear glasses do so because of presbyopia or "elder's eyes"—a loss of visual accommodation occurring after middle age, caused by diminished elasticity of the crystalline lens. Except for presbyopia, about 80% of older people have reasonably good sight until age 90 and beyond. In many cases at least one eye functions well, even though the other may lose vision.

There may be an increased slowness in visually adapting to darkness; for this reason, proper lighting is especially important, including night lights. Many older persons report visual difficulty related to glare. Night driving may need to be curtailed or, at least, the person may need to avoid looking directly at oncoming headlights while driving at night.

Psychologically, older persons greatly fear going blind and, consequently, tend to overestimate the possibilities of it happening. But actual vision impairment can be devastating, both in terms of psychological isolation and physical immobilization. With many people vision loss is gradual, and they are able slowly to compensate and adjust. A sudden loss of vision or a loss occurring when the person is feeble and unable to muster resources is usually the most difficult. The social restrictions and resultant sense of isolation for the blind or visually-impaired individual is generally greater than with the hearing-impaired. The public tends to stigmatize and stereotype those with vision problems more than those with hearing problems, probably because the handicap is more visible. Individual and group psychotherapy, as well as support groups for those with vision problems, can be highly effective in facilitating adjustment.

Rehabilitative solutions are becoming more varied and accessible.[88] A variety of low vision lenses, lights, and other optic assistive devices may help. Traditional rehabilitative and assistive efforts such as the teaching of Braille to totally blind individuals and the provision of large-type newspapers (for example, *The New York Times* and the *Reader's Digest*) and cookbooks for visually impaired individuals are still widely used today. The Library of Congress operates the Talking Books Program, which provides free tape players and record players, along with a large selection of books that have been read and recorded onto cassettes or phonograph records. In addition, many new technological devices have been developed. Hand-held magnifiers, some with light attachments, as well as concave mirrors and telescopic lenses permanently attached to the upper part of eyeglasses may be used to supplement low vision. Electronic devices that can translate print to voice output are getting better and more sophisticated. A variety of computers, calendars, thermometers, clocks, and rheostats also have voice capacity, using synthesized speech.

Volunteer readers should be available, as well as books or records on tape, stocked by public libraries.[89] Radio reading services and closed circuit television with lenses to enlarge the image on a cathode ray tube to aid in reading are available. A wide-angle mobility light (WAMO) can help persons with retinitis pigmentosa or other problems with night vision. Seeing-eye dogs and walking canes can assist those with severe visual problems.

Total blindness in both eyes, a relatively rare phenomena, even among the very old, requires special rehabilitation efforts that include (1) training the other senses; (2) training in skills and the use of assistive devices; (3) individual psychotherapy; and (4) group supports, including self-help groups. Family members or close friends should be included in training as well.[90]

The Directory of Services for Blind and Visually Impaired Persons in the U.S., 24th edition, is an exhaustive compendium of services, programs, self-help groups for specific sight disorders, and so forth around the country. It is available from the American Foundation for the Blind, 11 Pennsylvania Plaza, Suite 300, New York, NY 10001, (800) 232-3044.[91]

SEXUALITY IN OLD AGE

Societal Attitudes

Many people, young and old, are astonished at the idea of human beings making love in their seventies, eighties, and even beyond.[92] It is assumed that (1) older people do not have sexual desires, (2) they could not make love even if they did want to, (3) they are too fragile physically and it might hurt them, (4) they are physically unattractive and therefore sexually undesirable, and (5) anyway, the whole notion is shameful and decidedly perverse. There may also be anxieties on the part of adult children related to oedipal connections with their parents. (Many of us remain convinced that *our* parents were not interested in sex.) Yet, in work with older people it is clear that sex is a major concern in late life. Fear about loss of sexual prowess is a common preoccupation for the older man and can reach devastating proportions. Older women will often describe sexual desires, but many regard such feelings as undignified, if not depraved. Some older persons can freely accept their interest in sex, but their children and grandchildren may disapprove and make them feel guilty.

Older persons become the butt of jokes. Older men are frequently ridiculed as impotent or as "dirty old men." (A bumper sticker protesting this idea reads "I'm not a dirty old man. I'm a sexy senior citizen.") Older women fare even worse in the public eye. They are the neuters of our culture, who have mysteriously metamorphosed into sexual oblivion once they reach the age of 50 and beyond.

Homes for the aged, nursing homes, and mental institutions all add to the impression that older persons are sexless. There are seldom serious and dignified provisions for privacy; in fact, there seems to be an agreement that the aged must be prevented from having any sexual contacts. They are often rigidly segregated, men from women, with no visiting in each other's rooms. Conjugal visits with spouses are seldom provided for. Even husbands and wives living in the same institution may not be allowed to live or sleep together. Nursing staffs become anxious and upset when older persons, understandably, resort to masturbation. The problem is often no less difficult for older people who live with their children or in other people's homes. Federal regulations issued on June 1, 1978, provide some right to privacy in institutions, but only for married couples, and only in nursing homes that participate in federal Medicare and Medicaid programs.

The fear of death is another factor affecting sexuality. There are many symbolic associations between sexual activity and death—as in the French word for orgasm, *petit mort* or "little death." Fears of the occurrence of heart attacks or strokes during the course of sex may lead couples to acquire twin beds, separate bedrooms, and a habit of abstinence that may or may not be justified medically. Currents of anxiety, depression,

and hostility can accompany these fears as sexuality is inhibited.

Female longevity creates another baffling situation. Since 4.3% of older women have never been married, many others are widowed, often relatively early, and still others have husbands who are older than they and perhaps in poor health, there are many women without partners. What alternatives do they have? Compared to men, women as a group do not yet have the same cultural freedoms to socialize with younger members of the opposite sex. There are not enough older men available. Extramarital affairs are difficult for many to reconcile religiously or morally. Masturbation, although increasing in old age, is still frequently considered shameful or harmful. Thus women legitimately complain that they do not have suitable sexual expression or even information that is relevant to sexual needs in late life. Solutions include the eventual equalizing of the life expectancies of men and women through knowledge obtained from research, the equalizing of sex roles to give women the same opportunities as men, the encouragement of dating and relationships with younger men, the provision of accurate information about the benefits of masturbation, and the development of more lenient attitudes toward the homosexuality that already exists.[93]

Homosexuality as a life-style has both advantages and disadvantages in the later years. The stereotype of the aging homosexual is that of a lonely, bitter, isolated person. The reality, according to studies in this area, is much more complex and includes many close, satisfying relationships that have lasted 40 years or more.[94] Kimmel's study in the late 1970s of 14 aging gay men, ages 55 to 81, found older gays were used to taking care of themselves, with fewer role disruptions than older men with wives and families. On the negative side, gay men experienced both age and sexual-orientation discrimination, and the combination contributed to a tendency among older gay couples to withdraw from society. Lesbian women have a particular advantage as they reach mid-life and beyond, since partners who are their own age will have the same life expectancy, and in later life they move into a world that becomes increasingly female with each decade.

Bereavement, disablement, problems of inheritance and other legal issues, and ageism within the gay community itself can obviously all become problems for older gays. A program called Senior Action in a Gay Environment (SAGE), developed by the gay community in New York to offer free social services to older gay men and women, has become a model of supportive services to the gay community nationwide.

Specific sexual issues for male homosexuals and, increasingly, for the public at large, result from the AIDS epidemic beginning in the early 1980s. Although the majority of AIDS cases to date have been homosexual or bisexual men, AIDS treatment centers are beginning to find more women with AIDS. In addition, the number of AIDS patients over the age of 60 is rising. Early detection and treatment with drugs such as AZT and protease inhibitors can now prolong lives and improve the quality of life. More importantly, prevention of the disease through the practice of safe sex, including the routine use of condoms, the avoidance of exchange of body fluids (semen, blood, and possibly saliva), and testing of potential partners for the AIDS virus can save lives. Most cities have centers and services that can offer testing, information, support, and direct help in treating and preventing AIDS. The U.S. Public Health Service and most state health departments now provide information and referral services.

Research Findings

The data that have been accumulating on the sexuality of older persons have generally supported the view that sexual capacity has been underestimated except where illness or lack of a sexual partner is a factor. Kinsey can be considered the pioneer in modern studies of sexuality in older people. The aged constituted only a small part of his sample, but his findings were useful in beginning to demolish the notion of termination of sexuality in late life. It was found that most men at age 60 were sexually capable physically and

that there was little evidence of sexual decline in women even late in life.

Masters and Johnson's contributions included direct clinical observations of sexual performance as well as interviews. The Duke Longitudinal Study examined 250 people between ages 60 and 94 every three years (Palmore, 1970). Interestingly, these studies found that about 15% of older persons actually increased their patterns of sexual activity and interest as they aged. The Baltimore Longitudinal Study studied the sexuality of older men over a period of years.

Studies by Brecher (1984) as well as by Starr and Weiner (1981) queried the elderly directly about sexual behavior and feelings. Both found a high degree of interest in sexuality and continued sexual activity when a partner was available. Many older persons reported that sex was as satisfying or even more satisfying in later years.

Physical Characteristics of Sex in Old Age

Older Men.   Changes that occur with aging are often misinterpreted as evidence that older men are becoming impotent. "From a psychosexual point of view, the male over age 50 has to contend with one of the great fallacies of our culture. Every man in this age group is arbitrarily identified by both public and professional alike as sexually impaired."[95]

There are certain sexual changes associated with chronological aging. The older man ordinarily takes longer to obtain an erection and to achieve ejaculation. Manual stimulation of the penis may be necessary in the initial phase of lovemaking. But as Masters and Johnson point out, "one of the advantages of the aging process with specific reference to sexual functioning is that, generally speaking, control of ejaculatory demand in the 50–75 year age group is far better than in the 20–40 year age group."[96] Translated, this means that many older men can maintain a sexual erection and make love longer before coming to orgasm. This can be a decided advantage for female partners. There is also the advantage of lovemaking experience gained throughout a lifetime.

Older men will notice a reduction in the volume of seminal fluid, which explains the decrease in the pressure to ejaculate. Orgasm begins to be experienced in a shorter one-stage period, as compared to two stages in earlier life, but it remains pleasurable. There is, after age 50, a physiologically extended refractory period, meaning that the capacity for erection following ejaculation cannot be regained as quickly as in younger men. It may be 12 to 24 hours before sex is again possible. Couples who are aware of this may want to delay ejaculation in order to make love for a longer period of time. The penis will become flaccid more promptly after ejaculation; this is natural and not a sign of impairment.

A vital point to remember is that the older man does not lose his facility for erection as he ages unless physical illness or emotional anxiety interferes. For example, laboratory studies at Mount Sinai Hospital in New York City found that most men over 60 had penile erections with their sexual dreaming, including one who was 96. Many men over 60 are satisfied with one or two ejaculations a week or less. But others enjoy sex and satisfy a partner more frequently than that. The amount of sexual activity tends to reflect patterns established earlier in life. A consistent pattern of sexual expression also helps to maintain sexuality.

Older men are usually able to continue some form of physical sexual response until their seventies, eighties, and beyond. If they lose interest or become impotent, there can be a number of factors involved: boredom, fatigue, overeating, excessive drinking, medical and psychiatric disabilities (impotence can be one of the first signs of depression), and fear of failure. The last is common and often based on misinformation about what is normative in old age. Among physical causes of erectile dysfunction are atherosclerotic, cardiorespiratory, endocrine, genitourinary, hematological, neurological, and infectious disorders. Frequently, perineal prostatectomy and occasionally suprapubic and urethral prostatectomy can be factors. Drugs may also be responsible. Tranquilizers, antidepressants, and certain antihypertensive drugs, as well as alcohol have all been reported as inducing impotence. Papaverine, phentolamine, and/or prostaglandin E-1 are effective intracavernous pharmacotherapeutic agents. External vacuum devices are also widely used and effective.

In cases of intractable physical impotence caused by disease, injury, or in rare cases, by psychological factors which do not respond to other forms of treatment, surgical penile implants or prosthesis may be useful. Careful evaluation of both partners in a relationship is necessary to select appropriate candidates for implants. More often, erectile problems are not intractable and respond to medical treatments as well as various psychotherapies, including group, individual, couples, and sexual therapies.

Older Women. Biologically, the older woman experiences little sexual impairment as she ages. If she is in reasonably good health, she can expect to continue sex activities until late in life, assuming she has maintained a frame of mind that encourages this and has a sexual partner with whom to enjoy it. Menopause, also called "change of life" or "climacteric," occurs with the cessation of menstruation, usually between the ages of 45 and 50. Certain myths have surrounded menopause, including a fear of insanity, the ending of sexual desire and attractiveness, and the myths of inevitable depression, adverse physical symptoms, and defeminization. These have been disputed by research observations of the female climacteric. About 60% of women experience no remarkable physical or emotional symptoms with menopause, and many of those who do have minimal to moderate physical complaints. A small percentage have severe problems requiring a variety of medical and other interventions. Adverse psychological reactions such as depression occur for some, but these are not inevitable, and in fact often reflect a pattern of depression beginning earlier in life, unconnected to the menopause. Psychotherapy and various forms of group supports can provide relief. In severe cases, drug therapies may be successful.

The physiological situation of older women during and after menopause requires review. They commonly suffer from the effects of gradual steroid insufficiency, which causes a thinning of the vaginal walls. Cracking, bleeding, and pain (dyspareunia) during sexual intercourse can result. There may be vaginal burning and itching (estrogen-deficient vaginitis). The urethra and bladder can become more subject to irritation as they are less cushioned by the atrophied vaginal walls, and there can be burning or frequency of urination after sexual contact. The loss of sex steroids may also reduce the length and diameter of the vagina and may shrink the major labia. Estrogen replacement therapy can substantially reduce menopausal symptoms such as vaginal atrophy and dryness. The natural estrogen complex (conjugated estrogens, USP) has been in use for more than 40 years. It is inexpensive and can be helpful against osteoporosis (chronic backache, compression fractures, and "dowager's hump"), estrogen-deficient vaginitis, pruritus, and other aggravating symptoms. Studies of hormone replacement therapy published in 1975 and 1976 showed a somewhat increased risk of endometrial cancer, especially if estrogen was taken for more than one year. Since that time, new guidelines for use include smaller and shorter-term dosages, often combined with another female hormone, progestin (as a protection against endometrial cancer), and a greater clarity about contraindications. However, because of continuing concern about estrogen and breast cancer, long-term use of hormone replacement therapy remains controversial. On the positive side, recent studies have found that women on estrogen therapy were less at risk for the development of heart disease, osteoporosis, and other late life conditions. Possible benefits and risks must be carefully weighed for each patient. The National Heart, Lung, and Blood Institute conducted a double-blind, placebo-controlled, clinical trial in post-menopausal women of unopposed estrogen (estrogen alone) and estrogen/progestational agent combinations (called PEPI). This study supports the value of hormone replacement therapy. Further large-scale studies of the menopause are underway under the auspices of the National Institutes of Health's Women's Health Initiative.

Vaginal secretions that lubricate the vagina may decrease with age. But this does not seem to occur in women who maintain sexual stimulation on a regular basis once or twice a week from youth on, whether through self-stimulation or with a partner. As with men, a consistent pattern of sexual activity is beneficial to women in maintaining their sexual capacities. Muscle tone affecting the "grip" of the vagina on the penis during intercourse can be improved through special exercises (Kegel) designed originally for other gynecological problems.

Sex and Chronic Physical Conditions

The realization that people with chronic illnesses have sexual interests may be unexpected and even unwelcomed. It complicates the medical picture for doctors. The well spouse may not know how to respond. Yet patients may live for years with the help of medical treatment and want as normal a life as possible, including sex. Most current studies of sex concentrate on healthy populations rather than including people with disabling conditions. Sexual activity may be both therapeutic and preventive medicine. There is some evidence, for example, that sexual activity helps arthritis, probably because of adrenal gland production of cortisone. The sexual act is itself a form of physical activity, helping people stay in good physical condition. It can help to reduce both physical and psychological tensions.

Cerebrovascular accidents and coronary attacks can cause much concern, especially if patients and doctors do not discuss if and when sex can be safely resumed. The oxygen cost in sexual intercourse is equivalent to that in climbing a flight or two of stairs or walking briskly at a rate of two miles an hour. The heart rate ranges from 90 to 150 beats a minute, with an average of 120 beats—about the level for light to moderate physical effort. There is not yet a conclusive mass of data regarding sudden death during sex, but it probably occurs much less often than patients fear and somewhat more than the reported incidence (because of reluctance to report accurately). A conservative estimate is that less than 1% of sudden coronary deaths occur during intercourse. Potency may be affected psychologically because heart disease is not only frightening but also tends to undermine confidence in physical capacities. One could easily argue that the anxiety caused by restricting sex may be greater for some people than the actual physical risk from participating in it. A program of physical conditioning under a doctor's care is necessary in preparing for the safe resumption of sexual activities.

Diabetes mellitus is common in old age and causes impotence two to five times as often as in the general population, although sex interest and desire may persist. Impotence from poorly controlled diabetes usually disappears when control is established. But the adequately controlled diabetic man who develops impotence usually has a more permanent problem. The effects of diabetes on the sexuality of women have not yet been well studied, but current research suggests that sexuality is affected far less by diabetes in women than in men.

Pelvic surgery must be carefully planned to avoid unnecessary sexual impairment. Of men who have had prostatectomies, 70% remain potent. Three types of prostatectomy are performed:

1. *Transurethral resection of the prostate (TURP).* A thin, hollow, fiber-optic tube is inserted in the penis, an electric loop is maneuvered through the tube, and the gland is removed. The tissue sometimes grows back; therefore TURP is indicated chiefly when the prostate is not too enlarged, and for men over seventy.

2. *Perineal.* An incision is made between the scrotum and anus, removing most of the prostate. This procedure is used in the surgical treatment of cancer of the prostate.

3. *Suprapubic or retropubic.* The incision is made through the abdomen and is performed when the gland is very enlarged.

After a prostatectomy the semen is deposited in the bladder rather than ejaculated, resulting in "dry ejaculations." However, some semen may still pass through the penis or the prostate may regrow; therefore, a prostectomy is not a reliable form of birth control. Potency is rarely affected with the TURP and suprapubic approaches, and some men even have increased potency. Impotence may occur for psychological reasons. Nonpsychological, physical impotence is most often associated with the perineal approach.

In general, hysterectomies, with or without oophorectomy, do not produce long-term change in sexual desire or performance in women, although some women are especially sensitive to the loss of sexual sensations from the cervix and womb and may need to learn to focus more on clitoral stimulation and sensation. Women may experience a physiologically induced emotional lability and instability for a period of time, although this usually clears without medical treatment. Other psychological reactions include the fear of sexual impairment, fear of loss of sexual desire, and fear of becoming sexually unattractive. Like men, women tend to react emotionally to any subtractive surgery, especially if it is a major subtraction like hysterectomy. Mastectomies, ileostomies, and colostomies are other common surgical procedures that can lead to sexual concern and possible problems. The provision of information, counseling, and individual and group psychotherapies and support can all be immensely helpful in resolving psychological issues.

Peyronie's disease can interfere with sexual performance in men unless it responds to treatment or regresses spontaneously. The symptoms are an upward bowing of the penis, with a shift angled to the right or left. Hard tumors in the corpora cavernosa cause the symptoms, but the cause of these tumors is unknown. Intercourse may be difficult and painful or completely impossible. A variety of treatments may be used and the disease itself may regress in about four years. This disease has been thought to be rare, but judging from our own clinical experience, we suspect it is more common than is believed.

Mental Health Treatment Considerations

Sex, self-esteem, and self-image are closely related. A task of the mental health specialist is to help older people deal with their personal feelings, fears, and possible misunderstandings about sex in old age as well as to recognize and support the special developmental qualities of sex and intimacy that can occur in the later years. One of these special qualities we call "the second language of sex"—a growing capacity, seen in many emotionally healthy older persons, to develop intimacy and communication in a love relationship to new levels.[97] The capacity for sexual intercourse is only one of the measures of a successful relationship. Other forms of stimulation and arousal can be equally important. But perhaps most important is the quality of the emotional interaction between partners. If sexual activity and potency decline while interest remains high, the therapist and patient must consider whether improvement is possible in any or all of the areas—including physical capacity, other forms of stimulation that do not rely on erectile ability, and the emotional relationship itself. Physical examinations, medical treatments, marital counseling, individual and group psychotherapy, sex counseling and support groups may be indicated and can be successful.[98]

Masters and Johnson, in treating older people in their clinic, reported a higher incidence of referrals of men with sexual dysfunction than women, probably because of the need for erectile capacity in male sexuality. They reported a higher failure rate with their older patients, which they attributed to the length of time the problem existed and not the ages of the patients. Nonetheless, there was a more than 50% success rate even when the problem may have existed 25 years or longer.

> The fact that innumerable men and women have not been sexually effective before reaching their late fifties or early sixties is no reason to condemn them to continuing sexual dysfunction as they live out the rest of their life-span. The disinclination of the medical and behavioral professions to treat the aging

population for sexual dysfunction has been a major disservice perpetrated by those professions upon the general problem.[99]

Sex education for older people is important. Normal age changes need to be understood so that neither men nor women mistake such changes for loss of sexuality. Techniques of sexual activities especially pertinent to old age should be clarified. (For example, sex in the morning may be preferable for those older persons who fatigue easily.) The importance of masturbation when sexual partners are unavailable should be emphasized for those who do not find its practice personally upsetting. As discussed earlier, masturbation helps preserve potency in men and sexual functioning in women, releases tensions, stimulates sexual appetite, and contributes to general well-being. It must always be remembered that the current generation of older people was brought up to believe that masturbation is harmful physically and mentally. Such cultural and historic viewpoints cannot be lightly dismissed, but people may be responsive to new information.

Another cultural element is seen in the reluctance of some older women to go to a doctor for help with gynecological problems. Women with even advanced carcinoma of the vulva may delay asking for medical care. Some older women tolerate general prolapse of the uterus for long periods of time, and it is not unusual to find infection and edema from such untreated conditions. Women may need encouragement in accepting examinations on a regular basis.

Regular physical examinations, proper medical treatment, and adequate diet and exercise all help to preserve sexual capacities. As Masters and Johnson have so encouragingly reported, the two major requirements for enjoyable sexual activity until late in life are reasonably good health and an interested and interesting partner.

SELECTED READINGS

Abrams, R. C., & Alexopoulos, G. S. (1987). Substance abuse in the elderly: Alcohol and prescription drugs. *Hospital and Community Psychiatry, 38,* 1285–1287.

Adelman, R. D., & Butler, R. N. (1989). Elder abuse and neglect. In Kaplan, H. I., & Saddock, B. J. (Eds.), *Comprehensive textbook of psychiatry,* 5th ed. (pp. 2053–2056). Baltimore, MD: Williams & Wilkins.

Ade-Ridder, L. (1990). Sexuality and marital qualities among older married couples. In Brubaker, T. H. (Ed.), *Family relationships in later life,* 2nd ed. (pp. 29–48). Newbury Park, CA: Sage Publications.

Administration on Aging. (1996). Opening the door on elder abuse (special issue.) *Aging, 367.*

American Foundation for the Blind. (1993). *The directory of services for blind and visually impaired persons in the U.S.,* 24th ed. New York: Author.

Allers, C. (1990). AIDS and the older adult. *The gerontologist, 30,* 405–407.

Almvig, C. (1982). *The invisible minority: Aging and lesbianism.* Utica, NY: Institute of Gerontology.

American Association of Retired Persons. (1993). *A report on hearing aids: User perspectives and concerns.* Washington, DC: Author.

American Association of Retired Persons, Minority Affairs. (1995). *A portrait of older minorities.* Washington, DC: Author.

American Association of Retired Persons, Women's Initiative. (1994). *Facts about older women: Income and poverty.* Washington, DC: Author.

Anderson Jr., W. B. (1995). Eye: Clinical issues. In Maddox, G. L. (Ed.) *The Encyclopedia of aging* (pp. 354–357). New York: Springer.

Aravanis, S. C., Adelman, R. D., Breckman, R., et. al. (1993). *Diagnostic and treatment guidelines on elder abuse and neglect.* Chicago: American Medical Association.

Axin, J. (1989). Women and aging: Issues of adequacy and equity. *Journal of Women and Aging, 1*(3), 339–362.

Bandler, J. (1989, July). Family protection and women's issues in social security. *Social Work,* 307–311.

Barker, J. C. (1994). Recognizing cultural differences: Health-care providers and elderly patients. *Gerontology and Geriatrics Education, 15*(1), 9–21.

Barresi, C. M., & Stull, D. E. (Eds.) (1993). *Ethnic elderly and long-term care.* New York: Springer.

Bennett, G., & Kingston, P. (1993). *Elder abuse, concepts theories and interventions.* London: Chapman & Hall.

Beresford, T. P., & Gomberg, E. S. L. (1995). *Alcohol and aging.* New York: Oxford University Press.

Berger, R. M. (1982). *Gay and gray: The older homosexual.* Urbana, IL: University of Illinois Press.

Bienenfeld, D. (1987). Alcoholism in the elderly. *American Family Physician, 36*(2), 163–196.

Birren, J. E., Butler, R. N., Greenhouse, S. W., Sokoloff, L., & Yarrow, M. R. (1963). *Human aging: A biological and biobehavioral study.* U.S. Public Health

Service pub. no. 986. Washington, DC: U.S. Government Printing Office. (Reprinted 1971, 1974).

Blazer, D. G. (1995). Alcohol abuse and dependence. In Abrams, W. B., Beers, M. H., & Berkow, R. (Eds.), *The Merck manual of geriatrics,* 2nd ed. (pp. 1245–1248). Whitehouse Station, NJ: Merck & Co.

Blendon, R. J., Aiken, L. H., Freeman, H. E., & Corey, M. A. (1989). Access to medical care for black and white Americans, a matter of continuing concern. *Journal of the American Medical Association, 261,* 278–281.

Breckman, R., & Adelman, R. (1989). *Helping victims of elder mistreatment.* Newbury Park, CA: Sage Publications.

Brink, T. L. (Ed.). (1994). *The forgotten aged: Ethnic, psychiatric, and societal minorities.* Binghamton, NY: The Haworth Press.

Brink, T. L. (Ed.). (1992). Hispanic aged mental health. Binghamton, NY: The Haworth Press.

Brody, E. M. (1990). *Women in the middle: Their parent care years.* New York: Springer.

Browne, C., & Broderick, A. (1994, May). Asian and Pacific Island Elders: Issues for social work practice and education. *Social Work, 39*(3), 252–259.

Browne, C., Fong, R., & Mokuau, N. (1994). The mental health of Asian and Pacific Island elders: Implications for research and mental health administration. *Journal of Mental Health Administration, 21*(1), 52–59.

Burr, J. A., & Mutchler, J. E. (1993). Nativity, acculturation, and economic status: Explanations of Asian American living arrangements in later life. *Journal of Gerontology: Social Sciences, 48,* S55–S63.

Butler, R. N. (1975). *Why survive? Being old in America.* New York: Harper & Row.

Butler, R. N., & Lewis, M. I. (1993). *Love and sex after sixty,* revised ed. New York: Ballantine.

Canter, W. A., & Koretzky, M. B. (1989). Treatment of geriatric alcoholism. *Clinical Gerontologist, 9*(1), 67–69.

Carter, T. (1994, Sept.). Age related vision changes: A primary care guide. *Geriatrics, 49*(9), 37–45.

Castex, G. M. (1994, May). Providing services to Hispanic/Latino populations: Profiles in diversity. *Social Work, 39*(3), 288–296.

Chaneles, L. M., & Burnett, C. (1989). *Older offenders: Current trends.* Binghamton, New York: The Haworth Press.

Chatters, L. M. (1990). The family life of older black adults. *Journal of Health and Social Policy, 1,* 45–53.

Chatters, L. M., & Taylor, R. J. (1989, July). Life problems and coping strategies of older black adults. *Social Work,* 313–319.

Chen, Y. (1993). Improving the economic security of minority persons as they enter old age. In *Minority elders: Longevity, economics, and health.* Washington, DC: Gerontological Society of America.

Chung, M. (1989, September). Elderly Chinese living in the United States: Assimilation or adjustment. *Social Work,* 457–461.

Coke, M., & Twaite, J. A. (1995). The black elderly: Satisfaction and quality of later life. Binghamton, NY: The Haworth Press.

Comfort, A. (1978). *Sexual consequences of disability.* Philadelphia: George F. Stickley.

Commonwealth Fund Commission on Elderly People Living Alone. (1993). *The unfinished agenda: Improving the well-being of elderly people living alone.* New York: The Commonwealth Fund.

Commonwealth Fund Commission on Elderly People Living Alone. (1989, September). *Poverty and poor health among elderly Hispanic Americans.* New York: The Commonwealth Fund.

Congressional Caucus for Women's Issues. (1990, June 29). Women excluded from federally funded research, study finds. *Update, 10*(5), 1, 13.

Corso, J. F. (1995). Auditory perception. In Maddox, G. L. (Ed.), *The encyclopedia of aging* (pp. 95–97). New York: Springer.

Corso, J. F. (1995). Hearing. In Maddox, G. L. (Ed.) *The encyclopedia of aging* (pp. 449–452). New York: Springer.

Covey, H. C., & Menard, S. (1987). Trends in arrests among the elderly. *The Gerontologist, 27,* 666–672.

Cutler, S. J. (1995). Crime (against and by the elderly). In Maddox, G. L. (Ed.), *The encyclopedia of aging* (pp. 243–244). New York: Springer.

Daly, A, Jennings, J., Beckett, J. O., & Leashore, B. R. (1995, March). Effective coping strategies of African Americans. *Social Work, 40*(2), 240–248.

Daniels, R. S., Baumhover, L. A., & Clark-Daniels, C. L. (1989). Physicians' Mandatory Reporting of Elder Abuse. *The Gerontologist, 29*(3), 321–327.

Dodson, J. E. (Ed.). (1983). *Strengths of black families—An afrocentric educational manual: Toward a non-deficit perspective in services to families and children.* Nashville, TN: University of Tennessee, School of Social Work.

Douglas, K. C., & Fujimoto, D. (1995). Asian Pacific Elders: Implications for health care providers. *Ethnogeriatrics, 11,* 69–83.

Dowd, J. J., & Bengtson, V. L. (1978). Aging in minority populations: An examination of the double jeopardy hypothesis. *Journal of Gerontology, 33*(3), 427–436.

Dufour, M. C., Archer, L., & Gordis, E. (1992). Alcohol and the elderly. *Clinics in Geriatric Medicine,* 6(127).

Eastman, M. (1994). Old age abuse: A new perspective (2nd ed.) London: Chapman & Hall.

Fanon, F. (1967). *Black skin, white masks.* New York: Grove Press.

Feldman, M. D., Fillit, H., & McCormick, W. C. (1994). AIDS in the older patient. *Patient Care, 28,* 61–71.

Fillit, H., Fruchtman, S., Sell, L., & Rosen, N. (1989). AIDS and the elderly: A case and its implications. *Geriatrics, 44,* 65–70.

Flynn, E. E. (1996). Crime and age. In Birren, J. E. (Ed.), *Encyclopedia of gerontology* (vol. 1, pp. 353–359). San Diego, CA: Academic Press.

Fulmer, T. T., & O'Malley, T. A. (1987). *Inadequate care of the elderly.* New York: Springer.

Fulop, G., Reinhardt, J., Strain, J. J., Paris, B., Miller, M., & Fillet, H. (1993). Identification of alcoholism and depression in a geriatric medicine outpatient clinic. *Journal of the American Geriatrics Society, 41,* 737–741.

Garner, J. D., & Young, A. A. (Eds.). (1994). *Women and healthy aging: Living productively in spite of it all.* Binghamton, NY: The Haworth Press.

Gelfand, D. E. (1994). *Aging and ethnicity: Knowledge and services.* New York: Springer.

Gibson, R. C., & Jackson, J. S. (1992). The black oldest old: Health functioning and informal support. In Suzman, R., Willis, D., & Manton, K. (Eds.), *The oldest old* (pp. 129–147). New York: Oxford University Press.

Gomberg, E. S. L. (1996). Alcohol and drugs. In Birren, J. E. (Ed.), *Encyclopedia of gerontology* (vol. 1, pp. 93–101). San Diego, CA.: Academic Press.

Goodman, H. (1985, Spring/Summer). Serving the elderly blind: A generic approach. *Journal of Gerontological Social Work, 8*(3/4), 153–168.

Gordon-Salant, S. (1995). Hearing. In Birren, J. E. (Ed.), *Encyclopedia of gerontology* (vol. 2, pp. 643–653). San Diego, CA.: Academic Press.

Grad, S. (1996). *Income of the population 55 or older, 1994.* Washington, DC: U.S. Department of Health and Human Services, Social Security Administration, U.S. Government Printing Office.

Gran, L., & Susser, I. (1989). *Women in the later years: Health, social, and cultural perspectives.* Binghamton, NY: The Haworth Press.

Graham, K., Saunders, S. J., Flower, M. C., Timney, C. B., White-Campbell, M., & Pietropaolo, A. Z. (1994). *Addiction treatment for older adults: Eval-*

uation of an innovative client-centered approach. Binghamton, NY: The Haworth Press.

Greenwald, M. (1984). The Sage model for serving older lesbians and gay men. In *Homosexuality and Social Work* (p. 53–61). Binghamton, NY: The Haworth Press.

Guam, J. K., & Whitford, G. S. (1992). Adaptation and age-related expectations of older gay and lesbian adults. *The Gerontologist, 32*(3), 367–374.

Gulya, A. J. (1995) Ear disorders. In Abrams, W. B., Beers, M. H., & Berkow, R. (Eds.), *The Merck manual of geriatrics,* 2nd ed. (pp. 1315–1342). Whitehouse Station, NJ: Merck & Co.

Gutmann, D. (1987). *Reclaimed powers: Toward a new psychology of men and women in later life.* New York: Basic Books.

Harper, M. S. (Ed.). (1990). *Minority aging: Essential curricula content for selected health and allied health professionals.* (DHHS Publication no. HRS P-DV-90–4). Washington, DC: U.S. Government Printing Office.

Hartman, A. (1990). Aging is a feminist issue. *Social Work, 35*(5), 387–388.

Haug, M. R., Ford, A. B., & Sheafor, M. (Eds.). (1985). *The physical and mental health of aged women.* New York: Springer.

Haynes, C. L. (Ed.). (1993). *Women in midlife: Planning for tomorrow.* Binghamton, NY: The Haworth Press.

Hazzard, W. R. (1985). The sex differential in longevity. In Andres, R. Biermen, E. L., & Hazzard, W. R. (Eds.), *The principles of geriatric medicine* (pp. 72–81). New York: McGraw-Hill.

Herzog, A. R., Holden, K. C., & Seltzor, M. M. (Eds.). (1989). *Health and economic status of older women.* Amityville, NY: Baywood.

Ho, M. K. (1987). *Family therapy with ethnic minorities.* Newbury Park, CA: Sage Publications.

Indian Health Service (1995). *Trends in Indian health.* Washington, DC: U.S. Department of Health and Human Services, Indian Health Service.

Jackson, J. S. (1995). African American aged. In Maddox, G. L. (Ed.), *The encyclopedia of aging* (pp. 30–32). New York: Springer.

Jackson, J. S., Albright, J., Miles, T. P., Miranda, M. R., Nunez, C., Stanford, E. P., Yee, B. W. K., Yee, D. L., & Yeo, G. (Eds.). (1994). *Minority elders: Five goals toward building a public policy base.* Washington, DC: The Gerontological Society of America.

Jackson, J. S., Chatters, L. M., & Taylor, R. J. (1993). *Aging in black America.* Newbury Park, CA: Sage Publications.

Jackson, J. S., & Kalavar, J. (1994). Equity and distributive justice across age cohorts: A life-course family perspective. In Cohen, L. (Ed.), *Justice across generations: What does it mean?* Washington, DC: American Association of Retired Persons.

John, R. (1995). *American Indian and Alaska Native elders: An assessment of their current status and provision of services.* Rockville, MD: Indian Health Service.

John, R. (1991). *Defining and meeting the needs of Native American elders.* Final Report of the Administration on Aging Grant # 90AR0117/01 (11 volumes). National Technical Information Service, series PB91174284.

John, R., & Baldridge, D. (1996). *The National Indian Council on Aging Report: Health and long-term care for Indian elders.* Washington, DC: National Indian Policy Center.

Johnson, T. F. (Ed.). (1995). *Elder mistreatment: Ethical issues, dilemmas, and decisions.* Binghamton, NY: The Haworth Press.

Jones, F. C. (1973, January). The lofty role of the black grandmother. *The Crisis,* 19–21.

Kelly, J. (1977). The aging male homosexual: Myth and reality. *The Gerontologist, 17*(4), 328–331.

Kimmel, D. C. (1992). The families of older gay men and lesbians. *Generations, 16–17*(3), 37–38.

Kimmel, D., Raphael, S., Catalano, D. J., & Robinson, M. (1984). Older lesbians and gay men. In *Sourcebook on lesbian/gay healthcare.* San Francisco, CA: National Gay Health Education Foundation.

Kinsey, A. C., Pomeroy, W. B., Martin, C. R., & Gebhard, P. H. (1948). *Sexual behavior in the human male.* Philadelphia: W. B. Saunders.

Kinsey, A. C., Pomeroy, W. B., Martin, C. R., & Gebhard, P. H. (1953). *Sexual behavior in the human female.* Philadelphia: W. B. Saunders.

Kleinschmidt, J. J. (1996). An orientation to vision loss program: Meeting the needs of newly visually impaired older adults. *The Gerontologist, 36*(4), 534–538.

Kosberg, J. I., & Garcia, J. L. (1995). *Elder abuse: International and cross-cultural perspectives.* Binghamton, NY: The Haworth Press.

Kramer, B. J. (1995). Native-American aged. In Maddox, G. L. (Ed.), *The encyclopedia of aging* (pp. 671–673). New York: Springer.

Krause, N. (1993). Race differences in life satisfaction among aged men and women. *Journal of Gerontology: Social Sciences, 48,* S235–S244.

Kunitz, S. J., & Levy, J. E. (1991). *Navajo aging.* Tucson, AZ: The University of Arizona Press.

Kupfer, C. (1995). Ophthalmologic disorders. In Abrams, W. B., Beers, M. H., & Berkow, R. (Eds.), *The Merck manual of geriatrics,* 2nd ed. (pp. 1289–1314). Whitehouse Station, NJ: Merck & Co.

Lachs, M. S., & Pillemer, K. (1995). Abuse and neglect of elderly persons. *New England Journal of Medicine, 332,* 437–443.

Lazzari, M. M., Ford, H. R., & Haughey, K. J. (1996, March). Making a difference: Women of action in the community. *Social Work, 41*(2), 197–205.

Lee, J. A. (Ed.). (1991). *Gay midlife and maturity.* Binghamton, NY: The Haworth Press.

Lee, M. H. M., & Itoh, M. (1995). Rehabilitation: Self-help devices. In Abrams, W. B., Beers, M. H., & Berkow, R. (Eds.), *The Merck manual of geriatrics,* 2nd ed. (pp. 376–77). Whitehouse Station, NJ: Merck & Co.

Leighton, D. A. (1985). Special senses—aging of the eye. In *Textbook of Geriatric Medicine and Gerontology,* 3rd ed. (Ch. 21). Edinburgh: Churchill Livingstone.

Levin, J. S., & Taylor, R. J. (1993). Gender and age differences in religiosity among black Americans. *The Gerontologist, 33,* 16–23.

Lewis, M. I. (1985). Older women and health: An overview. In Golub, S., & Freedman, R. J. (Eds.), *Health needs of women as they age.* NY: The Haworth Press.

Lewis, M. I., & Butler, R. N. (1972). Why is women's lib ignoring old women? *International Journal of Aging and Human Development, 3*(3), 223–231.

Lieber, C. S. (1995). Medical disorders of alcoholism. *New England Journal of Medicine, 333,* 1058–1065.

Linet, O. I., & Ogrinc, F. G. (1996, April 4). Efficacy and safety of intracavernosal alprostadil in men with erectile dysfunction. *New England Journal of Medicine, 334*(14), 873–877.

Logan, S. M. L., Freeman, E. M., & McRoy, R. G. (1990). *Social work practice with black families.* New York: Longman.

Lopez, C., & Aguilera, E. (1991). *On the sidelines: Hispanic elderly and the continuum of care.* Washington, DC: National Council of La Raza.

Luckey, I. (1994, Feb.). African American elders: The support network of generational kin. *Families in Society: The Journal of Contemporary Human Services, 75*(2), 82–89.

Lum, O. M. (1995). Health status of Asians and Pacific Islanders. *Ethnogeriatrics, 11,* 53–67.

Maddox, G. L. (1995). Alcohol use. In Maddox, G. L. (Ed.), *The encyclopedia of aging* (pp. 53–54). New York: Springer.

Markides, K. S. (1994). Gender and ethnic diversity on aging. In Mannheimer, (Ed.), *Older Americans' almanac.* Detroit: Gale Research.

Markides, K. S., & Black, S. A. (1996). Race, ethnicity and aging: The impact of inequality. In Binstock, R. H., & George, L. K. (Eds.), *The handbook of aging and the social sciences,* 4th ed. San Diego: Academic Press.

Markides, K. S, & Mindel, C. H. (1987). *Aging and ethnicity.* Newbury Park, CA: Sage Publications.

Markides, K. S., & Rudkin L. (1996). Racial and ethnic diversity. In Birren, J. E. (Ed.), *Encyclopedia of gerontology* (vol. 2, pp. 371–376). San Diego, CA: Academic Press.

Martin, E. P., & Martin, M. (1983). The black extended family. In Dodson, J. E. (Ed.), *Strengths of black families—An afrocentric educational manual: Toward a non-deficit perspective in services to families and children* (pp. 160–167). Nashville, TN: University of Tennessee, School of Social Work.

Masters, W. H., & Johnson, V. E. (1966). *Human sexual response.* Boston: Little, Brown.

Masters, W. H., & Johnson, V. E. (1970). Human sexual inadequacy. London: J. & A. Churchill.

McDonald, L. (1996). Abuse and neglect of elders. In Birren, J. E. (Ed.), *Encyclopedia of gerontology* (vol. 1, pp. 1–10). San Diego, CA: Academic Press.

McGoldrick, M., Peonce, J., & Giordano, J. (Eds.). (1982). *Ethnicity and family therapy.* New York: Guilford Press.

Mercer, S. O. (1996, March). Navajo elderly people in a reservation nursing home: Admission predictors and culture care practices. *Social Work, 41*(2), 181–189.

Minkler, M., & Stone, R. (1985). The feminization of poverty and older women. *Gerontologist, 25*(4), 351–357.

Money, J. (1988). *Gay, straight, and in between.* New York: Oxford University Press.

Mooradian, A. D., & Greiff, V. (1990). Sexuality in older women. *Archives of Internal Medicine, 150,* 1033–1038.

Morioka-Douglas, N., & Yeo, G. (1990). *Aging and health: Asian/Pacific Island American elderly.* Stanford, CA: Stanford Geriatric Education Center.

Moscicki, E. K., Elkins, E. F., Baum, H. M., & McNamara, P. M. (1985). Hearing loss in the elderly: An epidemeology of the Framingham Heart Study Cohort. *Ear and Hearing, 6*(4), 184–190.

Mount Sinai/Victim Services Agency Elder Abuse Project. (1988). *Elder mistreatment guidelines for health care professionals: Detection, assessment and intervention.* New York: Mt. Sinai Medical Center.

Mui, A. C. (1996, November). Depression among elderly Chinese immigrants: An exploratory study. *Social Work, 41*(6), 633–645.

Muller, C. F. (1990). *Health care and gender.* New York: Russell Sage.

National Center for Health Statistics. (1995). Trends in the health of older Americans: United States, 1994. *Vital and Health Statistics,* Series 3, No. 30. DHHS Publication No.(PHS)95–1414. Hyattsville, MD: U.S. Deparment of Health and Human Services.

National Center for Health Statistics. (1995). Advance report of final marriage statistics, 1989 and 1990. *Monthly Vital Statistics Report, 43*(12), supplement. DHHS Publication No.(PHS)95–1120. Hyattsville, MD: U.S. Department of Health and Human Services.

National Institutes of Health. (1992, Dec. 7–9). *Impotence consensus development conference statement.* Bethesda, MD: National Institutes of Health.

Newman, E. S., Newman, D. J., & Gerwitz, M. (Eds.). (1984). *Elderly criminals.* Boston: Oelgeschlanger, Gunn & Harin.

Ory, M. G., & Warner, H. R. (Eds.). (1990). *Gender, health and longevity: Multidisciplinary perspectives.* New York: Springer.

Padgett, D. K. (Ed.). (1995). *Handbook on ethnicity, aging, and mental health.* Westport, CT: Greenwood Press.

Palmore, E. (1970). *Normal aging: Reports from the Duke Longitudinal Study, 1955–69.* Durham, NC: Duke University Press.

Parris, B. E., Meier, D. E., Goldstein, T., & Fein, E. D. (1995, April). Elder abuse and neglect: How to recognize warning signs and intervene. *Geriatrics, 50*(4), 47–51.

Perry, C. M., & Johnson, C. L. (1994). Families and support networks among African American oldest-old. *International Journal of Aging and Human Development, 38*(1), 41–50.

Pinderhughes, E. B. (1982). Family functioning of black Americans. *Social Work, 27,* 91–96.

Ponterotto, J. G., Casas, J, Suuzuki, L. A., & Alexander, C. M. (Eds.). (1995). *Handbook of multicultural counseling.* Thousand Oaks, CA: Sage Publications.

Preston, S. H., Elo, I. T., Rosenwaike, I., & Hill, M. (1996, May). African-American mortality at older ages: Results of a matching study. *Demography, 33*(2), 193–209.

Quinn, M. J., & Tomita, S. K. (1986). *Elder abuse and neglect: Causes, diagnosis and intervention.* New York: Springer.

Ramirez de Arellano, A. B. (1994). The elderly. In Molina, C. W., & Aguirre-Molina, M. (Eds.), *Latino health in the U.S.: A growing challenge.* Washington, DC: American Public Health Association.

Ripich, D. (Ed.). (1991). *Handbook of geriatric communication disorders.* Austin, TX: Pro-Ed.

Riley, M. W., Ory, M., & Zablotsky, D. (Eds.). (1990). *AIDS in an aging society: What we need to know.* New York: Springer.

Roberts, J. C. (1995). Eye: Structure and function. In Maddox, G. L. (Ed.), *The encyclopedia of aging* (pp. 357–359). New York: Springer.

Robertson, N. (1988). *Getting better: Inside Alcoholics Anonymous.* New York: William, Morrow and Co.

Robinson, J. B. (1989, July). Clinical treatment of black families: Issues and strategies. *Social Work,* 323–329.

Rosenthal, E. (Ed.). (1990). *Women, aging and ageism.* Binghamton NY: The Haworth Press.

Rosenzweig, R., & Fillit, H. (1992). Probable heterosexual transmission of AIDS in an aged woman. *Journal of the American Geriatrics Society, 40,* 1261–1264.

Scannapieco, M., & Jackson, S. (1996, March). Kinship care: The African American response to family preservation. *Social Work, 41*(2), 190–196.

Schiavi, R. C., Schreiner-Engel, P., Mandeli, J., Schanzer, H., & Cohen, E. (1990). Healthy aging and male sexual function. *American Journal of Psychiatry, 147*(6), 766–771.

Scialfa, C. T., & Kline, D. W. (1996). Vision. In Birren, J. E. (Ed.), *Encyclopedia of gerontology* (vol. 2, pp. 605–612). San Diego, CA: Academic Press.

Schiff, S. M. (1988, Summer). Treatment approaches for older alcoholics. *Generations,* 41–45.

Shanas, E., & Sussman, M. B. (1977). *Family, bureaucracy and the elderly.* Durham, NC: Duke University Press.

Silverstein, M., & Waite, L. J. (1993). Are blacks more likely than whites to receive and provide social support in middle and old age? Yes, no, and maybe so. *Journal of Gerontology: Social Sciences, 48,* S212–S222.

Social Security Administration, U.S. Department of Health and Human Services (1995). *Annual statistical supplement to the social security bulletin.*

Washington, DC: U.S. Government Printing Office.

Sotomayor, M. (1995). Hispanic elderly. In Maddox, G. L. (Ed.), *The encyclopedia of aging* (pp. 458–459). New York: Springer.

Stanford, E. P., Paddecord, K. M., & Lockery, S. A. (1990). Variations among the elderly in black, hispanic, and white families. In Brubaker, T. H. (Ed.), *Family relationships in later life* (pp. 212–241). Newbury Park, CA: Sage Publications.

Stanford, E. P., & Torres-Gil, F. M. (Eds.). (1991, Fall/Winter). Diversity: New approaches to ethnic minority aging. (Special Issue). *Generations, 15*(4).

Steffensmeier, D. J. (1987). The invention of the "new" senior citizen criminal: An analysis of crime trends of elderly males and elderly females, 1964–1984. *Research on Aging, 9,* 281–311.

Steinmetz, S. K. (1990). Elder abuse: Myth and reality. In Brubaker, T. H. (Ed.) *Family relationships in later life* (pp. 193–212). Newbury Park, CA: Sage Publications.

Stetten, D. (1981, August 20). Coping with blindness. *New England Journal of Medicine, 305,* 458–460.

Stock, R. W. (1996, April 18) Alcohol lures the old. *The New York Times,* C1–C2.

Taylor, R. J., & Chatters, L. M. (1991). Extended family networks of older black adults. *Journals of Gerontology, 46,* S210–S217.

Thompson, E. H. (Ed.). (1994). *Older men's lives.* Thousand Oaks, CA.: Sage Publications.

U.S. Bureau of the Census. (1996). 65+ in the United States. *Current Population Reports, Special Studies,* Series P-23, No. 190. Washington, DC: U.S. Government Printing Office.

U.S. Bureau of the Census. (1995). Population profile of the United States: 1995. *Current Population Reports,* Series P-23, No. 189. Washington, DC: U.S. Government Printing Office.

U.S. Bureau of the Census. (February 14, 1996). *U.S. population estimates by age, sex, race, and hispanic origin: 1990–1995.* PPL-41. Washington, DC: Population Projections Branch, Population Division, U.S. Bureau of the Census.

U.S. Bureau of the Census (1996). Marital status and living arrangements: March 1994, *Current Population Reports,* Series P-20, No. 484. Washington, DC: U.S. Government Printing Office.

U.S. House of Representatives Select Committee on Aging. (1989). *The quality of life for older women: Older women living alone.* Comm. pub. no. 100–693. Washington, DC: U.S. Government Printing Office.

Verbrugge, L. (1995). Sex differences in health. In Maddox, G. L. (Ed.), *The encyclopedia of aging* (pp. 850–854). New York: Springer.

Vestal, R. E. (1985). Clinical parmacology. In Andres, R., Bieman, E. L., & Hazzard, W. R. (Eds.), *Principles of geriatric medicine* (pp. 424–443). New York: McGraw-Hill.

Vestal, R. E., McGuire, E., Tobin, J. Andres, R., Norris, M., & Mesey, E. (1977). Aging and alcohol metabolism. *Clinical Pharmacology and Therapeutics, 21*(3), 343–354.

Wake, W. (1988). *Considering the special issues of older lesbians and gay men.* Unpublished paper. Available from author: Send a SASE to William Wake, BSN, P.O. Box 1782, Old Chelsea Station, New York, NY 10011.

Watson, W. H. (1991, Fall/Winter). Ethnicity, crime, & aging: Factors and adaptation. *Generations, 25*(4), 53–57.

Weber, N. D. (Ed.). (1992). *Vision and aging: Issues in social work practice.* Binghamton, NY: The Haworth Press.

Weinberg, A. D., & Wei, J. Y. (1995). *The early recognition of elder abuse.* Bayside, NY: American Medical Publishing Co.

Weinstein, B. E. (1994, August). Age related hearing loss: How to screen for it, and when to intervene. *Geriatrics, 49*(8), 40–45.

Wieland, D., Benton, D., Kramer, B. J., & Dawson, G. D. (Eds.). (1994). *Cultural diversity and geriatric care: Challenges to the health care professions.* Binghamton, NY: The Haworth Press.

Wilcott, J. F. (1991). *Aging and the auditory system: Anatomy, physiology and phychophysics.* San Diego, CA: Singular Publishing Group.

Wolf, R. S. (1992). Victimization of the elderly: Elder abuse and neglect. *Reviews in Clinical Gerontology, 2,* 269–276.

Wolf, R. S. (1994). What's new in elder abuse programming? Four bright ideas. *Gerontologist, 34*(1), 126–129.

Wolf, R. S. (1994, March). Elder abuse: A family tragedy. *Ageing International,* 60–64.

Wolf, R. S., & Pillemer, K. (1989). *Helping elderly victims: The reality of elder abuse.* New York: Columbia University Press.

Women Work! (1994). *Women work, poverty persists: A status report on displaced homemakers & single mothers in the United States.* Washington, DC: Women Work! The National Network for Women's Employment.

Wood, W. G. (1995). Alcoholism. In Maddox, G. L. (Ed.), *The encyclopedia of aging* (pp. 51–53). New York: Springer.

Yeo, G. (1995). Ethical considerations in Asian and Pacific Island elders. *Ethnogeriatrics, 11,* 139–152.

Yeo, G., & Hikoyeda, N. (1995). Asian and Pacific Islander American elders. In Maddox, G. L. (Ed.), *The encyclopedia of aging* (pp. 80–82). New York: Springer.

Young, J. J., & Gu, N. (1995). *Demographic and socio-economic characteristics of elderly Asian and Pacific Island Americans.* Seattle, WA: National Asian Pacific Center on Aging.

ENDNOTES

1. References on ethnic minority elderly can be found in the selected readings at the end of this chapter.
2. U.S. Bureau of the Census. (1996, February 14). *U.S. population estimates by age, sex, race, and hispanic origin: 1990–1995.* PPL-41. Washington, DC: Population Projections Branch, Population Division, U.S. Bureau of the Census.
3. U.S. Bureau of the Census. (1996, July). Population profile of the United States: 1995. *Current Population Reports,* series P-23, no. 189. Washington DC: U.S. Government Printing Office.
4. Jackson, J. J. (1985). Race, national origin, ethnicity, and aging. In Binstock, R. H., & Shanas, E. (Eds.), *Handbook of aging and the social sciences,* 2nd ed. (pp. 264–303). New York: Van Nostrand Reinhold.
5. Fanon, F. (1967). *Black skin, white masks.* New York: Grove Press.
6. Grier, W. H., & Cobbs, P. M. (1968). *Black rage.* New York: Basic Books.
7. Dr. William A. Reid, personal communication, 1972.
8. Jackson, J. S., & Gibson, R. C. (1985). Work and retirement among the black elderly. In Blau, Z. (Ed.), *Current perspectives on aging and the life cycle.* New York: JAI Press.
9. Castex, G. M. (1994, May) Providing services to Hispanic/Latino populations: Profiles in diversity. *Social Work, 39,* 288–296.
10. Markides, K. S., & Rudkin, L. (1996). Racial and ethnic diversity. In Birren, J. E. (Ed.), *Encyclopedia of gerontology* (vol. 2, pp. 371–376). San Diego, CA: Academic Press; Sotomayor, M. (1995). Hispanic elderly. In Maddox, G. L. (Ed.), *The encyclopedia of aging* (pp. 458–459). New York: Springer.
11. Commonwealth Fund Commission on Elderly People Living Alone. (1989, September). *Poverty and poor health among elderly Hispanic Americans.* New York: The Commonwealth Fund.
12. Torres-Gil, F. (1986). Hispanics: A special challenge. In Pifer, A., & Bronte, L. (Eds.), *Our aging society* (pp. 219–242). New York: W.W. Norton.
13. Kramer, B. J. (1995). Native-American aged. In Maddox, G. L. (Ed.), *The encyclopedia of aging* (pp. 671–673). New York: Springer.
14. *Ibid.*
15. John, R., & Baldridge, D. (1996). *The National Indian Council on Aging report: Health and long-term care for Indian elders.* Washington, DC: National Indian Policy Center.
16. Indian Health Service. (1995). *Trends in Indian health: 1995.* Rockville, MD: S. Department of Health and Human Services, Indian Health Service.
17. Mercer, S. O. (1996, March). Navajo elderly people in a reservation nursing home: Admission predictors and culture care practices. *Social Work, 41*(2), 181–189.
18. Ho, M. K. (1987). *Family therapy with ethnic minorities.* Newbury Park, CA: Sage Publications.
19. Young, J., & Gu, N. (1995). *Demographic and socio-economic characteristics of elderly Asian and Pacific Island Americans.* Seattle, WA: National Asian Pacific Center on Aging.
20. *Ibid.*
21. Browne, C., & Broderick, A. (1994, May). Asian Pacific Island elders: Issues for social work practice and education. *Social Work, 39*(3), 252–259.
22. *Ibid,*
23. From 1848 to 1882, over 100,000 Chinese men, as compared to 9,000 Chinese women, immigrated mostly to California and the Rocky Mountain states where they mined gold (they made up 25% of California's gold miners), worked on the railroad (helping to complete the first transcontinental railroad by 1869), and were employed in forestry. The Chinese Exclusion Act of 1882, which also disenfranchised Chinese immigrants and barred them from certain jobs, had as its most long-lasting effect the barring of wives and children from joining their men. By 1943 when the law was repealed, the ratio of males to females in New York's Chinatown was an incredible 17:1

(historical data from Tanzer, A. *The American experience of Chinatown's elderly,* unpublished paper, 1980).

24. The *Issei* (Japanese who were born and raised in Japan before immigrating to the United States) were discriminated against before World War II and placed in internment camps during the war. Despite adversities the *Issei* encouraged and supported the education of their children, the *Nisei,* the majority of whom now have professional and technical occupations.

25. Jackson, J. S. (1989). Race, ethnicity and psychological theory and research. *Journal of Gerontology: Psychological Sciences, 44*(1), 1–2; Gibson, R. G. (1989). Minority aging research: Opportunity and challenge. *Journal of Gerontology: Social Sciences, 44*(1), 2–3.

26. Yee, D. L. (1981, July–August). On Lok senior health services: Community-based long-term care. *Aging, 319–320,* 26–30.

27. Ho, M. K. (1987). *Family therapy with ethnic minorities.* Newbury Park, CA: Sage Publications.

28. *Ibid,* 177.

29. Boyd-Franklin, N. (1989). *Black families in therapy: A multi-system approach.* New York: The Guilford Press.

30. Kim, P. K., & Kim, J. (1989). Curriculum development for social work with Asian-American elderly. *Gerontology and Geriatrics Education, 10*(2), 89–98.

31. Die, A. H., & Seelback, W. C. (1988). Problems, sources of assistance and knowledge of services among elderly Vietnamese immigrants. *The Gerontologist, 28*(4), 448–452.

32. Ho, *Family therapy,* 69–112.

33. U.S. Bureau of the Census (February 14, 1996). *U.S. population estimates by age, sex, race, and hispanic origin: 1990–1995.* PPL-41. Washington, DC: Population Projections Branch, Population Division, U.S. Bureau of the Census.

34. AARP Women's Initiative. (1994). *Facts about older women: Income and poverty.* Washington, DC: American Association of Retired Persons.

35. Annual Statistical Supplement, 1995, to the Social Security Bulletin. Table no. 5.A3. Washington, DC: Social Security Administration.

36. Women Work! (1994). *Women work, poverty persists: A status report on displaced homemakers & single mothers in the United States.* Washington, DC: Women Work! The National Network for Women's Employment.

37. National Congress of Working Women of Wider Opportunities for Women. (1989). *Women, work and age: An overview.* Washington, DC: Wider Opportunities for Women.

38. U.S. Bureau of Labor Statistics, Current Population Survey, 1995 Annual Averages.

39. U.S. Bureau of the Census, March 1995, Current Population Survey.

40. National Congress of Working Women of Wider Opportunities for Women. (1989). *Women, work and age: An overview.* Washington, DC: Wider Opportunities for Women.

41. Social Security Administration. (1996, January). *Income of the population 55 or older, 1994.* Washington, DC: U.S. Government Printing Office.

42. *Ibid.*

43. U.S. Bureau of the Census (1996). Marital status and living arrangements: March 1994. *Current Population Reports,* Series P-20, No. 484. Washington, DC: U.S. Government Printing Office.

44. National Center for Health Statistics. (1995). Trends in the health of older Americans, 1994. *Monthly Vital Statistics Report, 43*(12), supplement. Hyattsville, MD: U.S. Department of Health and Human Services.

45. U.S. Bureau of the Census. (1996, February 14). *U.S. population estimates by age, sex, race, and hispanic origin: 1990–1995.* PPL-41. Washington, DC: Population Projections Branch, Population Division, U.S. Bureau of the Census.

46. U.S. Bureau of the Census (1996). Marital status and living arrangements: March 1994. *Current Population Reports,* Series P-20, No. 484. Washington, DC: U.S. Government Printing Office.

47. Verbrugge, L. (1995). Sex differences in health. In Maddox, G. L. (Ed.), *The encyclopedia of aging* (pp. 850–854). New York: Springer.

48. Gutmann, D. (1987). *Reclaimed powers: Toward a new psychology of men and women in later life.* New York: Basic Books.

49. Congressional Caucus for Women's Issues. (1990, June 29). Women excluded from federally-funded research, study finds. *Update, 10*(5), 1, 13.

50. Birren, J. E., Butler, R. N., Greenhouse, S. W., Sokoloff, L., & Yarrow, M. R. (1963). *Human aging: A biological and behavioral study.* U.S. Public Health Service Pub. No. 986. Washington, DC: U.S. Government Printing Office. (Reprinted 1971, 1974).

51. American Cancer Society. *Breast cancer facts & figures 1996.* New York: Author.

52. U.S. Bureau of the Census, November 1994 Current Population Survey, PPL-23.

53. See summary of data by Cutler, S. J. (1995). Crime (against and by the elderly) in Maddox, G. L. (Ed.),

The encyclopedia of aging (pp. 243–244). New York: Springer.

54. Brostoff, P., Brown, R., & Butler, R. N. (1972). The public interest: Report no. 6: Beating up on the elderly: Police, social work, crime. *Aging and Human Development, 3,* 319–322.

55. Butler, R. N. (1975). *Why survive? Being old in America.* New York: Harper & Row.

56. The following references on elder abuse are especially useful: Administration on Aging. (1996). Opening the door on elder abuse (special issue.) *Aging, 367;* Breckman, R., & Adelman, R. (1989). *Helping victims of elder mistreatment.* Newbury Park, CA: Sage Publications; Fulmer, T. T., & O'-Malley, T. A. (1987). *Inadequate care of the elderly.* New York: Springer; Parris, B. E., Meier, D. E., Goldstein, T., & Fein, E. D. (1995, April). Elder abuse and neglect: How to recognize warning signs and intervene. *Geriatrics, 50*(4), 47–51; Quinn, M. J., & Tomita, S. K. (1986). *Elder abuse and neglect: Causes, diagnosis and intervention.* New York: Springer; Wolf, R. S., & Pillemer, K. (1989). *Helping elderly victims: The reality of elder abuse.* New York: Columbia University Press.

57. Pillemer, K. A., & Finkelhor, D. (1988). The prevalence of elder abuse: A random sample survey. *The Gerontologist, 24,* 51–57.

58. National Center on Elder Abuse, American Public Welfare Association, 810 First Street, NE, Suite 500, Washington, DC 20002. Information can also be obtained from the National Clearinghouse on Elder Abuse and Neglect (CANE), University of Delaware, (302) 831-3235.

59. Wolf, R. S., & Pillemer, K. A. (1989). *Helping elderly victims.* New York: Columbia University Press.

60. Pillemer, K. A. (1988). Maltreatment of the elderly at home and in institutions: Extent, risk factors, and policy recommendations. In *Legislative agendas for an aging society: 1988 and beyond.* Proceedings of a Congressional Forum, House Select Committee on Aging (Pub. Nbr. 100664) and Senate Special Committee on Aging (Pub. Nbr. 100-J), Washington, DC: U.S. Government Printing Office.

61. Breckman, R., & Adelman, R. (1988). *Strategies for helping victims of elder mistreatment.* Newbury Park, CA: Sage Publications.

62. See: Covey, H. C., & Menard, S. (1987). Trends in arrests among the elderly. *The Gerontologist, 27,* 666–672; Cutler, S. J. (1995). Crime (against and by the elderly). In Maddox, G. L. (Ed.), *Encyclopedia of aging* (pp. 243–244). New York: Springer; Flynn, E. E. (1996). Crime and age. In Birren, J. E. (Ed.), *Encyclopedia of gerontology* (vol. 1, pp. 353–359). San Diego, CA: Academic Press; Steffensmeier, D. J. (1987). The invention of the "new" senior citizen criminal: An analysis of crime trends of elderly males and elderly females, 1964–1984. *Research on Aging, 9,* 281–311; Watson, W. H. (1991. Fall/Winter). Ethnicity, crime, & aging: Factors and adaptation. *Generations, 25*(4), 53–57.

63. Stock, R. W. (1996, January 18) Inside prison, too, a population is aging. *The New York Times,* p. C8.

64. Gomberg, E. S. L. (1996). Alcohol and drugs. In Birren, J. E. (Ed.), *Encyclopedia of gerontology* (vol. 1, pp. 93–101). San Diego, CA: Academic Press; Stock, R. W. (1996, April 18). Alcohol lures the old. *The New York Times,* C1–C2; Wood, W. G. (1995). Alcoholism. In Maddox, G. L. (Ed.), *Encyclopedia of aging* (pp. 51–53). New York: Springer.

65. During the 1950s, the World Health Organization and the American Medical Association declared alcoholism a disease. This, of course, raised the issue of whether personal responsibility (self-control) plays a role in addiction. For example, drug addiction is still treated as a crime rather than as a public health problem similar to alcoholism. There is great question as to the conceptual validity and the therapeutic wisdom of regarding alcoholism solely as a disease. A balance must be struck between that which the individual can control and that which is beyond his or her control.

66. As defined by the U.S. Department of Health and Human Services' National Institute on Alcohol Abuse and Alcoholism (NIAAA).

67. Beers and wines have a relatively higher concentration of various kinds of solids, which account for slower absorption. The alcohol in whiskey, brandy, vodka, and gin is absorbed more rapidly.

68. Federal Agencies concerned with alcoholism (and drug abuse) are: (1) Substance Abuse and Mental Health Services Administration (SAMHSA), a government agency within the U.S. Department of Health and Human Services responsible for administering federal grant programs to advance and support research, training, and service programs in the areas of alcoholism, drug abuse, and mental health. Within SAMHSA are the Center for Substance Abuse Prevention, the Center for Substance Abuse Treatment, and the Center for Mental Health

Services; (2) National Institute of Alcohol Abuse and Alcoholism, an institute within the National Institutes of Health; and (3) National Institute on Drug Abuse, also within the National Institute of Health.

69. Delirium tremens is an acute and sometimes fatal brain disorder (in 10% to 15% of untreated patients) caused by withdrawal or relative withdrawal from alcohol, usually developing in 24 to 96 hours. A history of excessive and unusually prolonged intake is present, and the symptoms of the syndrome include fever, tremors, ataxia, and sometimes convulsions, frightening illusions, delusions, and hallucinations. The condition is often accompanied by nutritional deficiencies. It is a medical emergency.

70. For the moving account of an older man's life as an alcoholic, see Straus, R. (1974). *Escape from custody: A study of alcoholism and institutional dependency as reflected in the life record of a homeless man.* New York: Harper & Row.

71. Canter, W. A., & Koretzky, M. B. (1989). Treatment of geriatric alcoholics. *Clinical Gerontologist, 9*(l), 67–69.

72. The American Hospital Association claims that 25% to 30% of all adult medicosurgical patients in metropolitan hospitals, regardless of diagnosis, have been found to be suffering from alcoholism.

73. Most towns and cities have an AA listing in the telephone book. If not, information may be obtained by writing to AA World Services Inc., 475 Riverside Dr., New York, NY 10115. There are no dues or fees for membership.

74. Robertson, N. (1988). *Getting better: Inside Alcoholics Anonymous.* New York: William Morrow.

75. Corso, J. F. (1995). Auditory perception. In Maddox, G. L. (Ed.), *Encyclopedia of aging* (pp. 95–97). New York: Springer; Gordon-Salant, S. (1995). Hearing. In Birren, J. E. (Ed.), *Encyclopedia of gerontology* (vol. 2, pp. 643–653). San Diego, CA: Academic Press; Gulya, A. J. (1995) Ear disorders. In Abrams, W. B., Beers, M. H., & Berkow, R. (Eds.), *The Merck manual of geriatrics,* 2nd ed. (pp. 1315–1342). Whitehouse Station, NJ: Merck & Co.; and Weinstein, B. E. (1994, August). Age related hearing loss: How to screen for it, and when to intervene. *Geriatrics, 49*(8), 40–45.

76. National Center of Health Statistics, Havik, R. J. (1996, September 19). Aging in the eighties: Impaired senses for sound and light in persons age 65 years and over. Preliminary data from the supplement in aging for the *National Health Interview Survey.* United States, January–June 1987, *Advance Data from Vital and Health Statistics.* No. 125, DHHS Pub. No. (PHS) 86–1250. Hyattsville, MD: Public Health Service.

77. Kovar, M. G. (1977). Elderly people: The population 65 years and over. In Department of Health, Education and Welfare, National Center for Health Statistics. *Health, United States 1976–1977.* Pub No. (HRA) 77–1232, Washington, DC: U.S. Government Printing Office.

78. Moscicki, E. K., Elkins, E. F., Baum, H. M., & McNamara, P. M. (1985). Hearing loss in the elderly: An epidemiology of the Framingham Heart Study cohort. *Ear and Hearing, 6*(4), 184–190.

79. Corso, J. F. (1995). Hearing. In Maddox, G. L. (Ed.), *The encyclopedia of aging* (pp. 499–552). New York: Springer.

80. Birren, J. E., Butler, R. N., Greenhouse, S. W., Sokoloff, L., & Yarrow, M. R. (1963). Interdisciplinary relationships: Interrelations of physiological, psychological, and psychiatric findings in healthy elderly men. In Birren, J. E., Butler, R. N., Greenhouse, S. W., Sokoloff, L., & Yarrow, M. R. (Eds.), *Human aging: A biological and behavioral study.* Pub. No. (PHS) 986. Washington, DC: U.S. Government Printing Office (reprinted as Pub. No. [HSM] 71–9051, 1971, 1974).

81. Gennis, V., Garry, P. J., Haaland, K. Y., Yeo, R. A., & Goodwin, J. S. (1991, November). Hearing and cognition in the elderly. New findings and a review of the literature. *Archives of Internal Medicine, 151*(11), 2259–2264.

82. Weinstein, B. E. (1994, August). Age related hearing loss: How to screen for it, and when to intervene. *Geriatrics, 49*(8), 40–45.

83. Information is also available from: National Information Center on Deafness (NICD), Gallaudet University, 800 Florida Ave. NE, Washington, DC 20002; National Institute on Deafness and Other Communication Disorders (NICD), National Institutes of Health, 31 Center Dr., MSC 2320, Bethesda, MD 20892; American Academy of Otolaryngology—Head and Neck Surgery, Inc. (AAO-HNS), One Prince St., Alexandria VA 22314; and the American Tinnitus Association, P.O. Box 5, Portland, OR 97207.

84. From Houston, F., & Royse, A. B. (1954). Relationship between deafness and psychotic illness. *The Journal of Mental Science, 100,* 990–993; see also Cooper, A. F., Kay, D. W. K., Curry, A. R., Garside, R. F., & Roth, M. (1974). Hearing loss in paranoid and affective psychoses of the elderly. *Lancet ii,* 851–854.

85. Kupfer, C. (1995). Opthamologic disorders. In Abrams, W. B., Beer, M. H., & Berkow, R. (Eds.), *The Merck manual of geriatrics,* 2nd ed. (pp. 1289–1314). Whitehouse Station, NJ: Merck & Co.

86. American Foundation for the Blind. (1996). *Facts about aging and vision.* Available from American Foundation for the Blind, M. C. Migel Library and Information Center, 11 Penn Plaza, Suite 300, New York, NY 10001.

87. Carter, T. (1994, September). Age related visual changes: A primary care guide. *Geriatrics, 49*(9), 37–45.

88. For a highly readable and useful personal description of learning about visual aids, see Stetten, D. (1981, August 20). Coping with blindness. *Sounding Board, New England Journal of Medicine, 305,* 458–460.

89. For more information on talking books and other library services, contact the National Library Service for the Blind and Visually Handicapped. 1291 Taylor St. NW, Washington, DC 20542, (800) 424-8567.

90. Lee, M. S., & Itoh, M. (1995). Rehabilitation: Section on "self-help devices in the home." In Abrams, W. B., Beer, M. H., & Berkow, R. (Eds.), *The Merck manual of geriatrics,* 2nd ed. (pp. 376–377). Whitehouse Station, NJ: Merck & Co.

91. For additional information and services contact: The National Eye Institute (NIE) of the National Institute of Health (NIH), 900 Rockville Pike, Building 31, Room 6A32, Bethesda, MD 20892-3655; The American Optometric Association, 243 North Lindbergh Blvd., St. Louis, MO 63141; The Lighthouse National Center for Vision and Aging, 111 E. 59th St., New York, NY 10022; The National Association for the Visually Handicapped, 22 W. 21st St. New York, NY 10010; The National Eye Care Project of the American Academy of Ophthalmology (AAO), P.O. Box 6988, San Francisco, CA 94120 (A helpline provides referrals for disadvantaged older people to free eyecare and information. Call (800)222-EYES); The National Society to Prevent Blindness, 500 E. Remington Rd., Schaumburg, IL 60173; and The Vision Foundation, 818 Auburn St., Watertown, MA 02172.

92. Butler, R. N., & Lewis, M. I. (1993). *Love and sex after sixty,* revised ed. New York: Ballantine.

93. Homosexuality per se was eliminated as a mental disorder by the American Psychiatric Association in DSM-II (1973). Thus homosexuality itself can no longer be medically labeled psychopathological; only when it is "egodystonic" (the individual does not accept being a homosexual), causing severe distress or disability, is it deemed a mental disorder.

94. A number of references on homosexuality and aging are included in the Selected Readings for this chapter.

95. Masters, W. H., & Johnson, V. E. (1970). *Human sexual inadequacy.* London: J. & A. Churchill, 316, 318.

96. *Ibid.*

97. Butler, R. N., & Lewis, M. I. (1993). *Love and sex After sixty,* revised ed. New York: Ballantine, 276–288.

98. As an example, a bachelor participating in the NIMH Human Aging Studies undertook intensive psychotherapy four times a week at age 65 and married for the first time. Another example is the English sexologist Havelock Ellis, who overcame lifelong impotence in his old age with the help of a loving and responsive woman (Calder-Marshall, A. [1959]. *The sage of sex: A life of Havelock Ellis.* New York: G. P. Putnam's Sons.)

99. From Masters, W. H., & Johnson, V. E. *Human sexual inadequacy.*

PART TWO

EVALUATION, TREATMENT, AND PREVENTION

Chapter 8

GENERAL TREATMENT PRINCIPLES

We are writing the treatment section of this book on two levels: one describing what we consider to be appropriate and ideal mental health care of older people and the other dealing with contemporary realities, far from ideal. Our aim is to keep in sight the direction for improvements, while also advising mental health personnel, older people themselves, and anyone involved in their welfare on how to make the best of what is now available.

There has been a steady growth in theory and practice in the mental health treatment of older persons, emphasizing the importance of active, restorative, and rehabilitative possibilities. Most important, the potentiality of reversibility has been demonstrated, both in the functional disorders and in some of the organic disorders, particularly delirium.

Prevention, comprehensive evaluations, and genuine therapeutic efforts have begun to be accepted as worthwhile activities on behalf of older persons.

CHANGES IN PERSPECTIVES TOWARD MENTAL HEALTH TREATMENT OF OLDER PERSONS

The body of theory surrounding mental health treatment of the elderly has slowly evolved from more general theory about human behavior. Beginning with psychiatry at the turn of the century, theories about abnormal behavior had a detached quality—observing and cataloging exterior behavior. Later, dominated by Freudian thinking, the focus moved to the inner life of humans—probing subjective experience and internalized modes of adaptation. Since World War II, psychiatry has moved out somewhat (but only *somewhat*) into the community—examining the influences of institutions and environmental conditions on human behavior, inner experience, and adaptations. This is reflected in the American Psychiatric Association's 1980 *Diagnostic and Statistical Manual* and its later revisions, which require consideration of social stresses as part of a psychiatric diagnosis. Biological psychiatry has made significant advances that have resulted in useful psychoactive medications. Recently some attention has been given to the inherent changes of the individual as he or she progresses through the life cycle. Thus, in about 90 years, psychiatry has looked at people's outward behavior, their inner life, their environment, their biology, and finally their passage through their finite existence—the life cycle. This includes a new interest in understanding old age.

American psychotherapist Carl R. Rogers's concept of humanistic psychology—emphasizing a person's own capacity for life-long growth and development rather than dwelling largely on the past—has been helpful in work with the elderly. Rogers and other founders of humanistic psychology, such as Abraham Maslow and Rollo May, have been called the "Third Force in Psychology" in order to distinguish their work from two other prominent schools of thought, psychoanalysis and behaviorism. Today their client-centered approach is widely used among therapists and counselors.

Cognitive psychotherapy, originally formulated by Aaron Beck, emphasizes finding solutions to definable, reality-based problems by means of interpretation, explanation, and practical information. It has been found to be especially useful with well-motivated, depressed older people who have few or no physically based mental impairments.

Other forms of psychotherapy include psychoanalysis and psychoanalytic psychotherapy, behavior therapy, hypnosis, group psychotherapy, psychodrama, family therapy, couples therapy, and brief or crisis therapy, all of which can be useful in work with older persons. These will be described more fully in Chapter 12.

There are also ongoing, exciting recent developments occurring in the neurosciences that are ultimately likely to make great contributions to understanding human behavior and to the treatment of mental disorders. Examples are the catecholamine hypothesis of the origins of affective disorders like depression (see Chapter 5) and the new understandings of the genetics and neurochemistry of Alzheimer's disease.

The Special Relevance of Life-Cycle Theory

A major direction in developing a psychology of old age has resulted in what has been called "life-cycle" theory. Social, biological, medical, and other changes have led to longer life and increased visibility of the stages of the life cycle. As a result, attention has begun to turn to the inherent psychological changes of the individual as he or she progresses through the life cycle. A science, or perhaps more humbly, a perspective and body of knowledge of the life cycle, is being born.

Improved public health and medical care have prolonged life in both the formerly dangerous years of infancy and the often frail years of late life. The middle years of life stand as a fulcrum and largely support the two ends of the life cycle—childhood and old age. This is true for individuals, when parents are responsible both for their children and for their own parents; it is true also in society, where middle-aged people hold the power, make the decisions, and produce the goods. We do not yet know to what extent normative, modal features of the life cycle account for the varying patterns of change and adaptation we see. A few investigators like Matilda White Riley have been engaged in disentangling the features of the successive phases of the life cycle from the contributions of such influences as social change, medical disease, and historical variation.[1] Butler (1968) introduced the term "average expectable life cycle" as a counterpart to Heinz Hartman's concept "average expectable environment"[2] to bring focus to the notion that there are average, normative experiences against which to measure individual patterns. If, for example, we see correlations of conservative behavior with age, are these a result of the conditions of youth carried forward in time, or are they intrinsic to aging? If we observe preoccupation with bowel function in aged persons, is it a result of the popular lore relating health with bowel function that was prevalent at the turn of the century or a consequence of the inherent character of old age? Are the declines in memory associated with aging to be interpreted as a consequence of brain disease, educational obsolescence, social anomie, depression, or the mysterious, inevitable, irreversible process called *aging?*

There is not yet a sufficiently sensitive methodology to weigh the relative significance of the many elements that are involved in the production of changes in people and adaptation to those changes. We believe the life cycle itself—the changes inherent in the rhythm of a life from birth to death—makes profound contributions to the variability. The study of human development has tended in the past to stop with adolescence. Recently social scientists have begun to study the psychology of mid-life. Persons involved in fact gathering and theoretical formulations now need to build up a head of steam and plunge through middle age to old age instead of losing interest after surveying the "achievement" of adulthood. Contemporary personality and developmental theories need enlargement and expansion to provide a full account of human nature. Such an effort would give further direction to the treatment of older people.

In clinical work and reflections, Butler speaks of the development of an *individual inner sense of the life cycle,* which is neither the same as the average expectable life cycle nor the same as a personal sense of identity, although it is related to both. It is a subjective feel for the life cycle as a whole—its rhythm, its variability, and the relation of this to the individual's sense of self. This inner sense seems to be a necessary personal achievement in order for individuals to orient themselves wherever they happen to be in the life cycle. It becomes particularly important as people age and begin to comprehend their own eventual end.

In adolescents, the middle-aged, and older persons, such a personal sense of the cycle of human life is a necessary adaptive mechanism. Understanding the kinds of changes to be expected and facing the reality and inevitability of these changes, including death itself, is important to individual security. A sense of the life cycle gives people the opportunity to prepare themselves, to plan and order their lives in more meaningful ways, and perhaps more important, to be assured that they are not alone in their experiences. All former and future generations and all of their fellow living human beings share many of the same basic realities. The understanding of this is part of what humans long for when they speak of searching for the meaning of life through religion or a personal philosophy of life. An inner sense of the life cycle—often unspoken—produces a profound

awareness of change and evolution—birth, maturation, aging, and death—and therefore a profound but nonmorbid realization of the precious and limited quantity of life. For older people it is not the same as "feeling old"; it is instead a deep understanding of what it means to be human.

One sees all kinds of people struggling for greater sensibility about life but, for various reasons, not being able to face what is there. There are adolescents who can comprehend the notion of suicide (perhaps because in killing oneself, one has active control over one's death) but cannot imagine death in old age or even that they themselves will grow old. Middle-aged persons often develop anxiety symptoms about aging and try to turn the clock back to youth by dressing and acting young. Even in old age, one sees Peter Pans—those who have never grown up to face their own age and the fact of death.

In our own work, we have seen what an inner sense of the life cycle can mean in old age. It can portend adaptation to inevitable changes in the best manner possible; or its absence can guarantee maladaptation, wherein the older person reacts with terror, dependency, and prolonged grief to personal change. The following case examples are illustrative.

A handsome, warm, and magnetic 78-year-old former politician, who had received many public awards, called for a psychiatric consultation, his voice full of despair. He had always been healthy and unusually vigorous until the previous summer, at which time he developed glaucoma. Shortly thereafter he began to notice weakness of his left arm. By means of a myelogram, electromyelographic studies, and other tests, it was determined that the patient had anterior horn cell disease.

He had been an unusually healthy man all his life, extremely vigorous, and very proud of his sexual prowess and attractiveness. He had been married three times and had had many private affairs.

However, until his recent problems, he had never taken seriously the fact that he could become old. Moreover, his much younger brother was suffering from severe chronic brain disorder and was residing in a nursing home; this fact began to preoccupy him.

Our patient remained somewhat busy in public life but had recently given up his last private love affair. During a warm and somewhat grief-stricken lunch together, the two quoted Ecclesiastes to each other: "Everything in its season. . . ."

Yet he never prepared for old age. He never thought about old age when he was younger; in fact he gave it little thought until his glaucoma. On the rare occasions when he did, he would say to himself, "Why shouldn't I live to be 100?" Whenever he, again rarely, thought about death, he wished for, and he thought that he would have, a quick sudden death. He had turned aside suggestions that he write his memoirs.

Now he felt helpless. His sense of omnipotence was under sudden siege and near collapse. He became extremely hypochondriacal. He not only went to physicians from a whole range of specialties but sought out possible quacks.

In summary, he had not experienced aging or the diseases associated with aging gradually. All was precipitous, with no stepwise intimations of mortality!

Although he had five children, he was not in any sense strongly involved with them, which suggests that he had not grown into or fulfilled the life-cycle task of parenthood.

Once engaged in psychotherapy, he became very much dependent on the therapist. Although the psychotherapist was obviously doing nothing "material," he believed the therapist was the only physician who was "doing anything" for him—in spite of the fact that the others had offered drugs and had conducted a variety of tests. Emphasis in psychotherapy was on consideration of the unfolding of the life cycle and on renunciation and restitution; that is, on grieving and accepting things as they were and finding other avenues for personal pleasure and development—particularly those pertinent to later life such as teaching, counseling, and leaving "traces." It was eventually necessary to reduce the number of sessions to help him resolve his dependency. He improved, but any lengthy separations from the therapist created setbacks, and he continued regular contacts as a way of maintaining his equilibrium.

In 1965 an 87-year-old former schoolteacher sustained a stroke from which she recovered except for a residual right hemiplegia. There was no aphasia. She had always been an extremely independent person, and she was quite agitated and depressed over what had happened to her. Unlike the previous patient, however, she did not respond with helplessness. She was a very courageous fighter, pulling herself up and down stairs for dinner each day. This was still true five years later at age 92. The therapist continued seeing her, although the agitated depression had gone. They seemed unable to give each other up. They would meet approximately once monthly, usually on Saturday afternoon, at which time at her insistence they would have a fine sherry or Madeira together. There were occasions when she would put herself to bed and seem to be failing. However, nothing would be amiss on physical examination, and it became clear that these episodes were related to the thought on her part that maybe she was just about to die. In view of her advanced age, this was not such an irrational idea. Then, after several days in bed, she would awaken to the realization that she was neither dead nor dying and would be back up functioning again.

At other times the therapist would simply tell her she was all right, whereupon she would agree and resume life. These episodes were characterized psychologically by great preoccupation with leaving things and with what the recipients would do with the objects of her legacy. It was very important to her that she not be falsely reassured about death but that respectful attention be given to her ideas about dying, death, burial, and the objects of her legacy—religious items, pictures of her parents, favorite old books, and so on. Unlike the previous patient, she had always had a sound sense of the evolving process of life, the life cycle. But her advancing age—or diseases—narrowed the opportunities in which she could express her personality. Thus she had to rely more and more on verbal or bodily expression of needs (rather than action). She had responsiveness in abundance from her daughter as well as from her therapist. She continued to do quite well.

In attempting to understand an individual's life cycle, it is useful to identify events that typically characterize a life. One way to approach this is to examine rites of passage or cultural observances of biological and social changes. Christenings, confirmations or bar mitzvahs, marriages, and burials are the most obvious, but there are countless others, all adding structure and meaning to lives. They lend predictability and help to ease the individual's movement from one stage to the next. Such rites help us to "know the score"; offer social supports from time of birth and early development; confirm our religious, sexual, occupational, and social identity; consecrate marriages as well as provide for their dissolution; and offer models for dealing with happiness and fulfillment as well as with failure, grief, loss, and eventual death. However, rites of passage, as with all other cultural institutions, are often out of tune with human needs as history unfolds. It is necessary to understand the nature of the particular life cycle in order to judge the validity of the rites of passage associated with it. Rites of passage undergo constant revision—and when the revision is delayed, complicated, incomplete, or aborted, humans flounder and suffer from the lack of a meaningful structure. An example in the present is the problem in handling grief that has resulted from increasing secularization and the loss of religious supports. Older people, and especially their children, often do not know what to do with grief. Should they cry, maintain a stoic front, deny it, become angry, or something else? For many there is no longer a structured and supportive mourning period. Some mourners pretend the loss never happened; others wait silently, hoping grief will go away. Yet we know theoretically what "grief work" is and what could be done to help find the best possible psychological resolution to loss. It remains for such knowledge to become part of popular psychology. People who no longer belong to an institutionalized religion must learn to do for themselves some of the work they formerly left up to the church or synagogue.

Other parts of the life cycle are changing as a result of alterations in biology and changes in the life span. Changes occur so quickly that people may be left bewildered. The bewilderment is greatest in those for whom the change is greatest. Small children born today have never experienced anything but accelerating change, and it has been suggested that change itself is an accepted way of life for them. But for the present generation of older people who remember a more slowly moving past, the contrast with the present can be horrifying, disconcerting, and disorienting, particularly if the older person feels or is in some way personally victimized by change.

New rites of passage are needed to support new developments. Recent and still-growing controls of the events of the life cycle bear comment. Flexibility of classic rites is needed to cope with birth control, liberalized abortion, genetic manipulation, sex prediction before birth—all of which could (and already do) allow considerable control over the occurrence and timing of birth and quality of children. The arrival of menstruation for girls has moved ahead thirty-six months in the last hundred years. The rite of marriage (which first became a sacrament in the ninth century A.D., when people seldom lived longer than 40 years) is being influenced by trial marriages, the ability to control births, and the notion of divorce by consent. The event of death is subject to greater control. Organ transplants, new thoughts about criteria for death (as a result of medical discoveries), interest in passive and active euthanasia—all produce legal, ethical, and medical considerations that will become part of the evolving rites surrounding death.

One feature of present life—retirement—has almost no formal rites of passage and no precedent historically. The institution of retirement is barely 100 years old and is a consequence of the lengthening of the life span for vast numbers of people. Many will spend 20 years or more in retirement. Similar demographic changes are occurring in other countries, some of which are responding more positively than we have. Our present lack of structured and meaningful rites for retirement has led to anomic nonparticipation of many people in American life.

Because of medical progress since the turn of the century, people are now free from many of the previously fixed biological states that have long controlled the culturally defined rites of passage. What such freedom means for the future is hard to fathom. But we do know that both present and future generations of older people need to have a secure place for themselves in a society that makes sense to them. Good mental health is not possible in chaos and meaninglessness.

OBSTACLES TO TREATMENT IN OLD AGE

Ageism and Countertransference

We have described the many negative attitudes toward older people by coining the general term *ageism*—the prejudices and stereotypes that are applied to older people sheerly on the basis of their age.[3] (Another term, *gerontophobia,* refers to a more rare "unreasonable fear and/or constant hatred of older people, whereas ageism is a much more comprehensive and useful concept.")[4] Ageism, like racism and sexism, is a way of pigeonholing people and not allowing them to be individuals with unique ways of living their lives. Prejudice toward older people begins in childhood[5] and is an attempt by younger generations to shield themselves from the fact of their own eventual aging and death and to avoid having to deal with the social and economic problems of increasing numbers of older people. It provides a rationalization for pushing older people out of the job market without devoting much thought to what will happen to them when they are no longer allowed to work. (Relatively recent U.S. retirement laws have ended mandatory retirement in the public and private sectors and are a powerful counterforce to this trend, but most other countries still maintain a fixed retirement age.) Ageism is the sacrifice of older people for the sake of "productivity" and the youth image that the working world feels compelled to project. A terrible awakening comes when these younger people themselves grow old and suddenly find that they are the victims of attitudes they once held against others.

Countertransference in the classic sense occurs when mental health personnel find themselves perceiving and reacting to older persons in ways that are inappropriate and reminiscent of previous patterns of relating to parents, siblings, and other key childhood figures. Love and protectiveness may vie with hate and revenge. Ageism takes this a step further. Mental health personnel not only have to deal with leftover feelings from their personal pasts, which may interfere with their perceptions of older persons, but they must also be aware of a multitude of negative cultural attitudes toward older persons, which pervade social institutions as well as individual psyches.

The Group for the Advancement of Psychiatry report, "The Aged and Community Mental Health," in 1971 listed some of the major reasons for negative staff attitudes toward treating older persons.[6] This list still holds true. Some items no doubt represent universal, timeless feelings about old age. Others are more culturally or historically specific to a particular time and place. These attitudes are the following:

1. The aged stimulate the therapist's fears about his or her own old age.
2. They arouse the therapist's conflicts about his or her relationship with parental figures.
3. The therapist believes he or she has nothing useful to offer older people because he or she believes they cannot change their behavior or that their problems are all due to untreatable organic brain diseases.
4. The therapist believes that his or her psychodynamic skills will be wasted when working with the aged, since they are near death and not really deserving of attention (similar to the triage system of the military, in which the sickest receive the least attention because they are least likely to recover).
5. The patient might die while in treatment, which could challenge the therapist's sense of importance.
6. The therapist's colleagues may be contemptuous of his or her efforts on behalf of aged patients. (One often hears the remark that gerontologists or geriatric specialists have a morbid preoccupation with death; their interest in older persons is therefore "sick" or suspect.)

Another factor in ageism and negative countertransference is what appears to be a human propensity for hostility toward the handicapped. There is often an unconscious overidentification with older people, especially those who are physically handicapped: They are thought of as defective, crippled, powerless, or castrated. Excessive sentimentality, sympathy, avoidance, or hostility may result. It is estimated that some 300 million people in the world have highly visible deformities. These cause emotional problems—in part because of the attitudes of society. In certain primitive cultures such "cripples" (and, we might add, old people) were often put to death. This "final solution" is not so obvious in present societies, but attitudes remain surprisingly similar.

Some people have described the treatment they have received as handicapped patients. An American writer, Eric Hodgins, in his book *Episode: Report on the Accident inside My Skull*[7] tells of his own doctor, an old friend of many years, who talked to others about him in the hospital room after his stroke as though Hodgins were no longer an aware human being. Hodgins's superb account is useful reading for all who work with patients of any age.

Publications in the field of mental health have long contained evidence of ageism. A respected and well-known clinical psychiatric textbook, as late as 1977, read:

> A dislike of change, a reduction in ambition and activity, a tendency to become constricted and self-centered in interests, an increased difficulty in comprehension, an increase in time and effort in adapting to new circumstances, a lessened sympathy for new ideas and views and a tendency to reminiscence and repetition are scarcely signs of senile dementia, yet they pass imperceptibly into mental destitution and personality regression. Many elderly people have little capacity to express warm and spontaneous feelings toward others. . . .
>
> The patient resents what he considers as interference by younger persons and may complain that he is being neglected. Some show a hostile but anxious and fearful dependence. Natural affections become blunted and may turn to hatred. A certain tendency to isolation occurs.[8]

There are half-truths in this statement in the case of persons with dementia. But more obvious is the pessimistic, patronizing view of old age, tempered only slightly by hints that some of the changes might be psychological reactions to loss and stress. Anyone reading such material was confirmed in his or her negative attitudes.

Reactions of Older Persons against Treatment

Force, deceit, or any other measure taken by mental health personnel "for the older person's own good," when it is against the wishes of that older person, cannot be justified morally or legally, except in those cases in which the person is a clear and present danger to the life of himself or others. Older people may resist mental health intervention in their lives for many reasons: desire for independence, fear of change, suspiciousness based on past experiences, realistic appraisal of the inadequacies of most "helping" programs for older persons, clumsy, insensitive, or patronizing intervention techniques on the part of mental health staff, and so forth. Many times older people will tenaciously hold on to what little they have rather than risk the unknown. They may prefer to live in their own homes despite crime, dilapidation, and isolation. They may resist medical examinations, surgery, and medications. Some have been known to keep guns to use on themselves or others if someone comes to take them to a nursing home— a fate feared by many as worse than death. Pride and desire for self-reliance, as well as depression and mental confusion, must be considered as factors in resistance.

One approaches the resistance of older persons just as one would the resistances of any age group—by gradual development of trust, provision of information, and a commitment to self-determination and civil rights. Members of the clergy can often be helpful in talking through problems and decisions, as can family members, neighbors, and friends. Whenever possible, the older person must be closely involved in any decision making about him- or herself. Action, rather than just verbalization by mental health staff, can bring satisfying results. An example is the case of an older, New York woman with mild intellectual impairment who refused to move out of her condemned apartment. No amount of talking could convince her. Finally a staff member offered to physically help her move and stay with her the first night. The old woman accepted. Her fears had been met with an appropriate response.

Another problem affecting treatment is the low self-esteem of some older people who have incorporated the negative cultural view of themselves. This reaction of the victims of discrimination has been called "self-hatred" and takes the form of depression, with passive giving up or active self-denigration. These elderly look at themselves as so many younger people see them and thus do not like what they see. Open discussions about ageism can help such people reexamine their self-views, particularly if at the same time they begin to experience new acceptance on the part of people around them. Age-integrated group therapy is especially useful in this regard.

Lack of Knowledge

We simply do not know enough about old age, especially about healthy old age. Most clinical experience and studies have been of the sick and institutionalized aged. Generally, older persons are not admitted to research and training centers. And most research experience has been limited to brief periods of contact—to short-term evaluation rather than to treatment.

One major consequence of this limitation is the lack of the more enduring, intensive relationship of treatment personnel and patients, which can be an important source of data about the older person as well as a check on one's evaluation of him or her. Indeed, referral for mental health treatment is not only relatively uncommon in the community, but when it does occur, it is usually late in the course of illness, again affecting the accumulation of basic knowledge for evaluation, as

well as decreasing the likelihood of therapeutic success.

Financial and Bureaucratic Impediments

Mental health care is expensive, especially when private psychiatrists, other psychotherapists, private-duty nurses, and private hospitalization are involved. Such care is far beyond the budget of most older people. Public care is occasionally adequate and at times exemplary, but usually it is a far cry from satisfactory. Until adoption of a comprehensive medical insurance plan for all U.S. citizens, the major method of obtaining care for older persons will continue to be the Medicare system. Medicare now covers only about 40% of the average older person's health expenses. The deductibles (that which the patients pay) are just that—deductions from the care of the aged. Older people often simply do not purchase the excluded items (including dentures, eyeglasses, outpatient drugs, physical examinations) because they cannot afford them. Unfortunately, the out-of-pocket proportion of the cost of medical care has actually risen for older people since the introduction of Medicare because of increases in physician's fees, hospital costs, long-term care, and other services that Medicare does not cover, as well as the general inflationary spiral. There is also no proof that the deductible features of Medicare deter unnecessary use of health services. Instead, the exclusions may actually increase the government's bill by discouraging preventive and early rehabilitative care and rewarding hospitalization. For example, some older people, with their doctor's collaboration, have themselves checked into a hospital simply to obtain a physical examination (basing it on some physical complaint) because routine physical examinations are not covered by Medicare on an outpatient basis.

Medical coverage for psychiatric disorders is unrealistically limited and was inserted in the Medicare legislation as a kind of afterthought. (The initial diagnostic work-up and medical management of psychotropic drugs are reimbursed at the usual 80% Medicare rate). There is a 190-day lifetime limit on treatment in mental hospitals; and the patient must pay approximately 50% of allowed charges for outpatient therapy given by a physician and, as of July 1990, by a psychologist or a social worker.

For the currently limited but growing numbers of older people in health maintenance organizations, patterns of coverage for mental health care are still uncertain.

Nursing homes unfortunately have gotten into the business of providing "care" for psychiatric patients; yet they are not in any sense of the word psychiatric institutions. The conditions for eligibility for extended care under the Medicare program are both inadequate and inadequately applied. As a result, tens of thousands of older patients, including those with psychiatric problems, are receiving no more than routine custodial care.

Many nursing home facilities are substandard. The frequent occurrence of fires in nursing homes is one consequence. Too often a nursing home can be defined as a place with few nurses and few of the characteristics of home. Social and restorative services hardly exist in many homes, and activity programs usually receive more advertising than implementation. It is rare for psychiatric or social work services to ever play a part in the nursing home program. Most commercial nursing homes as well as many voluntary homes do not provide a social work staff. In addition, nursing home care is not primarily funded by Medicare, but rather by Medicaid and public assistance. Medicaid pays about 42% of nursing home care. Medicare pays only 2%. Patients themselves pay 51%, and private health insurance picks up the remaining 5%.

New federal legislation, applied as of January 1, 1989, states, in effect, that nursing homes cannot care for patients who suffer from active psychiatric disorders or mental retardation. Some therefore began refusing admission to people seeking care solely because they are retarded or mentally ill, although states have varied in the speed with which they adopted these new federal regulations. However, from the perspective of this legislation, Alzheimer's disease is not considered to be an active psychiatric disease, and, therefore, Alzheimer's patients continue to be accepted in nursing homes.

Centralized information and referral services for provision of mental health care are lacking. Bureaucratic confusion abounds. The stress and frustration older people go through to collect Medicare and private health insurance must be experienced to be believed. We present a case that is not atypical in our work.

We attempted to assist one of our clients who was having difficulty collecting payments for psychotherapy. Medicare was sending payments in different amounts for the same service and the same fee, and Mrs. K wanted to know why. In addition, her supplementary major medical insurance with Blue Cross-Blue Shield was refusing to pay for psychiatric services even though the insurance agent handling the policy assured us our client was covered.

In a five-month period we made multiple calls to Medicare (Mrs. K had already spoken to eight different people in the Medicare office during the previous six months), asking for an explanation and a list of allowable charges. We were told that a computer was faulty, and an audit was being done.

Five months later Mrs. K received a notice that she had been overpaid $60 and that she must pay it back. There was still no explanation or list of allowable charges. Mrs. K refused to believe anything any longer and decided to ignore the $60, feeling sure another mistake had been made.

During the same five months we were told twice by Blue Cross-Blue Shield that Mrs. K was eligible for psychiatric services and three times that she was not. We were twice asked to resubmit everything (previous material had been lost, couldn't be transferred from one part of BC-BS to another, etc.). After five months of work on our part, Mrs. K still had not been paid. Like the carrot on a stick, there was a constant promise of resolution—"in a month or six weeks."

We checked with Mrs. K ten months after our first contact. She had finally been paid by BC-BS. She had never paid Medicare the $60 and was never billed for it. She continued to receive different payments from Medicare for the same service and said, "but I don't question it anymore—as long as I get *something back." Medicare never sent a list of allowable charges, and BC-BS said they could not furnish her with a list of covered services or allowable charges for people who also had Medicare, because "each case is considered separately."*

When an older person with anxiety, anger, and frustration about public and private health insurance programs comes to the attention of mental health personnel, the following are possibilities to consider before simply deciding that the person is "acting dependent" or that he or she "can't cope":

1. It is often difficult to reach the proper insurance or government official by phone.
2. Clients are shifted from one person to another person and tend to give up before they reach the "right" person.
3. Phone calls are often not returned; neither are messages received. Materials that are promised may not be sent.
4. Conflicting information may be given. Many health insurance employees do not know their own office procedures or the specifics of the programs they serve.
5. Records seem, routinely, to get lost. Then the client must begin all over again.
6. There may be no explanation about payments or inconsistent payments, especially in Medicare.
7. When a mix-up occurs, clients often hear an insurance representative say, "It's out of my hands" (in the computer, another office, etc.); there is seldom any avenue to retrieve it promptly.
8. Even when insurance or government personnel are pleasant and interested, they often give the impression of being helpless in straightening out problems efficiently. Thus the older person is made to feel guilty about complaining or causing a fuss.

As we mentioned in Chapter 2, one of the new, major, time-consuming functions emerging for middle-aged offspring is helping their older parents deal with and untangle bureaucratic red tape in order to collect the benefits to which they are entitled. To assist older persons and their relatives

in general, federal and state agencies should work toward

1. Centralizing or unifying offices in each locality to which older people must go for assistance under various federal and state programs.
2. Developing a common application form for various programs.
3. Arriving at uniform definitions.
4. Unifying and simplifying procedures for determining eligibility and recertification of eligibility under various programs (for example, as of October 1, 1990, physicians are required to submit Medicare claims for their patients).
5. Unifying hearing and appellate procedures for various benefit programs.

PROGRESS TOWARD DEVELOPING PROFESSIONAL INTEREST AND SKILLS IN PROVIDING MENTAL HEALTH CARE TO THE ELDERLY

Psychiatrists and Other Physicians

In the mental health field, ageism has become professionalized—often to the point where it is not recognized. In some of the earliest investigations on this subject, Gibson noted in 1970 that psychiatrists were pessimistic about the treatability of older persons.[9] In reviewing the records of 138 patients over 65 who were admitted to a private hospital during a three-year period, it was found that the prognosis was considered poor in 80% of the patients; yet 60% were discharged as improved to their homes within 90 days. Even earlier, Gallagher et al. in 1965 found age correlating with therapeutic pessimism.[10] Of patients between 15 and 29 years of age, 66.7% received psychotherapy; of patients who were 30 to 39, 38.5% did; and of those 40 to 65, only 15.4% did.

A study of 179 psychiatrists, published in 1980, corroborates findings from earlier studies. The study indicates that

1. Psychiatrists regarded older patients as less ideal to work with than younger patients with identical symptoms.

2. The prognosis for older persons was considered poorer than that for young persons, even though the data (admittedly limited) on the prognosis of older persons do not support this conclusion.

3. Psychiatrists were much less likely to use psychotherapy, especially with older depressed women, than they were with younger persons. Instead they gave drugs, with the implication that psychotherapy would not be worthwhile.[11]

A 1987 study of primary care settings by German et al. found that despite the prevalence of emotional and psychiatric problems in the older generation, physicians in general practice are less likely to diagnose mental disorders among older persons than they are in younger persons. There is a tendency to confuse certain symptoms with general signs of aging; diagnostic mistakes also occur due to confusion over drug side effects.[12] In an accompanying editorial, Glass termed this tendency to attribute psychiatric symptoms either to changes expected to come with age or to concomitant physical disorders "a subtle form of ageism on the part of some primary care providers."[13] Interestingly, one early study found that older psychiatrists who see a higher proportion of older patients, advocate more comprehensive treatment and find older patients more interesting and gratifying.[14]

The American Geriatrics Society has pointed out that community surveys suggest that 1% or fewer of the elderly receive psychiatric care. More specifically, only 4% of community mental health center patients are over age 65; fewer than 4% of patients seen by private practitioners are elderly; and less than 1.5% of all community-based mental health care goes to the older population.[15] German et al. note that the elderly's limited use of mental health specialty care is also influenced by the stigma the elderly themselves attach to mental illness, namely that it denotes a morally weak person and may result in becoming an outcast.[16]

Although the 1980 Mendenhall psychotherapy study reports that the average psychiatrist spends only 5.3% total patient time on patients over 65,[17]

over 2,000 psychiatrists now identify themselves as having a primary interest in older patients (the extent of their knowledge or ability to work with older persons is unknown). The recent development of geriatric psychiatry (Great Britain's comparable development is called "psychogeriatrics") is evident in Sanford Finkel's organization of the American Association for Geriatric Psychiatry (AAGP) in 1978.[18] More than 400 physicians joined the AAGP in its first year, and by 1996 membership had increased to 1,400.

Many believe that geriatric psychiatry probably should not become a practice specialty in and of itself since all psychiatrists may have older people as patients and all of them will need to know the principles of geriatric psychiatry. From this point of view, the major goal for geriatric psychiatry should be academic, to train the teachers and researchers whose responsibility it is to train future generations of psychiatrists.

Leaders in the field of geriatric psychiatry have begun to emerge. In addition to contributing to the development of treatment approaches, Berezin, Busse, Eisdorfer, Gaitz, Gitelson, Goldfarb, Greenleigh, Grotjahn, Pfeiffer, Rothschild, Simon, Thompson, and Weinberg are among the U.S. psychiatrists whose work has stimulated research into the psychopathology and psychodynamics of aging.

Liaison psychiatry has also become important, particularly in hospitalized populations of older people, because it addresses the interpersonal, psychological, and psychosocial needs of patients whose illnesses are primarily nonpsychiatric. Together with the medical-surgical physicians and nonphysician staff, the liaison psychiatrist attempts to augment the diagnosis, treatment, and management of the patient. Although consultation usually consists of a brief intervention by a liaison team with a biophysical approach to illness, it sometimes leads to a recommendation for more in-depth psychotherapy.

Major labor needs exist in both the present and the future for both psychiatry and primary care medicine.[19] In 1979 the American Psychiatric Association showed a commitment to aging by establishing a Council on Aging. The American Board of Medical Specialties, based on the recommendations of the American Boards of Psychiatry and Neurology (ABPN) agreed to give examinations beginning in 1991 to those interested in receiving a Certificate of Added Qualification in Geriatric Psychiatry, following the American Board of Internal Medicine and the American Academy of Family Practice's development of a certificate of competence in geriatrics. (Applications for the ABPN examination can be obtained by calling 847-945-7900. The Beeson Report of the Institute of Medicine, *Aging and Medical Education,* was an important catalyst toward high-quality geriatric medicine, along with the National Institute on Aging's Geriatric Medicine Academic Awards, open to departments of internal medicine, family medicine, and psychiatry.[20]

On the whole, however, psychiatry as a practice specialty has not kept pace with the theoretical aspects of the discipline. Private psychotherapy, analytic practice, and psychopharmacology remain psychiatry's main preoccupations, with little active participation in the broader field of community psychiatry. Meanwhile, other disciplines have become more involved than ever in mental health work. Nurses, social workers, psychologists, pastoral counselors, paraprofessionals, and members of still-forming specialties are doing much of the work traditionally thought of as psychiatry in the past. Financial reimbursement by insurance companies and government programs of mental health services to the elderly do not yet adequately reflect this new reality. Psychologists and social workers are becoming increasingly recognized as independent vendors of mental health services.

Psychologists

The American Psychological Association's task force on training and aging updated a report on graduate education in August 1985.[21] Those U.S. and Canadian universities with psychology-related doctoral programs as listed in the American Psychological Association's publication *Graduate Study in Psychology for 1983–1984* were queried. Of these, 303 academic units responded. About 21%, 65 units, provided a specialization in adult development and aging. Another 76, or about 33%, were without specialization, but had at least one full-time faculty member with a primary interest in adult development and aging and had at least one course in this area. Thus, apparently 46% of the academic units have no faculty, courses, or programs related to aging.

As of July 1990, under Public Law 101–231, psychologists became reimbursable as independent vendors for their mental health services to the elderly (Medicare Part B outpatient mental health benefits). They also have pressed for the right to prescribe medication and to admit patients to psychiatric hospitals on their own, rather than under the supervision of psychiatrists. These rights, especially for prescribing medications, have been questioned by many and are currently under review in numerous jurisdictions.

Nurses

Nurses have, of course, always taken care of older people, and those in the nursing field have been showing increasing interest in such care.[22] Nurses who have taken leadership with regard to aging are Faye G. Abdullah, Doris Alford, Sister Rose Therese Bahr, Anna M. Brock, Myrtle I. Brown, Sister Erika Bunke, Irene M. Burnside, Sally Busck, Barbara Davis, Priscilla Ebersole, May Futrel, Laurie M. Gunter, Barbara W. Hansen, Jacqueline Heppler, Lois Knowles, Mathy Mezey, Helen Monea, Dorothy Moses, Maxine Patrick, Valencia Prock, Joan Quinn, Sister Marilyn Schwab, Doris Schwartz, Eldonna Shields, Edna M. Stilwell, Virginia Stone, Mary O. Wolanin, and May Wykie. Nurses are usually the first medical contact older people have (67% of RNs work in acute care hospitals and 6% in nursing homes; the rest are in clinics, private doctors' offices, and public health programs, with a few in private practice).[23] Therefore their training, skills, and sensitivity are crucial in creating positive and effective health care for the old. Because of their pioneering work as a profession in the field of aging, we have compiled a historical summary of their activity (Table 8.1). In the 1970s nurses began moving away from primary emphasis on a medical model to a nursing model, emphasizing health and prevention of illness as well as care during illness (rising out of the tradition of the public health nurse). At the same time they began to move away from their previous focus on institutionalized older persons to care in other settings, such as home care. Leadership in teaching nurses to work with other professions in a multidisciplinary approach to the problems of old age became a focus of the nursing profession.

Certification as a geriatric nurse recognizes the registered nurse who practices in a health care setting or performs health care functions where the primary responsibility is the care of the aged, where actions are focused on a particular patient in a case management style, and where there is personal responsibility and accountability to the patient for the outcome of such actions. Only those who are in the clinical practice of nursing qualify for such certification. Consultants, researchers, administrators, and educators are eligible to seek certification if they are also in clinical practice and can meet the criteria as specified.[24] As of October, 1995, the American Nurses' Credentialing Center listed 11,081 certified gerontologic nurses and 1,941 certified gerontologic nurse practitioners.

There are now a number of nursing schools that offer gerontological courses at the undergraduate and graduate levels. Duke University was the first to offer a master's degree in gerontological nursing, under the direction of Dr. Virginia Stone. Several schools have geriatric nurse practitioner programs,[25] but lack of interest and resistance against work with older persons remains.

Unfortunately, the broadening role of nurses—for example, as nurse practitioners—combined with modest pay, low status, and often difficult working conditions (largely because it has been a "female" profession) continue. There are increasing needs for nursing in certain areas, notably AIDS, drug addiction, and Alzheimer's disease.

Furthermore, cutbacks in federal funds for nursing research in the 1980s and early 1990s hamper the discovery of new techniques for caring for older persons on the most practical levels of care. However, the new National Institute for Nursing Research at the National Institutes of Health, in collaboration with the National Institute on Aging, contributes new knowledge for the care of older persons.

Social Workers

Social workers provide the majority of mental health care to persons of all ages in the United States, and in rural areas they are often the sole providers of services. Clinical social workers are recognized in federal law as autonomous providers of mental health care under CHAMPUS (Civilian Health and Medical Benefits Program of the Uniformed Services), FEHBP (Federal Employee Health Benefits Program), and in risk-sharing HMOs (Health Maintenance Organizations) funded through Medicare. Under the FEHBP program, private insurance carriers, including Aetna, Blue Cross/Blue Shield, Prudential, Mutual of Omaha, Harvard Community Health Plan, Kaiser Permanente, and the Health Insurance Plan of Greater New York, reimburse clinical social workers for treatment of federal employees, retirees, and their dependents. In addition, all states legally regulate social workers in an effort to ensure standards of qualification and demonstrated competence and many require licensing. With regard to specific mental health care of the elderly, a law authorizing direct reimbursement of clinical social work and psychological services under Medicare Part B outpatient mental health benefits took effect July 1990. Qualified social workers no longer have to work under the supervision of a physician for the purposes of psychotherapy.

Geriatric social work has been consistently described by social policy analysts and forecasters as a field with significant growth potential. Yet the profession has been slow in responding to the growing numbers of older persons and their need

TABLE 8.1 The pioneering involvement of the nursing profession in work with older persons

1943–1948—Two articles appeared in *American Journal of Nursing,* giving geriatric nursing direction and value and viewing geriatric nursing as a potential speciality.

1950—First nursing textbook for care of the elderly published (Newton, K. [1950]. *Geriatric nursing.* St. Louis: C. V. Mosby).

1950 on—Nursing literature about nursing and the aged proliferated.

1955—American Nurses' Foundation established to promote nursing research, much of which has been concerned with care of the aged.

1958—American Nursing Association (ANA) became first health profession to support health insurance for elderly (culminated in Medicare in 1965).

1959—ANA testified before U.S. Senate Subcommittee on Aging about low standards of care in nursing homes and also recommended expansion of home care programs.

1960—ANA adopted statement on standards for nursing care in nursing homes.

1961—ANA formed conference group for geriatric nurses, which met for first time in 1962 (70 nurses).

1966—Conference group became one of five clinical divisions in the ANA.

1966—A professional publication, *Geriatric Nursing,* appeared (discontinued in 1968).

1970—ANA published its standards of geriatric nursing practice. These were revised in 1976 (see *Standards: Gerontological nursing practice,* 1976, American Nurses' Association, 2420 Pershing Rd., Kansas City, Mo. 64108). These were designed for all areas of nursing practice, not just for "gerontological nurses."

1972—ANA committee formed to develop program to certify nurses for work with the aging. First group of nurses (74) was certified in 1974. In 1980 there were over 280 such nurses. (Nurses must be RNs. Training is nine months to one year, offered by at least nine nursing programs around the United States.)

1973—National project of continuing education on geriatric nursing started.

1974—Geriatric nurse practitioner programs were being developed.[†]

1974 on—Department of Health, Education, and Welfare made grants to nursing schools to develop curricula on aging. By 1976, 9% of nursing schools had required courses in gerontological nursing.

1974 on—Nursing textbooks on aging began to appear.

1975—Membership in ANA gerontological (formerly geriatric) group rose to 30,000.

1975—ANA published *Nursing and Long-Term Care: Toward Quality Care for the Aging,* report from the American Nurses' Association, Committee on Skilled Nursing Care, prepared for the Subcommittee on Long-Term Care of the U.S. Senate Committee on Aging.

1975—*Journal of Gerontological Nursing* appeared.

1975—Nurses' Training Act gave special emphasis to work with older persons.

1980—Four doctoral nursing programs had either an individualized program or a major in gerontological nursing. Twenty-three universities had master's degree nursing programs with specialization in geriatric/gerontological nursing.[‡] About 100 baccaulaureate nursing programs included specific focus on geriatrics.

1985—Creation of the National Center for Nursing Research at the National Institutes of Health. (The National Institute on Aging collaborates with the center.) It is now a national institute.

Source: Adapted from Reif, S. D., & Hoffman, T. Have nurses made a difference: A historical perspective, paper presented at a conference for gerontological nurses entitled *Nurses Make a Difference,* St. Paul, Minn., Oct. 6, 1977; Brimmer, P. F. (1979). Past, present and future in gerontological nursing research, *Journal of Gerontological Nursing* 5(6):27–31; and Martinson, I. M. *Gerontological nursing,* presentation to the National Institute on Aging, Bethesda, Md., Oct. 1980. Reprinted by permission.

[†]*Guidelines for the preparation of geriatric nurse practitioners* and *Guidelines for short term continuing education programs preparing the geriatric nurse practitioner,* 1974, American Nurses' Association, 2420 Pershing Rd., Kansas City, MO 64108.

[‡]See Brower, T. H. (1977). A study of graduate programs in gerontological nursing, *Journal of Gerontological Nursing* 3(6):40–46, for a more complete account of graduate programs.

for services. In particular, there are few social workers trained to work clinically with the mental health problems of the old.

Two extraordinary social workers, Harry Hopkins and Wilbur Cohen, set the stage for Social Security and other welfare entitlements affecting the elderly and others. Other leaders in the field of gerontological social work include Walter M. Beattie, Jr., Marie L. Blank, Margaret Blenkner, Elaine M. Brody, Helen Turner Burr, James J. Burr, Rose Dobrof, Rebecca Eckstein, Monseignor Charles Fahey, Roberta R. Greene, Bernice Harper, Theodore Isenstadt, Hobart C. Jackson, Rosalie Kane, Wilma Klein, Ruth Knee, Virginia Lehmann, Inabel Lindsay, Helen Lokshin, Louis Lowy, Jean M. Maxwell, Robert Morris, Helen Padula, William Posner, Ollie A. Randall, Herbert Shore, Barbara Silverstone, Barbara Soloman, Cleo Tavani, Sheldon S. Tobin, Edna Wasser, Ruth Webber, and Ellen Winston.

A 1986 report on social work services for the aged by Roberta Greene of the National Association of Social Workers summarizes the situation for geriatric social work generally:[26]

• In 1986 an estimated 18 to 21% of the 103,000 members of the National Association of Social Workers (NASW), holding either Master's or Bachelor's degrees in social work, worked with the elderly either full- or part-time. One-third to one-half of these worked in hospitals. (Figures do not exist for geriatric social workers who are not members of NASW. Overall, in 1985, 438,000 persons were filling jobs with the title of "social worker." Not all have master's or bachelor's degrees in social work, and a good number have no social work training whatsoever).

• Of 6,302 *hospitals* in 1984, 83% had a social work department. The need for social workers has grown because of Medicare's introduction of a new method of reimbursement, popularly known as the "DRGs" (Diagnostic Related Groups), which pays a specific amount per diagnostic category. This has meant that social workers often play a critical role in discharge planning in order that patients can be moved out of hospitals as quickly as possible. A Medicare requirement that adequate discharge planning for the elderly must be provided has reinforced the importance of sound discharge planning, including provision of long-term home or institutional care. Unfortunately, pressure for focus on discharge often does not allow adequate attention to mental health care.

• Social work is a major provider of outpatient psychiatric clinic services; nearly 11,000 of 28,000 professional staff in *community mental health centers* and major *outpatient facilities* in 1985 were social workers. However, services for the elderly in such centers are minor since a disproportionately small portion of the clientele is elderly.

• Social workers work in the nearly 800 *Area Agencies on Aging,* which are beginning to provide more direct services for the elderly.

• *Family service agencies* are underused by the elderly. In 1985, about one-half of the 228 Family Service Agencies reported that older persons represented only 3% of their clients.

• The nation's 23,000 *nursing homes* reported few full-time or part-time social workers (not all professionally trained). The institutionalized aged have been a particularly underserviced or totally unserved population. However, effective October 1990, as part of the Omnibus Reconciliation Act of 1987, skilled nursing facilities with more than 120 beds must have at least one social worker with at least a Bachelor's degree in social work or the equivalent.

• Three thousand social workers are employed by the Veterans' Administration. In 1990 one in four veterans was 65 years of age or older. By the year 2000, it will be one in three. Because of the large numbers of young men in service in World War II, 63% of the entire U.S. male population over age 65 will be veterans in the year 2000. Thus *veterans' hospitals* and other facilities already are and will continue to be significant employers of geriatric social workers until the population of veterans thins out.

In 1988 the National Association of Social Workers created a subcommittee on aging as part of its Commission on Family and Primary Associations in order to help improve awareness of the increasing demand for social workers in the field of gerontology. A major recommendation of the subcommittee was to begin collecting data on the size, characteristics, and trends of aging services within the profession, as well as developing a vehicle for conducting labor force studies and a clearinghouse for research data on aging.

From 1983 to 1985, the Council on Social Work Education, with funds from the Administration on Aging, sponsored several projects on improving social work education in work with the aging. The purpose was to integrate gerontology into social work curricula and to develop a model curriculum for gerontological specialization at the graduate level.[27] Robert Schneider and Nancy Kropf coedited a curriculum series in gerontology for bachelor of social work programs,[28] and Roberta Greene of the National Association of Social Workers completed a continuing education curriculum for social workers already in the field of aging.[29]

Training in the field of aging has improved slowly, but is still unavailable in many social work programs. A 1988 survey found that out of 100 master's of social work programs that responded, only 34% offered a concentration in aging and an additional 33% offered at least one course in aging. Out of 372 bachelor's of social work programs that responded, only 9% offered a concentration in aging and an additional 11% offered at least one course in aging.[30] In addition, most full-time faculty in these programs have no formal training in gerontology. The conclusion to be drawn here is that schools are relying on outside lecturers and on-the-job training of faculty to present the gerontological programs.

Counselors

A valuable, expanding resource of capable counselors can be found in other areas. Within the American Counseling Association[31] are various counselors: mental health, school, employment, and so forth. Counselors work in a variety of set-tings, including community mental health centers, as professionals, and paraprofessionals. Standards-setting, state licensure, and third-party reimbursement are current issues confronting counselors. The AACD had a two-year cooperative agreement with the Administration on Aging to support the National Project on Counseling Older People. Through this project, various service providers who work with older persons—social service aides to administrators and attorneys—were to be provided continuing education in basic gerontological counseling skills.

Paraprofessionals

Paraprofessionals are also known as "new professionals," "nonprofessionals," "lay therapists," "community workers," "community aides," "indigenous workers," and even, condescendingly, "subprofessionals." The abundance of names points to the vagueness of the concept and the disagreement about roles. We prefer the term "paraprofessional" because its Greek roots mean "along side of" professionals, implying a working together rather than working "beneath" other staff members. Paraprofessionals should and will play increasingly more important roles in evaluation and treatment of older persons.

Paraprofessionals such as home health workers are often paid minimum wages and ironically, though health providers themselves, often receive no fringe benefits, including health insurance. Like nurses' aides, these workers are often hired off the street and are frequently young immigrants with language and culture different from their clientele. They usually lack pre-service training and are not given in-service training, let alone a career path to follow. All this is disadvantageous both to home health workers and patients. Training and supervision are crucial to growth and utilization of inherent skills. Reasonable and uniform standards of performance ensure better treatment capabilities.

In the future, various new careers are likely to evolve—one example, a "personal care worker" who would be trained to absorb a variety of functions now distributed among members of many occupations, from home health aide to home-maker to occupational therapy assistant. This would avoid the jurisdictional disputes that now arise, as shown by the homemaker who will not or cannot change a cancer dressing, the home health aide who will not clean the kitchen, and so on.

Community Mental Health Workers

Community mental health centers failed to become a major resource for the elderly. Only half of the 600 centers existing in the 1980s had services designed especially for the elderly and only 4 to 5% of all clientele at these centers were age 65 or older. Some of the reasons for low usage were (1) community mental health centers were often not easily physically accessible to the elderly, (2) few staff members had specific training in work with the elderly, (3) most did not coordinate their work with the available health and social services for the elderly, for example, Area Agencies on Aging.[32] However, those centers that did have specialized programs with trained staff and coordination with area services reported a significantly higher utilization rate by the elderly.[33] (See Chapter 10)

STAFF CONSIDERATIONS

What Kind of People Work with Older Persons?

It has been suggested that few mental health personnel actively choose to work with older people and that most of them fall into the work by chance. Professionals tend to deny having an original, personal attraction to the field, preferring to say they have responded to a "need" in society or to an intellectual curiosity about aging. Directors of institutions for older people will state that most of their employees developed interests and satisfactions after beginning their work. We suggest that these may be subtle denials, concealing a reluctance to admit an interest in old age—a reluctance fostered by the societal devaluation of the aged and by the often heard professional opinion that an interest in

aging represents a morbid preoccupation with decline and death. Naturally chance plays a part in determining career opportunities. But conscious or unconscious personal factors are as important in choosing and remaining in the field of aging as they are in any other human decisions. We offer the following as a number of possible emotional motivations for working professionally with older people.

1. Particularly warm relationships in childhood with grandparents, who then leave their grandchildren a legacy of natural sympathy and interest in older people

2. Early dependence on grandparents (i.e., the "grandmother's children" who were not reared by their own parents) or on older persons (i.e., children of parents who were already older than average when they had children or children of a young mother and a much older father)

3. Death or painful illness of an important older person when a child is young and extremely impressionable (Studies of physicians, for example, have shown that a significant number experienced an early death of a loved person. Medicine then became a way of gaining power over death and the helpless feelings of childhood.)

4. Unconscious counterphobic attempt to conquer fears of aging and death

5. Conscious attempt to prepare for old age, especially if the models of parents or grandparents are unacceptable (A 58-year-old social worker interested in working professionally in the field of the aging joined one of our age-integrated therapy groups to prepare, as she said, for old age. She was terrified at seeing herself become more and more like her mother, whom she viewed as a bitter, disillusioned old woman. She felt helpless in the grip of the model her mother presented her.)

6. Personal sense of inferiority that causes identification with older people, who are culturally defined as inferior

7. Guilt and subsequent reaction formation for feelings of fear and revulsion toward the aged

8. Admiration for and identification with someone working in the field of aging

The importance of determining one's personal motivation is obvious. A mental health specialist must know from where he or she is starting emotionally, in order to help others more effectively.

STAFF TRAINING

General therapeutic principles should be applicable in all settings—private offices, community mental health centers, hospital wards, service agencies—where older people are seen in a mental health context. Intrapsychic phenomena, mechanisms of defense, developmental theory, the structure of grief, and the dynamics of dependency are some of the key areas of knowledge. Everyone, including the paraprofessionals, should have a working knowledge of this material. Even difficult concepts can be presented in in-service training in a clear, simplified, but accurate manner.[34]

Mental health personnel working as a team can teach each other from their collective backgrounds. Anyone with special training or skills should, ideally, share such knowledge openly rather than retaining it as secret prerogatives. Psychiatrists, psychologists, and nurses have particular bodies of information to teach others, but they need to learn much more about social, economic, and cultural considerations and thus will have to be students as well. Social workers can use increased skills and knowledge in understanding and recognizing medical symptoms and in sharpening diagnostic skills. Paraprofessionals are usually weak on formal knowledge of psychopathology and psychodynamics but may be exceedingly sensitive about environmental conditions and cultural factors. A successfully working team will eventually end up sharing a mutual body of knowledge, with the final product being qualitatively more useful than the sum of its parts. Individual disciplines can maintain their individual skills while at the same time gaining from and adding to a larger whole. The danger, of course, lies in the competition and power struggles that seem to arise naturally under such circumstances. These reactions should be anticipated and a plan

of action agreed on before they occur. There is no reason why human beings who have chosen a career of helping others should not be able to help themselves in working peacefully and constructively with their colleagues. Much is known theoretically about group behavior. It remains for us to apply it in our dealings with each other as mental health practitioners.

In working specifically with the aged, it is safe to assume that all staff members will have some attitudes toward older people that are unclear untrue, and even prejudicial. Major tasks in staff training are to clear up uncertainty and misinformation and to make personnel aware of negative countertransference and ageist feelings. Sometimes this can be accomplished by simply providing accurate information. At other times it may require sensitivity training of a sort that brings a staff member's feelings to his awareness and invites and stimulates him to reexamine them. Supervisory sessions, both group and individual, are useful. For the sake of learning, it is wise to see many kinds of older people in many different settings and circumstances. It is also desirable to have had work experiences with persons from all age groups—a life-cycle view is helpful.

In-service training, planning, and problem-solving programs are ways of wrestling with staff conflicts and antagonisms when they arise, providing a forum for resolving countertransference, setting policy and programs, and planning formal and informal learning experiences. Outside teachers and consultants can be used to avoid inbreedings of ideas and outlook. Staff members generally rebel at the thought of extensive outside reading, which should be kept at a minimum and carefully selected for clarity and direct usefulness.[35]

Ideally, research should be built into any ongoing program. Any unusual observations of the older person or his or her family, responses to drugs, or other pertinent information should be recorded in observation books kept available for that purpose, as well as in the person's individual records. Such a practice can result in serendipitous findings that would otherwise be lost and may add to an accumulating body of general knowledge about older people. Another form of research is a routine, periodic reevaluation of the program or service itself. Both of these research methods can be uncomplicated, do-it-yourself ways of learning more and of revitalizing services. Cooperative and more sophisticated research can be arranged among various similar institutions or services in an area. Grants can be obtained for applied research studying delivery systems. The National Institute of Mental Health in Rockville, Maryland, can be contacted for ideas and support.

TREATMENT POINTS TO REMEMBER

What's in a Name?

What we call someone often defines how we will treat him or, at least, how we view him. What should an older person be called? Some of the names one hears are *aged, elderly, senior citizen, retiree, gramps, granny, old biddy, old fogy, old gal,* or simply *old.* If the older person comes for mental health care, is he or she a patient? A client? A "health consumer"? In our experience, people prefer the simplest and most dignified title. *Older person* can be used for anyone from a 60-year-old to a 90-year-old. *Elderly* is accepted in advanced old age—the seventies and eighties. *Aged,* to some, has implications of decrepitude and is not as favored. We have used the terms *older person* most frequently and *elderly* less often and have referred to the older person as *patient* only when it was confusing not to do so. *Patient* implies a limited role in relationship to a doctor or therapist, and we are interested in presenting the older person as a whole. Viewing someone as a patient encourages his or her self-evaluation as dependent and inferior.

In contacts with older persons, it is important to address them respectfully as Mr. or Mrs. unless they specifically ask to be called by their first names. Young students, interns, and trainees are especially tempted to use first names brashly, either through habit or as an attempt to overcome feelings of intimidation. Older people may find this insulting. African Americans and other mi-

nority elderly may be especially sensitive. The presumptuous use of first names or nicknames implies a careless, thoughtless, even contemptuous attitude toward the feelings of older people, who grew up at a time when this was a demeaning and disrespectful gesture. In the case of the African American elderly, they have too long been known only as "James" while the white person was "Mr."

There is also the habit, especially rampant in medical schools, of students and interns to refer to older patients as *gomers* (meaning get out of my emergency room!), *turkeys, gorks, dirtballs, trolls,* and the apparent all-time favorite, *crocks.* Students are too often socialized into being impatient and bored with the old, as well as resentful and fatalistic about the physical and mental deterioration found in many of the older people they see. Medical schools must begin to offer sensitivity training as well as more formal geriatric education in the early years of medical school to counter these tendencies.

Who Decides?

Treatment is a collaboration among older people, their families, and mental health personnel. Decisions should be mutually agreed on unless physical or mental incapacity prevents this. Some treatment personnel use contracts between the patients and themselves, stating specific goals of treatment, as well as the cost and length of sessions, measures for renegotiation after a stipulated period, and provisions for cancellation.

Need for Full Attention to Physical Complaints

It is very important emotionally for the older person to feel that everything possible is being done medically, even when there is really little that can be done. To exhaust the limits of the possible is very reassuring. The arthritic pain, the hypertensive flare-up, the constipation, nerves, irritable colon syndrome, unsightly varicose veins, stress incontinence, estrogen-deficient vaginitis, urinary tract infections, dry and itchy skin, gout,

Parkinsonism, osteoporosis, cold extremities, painful calves, fatigue, edema, irregular pulse, headaches, dizziness, shortness of breath, and confusion are all common complaints that must be treated with seriousness and competence. Often, side effects from the treatments must also be treated. For instance, magnesium-aluminum hydroxide helps alleviate gastric distress associated with prolonged salicylate therapy for arthritis.

It is extraordinarily painful for a human being to be sold short, to be considered unreachable, beyond help, having received the "maximum benefits" of physical therapy and other treatment. Imagine the sense of numbing despair. It is equally true, of course, that action for the sake of action can be a pointless charade. Therefore, to avoid premature dismissal or pointless continued care, a continuing collaboration is necessary with objective assessment, including assessment of the person's morale. Treatment should never be discontinued in a vacuum, without explanation from the professional and some acceptance from the patient. To do so is to risk depression and despair.

Because Medicare does not cover physical checkups, mental health personnel often do not have ready access to knowledge concerning the patient's physical condition and must necessarily be alert to signs of physical illness. For example, early signs of peripheral vascular disease (arteriosclerosis obliterans) such as mild calf pain, loss of hair on toes, slow or unusual toenail growth, cold sensitivity, and shiny skin may be presented as part of an older person's complaint and should be investigated medically.

As an additional consideration, older people often have a dilemma with regard to their family doctor. Usually the doctor is older than the patient. As the patient gets older that is often disadvantageous. It would be ageist to recommend against the older, experienced doctor; but the potential reality of retirement, disability, or death of such a physician must not be overlooked. One direction to take is to build a parallel relationship with a younger colleague of the doctor. Membership in a group practice is another solution.

Psychoanalytic Theory as It Applies to Older People

Psychoanalytic theory provides a valuable means of viewing old age. The ego, the id, the superego, and the ego ideal are useful constructs. In the presence of brain damage, impulses may overrun inhibitions; that is, the id may overpower the superego and the ego, executive functions having been damaged. Incomplete fulfillment of an individual's ego ideal occupies an important part of the content of the life review in both the brain-damaged and the unaffected individuals. In the person not brain-damaged, considerations pertinent to ego psychology indicate the continuing capacity of the older ego to grow and the superego to become more flexible. The notion of the weakening of the id or libido (vitality) with age is reminiscent of Aristotle's observation contained in the *Rhetoric* that older persons love and hate less strongly. We do not yet know enough about outer influences on ego structure or even the id to be certain how intrinsic any observed weakening of the id or ego may be.

The full range of transference possibilities can be seen in older persons as with any age group. One may see role reversal, with the older person taking the role of parent to the therapist. Coercive, dominating, or patronizing behavior may occur. For older people who manifest helplessness, the therapist may be imbued with magical powers.

How to Estimate Treatability

When in doubt, treat judiciously and see if improvement occurs. This is, of course, obvious with respect to brain disorders like delirium but should also be applied elsewhere. Improvements can occur in people who are considered hopeless. Overt behavior is too often taken as innate rather than adaptive. On the other hand, patients with apparently positive treatment possibilities may not respond well at all because of hidden, underlying processes. Treatment should be used to both rule in and rule out a diagnosis and should not be separated from evaluation.

When Not to Argue

Older people often have long-standing personal habits which may at first glance appear idiosyncratic, old-fashioned, useless, or even an interference with mental or physical health care. But take another look. Such habits frequently provide an important sense of identity, security, and comfort, especially under stress. Examples are strong food preferences, sleep rituals, and use of laxatives or other self-prescribed medications. The older and more frail the person, the more important it is not to disturb personal habits unless they present a major threat to health and well-being.

Arguing or cajoling the elderly into a shift of long-standing behavior is usually counterproductive and may be outright cruel or harmful in its impact. Health professionals faced with what may seem to be "egocentricities" of the elderly are well advised to graciously yield the right-of-way unless there is clear reason for not doing so. The elderly should be granted the luxury of their special demands, especially when they are under stress. To do so communicates respect, caring, acknowledgment of individual differences and a desire to respond to personal needs. For some of the most frail, it can mean the difference between maintaining psychic balance or being toppled into confusion and alienation.

Use of Nonverbal Communication

Because of the greater likelihood of physical impairments, nonverbal communication can facilitate treatment and in some cases become a dominant part of the relationship. Persons who are hard-of-hearing need to be able to see the lips of the person talking to them in order to "read" them. We all do this to some degree, but the hard-of-hearing often need special training. It may be necessary to speak very close to the ear, and it is important to learn if one ear is better than the other. Eye contact also is useful in relating; one can learn to "read" the eyes of a stroke victim or of someone with throat problems or certain forms

of aphasia. Older people seem to be very alert and responsive to the tone and inflection of an interviewer's voice—able to judge rather accurately the personality behind the voice. Touch or tactile communication becomes extremely important. There is often a desire to be literally "in touch" with the person speaking. People who are very sick may respond more to holding hands than to talking. Shared tears of happiness or sadness on the part of both mental health personnel and older people are common and can be therapeutic. When the older person is physically unable to talk, interviews can be carried out via intuition: The therapist surmises what is on the older person's mind and verbalizes it for him; then the person signals in some way (a smile, nod, frown) if he is being understood. Affection from an older person should be accepted graciously and warmly—and returned—when appropriate. A kiss on the cheek, an embrace, or a pat on the hand for the therapist may become part of the ritual of therapy.

Patience is needed for those struggling to speak. We never shall forget the 75-year-old woman who had had a stroke and was attempting to express her feelings about her suffering. She struggled mightily for a number of minutes, but the words just would not come. Finally everything fell momentarily into place and she shouted "Shit" to the heavens, with a triumphant voice and a gleam in her eye—summing up her feelings succinctly. We and she alike considered it a therapeutic victory.

"Listening" as a Form of Therapy

Listening is an important ingredient in therapy with older persons. Some older people have a great need to talk, and their talking should not be dismissed as a bore or garrulousness. Reminiscence has meaning for the life review that occurs in nearly all people. Feelings of guilt that result from such reminiscing should not be treated as irrational, to be patched up by patronizing reassurance. Guilt is as real in old age as in any other age and must be dealt with therapeutically.

Race and Culture—Language Differences

In Chapter 7 and elsewhere we emphasize the importance of racial, cultural, and ethnic backgrounds in diagnosis and treatment. We wish to add here the problems of language differences, whether these be regional dialect, slang or accent differences, or use of a totally different language—such as Chinese, German, or Spanish. Members of minority groups should be employed in every level of mental health care. Bilingual interpreters having skill in slang or dialect interpretation, as well as actual dual language ability, should be used to train staff, provide direct interpretation, and help older members of minority groups obtain needed services. In addition, hospitals and services that hire foreign personnel, including doctors, have a responsibility to train them adequately in English or provide interpreters. Older persons should not have to bear the burden of treatment personnel's language handicaps.

Myth of Termination of Treatment

Older persons need the opportunity for continuing support and easy availability of services, even when a particular problem has been resolved. Traditional psychiatric and social work has as a goal the eventual termination of mental health care, and there is a considerable literature on countertransference and the problem of termination of treatment. With older people it may be necessary and totally appropriate to continue treatment and care, varying it according to changing conditions until a quite different termination—death.

Three Directions to Move in Treatment

Older people need a *restitution capacity,* the ability to compensate for and recover from deeply felt losses. They also need the *opportunity for growth and renewal,* which represent the opposite of obsolescence and stagnation. This can be defined as the effective striving toward discovery and utilization of innate potential. It can mean a rediscovery or even a first discovery of the self. Jung has written of individuation as one of the tasks of late life. Consequent to a successful psychotherapeutic process (or occurring naturally in a private life review) one may see either the emergence of a qualitatively different personality or a renewal.

> I for one have never touched bottom in self, nor even struck against the surface, the outlines, the boundaries of the self. On the contrary, I feel the self as an energy only which expands and contracts—Bernard Berenson at 83

And, finally, older people require *perspective,* the ability to see themselves and their lives as a whole rather than fixating on any particular aspect. This is the ability to perceive one's place in the world, free from distortion, extending to both the outer and the inner world. It is the sense of "putting one's house in order." Inherent in perspective is a time framework that includes both past and future. It is longitudinal rather than merely situational. The end result is to make acceptable sense out of one's life.

We discuss other treatment directions in later chapters: what to do when that which is "possible" becomes limited; the psychotherapy surrounding death, loss, and their emotional trappings; and advocacy—including the therapist as advocate.

RIGHT TO TREATMENT

The right to treatment is more than a moral obligation—it is now a legal right and requirement. The Age Discrimination Act of 1975 mandates against discrimination toward older persons in the delivery of mental health services. Mental health personnel have too long had the unjustified luxury of deciding whether to offer services or being able to weigh the wisdom of expending resources. Enforcement of the Age Discrimination Act could significantly reduce discrimination in mental health services to the elderly.

SELECTED READINGS

Aaron, H., & Schwartz, W. B. (1990). Rationing health care: The choices before us. *Science, 247,* 418–422.

AGS Public Policy Committee. (1993). *American Geriatrics Society position statement: Mental health and the elderly.* New York: American Geriatrics Society.

American Nurses Association, Council on Gerontological Nursing. (1987). *Standards and scope of gerontological nursing practice.* Kansas City, MO: American Nurses Association.

Ansello, E. F. (1976). Ageism and picture books. *Interracial Books for Children Bulletin, 7,* 4–10.

Ansello, E. F. (1977). Age and ageism in children's first literature. *Educational Gerontology, 2,* 255–274.

Aries, P. (1962). *Centuries of childhood: A social history of family life* (translated by R. Baldick). New York: Alfred A. Knopf.

Barusch, A. S., Greene, R. R., & Connelly, J. R. (1990). *Strategies for increasing gerontology content in social work education.* Washington, DC: Association for Gerontology in Higher Education.

Bazelon, D. (1975). Lake vs. Cameron. In Allen, R. C., Ferster, E., & Rubin, J. G. (Eds.), *Readings in law and psychiatry.* Baltimore, MD: John Hopkins University Press.

Beck, A. T. (1976). *Cognitive therapy and the emotional disorders.* New York: International Universities Press.

Birnbaum, M. (1965). Some comments on the right to treatment. *Archives of General Psychiatry, 13,* 33–45.

Butler, R. N. (1988). A U.S. view—Life after cost containment: Perspectives on meeting the health care needs of older people. In Binns, T. B., & Firth, M. (Eds.), *Health care provision under financial constraint.* Royal Society of Medicine International Congress and Symposium Series No. 115, Royal Society of Medicine Services.

Butler, R. N. (1989, May). Dispelling ageism: The cross-cutting intervention. In Riley, M. W., & Riley, J. W., Jr. (Eds.), The quality of aging: Strategies for interventions. *Annals of the American Academy of Political and Social Science, 503,* 163–175.

Butler, R. N. (1990). A disease called ageism (editorial). *Journal of the American Geriatrics Society, 38,* 178–180.

Butler, R. N. (1990). Perspectives on psychogeriatrics: Message to the 21st century. *International Psychogeriatrics, 2*(1), 9–12.

Committee on Leadership for Academic Geriatric Medicine. (1987). Report of the Institute of Medicine: Academic geriatrics for the year 2000. *Journal of the American Geriatrics Society, 35,* 773–791.

Erikson, E. H., Erikson, J. M., & Kivnick, H. Q. (1987). *Vital involvement in old age.* New York: W. W. Norton.

Frankl, V. (1963). *Man's search for meaning* (original, 1959). New York: Washington Square Press.

Fries, J. F. (1984). The compression of morbidity: Miscellaneous comments about a theme. *The Gerontologist, 24,* 354–359.

Fulop, G., Reinhardt, J., Strain, J., Paris, B., Miller, M., & Fillit, H. (1993). Identification and depression in a geriatric medicine outpatient clinic. *Journal of the American Geriatrics Society, 41,* 737–741.

Green, R. R., Barusch, A. S., & Connelly, J. R. (1990). *Social work and gerontology: Status report.* Washington, DC: Association for Gerontology in Higher Education.

Gruman, G. J. (1978). Cultural origins of present-day "age-ism": The modernization of the life cycle. In Spicker, S. F., Woodward, K. M., & VanTassel, D. D. (Eds.), *Aging and the elderly: Human perspectives in gerontology.* Atlantic Highlands, NJ: Humanities Press.

Hartman. H. (1985). *Ego psychology and the problem of adaptation.* New York: International Universities Press.

Hodgins, E. (1985). *Episode: Report on the accident inside my skull.* New York: Atheneum Press.

Hollingshead, A. B., & Redlich, F. C. (1958). *Social class and mental illness.* New York: John Wiley & Sons.

Holosko, M. J., & Feit, M. D. (Eds.) (1995). *Social work practice with the elderly,* 2nd edition. Canadian Scholars' Press.

Jung, C. G. (1933). The stages of life. In *Modern man in search of a soul* (pp. 109–131). New York: Harcourt, Brace and World.

Levin, S., & Kahana, R. (Eds.). (1967). *Psychodynamic studies on aging: Creativity, reminiscing and dying.* New York: International University Press.

Lieber, C. S. (1995). Medical disorders of alcoholism. *New England Journal of Medicine, 333,* 1058–1065.

Maslow, A. (1971). *The farther reaches of human nature.* New York: Viking Press.

Mellor, M. J., & Solomon, R. (Eds.). (1992). *Geriatric social work education.* Binghamton, NY: The Haworth Press.

Meyer, C. H. (1986). *Social work with the aging.* Washington, DC: National Association of Social Workers (NASW) Press.

Palmore, E. (1972). Gerontophobia Versus Ageism. *The Gerontologist, 12,* 213.

Parham, I. A. (1993). *Gerontological social work: An annotated bibliography.* Westport, CT: Greenwood.

Paulin, J. E., & Walter, C. A. (1992). Retention plans and job satisfaction of gerontological social workers. *Journal of Gerontological Social Work, 19*(1), 99–114.

Peterson, D. A. (1990). Personnel to serve the aging in the field of social work: Implications for educating professionals. *Social Work, 35*(5), 412–415.

Reed, C. C., Beall, S. C., & Baumhover, L. A. (1992). Gerontological education for students in nursing and social work: Knowledge attitudes, and perceived barriers. *Educational Gerontology, 18*(6), 625–636.

Rich, T. A., Connelly, J. R., & Douglas, B. (1994). *Standards and guidelines for gerontology programs.* Washington, DC: Association for Gerontology in Higher Education.

Riley, M. W. (1980). *Aging from birth to death and social change.* Paper presented for a session on New Frontiers in Science. San Francisco, CA: American Association for the Advancement of Science.

Rogers, C. R. (1980). *A way of being.* Boston: Houghton Mifflin.

Rowe, J. W., Grossman, E., Enriqueta, B., & the Institute of Medicine Committee on Leadership for Academic Geriatric Medicine. (1987, May 28). American geriatrics for the year 2000. *New England Journal of Medicine, 316,* 1425–1428.

Schell, E. (1993). The origins of geriatric nursing: The chronically ill elderly in almshouses and nursing homes, 1900–1950. *Nursing History Review, 1,* 203–216.

Swanson, E. A., & Tripp-Reimer, T. (Eds.). (1996). *Advances in gerontological nursing. Volume 1: Issues for the 21st century.* New York: Springer.

Widner, S., & Zeichner, A. (1991). Alcohol abuse in the elderly: Review of epidemiology, research, and treatment. *Clinical Gerontologist, 11*(1), 3–18.

ENDNOTES

1. Riley, M. W. (1980). *Aging from birth to death and social change.* Paper prepared for a session on New Frontiers in Science, American Association for the Advancement of Science, San Francisco.

2. Hartman, H. (1985). *Ego psychology and the problem of adaptation.* New York: International Universities Press.

3. First described by Butler, R. N. (1969). The effects of medical and health progress on the social and economic aspects of the life cycle. *Industrial Gerontology, 1,* 1–9; see also Butler, R. N. (1990). A disease called ageism. *Journal of the American Geriatric Association, 38,* 178–180.

4. Palmore, E. (1972). Gerontophobia versus ageism. *The Gerontologist, 12,* 213.

5. Ansello, E. F. (1976). Ageism and picture books. *Interracial Books for Children Bulletin, 7,* 4–10; and Ansello, E. F. (1977). Age and ageism in children's first literature. *Educational Gerontology, 2,* 255–274.

6. Group for the Advancement of Psychiatry, Committee on Aging. (1971, November). *The aged and community mental health: A guide to program development.* (vol. 8, series no. 81). New York: Brunner-Mazel.

7. Hodgins, E. (1964). *Episode: Report on the accident inside my skull.* New York: Atheneum Press.

8. From Noyes, A., & Kolb, L. (1977). *Modern clinical psychiatry,* 9th ed. Philadelphia: W. B. Saunders, 289.

9. Gibson, R. W. (1970). Medicare and the psychiatric patient. *Psychiatric Opinion, 7,* 17–22.

10. Gallagher, E. B., Sharaf, M. R., & Levinson, D. (1965). The influence of patient and therapist in determining the use of psychotherapy in a hospital setting. *Psychiatry, 28,* 297–310.

11. Ford, C. V., & Sbordone, R. J. (1980). Attitudes of psychiatrists toward elderly patients. *American Journal of Psychiatry, 137,* 571–575.

12. German, P. S., Shapiro, S., Skinner, E. A., VonKorff, M., Klein, L. E., Turner, R. W., Teitelbaum, M. L., Burka, J. B., & Burns, B. J. (1987, January 23/30). Detection and management of mental health problems of older patients by primary care providers. *Journal of the American Medical Association, 257,* 489–493.

13. Glass, R. M. (1987, January 23/30). Psychiatric megatrends and the elderly. *Journal of the American Medical Association, 257,* 527–528.

14. See Garetz, F. K. (1975). The psychiatrist's involvement with aged patients. *American Journal of Psychiatry, 132,* 63–65.

15. AGS Public Policy Committee. (1993). *American Geriatrics Society position statement: Mental*

health and the elderly. New York: American Geriatrics Society.

16. Garetz (1975).

17. University of Southern California, Division of Research in Medical Education. (1978). *Psychiatry practice study report.* Los Angeles: University of Southern California.

18. The American Association for Geriatric Psychiatry (AAGP) publishes a booklet listing its membership. It can be obtained by writing the AAGP, 7910 Woodmont Ave., Bethesda, MD, 20814.

19. Kane, R., Solomon, D., Beck, J., Keelor, F., & Kane, R. (1980). The future need for geriatric manpower in the United States. *New England Journal of Medicine, 302,* 1327–1332.

20. For a valuable assessment of these areas, see Committee on Leadership for Academic Geriatric Medicine. (1987). Report of the Institute of Medicine: Academic geriatrics for the year 2000. *Journal of the American Geriatric Society, 35,* 773–791.

21. Educational Committee of Division 20 (Adult Development and Aging), Washington, D.C., August 1985, American Psychological Association (APA). In 1996, the APA had a membership of 142,000 psychologists, with divisions in 49 subfields of psychology.

22. For example, see Irene M. Burnside's excellent book: *Nursing and the aged,* 3rd ed. New York: McGraw-Hill, 1988.

23. There were an estimated 2.2 million RNs in 1992, and 83% of these (1.8 million) were in active practice. See the U.S. Dept. of Health & Human Services, U.S. Public Health Service, HRSA. (1992, March). *The Registered Nurse Population: Findings from the National Sample of Registered Nurses.*

24. Geriatric nursing was the first nursing area to give certification exams. In addition, certification of clinical specialists began in October 1989. Candidates who achieve a passing score on the examination must submit additional documentation on their practice, reference vouchers, and evidence of continuing education. Case studies, clinical research, or a pilot project complete the requirements. Information on certification can be obtained from the American Nurses' Credentialing Center 600 Maryland Ave, SW, Suite 100W, Washington, DC 20024, (800) 274-4262.

25. See Standards of geriatric nursing practice (Appendix A) and Guidelines for short-term continuing education programs preparing the geriatric nurse practitioner (Appendix B). In Burnside, I. M.

(1988). *Nursing and the aged,* 3rd ed. New York: McGraw-Hill.

26. Greene, R. (1986). The growing need for social work services for the aged in 2020. In Vourlekis, B., & Leukefeld, C. (Eds.), *Making our case: A resource book of selected materials for social workers in health care.* Silver Spring, MD: The National Association of Social Workers.

27. The assessment, *The Current Status of Gerontology in Graduate Social Work Education,* and a four-volume work, *The CSWE Series in Gerontology,* are available from the Council on Social Work Education, 1600 Duke Street, Suite 300, Alexandria, VA 22314-3421.

28. Schneider, R., & Kropf, N. (Eds.). (1989). *Integrating gerontology into the BSW curriculum* (Vol. 1) and *Essential knowledge and skills for baccalaureate social work students in gerontology* (Vol. 2). Joint publication of the Council on Social Work Education, Washington, DC, and Virginia Commonwealth University School of Social Work, Richmond, VA.

29. Greene, R. (1988, April). *Continuing education for gerontological careers.* Washington, DC: Council on Social Work Education (1744 R St.).

30. Lubben, J. E., Damon-Rodriguez, J., & Beck, J. C. (1992). A National Survey of Aging Curriculum in Schools of Social Work. In Mellor, M. J., & Solomon, R. (Eds.), *Geriatric social work education.* Binghamton, NY: The Haworth Press.

31. American Counseling Association, 5999 Stevenson Ave., Alexandria, VA 22304, (800) 347-6647. (Note especially the division called the American Mental Health Counselors Association.)

32. Light, E., Lebowitz, B. D., & Bailey, F. (1986). CMHCs and elderly services: An analysis of direct and indirect services and service delivery sites. *Community Mental Health Journal, 22,* 294–302.

33. Lebowitz, B. D. (1988, July). Correlates of success in community mental health programs for the elderly. *Hospital and Community Psychiatry, 39*(7), 721–722.

34. For example, for general interviewing principles presented simply and clearly, we recommend Garret, A. (1982). *Interviewing—Its principles and methods* (3rd ed. revised by E. P. Zuki & M. Mangold). New York: Family Service Association of America.

35. For a beginning look at possible teaching materials, see references at the end of each chapter, as well as lists of films and fiction in Appendix E at the end of the book.

CHAPTER 9

DIAGNOSTIC EVALUATION: HOW TO DO A WORKUP

THE PURPOSE OF DIAGNOSTIC EVALUATION
THE ROLE OF GERIATRIC ASSESSMENT
HOW COMPREHENSIVE SHOULD
AN EVALUATION BE?

CONDITIONS FOR A GOOD EVALUATION
A BASIC EVALUATION

This chapter brings us to the core of mental health care of the elderly, namely the need to establish a sound treatment plan based on a comprehensive diagnostic evaluation of each older individual who is in need of such care.

THE PURPOSE OF DIAGNOSTIC EVALUATION

In its simplest sense, the mental health diagnostic evaluation is a method of looking at the problems of older people, arriving at decisions that are as accurate as possible as to what is wrong, and concluding what can be done to try to alleviate or eliminate these problems. The older person, together with mental health personnel, tries to discover whether the problems are *intrinsic* (i.e., originating from long-term personality traits or emotional reactions to personal situations) and/or *extrinsic* (i.e., secondary to environmental or social causes); whether there are physical components; and whether the problems represent a new, first-time experience, an old experience with new implications, or something new superimposed on already existing difficulties. Gathering together and assessing the many factors that affect the emotional life of an older person is the process by which such evaluation is carried out. Evaluators

use historical data from the person's past; current medical, psychiatric, and social examinations; and their own personal interactions with the individual to get a many-sided and, one hopes, coherent picture of what is happening.

THE ROLE OF GERIATRIC ASSESSMENT

Much of what will be described in this chapter for the elderly in general is gradually becoming formalized, especially for the very frail elderly, under the concept of comprehensive *geriatric assessment* (GA), defined in 1988 by the National Institutes of Health Consensus Development Conference in Geriatric Assessment as:

> a multidisciplinary evaluation in which the multiple problems of older persons are uncovered, described, and explained, if possible, and in which the resources and strengths of the person are catalogued, need for services assessed, and a coordinated care plan developed to focus interventions on the person's problems.[1]

Studies of the frail elderly are beginning to document the benefits of comprehensive assessment. Such benefits include improved diagnostic accuracy, more appropriate choice of living location, improved functional and mental status, reduced medications, decreasing use of nursing homes and acute care services, prolonged survival, and more appropriate use of health care services with generally reduced health care costs.[2]

Geriatric assessment, in this more formal sense, usually involves a multidisciplinary team of professionals working together on the assessment, a distinct set of criteria for evaluating the elderly in settings that range from inpatient and outpatient to at-home locations, and three levels of intensity of assessment—brief, intermediate, or comprehensive—based on patient needs. In the remainder of this chapter, we shall broaden these concepts to include assessment of all the elderly seeking mental health care.

HOW COMPREHENSIVE SHOULD AN EVALUATION BE?

We recognize the range of opinion regarding the length, style, and content of an evaluation and the methods by which it should be conducted. A number of variations can be justified on the basis of the treatment method and setting under consideration as well as the individual's specific request for help. For example, an older person wanting only brief assistance in dealing with feelings about retirement may not require the same workup as the person needing evaluation for placement in a nursing home. But in general we believe that a comprehensive evaluation has much to recommend it. There is an astounding lack of uniformity in what happens when an older person meets with mental health practitioners or institutional facilities. There may be a failure to gather even routine information. An individual may or may not get treatment, which may or may not be based on a solid evaluation and recommendation. Busy agencies and personnel with limited resources plead that their hands are tied. Yet even the shoddiest medical facility or the busiest family doctor would not be able to deal quite as cursorily with patients if they presented physical (rather than emotional) complaints—at least some minimal workup would be done.

Court suits have been instituted claiming the "right to treatment" for persons requiring mental health care, particularly in the case of the poor. Such suits have been helpful in forcing more meaningful standards of treatment. The older person not only has a right to expect treatment, as opposed to custodial care or no care, but also to expect that it be based on a thorough evaluation.

The following categories of treatment encompass the major services to older persons in terms of evaluation:

- Emergency-crisis intervention
- Evaluation for brief services
- Evaluation for extended, comprehensive services
- Evaluation for referral elsewhere (for example, a mental health evaluation for referral to a psychiatric hospital or nursing home)
- Evaluation for legal purposes (psychiatric commitment, guardianship, etc.)

In all these categories a complete evaluation is indicated for optimal and often time-saving intervention. An emergency, of course, requires attention to the immediate crisis, but with older people a crisis often points to underlying problems and requires extended periods of recovery. Thus, an evaluation can be begun as soon as the emergency subsides. The evaluation should ideally fulfill a *preventive, screening* function as well as a diagnostic one.

As with all ages, the problem first presented by older persons is often not their major or only difficulty. They may be reluctant to reveal intimate matters or be fearful of appearing demanding and complaining. They may sometimes deny actual problems or be totally unaware of their presence. The interviewer, as with any age group, must be alert to any clues and must gently and sensitively help older persons provide as full a picture of their situation as possible. But with the elderly (as discussed in the previous chapter), the interviewer may have less patience than with younger subjects and, consequently, may fail to do this properly. (See Chapter 8 for staff training techniques.)

On the basis of the evaluation, decisions must be made as to reasonable, reachable treatment goals: Can the problem at hand be reversed or merely ameliorated? Should treatment be aimed at total recovery, partial restitution, maintaining the status quo, or—of equal importance—supporting the person during some inevitable decline? Is environmental change indicated? Would direct medical treatment be useful? Or, does the individual need psychotherapy?

The issue of the availability of personal, hospital, and community resources is an ever-present and often frustrating factor in working with and planning for the care of older people. It is, of course, necessary to know what resources are available for treatment purposes: the older person's own emotional and physical capabilities, the supports in his or her family and social structure, and the kind of services and support available in the community. Then, there is the problem of access to needed services. For example, it is increasingly evident that older people make good use of individual psychotherapy; yet it is seldom offered, even when they can afford to pay. In some cases such services are not available for any age group, and older persons are excluded along with everyone else. However, in many instances, a service may be offered to the general public but older people find themselves put at the bottom of the waiting list or totally denied access to what is theoretically available. This is an example of *institutionalized ageism*—discrimination on the basis of age. All too many mental health personnel, because of training and background, assume that certain services are not applicable for older people and thereby deny treatment possibilities. We hope that Part Two of this book will help to overcome the pessimism that has prevailed regarding rehabilitation and treatment in the later years and especially in very old age.

CONDITIONS FOR A GOOD EVALUATION

Once the goals of the evaluation are set and the available resources are known, the mental health professional is ready to proceed with the actual evaluation of the older person. Whether in the person's home, a clinic, hospital room, or private office, the evaluation should build on the following ten principles:

1. Purpose
2. Rapport
3. Authorization and consent
4. Confidentiality
5. Setting
6. Time
7. Extent and structure of evaluation
8. Impressions and feedback
9. Documentation and information sharing
10. Follow-up visit

Purpose

An explanation of the purpose of the evaluation lays out the guidelines for the work between mental health personnel and the elderly. Older persons must understand precisely why they are seeing a mental health specialist and what they can expect during and as a result of the evaluation. They also have the right to know who is interviewing or examining them (a psychiatrist, a social worker, a visiting nurse, etc.). And, finally, they deserve an intelligible explanation, in lay person's language, of the desired result of the evaluation.

Rapport

It is a standard mental health principle that the first contact for evaluation is also the first therapeutic treatment hour; the two cannot be separated. Unfortunately, for many older people it may be the first and last time they will have a structured opportunity to talk about their problems and feelings. As discussed more fully in Chapter 8, the older person needs to sense certain things in order to feel comfortable about revealing him- or herself. The individual must perceive that (1) the interviewer is not repulsed or frightened by the physical or mental changes in old age but can accept these changes as a matter of fact and can see through them to the person inside, (2) the interviewer knows what he or she is talking about when dealing with old age (the psychological aspect of being old), (3) the interviewer understands the social problems of old age, having a broad and accurate knowledge of conditions as they exist for the majority of older persons, and (4) the interviewer has the professional skills and empathy that will inspire older people to trust him or her with their confidence, in the expectation that help will follow.

Authorization and Consent

The obtaining of authorization and consent must be high on the list of principles for a thorough geriatric evaluation. Ethical and legal protections for both older people and for health care professionals are provided by obtaining informed consent for an evaluation. But there are other motivations as well. Mental health evaluations can be thwarted before they begin simply because the older person was either unaware of the impending interview or was even vehemently opposed to it. Patients need to be clear about what is being proposed and must give their consent whenever their mental or physical health status makes this possible. Even severely demented older persons should be given the opportunity to understand, however dimly, why another health care worker has entered their world. A brief introduction to the worker and to the evaluation process almost always helps orient and prepare them for the tasks ahead.

Confidentiality and Privileged Communication

Confidentiality is a critical element in gaining an accurate history and in establishing and maintaining rapport. *Privilege* is the legal right of the person to privacy of communication. With the advent of the team concept, using paraprofessionals and peer review, the legal situation has not yet been clarified. In most states a patient can sue the physician who does not preserve privileged communication, but what about the nurse, the social worker, the nursing assistant, and others? The increase in insurance forms and computer use complicates the picture. It is essential that practitioners recognize the seriousness of protecting the client's privacy. For instance, a designing relative may be trying to get possession of an older person's house and attempt to gain information toward that end from mental health personnel. It is well known that the privacy of the poor who are served in community mental health centers, public clinics, and the like is less protected than that of the privately paying person. Legal suits may help curb such practices.

It is always helpful to spell out confidentiality in detail. A few of the typical questions elderly persons may have include the following: Who will be informed about the results of the evaluation? What will be written in the record? Who will have access to that information? What will my family hear about this? Will I be seen by students as well? Time given to carefully answering these and any other related questions is well spent in terms of improved patient understanding and comfort.

Setting

All persons should be interviewed wherever possible in dignified, private surroundings—not on the run, in public hallways and open clinic areas. The office should not present barriers to successful and safe evaluation of the older person. Lighting should be sufficient (remembering that age-related yellowing of the eye lens blocks two-thirds of the light that used to reach the retina), and back lighting behind the interviewer should be avoided because the older person may have difficulty seeing the interviewer's face.

Time

Older persons, especially the frail elderly, can be more easily overcome by the challenges of tests and measurements; therefore, one must proceed carefully and cautiously in order not to upset their physical and mental equilibrium. They should be given more time when there is evidence of intellectual slowing, whether this be caused by depression or organic changes. Interviews and examinations should be unhurried and relaxed. Instructions of any kind should be written out after they have been given verbally. When organicity, severe depression, or paranoid reactions are suspected, there must be several sessions, preferably at different times of day, to take into account variation in general and cerebral circulation. Early morning confusion—before the older person has shaken off sleep—can be mistaken as chronic, fixed disorientation. There is also a "sundown syndrome"—the increased disorientation and agitation at night resulting from loss of visual orientation when daylight is gone or electric lights are turned off. If this is organically based, it has been called "senile nocturnal agitation."

Special Conditions

The Hard-of-Hearing.   When hearing loss is a problem, interviews should take place in settings with minimal background noise. Presbycusis, one common hearing disorder in old age, produces hearing loss and selectively impairs high tones and consonant perception. Accordingly, if the voice is to be raised, it should be kept at low pitch and consonants should be especially clearly articulated. The interviewer should feel free to ask directly about the hearing loss. This will be seen by most older people as a sign of sensitivity and concern. If one ear is better than the other for an older person, the interviewer should sit near and speak into that ear. The voice volume should be constant and distinct, with no trailing off at the end of a sentence. The expression on the patient's face should be noted to be certain that he or she is hearing and understanding. Many older people read lips to augment their hearing; it is difficult for them if the interviewer's face is not turned toward them or his or her mouth is covered. Beards and mustaches can be a problem for lip-readers.

Persons with Stroke.   Just as with the hard-of-hearing, the interviewer should sit on the "good" side of the stroke patient, since there may be damage to hearing and vision on the other side. When the patient has difficulty speaking (aphasia), the interviewer should allow him or her to struggle to speak. The word should be supplied only when absolutely necessary. The person should be reassured that the interviewer wants him or her to try

to talk. If words won't come, the person can try to write on a large pad or a blackboard. When asking questions, the interviewer should phrase them so the patient can respond yes or no or shake his or her head. Above all, it should *not* be assumed that the patient's intelligence has been affected. Stroke victims frequently complain that people routinely treat them as though they are intellectually impaired.

Recognizing the Goldstein Catastrophic Reaction.[3]   The *Goldstein catastrophic reaction* describes the tendency of brain-damaged persons to become flooded with anxiety and irritability when confronted with a task they cannot handle. Weinberg's "exclusion of stimuli" may have a similar basis.[4] Any examination may provoke this reaction and thus complicate or delay findings. The careful, skilled interviewer can alleviate unnecessary stress by being sensitive to the reaction of the person. (It is also, of course, important to note the presence of this reaction in diagnosing brain damage.)

When talking to a brain-damaged older person, an interviewer should be sure to get the person's attention, speak slowly with good light on the interviewer's face, and use short, meaningful sentences with appropriate gestures. If the answer seems to be inappropriate, the interviewer may try rephrasing the question in several different ways. For example, "Did you take your pill?" might be varied by saying, "What medicine have you taken today?" The purpose of all of this (and the interviewer can develop other techniques through trial and error) is to try to tap into the remaining intellectual capacity of the older person through any device that works with that individual. Only careful observation will tell if the interviewer is succeeding.

Extent and Structure of Evaluation

A brief preview of actual procedures the older person will encounter in the course of a mental health evaluation is usually helpful both in orientation and enlisting cooperation. This is in addition to the description of the overall purpose of the evaluation described earlier. It is all too common for an interviewer to assume incorrectly that the patient already knows the procedures to be followed or that the person requesting the evaluation has previously explained the routine. In any case, neither scenario generally is accompanied by accurate information, particularly in relation to mental health evaluations, because very few patients really know what goes into such an evaluation and because routines vary so much from one setting to the next.

It is also important to provide details about logistics of the evaluation. For example, several visits may be required, and in some cases, other individuals are involved (i.e., personnel to administer psychometric testing). Whenever possible, such logistics of scheduling should include the involvement of patients in planning, giving them some opportunity for a sense of control (i.e., when follow-up testing will be done, whether the patient would rather be tested in the room or in a clinic setting, etc.). While such control may seem trivial to the interviewer or may be tightly truncated by a busy schedule, any flexibility offered to the older person may be welcomed. Finally, the issue of billing is often overlooked in detailing the structure of an evaluation. Since financial concerns are so frequently a part of an elderly person's worries, it is well worth beginning to discuss the subject as soon as possible, providing assistance in planning how bills will be paid.

Impressions and Feedback

One of the greatest fears of older patients as they are being evaluated by mental health personnel is that they will be thought "crazy" or otherwise seriously disturbed. After all, someone did request a mental health evaluation. That fear can frequently be allayed with simple feedback, especially of positive findings, during the evaluation. Not only does this feedback humanize the evaluation process, but it also allows the patient to relax and thereby discuss issues more freely than might otherwise have been likely. When the evaluation

is drawing to an end, a summary review of the information gathered (even just repeating the clinical history in capsule form to verify the factual content) and a brief outline of some preliminary impressions, being careful to focus on strengths as well as problems, is usually welcomed by the patient. Further study or conference with other mental health personnel may be necessary before the final recommendations can be offered, but in the meantime, a sense of the possible outcomes once more helps to focus the patient and allay persistent fears about the process.

Documentation and Information Sharing

In the case of evaluation requests from other health or social service providers, once all the sources of information have been gathered and the data generated during an evaluation have been discussed with appropriate colleagues, it is time for delivering the formal evaluation results to the original requester. While written forms are usually required and are often the principal means of communication between consultants, direct contact in person or at least by telephone is also highly recommended. This time-consuming procedure may seem burdensome but it ensures immediate transmission of the consultation to the appropriate source, thereby avoiding the frequent delayed impact of mail services and notes left in medical charts. Further, it encourages discussion between health personnel, once more personalizing the process for the patient and increasing the likelihood of a successful outcome.

Follow-Up Visit

A brief follow-up visit with the interviewer is often valuable, if only to inform the patient that the evaluation has been completed and the recommendations are ready. Depending on the situation, this visit may be expanded to include a detailed review of the findings, a large family meeting, or even a continued relationship in ongoing therapy. If and when the family is to be involved in the follow-up process, it is usually wise to first meet with the patient alone and preview the findings. This enables the patient to digest the results privately and to once again give consent before intimate details or test results are discussed with others.

A BASIC EVALUATION

A basic mental health evaluation should include a core collection of material: (1) basic personal information, (2) medical assessment, (3) psychiatric assessment, (4) sociocultural assessment with the older person including his or her relatives and, if possible, on-the-spot evaluation of the home environment where indicated. In addition, any number of special evaluations (for example, special medical tests or nutritional evaluation) may be deemed valuable in arriving at a clear understanding of the older person.

Basic Personal Information

The question of how to collect background information or histories for use in mental health evaluations has always been a controversial and confusing one. This is largely because mental health, as we define it today, encompasses every aspect of a person's life, and the task of collecting and assimilating so much information boggles the mind. Add to this the need to take a longitudinal life cycle view, as in the evaluations of older people, and the problem grows. In an era of specialization, medical doctors have tended to limit themselves to the body and its ills, traditional psychiatrists to "inner" problems (although this is hopefully becoming less true—the trend is toward a more comprehensive biomedical and psychosocial approach), traditional social service workers to "outer" difficulties, and members of the clergy to spiritual life. However, mental health personnel, who can be from any of these professions and more, must familiarize themselves with the whole picture in order to prescribe and carry out sound treatment. Collection of basic background information should be done in a manner that ensures comprehensiveness without being rigid. The goal is a high-quality evaluation, whether it takes place in a private hospital, a public clinic, a doctor's office, or a nursing home.

In its most complete form, personal history taking should be flexible in format, transferable to other professionals (with appropriate permission), and psychologically organizing for both the patient and the clinician alike. In addition, this body of information can provide a rich source of knowledge about older people for research purposes, as there are still tremendous gaps in our understanding of old age. As a result of our own work experiences in various hospitals, welfare departments, community mental health clinics, nursing homes, research, and private practice, we (RNB and MIL) have devised a method of collecting data that combines an adaptable format with a thorough content. (See the Personal Mental Health Data Form in Appendix G.) This form can be compiled either piecemeal or all at once, and at any time during contact with a patient. For example, when seeing a person in crisis, one must deal with the immediate situation and may not be able to obtain much background data until the crisis subsides. When we know we will be seeing a person over a period of time, we generally fill out the form with the older person ourselves in an unhurried manner as the data accumulate. However, in a period of crisis or shortage of time, a relative may complete the form, either at home or in the office. (Material, of course, is not as rich as when the patient is directly involved.)

In other cases, it is appropriate and even highly therapeutic for the patient to fill out the form alone. Patients report that filling out the form is a life review process that is helpful to them in evaluating themselves and planning for the future. We would generally not recommend this for patients with obvious severe organic brain disorders, poor eyesight, or severe hand tremors or for those who would become frustrated without help. It can, on the other hand, be extremely useful for hard-of-hearing patients, with whom interviewing is difficult, and for those who pride themselves on their independence.

We also ask patients who are entering group therapy to fill out the form themselves if they are being seen by us in only one individual, pregroup session.

A completed personal history form is like a baseline electrocardiogram: It indicates the person's present situation and provides a standard against which to measure changes in the future. It is often not accurate to think in terms of eventual "discharge from treatment" for older people in the same way as for the young. Since many will need various kinds of service the rest of their lives, it saves time to collect adequate information right from the start. Mental health personnel need to review their own thinking and attitudes about the quality of evaluation given to older people. A sloppy, haphazard approach can be rationalized neither as time-saving nor as humane care.

Another means of assessment is the Older Americans Resources and Services (OARS) methodology, produced under the direction of Dr. Eric Pfeiffer at Duke University. OARS's objectives are to develop models for mental health care, social services, and multidimensional techniques for evaluating the functional status of older people.[5] Also see the discussion on the Patient Appraisal and Care Evaluation (PACE) instrument in Chapter 11.

Several other geriatric assessment instruments have been developed over the last few years including the Comprehensive Assessment and Referral Evaluation (CARE),[6] the Association of Gerontopsychiatry System,[7] and the Cambridge Mental Disorders of the Elderly Examination (CAMDEX).[8] Each of these evaluations provides personal data forms and instructions for semistructured interviews with elderly patients and their families, which in turn could lead to improved history taking, concurrent medical diagnoses, and careful differentiation of psychosocial problems. With the CAMDEX, in particular, the procedure has been well accepted by the older patients interviewed and found to have high interrater reliability among professionals. Reliability is an important issue when such a scale is used for research purposes.

Medical Assessment

While the focus of a mental health evaluation is usually on psychiatric symptoms, it is not uncommon in the elderly that these symptoms are secondary to underlying medical problems. With respect to depression alone, the list of medical conditions and drugs associated with depressive symptoms in the elderly is impressive. Frequently, these medical conditions are either not diagnosed adequately or the association with depression is not recognized. Therefore, it is the responsibility of the mental health professional to make these connections, and the most essential starting point is the medical evaluation.

Much has been written about medical evaluation of the elderly.[9] Of greatest importance is the routine medical history and physical. The greatest clues regarding concurrent medical problems arise here. The diagnosis is then confirmed by the laboratory evaluation. While esoteric tests are sometimes required, a basic laboratory screening is often all that is needed. As part of a standard laboratory evaluation, patients should undergo the following:

- Complete Blood Count (Hematocrit, Hemoglobin, Mean Corpuscular Volume, White Blood Count, and Platelet Count)
- Erythrocyte Sedimentation Rate
- Chemistry Profile (Serum Sodium, Potassium, Bicarbonate)
- Fasting Blood Sugar
- Thyroid Profile (Thyroxine, T3 Resin Uptake, and TSH)
- Liver Function Tests (LDH, SGOT, and Bilirubin)
- Serum Phosphorous and Magnesium
- VDRL
- B_{12} and Folate Level
- Serum Cholesterol and Triglycerides
- Chest X-Ray
- Electrocardiogram (EKG)
- Urinalysis
- Stool for Occult Blood
- Visual and Hearing Screening
- EEG and CT Scan (when indicated)

How recently these tests should have been completed depends on the condition being considered and the rate of change with the individual patient. In any case, it is imperative that the mental health professional be certain that these basic medical checkpoints have not been overlooked. Otherwise, the mental health assessment that follows can be seriously flawed due to an undiagnosed medical problem.

A thorough physical examination is mandatory. Even more than with younger adults, a thorough neurologic evaluation should be included in this examination.[10] In addition to a medical history, recent reports from the patient's family doctor or other involved physicians are also invaluable. The latter reports are often obtained verbally by phone but should be summarized in written form in the patient's record. It must be known what drugs are being taken, for what condition, for how long, and what, if any, have been the side effects, especially adverse reactions.

Hearing tests, a visual examination with a check of eyeglasses, and a dental examination are obviously important for older people. Nutrition and sleeping habits must be noted. Because of widespread poverty among older persons, sometimes combined with the physical incapacity to care for themselves, many suffer from malnutrition in subtle or gross forms.[11] Malnutrition and dehydration therefore are among the major medical problems to recognize. Dehydration without malnutrition is also common. Subtle changes in nutrition and exercise programs can, in fact, affect both mood and cognition, even in the otherwise healthy elderly.[12] The interviewer should also be familiar with changes over time in touch, pain sensitivity, and other functions.[13]

Optional and Research Testing. Electroencephalography (EEG or brain wave test) is the process of making a graphic record of the electrical activity of the brain. For the purposes of clinical evaluation and study, EEG waves are subdivided into four basic forms (delta, theta, alpha, and beta) according to the frequency of the waves. Some EEG slowing, particularly in the

alpha rhythm, is commonly seen in normal elderly subjects when compared to young normals. Women may show less delta and more beta than men, and there are some suggestions that these changes are not always symmetrical across the brain surface.[14] More commonly, EEG or the newer computerized "mapping" EEG techniques have been employed to differentiate normal populations from organically impaired individuals, especially those with Alzheimer's disease where decreases in alpha activity and increases in delta activity are well documented.[15] It should be pointed out, however, that while this technique is usually effective in differentiating groups of Alzheimer patients from groups of normal or depressed patients, it is not especially accurate with individual patients because of the large variation between subjects. In fact, there is even some recent controversy as to whether the EEG changes progress during the course of Alzheimer's disease.[16]

Introduced in 1973, computerized axial tomography (CT) is a technique for evaluating brain pathology. It is based on two principles: (1) tomography, that is, radiological serial sectioning, and (2) computerization, that is, the rapid integration of thousands of pictures via computer. A narrow beam of x-rays passes through the head rapidly in a series of thin "slices," hitting radiation detectors that feed signals into a high-speed computer. The technique is noninvasive (unlike the injection of radioactive isotopes for x-ray purposes) and uses no more radiation than is required for a traditional x-ray film of the skull. X-ray films are only two-dimensional and thus flat, as compared to the multidimensionality of a CT scan. This technique has essentially replaced the higher risk and unpleasantness of pneumoencephalography, in which air is injected into the central nervous system. It also has greatly reduced the need for angiography, isotope scanning, and some exploratory surgery. Numerous CT studies over the past decade have revealed a generalized reduction in brain size with increasing age. These age-related changes are noted either in the overall brain volume or in the ventricular size, and they are found to be markedly exaggerated in patients with Alzheimer's disease,[17] though as with the EEG, the technique is diagnostic only when differentiating groups of patients.

Magnetic resonance imaging (MRI) is a relatively new procedure which also allows cross-sectional views of the brain but without the ionizing radiation required for CT and other brain-imaging techniques. The MRI is based on the principle that atomic nuclei have an angular momentum associated with their spin, which creates a small magnetic field. The technique is quite complex but essentially relies on the measurement of relaxation times (labeled T1- or T2-"weighted") following radio-frequency excitation of magnetized tissues.[18] While the clinical advantages of MRI over CT and other noninvasive procedures are still being debated and studied, it is already clear that MRI has many applications for diagnosing brain disorders in the elderly.[19]

Since the original introduction of the nitrous oxide method by Kety and Schmidt in 1948, there has been continued interest in the measurement of cerebral blood flow and its relationship to intellectual functioning. More recently, the xenon inhalation technique has allowed safer and repeated testing of subjects with group differentiation of elderly patients with multi-infarct dementia, Pick's disease, and Alzheimer's disease.[20]

With positron emission tomography (PET) scanning, another level of brain imaging can be obtained. This technique is built on the discovery by Sokoloff that the glucose analog, 2-deoxy-glucose could be radiolabelled and taken up into brain cells much like glucose. When trace amounts of radioactive 2-deoxy-glucose is injected into a patient and is absorbed by the brain cells, these isotopes soon emit positively charged particles called positrons, which collide with negatively charged electrons normally present in the cells. Each collision produces high-energy particles called photons, whose speed and path are recorded in the PET scan. A computer processes the information in color on a screen, showing biochemical activity in the living brain. Thus, with computerized tomography, one can see structure

(anatomy and pathology), but with positron emission transverse tomography one can study function and metabolism.

Using the 2-deoxy-glucose PET approach, changes in cortical glucose metabolism have been documented in Alzheimer's disease and multi-infarct patients compared to controls.[21] In addition, asymmetries in cortical measurements of Alzheimer patients have supported the clinical observations of diagnostic heterogeneity and have led to theories of metabolic uncoupling in various brain regions.[22] Further PET studies with more specific brain markers such as neurotransmitter receptor labels will certainly greatly add to our knowledge of central nervous system function in the elderly.[23]

With single photon emission computerized tomography (SPECT) scans, yet another related imaging technique, the methodology is now available to study specific brain chemical systems such as the important cholinergic system in living Alzheimer's disease patients.[24] As with all of these brain-imaging techniques, however, we must be cautious. These methodologies are primarily research tools that are not even clinically available in most cases, and they must first be proven to be of further diagnostic value before eventually becoming part of the standard clinical evaluation.

Summary of Medical Assessment.   In its best form, the medical evaluation should be comprehensive, multiphasic, continued at regular intervals, and when feasible, computerized. It is hoped there will soon be a baseline body of quality data available through automated technology and telemetry (to send information quickly, long distance) to aid in diagnosis. Heart disease, diabetes, glaucoma, emphysema, and cancer are particular foci. Indeed, after age 45 there should be regular medical checkups for the healthy and more frequent ones for the ill. Unfortunately, Medicare does not cover routine checkups, making it difficult for older persons to take advantage of the early detection and prevention possible through regular physical examinations.

Another difficulty for older people is lack of knowledge about health, medicine, and their own bodies. For obvious reasons they know less than later generations will know. Physicians have not been the major source of health education that they could be for older people. Often they are reluctant to impart information—saying it takes too much time, there is no good purpose to it, and so on—while older persons remain unenlightened as to what is being done to them. Many, for example, are given medication without knowing what it is for or what the side effects may be. Numerous other examples could be given of medical care administered in a manner that produces needless anxiety and emotional anguish.

Besides the usual diagnostic benefits, medical evaluation has two particularly important functions for the older patient. First, the examination is essential for the detection and early treatment of reversible delirium. These syndromes must be diagnosed early or they can become complicated, losing their reversibility. Second, the medical examination helps to "rule in" the functional disorders by ruling out physical causes. Thus mental health personnel may begin to suspect the possibility of a functional disorder (depression, paranoid states, etc.) and are more inclined to explore psychogenic processes.

Psychiatric Assessment

Who Does a Psychiatric Assessment?   Psychiatrists are by no means the only people qualified to do psychiatric evaluations. In community mental health centers, psychiatric hospitals, and elsewhere, a team of people from many disciplines may arrive at a joint evaluation. In addition, well-trained paraprofessionals can learn to assess the psychiatric condition of patients. With inadequate psychiatric coverage in most public and many private facilities, such skills can and should be learned by others. Responsible supervision and competent training can ensure quality care, regardless of the primary discipline. The introduction in recent years of more structured diagnostic

interview instruments such as the Diagnostic Interview Schedule (DIS),[25] the Schedule for Affective Disorder and Schizophrenia (SADS),[26] and the Structured Clinical Interview for DSM-IIIR (SCID)[27] allow the broader use of clinical skills for both patient care and research purposes.

What Constitutes a "Diagnosis"?   A psychiatric diagnosis is not simply a matter of psychiatric nomenclature that an evaluator, by the process of elimination, plucks out of the American Psychiatric Association's *Diagnostic and Statistical Manual.* One must know the psychological strength of persons (for example, their defenses and personality assets); their physical capabilities; and the familial, social, and cultural climate and structure of their lives. The direct and immediate environmental influence on people's lives is finally receiving its due share of importance along with the more traditional emphasis on early developmental and constitutional factors of personality. It is vital also to recognize the vast implications of prejudice in its institutional and personal forms as they affect the lives of African American, Asian American, American Indian, Latino, and other minority and ethnic elderly. (See Chapters 1 and 7.) The serious mental disorders and the emotional reactions seen in old age are multicausal.

A problem may not only have many causes; it may itself be multiple, that is, a combination of many problems, as is often the case with the diagnosis of dementia with superimposed delirium. Another serious and frequent oversight is the failure to recognize the emotional component or overlay to physical illness of the body or brain. Mental health personnel must search for possible combinations of problems where some may be less obvious than others but no less damaging. Thus, diagnosis is best viewed as a continuing, dynamic assessment, particularly in the case of older persons. Old age, indeed life at any age, is more similar to a motion picture than a still photograph; it is constantly changing. Because of this ongoing, altering process, evaluation, too, must be continuous, with treatment intervention varied accordingly.

Some Principles of Psychiatric Assessment. The traditional psychiatric assessment derives from the medical model; it can be an unimaginative, tedious, rigid procedure of limited usefulness in mental health care of the elderly unless attention is given also to psychodynamics and socioeconomics. A completed personal data form such as we have described can provide background and direction for the psychiatric interview. But the psychiatric perspective itself is also essential. One must be ever alert, perhaps more for older people than any other age group, to the possible presence of reversible delirium and functional disorders, both of which can be treated if properly diagnosed. A psychiatric look at the everyday crises of living, too, can be valuable. Much that is swept under the rug as old age, or even viewed as reaction to environmental stress, may have a psychiatric component that rightly deserves clarification and treatment.

In conducting a psychiatric examination, it is obviously not wise to be bound to a rigid routine. Rather, one must continue to build skill in observation, perception, and intuition (for hypothesis making), while at the same time taking a comprehensive approach. The degree of comprehensiveness—the width and depth—of the study will vary according to time pressures, purposes, motivation, and unfortunately, the patient's economic status and ability to pay.

Without reviewing all the general techniques of psychiatric examination, those components of the examination that are found to be especially pertinent to older people will be stressed. For instance, the appearance and general behavior of the person can offer significant clues: Does she walk like an "old" person, or does her walk belie her age? Does he dye his hair and pretend to be youthful? Is there a peculiar gait (for instance, the distinctive Parkinsonian "march," the *marche à petits pas* with its characteristic short shuffling steps, the patient leaning forward so that the gait is propulsive, the arms not swinging)? Does she look blank-faced (indicating organicity or depression)? An ironed-out, masklike face may point to Parkinsonism. Is he slow-moving in speech and action, distractable, flighty, incoherent, or irrelevant? Does she speak *sotto voce,* quietly, while looking about suspiciously (possible paranoid feature)? Is the appearance one of premature age and debilitation (there may be a basic physical process or illness underlying the psychiatric symptomatology)? One must also be aware of behavior that might be inappropriate for younger people but is "normal" in old age—a good example is the fact that an older person may arrive an hour or more early for an interview. This should not instantly be given the label "obsessive-compulsive." Older people often are highly time-conscious and want to compensate for any unavoidable delays along the way that may be hard for them to cope with; thus they tend to overcompensate by starting very early.

The Psychiatric Examination. The psychiatric examination generally begins with questions about what brought the person for evaluation and possible treatment—what is the chief problem or complaint. The history of the problem in the person's own words is next. Family and chronological life histories follow. Careful questioning is necessary to discover how the older person feels about his family: Does he see himself as a burden? Is he angry at them? Do they indicate annoyance with him? At every step, care must be taken to watch the nonverbal communications and revelations of the unconscious. The interviewer should try to record important aspects of the person's description in his or her own exact words, not only for any later medico-legal reasons but also for later reflection on psychodynamics.

The examiner must also be especially alert for "new" and "peculiar" behavior—keeping in mind the immediacy of the life situation as well as the life history. Immediate precipitants are crucial in old age when change, loss, and deprivation are so powerful in their effects. Certain symptoms in old age practically guarantee medical and/or psychiatric problems. Persons with organic brain disorders and severe depressions may survive—even function well—in the community, and then suddenly a change in their lot can make the underlying pathologic condition more visible. Wandering at night, evident confusion, and incontinence are examples of problems that are usually organic in nature—all of which can, however, be behavioral in origin. Wandering, for instance, may have as its psychogenic root the need to escape. Incontinence may be an expression of anger. Whatever the psychological underpinnings, these symptoms may have behavioral or pharmacologic interventions if properly evaluated and diagnosed.

The alert facade or appearance and normal-looking social habits can be deceptive, masking the presence of severe brain damage. Korsakoff's syndrome and the dementias are conditions in which an observer can be misled by first impressions of mental capacity.

Two sisters were admitted to the National Institute of Neurological Diseases and Blindness for studies of familial essential hypercholesterolemia and general research studies. One was 57, the other 55. They were anxious, depressed, fearful, restless, and perplexed. Verbal productivity was somewhat decreased. There was slurring of speech as well as delay in responses and little spontaneity of thinking. They had difficulty finding words, they were distractable. In these patients, there was perseveration of ideas, but not of words.

In spite of all of this, they appeared outwardly intact. Their personal habits and conduct were fine. The successful social facade, however, fell away drastically when tested in the mental status examination. They knew all the "right things" to say. They just didn't know such simple facts as what day it was.

Intellectual deficiency, memory loss, acalculia, inability to abstract proverbs, and impaired judgment were present. Both began to show signs of illness in their early fifties. Their courses were insidious and progressive. There was a family history of Alzheimer's disease. Four of five siblings showed signs of mental decline. Our studies showed evidence of reduced cerebral blood flow and oxygen consumption. Autopsies later confirmed the diagnosis of Alzheimer's disease.

The Search for a Psychological Baseline against Which to Measure "Illness"

Studies of Community-Resident "Healthy" Older Persons.   If we are to recognize what is problematic for an older person, we must first be able to recognize what is emotionally healthy behavior. Busse's group (Palmore, 1970) and the NIMH group (Birren et al., 1963) are among those who have evaluated healthy community-dwelling older persons. In the NIMH studies, begun in 1955, physical and emotional health was a criterion in selection for study. Part of the purpose in such work was to obtain a baseline for evaluating older people that consisted of a composite of the statistical norm (the average) and the healthy (the ideal). A longitudinal view of the life cycle is necessary and, indeed, has begun to receive attention. Senescence as a developmental stage or process in the course of the life cycle has a psychology of its own, which thus far has only been crudely delineated.

Evaluation of the Effects of Lifelong Personality.   The list given here, resulting from the NIMH studies of the healthy elderly, indicates the contribution of some aspects of lifelong personality to the psychological nature of older people.

1. Adaptive qualities for later life
   a. Candor, ease of relationships, independence, affirmation, positive self-concept, sense of usefulness
   b. Defense mechanisms: insight, denial, use of activity
2. Maladaptive qualities for later life
   a. Paranoid isolation
3. Maladaptive in early life—adaptive in later life
   a. Obsessive-compulsive features
   b. Schizoid mechanisms
   c. Dependent personality

Both adaptive and maladaptive features are brought by the person into old age. We must caution observers, however, that only through a careful knowledge of life history can differentiation be made between those qualities possessed by the individual throughout life and those that first came into being in old age through a reorganization of personality. For example, the Swedish film *Wild Strawberries* reflects the potential of an older man, set in his ways, to make rather basic changes in his personality late in life.

Lifelong personality traits that are useful in old age include a sense of self-esteem, candor, ability to relate easily with others, independence and self-motivation, and a sense of usefulness. Measures of ego strength (the ego's function as the moderating and reality-testing component of the personality) enable judgments to be made regarding the capacity to cope and adjust. Some defense mechanisms (by which the ego copes) are more useful than others. Naturally, insight is a valuable aid in alleviating anxiety and guilt by realistically appraising the changed circumstances of life and body. Denial can be beneficial if it does not interfere with needed medical or emotional care and if it facilitates relationships and activities. Older people who use appropriate activity, ranging from the creative to merely "keeping busy" in order to counteract fear or depression, also have a defense that is an asset. Less adaptive are the counterphobic defenses, wherein some older people undertake excessive and dangerous activities in order to prove their continued prowess, youthfulness, and fearlessness.

In judging the adaptations of older persons, it is vital to remember that they commonly deal with more stresses (in actual number, frequency, and profundity) than any other age group. Thus evaluation of restitutive attempts must be viewed with this in mind. Sometimes maintenance of the status quo may be all that is possible; indeed, this may be a triumph under some circumstances. A pride in present accomplishments, no matter how small, is appropriate.

Paranoid personality features have a particular maladaptiveness in old age, since so much happens to reinforce the notion that the problems are all "out there." In addition, hearing and other sensory losses increase the inability to deal with threatening forces and compound the isolation of the person with paranoid tendencies. A defensive use of perceptual loss, such as "hearing what one wants to hear," may be present. Tendencies to use age, disease, or impairment as a defense (by acting more helpless than is warranted) are common problems. Personality characteristics of rigidity, despair, depression, and the whole range of psychopathological reactions can further hamper adaptation to old age.

As we state in Chapter 5, certain psychopathology can become increasingly adaptive as people age. Obsessional maneuvers fill the emptiness of retirement; schizoid detachment apparently insulates against loss; dependency can result in a welcoming of greater care and help from others.

Diagnostic Attention to the Inner Experience of Old Age.   Aside from the complex of reality factors and the influences of the individual personality, there are inner reactions to old age that seem to be part of the developmental work of late life. One of these inner processes, the life review, appears to be a universal occurrence. (See Chapters 5 and 12.) The life review takes place through reminiscence accompanied by feelings of nostalgia, regret, and pleasure. Complications that can occur are extreme emotional pain, despair, guilt, obsessive rumination, panic, and suicide. A resolution or working through of the life review may bring atonement, serenity, constructive reorganization, and creativity.

The Holmes Social Adjustment Rating Scale (Table 9.1) provides a constructive approach to evaluating the impact of various life events on persons of all ages, moderated, of course, by the individual character of the person.

Problems Commonly Misdiagnosed or Overlooked.   We have listed a series of conditions more fully described in Chapter 6 that require special diagnostic attention from physicians conducting medical/psychiatric assessments as well as other mental health personnel involved in evaluation of the elderly. These conditions, summarized here and commonly overlooked, are often

TABLE 9.1   The social readjustment rating scale

LIFE EVENT	MEAN VALUE	LIFE EVENT	MEAN VALUE
1. Death of spouse	100	23. Son or daughter leaving home	29
2. Divorce	73	24. Trouble with in-laws	29
3. Marital separation	65	25. Outstanding personal achievement	28
4. Jail term	63		
5. Death of close family member	63	26. Wife begin or stop work	26
6. Personal injury or illness	53	27. Begin or end school	26
7. Marriage	50	28. Change in living conditions	25
8. Fired at work	47	29. Revision of personal habits	24
9. Marital reconciliation	45		
10. Retirement	45	30. Trouble with boss	23
11. Change in health of family member	44	31. Change in work hours or conditions	20
12. Pregnancy	40	32. Change in residence	20
13. Sex difficulties	39	33. Change in schools	20
14. Gain of new family member	39	34. Change in recreation	19
15. Business readjustment	39	35. Change in church activities	19
16. Change in financial state	38	36. Change in social activities	18
17. Death of close friend	37	37. Mortgage or loan less than $10,000	17
18. Change to different line of work	36		
19. Change in number of arguments with spouse	35	38. Change in sleeping habits	16
		39. Change in number of family get-togethers	15
20. Mortgage or loan over $10,000	31	40. Change in eating habits	15
21. Foreclosure of mortgage or loan	30	41. Vacation	13
		42. Christmas	12
22. Change in responsibilities at work	29	43. Minor violations of the law	11

Source: Holmes, T. H., & Rahe, R. H. (1967). The social readjustment scale, *Journal of Psychosomatic Research, 11,* 213. Reprinted by permission of Pergamon Press. See the article for complete wording of items.

recoverable and treatable. Table 9.2 lists reversible causes of mental impairment. Look especially for the following:

1. Delirium
   a. Alone
   b. Superimposed on dementia
2. Depressive reactions simulating organic brain disorders
3. Paranoid states without organic brain disease
   a. Generalized
   b. Circumscribed
   c. Chronic paranoid state with superimposed, reversible crises
4. Subdural hematomas leading to confusional states
5. Drug reactions
6. Suicide risk factors

Delirium.   Delirium usually develops quickly, is typically fluctuating in severity, and can be caused by a large number of possible reversible organic

TABLE 9.2   Reversible causes of mental impairment

CAUSE	DEMENTIA	DELIRIUM	EITHER OR BOTH
Therapeutic drug intoxication			Yes
Depression	Yes		
Metabolic			
a. Azotemia or renal failure (dehydration, diuretics, obstruction, hypokalemia)			Yes
b. Hyponatremia (diuretics, excess antidiuretic hormone, salt wasting, intravenous fluids)			Yes
c. Hypernatremia (dehydration, intravenous saline)		Yes	
d. Volume depletion (diuretics, bleeding, inadequate fluids)			Yes
e. Acid-base disturbance		Yes	
f. Hypoglycemia (insulin, oral hypoglycemics, starvation)			Yes
g. Hyperglycemia (diabetic ketoacidosis, or hyperosmolar coma)		Yes	
h. Hepatic failure			Yes
i. Hypothyroidism			Yes
j. Hyperthyroidism (especially apathetic)			Yes
k. Hypercalcemia			Yes
l. Cushing's syndrome	Yes		
m. Hypopituitarism			Yes
Infection, fever, or both			
a. Viral			Yes
b. Bacterial			
Pneumonia, Pyelonephritis, Cholecystitis, Diverticulitis		Yes	
Tuberculosis			Yes
Endocarditis			Yes
Cardiovascular			
a. Acute myocardial infarct		Yes	
b. Congestive heart failure			Yes
c. Arrhythmia			Yes
d. Vascular occlusion			Yes
e. Pulmonary embolus		Yes	
Brain disorders			
a. Vascular insufficiency			
Transient ischemia		Yes	
Stroke			Yes
b. Trauma			
Subdural hematoma			Yes
Concussion/contusion		Yes	
Intracerebral hemorrhage		Yes	
Epidural hematoma		Yes	
c. Infection			
Acute meningitis (pyogenic, viral)		Yes	
Chronic meningitis (tuberculous, fungal)			Yes
Neurosyphilis			Yes

(continued)

TABLE 9.2   *(Continued)*

CAUSE	DEMENTIA	DELIRIUM	EITHER OR BOTH
Subdural empyema			Yes
Brain abscess			Yes
d. Tumors			
Metastatic to brain			Yes
Primary in brain			Yes
e. Normal pressure hydrocephalus	Yes		
Pain			
a. Fecal impaction			Yes
b. Urinary retention		Yes	
c. Fracture		Yes	
d. Surgical abdomen		Yes	
Sensory deprivation states such as blindness or deafness			Yes
Hospitalization			
a. Anesthesia or surgery			Yes
b. Environmental change and isolation			Yes
Alcohol toxic reactions			
a. Lifelong alcoholism	Yes		
b. Alcoholism new in old age			Yes
c. Decreased tolerance with age producing increasing intoxication			Yes
d. Acute hallucinosis		Yes	
e. Delirium tremens		Yes	
Anemia			Yes
Tumor—systemic effects of nonmetastatic malignant neoplasm			Yes
Chronic lung disease with hypoxia or hypercapnia			Yes
Deficiencies of nutrients such as vitamin B_{12}, folic acid, or niacin	Yes		
Accidental hypothermia		Yes	
Chemical intoxications			
a. Heavy metals such as arsenic, lead, or mercury			Yes
b. Consciousness-altering agents			Yes
c. Carbon monoxide			Yes

Source: NIA Task Force. (1980). Senility reconsidered; treatment possibilities for mental impairment in the elderly, *Journal of the American Medical Association,* 244(3), 261–262.

conditions such as drug intoxication or metabolic and infectious disorders. Emergency diagnosis and treatment is imperative in every situation in order to achieve the highest possible rate of reversal and avoid the permanent damage that can result if the condition is allowed to fulminate.

Depressive Reactions Simulating Organic Brain Disorders.   Depressions may be masked as organic states. Observe the content of thought and the sense of interpersonal responsibilities. Listen for feelings of worthlessness. Look for specific events or stimuli that may have precipitated the feelings of depression. Many depressive episodes in old age are realistic responses to loss. When this is the case, there may be a relief of symptoms when actual loss or threat is relieved, compensated for, or replaced; this is not so with purely organic disorders. It must not be forgotten, however, that depression and organic brain disorder can coexist. The following letter from the relative of an older woman to a therapist is an example of the kind of evidence often presented:

In order to help you [the therapist] with your evaluation of her problems, I [her relative] thought it best to let you know what I have observed in her behavior, attitude, appearance, and general demeanor the last six months. She puts clothes on backwards, inside out, sometimes leaving night clothes underneath street clothes, and shoes on the wrong feet. She has lost interest in books, television, letter writing. When in my home she follows me constantly. When she can't find me, she goes all over house and garden looking for me and calling my name. She is extremely restless no matter what the situation—she cannot wait for anything, which is one reason we were an hour early for your appointment. When she is in her own apartment and not having dinner in the communal dining room, she is on the phone dialing me every 10 minutes for hours on end. If my husband and I are out, she then dials my friends until our return. She has a habit of making loud "sighs" in my presence and says aloud, "I don't know what I'm going to do." At this time she has made no effort to make new friends at the residential home for older people where she now lives although outwardly she is an extremely friendly and gregarious person.

The diagnosis was that of organic brain disorder with a concurrent depression.

Paranoid States without Organic Brain Disorder. Look for ideas of ruin and for delusions of noxious fumes, delusions of marital infidelity, and the like. Note isolated evidences of projection as well as comprehensive delusional systems. Be aware of the possibility of *folie à deux,* in which paranoid delusions may be shared by two people—most often mother and daughter, two sisters, or husband and wife. Check for hearing loss, which is associated with suspiciousness and paranoid states.

Subdural Hematomas Leading to Confusional States. Falls and fractures are common in old age. Persons over 65 account for over 70% of all fatal falls and 30% of all pedestrian fatalities. Subdural hematomas are collections of blood between the dura mater (the hard outer membrane over the brain) and the skull. They may be clinically silent. Again, a careful history may elicit a story of head injury (although the person may not remember falling because of memory loss), concussion, perhaps coma, delirium, or a syndrome (Korsakoff's) marked by fabrication and confabulation. Papilledema (swollen optic nerve head) and possibly headaches are more common in younger persons. Mental symptoms such as somnolence (sleepiness), confusion, memory loss, and hemiparesis (paralysis on one side) are more common in older persons. The hematomas of older persons are thicker than those in younger persons. This may be because of the decreasing weight of the brain that occurs with age, thereby increasing the space between the brain and the skull and making room for the hematoma to expand without increasing intracranial pressure. Subdural hematomas, as well as brain tumors, hypertension, and extracerebral vascular occlusion or narrowing, can often be successfully treated—provided they are discovered via CT scan and other diagnostic measures.

Drug Reactions. The wide use of drugs among the elderly, from tranquilizers to anti-depressants, has increased the potential for negative drug reactions. Drugs may make a differential diagnosis between functional and organic disorders exceedingly difficult, and discontinuation of the medications during an evaluation period may be required. A fuller discussion of drug reactions can be found in Chapter 13.

Suicide Risk Factors. Older people account for approximately one-fourth of all reported suicides. Therefore, a mental health evaluation should give serious consideration to behavior that might indicate self-destructive tendencies. More than any other therapeutic intervention available to mental health professionals, accurate diagnosis of suicidal intentions can directly save a life.

Although suicide in old age has already been discussed at some length in Chapter 5, we wish to list here (not necessarily in order of frequency or importance) some of the major diagnostic risk factors for suicide in old age:

- Depression (with no anger outlet)
- Withdrawal
- Bereavement (especially within first year after loss)
- Isolation: widowed; single
- Expectation of death from some cause
- Less organization and complexity of behavior than previously
- Induced helplessness
- Institutionalization
- Physical illness
- Alcoholism
- Desire and rational decision to protect survivors from financial disaster
- Philosophical decision: no more pleasure or purpose
- Meaninglessness of life
- Decreased self-regard
- Organic mental deterioration
- Changes in sleep patterns: severe nightmares
- White males (a higher rate of suicide than in any other group)

A threat to commit suicide is relatively uncommon in the elderly; they tend to simply kill themselves. Nonetheless, one must be alert for indirect or veiled threats or previous suicide attempts. Self-destruction can be abrupt or drawn out over long periods of time (not eating, not taking medication, alcoholism, delay in seeking treatment, excessive risk taking).

Mental Status, Memory, and Psychological Tests

The mental status examination should not be conducted in the absence of a thorough appreciation of what the patient is feeling and thinking. Be certain the patient can hear you and explain that you are going to ask about feelings, thinking, and cognition. Because of their variability, these functions must be appraised with delicacy. Although there have been advances in recent years in psychiatric techniques for rating or measuring the psychological functioning, mental status, and symptoms of older persons, much work remains to be done. Neuropsychology is making a great contribution. The differentiation of age-related behavior from lifelong behavior (as well as disease-determined, culturally deprived, and other behavior) must be borne in mind.

A number of brief screening instruments for cognitive impairment are available. Folstein's Mini Mental Status Examination[28] or MMSE (Tables 9.3 and 9.4) is probably the most widely used instrument in both clinical and research settings because of its ease of administration, although it does have significant limitations. For example, orientation is not necessarily a sensitive indicator of mental dysfunction. Visual and auditory deficits (as well as aphasia) may lead to misdiagnosis. The Mattis Dementia Rating Scale[29] is also a very good screening instrument, which more systematically examines a variety of cognitive skills. The Blessed[30] mental status exam developed in Great Britain is less frequently used today, but if used, gives a quick but crude impression of mental capacities. Rarely used now, the Mental Status Questionnaire[31] of Kahn and colleagues (Tables 9.5 and 9.6) is also available. It is presented here only so readers will know of this historic first step in the development of more effective measurements.

Central nervous system functioning is too complex to be left to a "simple test" except as a crude screening device. As valuable as brief mental status exams may be when screening large populations or when monitoring the potential effects of medications in geriatric patients, a more detailed exam is often indicated. No self-respecting cardiologist would use a mini cardiac status to evaluate a serious heart problem. Just as a malfunctioning heart requires a comprehensive exam, so too does the malfunctioning brain—the most complex part of the human body and the wellspring of personal and social adaptation. If, for example, a first meeting with an older patient brings

TABLE 9.3 "Mini-mental state"

MAXIMUM SCORE	SCORE	
		Orientation
5	(_____)	What is the (year) (season) (date) (day) (month)?
5	(_____)	Where are we (state) (county) (town) (hospital) (floor)?
		Registration
3	(_____)	Name 3 objects: 1 second to say each. Then ask the patient all 3 after you have said them. Give 1 point for each correct answer. Then repeat them until he learns all 3. Count trials and record. ☐ Trials
		Attention and calculation
5	(_____)	Serial 7's. 1 point for each correct. Stop after 5 answers. Alternatively spell "world" backwards.
		Recall
3	(_____)	Ask for the 3 objects repeated above. Give 1 point for each correct.
		Language
9	(_____)	Name a pencil, and watch (2 points). Repeat the following "No ifs, ands or buts." (1 point) Follow a 3-stage command: "Take a paper in your right hand, fold it in half, and put it on the floor." (3 points) Read and obey the following: Close your eyes (1 point) Write a sentence (1 point) Copy design (1 point)
	_____	TOTAL SCORE Assess level of consciousness along a continuum

Alert	Drowsy	Stupor	Coma

Source: Folstein, M. F., Folstein, S. E., & McHugh, P. R. (1975). "Mini-Mental State," a practical method for grading the cognitive state of patients for the clinician. *Journal of Psychiatric Research, 12,* 189–98. Copyright 1975, Pergamon Press. Reprinted by permission.

up questions of intellectual decline, it is important to refer for a detailed examination of neuropsychological abilities, including attention, memory, language, abstraction, judgment, orientation to time, place, and person, and other elements of mental functioning such as visual and spatial skills and calculations. Such an exam not only provides an opportunity to diagnose Alzheimer's Disease, multiinfarct dementia or other less obvious reasons for cognitive change,[32] but also gives a baseline for later comparisons.

By now a variety of normed and well-validated neuropsychological tests exists for diagnosing older people. Verbal learning tests such as the California Verbal Learning Test[33] are among the most sensitive memory tests available. The revised Wechsler Memory Scale[34] allows evaluation of both verbal and visual memory. Visual memory can also be tested with the Benton Visual Retention Test.[35] Language functions can be tested by the naming of objects, repeating of a phrase, reading and writing samples, and ability to follow oral

TABLE 9.4   Instructions for administration of "Mini-Mental State" examination

---

Orientation

1. Ask for the date. Then ask specifically for parts omitted, e.g., "Can you also tell me what season it is?" One point for each correct.
2. Ask in turn "Can you tell me the name of this hospital?" (town, county, etc.) One point for each correct.

Registration

Ask the patient if you may test his memory. Then say the names of 3 unrelated objects, clearly and slowly, about 1 second for each. After you have said all 3, ask him to repeat them. This first repetition determines his score (0–3) but keep saying them until he can repeat all 3, up to 6 trials. If he does not eventually learn all 3, recall cannot be meaningfully tested.

Attention and calculation

Ask the patient to begin with 100 and count backwards by 7. Stop after 5 subtractions (93, 86, 79, 72, 65). Score the total number of correct answers.

If the patient cannot or will not perform this task, ask him to spell the word "world" backwards. The score is the number of letters in correct order, e.g., dlrow = 5, dlorw = 3.

Recall

Ask the patient if he can recall the 3 words you previously asked him to remember. Score 0–3.

Language

Naming: Show the patient a wrist watch and ask him what it is. Repeat for pencil. Score 0–2.

Repetition: Ask the patient to repeat the sentence after you. Allow only one trial. Score 0 or 1.

3-stage command: Give the patient a piece of plain blank paper and repeat the command. Score 1 point for each part correctly executed.

Reading: On a blank piece of paper print the sentence "Close your eyes," in letters large enough for the patient to see clearly. Ask him to read it and do what it says. Score 1 point only if he actually closes his eyes.

Writing: Give the patient a blank piece of paper and ask him to write a sentence for you. Do not dictate a sentence, it is to be written spontaneously. It must contain a subject and verb and be sensible. Correct grammar and punctuation are not necessary.

Copying: On a clean piece of paper, draw intersecting pentagons, each side about 1 inch, and ask him to copy it exactly as it is. All 10 angles must be present and 2 must intersect to score 1 point. Tremor and rotation are ignored.

Estimate the patient's level of sensorium along a continuum, from alert on the left to coma on the right.

Source: Folstein, M. F., Folstein, S. E., & McHugh, P. R. (1975). "Mini-Mental State," a practical method for grading the cognitive state of patients for the clinician. *Journal of Psychiatric Research, 12,* 189–98. Copyright 1975, Pergamon Press. Reprinted by permission.

commands. Subtests of the revised Wechsler Adult Intelligence Scale (WAIS)[36] can be used to examine attention, conceptualization, and visual and spatial skills. The neuropsychological examination may take about two hours depending upon the patient. It almost always is associated with another 45 minutes of interviewing to take the history from the point of view of both the patient and family. With the rise of managed care there is pressure to reduce referral for neuropsychological testing, as there is for any specialty testing. But the argument can be justifiably made that a neuropsychological assessment will save money as a result of improved management due to early detection, and by minimizing non-compliance with treatment plans.

When do you refer the patient to the neuropsychologist for a more comprehensive examination?

1. For early detection of dementia.
2. When you are not quite clear about the differential diagnosis (e.g., Alzheimer's vs. brain tumor, Parkinson's disease, etc.)
3. Differentiation from or recognition of concurrent depression.
4. Need to treat the emotional and social context.
5. Help the patient overcome the denial of deficits. It is also helpful to the family, which may need to see the data to help them confront the deficits in the older person. This may lead to less anger at the patient by the family who now understands the deficits better.
6. At times it is important to monitor the disorder in a longitudinal fashion by repeat testing.

When would you not refer a patient to a neuropsychologist, or delay neuropsychological testing?

1. When the individual is barely testable because of too much deterioration. The only reason for some testing at this stage might be to assist the family in management.
2. When the patient is clearly severely depressed so as to require immediate inpatient or outpatient treatment. He/she should still be tested later to determine if dementia is also present.

TABLE 9.5   Mental Status Questionnaire

MENTAL STATUS QUESTIONNAIRE—"SPECIAL TEN"

1. Where are we now?
2. Where is this place (located)?
3. What is today's date—day of month?
4. What month is it?
5. What year is it?
6. How old are you?
7. What is your birthday?
8. What year were you born?
9. Who is President of the United States?
10. Who was President before him?

Source: Modified from Kahn, R. L., Goldfarb, A. I., & Pollack, M. (1964). The evaluation of geriatric patients following treatment. In Hoch, P. H., Zubin, J., (Eds.), *Evaluation of psychiatric treatment.* New York: Grune & Stratton. Reprinted by permission.

TABLE 9.6   Rating of mental functional impairment by Mental Status Questionnaire

NO. OF ERRORS	PRESUMED MENTAL STATUS
0–2	Chronic brain syndrome absent or mild
3–8	Chronic brain syndrome moderate
9–10	Chronic brain syndrome severe
Nontestable	Chronic brain syndrome severe*

Source: Modified from Kahn, R. L., Goldfarb, A. I., & Pollack, M. (1964). The evaluation of geriatric patients following treatment. In Hoch, P. H., Zubin, J., (Eds.), *Evaluation of psychiatric treatment.* New York: Grune & Stratton. Reprinted by permission.

*In the noncooperative person without deafness or insuperable language barriers.

Candor is important in discussing the results of testing with the patient and family, since it helps them to prepare for the future. For example, it is difficult to send the patient to an Alzheimer's Disease Association support group without some explanation. It is very rare that a patient would become acutely depressed or suicidal because he/she was told frankly the findings of neuropsychological testing.

The Raven Progressive Matrices, utilizing geometric figures, is presumably culture-free, but there is some debate on this issue. Another popular test is the Kent E-G-Y,[37] a 10-item, quick-screening test for intelligence. Some people, such as Goldfarb, find M. Bender's Double Simultaneous Tactual Stimulation (Face-Hand) Test[38] of value in the important differential diagnosis between organicity and depression. The Face-Hand Test (Table 9.7) is also of value in attempting to determine the degree of brain damage. The failure to properly report touch on the back of the hands is a valid and reliable suggestion of brain damage or senile brain disease. The errors made are failure to report the touch at all (extinction), displacement of the hand touch to another part of the person's body, and exsomesthesia (the touch somewhere "out there" or "over there"). The number of errors

TABLE 9.7 Order of stimulation used in Face-Hand Test

1. Right cheek—left hand
2. Left cheek—right hand
3. Right cheek—right hand
4. Left cheek—left hand
5. Right cheek—left cheek
6. Right hand—left hand
7. Right cheek—left hand
8. Left cheek—right hand
9. Right cheek—right hand
10. Left cheek—left hand

Source: Modified from Bender, M. B., Fink, M., & Green, M. (1951). Patterns in perception in simultaneous tests of the face and hand, *Archives of Neurology and Psychiatry* 66:355–62.

is recorded for the test done with the eyes closed and then for the test repeated with the eyes open.

On a more subjective level, projective tests elicit spontaneous and personal responses to a vague stimuli, thus giving valuable psychological insight into the person being tested. The Rorschach Inkblot Test is a series of 10 cards, each containing a different inkblot to which the patient associates whatever thoughts may come to mind.[39] This provides information on the formal organization of the personality and some of its unconscious features. The Thematic Apperception Test (TAT) stimuli are more suggestive but still unspecific. The test consists of 20 pictures to each of which the patient associates a story. The Sentence Completion Test is a group of unfinished sentences that the patient is asked to complete with the first thought that comes to mind.

Although we do not necessarily believe that psychological tests must be done in every case, they can be most useful when indicated. When there is uncertainty about the differential diagnosis of organic brain damage versus depression, such tests can be invaluable; but one should not forget that the patient with an organic problem can still be depressed. A patient with chronic organic brain disorder generally produces lower test scores than one with acute brain disorder; however, at the height of the acute reversible crisis (for

example, delirium), the patient is likely to be untestable.

The Life Satisfaction Measure of Neugarten et al. isolates five components of an individual's positive life satisfaction:[40] (1) taking pleasure from the round of activities that constitutes everyday life, (2) regarding life as meaningful and accepting resolutely that which life has been, (3) feeling success in achieving major goals, (4) holding a positive image of self, and (5) maintaining happy and optimistic attitudes and moods. Lawton's Morale Scale was specially designed to assess morale of the aged.[41] This scale determines self-perceptions of mood, adjustment, and well-being. The Minnesota Multiphasic Personality Inventory (MMPI) assesses personality structure and diagnostic classification through a paper and pencil inventory. Of the nine dimensions of the personality that are measured, the aged do not appear to deviate from other age groups except in the D scale, which measures depression.

Multiple scales measure mood in adult populations.[42] Unfortunately, very few mood scales are designed specifically for the elderly or organically impaired.[43] Since memory impairments are so commonly associated with depression in the elderly,[44] the clinician must carefully review whether subjective self-ratings versus objective measures are the appropriate tests for individual subjects.[45]

Diagnostic Use of Mirror and Self-Drawings.

Any technique that is useful in eliciting rich, spontaneous information and response from older people can become part of the diagnostic repertoire. Such techniques may be discovered by accident. Clinical experiences by the author (RNB) of observing certain older people communicating with their mirror images led to investigation of self- and body concepts through the experimental use of the mirror and self-drawings. These techniques were introduced as cues for a collaborative self-exploration with the older person as an *active* participant—how does he view himself now, how did he in the past, and what does he see in his future?

Mirror. To help illustrate the psychological significance of an individual's mirror image, let us quote from a Tolstoy short story, *The Death of Ivan Ilych* (1886).

> And Ivan Ilych began to wash. With pauses for rest, he washed his hands and then his face, cleaned his teeth, brushed his hair, and looked in the glass. He was terrified by what he saw, especially the limp way in which his hair clung to his pallid forehead. While his shirt was being changed he knew that he would be still more frightened at the sight of his body, so he avoided looking at it.

Asking an older person to look into a mirror and tell about what is seen is an exceptionally excellent way of acquiring data about body images and reactions to changes with age. The mirror is a powerful trigger or cue to thoughts and observations about self and changes in self. The clinician often obtains much richer data in less time than by elaborate verbal questioning about physical, personality, and other changes. The range of reactions may be accounted for by (1) reality factors in appearance, (2) personality factors, whether lifelong or in reaction to old age, and (3) organic factors. The following outline provides details:

1. Reality factors in appearance
   a. Skin-wrinkling; pigmentation; flabbiness; leathering
   b. Bodily movements—slowing
      (1) Physical impairments
      (2) Arthritis
      (3) Palsies—tremors
   c. Facial changes—palsies; wrinkling
   d. Hair—balding; graying
   e. Eyes—opacities of the lens
   f. Teeth—absence; discoloration
   g. Cartilage growth—ears; nose
   h. Chest—increased diameter; breathing rate
   i. Abdomen—protuberance
   j. Weight—loss; shrunken
2. Personality factors
   a. Lifelong
      (1) Focal emphasis on (cathexis of) parts versus whole—for example, nose; profile versus frontal view; sexual organ
      (2) Character—narcissism, self-hate, etc.
      (3) Identity—crisis

   (4) Mood-depression, hypomania, etc.
   b. Old age
      (1) Fear, anxiety, and/or tension over aging and death
      (2) Denial of aging changes
3. Organic factors
   a. Perceptual factors
      (1) Vision affected (can be defensive; cf., exclusion of stimuli—Weinberg)
   b. Organic factors
      (1) Organic brain damage: "Not me"
      (2) Disorientation for person

As is known, cartilage continues to grow in old age, so the ears and nose may consequently become more prominent, but these changes are not mentioned as often as wrinkling, sagging around the eyes, hair loss, and general appearance of "oldness." On the other hand, most healthy older people find it difficult to see themselves as having essentially changed. Of course, much turns on the term "essentially." It appears that they are in effect recognizable to themselves, and in their own minds they have not drastically altered in their character and nature in the course of time; their identity has remained solid. A sudden and rapid deterioration and change of appearance can cause an identity crisis or reaction, even in otherwise healthy people. Adjustment and acceptance are much easier when physical change comes slowly. A clue to shaky identity or difficulty in adapting to changes can be seen in people who reject their mirror image.

A middle-aged woman who expressed a profound fear of aging could not accept her mirror image as herself. She regarded the image as something foreign and experienced her "real" self as being on the inside of her body, feeling and reacting, while people responded to her "foreign" outside image in a way that was unacceptable to her.

Personality factors before the mirror can be strikingly obvious. People exhibiting defensive preoccupation with themselves (narcissism) are pleased and attracted by their image, whereas those who are ashamed and guilty shun the mirror, reject their images, become anxious. A focal emphasis on or cathexis of a particular body part (for example, the nose) is observed and provides diagnostic clues. Usually a part rather than the whole is seen by the older person. Other common reactions are fear, shudders, suddenly occurring thoughts about aging and approaching death, or, conversely, a denial of aging changes and denial of fear of death.

Organic factors can affect the mirror reactions. Persons with organic brain damage may insist the image is "not me" or illustrate vividly a "disorientation for person" by not recognizing the person in the mirror. Perceptual impairments of vision can be actual or defensive in nature, the latter recalling Weinberg's concept of exclusion of stimuli, in which the person blocks out images that are too painful.

Self-Drawings. Some classic examples of the emotion-laden quality of self-drawings are the variety of self-portraits done by well-known artists (many using their mirror image). A museum exhibit displayed such portraits with expressions ranging from pleased and serene to displeased and tortured. Goya made his self-portrait defiantly ugly and troubled, not bothering to idealize himself or impress his audience. Cézanne dressed himself in overalls and a lumpy, battered hat, beneath which he seemed to be shy and retiring. The self-portrait of Dürer was exquisitely and lovingly drawn.

Self-drawings by patients are revealing, whether done in front of the mirror or by themselves. The technique is to focus the person directly on himself. Self-drawings of older persons with and without the mirror often suggest a self-view of dissolution, sometimes bizarre; they do not appear, as some have said, similar to the drawings of children. The illustrations in Figure 9.1 show examples of self-drawings of normal older men.

Barring severe hand tremors or profound visual problems that would affect expression, drawing provides other clues to the feelings of older people. Things to look for in drawings are the size of the image and placement of figures on the page, amount and kind of detail, underemphasis or overemphasis of a body part, omissions, facial expressions, activity or inactivity of the figure, and the general emotional quality of the picture.

"Draw Your Insides." "Draw your insides" is an interesting device because of the preoccupation of so many older people with their bodily ailments and changes. One can get clues about the emotional impact of such changes by observing the older person's response in this kind of drawing. Shown in Figure 9.2 is the figure provided for male subjects. A female figure should be provided for women.

Items most commonly drawn are intestines, heart, lungs, and stomach. Placement and size of these organs in the drawing can give indications of their meaning emotionally. In experimental tests, 20% of inner body parts were drawn as protruding out from the body or as completely outside, suggesting possible mental confusion and organicity.

Since comparative data for other age groups or various diagnostic entities are not available, no concise inferences can be drawn from findings; indeed, anatomical knowledge may be limited in the older population simply because many of them did not receive as much educational emphasis on biology and health as more recent generations have. But the draw-your-insides procedure, along with mirror reactions and self-drawing, produces rich emotional data without being unduly threatening. In the same way, reviews of family photo albums and scrapbooks can provide stimulation and diagnostic clues, while often giving immense pleasure to the older person in the process.

Personality. One of the major advances in personality psychology in recent years has been the widespread recognition that most personality traits familiar to laypersons and conceived by personality theorists can be described in terms of five basic dimensions or factors (the Five Factor Model or FFM).[46] The Revised NEO Personality Inventory (NEO-PI-R)[47] is a 240-item questionnaire designed to measure the five factors as well as some of the more specific traits that define them. For example, the broad *Agreeableness versus Antagonism* factor includes scales measuring

SUBJECT 16

In front of mirror ▶

Subject 16.   *This 76-year-old retired merchant's counterphobic activity helped him to ward off depressive symptoms. Although emphasizing his physical well-being, his self-drawing suggests incompleteness. Character trait disorder.* Subject 20.   *This 78-year-old retired clerk has recurrent nightmares related to death. He describes himself as a "silent worrier." No psychiatric diagnosis.*

SUBJECT 20

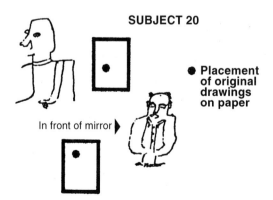

● **Placement of original drawings on paper**

In front of mirror ▶

Subject 19.   *This 75-year-old physically healthy man did not have diagnosable psychopathology. He first drew a female figure in the "draw-a-person" test; his second draw-a-person figure is essentially the same as his self-drawings.*

(continued)

FIGURE 9.1   Self-drawings of normal older men.
(*Source:* Butler, R. N. (1963). *Geriatrics, 18,* 220–232. Reprinted by permission.)

FIGURE 9.1   **Continued**

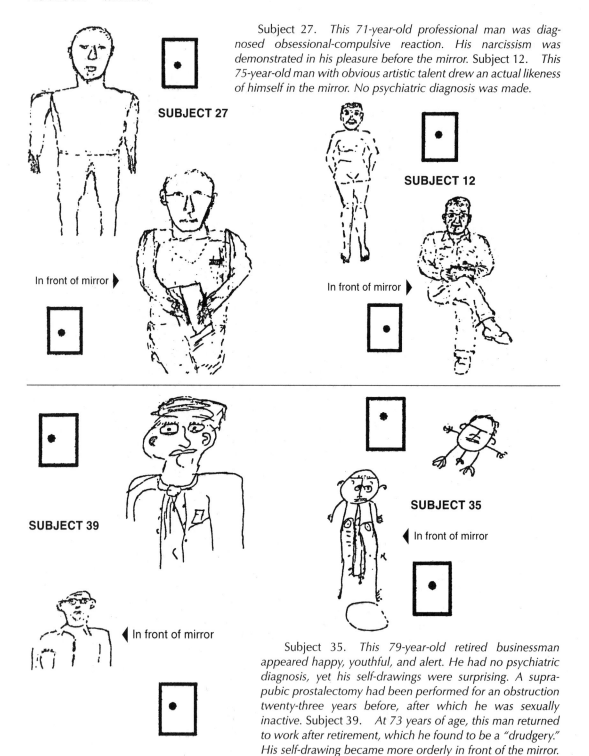

Subject 27.   *This 71-year-old professional man was diagnosed obsessional-compulsive reaction. His narcissism was demonstrated in his pleasure before the mirror.* Subject 12.   *This 75-year-old man with obvious artistic talent drew an actual likeness of himself in the mirror. No psychiatric diagnosis was made.*

SUBJECT 27

SUBJECT 12

In front of mirror ▶

In front of mirror ▶

SUBJECT 39

SUBJECT 35

◀ In front of mirror

◀ In front of mirror

Subject 35.   *This 79-year-old retired businessman appeared happy, youthful, and alert. He had no psychiatric diagnosis, yet his self-drawings were surprising. A supra-pubic prostalectomy had been performed for an obstruction twenty-three years before, after which he was sexually inactive.* Subject 39.   *At 73 years of age, this man returned to work after retirement, which he found to be a "drudgery." His self-drawing became more orderly in front of the mirror.*

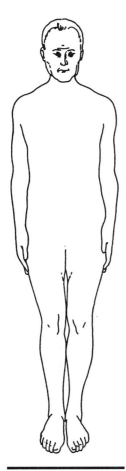

FIGURE 9.2 Figure given to a male patient when he is asked to draw his insides.

trust, straightforwardness, altruism, compliance, modesty, and tender-mindedness. Each item in the NEO-PI-R is answered on a five-point scale from "strongly disagree" to "strongly agree." The instrument has a sixth-grade reading level and usually takes 30 to 40 minutes to complete. It can be administered in groups or individually, by computer, or orally. A Spanish version is available for assessing Hispanic Americans.

The NEO-PI-R is one of the few personality inventories developed and validated on adult samples spanning the entire age range. Research comparing self reports with peer and spouse ratings has demonstrated that both the first-person and third-person versions of the instrument yield valid scores.[48] The NEO-PI-R has been used in research on personality change in dementia,[49] predictors of caregiver burden,[50] correlates of psychological well-being,[51] psychotherapy outcome,[52] and stress and coping in aging men and women.[53]

Socioeconomic Assessment

Work at the NIMH and elsewhere has documented effects of the social support system on the older person's psychological and behavioral attitudes.[54] "As the environment showed qualities of deprivation or displacement of the person (in loss of intimate persons, loss of income, in cultural displacement), the attitudes and behaviors of the aged showed more deteriorative qualities. Losses of significant persons were especially associated with deteriorative functioning,"[55] and further, "findings of this study lead to the suspicion that psychological reactions to the loss of friends and other environmental supports may amplify if not initiate changes in the older nervous system and thereby the rest of the organism."[56]

Having intimate friends in whom one can confide is very important. It must be recognized, however, that social isolation per se is not always causative of emotional and mental reactions in old age. Persons who have lived isolated lives throughout the years—"loners"—are not necessarily more susceptible to the occurrence of late-life psychopathology. It is those persons who become isolated relatively late in life, through no choice of their own, who have the most difficulties.

A socioeconomic evaluation should include general background information concerning details of family structure, housing, work or retirement, friendship patterns, economic circumstances, social roles, activities, and interests. (See examples in the personal mental health data form in Appendix G.) Interviews with the older person and members of his or her family can provide valuable insight into the contribution of social factors to the patient's problem and into potential assets that can aid and support treatment. An assessment should include the amount and quality of love and affection that exist between the family and the older person.

The evaluation of the family itself is crucial, since the genesis, precipitation, and maintenance of disorders may derive from a family context. The older person may be expressing what is really a familywide pathology in which he or she is the scapegoat or the victim of ancient angers. Sometimes the "problem" of the older person is the means by which a son or daughter seeks treatment when unable to ask for it directly. A skilled evaluator may be able to detect this phenomenon and help the younger family members obtain treatment themselves. In other situations the older person may exploit the family; for example, the domineering parent who becomes even more tyrannical in old age by playing on guilt feelings of children toward the aging and decline of a parent. A prideful overemphasis on independence and a manipulation of others through passivity are other patterns of behavior in older persons that can cause family conflict. Older people must not routinely be judged helpless or fragile. Indeed, a fair number of them wield substantial influence over family and friends.

In working with the total family, it is imperative to share evaluation findings as openly as possible with all members, guided by permission from the older person and by judgment as to the effects of such sharing. Family therapy involving the older person may be indicated—couples' therapy with the patient and spouse can be beneficial even in marriages that have been difficult for years or have deteriorated. At times, the family approach is used as a rationale to exclude the older patient (usually the result of counter-transference problems on the part of treatment personnel).

There is no point seeing the patient—you know his memory is gone. He feels rejected—I find it more useful to see the son and daughter-in-law.

One must recognize the vast implications of race and racism in the lives of older African Americans, Asian Americans, Native Americans, Latinos, and members of other groups. A knowledge of cultural patterns and traditions and the discriminatory practices and prejudices experienced in a lifetime are fundamental parts of a thorough evaluation. This applies also to ethnic origins, since so many older persons are immigrants. However, a note of caution is warranted here: At times, race or ethnic origin may be used to rationalize another form of prejudice. For example, the older African American can be denied psychiatric care because his or her problems are viewed as social or racial, while intrapsychic problems remain unnoticed. People in every culture develop internalized emotional difficulties that are not necessarily directly attributable to the social condition and that require treatment.

Treatment should ideally be planned to coincide with those cultural elements that are familiar and valued by the older person. An elderly African American man in a nursing home might prefer "soul food," whereas a Norwegian immigrant could long for "lute-fisk." Patient comfort, satisfaction, and dignity are important in a positive treatment program.

Not least among the steps in an adequate evaluation is determining the patient's health care coverage and economic circumstances. Pending the introduction of a truly comprehensive national health insurance, it is usually necessary to appraise the patient's "ability to pay" for treatment, although this notion of personal financial responsibility is generally obsolete, given the realities of escalating costs and, for older persons, the denial of adequate income programs and job opportunities. Third-party medical payments include Medicare and Medicaid (Table 9.8). Insurance to supplement Medicare may also be available. A routine check should be made to determine whether the older person is a member of one of the national organizations that sell such supplementary insurance. The National Council of Senior Citizens and the American Association of Retired Persons offer policies, as do the so-called

TABLE 9.8 Government health programs

HEALTH INSURANCE FOR THE AGED—HOSPITAL INSURANCE
(Popular name: Medicare—Part A)

This program provides hospital insurance protection for covered services to any person 65 or over who is entitled to Social Security or Railroad Retirement benefits. A dependent spouse 65 or over is also entitled to Medicare, based on the worker's record. The covered protection in each benefit period includes hospital inpatient care, posthospital extended care, hospice care (210 days), and home health visits by nurses or other health workers from a participating home health agency. It does not include doctors' services.

Under Social Security, workers, their employers, and self-employed people pay a contribution based on earnings during their working years. At age 65, the portion of their contribution that has gone into a special Hospital Insurance Trust Fund guarantees that workers will have help in paying hospital bills.

HEALTH INSURANCE FOR THE AGED—SUPPLEMENTARY MEDICAL INSURANCE
(Popular name: Medicare—Part B)

Social Security's medical insurance program helps pay for doctor bills, outpatient hospital services, medical supplies and services, home health services, outpatient physical therapy, and other health care services.

Medical insurance is not financed through payroll deductions and is not based on earnings or period of work. As a voluntary supplemental extension of Medicare's hospital insurance protection, it helps pay for many of the costs of illness not covered by hospital insurance.

MEDICAL ASSISTANCE PROGRAM
(Popular name: Medicaid Title XIX)

This program provides grants to states to administer medical assistance programs that benefit (1) the needy—all Supplemental Security Income recipients and public assistance families with dependent children—and those who would qualify for that assistance under federal regulations, (2) at a state's option, the medically needy—people in the four groups mentioned above who have enough income or resources for daily needs but not for medical expenses, and (3) all children under 21 whose parents cannot afford medical care.

State plans must include at least five basic services for the needy, and a similar or less extensive program for the medically needy. Family planning services may be included in both.

---

nonprofit Blue Cross–Blue Shield plans and the commercial insurance carriers. One must be on the lookout against fly-by-night, fraudulent Medicare supplements that have been sold to older people. A check of the additional income resources listed on a personal mental health data form (see Appendix G) and information about average living expenses will help to complete the financial assessment.

Older people, like others, may be sensitive to questions about finances, fearing that they will be billed unjustly for treatment or simply resenting an intrusion into their privacy. Some are ashamed to admit their meager incomes and out of pride

may refuse to accept financial benefits to which they are entitled. Every effort should be made to help them exploit all possible outside resources in order to protect their own incomes during treatment.

Medicare coverage may be expanded and will probably be incorporated within a national health insurance plan. In the meantime, actual coverage is limited to about 40% of the health bill of older persons. It is important to note that only Medicare Part A is an entitlement, paid for from a portion of the payroll tax on workers. Part B is voluntary, not automatic. Enrollees who opt for Part B pay a monthly premium ($42.50 in 1996), usually deducted from their Social Security check. Approximately 5% of those who are eligible decide not to opt for Part B, primarily because they cannot afford it. Confusion and ambivalence may be present. Some are opposed ideologically to the concept of Social Security; others mistakenly believe Medicare automatically covers all costs; and still others just do not understand it.

In 1989, the controversial Catastrophic Coverage Act was enacted and then repealed. Although it attempted to revamp and expand Medicare and close a few of the gaps in coverage, it still failed to cover the greatest single source of catastrophic costs: long-term custodial care, which accounts for 90% of nursing home care. A major criticism of the act, leading to its repeal, was that, rather than everyone's payroll taxes being increased, the elderly themselves paid for the new benefits.

The Medicare Catastrophic Coverage Repeal Act did maintain a small portion of these "new" benefits: protection from impoverishment for spouses of nursing home patients, coverage for Papanicolaou smears, and state Medicaid buy-in of Part B, which covers Medicare premiums and co-payments for those below the official poverty level. But for the most part, Medicare looks like it did before 1989.

Congress also initiated physician payment reform in 1989, partly sparked by the continuing annual 16% increase in fees over the previous decade. The new plan limits the amount patients can be charged above the Medicare-approved fees. It also establishes a budget methodology and limit on total Medicare spending for physician services. Moreover, as of October 1, 1990, physicians have been required to bill Medicare for all services they provide. This is helpful, of course, for those patients who find it difficult to complete the often incomprehensible claim forms. Perhaps most important is a revised fee schedule, which places more emphasis on primary and preventive care through enhancement of evaluation and management payment than on surgical, diagnostic, and treatment procedures. Moreover, doctors practicing in inner cities and rural areas receive a 10% bonus. The resource-based relative value scale (RBRVS), as the reforms are called, does not, however, reflect the complexity of care for the frail elderly. It is necessary to address at least two additional reforms: (1) appropriate reimbursement for the extraordinary time required for care of the elderly under RBRVS; and (2) the explicit establishment of a geriatric assessment code.[57]

One of the financial resources for the chronically mentally ill patient is Social Security disability. It provides coverage for nonworkers and workers forced to retire by injuries or health infirmities before they have reached age 65. Those signed up as disabled are automatically eligible for Medicare Part A (hospitalization benefits); if impoverished, they also are eligible for Part B (doctors' benefits) through Medicaid. All of these programs can help support patients, but only if there have been adequate services to get them registered. Mental health personnel often lack systematic training in the ever-changing and complicated system of available benefits.

Managed Care

With the revolutionary changes in the health care system in the 1990's, there have been cuts in the growth of Medicare and Medicaid expenditures, a growing importance in market forces, and an increase in the number of health maintenance organizations (HMOs) and the number of people enrolled in them. By 1996 approximately 10% of Medicare beneficiaries were enrolled in managed care organizations nationally. In some sections of the country, the percentage is much higher. In San Diego County, California, for example, some 30% of Medicare beneficiaries were signed up in managed care plans. By federal arrangement, health maintenance organizations (HMOs) receive 95% of the usual Medicare fee on a capitated basis. However, where possible, HMOs market to the "young-old" (those aged 65 to 75) and try to avoid enrolling frail older persons. Eventually, however, the companies will experience "aging in" of the currently young-old enrollees, and costs will rise. HMOs have emerged that provide various services along a continuum of needed care, from home care, sub-acute care, community care, and rehabilitation, and some companies have been trying to achieve integrated care that sews together all these services in a seamless fashion. By and large, however, there have been great difficulties in coordinating mental health and medical care services in managed care plans partially due to the practice of "carving out," or subcontracting, mental health services. With respect to the geriatric, psychiatric patient it has been argued that "managed care" has really become "managed cost."

On-the-Spot Home Evaluation.   Outreach services such as home visiting by mental health personnel are still insufficient in the United States. The physician, the psychiatrist, the psychologist, the social worker, the nurse, and the paraprofessional all should make use of home visiting to keep in touch with the realities of life of older persons from various backgrounds—urban, suburban or rural. Measures of activities of daily living (ADL) in various settings are valuable.[58]

To see how older people of all socioeconomic classes live is a first-rate diagnostic tool. Extreme privation is not unusual. For example:

The old man lived in an unpainted, roach-infested, windowless closet, sleeping on a urine-smelling mattress that could not be fully extended because of the small size of the closet.

With 95% of older persons residing in the community, a home evaluation is a logical way to get a sense of the day-to-day existence of the patient. One looks for pets (companionship), a calendar (to what month is it turned?), a clock (is it running and set properly?), odors (gas leaks, spoiled food, signs of incontinence), food supply (is the person eating regularly and adequately?), mementoes (what does the person consider important?), family pictures, temperature of house (potential accidental hypothermia resulting from a cold home), and medication cabinet and night stand (to see what and how prescription and nonprescription drugs are being taken). The safety

and security of the home, the ability of the person to get around the house, and the presence of others can be assayed. (It is not uncommon to find an older person caring for someone who may be even sicker than he or she.) A realistic evaluation of the fear of crime and financial and physical limitations to transportation can be made.

The older person's community resources should be included in the evaluative process, both to determine what the community has to offer and to engage community services in ongoing evaluations of patients. A homemaker working in a patient's home may be able to furnish a picture of the person's day-to-day life. Visiting nurses, workers in Meals-on-Wheels programs, occupational therapists, and others can offer their particular viewpoints. See Chapter 10 for a fuller discussion of community services and contributions to the mental health care of the at-home elderly.

Legal Issues

Forensic (legal) psychiatry is a field of psychiatry concerned with legal issues, hearings, and trials, including insanity pleas, commitment procedures, theories, and laws dealing with criminal responsibility, guardianship, conservatorship, confidentiality, competence to stand trial, and the legal definition of "insanity."

Questions of competency and informed consent with the elderly have received increasing attention in the legal system in recent years.[59] Medical doctors, especially psychiatrists, may be called on to evaluate an older person's need for involuntary commitment to an institution or to ascertain aspects of competency (contractual or testamentary capacity). Human beings have a fundamental right to make their own decisions, enter into contracts, vote, make a will, and refuse medical or psychiatric treatment. Each of these decisions represents the individual's control over his or her own life, with the understanding that the consequences may be unfortunate as well as fortunate, folly as well as wisdom. Limitations of such rights or freedom ideally come about only when illnesses invalidate the capacity to make choices or, in the case of legal commitment, when the older person is a danger to him- or herself or to others, physically, or is in clear and present need of immediate care or treatment. Older people also need protection when they are vulnerable to exploitation by others.

In examining an older person for forensic (legal) purposes, the examiner should spell out that fact in detail. The person needs to know that he or she can be represented by an attorney and that statements to the examiner will *not* be protected either by privilege (the legal concept) or by confidentiality (the relationship). What is the test of incompetency? "Understanding" is the crucial criterion: The person must have sufficient mental capacity to *understand* the nature and effect of the *particular* transaction in question. The psychiatric diagnosis is not considered in courts of law to be as important as judgment. Commitment to a mental hospital for psychiatric reasons is not necessarily equivalent to incompetency.

Contractual capacity (the ability to make contracts) is related to the degree of judgment required—selling a major business is a complex situation that may require a greater degree of judgment than selling a car. One problem sometimes emerging in contractual cases is that in which an older person's judgment may, indeed, be adversely affected by mental or physical disorders, but this fact is unknown to the other party in the contract.

A 69-year-old woman was profoundly depressed but outwardly cheerful. She sold her $75,000 home for $55,000. It was a bona fide sale, so there was no later recourse.

The concept of the "lucid interval" is a vague and difficult one, implying the capacity to exercise sound judgment at one time and not another. The multicausal aspects of the emotional and mental disorders of old age indicate the possibility of such intervals. For example, a person with cerebral vascular insufficiency may do well until severe emotional stress (for example, death of a spouse) compromises the equilibrium; after a period of time, he or she may again stabilize and be considered "lucid." An evaluator must be extremely thorough in examining the older person for such a possibility.

Testamentary capacity (the ability to make a will) requires that the testator (person who makes the will) be "of sound mind and memory," knowing the condition of the estate, his obligations, and the import of the provisions of the will. The psychiatric examiner must consider whether the older person is unduly suggestible or under "undue influence" from others. Severe depression and paranoid states, as well as organic brain disorders, may affect the capacity to write a will; however, diagnosis of psychosis, adjudication of guardianship, or commitment per se does not invalidate a will. Extreme age, mental sluggishness, and defective memory do not render a testator incapable of making a will if he is able to recall to mind his property. Alcoholism, addictions, and unusual beliefs (for example, spiritualism) do not by themselves invalidate wills. When there is any doubt of testamentary capacity or when a contesting of the will is anticipated, it is wise of the testator to arrange for a comprehensive medical and psychiatric evaluation while he or she is alive, with a careful and complete report filed before death. It may also be wise to audiotape or videotape the testator with his or her attorney present. With the help of this technology, not only is the will clearly spelled out, but aspects of the will that are likely to be disputed can be explained. By so doing, further grief and turmoil, as in the following example, can be prevented for the family.

An 87-year-old man married his nurse and rewrote his will. Other members of the family challenged his mental soundness and pushed for a postmortem examination of his brain, resulting in bitterness and anguish for everyone concerned.

Guardianship, the appointment of a committee for a person or the person's estate, should be solely for the person's benefit and protection. The test is whether the person can or cannot protect himself or arrange his own affairs. Emotional disability, as well as intellectual impairment, is important. (Guilt or feelings of worthlessness may lead a person to give everything away.) Injudicious management and improvidence are difficult to evaluate and are not precisely correlated with intellectual debility. Laws are unclear on many points, and there is an all-or-nothing quality, whereas a continuum or scale of impairment would be more appropriate. It is here that the current use of a durable power of attorney (whereby an individual assigns someone the right to manage the individual's affairs if and when he or she becomes significantly impaired, such as through a dementing process) may well play an increasing role in the future. Certain disabilities are not considered at all by the law—visual and auditory impairments, loss of speech, and others.

Poor people are disadvantaged because of the legal costs of conservatorships;[60] since few states provide for public guardianship (the poor man's conservatorship), estates are easily eroded. The poorly educated and the uninformed are not protected, and the Roman injunction *caveat emptor* ("let the buyer beware") holds sway to a greater degree in old age than ever before.

In 1989 the Social Security Administration estimated that it appointed third-party representatives for 4.7 million beneficiaries unable to manage their own financial affairs due to mental illness, homelessness, or drug addiction. Unfortunately, a small percentage of these incompetent beneficiaries are believed to be defrauded by their representatives, whose job is to receive the benefit checks and pay the beneficiaries' living expenses.

Involuntary commitment is examined more thoroughly in Chapter 11, but we wish to discuss here the question of court cases for mental patients and older people in general. In what passes for kindness, it is often argued that court appearances are too disturbing for the older patient. Even when a hospitalized person decides to call for a jury trial, the hospital psychiatrist may back away and discharge the patient first. We believe there are serious faults with these attitudes. They

conceal from the public, from the person involved, and from the psychiatrist and mental health personnel the realities of legal processes and of property and personal rights. Patients often learn from the painful court proceedings; it becomes clear what the situation really is, and the process can have therapeutic effects. Our traditional overestimation of the fragility of patients and, indeed, our paternalism and infantilization can deny people their rights and the opportunity for self-expression.

Court appearances may also assist mental health personnel in sharpening up their diagnostic thinking. A few embarrassing moments under cross-examination in a court of law can be a humbling experience and worth hours of postgraduate training or review. Psychiatrists and other staff who complain of wasting time in court might be well-advised to keep eyes and ears open, taking the occasion to learn something more about the human condition as it unfolds in a courtroom.

The adversary system does have its cruelties, and one might argue for dispassionate commissions wherein commitment, competency, and contractual and testamentary capacities are evaluated. We would support the use of independent commissions comprised of physicians, mental health personnel, and lawyers but subject to administrative and judicial reviews. Hearings must include patients, well-represented by counsel. The amount of time provided must be adequate, not just a token. We also believe, along with others, that the various capacities under consideration (contractual, testamentary, etc.) should be considered separately and in their special contexts, rather than under a global concept called "competence."

In summary, the legal issues surrounding the protection of the elderly and their families are leading to the gradual evolution of a comprehensive system of law and precedent. Several excellent books by Strauss et al. (1990) and Regan (1990) are useful for the elderly and their families, as well as for mental health personnel in surveying these developments. But much remains to be done to make certain that the rights and privileges of each older person are safeguarded at the same time that actions are taken legally to provide supports and protections when the older person is no longer capable of self care. All of this effort must be balanced with protection of the needs and rights of family members and of the community at large.

SELECTED READINGS

Albert, M. S., & Moss, M. B. (Eds.). (1988). *Geriatric Neuropsychology.* New York: Guilford Press.

American Association for Geriatric Psychiatry. (1988). *Essentials for geriatric psychiatry, a guide for health professionals.* Lazarus, L. W., Jarvik, L. F., Foster, J. R., Lieff, J. D., & Mershon, S. R. (Eds.). New York: Springer.

Ames, L. B., Metraux, R. W., Rodell, J. L., & Walker, R. N. (1974). *Rorschach responses in old age.* New York: Brunner/Mazel.

Anthony, K., Procter, A. W., Silverman, A. M., & Murphy, E. (1987). Mood and behavior problems following the relocation of elderly patients with mental illness. *Age and Ageing, 16,* 355–365.

Applegate, W. B., Blass, J. P., & Williams, T. F. (1990, April 26). Instruments for the functional assessment of older patients. *The New England Journal of Medicine, 322*(17), 1207–1214.

Bender, L. (1938). *A visual-motor gestalt test and its clinical use.* Research Monograph No. 3. New York: American Orthopsychiatric Association.

Bender, M. B., Fink, M., & Green, M. (1951). Patterns in perception in simultaneous tests of the face and hand. *Archives of Neurology and Psychiatry, 66,* 355–362.

Benton, A. (1974). *Revised visual retention test,* 4th ed. New York: Harcourt-Brace, Jovanovich.

Birren, J. E., Butler, R. N., Greenhouse, S. W., Sokoloff, L., & Yarrow, M. R. (Eds.). (1963). *Human aging: A biological and biobehavioral study.* Pub. no. (PHS) 986. Washington, DC: U.S. Government Printing Office. (Reprinted as Pub. No. [HSM] 71–9051, 1971, 1974).

Blessed, G., Tomlinson, B. E., & Roth, M. (1968). The association between quantitative measures of dementia and of senile change in the cerebral grey matter of elderly subjects. *British Journal of Psychiatry, 114,* 797–811.

Busse, E. W. (Ed.). (1996). *APA textbook of geriatric psychiatry,* 2nd ed. Washington, DC: American Psychiatric Association Press.

Butler, R. N. (1963). The facade of chronological age. *American Journal of Psychiatry, 119,* 721–728.

Butler, R. N. (1963). The life review: An interpretation of reminiscence in the aged. *Psychiatry, 26,* 65–76.

Butler, R. N. (1963). Self-drawings of normal older men. *Geriatrics, 18,* 220–232.

Butler, R. N., & Hyer, K. (1989). Reimbursement reform for the frail elderly. *Journal of the American Geriatrics Society, 37,* 1097–1098.

Coblenz, J. M., Mattis, S., Zingesser, L. H., Kasoff, S. S., Wisniewski, H. M., & Katzman, R. (1973, November). Presenile dementia: Clinical Aspects and Evaluation of Cerebrospinal Fluid Dynamics. *Archives of Neurology, 29*(5), 299–308.

Costa, P. T., Jr., & McCrae, R. R. (1992). *Revised NEO Personality Inventory (NEO-PR-R) and NEO Five-Factor Inventory (NEO-FFI) Professional Manual.* Odessa, FL: Psychological Assessment Resource.

Costa, P. T., Jr., & McCrae, R. R. (1992). Trait Personality Comes of Age. In Sonderegger, T. B. (Ed.), *Nebraska symposium on motivation: Psychology and aging* (pp. 169–204). Lincoln, NE: University of Nebraska Press.

Costa, P. T., Jr., Somerfield, M. R., & McCrae, R. R. (1995). Personality and coping: A reconceptualization. In Zeidner, M., & Endler, N. S. (Eds.), *Handbook of coping.* New York: John Wiley & Sons.

Crook, T., Bartus, R. T., Ferris, S. H., Whitehouse, P., Cohen, G. D., & Gershon, S. (1986). Age associated memory impairment: Proposed diagnostic criteria and measures of clinical change. Report of a National Institute of Mental Health work group. *Developmental Neuropsychology, 2,* 261–276.

Daniels, N. (1988). *Am I my parents' keeper? An essay on justice between the young and the old.* New York: Oxford University Press.

Delis, D. C., Kramer, J. H., Kaplan, E., & Ober, B. A. (1987). *California verbal learning test (Adult version).* San Antonio, TX: Psychological Corp., Harcourt-Brace, Jovanovich.

Delp, H. A. (1953). Correlations between the Kent E-G-Y and the Wechsler Batteries. *Journal of Clinical Psychology, 9,* 73–75.

Digman, J. M. (1990). Personality structure: Emergence of the five-factor model. *Annual Review of Psychology, 41,* 417–440.

Duara, R., Grady, C., Haxby, J., Sundaram, M., Cutler, N. R., Heston, L., Moore, A., Schlageter, N., Larson, S., & Rapoport, S. I. (1986). Positron emission tomography in Alzheimer's Disease. *Neurology, 36,* 879–887.

Dubler, N. N. (1995). Legal issues. In Abrams, W. B., Beers, M. H., & Berkow, R. (Eds.), *The Merck manual of geriatrics,* 2nd ed. (pp. 1379–1392). Whitehouse Station, NJ: Merck & Co.

Folstein, M. F., Folstein, S. E., & McHugh, P. R. (1975). "Mini-mental state," a practical method for grading the cognitive state of patients for the clinician. *Journal of Psychiatric Research, 12,* 189–198.

Goldfarb, A. I. (1964). The evaluation of geriatric patients following treatment. In Hoch, P. H., & Zubin, J. (Eds.), *Evaluation of psychiatric treatment* (pp. 271–308). New York: Grune & Stratton.

Goldstein, K. (1942). *Aftereffects of brain injuries in war and their evaluation and treatment.* New York: Grune & Stratton, 71–73, 77–78, 93.

Goldstein, K., & Scheerer, M. (1941). Abstract and concrete behavior. *Psychological Monograph, 53*(2), 239.

Gottlieb, G. L. (1995). Financial issues in geriatric psychiatry. In Kaplan, H. I., & Sadock, B. J. (Eds.), *Comprehensive textbook of psychiatry/IV* (vol. 2, pp. 2656–2661). Baltimore, MD: Williams and Wilkins.

Gurland, B. J., & Wilder, D. E. (1984). The CARE interview revisited: Development of an efficient systematic clinical assessment. *Journal of Gerontology, 39,* 129–137.

Hachinski, V. C., Iliff, L. D., Zilhka, E., Du Boulay, G. H., McAllister, V. L., Marshall, J., Russell, R. W. R., & Symon, L. (1975). Cerebral bloodflow in dementia. *Archives of Neurology, 32,* 632–637.

Holmes, T. H., & Rahe, R. H. (1967). The social readjustment rating scale. *Journal of Psychosomatic Research, 11,* 213–218.

Hooker, K., Frazier, L. D., & Monohan, D. J. (1994). Personality and coping among caregivers of spouses with dementia. *The Gerontologist, 34,* 386–392.

Jutagir, R. (1993). Geropsychology and neuropsychological testing: Role in evaluation and treatment of patients with dementia. *The Mount Sinai Journal of Medicine, 60,* 528–531.

Kane, R. A., Kane, R. L., & Rubenstein, L. Z. (1989). Comprehensive assessment of the elderly patient. In Petersen, M. D., & White, D. L. (Eds.). *Health care of the elderly* (pp. 475–519). Beverly Hills, CA: Sage Publications.

Katz, I. R., & Alexopoulos, G. S. (Eds.). (1996, Fall). Consensus update conference: Diagnosis and treatment of late-life depression, proceedings of the Geriatric Psychiatry Alliance—January 20, 1996. *The American Journal of Geriatric Psychiatry, 4*(4), supplement 1.

Katz, S., Downs, T. D., Cash, H., & Grotz, R. C. (1970). Progress and development of the index of ADL. *The Gerontologist, 10,* 20–30.

Kent, G. H. (1946). *Kent E-G-Y test: Series of emergency scales. Manual.* New York: The Psychological Corporation.

Kramer, A. M. (1995, April 13). Health care for elderly persons—Myths and realities. *New England Journal of Medicine, 332*(15), 1027–1029.

Lachs, M. S., Feinstein, A. R., Cooney, L. M., Drickamer, M. A., Marottoli, R. A., Pannill, F. C., & Tinetti, M. E. (1990, May 1). A simple procedure for general screening for functional disability in elderly patients. *Annals of Internal Medicine, 112*(9), 699–706.

Lawton, P. (1975). The Philadelphia Geriatric Center Morale Scale: A revision. *Journal of Gerontology, 30,* 85–88.

Lebowitz, B. D., & Gottlieb, G. L. (1995). Clinical research in the managed care environment. *American Journal of Geriatric Psychiatry, 3,* 21–25.

Lubitz, J., Beebe, J., & Baker, C. (1995, April 13). Longevity and Medicare expenditures. *New England Journal of Medicine, 332*(15), 999–1003.

McCrae, R. R., & Costa, P. T., Jr. (1991). Adding *Liebe und Arbeit:* The full five-factor model and well-being. *Personality and Social Psychology Bulletin, 17,* 227–232.

McKhann, G., Drachman, D., Folstein, M., Katzman, R., Price, D., & Stadlan, E. M. (1984). Clinical diagnosis of Alzheimer's Disease: Report of the NINCDS-ADRDA work group under the auspices of the Department of Health and Human Services Task Force on Alzheimer's Disease. *Neurology, 34,* 939–944.

Monk, A. (Ed.). (1990). *Health care of the aged.* Binghamton, NY: The Haworth Press.

Moon, M. (1996). *Medicare now and in the future,* 2nd ed. Washington, DC: The Urban Institute Press.

Miller, T. (1991). The psychotherapeutic utility of the five-factor model of personality: A clinician's experience. *Journal of Personality Assessment, 57,* 415–443.

National Institute on Aging Task Force. (1980). Senility reconsidered: Treatment possibilities for mental impairment in the elderly. *Journal of the American Medical Association, 244–263.*

National Institute of Mental Health. (1979). *The diagnostic interview schedule.* Washington, DC: Center for Epidemiologic Studies, National Institute of Mental Health.

National Institutes of Health. (1988). National Institutes of Health consensus development statement: Geriatric assessment methods for clinical decision-making. *Journal of the American Geriatric Society, 36,* 342–347.

National Institutes of Health Consensus Development Conference. (1991, November 4–5). Diagnosis and treatment of depression in late life. Reprinted from: *NIH Consensus Development Conference Consensus Statement, 9,*(3). Bethesda, MD: NIH.

National Institutes of Health, Office of the Medical Applications of Research. (1992). Consensus development panel on late life: Diagnosis and treatment of depression in late life. *Journal of the American Medical Association, 268,* 1018–1024.

Neugarten, B. L., Havighurst, R. J., & Tobin, S. S. (1961). The measurement of life satisfaction. *Journal of Gerontology, 16,* 134–143.

Palmore, E. (1970). *Normal aging: Reports from the Duke Longitudinal Study, 1955–1969.* Durham, NC: Duke University Press.

Pfeiffer, E. (1975). A short portable mental status questionnaire for the assessment of organic brain deficit in elderly patients. *Journal of the American Geriatrics Society, 23,* 433–441.

Rapoport, S. I., Horwitz, B., Haxby, J. V., & Grady, C. L. (1986). Alzheimer's Disease: Metabolic uncoupling of associative brain regions. *Canadian Journal of Neurological Sciences, 13,* 540–545.

Regan, J. (1990). *The aged client and the law.* New York: Columbia University Press.

Rosen, W. G., Mohs, R. C., & Davis, K. L. (1984). A new rating scale for Alzheimer's Disease. *American Journal of Psychiatry, 141,* 1356–1364.

Rubenstein, L. Z., Campbell, L. J., & Kane, R. L. (Eds.). (1987). Geriatric assessment [Special issue]. *Clinical Geriatric Medicine, 3*(1).

Rubenstein, L. Z., Josephson, K. R., Wieland, G. D., Pietruszka, F., Tretton, C., Strome, S., Cole, K. D., & Campbell, L. J. (1987). Geriatric assessment on a subacute hospital ward. *Clinical Geriatric Medicine, 3*(1), 131–143.

Schoenfeld, B., & Tuzil, T. J. (1979). Conservatorship: A move towards more personalized protective services. *Journal of Gerontology and Social Work, 1,* 225–234.

Sheikh, J. I., & Yesavage, J. A. (1986). Geriatric depression scale (GDS): Recent evidence and development of a shorter version. In Brink, T. L. (Ed.), *Clinical gerontology* (pp. 165–173). Binghamton, NY: The Haworth Press.

Shore, J. H., Breakey, W., & Arvidson, B. (1981). Morbidity and mortality in the commitment process. *Archives of General Psychiatry, 38,* 930–934.

Siegler, I. C., Dawson, D. V., & Welsh, K. A. (1994). Caregiver ratings of personality change in Alzheimer's Disease patients: A replication. *Psychology and Aging, 9,* 464–466.

Spitzer, R. L., Williams, J. B. W., Gibbon, M., & First, M. B. (1988). *Structured clinical interview for DSM-IIIR: Patient version (SCID-P, 6/1/88).* New York: Biometrics Research Department, New York Psychiatric Institute.

Strauss, P., Wolf, R., & Shilling, D. (1990). *Aging and the law.* Chicago: Commerce Clearing House.

Sunderland, T., Alterman, I. S., Yount, D., Hill, J. L., Tariot, P. N., Newhouse, P. A., Mueller, E. A., Mellow, A. M., & Cohen, R. M. (1988). A new scale for the assessment of depressed mood in demented patients. *American Journal of Psychiatry, 145,* 955–959.

Wechsler, D. (1955). *WASI Manual: Wechsler Adult Intelligence Scale.* New York: The Psychological Corporation.

Wechsler, D. (1981). *Wechsler Adult Intelligence Scale* (Revised). San Antonio, TX: Psychological Corporation, Harcourt-Brace, Jovanovich.

Wechsler, D. (1987). *Wechsler Memory Scale* (Revised). San Antonio, TX: Psychological Corporation, Harcourt-Brace, Jovanovich.

Weinderg, J. (1956) Personal and social adjustment. In Anderson, J. E. (Ed.), *Psychological aspects of aging* (pp. 17–20). Washington, DC: American Psychological Association.

Williams, M. E. (1990, May 1). Why screen for functional disability in elderly persons? *Annals of Internal Medicine, 112*(9), 369.

Yesavage, J. A. (1986). The use of self-rating depression scales in the elderly. In Poon, L. W. (Ed.), *Handbook for clinical memory assessment* (pp. 213–217). Washington, DC: American Psychological Association.

Yesavage, J. A., Brink, T. L., Rose, T. L., Lum, O., Huang, V., Adey, M., & Leirer, V. O. (1983). Development and validation of a geriatric depression screening scale: A preliminary report. *Journal of Psychiatric Research, 17,* 37–49.

ENDNOTES

1. National Institutes of Health. (1988). National Institutes of Health consensus development statement: Geriatric assessment methods for clinical decision-making. *Journal of the American Geriatrics Society, 36,* 342–347.

2. Kane, R. A., Kane, R. L., & Rubenstein, L. Z. (1989). Comprehensive assessment of the elderly patient. In Petersen, M. D., & White, D. L. (Eds.), *Health care of the elderly.* Beverly Hills: Sage Publications; Rubenstein, L. Z., Campbell, L. J., & Kane, R. L. (Eds.). (1987). Geriatric assessment. *Clinical Geriatric Medicine, 3*(l); and Rubenstein, L. Z., Josephson, K. R., Wieland, G. D., Pietruszka, F., Tretton, C., Strome, S., Cole, K. D., & Campbell, L. J. (1987). Geriatric assessment on a subacute hospital ward. *Clinical Geriatric Medicine, 3*(l), 131–143.

3. Goldstein, K. (1942). *Aftereffects of brain injuries in war and their evaluation and treatment.* New York: Grune & Stratton, pp. 71–73, 77–78, 93.

4. Weinberg, J. (1956). Personal and social adjustment. In Anderson, J. E. (Ed.), *Psychological aspects of aging.* Washington, DC: American Psychological Association.

5. Pfeiffer, E. (Ed.). (1975). Multidimensional functional assessment: The OARS methodology. Durham, NC: Duke University Press, Center for the Study of Aging and Human Development.

6. Gurland, B., Kuriansky, J., Sharpe, L., Simon, R., Stiller, P., & Birkett, P. (1977). The Comprehensive Assessment and Referral Evaluation (CARE): Rationale, development and reliability. *International Journal of Aging and Human Development, 8,* 9–42; Golden, R. R., Teresi, J. A., & Guriand, B. J. (1982–1983). Detection of dementia and depression cases with the comprehensive assessment and referral evaluation interview schedule. *International Journal of Aging and Human Development, 16,* 241–254.

7. Kanowski, S., Kruger, H., & Kuhl, K. P. (1985). The AGP system: Assessment of symptoms in psychogeriatric patients. In Traber, J., & Gispen, W. H. (Eds.). *Senile dementia of the Alzheimer type* (pp. 44–59). Berlin: Springer-Verlag.

8. Roth, M., Tym, E., Mountjoy, C. Q., Huppert, F. A., Hendrie, H., Verma, S., & Goddard, R. (1986). CAMDEX: A standardized instrument for the diagnosis of mental disorder in the elderly with special reference to the early detection of dementia. *British Journal of Psychiatry, 149,* 698–709.

9. Kennie, D. C. (1983). Good health care for the aged. *Journal of the American Medical Association, 249,* 770–773; Fisk, A. A. (1983). Comprehensive health care for the elderly. *Journal of the American Medical Association, 249,* 230–236; Larson, E. B., Reifler, B. V., Sumi, S. M., Canfield, C. G., & Chinn, N. M. (1985). Diagnostic evaluation of 200 elderly outpatients with suspected dementia. *Journal of Gerontology, 40,* 536–543.

10. Granacher, R. P. (1981). The neurologic examination in geriatric psychiatry. *Psychosomatics, 22,* 485–499.

11. One should not overlook the possibility of pellagra in the workup. The complete syndrome of this vitamin deficiency disease may not be present. One can look for redness of the mouth and tongue (more obvious in acute cases), skin changes, and—of special interest to mental health personnel—evidence of intellectual changes in a chronic brain disorder.

12. Goodwin, J. S., Goodwin, J. M., & Garry, P. J. (1983). Association between nutritional status and cognitive functioning in a healthy elderly population. *Journal of the American Medical Association, 249,* 2917–2921; Wurtman, R. J. (1984). The ultimate head waiter: How the brain controls diet. *Technology Review,* July, 42–51.

13. Kenshalo, D. W. (1977). Age change in touch, vibration, temperature, kinesthesis, and pain sensitivity. In Birren, J. E., & Schaie, K. W. (Eds.), *Handbook of the physiology of aging,* New York: Van Nostrand Reinhold.

14. Torres, F., Faora, A., Loewenson, R., & Johnson, E. (1983). The encephalogram of elderly subjects revisited. *Electroencephalography and Clinical Neurophysiology, 56,* 391–398; Duffy, F. H., Albert, M. S., McAnulty, G., & Garvey, A. J. (1984). Age-related differences in brain electrical activity of healthy subjects. *Annals of Neurology, 16,* 430–438; Giaquinto, S., & Nolte, G. (1986). The EEG in the normal elderly: A contribution to the interpretation of aging and dementia. *Electroencephalography and Clinical Neurophysiology, 63,* 540–546.

15. Celesia, G. G. (1986). EEG and event-related potentials in aging and dementia. *Journal of Clinical Neurophysiology, 3,* 99–111; Brenner, R. P., Ulrich, R. F., Spiker, D. G., Sclabassi, R. J., Reynolds, C. F., Marin, R. S., & Boller, F. (1986). Computerized EEG spectral analysis in elderly normal, demented and depressed subjects. *Electroencephalography and Clinical Neurophysiology, 64,* 483–492; and

Leuchter, A. F., Spar, J. E., Walter, D. O., & Weiner, H. (1987). Electroencephalographic spectra and coherence in the diagnosis of Alzheimer's-type and multi-infarct dementia. *Archives of General Psychiatry, 44,* 993–998.

16. Rae-Grant, A. D., Blume, W. T., Lau, K., Fisman, M., Hachinski, V., & Merskey, H. (1986). The EEG in Alzheimer-type dementia: Lack of progression with sequential studies. *Canadian Journal of Neurological Sciences, 13,* 407–409.

17. McGeer, P. L. (1986). Brain imaging in Alzheimer's disease. *British Medical Bulletin, 42,* 24–28.

18. Kramer, D. M. (1984). Basic principles of magnetic resonance imaging. *Radiologic Clinics of North America, 22,* 765–778.

19. Agee, O. F. (1988). MRI vs. CT for diagnosing brain disorders in the elderly. *Geriatrics, 43,* 25–38.

20. Hachinski, V. C., Iliff, L. D., Zilhka, E., Du Boulay, G. H., McAllister, V. L., Marshall, J., Russell, R. W. R., & Symon, L. (1975). Cerebral blood flow in dementia, *Archives of Neurology, 32,* 632–637; Ingvar, D. H., Brun, A., Hagberg, B., & Gustafson, L. (1978). Regional cerebral blood flow in the dominant hemisphere in confirmed cases of Alzheimer's disease, Pick's disease, and multi-infarct dementia: Relationship to clinical symptomatology and neuropathological findings. In Katzman, R., Terry, R. D., & Bick, K. L. (Eds.), *Alzheimer's disease: Senile dementia and related disorders* (pp. 203–211). New York: Raven; and Deutsch, G., & Tweedy, J. R. (1987). Cerebral blood flow in severity-matched Alzheimer and multi-infarct patients. *Neurology, 37,* 431–438.

21. Foster, N. L., Chase, T. N., Mansi, L., Brooks, R., Fedio, P., Patronas, N. J., & Di Chiro, G. (1984). Cortical abnormalities in Alzheimer's disease. *Annals of Neurology, 16,* 649–654; Kuhl, D. E., Metter, E. J., & Riege, W. H. (1985). Patterns of cerebral glucose utilization in depression, multiple infarct dementia, and Alzheimer's disease. *Research Publications/Association for Research in Nervous and Mental Disease, 63,* 211–226; Duara, R., Grady, C., Haxby, J., Sundaram, M., Cutler, N. R., Heston, L., Moore, A., Schlageter, N., Larson, S., & Rapoport, S. I. (1986). Positron emission tomography in Alzheimer's disease. *Neurology, 36,* 879–887.

22. Rapoport, S. I., Horwitz, B., Haxby, J. V., & Grady, C. L. (1986). Alzheimer's disease: Metabolic uncoupling of associative brain regions. *Canadian Journal of Neurological Sciences, 13,* 540–545.

23. Mayberg, H. S., Robinson, R. G., Wong, D. F., Parikh, R., Bolduc, P., Starkstein, S. E., Price, T., Dannals, R. F., Links, J. M., Wilson, A. A., Ravert, H. T., & Wagner, H. N. (1988). PET imaging of cortical S_2 serotonin receptors after stroke: Lateralized changes and relationship to depression. *American Journal of Psychiatry, 145,* 937–943.

24. Holman, B. L., Gibson, R. E., Hill, T. C., Eckelman, W. C., Albert, M., & Reba, R. C. (1985). Muscarinic acetylcholine receptors in Alzheimer's disease: In vivo imaging with iodine 123-labeled 3-quinuclidinyl-4-iodobenzilate and emission tomography. *Journal of the American Medical Association, 254,* 3063–3066.

25. National Institute of Mental Health. (1979). *The diagnostic interview schedule.* Washington, DC: Center for Epidemiologic Studies, National Institute of Mental Health.

26. Spitzer, R. L., & Endicott, J. (1978). *NIMH Clinical Research Branch collaborative program on the psychobiology of depression: Schedule for affective disorders and schizophrenia (SADS).* New York: Biometrics Division, New York State Psychiatric Institute.

27. Spitzer, R. L., Williams, J. B. W., Gibbon, M., & First, M. B. (1988). *Structured clinical interview for DSM-IIIR: Patient version (SCID-P, 6/1/88).* New York: Biometrics Research Department, New York State Psychiatric Institute.

28. Folstein, M. F., Folstein, S. E., & McHugh, P. R. (1975). Mini-mental state, a practical method for grading the cognitive state of patients for the clinician. *Journal of Psychiatric Research, 12,* 189–198.

29. Coblenz, J. M., Mattis, S., Zingesser, L. H., Kasoff, S. S., Wisniewski, H. M., & Katzman, R. (1973, Nov.). Presenile dementia: Clinical aspects and evaluation of cerebrospinal fluid dynamics. *Archives of Neurology, 29*(5), 299–308.

30. Blessed, G., Tomlinson, B. E., & Roth, M. (1968). The association between quantitative measures of dementia and of senile changes in the cerebral grey matter of elderly patients. *British Journal of Psychology, 114,* 809.

31. Kahn, R. L., Goldfarb, A. I., & Pollack, M. (1964). The evaluation of geriatric patients following treatment. In Hoch, P. H. & Zubin, J. (Eds.), *Evaluation of psychiatric treatment.* New York: Grune & Stratton.

32. Jutagir, R. (1993) Geropsychology and neuropsychological testing: Role in evaluation and treatment of patients with dementia. *The Mount Sinai Journal of Medicine, 60,* 528–531.

33. Delis, D. C., Kramer, J. H., Kaplan, E., & Ober, B. A. (1987). *California verbal learning test (adult version).* San Antonio, TX: Psychological Corp., Harcourt,-Brace, Jovanovich.

34. Wechsler, D. (1987). *Wechsler memory scale (revised).* San Antonio, TX: Psychological Corp., Harcourt-Brace, Jovanovich.

35. Benton, A. (1974). *Revised visual retention test* (4th ed.). New York: Harcourt-Brace, Jovanovich.

36. Wechsler, D. (1981). *Wechsler adult intelligence scale* (revised). New York: Harcourt-Brace, Jovanovich.

37. Kent, G. H. (1946). *Kent E-G-Y test: Series of emergency scales. Manual.* New York: The Psychological Corporation. See Delp, H. A. (1953). Correlations between the Kent E-G-Y and the Wechsler batteries. *Journal of Clinical Psychology, 9,* 73–75.

38. Bender, M. B., Fink, M., & Green, M. (1951). Patterns in perception in simultaneous tests of the face and hand. *Archives of Neurology and Psychiatry, 66,* 355–362.

39. Ames, L. B., Metraux, R. W., Rodell, J. L., & Walker, R. N. (1974). *Rorschach responses in old age.* New York: Brunner/Mazel.

40. Neugarten, B. L., Havighurst, R. J., & Tobin, S. S. (1961). The measurement of life satisfaction. *Journal of Gerontology, 16,* 134–143.

41. Lawton, P. (1975). The Philadelphia Geriatric Center morale scale: A revision. *Journal of Gerontology, 30,* 85–88.

42. Kearns, N. P., Cruickshank, C. A., McGuigan, K. J., Riley, S. A., Shaw, S. P., & Snaith, R. P. (1982). A comparison of depression rating scales. *British Journal of Psychiatry, 141,* 45–49.

43. Yesavage, J. A., Brink, T. L., Rose, T. L., Lum, O., Huang, V., Adey, M., & Leirer, V. O. (1983). Development and validation of a geriatric depression screening scale: A preliminary report. *Journal of Psychiatric Research, 17,* 37–49; and Sunderland, T., Alterman, I. S., Yount, D., Hill, J. L., Tariot, P. N., Newhouse, P. A., Mueller, E. A., Mellow, A. M., & Cohen, R. M. (1988). A new scale for the assessment of depressed mood in demented patients. *American Journal of Psychiatry, 145,* 955–959.

44. Plotkin, D. A., Mintz, J., & Jarvik, L. F. (1985). Subjective memory complaints in geriatric depression. *American Journal of Psychiatry, 142,* 1103–1105.

45. Yesavage, J. A. (1986). The use of self-rating depression scales in the elderly. In Poon, L. W. (Ed.). *Handbook for clinical memory assessment* (pp. 213–217). Washington, DC: American Psychological Association.

46. Digman, J. M. (1990). Personality structure: Emergence of the five-factor model. *Annual Review of Psychology, 41,* 417–440.

47. Costa, P. T., Jr. & McCrae, R. R. (1992a). *Revised NEO Personality Inventory (NEO-PI-R) and NEO Five-Factor Inventory (NEO-FFI) Professional Manual.* Odessa, FL: Psychological Assessment Resource.

48. Costa P. T., Jr. & McCrae, R. R. (1992b). Trait psychology comes of age. In Sonderegger, T. B. (Ed.), *Nebraska symposium on motivation: Psychology and aging* (pp. 169–204). Lincoln, NE: University of Nebraska Press.

49. Siegler, I. C., Dawson, D. V., & Welsh, K. A. (1994). Caregiver ratings of personality change in Alzheimer's disease patients: A replication. *Psychology and Aging, 9,* 464–466.

50. Hooker, K., Frazier, L. D., & Monahan, D. J. (1994). Personality and coping among caregivers of spouses with dementia. *The Gerontologist, 34,* 386–392.

51. McCrae, R. R. & Costa, P. T., Jr. (1991). Adding *Liebe und Arbeit:* The full five-factor model and well-being. *Personality and Social Psychology Bulletin, 17,* 227–232.

52. Miller, T. (1991). The psychotherapeutic utility of the five-factor model of personality: A clinician's experience. *Journal of Personality Assessment, 57,* 415–443.

53. Costa, P. T., Jr., Somerfield, M. R., & McCrae, R. R. (1995). Personality and coping: A reconceptualization. In Zeidner, M. & Endler, N. S. (Eds.) *Handbook of Coping.* New York: John Wiley & Sons.

54. Birren, J. E., Butler, R. N., Greenhouse, S. W., Sokoloff, L., & Yarrow, M. R., (Eds.) (1963). *Human aging: A biological and behavioral study.* Pub. No. (PHS) 986. Washington, DC: U.S. Government Printing Office (reprinted as Pub. No. [HSM]71–9051, 1971, 1974); Hiatt, L. G. (1985). Understanding the physical environment. *Pride Institute Journal of Long-Term Home Health Care, 4,* 12–22; and Anthony, K., Procter, A. W., Silverman, A. M., & Murphy, E. (1987). Mood and behavior problems following the relocation of elderly patients with mental illness. *Age and Aging, 16,* 355–365.

55. Birren et al., *Human aging,* 31.

56. *Ibid.,* 316.

57. Butler, R. N., & Hyer, R. N. (1989). Reimbursement reform for the frail elderly. Editorial, *Journal of the American Geriatrics Society, 37,* 1097–1098.

58. Katz, S., Downs, T. D., Cash, H., & Grotz, R. C. (1970). Progress and development of the index of ADL. *The Gerontologist, 10,* 20–30; and Clark, G. S. (1984). Functional assessment in the elderly. In Williams, T. F. (Ed.), *Rehabilitation in the aging* (pp. 111–124). New York: Raven Press.

59. Shore, J. H., Breakey, W., & Arvidson, B. (1981). Morbidity and mortality in the commitment process. *Archives of General Psychiatry, 38,* 930–934; Pecora, A. K. (1982, April). Medical treatment of mentally disabled adults: Limitation on the spouse's right to consent. *Maryland State Medical Journal, 54–55;* and Drane, J. F. (1984). Competency to give an informed consent: A model for making clinical assessments. *Journal of the American Medical Association, 252,* 925–927.

60. See discussion of role of social service as conservator and New York State's Conservatorship Law of 1973 in Schoenfeld, B., & Tuzil, T. J. (1979). Conservatorship: A move towards more personalized protective services. *Journal of Gerontology and Social Work, 1,* 225–234

CHAPTER 10

HOW TO KEEP PEOPLE AT HOME

Home care is the term used for the professional or personal services provided to older persons on a recurring or continuing basis at home as treatment of chronic physical or mental impairment. The term *long-term care* has often been used primarily in connection with institutionalization but, in fact, it also covers care in the older person's home or any other location. Furthermore, home care involves more than just care for chronic impairments. For example, an older person may have an acute episode of illness or disability, or a time-limited recuperation after acute hospitalization that can be managed at home. This chapter will focus on both acute and long-term care in the home. In the next chapter, we concentrate on care in institutions.

WHO NEEDS HOME CARE?

According to a Commonwealth Fund Commission study of community-dwelling elderly, impairment among the elderly is distributed as follows: Of a total of 30.8 million elderly in 1989, 77% (23.8 million) have no impairment, 13% (3.9 million) are moderately impaired, and 5% (1.6 million) are

severely impaired. Another 5% (1.5 million) of the elderly are impaired enough to be in nursing homes. The salient point for our home-care discussion is that 18% of all elderly, or 5.5 million persons, are moderately to severely impaired and remain in homes in the community. (Figure 10.1.)

The most dependent of the home-dwelling elderly are obviously those with severe impairment. Of the 1.6 million severely impaired elderly living in the community, 22% have both severe physical and cognitive impairment, 32% have severe cognitive impairment only, and 46% have severe physical impairment only. (Figure 10.2.)

What kinds of activities do impaired older persons need help with at home? The activities of daily living (ADLs) are the basic tasks of everyday life, such as eating, bathing, toileting, and moving in and out of chairs and bed. A number of different ADL measurements have evolved to estimate both the incidence and prevalence of disability generally as well as to aid in the evaluation of an individual's need for help.[1] The figures we have used in this chapter are based on the 1982 National Long Term Care Survey. Table 10.1 shows the

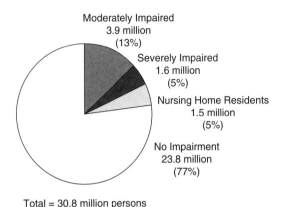

Moderately Impaired
3.9 million
(13%)

Severely Impaired
1.6 million
(5%)

Nursing Home Residents
1.5 million
(5%)

No Impairment
23.8 million
(77%)

Total = 30.8 million persons

FIGURE 10.1   Distribution of elderly population by impairment, 1989

Source: The Commonwealth Fund Commission on Elderly People Living Alone. (1989). *The estimated costs of a proposed home care program* (Background Paper Series No. 16). New York: The Commonwealth Fund. Reprinted by permission.

specific activities of daily living most needed by three separate groups of persons with different levels of impairment. Of the cited impairments, the most frequent limitation was difficulty in walking.

Some 44% of persons who are most impaired in ADLs have cognitive impairment that is contributing to or causing disability. Cognitive impairment is also present in less ADL-impaired people, though it plays a smaller role. (Figure 10.3.)

LIVING ALONE

A significant proportion of the elderly live alone at home. In 1993 32.5%, or about 10 million people age 65 or older, lived independently of other family members. A small number of these (2.3%) lived with nonrelatives. The remainder, 30.2% of the elderly lived alone. 55% of the elderly were married and living with their spouses, while 12.5% lived with other relatives. Older women, mostly widowed, represented the vast majority of those living alone.[2]

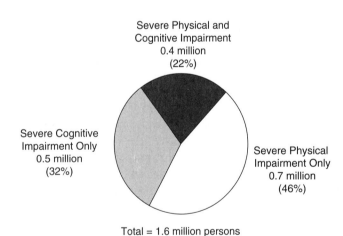

Severe Physical and
Cognitive Impairment
0.4 million
(22%)

Severe Cognitive
Impairment Only
0.5 million
(32%)

Severe Physical
Impairment Only
0.7 million
(46%)

Total = 1.6 million persons

Severe Physical Impairment: human assistance with two or more ADLs

Severe Cognitive Impairment: five or more errors on SPMSQ or reported senile

FIGURE 10.2   Distribution of the severely impaired community-dwelling elderly population, 1989

Source: The Commonwealth Fund Commission on Elderly People Living Alone. (1989). *The estimated costs of a proposed home care program* (Background Paper Series No. 16). New York: The Commonwealth Fund. Reprinted by permission.

TABLE 10.1   Functional limitations of persons aged 65 and over by age, and living arrangement: 1991 (in thousands)

	AGED 65+			AGED 85+
	TOTAL	**LIVING ALONE**	**LIVING WITH OTHERS**	
Total Population	30,748	9,634	21,214	2,430
Percent with difficulty*				
Walking	14.3	18.1	12.6	34.9
Getting outside	15.9	20.7	13.8	44.8
Bathing or showering	9.4	11.2	8.7	30.6
Transferring**	9.0	10.9	8.2	21.9
Dressing	5.8	6.3	5.6	16.1
Using toilet	4.2	4.8	3.9	14.2
Eating	2.1	2.2	2.0	4.1
Preparing meals	8.6	9.1	8.4	27.6
Managing money	7.1	8.4	6.5	26.2
Using the telephone	7.1	7.1	7.1	21.4
Doing light housework	11.4	13.6	10.4	30.8
Percent of total receiving help*				
Walking	5.9	4.9	6.4	16.8
Getting outside	13.2	17.2	11.4	42.3
Bathing or showering	5.9	5.0	6.3	20.9
Transferring**	3.9	2.7	4.5	11.0
Dressing	3.9	2.7	4.4	11.1
Using toilet	2.6	1.9	2.9	7.8
Eating	1.1	0.8	1.2	2.5
Preparing meals	7.5	7.0	7.8	25.4
Managing money	6.4	7.4	5.9	24.6
Doing light housework	8.9	9.6	8.7	27.3

Source: U.S. Bureau of the Census (1996). 65+ in the United States. *Current Population Reports,* Special Studies, Series P-23, no. 190. Washington, DC: U.S. Government Printing Office.

 *Difficulty due to a physical or mental health condition

 **Getting in or out from a bed or chair

***Receiving help with the specified difficulty

Many of the eight million elderly living alone were not at all disabled, in poor health, suffering from lack of medical care, or lacking family or companionship. Seventy percent had children, and many of these lived near at least one child, saw their children regularly, and spoke frequently with them by phone. Many also have networks of social contacts from long years of living in the same location or from moving to retirement communities with active social programs. But almost 30% had no living children, and an additional 19% had only one child. Thus, this group represents a particularly vulnerable population when illness or disability strikes, since family members provide most home-care supports.[3]

To illustrate the importance of families, of all those living alone, most felt they had someone to help them for a few days if they needed care. Sixty-nine percent would turn to their families, and 17% had someone else. But 14% had no one. If the need

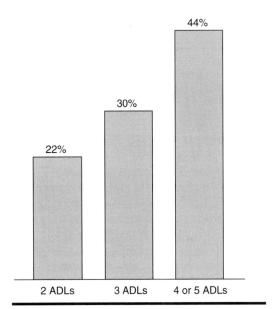

FIGURE 10.3   Percent of ADL impaired community-dwelling elderly persons with cognitive impairment, 1989

Source: The Commonwealth Fund Commission on Elderly People Living Alone. (1989). *The estimated costs of a proposed home care program* (Background Paper Series No. 16). New York: The Commonwealth Fund. Reprinted by permission.

for care lasted a few weeks or more, 67% could still rely on their families, but 24% said they had no one to care for them. Only 10% could turn to others outside of their families for lengthy care.[4]

The functional capacity of those living alone provides a framework for assessing the need for home-care services. According to the 1984 National Health Interview Survey, 60% of those living alone had no limitations in their usual activities, 17% had some outside limitations but could perform their usual activities, 16% were limited in some way in their usual daily activities, and 8% were unable to perform their usual daily activities.[5]

HOW IMPORTANT IS "HOME"?

Home is extraordinarily significant to many older persons. It is part of their identity, a place where things are familiar and relatively unchanging, and a place to maintain a sense of autonomy and con-

trol. Some insist on remaining at home regardless of the cost to their emotional and physical health and personal security. Such tenaciousness can be attributed to a desire for freedom and independence; a fear of loss of contact with familiar and loved people, places, and things; a fear of dying, because of the reputation of hospitals and nursing homes as places "where old people go to die"; and a trepidation about change and the unknown, which frightens people of all ages. In this nation of homeowners, where about 70% of older people own their homes, the idea of a home of one's own is deeply ingrained; communal or institutional living is often viewed as a loss of personal liberty and dignity.

The notion of home can refer to many things, from the four walls surrounding a person, to the neighborhood in which one's house is located, or to the possessions that make one feel at home. The meaning of the word *home* may include other individuals living with a person, as well as neighbors, pets, and plants. It can either be a place where one has lived a good part of one's life or a new place, as when older people move into a retirement community or leave the farm for a home in town. Thus the concept of home is unique to each individual.

Home can also be a euphemism. In our eagerness to recognize the importance of the feeling of home, we must not overlook those older people who dislike their living conditions, who have never felt "at home" where they are, and who are eager to move somewhere else—even to an institution. They may live in a dilapidated rooming house in a bare room with a lone light bulb suspended from the ceiling, in a boarding house with skimpy meals, in a cheap "retirement hotel" where the bath is shared with drug addicts, alcoholics, or street drifters.

Some older people are themselves homeless. They sleep on park benches or in subways, bus and train stations, bowery missions, doorways. Since the 1980s, such homelessness has become a major public issue. According to the National Coalition for the Homeless, estimates of the number of homeless in the United States are extremely inaccurate and tend to be low. One study, conducted by Bruce Link of Columbia University, examined the number of people who were homeless over a period of time to estimate that between 4.95 million and 9.32 million people experienced homelessness at some time during the second half of the 1980s. Another study conducted by the Urban Institute put the number of homeless people of all ages in the United States at between 500,000 and 600,000, using a "point in time count" during one week in 1988. The survey found 20% had been "deinstitutionalized," that is, removed from mental hospitals. Many of these are older persons.[6]

Alternatively, home may be fine physically but miserable emotionally because of family circumstances. An in-law problem may result when an older person moves in with a married son or daughter:

One 69-year-old woman was living with her son and daughter-in-law. The mother and daughter-in-law had never gotten along and couldn't tolerate talking to each other. The mother was discouraged from participating in housework. She therefore would remain in her pajamas all day, watching television. When her son was due home, she would dress, put on her makeup, and become warm and friendly. She and her daughter-in-law vied for his attentions. The mother complained that she was not invited to help the family and was considered a burden. The daughter-in-law stated that the mother expected total care. The son, caught in the middle between the two women in his life, finally asked his mother to leave.

Many situations with an older parent in the home fortunately work out much more satisfactorily. But one must avoid falling prey to one's own slogans, such as "keep people in their own homes," when this may be totally inappropriate and even cruel.

The periodic cry of reformers, "return institutional patients to the community," also needs to be examined with careful skepticism. What kind of community? What kind of home will be involved? Successful adjustment and adaptation is no more ensured in the community than anywhere else. Each decision concerning home care versus institutional care must be based on the older person's needs, but both alternatives should be as attractive and as therapeutic as possible. In general, care centered around the home offers the best treatment location except when people are physically dangerous to themselves or others, or require inpatient medical treatment. But it is beneficial only when the home is an adequate place to begin with or can be made adequate by selected interventions and community supports.

ADVANTAGES OF HOME CARE

One of the obvious advantages of home care is that most older people prefer it. Care at home offers better morale and security as long as proper services are given to provide comfort, support, and direct treatment of physical and emotional ills. Relatives and service personnel, such as homemakers and home health aides, can often give more individualized care than nursing staffs in institutions. Families tend to become intimately involved in treatment. Familiar surroundings are reassuring, and the older person does not have to be separated from family members, friends, possessions, and pets. Earlier intervention is possible, since it is not necessary to wait until hospitalization to begin treatment, and hospital beds can be saved for those who are more critically ill. Older people who are very ill or who are not ambulatory are not forced to leave home and travel to get treatment. Physicians, nurses, social workers, and members of all other disciplines involved in home care become more familiar with community resources, learn to use them more fully, and act as monitors and advocates who note services not presently available. Older people and their families can receive not only medical and psychiatric home care but also social and economic help.

The older person and the people in his or her life have a different perception of illness and treatment in the process of home care. Instead of being whisked off to the hospital or an institution, people remain where their care can be observed and participated in. It becomes evident to family members and older people themselves that mental or physical illness can be lived with as long as the stress on caregivers does not become too great. Life does not have to stop or become totally disrupted, and rehabilitation and recovery may be seen occurring even in a proportion of the very old and sick.

It should also be mentioned that home care is a growing consumer market that is creating many new jobs and a whole new service industry. It will eventually open up the mental health professions to an influx of new personnel and new ideas. Some day, home services (and nursing homes themselves) may be operated as social or public utilities, well regulated and run in the public interest. New professions, having a broader base of skills than is now seen, may evolve.

THE INITIAL REQUEST FOR MENTAL HEALTH EVALUATION

Requests for mental health care services may come from a variety of referral sources that include the following:

- Self-referral
- Family
- Friends and neighbors
- Members of the clergy
- Physicians—often internists
- Visiting nurse service
- Welfare department
- Community agencies
- Police

The more isolated the older person, the more likely it is that his or her difficulties will remain unnoticed until an emergency occurs and the police are called. Health inspectors, shopkeepers, and service workers such as meter readers, mail carriers, and hotel and apartment clerks may be the link that connects the isolated older person with the police after something obviously begins to go wrong.

FACTORS TO CONSIDER REGARDING HOME CARE

The decision to provide treatment in the home is influenced by the older person's self-care capacities, by the environmental resources the older person has, by the care-giving situation, including family and friends, and by the services and choices of care available in the community.

Activities of Daily Living

In terms of the individual older person, one must know if he or she is physically and mentally capable of self-care, either alone or with assistance. A diagnosis of an older person's physical or mental condition has proven to be a poor predicator of the use of home care. Therefore, researchers and health practitioners have turned to assessment of the actual *functioning* of the older person in his or her environment. The list below gives the most important of the functional skills needed for living at home, particularly if the person is alone part or all of the time.

- Orientation to time, place, person
- Cooking and feeding
- Bathing
- Dressing
- Grooming
- Toileting
- Continence
- Transferring from bed to chair
- Standing and walking
- Climbing stairs
- Fire and accident security
- Shopping
- Money management
- Ability to follow instructions (for example, medication)
- Ability to seek assistance when needed
- Social participation

As discussed earlier in this chapter, measurements of the capacity for performing the ADLs have evolved, making it possible to obtain a comprehensive picture of what a person can or cannot do. The Interagency Forum on Aging-Related Statistics (1989) provides a useful analysis of the various ADL measures and their applications in 11 recent national surveys.[7] Increasingly, ADL dependency measures are used to determine whether an individual qualifies for certain benefits and services, including home-care services. They have also been found to be significant predictors of admission to a nursing home, use of home care, use of hospital services, living arrangements, overall Medicare and Medicaid expenditures, insurance coverage, and mortality.

The most frequently used measure of functional ability is the Katz Activities of Daily Living Scale, which covers bathing, dressing, transferring, toileting continence, and eating.[8] Other scales are available as well. In addition, measures have been developed to help capture an even wider range of activities necessary for independent community living. Called the "instrumental activities of daily living" (IADLs), these measures address the capacity to handle personal finances, meal preparation, shopping, traveling, doing housework, using the telephone, and taking medications.[9]

Resource Assessment

Assessment of the adequacy of an older person's resources is another consideration. How adequate are transportation, socializing opportunities, quick availability of emergency medical care, neighborhood safety, financial security? Can the rent or mortgage and the utilities, repair costs, and property taxes be paid? Does the older person have the inner resources to manage on his or her own? Are there interests and activities? Personal relationships? Sexual outlets when desired? Religious and spiritual supports?

Assessment of Family and Other Informal Caregivers

One must also consider those people with whom the older person will be living or on whom they will be relying. Does home include other family members, roomers, or companions? Is it possible to feel at home in someone else's home, perhaps with sons or daughters? Can sharing and intergenerational living work in the average family? Or would the older person be more content in a communal arrangement with other elderly persons or with an intergenerational mix of people? Relatives

or friends with whom an older person lives may not be willing or able to care for the person at home when illness or disabilities increase. Sometimes there are no comfortable or easy solutions as the needs of the elders clash with those of younger family members. However, in many situations, families will make every sacrifice to keep an older person at home and may, in fact, need help in reconsidering whether this is the wisest course of action. In other cases families need support and opportunity for respite if they do decide on home care.

Eighty to ninety percent of home care of the sick or frail elderly is provided by families, and 70 to 80% of that family care is by women. In a nationally representative probability sample of informal caregivers of elderly who are dependent in ADLs, 71.5% of 2.2 million caregivers in the United States were women, with an average age of 57.3 years. Of all caregivers, 23% were wives; 29% were daughters; 20% were other females; 13% were husbands; 8.5% were sons; and 7% were other males. (Note: The figure of 2.2 million caregivers is an underestimate of informal care-giving, since much family assistance is given to older people who need assistance but are not yet frail or sick enough for the ADL categories.) Many caregivers (31.5%) were in vulnerable economic circumstances due to poverty or near-poverty, produced or compounded by the costs of care-giving. Fewer than 10% purchased services to assist them in their work. About 9% of all caregivers had left the labor force to care for a relative or friend, and of the one million caregivers still in the work force, one-fifth cut back on hours, nearly 30% rearranged their schedules, and almost 19% took time off without pay. Wife and daughter caregivers were more likely than husband and son caregivers to take any of these measures.[10]

Looking at aging from the point of view of the caregivers of the elderly, most of whom, as we see, are female, is an emerging public policy issue. In the past, most of the literature on care of the elderly focused on the elderly themselves—their medical and social needs, their financial capacity to pay for care, their preferences and predilections regarding care—as well as the services in place or proposed for the future. In recent years attention has begun to broaden to include concern for the needs of caregivers—the physical burdens that the care of the elderly imposes, the emotional stresses common to care-giving, the financial costs to the caregiver, and the services that would need to be provided if care-giving were to become a more viable, and when possible, a more positive, enriching experience for all concerned.

What happens as the "women in the middle" (ages 40 to 55) become employed in the paid work force in increasing numbers? Brody sees a caregiving shift toward the "young-old" women, ages 55 to 74, who become responsible for the care of the old-old—those over 75. However, even young-old women are themselves increasingly in the paid work-force.

Women over age 50 are in danger of becoming a new high-risk group for "burnout" or stress because of their many roles: wife and possibly caregiver to the husband when he is ill, out-of-home worker, parent, grandparent, and caregiver to parents or the husband's parents.[11] A number of studies point to the fact that a substantial subgroup of caregivers have competing family and employment demands in addition to care-giving roles.[12] This is true of many of the daughter-caregivers as well as a number of the wife-caregivers, who may also be responsible for the care of children at home and/or work in the outside labor force. One-quarter of care-giving daughters and one-third of other care-giving females had children under the age of 18 in their households. A 1984 report on care-giving by the National Association of State Units on Aging found "the role conflict among working/caregiving women is complex. The multiple roles assumed include employee, parent, spouse, filial caregiver and, sometimes, grandparent. The combination of multiple roles and value conflicts makes the working/caregiving woman a high risk health group.[13]

Measurements of caregiver strain are being developed. Examples are Robinson's *Caregiver Strain Questionnaire* and Zarit, Reaver, and Bach-Peterson's *The Burden Interview.*[14]

The 1979 Health, Education, and Welfare Task Force on Implementation of the Report to the President from the President's Commission on Mental Health pointed out that women, one-half of whom are in the work force, cannot be expected to shoulder the entire burden of care-giving to the young, old, and sick. The report recommended that government at local, state, and federal levels continue to develop formal support systems to supplement the informal supports provided by women.

Major gaps exist on many questions concerning caregivers. Measurements of all forms of stress on caregivers are crude and inconclusive. There is little documentation, pro or con, regarding the "woodwork effect"—namely the widespread fear that providing more resources to families will cause them to "come out of the woodwork" and overburden the system of supports. Nor is there yet enough research-based clarity about the worry that families will withdraw supports to the elderly if they are available elsewhere. There is little accurate information beyond demographic evidence about the actual wishes and needs of both caregivers and care recipients. Little is known about the viability of service exchanges and bartering of care services. And finally, there is still relatively little acceptance and understanding of the economic value of the care-giving services that women provide and of the fact that if they can no longer manage the burden, the alternatives will neither be inexpensive nor uncomplicated.[15]

The literature on the subject of the cost-effectiveness and cost-benefit of institutional versus home-based eldercare has been summarized by Weissert et al. (1988).[16] Long a topic of conjecture, home care was first thought to be a less expensive form of care for the frail and disabled elderly. But a look at the literature reveals that home- and community-based care, together with the services that support them, actually raise overall health-care service costs. Nor does home care produce a marked improvement in health status of the elderly or in delaying institutionalization. What it does produce is an improved degree of satisfaction and contentment among the elderly. But what happens to the caregivers? Studies of the economic and social costs to caregivers would help clarify this question and reveal what price caregivers are paying for the enhanced contentment of the elderly.[17] Such information would improve policy decisions about provision of support and respite to caregivers if home care continues to be seen as a desirable and important part of a comprehensive program of care for the elderly.

While it is true that home care is more expensive than institutional care if it is provided on a 24-hour-per-day basis, it is important to recognize that home care (and community care) should be and is provided in "dosage" form in accord with need, for example, severity of the condition (as measured by ADLs) and the character of the patient (degree of cooperativeness). Thus, home care is not all-or-nothing. There should be a "trigger" or "circuit-breaker" mechanism that is set off when the costs of care in the community attain 75% of institutional care costs. It is then time for reassessment and, depending upon the results, possible decision time for institutional admission. (From our perspective, the residual 25% is a crude measure of the caregiver strain or burden "cost," not usually measured.)

Availability of Home Health Services—What *Really* Exists and What *Ideally* Should Exist

Any truly serious national effort to keep people in their own homes requires provision for direct home delivery of health, including mental health, services. The middle class as well as the poor suffer from the unavailability of such services. Home care should be available to the chronically ill, to those recuperating from hospitalization, to those who may be acutely ill but can be treated outside a hospital, and finally to all those older people who simply need some help here and there to fill in the gaps left by various losses or declining functions. The U.S. health care system is gradually incorporating home care into the overall system of health care. For example, U.S. hospitals have become well aware of the need for home care; in 1988, 35% had home-care departments, compared to only 6.5% in 1976. We will describe the services we believe are essential if home care is to be a comprehensive approach to the treatment and prevention of mental illness. Evaluations, treatment plans, and coordination of care by some responsible person or group are, of course, essential. (Such services, known as *geriatric assessment* and *case management* or *care coordination* will be discussed shortly.)

Home care is not a radical new idea, but rather a return to some of the sound principles of the past, strengthened by newer medical and psychiatric understanding and techniques. In the past the family doctor, by means of the house call, took care of physical problems for the homebound elderly, while members of the clergy attended to spiritual and emotional matters, buttressed by neighbors and nearby family members. However, doctors and the clergy moved away from home visits, and crime, especially in urban areas, frightened away other health service providers who had formerly performed direct community work. Now only two major groups routinely make house calls: public health nurses and social workers. Much to their credit, members of these professions—usually women—continue working unarmed and often alone in high crime areas where the poor and many urban older persons reside. Fortunately, some physicians, psychiatrists, and related professionals are becoming interested and involved once again in community work, particularly through community mental health centers and outreach programs. Paraprofessionals of all kinds entered the home-care field with the community mental health movement. But overall, nurses and social workers are the most prominent professional home-health workers, and they are likely to be the central coordinating figures in any plans for provision of home care.

Services for older people include basic maintenance services, supportive services, remedial and restorative services, and life-enrichment services. The outline here summarizes the range of services that should be part of a repertoire of home care.

Geriatric assessment
Case management/Care coordination
Mental health intake, screening, and evaluation
Mental health care
Physician's services
Nursing services
Homemaker-home health aides
Physical therapy
Occupational therapy
Speech therapy
Inhalation therapy
Dental care
Nutrition service (Meals-on-Wheels, group dining, food distribution programs)
Health education, including self-care and prevention of illness
Laundry service
Social services
  Information and referral
  Financial support
  Legal services
  Personal needs (transportation, telephone reassurance, letter writing services, bill-paying services, grooming, shopping, companions, friendly visitors, pets)
  Family "respite" services
  Caregiver training
  Night sitters (for short-term illnesses)
  Home safety and other preventive services
  Chore services (handyman) or home maintenance repairs
  Recreation (community center, senior center)
  Employment and volunteer work (VISTA, Senior Aides, SCORE, Peace Corps, Foster Grandparent, Green Thumb, etc.)
  Education (home library service, reader services, academic courses)
Religious support (clerical or pastoral counseling, "practical" ecumenism)
Police assistance

Outpatient care in clinics, community mental health centers, day hospitals, day-care centers
Alzheimer's service centers
Multipurpose senior centers
Protective services
Screening before hospital admission

Many communities will not have all or even most of these resources. Some can be created at little or no cost by volunteer groups; others can be lobbied for in state legislatures. Pressure can be put on professional groups and voluntary agencies to make their services available or to create new services.

Coverage under Medicare and the private insurance programs for older people encourages hospitalization rather than home care. The very poor may be able to obtain home-care services through Medicaid, the state welfare program (some states like New York are much more adequate than others), but self-supporting middle-class people tend not to be able to afford such services. Free care or care based on the ability to pay is sporadically available through charitable agencies and United Way organizations. There has been an increase of limited home-care support under Medicare in the 1980s, particularly after implementation of DRGs.

Six current sources of financial support for home health care services are included in the following list.

1. *Medicare.* Medicare can pay for home health visits only if all of the following four conditions are met: (1) the care needed includes intermittent skilled nursing care, physical therapy, or speech therapy; (2) the person is confined to his or her home; (3) a doctor determines that home health care is needed and sets up a home health plan; and (4) the home health agency providing services is participating in Medicare.

2. *Medicaid.* Medicaid payments depend on what individual states allow. New York state offers particularly comprehensive Medicaid coverage for home care. Overall, however, less than 3% of the

$15 billion in Federal Medicaid expenditures went to home care in 1990. A much higher proportion was used for skilled nursing home care.

3. *Social Services.* Under Title XX (SSA), state funds are available for social services.

4. *Older Americans Act.* Under Title III (OAA), payments are made to states for distribution to local branches of Area Agencies on Aging (AAA). Title VII also provides monies for home-based services.

5. *Veterans Administration.* The VA provides aid and assistance grants for purchase of home health services to families caring for disabled veterans. The VA also furnishes these services directly, usually through a VA hospital.

6. *Internal Revenue Service.* The IRS provides for an exemption under the income tax law for families purchasing medically prescribed home health care for a dependent parent.

The organization and delivery of comprehensive geriatrics to Medicare-only and Medicare-Medicaid beneficiaries are being tested in four social and health maintenance organizations (SHMOs) with about 15,000 enrollees. SHMOs unify health and social services under the direct financial management of a provider of services who carries the risk. The SHMO adds long-term care benefits to the hospital and medical benefits ordinarily provided by health maintenance organizations under capitation arrangements. The SHMO participant pays a monthly premium for a specified dollar amount of home care and nursing services; hospital and medical services are covered entirely by payments from Medicare and Medicaid. The SHMO may add preventive and other benefits as savings allow in the provision of regular Medicare services. Like health maintenance organizations (HMOs), the SHMOs are considered a prepaid health care alternative to the standard fee-for-service Medicare coverage. The four SHMOs are:

- Kaiser Permanente, Portland, OR: *Medicare Plus II*
- Metropolitan Jewish Geriatric Center, Brooklyn, NY: *Elderplan*
- Ebenezer Society–Group Health Inc., Minneapolis, MN: *Seniors Plus*
- Senior Care Action Network, Long Beach, CA: *SCAN Health Plan (SHP)*

USE OF THE HOME FOR SCREENING AND EVALUATION

Ideally, older people would be kept at home even after a request or referral for mental health services is made. Part or all of the evaluation could be done at home, except for technical (usually medical) examinations that require a specific setting. Even when most of an evaluation must be carried out elsewhere, it is important that a direct evaluation of the person's home situation be made.

In planning a program of home care, one must be clear about the objectives, whether rehabilitation, maintenance of the status quo, or support during decline and eventual death. Older people themselves should voice their opinions about the kind of mental health and physical care they want. Change is the most constant factor in the treatment of older persons. Treatment must be constantly evaluated for its appropriateness and be altered whenever circumstances change in the direction of either improved functioning or greater illness. It can be as harmful to overtreat someone who is struggling to recover as it is to undertreat someone who truly needs help. Dependency and loss of functioning can result if people of any age are overprotected and coddled when they do not need it. Deterioration and complications can result when care is not adequate.

After an evaluation of the specific nature of a person's problem has been completed (Chapter 9 describes the process of evaluation in detail), a mutually agreeable decision must be made among family members, the older person, and mental health personnel as to the nature and location of treatment. Does mental health care include such diverse services as provision of adequate income, homemakers, or even podiatry (foot treatment)? A comprehensive, broad concept of care includes whatever has to be done. The goal is to attempt to preserve any aspects of the older person's life that contribute to his or her physical and emotional well-being.

THE ROLE OF GERIATRIC ASSESSMENT AND CARE COORDINATION

Geriatric assessment is a multidisciplinary team approach, used far less in the United States than in various other countries, that employs combinations of physicians, nurses, social workers, psychologists, and others in an evaluation of an elderly patient by his or her capacity to function rather than by assessment of specific body organs, body systems, and diseases. Such an evaluation discovers and explains the older person's multiple problems, resources, strengths, and need for services. Once this is done, a coordinated care plan is developed, focusing on possible interventions. In addition, the geriatric assessment may identify problem areas requiring more detailed evaluation by other medical and nonmedical professionals such as clinical psychologists, dentists, nutritionists, or podiatrists.

This assessment process alerts mental health staff to an elderly person's true ability to function independently in the community. It also informs them about certain nonmedical needs of the patient, such as Medicaid eligibility, respite care for their caregivers, and Meals-on-Wheels.

Many inpatient studies have shown how effective this interdisciplinary approach can be. The Veterans Administration Hospital, for example, has seen reduced hospital stays, reduced readmissions, and lower mortality and morbidity rates. Team-oriented outpatient assessment was found to facilitate the delivery of high-quality care to the elderly and even possibly to decrease health care costs by supporting the elderly's functional capacity.[18]

A number of recent efforts have been made to establish methods for comprehensive evaluation of older persons prior to admission into any program—institutional or noninstitutional—with the ultimate goal of helping to keep them at home. In contrast to other societies, the United States has been slow in developing such a technique. For example, 75% of Australian elderly have access to geriatric assessment, compared to perhaps 10% of U.S. elderly.

Case management is another relatively new concept in the care of older persons. (In our experience, many older people don't like the term *case management.* They do not wish to think of themselves as "cases," nor do they like to be "managed." A better term might be *service coordination* or, when both coordination and psychotherapy are combined, as is often the case with social workers, *care coordination* might describe the role.) To obtain all the needed services for a client, a care coordinator acts as the link between client and affordable health and social service providers, such as home health care agencies or adult day-care centers. Care coordinators can be social workers, nurses, psychologists, or other geriatric specialists. A care coordinator conducts a comprehensive needs assessment, develops an overall care plan, coordinates and monitors the delivery of services, and frequently does reassessments. The hallmark of care coordination is "to hold one person responsible for overcoming fragmentation in the service delivery system." Social work care coordination also adds a clinical, social case-work or counseling approach for dealing with emotional problems surrounding illness and disability.[19] (Roberta Greene provides a comprehensive discussion of care coordination from a social work perspective.[20])

One governmental study, the Long-Term Channeling Demonstration program, attempted to document the value of assessment and care coordination.[21] Although no savings were demonstrated, the results indicated that there was a higher degree of life satisfaction for patients and families with care coordination and an integration of services. Over the past 10 years, approximately 600 for-profit care coordination agencies have developed. They essentially act as surrogates for children or other relatives who may lack the skills, time, geographic proximity, or emotional capacity to provide the services an older person needs.

One especially troublesome situation adult children confront is handling the needs of parents or other relatives in a distant location. Aging Network Services, one of the country's leading care-coordination referral services, has ties to 250 private-practice geriatric social workers nationwide who find suitable paraprofessionals for the elderly and are also available for future consultation.[22]

As an example of care coordination, the "Living at Home Program" took place at 20 sites throughout the United States from 1986 to 1989 and was supported by 39 foundations, including the Commonwealth Fund (of which Dr. Robert N. Butler was the advisory committee chairman) and the Pew Memorial Trust. The program explored ways to help people remain at home for as long as possible. Hoping to make a significant improvement in the quality of life for a substantial number of older people, the program provided each elderly person with a broad range of services. These were coordinated through a care coordinator skilled both in understanding the unique needs of each elderly individual, and in securing the necessary services. What differentiated this program is that the care coordinator developed, orchestrated, assessed, and ensured the satisfactory provision of each individually tailored set of services (medical, financial, legal, and social) from *multiple* participating agencies, including volunteer services, not just a single agency. Many of the original 20 sites in the program are continuing to operate under new funding provided by a variety of sources, giving hope to the idea that through care coordination, many existing community programs can be well utilized.

Private care coordination can be expensive and, unfortunately, is not covered by Medicare, Medicaid, or private insurance. The first assessment (including a home visit, a meeting with the physician and relatives, and a written care plan) ranges from $100 to $300 in 1996; continuing consultation can cost anywhere from $40 to $150 an hour. Religious charities, hospitals, and other nonprofit organizations also provide care-coordination services, usually at a lower cost; however, staffers tend to have more than twice the number of elderly in their caseloads.

Since care coordination is generally unregulated, one should check credentials and references carefully when looking into such services. At minimum, care coordinators should have a master's degree in either social work or another human-services area, as well as geriatric experience.[23]

HOME DELIVERY OF SERVICES

All the services mentioned in this chapter are considered by us as part of mental health care. In addition, the specific services of psychiatrists, social workers, and all other members of mental health teams should be routinely available in people's homes. The two major types of psychiatric outreach care are emergency care (usually for persons making suicide threats and attempts or for those wandering in the streets as a result of brain damage or functional psychosis) and ongoing therapy for those who find it difficult to leave home. Evaluations for mental health services as well as screening for institutional admissions can be done in homes.[24] Screening should, of course, emphasize keeping people out of institutions, when appropriate, by use of community and home care. Mental health services are discussed more fully in Chapter 12. With outreach services one sees many people who would never appear at clinics and would only be seen in hospitals as a result of an emergency. A discussion of specific home delivery of health, mental health, and social support services follows.

Physicians' Services

Physicians should be on call for emergency home visits on a 24-hour basis and for ongoing medical evaluation and management of patients. Contact may vary from brief intensive care to weekly or monthly medical supervision and treatment. Laboratory services can also be provided. Specimens—blood, urine, feces, and so on—can be obtained from the person at home and analyzed in the laboratory. Electrocardiograms and other selected studies can be made in the home.

There are two major problems standing in the way of home medical care: doctors' reluctance to make house calls and a lack of financial resources that might make it possible to overcome this reluctance by offering incentives. In most cases doctors believe they can treat a patient better in an office or in a hospital emergency room and that the house calls take too much time. "It is rare that a house call is justified" is a common viewpoint. But doctors who do make house calls provide an enormous sense of security for the older person who may be worried about health or unable to leave home for care of aggravating but noncritical illnesses.

Mrs. H, a woman of 85 years, lives in a public housing project with her daughter's family. She is confined to her second-floor room because of arthritis and a disabled hip. She seldom sees a doctor because her son-in-law has a heart condition that prohibits him from carrying her down the stairs. In addition, her daughter must take off a day's work to transport her in the family car. Mrs. H does not want to put an extra burden on them, so she seldom mentions her aches and pains. She wept with disbelief and happiness at the sight of the physician from the neighborhood community mental health service who came to see her in her room.

Doctors are not well-distributed geographically. Some areas—especially poor urban areas and many rural areas—typically have few doctors and other health personnel. In Washington, D.C., a predominantly African American city, 90% of doctors are located west of Rock Creek Park, which essentially divides white (west) from black Washington, where some 60% of the African American population lives.

Specialization by doctors is another problem for older people. Older people frequently look in vain for a "family doctor." Although there has been insufficient congressional emphasis on geriatrics, in the 1970s congressional legislation aimed at encouraging doctors to enter family practice. Geriatric medicine has not been recognized as a practice specialty in the United States, although 40% of internists' patients are older peo-

ple with whom they spend 60% of their time. In spite of the fact that older people are medically underserved, a 1980 report by the Graduate Medical Education National Advisory Committee (GMENAC), concerned about a possible oversupply of physicians, failed to consider the impact of the growing number of older people and the consequent growing need for geriatricians. Others have recognized that physicians in nearly all specialties need special training in geriatric medicine, in addition to their regular training; this would open up a whole new area of expertise as well as a new clientele.[25]

Although there has been insufficient congressional emphasis on geriatrics, in 1986 Congress established the Institute of Medicine Committee, which investigated the supply and demand for academic geriatricians. In addition, they evaluated potential strategies for bringing academic training capacity to needed levels.[26] In 1988, for the first time, the American Board of Internal Medicine and the American Academy of Family Practice gave examinations for added competence in geriatrics. The American Board of Neurology and Psychiatry also agreed to offer examinations for special competence in geriatric psychiatry. Postgraduate training (fellowships) in geriatrics must include geriatric psychiatry, especially psychopathology, mental status testing, and psychopharmacology.

Nursing Services

The services included under home nursing care are those of *registered nurses* (RNs), whose two specialties pertinent to older persons are public health nursing and psychiatric nursing; *licensed practical nurses* (LPNs); and *home health aides*. Registered nurses are qualified to assess patients, develop a care plan, and carry out skilled nursing functions. LPNs and home health aides are supervised by registered nurses.

We shall attempt to clarify the work of each of these groups as they care for older persons. *Public health nurses* are RNs, and sometimes LPNs, who work for tax-supported city or county health departments. They visit families in their homes, provide direct nursing care, give health guidance, participate in communicable disease control programs, and staff public health clinics. They may give emergency care as well as care for acute and chronic illness. Public health nurses can instruct people in the use of community health and social resources and make authorized investigations of convalescent homes, nursing homes, and other institutions. Referrals usually come from public health clinics or city and county hospitals as well as other public agencies. There is a heavy concentration of poor and inner-city people as clientele. Services are free of charge to those eligible.

The over 400 Visiting Nurse Associations are among the 15,000 home care agencies throughout the country. They are freestanding, nonprofit organizations governed by a community board of directors, or divisions of large national nonprofit organizations such as the United Way. Part of their mission is to take care of everyone regardless of their ability to pay. They are financed by tax-deductible contributions and earnings. Like the large proprietary national home care chains, they offer a full range of home care services and categories of employees. During this time of significant change in the industry, many Visiting Nurse Associations are being bought up by hospital-based systems. For example, Michigan used to have twelve Visiting Nurse Associations—now there are only two.

Visiting nurses provide almost the same services as public health nurses but tend to have smaller caseloads and can devote more time to individual patients. Public health nurses may each have several hundred patients as well as responsibilities in clinics and schools. In some communities, visiting nurses and public health nurses have merged their staffs and functions, while in others they work separately. Both groups wear similar blue uniforms, and community familiarity with these uniforms gives them protection as they work in high crime neighborhoods. Visiting nurses try to go into such areas unless deemed extremely unsafe. Escorts are often hired and if night visits are required, security personnel ac-

company them. Public health nurses are accompanied by other health care workers whenever safety is in question.

Visiting nurses do more direct home nursing, while public health nurses carry an added responsibility for preventive and community work. Referrals to visiting nurses come from private doctors and private hospitals and are initiated by patients themselves or their families or are made by overloaded public health nurses. Visiting nurses care for both poor and middle-class patients. Older people are required to pay a fee adjustable to their income or may be eligible for free service through one of the organizations contracting with the VNA and the third-party payments of Medicare and Medicaid.

Licensed practical nurses work under the supervision of RNs and perform many of the same nursing skills. *Home health aides* also provide simple nursing care, which will be discussed later. For those who can afford very expensive services, a number of agencies supply *private duty RNs, LPNs,* and *nurses aides* for up to 24-hour total nursing care.[27]

Home nursing services enable older people to leave hospitals sooner and keep them at home longer before institutionalization. Some of the common ailments for which persons are treated are strokes, cerebrovascular accidents, arthritis, cancer, hip fractures, paraplegia, and minimal to moderate dementia. Teaching a procedure, such as self-administration of insulin for diabetes, is another nursing function. Family members can be taught to do a variety of tasks, including physical therapy. Helping the patient with problems of incontinence, bedsores, care of teeth and mouth, bathing and skin care, grooming, and feeding are other tasks of nursing personnel. Home nurses are also trained to look at the patient's family from a life-cycle perspective: If there are grandchildren, are they immunized? Is the daughter-in-law (for example) receiving prenatal care if she is pregnant? What can be done about the son's chest pains? All this is in addition to the original reason for the visit, which was to serve the older patient.

Social Work Services

Earlier we discussed the multiple roles of social workers as community workers, members of geriatric assessment teams, care coordinators, hospital discharge planners, agency intake workers and caseworkers, and the like.[28] They also are responsible for much of the planning and coordination of the social services to be described next.

Home Health Aides and Homemakers/Home Care Aides

The responsibilities of home health aides can differ from state to state, depending on nurse practice laws. Nurses delegate to home health aides, so the nurse's license covers the home health aides working under her supervision. Home health aides are defined as those who provide physical care to patients at home. They work under a medically supervised plan of care to assist the client and family with household management and personal care such as bathing, dressing, and toileting. They can help with assistive devices and respond to appropriate client instructions consistent with their training. In addition, they can assist with nonsterile wound care, self-administered medications, simple procedures, and prescribed exercises.

Homemakers, or *home care aides,* as the National Association for Home Care has renamed them, are defined as those who provide housekeeping services. They assist with environmental services such as laundry, cleaning, shopping, and meal preparation in order to maintain a safe, sanitary, and healthy home environment.

Home health aide services are covered by Medicare, whereas homemaker services generally are not covered, unless they are directly related to required and approved medical care. The home health care benefit under Medicare Part A includes intermittent skilled nursing care, home health aide services, physical therapy, speech therapy, and occupational therapy. While there are no deductibles, co-insurance payments, or limits on the number of visits under the home health care

benefit, only 80% of the approved cost of durable medical equipment is covered.

Home health aides and homemakers/home care aides are always employed by an agency, organization, or administrative unit which selects, trains, and supervises them. Olsten Kimberly Quality Care and Interim Health Care are examples of such agencies. Referrals to home care agencies may be obtained from physicians, nurses, social workers, and health institutions. According to the National Association of Home Care, in 1995 there were approximately 17,561 home care agencies in the U.S. Of these, 8,747 are Medicare-certified home care agencies, 1,795 are Medicare-certified hospices, and 7,019 are home health agencies, home care aide organizations, and hospices that do not participate in Medicare.[29] For Medicare-certified agencies, there are 12 federal conditions of participation, which include aide training requirements. If the government cites an agency for violating one of these 12 conditions, the agency can lose its ability to train home health aides. Private agencies have no government regulations, but they can choose to be approved by the Community Health Accreditation Program (CHAP) of the Joint Commission on Accreditation of Healthcare Organizations (JCAHO).

According to Cindy Stonerock, editor of the *Home Health Aide Digest,* hospital-based and proprietary agencies are growing faster than any other type of agency. Proprietary agencies now comprise 40% and hospital-based agencies about one-quarter of all certified agencies. One-third of home care agencies are located in six states: California, Florida, Illinois, New York, Pennsylvania, and Texas.

Payment sources for home care include private insurance, Medicare, Medicaid, Older Americans Act, Social Services Block Grants, Workers Compensation, the Veterans Administration, health maintenance organizations, CHAMPUS, social services organizations, and private payments. Some agencies offer a sliding scale so a family need pay only what it can afford.

The U.S. Department of Labor indicates that positions for homemakers/home care aides will increase from 179,000 in 1994 to 391,000 in 2005. Positions for home health aides are expected to rise from 420,000 in 1994 to 848,000 in 2005. Despite these upward trends, many communities across the nation are without home health aide and home-maker services. Furthermore, home-care workers are too often undertrained and underpaid, according to the Home Care Aide Association of America. Minimal wages, a lack of health benefits, and limited options for career path development contribute to high turnover rates among home-care workers even as the demands for home-care services keep growing.

Physical, Massage, Occupational, and Speech Therapies

Occupational, physical, and speech therapies are partly reimbursable under Medicare, but severe restrictions limit their use. Thus patients may receive a great deal of rehabilitative work in hospitals following bone and joint diseases and strokes, but the investment is lost because home-care follow-up is not given. Massage therapy is seldom reimbursed.

Physical Therapy.   Physical therapy is a critical piece of both rehabilitation and prevention of decline in older persons. Many persons with neuromusculoskeletal problems can benefit from an individually prescribed program of physical therapy. Common problems are paralysis, weakness or pain affecting the musculoskeletal system, cardiovascular accidents, arthritis, degenerative brain conditions, and trauma. Stroke patients and fracture patients of all kinds, especially, should be seen as soon as possible by a physical therapist to increase the possibility of recovery. Patients debilitated after long bouts of illness are also prime candidates for physical therapy.

The physical therapist should be responsible for providing and teaching the use of any equipment and appliances necessary for rehabilitation, in addition to the actual provision of therapy. Physical exercise on a daily basis should be introduced, following an appropriate medical evaluation, if the older person does not exercise regularly. Two

kinds of exercise are usually indicated: one to keep the body and its muscles and joints limber and the other to increase the endurance and capacity of the cardiovascular system.

Physical therapists are licensed in every state, and their services are generally available in all hospitals, rehabilitation centers, nursing homes, home-care agencies, and physical therapy private practice offices.[30]

Massage Therapy.   As an adjunct to physical therapy, massage, one of the oldest forms of healing, is beneficial in later life. In China, it has been used since the Han dynasty, about 200 B.C., for relief of pain and chills, and Hippocrates recognized its positive effect on muscles and joints. Massage may hasten and improve the convalescent periods after illness or surgery. It may be used to enhance vitality, relax muscle tension, improve circulation, reduce edema and induration, and stretch adhesions from surgery. It is especially beneficial for bed-ridden patients, since it helps maintain circulation and muscle tone. Massage has psychological value in providing "touching" from one person to another, conveying essential feelings of caring and belonging. We believe that the healing and comforting quality of touch may make massage the physiological equivalent to psychotherapy. It can be taught to spouses and other family members of the older person.

The United States is the only developed country that does not consider massage an official part of its health care system. In fact, it is also the only country in the world where people mistake the word "massage" as synonymous with illicit sexual activity. Fortunately, this image is being replaced with a more positive one. Membership in the American Massage Therapy Association has increased five-fold between 1985 and 1996, from 5,000 to 25,000. In addition, the number of AMTA-accredited schools grew from 32 approved schools (actual accrediting began in the 1990s) to 65 in the same 11 year period.

Since only 25 states require that massage therapists be licensed, it is important that consumers check the credentials of any therapist they may be considering, namely whether and where the therapist attended school and the number of hours of instruction received. If the school is registered with the American Massage Therapy Association, 820 Davis St., Suite 100, Evanston, IL 60201-4444, (773) 761-2682, it is a good indicator that the therapist is legitimate; not all schools are registered with the AMTA, but those that are must require a minimum of 500 hours of instruction. Basic training must be in Swedish massage, which involves heavy strokes toward the heart. However, many massage therapists also incorporate acupressure, or *shiatsu* (pressure massage on acupuncture points) and reflexology (massage of acupuncture points on the foot) with basic Swedish techniques. The Feldenkrais method of body therapy includes gentle manipulation of the limbs with the aim of realignment of the skeletal system. The Alexander method focuses on alignment of the head, neck, and shoulders. More controversial techniques include polarity therapy (described as a "balancing of energy systems") and Rolfing (a probing, "deep tissue" treatment to purge long-held emotional tensions).

Occupational Therapy. Occupational therapy (O.T.) is often stereotyped as "arts and crafts" or is considered infantilizing or paternalistic. This is unfortunate. Properly prescribed O.T. is of great value in maintaining or restoring self-mastery. According to the Occupational Therapy Association, occupational therapy is concerned with a person's ability and capacity to perform tasks of daily living that enable the person to be productive and maintain a satisfying life. Through the use of activities, selected according to the patient's abilities and health needs, the occupational therapist evaluates the individual's capacities related to psychological and social functioning, motor and sensory integrative functioning, and cognitive and performance abilities. Occupational therapists seek to teach, restore, and maintain the occupational performance skills, behaviors, and attitudes crucial to independent and healthy functioning. Home and daily family role demands,

work and play needs, and social or community factors that impede or contribute to health form the primary perspective of occupational therapy practice.

At its best, O.T. is geared toward helping the individual improve functioning in any way possible, as defined by the person, the family, and the therapist. This can be done through any form of therapeutic activity that encourages self-expression and use of those resources available to the individual. For example, one occupational therapist used the "life review" concept in her O.T. group program to encourage older people to examine their lives in a constructive way.[31]

Speech Therapy. Many speech-language disorders accompany medical conditions, such as Parkinson's disease and Alzheimer's disease, commonly found in older persons. Since communication impairment can interfere with an older person's daily functioning, independence, and self-maintenance, and possibly lead to decreased interactions with others, making the older person feel isolated, the assistance of a speech therapist (or speech-language pathologist) may become necessary. Speech therapists are trained to diagnose speech, language, and swallowing disorders and provide appropriate treatment, including, when necessary, instruction in how to use speech aids and prosthetic speech devices. It is generally recommended that physicians refer patients directly in order to make certain that a qualified speech-language pathologist is chosen and that services will be reimbursable under government and private insurance plans.[32]

Dental Services

"Visiting dentists" are available in some areas and should be provided for all older people who find it difficult to leave their homes. Dental hygienists may also be willing to make home or nursing home visits. Dentistry is not covered by Medicare, even though it is a critical element of nutrition and general health.

Nutrition Services

Food stamps, governmental supplemental food programs, Meals-on-Wheels, group dining, and homemaker/home health aides who shop for and prepare food are some of the means of combating the hunger and malnutrition found in many older people. The best medical prescription for countless older persons would be a prescription for proper food rather than drugs. Reversible (and ultimately irreversible) brain syndromes can result from malnutrition. It is imperative to examine for evidences of malnutrition and hypovitaminosis even in the affluent, whose eating habits may be poor. Low-income older persons must scrimp on food. Psychological conditions—loneliness, depression, apathy, confusion—can induce malnutrition, which in turn furthers these symptoms. Physical disabilities can keep people from shopping and cooking.

Congress first passed legislation in 1972 for a national program for one nutritiously planned hot meal a day, five days a week, to people over 60 years of age. The meals are served in the form of group dining in schools, churches, synagogues, and community centers and are also delivered to people's homes. The federal government provided 90% matching money, with state and local governments or private nonprofit organizations providing the remaining 10%. Although the measure emphasized that the projects be located in low-income areas, having a low income is not a requirement and there is no eligibility test. According to the Administration on Aging, in 1994 under Title III 127 million meals were served to 2.3 million older persons at congregate facilities, and 113 million meals were delivered to 877,000 home-bound older persons. Under Title VI, which applies to Native American populations, 1.3 million meals were served to 41,000 people in congregate facilities, and 1.5 million meals were delivered to home-bound older Native Americans.

The Food Stamp Act was passed by Congress in 1964 to provide food for needy families. The program is part of the department of Agriculture. Low-income people purchase stamps at less than face value and redeem them for food in standard food stores. Of the more than 20 million registered in 1994, only about 7% were aged 60 and over; however, 16% of food stamp households have at least one member aged 60 and over. This difference is due to the typically small size of elderly households (74% were single person households), and their relatively higher income in comparison to other food-stamp recipient households of equal size.[33] Food stamps can also be used for Meals-on-Wheels, but not for group dining.

Nutritionists are available to consult with referring health care personnel, patients, and families about general food needs, special diets, food preparation, food shopping, and the like. A trained nutritionist can be located through local dietetic associations (in the phone directory) or by calling the national headquarters of the American Dietetic Association ([800] 621-6469). The designation of *licensed dietition* (LD) means the person has met state standards. For states without licensing, the *registered dietition* (RD) is the nearest equivalent. A qualified nutritionist should be able to perform a nutritional assessment that includes physical measurements, dietary analysis, the ordering of appropriate laboratory tests, a treatment plan, diet prescription, and follow-up. Since malnutrition among the elderly can be caused by unnecessary or poorly understood dietary restrictions, follow-up visits are especially important.[34]

Social Services

Social services are services that are not strictly medical or psychiatric, but instead represent economic and social supports. In the past, social service has been synonymous with social work, but this is no longer true. Many other professions have become involved: members of the clergy, police officers, nurses, government officials, volunteers, paraprofessionals, and physicians who are actively working in the community. In home care, however, it is still most often the social worker who works together with nursing personnel to coordinate a program designed for an individual.

Many homemaker/home health aide services are administered by professional social workers. Over 60% of certified home health agencies offer social services.

Information and Referral.   How does the older person find out about social services? Some cities have information and referral services especially for the elderly. If not, local or state commissions or advisory committees on aging may be helpful. Social services, human resources, or welfare departments (the names vary in municipalities and states) usually have information numbers to call. The same is true of local health and welfare councils and local mental health associations. Social Security district and branch offices can provide information. Family Service agencies are another resource.[35]

Some of the agencies and institutions furnishing direct social service to older people are welfare offices, voluntary agencies (the Hearing Aid Society, Societies for the Blind, etc.), public health departments, including community mental health centers, hospitals (both medical and psychiatric), visiting nurse services, nursing homes, employment offices, departments of vocational rehabilitation, religious organizations, and the police.

Financial Support.   Regardless of potential benefits of home care, one must be realistic about whether a person can survive financially. All sources for financial support must be explored for the older person at home, including free or low-cost services and any pensions or financial assistance for which he or she might be eligible. It is not unusual to find older people who do not know they are eligible for Medicare, Medicaid, Supplemental Security Income, Veterans benefits, and even Social Security benefits. Federal tax laws no longer allow a double income tax exemption for people over 65 years of age and two double exemptions for a married couple. For the blind, an exemption is allowable.

For homeowners, it is important to understand the upkeep and property tax situation. Many older homeowners face financial crises and may be forced to sell their homes. (Those seniors who own their own homes may consider a home equity conversion loan, which allows them to use the equity they have built up in their homes to help them pay for long-term care.) Older renters often experience substantial rent increases, partly necessitated by property tax increases. Energy costs in the late 1970s and early 1980s spiraled, and many older persons were forced to cut back on heat, air conditioning, light, and other energy expenses. One effect was an increase in accidental hypothermia—lowering of body temperature to such an extent that coma and even death can result. Older people are particularly susceptible to temperature changes because their bodies no longer regulate temperature as well as they did in the past.[36]

For the very poor, welfare is usually the last resort. Supplemental Security Income (SSI) is not enough for decent subsistence, and 50% or more of especially poor older persons do not receive SSI. They may not be eligible (SSI is a state-federal program), or they may not be registered even if they are eligible. Money for food must often be sacrificed for medical care and medical supplies as well as other crucial living expenses. Clothing is not a part of many welfare budgets; neither are household articles and furniture.

Personal Needs (Companions, Pets, Telephones, Shopping, Transportation, Grooming, etc.). Older persons may need live-in or part-time companions, help with shopping and transportation, instructions or direct help with grooming (home visits from beauticians and barbers can do wonders for mental health), and appliances and aides to support or compensate for various disabilities (special handles near toilet and tub, wheelchairs, wide door frames, etc.).

A telephone can mean a longer life. The National Innovations Center of London, England, reported in 1972 that people without a phone had significantly higher mortality. In increasing numbers of urban, suburban, and rural areas, telephone reassurance services have been established under the auspices of private and public agencies. Volunteers often work the phones and check to see if older people living alone are all right. "Hot lines" are for emergencies. "Warm lines" are to offer comfort and support. Special telephones are available for the hard-of-hearing. "Memory" telephones allow a phone to be programmed with a dozen or so most-used phone numbers so an older person can simply push one button per call rather than dialing seven digits.

Given the state of loneliness and isolation affecting significant numbers of older people, pets can contribute directly to mental wellbeing.[37] Dogs and cats are the most favored pets, in that order. For the older person, a dog may have the added advantage of providing some protection. Size, the need for exercise, and economy are three key points in selection. A large dog requires a daily walk and eats a great deal. On the other hand, a small dog like a poodle can be expensive to maintain because of necessary grooming every six weeks to avoid skin problems, sore feet, and eye problems. Poodles and certain other dogs have the advantage of not shedding, helpful to allergic persons and to housekeeping. One can acquire a dog from the Humane Society or an animal shelter free or at a modest cost, depending on locale. A female dog is usually more tractable. The bark of a dog may fend off an intruder. In England one can get house insurance at lower premiums if one owns a dog, and in the United States a dog is tax deductible if obtained *after* a robbery. Although the majority of older persons are homeowners, and can make independent decisions regarding their desire for pets, older persons in rental housing may be limited as to the size and type of pet they can have, and many landlords forbid pet ownership altogether.

Cats are easier to train than dogs and cost less to maintain. Birds bring pleasure to many older people. Canaries, finches, and parakeets are especially popular. Perhaps the easiest, least expensive, and least time-consuming pets to care for are fish. Plants sometimes fulfill the role of pets in the lives of many older people.

Experimental programs like "Pets on Wheels" bring pets to nursing homes during the day through the use of volunteers. The A.S.P.C.A. in New York City has a program of placing homeless pets with older persons who want pets. A new idea is the provision of "pet day care" by elderly persons at home who will care for working families' pets during the day for a small fee. *Pets and the Elderly* is a "how to" book extolling the positive effects of pets.[38]

Family Respite Services. Although home care may be the treatment of choice for most older persons, it can place such a strain on other family members in the household that care is undermined and the family's own mental health compromised. Any program of care must therefore consider regular social supports to the families themselves.

"Respite" services (more available in England than here) are a great relief to families and can make it possible for the generations to live together under even stressful circumstances. Such respite includes sending someone to care for the older person at home so the family can take holidays, weekends, and vacations by themselves. At times of particular stress, or when the older person needs more attention, it should be possible to admit the individual briefly to an institution to give the family a chance to rest and recover. This also helps to acquaint the older person with institutional life and reduces the symbolic and real associations of institutions as places of no return. Day and night sitters should be available when the family wants to go out or when the older person requires inordinate attention at night, exhausting family members. Home appliances and aids— wheelchairs, special handles and bars to assist walking, or anything else that alleviates undue dependency or physical stress on the family—can make care easier. The availability of psychiatric, medical, and social assistance on an emergency or routine basis can provide significant relief to a family.

Caregiver Training and Support. Caregiver support groups and training programs (such as employee assistance programs in corporations and nonprofit institutions) have begun to help families cope with the often-present stress resulting from caregiving. Such groups and programs are designed to teach care-giving techniques that not only ease caregivers' anxieties and mental and physical strain, but also benefit the care recipients. (See Corporate Sector Efforts, at the end of this chapter). An updated state-by-state listing of more than 750 self-help groups in 49 states, called *Caregiver Support Groups in America,* is available from the National Council on Aging.[39] Hospitals have begun to provide information, training, and support to both employees and families of patients.[40] The National Alzheimer's Disease Association has one of the most advanced programs for supporting and educating caregivers through its nationwide network of groups and programs for families. Research directions for treatment of Alzheimer's disease and family stress have been developed under the direction of the National Institute of Mental Health in 1989.[41]

We learned of several unique caregiver techniques used in a Japanese day treatment center for Alzheimer's patients[42]: The first involved use of one-way mirrors in order that Japanese family members could observe their elderly relative interact in the center. This was found to be very reassuring to families as they frequently saw their older family member showing more responsiveness than was seen at home. It also allowed them to compare notes with center staff about home versus center behavior. The second technique was a "patient notebook" in which the family wrote observations during the patient's evening hours at home and the center staff wrote comments in the same notebook during the day. This process of writing notes back and forth to each other greatly enhanced communication between family and staff and provided valuable information and a sense of collegial support for both.

Home Safety.   Accidents both in and out of the home are an area of legitimate concern. Studies show that 30 to 60% of individuals age 65 and over will experience at least one fall in a given year.[43] Among older people, accidents are the seventh leading cause of death, claiming 27,784 vic-

tims in 1993. Although they make up only 13% of the population, in 1993 30.7% of all accidental deaths happened to people age 65 and older.[44] Accidents that do not result in death can have permanent physical and emotional repercussions and may end the older person's independence of movement. A fall may so seriously undermine self-confidence that mobility is curtailed.

Falls lead as the cause of accidental injuries and deaths.[45] There is a dramatic upsurge of falls for those over 75. To get an idea of the impact of falls leading to hospitalization and nursing home admissions, consider the following:

1. People over 60 make up almost one-fourth of all hospital admissions for injuries due to falls.
2. Even more significantly, the group just described is responsible for over 80% of all hospital stays for falls. Older people also require longer periods to recover than younger people.
3. Forty percent of all older people admitted to hospitals with hip fractures die within one year; another 25% have mobility limitations.
4. Hip fractures alone are responsible for the admission of 4.4% of all nursing home residents.
5. Another 3.6% of nursing home admissions are the result of bone fractures other than hip fractures.
6. Repeated falls or immobility account for up to one-third of all nursing home admissions.
7. The median length of stay in a nursing home for a hip fracture is 85 days. One-third of hip fracture patients stay six months or more. About one-fourth never leave until their death.

Most falls occur in the home. Losses in muscle strength and coordination (often resulting from failure to actively maintain physical conditioning), sense of balance, and speed of reaction are factors. Reduced blood flow and oxygen to the brain can result in dizziness and faintness. Older people should beware of abrupt moves of the head because of changes in the balancing mechanism of the inner ear. Some people suffer "drop attacks"—sudden and unexpected falls without loss of consciousness but with loss of muscle power of body and legs. Drugs, especially sedatives and tranquilizers, may confuse and slow response. For example, phenothiazine medications may cause falls following a drop in blood pressure when standing up (postural hypotension). See Chapter 13 for further details.

The home should be made as safe as possible. Staircases are especially dangerous at the top and bottom steps. Steps should be highly visible and have good illumination, nonskid treads, and handrails. Slippery floor coverings should be eliminated. Linoleum, small mats, and sliding rugs are offenders. Nonskid floor waxes, wall-to-wall carpets or rubber-backed rugs, and tacking are wise. Corrugated shoe soles help. Nonskid mats and grab rails should be used in bathtubs and near toilets and beds. One must also be alert to the disorientation that can follow a move to a new residence.

A 73-year-old carpenter moved to Florida after living in his home for 36 years. He was accustomed to turning to the left from his bedroom door to enter the bathroom. Needing to urinate, he had to get up several times a night. In his new home a stairway was to the left. Several nights after moving, he fell down the stairs and fractured his hip.

Burns, cuts, and poisonings are other hazards. Especially dangerous practices like smoking in bed should be stopped. Room heaters and heating pads must be carefully controlled. Fires can occur when a person is cooking while wearing long sleeves or bed clothes. Medicine bottles must be read with caution; it is recommended that they be read *twice* before medicine is taken and *once* afterward to make certain the medication is correct *and* is being taken at the correct time.

The number of drivers age 65 and older has doubled in the last twenty years to about 13 million. By the year 2020 it is expected to double again.[46] Approximately two-thirds of those 65 and older are licensed to drive, accounting for 12% of all licensed drivers. Interestingly, because they drive less these older drivers have lower accident rates per person than younger drivers. However, both normal physiological changes as-

sociated with aging—losses of visual and auditory acuity, slower reflexes, poor night vision, and arthritic limitations on neck movements—as well as diseases that commonly affect the elderly can affect the ability to drive a car.

The loss of an older person's driver's license and the capacity to drive is often a very touching and powerfully disturbing experience—a blow to self-esteem as well as mobility. It represents not only a major life change for someone who has driven, but a real loss of control. Reuben et al. suggest that the elderly be given a functional assessment based on the skills necessary for driving, conducted either by a simulated or actual road test.[47] A National Research Council study also stresses functional assessment to ensure public safety, but using such an evaluation for all age groups, not for just the elderly. Age alone is a poor predictor of any individual's performance and certainly not sufficient to restrict older drivers' licenses. In addition, in keeping with the reality of an aging society, we must alter the signs and the physical dynamics of streets and highways, such as curves and timing of traffic light changes.

Friendly Visiting and Outside Contact. The world must be brought inside to the bed-ridden and the homebound. Many voluntary organizations, including the Salvation Army, provide friendly visitors programs, through which visits are made to isolated individuals. Studies indicate that such visiting has a positive effect on the mental health of those who must stay in bed or in their homes. Frequent contacts with family, friends, and neighbors help keep emotions responsive and minds interested. Television (including the use of video cassettes), radio, phonographs, and newspapers can be rich sources of enjoyment. Older people have been known to sacrifice food to pay for television repairs because television is so important to them. Some people leave their television on all day ("like a friend in the house") or sleep with it on at night. Large screens are a visual help, and volume can be adjusted for hearing difficulties. Television and radio offer recreation, education, and religious services. One man described watching television as rather like sitting on the park bench and watching the world go by, a continuous nonstop show. Another spoke of the sense of having world events at his fingertips; he had two sets, one on top of the other, which he watched simultaneously. People call or write to broadcasting stations, avidly follow their favorite newscasters and masters of ceremonies, and participate in audience talk and game shows.

Recreation, Education, and Employment. The most broadly accepted definition of therapeutic recreation describes it as a process that utilizes recreation services for purposive intervention in some physical, emotional, or social behavior to bring about a desired change in that behavior and to promote the growth and development of the individual. Recreation specialists use recreation as a medium to assist disabled people to change certain physical, emotional, or social characteristics so they may live their leisure life-styles as well and as independently as possible.[47] Treatment settings include acute care hospitals, physical rehabilitation centers, prisons, skilled care facilities, mental health centers, and the community.[48]

For those who can leave their homes, senior centers and community centers may offer a variety of possibilities. Increasing numbers of senior centers no longer simply supply recreation; they now also provide a range of social and health services.[49] A number of centers offer some kind of health education in addition to direct medical services, which include professional clinics, screening programs, immunizations, and physical examinations. They may have activities a few hours each week or may be open all day, five days a week. Shows, parties, music, beauty salon appointments, handicrafts, candle making, cooking, flower arranging, trips, discussion groups (also group therapy), games, television watching, walks, group shopping trips, and special programs for the blind are some of the activities in a well-functioning center. Some centers even offer vacations.

Continuing their education is an interest expressed by many older people. Some communities

offer home library services. Inexpensive or free correspondence courses should be offered by high schools and colleges, and older people could be encouraged to enroll in regular academic classes if scholarships and low fees were possible. For example, Vartan Gregorian as president of Brown University suggested that graduates be allowed to return to Brown, free of charge, to take courses throughout their lives. Elementary and junior and senior high schools located in communities where older people live could remain open after the regular class day and provide recreation, education, and food service.

Colleges could furnish curricula especially designed for older people; some are already doing this. In the summer of 1975, five New Hampshire colleges, in a small pilot project, opened their campuses to "hostelers" of retirement age. The result was the Elderhostel program, now found at about 2,000 colleges, universities, and other institutions which offer their classrooms, dormitories, and staff for week-long programs to people age 55 and older.[51] Older people can take a wide variety of courses, live in dormitories on campus, and generally enjoy student life at reasonable costs during the off-seasons of vacation time and summers. In 1981, the first foreign programs were offered—16 in Great Britain and four in Scandinavia—arranged in connection with partner organizations abroad. Today the Elderhostel program has expanded to over 70 different countries. In 1995, 295,000 older persons took courses through the program.

The New School for Social Research's program called the Institute for Retired Professionals of New York City draws professionals and community leaders into study programs that are administered and taught by older persons.

About one-third of the 3,000 colleges and universities in the United States (a 10% increase since 1970) are now offering some kind of continuing education aimed at those over 25. The returning adult is welcomed at a time when college enrollments of younger students are slipping. Many of the returnees are middle-aged women reentering the job market. But increasingly, as it has become clear how eager older people are to continue their education, schools have begun to encourage elderly students as well. The American Association of State Colleges and Universities sees universities developing into "three-tiered" institutions, serving the traditional student, the middle-aged student, and retirees.

In their book, *You Are Never Too Old to Learn,* Cross and Florio report on a survey taken by the Academy for Educational Development.[52] Program directors at several hundred colleges and universities with large numbers of older students were asked to identify the most popular subjects with these students. The nine most popular subjects were history, psychology, health, foreign languages, literature, painting, creative writing, religion, and needlework. Philosophy, preretirement planning, and physical fitness were tied for tenth place.[53]

Employment and volunteer work allow older persons to supplement their incomes and involve them in absorbing activities that benefit them and the community. In Bethesda, Maryland, the Over 60 Counseling and Employment Service of the Montgomery County Federation of Women's Clubs, Inc. developed a program that provides job opportunities for older men and women—acting as companions for other older persons, caring for children, doing yard work and carpentry, and so on. Other scattered programs have trained unskilled older persons as family aides. The Retired Senior Volunteer Program (RSVP),[54] the Foster Grandparents Program and the Senior Companions Program are now divisions of the National Senior Service Corps which, together with AmeriCorps*VISTA (Volunteers in Service to America), forms the federally funded Corporation for National Service. Senior Aids, Service Corps of Retired Executives Association (SCORE), The Peace Corps, Green Thumb, Mature-Temps, and other employment and volunteer programs are also designed for, or accommodate, older persons.

Those with handicaps must be given every opportunity to take part in such activities. Section 504 of the 1973 Rehabilitation Act states:

No otherwise qualified handicapped individual in the United States . . . shall, solely by reason of his handicap, be excluded from the participation in, be denied the benefits of, or be subjected to discrimination under any program or activity receiving Federal financial assistance.

The purpose of the Act was to ensure that federally funded programs and activities were accessible to handicapped persons. The objectives are to ensure equal opportunity, equal access, and equally effective services and treatment for handicapped individuals.

In 1990, the Americans with Disabilities Act was passed, extending the above concept throughout the public and private sectors; even businesses or agencies that do not receive federal funds are required to comply. Called the most sweeping civil rights act in two decades, the bill bars employment discrimination against people with physical or mental disabilities, requires access to public buildings, telephone service, mass transportation, and government services for the millions of Americans with disabilities.

Religious Support

Members of the clergy of all faiths are involved in the care of older people. Some concentrate only on spiritual aspects, while increasing numbers of others become directly involved in social services, counseling, and other secular activities. Many older people are deeply religious, and members of the clergy can become an integral part in planning and providing for their care. The clergy has traditionally formed one of the few professional disciplines whose members are specifically trained to care for the dying. Home visiting with the sick and infirm is also common practice, and members of the clergy are an important source of referral to other health professionals for medical and psychiatric problems.

Religious groups have for centuries given special attention to older people. Some of the best, as well as worst, examples of homes for the aged and old-age-oriented community activities can be found under their auspices. But the need to maintain doctrinal differences has led to fragmentation of services. Each denomination builds its own little island of concern, isolated from everything else. A "practical ecumenism" could allow churches and synagogues to protect their identities yet pool their resources in a planned effort to help older persons.[55] For example, buying necessary supplies together for homes for the aged could sharply cut costs. Pooling skilled personnel would increase the range of services each home could give. Cooperative planning of vital community programs such as Meals-on-Wheels[56] and friendly visitors could reach many more people, with the churches of all denominations acting as neighborhood bases for all older persons, regardless of denomination. A national church program including all denominations could register all eligible older people for health programs, coordinate food programs, provide friendly visitors and telephone reassurance, set up information and referral services nationally, help coordinate home-care programs, and much more. Members of the clergy could receive special training for work with older persons. Religious groups should use their power and influence for improvement of older people's economic and social conditions.

Home Hospice Services

Home hospice care has become an important part of the hospice movement in the United States. Patients are considered for such care during the last days of their lives if no treatment will significantly alter the disease, and the desire is to make the patient as comfortable as possible at home. In 1982 financing for hospice care was included under Title 18 of the Social Security Act. Home nursing, psychological counseling, nutritional evaluation, home support services, and a number of other services may be available, as well as bereavement counseling for family members. Usually home care is monitored by a home health care team connected with a hospital. The patient may be readmitted to the hospital for the last 24 to 36 hours of life. Both patients and their families generally agree that such care enhances the quality of life remaining, compared to more traditional hospital care.

New Housing Arrangements

Although the vast majority of older persons continue to live in private single family houses or apartments, many must seek alternatives when independent living becomes difficult or undesirable. In addition, federal rent subsidies and support of new housing has fallen dramatically, making independent living more difficult for those on fixed incomes. Fortunately, the available continuum of alternatives to nursing homes is exploding. Assisted living and other types of supportive and alternative housing are expanding, largely as a result of private market forces.

Assisted Living. *Assisted living* is generally defined as a residential program that also provides or arranges supportive and recreational services including meals and health care, in addition to around-the-clock monitoring and assistance for those who need help with activities of daily living (ADLs). This broad definition includes a variety of programs that fall between individual homes and institutional programs, such as nursing programs, under a variety of names, due partly to individual state regulations and definitions.

Programs that offer assisted living are not new; however, this option has become more popular with the recognition of the fact that many older people need help with activities of daily living, but do not need skilled nursing care and therefore can maintain a higher level of independence. Also, pressure to diminish Medicaid expenditures on nursing facilities has increased support of assisted living programs, which are primarily paid for privately. Oregon, by using Medicaid to fund services and Supplemental Security Income to cover housing costs, has implemented a model program that makes assisted living available to low-income people who would otherwise be in nursing homes at a much higher cost.

The philosophy of assisted living also implies service that is, according to the American Association of Homes and Services for the Aged, "consumer-driven, flexible, individualized and maximizes consumer independence and dignity."[57] It is also implied that the atmosphere in assisted living facilities will be "home-like."[58] The degree to which independence and comfort is maintained, however, varies by facility and state.

Although there are no reliable figures on the assisted living industry, 1993 estimates published by the Assisted Living Facilities Association of America suggest that 30,000 to 40,000 facilities serve approximately one million older people.[59]

Congregate Housing.   Congregate housing programs are residential facilities where older people live in their own private apartments and services are provided, such as meals (often one a day), transportation, housekeeping, and health clinics. Often residents can receive some help with activities of daily living. However, unlike assisted living facilities, 24-hour-a-day assistance is not provided.

A number of states have developed programs to promote congregate housing by setting standards and licensing, by funding services at housing locations, and by making loans and grants available to build new housing. In the early 1990s the federal government promoted congregate housing by providing funding for service coordinators and services at a variety of government supported housing projects. However, in 1996 this program was eliminated due to budgetary pressures. Still, congregate housing is a cost-effective alternative for many low-income older people.

Shared Living Concept or Home Sharing.   The shared living concept centers around a living arrangement where two or more unrelated adults share a home or apartment, usually to save money. In addition, shared housing can bring companionship, increase safety, and minimize household chores. This arrangement has been particularly popular among older people who, in many cases, share dwellings with middle-aged or younger people. There are two types of shared housing. Match-ups, where homeowners share their home with a border or roommate who pays rent, are by far the most common. Group-shared residences are cooperative arrangements where two or more people share a home or apartment. The popularity of shared housing has increased rapidly. The U.S. Census reported that in 1980 670,000 older people were sharing homes, 35% more than a decade earlier. As of the 1990 census, almost 970,000 people age 45 and older lived as roommates, with an additional 1,215,900 living as unmarried partners.[60] The number of programs nationwide that match prospective home sharers rose from 50 in 1981 to over 350 in 1996.

Shared housing can also lower costs to communities and consumers. A shared home is for many an alternative to institutionalization. The National Shared Housing Resource Network (NSHRN) in Baltimore, Maryland,[61] an information clearinghouse founded by Maggie Kuhn, who also founded the Gray Panthers, estimates that the cost to the average home-sharing program to place one person ranges from $500 to $2,000, whereas a unit of public housing can cost more than $70,000. Prospective home sharers pay only a small fee to apply to a program, and an additional fee if a match is found. In shared housing arrangements, rents are often lower than market price. Homeowners who share their homes may use the extra income to maintain their residences or to buy services such as home health care, allowing them to remain independent.

Many states provide some funds for shared housing, but the government needs to play a larger role. For example, older homeowners are often dissuaded from participating in home sharing because they risk having their assistance checks (e.g., food stamps, Supplemental Security Income, rental assistance) reduced due to an increase in their total household income. The sharing of public housing units has been allowed since 1978, with rents based on individual incomes, and with individual leases.

Continuing   Care   Retirement   Communities.
Continuing care retirement communities (CCRCs)
offer a broad spectrum of housing options and social, health care, and personal services, ranging
from independent living to 24-hour nursing care.
Entry fees are required for many, in addition to a
monthly fee for specific services. Agreements are
either made for a specific period or for the rest of
the resident's life. Most such housing is too expensive for more than a small proportion of the
older population.

In 1996, the American Association of Homes
and Services for the Aging (AAHSA) noted that
approximately 350,000 residents were living in
1,100 CCRCs throughout the United States. The
average age of residents in CCRCs is 81, 75% of
residents are women, and 70% are single.[62] Approximately 98% of CCRCs are still sponsored by
religious groups or other nonprofit organizations.
However, the private sector has recently entered
the industry. The Marriott Corporation is currently developing over 150 CCRCs. Thirty-seven
states regulate financial aspects of CCRCs and all
states regulate the health care they provide, yet
there are vast differences in the quality of services
provided.[63] The Continuing Care Accreditation
Commission, sponsored by AAHSA, is the only
accrediting body for CCRCs. As of July, 1996,
under 200 CCRCs were accredited.[64]

Others.   A variety of boarding homes, retirement
hotels, and other facilities, which offer a variety
of services and a somewhat protected environment, can be found here and there. So-called
"granny flats" or "echo flats" are small units that
can be attached to larger structures, such as adult
children's homes, and are used to house older
family members.

OUTPATIENT CARE

Outpatient services (or ambulatory care) is the
term for care given to people who live in the community rather than in institutions. This care is provided by hospital outpatient clinics, neighborhood
health and mental health centers, family agencies,

day hospitals, and adult day-care centers. Outpatient services may be given in or outside of the
home, either by bringing the person to the services
or taking the services to the person. Since we have
already described home care, this section emphasizes the facilities where people can go for outpatient care rather than having it brought to them.

Under Medicare, coverage of psychotherapy
is unlimited in terms of length of care, but it is
subject to review. Clinical psychologists now receive the same scheduled fee allowances from
Medicare Part B as physicians, and clinical social
workers are reimbursed at 75% of that rate.
Spurred in part by the Senate's passage of the
Domenici-Welstone mental illness parity provision in 1995, which requires many large insurance
providers to offer equal lifetime and annual payment limits for mental and physical health care, a
push for increased parity between physical and
mental services is underway. Currently Medicare
enrollees must pay a 50% co-payment for psychological services. In the near future, however,
Medicare is expected to offer the same coverage
of 80% for both psychological and physical care
services.

Hospital emergency rooms are the major 24-
hour facilities available for medical and psychiatric emergencies. In addition, hospitals generally
offer *outpatient medical clinic care;* some have
outpatient psychiatric clinics as well. Currently
only 2% of patients in outpatient psychiatric clinics are over 60 years of age. Few of the clinics offer
the services necessary for older people, especially
psychotherapy. In an effort to offer integrated and
comprehensive services, the Phyllis and Lee Coffey Outpatient Geriatrics Clinic of the Department
of Geriatrics of Mount Sinai Medical Center provides full services (including psychiatric) to nearly
1,000 patients with an average age of 80 who have
multiple, complex, and interacting acute and
chronic psychosocial and physical conditions.

Community mental health centers (CMHCs)
represent another potential, but unrealized, resource for older persons. In 1961, proposals regarding the establishment of community mental
health centers were made and published by the

Joint Commission on Mental Illness and Health. The Federal Community Mental Health Centers Program was enacted by Congress in 1963 and amended in 1965, 1967, and 1975. The community mental health center was required to offer a minimum of five services, four of which were direct clinical activities: inpatient care, outpatient care, partial hospitalization (such as day care), and around-the-clock emergency service. The fifth required program element was community education and consultation services oriented toward prevention. In addition, Public Law 94-63, the Public Health Service Act of 1975, required that the community mental health centers provide "a program of specialized services for the mental health of the elderly, including a full range of diagnostic, treatment, liaison, and follow-up services." Community mental health centers were responsible for specific catchment areas, but certain of the center programs (such as those for children, older persons, and drug addicts) served several catchment areas.

The passage of the 1980 Mental Health Systems Act was aimed at correcting the many inadequacies found in the Community Mental Health Center Program by the 1979 President's Commission on Mental Illness, chaired by Rosalynn Carter. The act was designed to improve the delivery of mental health care in the United States, addressing such issues as the needs of the chronically mentally ill to cope in the community and prevention and improvements in state mental health systems. Although it was never adequately funded by Congress, the act contained the following potentially valuable features:

1. More community care will be provided for those who have been underserved by the current CMHC program—namely, the old, the young and adolescent, the chronically mentally ill, and certain racial and ethnic minorities. Projects can be specifically targeted for these groups.

2. All federal funding for community care must go through the states, which will act as service coordinators and program evaluators. There will be no direct federal funding to local commu-

nities as in the 1963 CMHC Act. The purpose is to return authority to the states and avoid a two-tiered federal-state system of authorization and review.

3. However, none of the money authorized can go to state hospitals. All of it must go to community-based care; thus, states are being required to commit themselves to community care of chronic-care patients if they want federal funds. This Act was supported by block grants under the Reagan administration. Thus, there is no targeting on a national basis.

Community Mental Health Centers have been adversely affected by the change in the law that led to block grants going to the states. States can elect to use their funds in a variety of ways including combining them with Medicaid to contract with private providers. Such contracts are part of the general privatization movement and make questionable the future of public mental health at both the state and federal level. The Veteran's Administration has designated patients for "behavioral health care" or total care for the chronic mentally ill. Therefore, individuals with psychiatric disorders also have their physical problems managed, all on a capitated basis. The effectiveness of this approach remains to be proven.

Both public and private agencies participated in the establishment of community mental health centers. It should be pointed out that whatever the nature of its sponsorship, the typical community mental health center was supported through a combination of public and private funds. Public monies met 75% of the total operating costs of typical centers during the first year of operation. Private funds derived from varying combinations of patient payments, third-party payments made in behalf of patients, and voluntary contributions.

By 1987 some 700 centers were operating. However, mental health service needs of older persons frequently were unmet.[65] Older people made up only 4% to 5% of community mental health center clientele.[66] The centers were never adequately funded, housed, and staffed. No standards

existed. Inservice training and personnel development lagged. Racism and stereotypes about "the
poor" were negative influences.

Day hospitals for patients with psychiatric
problems enable persons to come to the hospital
for any indicated treatment during the day and return home at night. This provides a degree of care
intermediate between outpatient therapy and total
institutional care. It is particularly useful for former mental hospital patients and persons with significant organic mental impairment. In this way
families obtain substantial support in keeping an
older person at home. Nursing and old age homes
should offer similar partial care. One of the greatest problems with day hospital programs is the
need for transportation, particularly in rural areas.
In England, ambulances are used to transport people. Taxis (paid for by Medicaid in some states),
volunteers' cars, and staff cars may be used. An
ideal day hospital service has a staff-to-client ratio
not exceeding one-to-eight and should offer medical care, individual and group psychotherapy,
drug therapy, occupational and physical therapy,
entertainment, education, a library, a store, beauty
and barber shops, free lunches, baths, some form
of patient government, and plenty of opportunities
for congenial socializing. Day hospitals can ease
the return of former mental hospital patients to
community life and monitor the physical condition and reactions to medications of all patients.
Relatives, friends, and community volunteers
should have free access to these facilities.

Day-care centers offer day care in a nonhospi-
tal setting (often in a YMCA or a church) but provide many of the same social and recreational
services as day hospitals.[67] *Adult day-care centers*
serve those who are not strong enough to stay
home alone, yet do not need constant care. In
1970, only a dozen or so adult day-care centers
existed in the United States; by 1996, about 3,000
such centers served more than 60,000 people. Basically, there are two types of centers: those focused on medical needs and those focused on
social needs.

The first recreational day center for the aged,
the William Hodson Community, was set up in

1944 as part of New York City's Department of
Public Welfare.[68] This center emphasized self-
government, poetry, music, drama, woodwork,
painting, birthday parties, discussion groups,
counseling, and an added fillip in the form of
country vacations. Various other groups now offer
similar programs. Depending upon location and
services offered, the National Council on the
Aging described the average daily cost of adult
day care in 1996 as ranging from $30 to $125.
Medical centers may exceed $80 a day, while
transportation may run another $7 a day. Yet these
costs are lower than the average $100 daily cost
of nursing home care or the $15 to $30 per hour
charge for private nursing care. Unfortunately,
Medicare Part A does not cover adult day care.
Medicare Part B does cover outpatient medical
and therapeutic services at day-care centers if the
centers are Medicare approved vendors.

Families seeking day care for an older person
should visit a center first, for although 42 states
have set up quality standards for such centers,
fewer than half require licensing. A search for
adult day-care centers can begin by contacting the
area Agency on Aging or a local health or social
services department.[69]

MULTIPURPOSE SENIOR CENTERS

Former Congressman John Brademas (D-Ind.) introduced legislation in December 1971 to autho-
rize construction of multipurpose senior citizen
community centers. A revolving fund was to be
established to ensure mortgages for such centers.
The National Council on Aging estimates that
2,000 to 2,500 centers existed in 1990. The senior
center movement illustrates the continuing debate
over the development of comprehensive versus
categorical programs: whether the services
needed by older people should be assured within
comprehensive programs for people of all ages or
be provided in specialized ways. Philosophically,
socially, and psychologically, integration of services for all age groups is the more desirable. Experience demonstrates, however, that older people
get lost in the shuffle, and fall through the cracks.

Until there is a change in the cultural sensibility so that older persons are not ignored, it is necessary to press for special, highly visible programs aimed specifically at the elderly.

Multipurpose senior centers can provide a range of services beyond the walls of their facilities. Social workers and aides (paraprofessionals, who are sometimes called "geriatric aides") and friendly visitors may visit the homes of clients. Residential homes may be organized. Group shopping trips by bus, for check-cashing as well as shopping, may be chaperoned. Little House in Menlo Park, California, has been a pioneer example of a multipurpose senior center since 1949.

PROTECTIVE SERVICES

Protective services is the name for a group of services given to persons who are so mentally deteriorated or disturbed as to be unable to manage their affairs in their own best interest and who have no responsible relatives or friends able and willing to act on their behalf. Social work, legal, medical, psychiatric, nursing, homemaking, and home health aide services may be provided. Small amounts of cash may be available for use in certain situations.

Federal legislation was enacted to permit state welfare offices to set up protective service programs, for which the federal government covers 75% of the cost.[70] Adult protective services programs have been developing more rapidly since the passage in 1974 of Title XX of the Social Security Act. The Omnibus Reconciliation Act of 1981 amended provisions of Title XX; it also created the Social Services Block Grant Program, through which adult protective services are federally funded. Federal guidelines, however, are broad, allowing states freedom in shaping their policies and program directions.[71] Every state has an organized program of service and intervention.

Protective services clients often need assistance because of some mental condition such as paranoid ideas, organic brain syndrome, overwhelming anxiety, or severe personality disorder. Most of these clients are best helped by social workers and nurses who are generalists in the sense that they handle their clients' problems with the support of medical, legal, and psychiatric consultations and can call on homemakers, visiting nurses, and paraprofessionals for help. A typical case illustrates the importance of such services to mental health.

A mildly confused older woman developed paranoid ideas about the gas company, which resulted in her not paying her bills for several months. She was threatened with having the gas turned off, which would leave her without heat in midwinter. Had she been without help, her gas probably would have been turned off; after a while police and medical help would have been called for, and her eventual transfer (probably in a very deteriorated condition) to an inpatient psychiatric ward would have been necessary. With protective services, the crisis with the gas company was averted. A casework aide, under the supervision of a social worker, was able to gain the woman's confidence enough to convince her to pay the gas bill. Since she had no money for an immediate payment, protective services made a partial payment of the bill and arranged with the gas company for the woman to pay the rest later. Continuing contact with the protective service worker enabled the woman to continue living in her own home. A homemaker was also provided for a few hours a week. All these helpers used psychiatric consultants to help them react appropriately to the client's psychiatric condition.

The protective service and the community mental health approaches are closely related in that both provide a variety of services to meet a person's needs while the person remains in his or her home, thus utilizing less-than-total-care institutions whenever it is in the person's best interest. The older person is seen not just as having a certain illness but in the context of psychological, social, physical, and economic conditions. Also, psychiatric needs may be met without requiring the person to accept the idea that he or she is a "mental patient."

In 1962 the Social Security Administration made a grant to the Benjamin Rose Institute of Cleveland, one of the few agencies providing extensive protective services to older people, for a research and demonstration project. It is important to note that the early work of Margaret Blenkner, director of this research, continues to be relevant to our understanding of the possible danger of intervening too quickly or too globally with protective services.[72] Any reduction in the autonomy of elderly people must be done with great care and caution.

No figure has been established for how many people need protective services. The number who have mental impairment is substantial, and this applies to people in institutions as well as in the community. Early studies showed that about 50% of institutionalized populations had mental impairment.[73] Later studies suggest that one-sixth of the noninstitutionalized elderly population— three million people—has some degree of mental impairment. Even if these figures include unrecognized or simulated depression, rather than organic impairment, for practical purposes this describes a vulnerable population. Some of the earliest studies concerning "certifiable" persons in the community estimated that 5% need protective services.[74] Less stringent later studies have estimated up to 16%, although studies are not strictly comparable because of varied criteria.

In Blenkner's approach, social casework was the core service and the directive was "do, or get others to do, whatever is necessary to meet the needs of the situation." Rapport, trust, mutual respect between the elderly and health personnel are necessary. Gradualism (nonprecipitous, careful intervention) is a guiding concept; it is not necessary or even desirable to think in terms of completing a case, except as nature dictates through death. The following are some principles crucial to protective services.

1. Entrust client or patient with decision-making power.
2. Establish trust and rapport; before all else, do not violate that trust.
3. Use gradualism—do things nonprecipitously and carefully.
4. Do not kill with kindness.

5. Work with assets.
6. Respect resistance.
7. Do not move people if it can be avoided and if it is against their will.

Blenkner's intriguing work found that the protected group as compared to the control group had higher rates of institutionalization and death. This was attributed to hopelessness (we would add helplessness) engendered by things being done for people. Members of the protected group were institutionalized earlier than they would otherwise have been and "contrary to intent . . . [protective intervention] did not . . . prove protective of the older person although it did relieve collaterals and community agents." It is essential that studies be designed to confirm or refute the Benjamin Rose studies. In the meantime, "We should . . . question our present prescriptions and strategies of treatment. Is our dosage too strong, our intervention too overwhelming, our takeover too final?"[75]

In a 1985 literature review, Zhorowsky concludes that social work must take a renewed look at protective services. The protective services literature has focused on the individual person unable to manage his or her own affairs. But this definition has begun to be broadened to include protection of the older person from neglect or abuse by others, thereby moving protective services into major new areas. Zhorowsky also describes the relatively new protective service laws in many states that give designated social workers broad powers of intervention even when an older person or caretaker is resistant. The need to balance older people's well-being with that of their civil rights and their need for autonomy represents a delicate social work practice issue that is still problematic.[76]

MODELS OF MULTIPLE SERVICE PROGRAMS

New York State's Nursing Home without Walls Program (also known as the Lombardi Program, named after its originator, New York State Senator Tarky Lombardi), established in 1977, is a viable alternative to institutional care, both providing and coordinating the delivery of nursing-home level services to the chronically ill and disabled so they may be cared for at home. A comprehensive range of health, social, and environmental services is tailored to patients' individual needs and managed on a 24-hour, seven-day-a-week basis. Care is provided by approved hospitals, residential health care facilities, and certified home health agencies and is available to any patient determined medically eligible for placement in a skilled or intermediate care nursing facility and who can be appropriately maintained at home. NHWW has allowed families to remain together and has provided care in a more personalized and compassionate manner. Many patients already hospitalized have been able to return home; at-risk community residents have avoided further deterioration; some patients have been rehabilitated. At the same time that it helps meet the increasing need for long-term care, NHWW helps contain the high costs to public and private payers. Patient care costs are approximately half of what institutional facilities charge for comparable care. Lombardi services cannot cost over 75% (or in some cases 100%) of the average cost of care in a residential health care facility.

The Minneapolis Age and Opportunity Center (MAO) is a comprehensive program of health and social services founded by its president, Daphne Krause, in 1969.[77] It is a nonprofit organization governed by seniors. The purpose of MAO is to give older frail and younger handicapped people an alternative form of care, with direct home-care network services. The goal is independence. Services include daily meal deliveries; homemaker and home health aide services (including bathing, housework, and laundry); transportation to medical services, counseling; special health counseling; legal services; employment services; nursing services; once-a-day telephone reassurance; and a "food closet" for emergency or supplementary food. Contacts between the old and young are encouraged. A free clinic was opened in 1973, sponsored by Abbott-Northwestern Hospital, with Medicare accepted as full payment for fees.

This clinic offers preventive medical services, diagnosis and treatment services, emergency service, counseling service on health matters, and inpatient service where needed. The hospital provides health care personnel and equipment, and MAO supplies volunteers and professionals for the wide range of services described earlier. Funding for MAO has been provided by Medicare, county welfare, private donations, and other sources.

The Council for the Jewish Elderly (CJE) of Chicago is a social agency with transportation, outreach, and homemaker services, Meals-on-Wheels, storefront area service centers, a senior work center, apartments, and liaisons with two hospitals. Another program with a more distinct ethnic orientation is that of the On Lok Senior Health Center for older Chinese, Filipinos, and Italians.

CORPORATE SECTOR EFFORTS

Corporate sector efforts have focused on the caregiving aspects of home care. Private sector employers are beginning to provide special benefits to employee caregivers, partly to attract women into the work force and partly to protect the existing work force from work/home conflicts arising from the growing demand for family elder care. Studies indicate that 20 to 25% of a typical employer's work force is providing some form of elder care for either a parent, a grandparent, or a spouse.[78]

Employee benefits for long-term care include long-term care insurance and caregiver assistance programs, both direct and indirect.[79] Indirect caregiver benefits are potentially beneficial to all employees. They include flex-time, personal leave policies, job sharing, employee assistance programs, and dependent care reimbursement (or flexible spending) accounts. Direct programs focus especially on employees providing elder care. They include information programs, referral programs to helpful resources, direct service programs of group support and individual counseling, occasional programs to provide access to adult day-care programs for older relatives, and subsidies for respite care.

In 1989, Ford Motor Company became the first major U.S. company to introduce an employer-financed long-term-care health plan covering both home and institutional care. Some other companies, such as Proctor and Gamble, offer employees the opportunity to purchase long-term-care insurance at special group rates. Travelers Life Insurance Company offers an array of elder care benefits under a flexible benefit program called Family Care (which also includes child care). The three basic components are financial assistance, time off, and information on referral services.

The Washington Business Group on Health and the U.S. Administration on Aging have sponsored efforts by business coalitions and government aging units in eight states to collaborate on programs for older adults and their caregivers.

A 1989 New York Business Group on Health study explored 37 companies' responses to the needs of employees who provide elder care. The study found that employers are becoming aware of the need for changes in personnel policies (flexible work schedules, leaves of absences, and so forth), financial benefits, caregiver information, caregiver support, and support to community agencies providing caregiver services.[80]

THE PEPPER COMMISSION

The Pepper Commission, officially the U.S. Bipartisan Commission on Comprehensive Health Care (established by the Medicare Catastrophic Coverage Act), issued recommendations to Congress in 1990. Its key recommendations have not been enacted into law. Support for home and community-based care for the severely disabled of all ages would be greatly increased under the Commission's plan. All those who need assistance with three or more personal activities of daily living (i.e., eating, bathing, toileting, dressing, and transferring) or who have severe cognitive impairment due to developmental disabilities or Alzheimer's disease or a related disorder would be eligible for care. Care coordinators would determine the amount and mix of services needed, including home health care, personal care, homemaker chore services, adult day care, and respite care. Beneficiaries would pay 20% of the costs. The rest would be provided by the federal government. Special subsidies would be available for those who were unable to pay the co-insurance of 20%.[81]

SELECTED READINGS

American Association of Homes and Services for the Aging, Public Affairs. (1996). *Assisted living: Background*. Washington, DC: Author.

American Association of Homes and Services for the Aging, Public Affairs. (1996). *Continuing care retirement communities: Background*. Washington, DC: Author.

American Association of Retired Persons. (1990). *Home health care benefits covered by Medicare: A chart book*. Washington, DC: Author.

Ayers, R. E. (1990, February). The physical therapist's role in geriatric care. *Geriatrics, 45*(2), 83–84.

Barer, B. M. (1992). The relationship between homebound older people and their home care workers, or "the pas de deux" of home care. *Journal of Gerontological Social Work, 19,* 129–147.

Barer, B. M., & Johnson, C. L. (1990). A critique of the caregiving literature. *The Gerontologist, 30*(1), 26–29.

Barker, W. H. B. (1987). *Adding life to years: Organized geriatrics services in Great Britain and implications for the United States*. Baltimore: Johns Hopkins University Press.

Bass, D. M., & Bowman, K. (1990). The transition from caregiving to bereavement: The relationship of care-related strain and adjustment to death. *The Gerontologist, 30*(1), 35–42.

Berkman, L. F. (1986). Social networks, support, and health: Taking the next steps forward. *American Journal of Epidemiology, 123, 559–562.*

Blenkner, M., Bloom, M., Wasser, E., & Nielsen, M. (1971). Protective services for old people: Findings from the Benjamin Rose Institute Study. *Social Casework, 24,* 483–522.

Branch, L. G., & Stuart, N. E. (1984). A five-year history of targeting home care services to prevent institutionalization. *The Gerontologist, 24,* 387–391.

Brickel, C. M. (1986). Pet-facilitated therapies: A review of the literature and clinical implementation considerations. In Brink, T. L. (Ed.), *Clinical gerontology: A guide to assessment and intervention* (pp. 307–332). Binghamton, NY: The Haworth Press.

Brickner, P. W., Lechich, A. J., Lipsman, R., & Scharer, L. K. (1987). Long-term health care: Providing a spectrum of services to the aged. New York: Basic Books.

Brody, E. M. (1985). *Mental and physical health practices of older people: A guide for health professionals.* New York: Springer.

Brody, E. M. (1990). *Women in the middle: Their parent-care years.* New York: Springer.

Buchwalter, K. C., Smith, M., Zenenbergen, P., & Russell, D. (1991). Mental health services of the rural elderly outreach program. *The Gerontologist, 31,* 408–412.

Carcango, G. J., & Kempes, P. (1988). The evaluation of the national long-term care demonstration 1. An overview of the channeling demonstration and its evaluation. *Health Services Research, 23*(1), 1–22.

Chalfie, D. (1995). *The real Golden Girls: The prevalence and policy treatment of midlife and older people living in nontraditional households.* Washington, DC: American Association of Retired Persons, Women's Initiative.

Clark, L. W. (1990, February). Specialists for the communicatively impaired. *Geriatrics, 45*(2), 72–75.

Clemmer, E. (1995, February). Assisted living and its implications for long-term care. *AARP Public Policy Institute Issue Brief, 20.* Washington DC: American Association of Retired Persons.

Commonwealth Fund Commission on Elderly People Living Alone. (1989, May). *Help at home: Long term care assistance for impaired elderly people.* Baltimore, MD: Commonwealth Fund Commission on Elderly People Living Alone. Available from Center on Elderly People Living Alone, Public Policy Institute of AARP, 1909 K Street N. W., Washington, DC 20049.

Commonwealth Fund Commission on Elderly People Living Alone. (1987, November 20). *Medicare's poor.* Baltimore, MD: Author. Available from Center on Elderly People Living Alone, Public Policy

Institute of AARP, 1909 K Street N. W., Washington, DC 20049.

Council on Scientific Affairs. (1990, March 2). Home care in the 1990's. *Journal of the American Medical Association, 263*(9), 1241–1244.

Cusak, O., & Smith, E. (1984). *Pets and the elderly.* Binghamton, NY: The Haworth Press.

Eliopoulos, C. (1990). *Caring for the elderly in diverse care settings.* Philadelphia: J. B. Lippincott.

Fishman, P. (1990, February). A physician's guide to locating a qualified nutritionist. *Geriatrics, 45*(2), 61–65.

Flattan, K., Wilhite, B., & Reyes-Watson, E. (1987). *Recreation activities for the elderly.* New York: Springer.

Gallo, J. J., Reichel, W., & Anderson, L. (1988). *Handbook of geriatric assessment.* Rockville, MD: Aspen Publishers.

Greene, R. R. (1990). Case management: An arena for social work practices. In Vourlekis, B., & Greene, R. (Eds.), *Social Work Case Management.* New York: Aldine de Gruyter.

Gulyas, R. A. (1995, October). *AAHSA's position on assisted living.* Washington, DC: American Association of Homes and Services for the Aging.

Hamlet, E., & Read, S. (1990). Caregiver education and support group: A hospital based group experience. *Journal of Gerontological Social Work, 15*(½), 75–88.

Health Care Financing Administration. (1996). *Your Medicare handbook 1996.* Baltimore, MD: Health Care Financing Administration, U.S. Department of Health and Human Services.

Hunter College/Mount Sinai Geriatric Education Center (GEC), Levenson, D. (Ed.). (1990). Getting the job done: Helping hands in geriatric primary care. A Mount Sinai special series. *Geriatrics, 45*(2), 58–84.

Interagency Forum on Aging-Related Statistics. (1989, October). *Measuring the activities of daily living among the elderly: A guide to national surveys.* Prepared by Wiener, J. M., & Hanley, R. J., The Brookings Institution. Federal Forum: Final Report.

Kane, R. A., & Kane, R. L. (1987). *Long-term care.* New York: Springer.

Katz, S., & Stroud, M. W. (1989). Functional assessment in geriatrics, a review of progress and directions. *Journal of the American Geriatrics Society, 37,* 267–271.

Lachs, M. S., Feinstein, A. R., Cooney, L. M., Jr., Drickamer, M. A., Marottoli, R. A., Pannill, F. C., & Tinetti, M. E. (1990). A simple procedure for general screening for functional disability in elderly patients. *Annals of Internal Medicine, 112,* 699–706.

Lewin/IFC & Brookings Institution. (1989). *The estimated cost of a proposed home health care program.* Report prepared for the Commonwealth Fund Commission on Elderly People Living Alone. Background Paper Series no. 16.

Liebenson, D. S. (Ed.). (1990). *The case management resource guide.* Irvine, CA: Center for Consumer Health Care Information.

Maki, B. E., & Fernie, G. R. (1996). Accidents: falls. In Birren, J. E. (Ed.), *Encyclopedia of gerontology* (vol. 1, pp. 11–18). San Diego, CA: Academic Press.

Monk, A. (Ed.). (1990). *Handbook of gerontological services,* 2nd ed. New York: Columbia University Press.

Morrison, I. Bennet, R., Frisch, S., & Gurland, B. (Eds.). (1986). *Continuing care retirement communities.* Binghamton, NY: Haworth Press.

National Association for Home Care. (1995). *Basic statistics about home care, 1995.* Washington, DC: National Association for Home Care.

National Center for Health Statistics. (1986). Aging in the eighties, age 65 years and over and living alone, Contacts with family friends and neighbors. *Advance Data from Vital and Health Statistics.* No. 116, DHHS Pub. No. (PHS) 86–1250. Hyattsville, MD: Public Health Service.

National Center for Health Statistics. (1987). Aging in the eighties, functional limitation of individuals age 65 and over. *Advance Data from Vital and Health Statistics.* No. 133, DHHS Pub. No. (PHS) 87–1250. Hyattsville, MD: Public Health Service.

National Center for Health Statistics. (1988). Aging in the eighties, people living alone—Two years later. *Advance Data from Vital and Health Statistics.* No. 149, DHHS Pub. No. (PHS) 82–1250. Hyattsville, MD: Public Health Service.

National Center for Health Statistics. (1993). Health data on older Americans: United States, 1992. *Vital and Health Statistics,* Series 3, No. 30. DHHS Publication No. (PHS) 93–1411. Hyattsville, MD: U.S. Department of Health and Human Services.

National Center for Health Statistics. (1995). Trends in the health of older Americans: United States, 1994. *Vital and Health Statistics,* Series 3, No. 30. DHHS Publication No. (PHS) 95–1414. Hyattsville, MD: U.S. Department of Health and Human Services.

National Council on the Aging. (1990). *Caregiver support groups in America.* Washington, DC: National Council on the Aging.

National Long Term Care Survey. (1982). Funded by the Health Care Financing Administration and the Office of the Assistant Secretary for Planning and Evaluation, U.S. Department of Health and Human Services.

New York Business Group on Health. (1989, February). *Assisting employee caregivers: Employers' "eldercare" programs.* New York: New York Business Group on Health.

New York State Senate Health Committee. (1988, December). *Nursing homes without walls program—a decade of quality care at home for New York's aged and disabled.* Albany, NY: New York State Senate.

Regan, J. J. (1990). *The aged client and the law.* New York: Columbia University Press.

Reuben, D. B., Silliman, R. A., & Traines, M. (1988). The aging driver: Medicine, policy and ethics. *Journal of the American Geriatrics Society, 36,* 1135–1142.

Rubenstein, L. Z., & Kaiser, F. E. (1989). *Home care service needs for the frail elderly population.* Report prepared for the Commonwealth Fund Commission on Elderly People Living Alone. Background Paper Series no. 18.

Sheehan, S. (1983, November 28). A reporter at large: Kate Quinton, part 2. *The New Yorker,* pp. 56, 104.

Snyder, M., Egan, E., & Burns, K. R. (1995, March/April). Efficacy of hand massage in decreasing agitation behaviors associated with care activities in persons with dementia. *Geriatric Nursing,* 60–63.

Solomon, D., Chairman. (1988). National Institutes of Health Consensus Development Conference Statement: Geriatric assessment methods for clinical decision making. *Journal of the American Geriatrics Society, 36,* 342–347.

Somers, A. R. (1995). Continuing care retirement community. In Maddox, G. L. (Ed.), *The encyclopedia of aging* (pp. 224–227). New York: Springer.

Sommers, T., & Shields, L. (1987). *Women take care.* Gainesville, FL: Triad.

Spector, W. D., Katz, S., Murphy, J. B., & Fulton, J. P. (1987). The hierarchical relationship between activities of daily living and instrumental activities of daily living. *Journal of Chronic Diseases, 40*(6), 481–489.

Strauss, P. J., Wolf, R., & Shilling, D. (1990). *Aging and the law.* Chicago: Commerce Clearing House.

Streib, G., Folts, E., & Hilker, M. (1984) *Old homes—New families: Shared living for the elderly.* New York: Columbia University Press.

Transportation Research Board. (1988). *Transportation in an aging society: Improving mobility and safety for older persons,* vol. 1. (Special Report 218). Washington, DC: National Research Council.

Tully, C. T., & Jacobson, S. (1994). The homeless elderly: America's forgotten population. *Journal of Gerontological Social Work, 22*(¾), 61–81.

U.S. Bipartisan Commission on Comprehensive Health Care (The Pepper Commission). (1990, March, 2). *Recommendations to the Congress.* Washington, DC: U.S. Government Printing Office.

U.S. Bureau of the Census (1996). 65+ in the United States. *Current Population Reports, Special Studies,* Series P-23, No. 190. Washington, DC: U.S. Government Printing Office.

U.S. Bureau of the Census (1996). Marital status and living arrangements: March 1994. *Current Popula-*
tion Reports, Series P-20, No. 484. Washington, DC: U.S. Government Printing Office.

U.S. Senate Special Committee on Aging. (1971). *Mental health care and the elderly: Shortcomings in public policy.* Washington, DC: U.S. Government Printing Office.

U.S. Senate Special Committee on Aging. (1972). *Home health services in the United States.* Washington, DC: U.S. Government Printing Office.

U.S. Senate Special Committee on Aging. (1989). *Developments in aging: 1988* (Report 101–4, vol. 1). Washington, DC: U.S. Government Printing Office.

Weissert, W. G., Cready, C. M., & Pawelak, J. E. (1988). The past and future of home- and community-based long-term care. *The Milbank Quarterly, 66*(2), 309–369.

ENDNOTES

1. ADL disability rates are much "softer" measures than, for example, mortality rates, because of the different methods of measurement involved. However, ADL estimates can differ for good reasons and there is no "right" estimate. See Interagency Forum on Aging-Related Statistics. (1989, October). *Measuring the activities of daily living among the elderly: A guide to national surveys, final report.* Prepared by J. M. Wiener & R. J. Hanley, The Brookings Institution.

2. Data excludes older persons in institutions. See U.S. Bureau of the Census. (1996). Marital status and living arrangements: March, 1994. *Current Population Reports,* Series P-20, no. 484. Washington, DC: U.S. Government Printing Office.

3. National Center for Health Statistics, M. G. Kovar. (1986, May 9). Aging in the eighties: age 65 years and over and living alone, contacts with family, friends and neighbors. *Advance Data from Vital and Health Statistics.* No. 116, DHHS Pub. No. (PHS) 86–1250. Hyattsville, MD: Public Health Service.

4. *Ibid.*

5. *Ibid.*

6. Homelessness Information Exchange, National Coalition for the Homeless. (1994, September). *How many people are homeless in the U.S.?, 1994.* Available from the National Coalition for the Homeless. 1612 K St. NW, #1004, Washington, DC 20006.

7. Interagency Forum on Aging-Related Statistics. (1989, October). *Measuring the activities of daily*
living among the elderly: A guide to national surveys.* Prepared by J. M. Weiner, & R. J. Hanley. Washington, DC: The Brookings Institution, October.

8. Katz, S., Ford, A., Moskowitz, R. W., Jackson, B. A., & Joffe, M. W. (1963, September 21). Studies of illness in the aged. *Journal of the American Medical Association, 185*(12), 914–919.

9. Lawton, M. P., & Brody, E. (1969). Assessment of older people: Self-maintaining and instrumental activities of daily living. *Gerontologist, 9,* 179–186.

10. Stone, R., Cafferata, G. L., & Sangl, J. (1986). *Caregivers of the frail elderly: A national profile.* National Center for Health Services Research, Public Health Services, U.S. Department of Health and Human Services. Rockville, MD: National Center for Health Services Research.

11. Brody, E. M. (1985). Parent care as a normative stress. *The Gerontologist, 25,* 19–29.

12. Bianchi, S. M., & Spain, D. (1986). *American women in transition: The population of the United States in the 1980s.* A Census Monograph Series. New York: Russell Sage Foundation; Sommers, T., & Shields, L. (with contributing authors). (1987). *Women take care.* Gainesville: Triad Publishing; and Stone, R., Cafferata, G. L., & Sangl, J. (1987). Caregivers of the frail elderly: A national profile. *The Gerontologist, 27*(5), 616–626.

13. National Association of State Units on Aging. (1984, June). *A synthesis of issues and findings on primary care-givers: Support systems.* Report prepared by NASUA for the Office of Human

Development Services. Washington, DC: Department of Health and Human Services.

14. See Zarit, S., Reever, K., & Bach-Peterson, J. (1980). The burden interview. *The Gerontologist, 20*(6), 651; and Robinson, B. (1983). The caregiver strain questionnaire. *Journal of Gerontology, 38*(3), 334.

15. Lewis, M. L. (1989). *Economic perspectives on calculating the costs of women family members providing home eldercare.* Unpublished paper. New York: Mount Sinai Medical Center.

16. Weissert, W. G., Cready, C. M., & Pawelak, J. E. (1988). The past and future of home- and community-based long-term care. *The Milbank Quarterly, 66*(2), 309–369; and Wissert, W. G. (1985, Summer). The cost-effectiveness trap. *Generations,* 47–50.

17. Pannger, L. (1983, June). *The forgotten costs of informal long-term care.* Report contract no. HHS-100–80–0158. Washington, DC: Department of Health and Human Services.

18. See Rubenstein, L. Z., Wieland, G. D., English, P., Josephson, K., Sayre, J., & Abrass, I. B. (1984). The Sepulveda VA Geriatric Evaluation Unit: Data on four-year outcomes and predictors of improved patient outcomes. *Journal of the American Geriatrics Society, 32,* 503–512; and Rubenstein, L. Z., Josephson, K., Wieland, G. D., English, P., Sayre, J., & Kane, R. L. (1984). Effectiveness of a geriatric evaluation unit. *New England Journal of Medicine, 311,* 1664–1670.

19. Greene, R. R. (1990). Case management: An arena for social work practice. In Vourlekis, B., & Greene, R. (Eds.), *Social case management.* New York: Aldine de Gryter.

20. *Ibid.*

21. See *Long-term care for the 80's: Channeling demonstrations and other initiatives.* Hearing before the Subcommittee on Health and Long-Term Care of the Select Committee on Aging. U.S. House of Representatives. 96th Congress, February 27, 1980. Committee Publication No. 96–234.

22. Aging Network Services is located at 4400 East West Highway, Suite 907, Bethesda, MD 20814, (301) 657-4329.

23. For referrals to private care coordinators, contact the National Association of Professional Geriatric Care Managers, 1604 N. Country Club Road, Tucson, AZ 85716, (602) 881-8008. The association will provide up to three referrals in your area over the phone or will send a list of local care coordinators upon request. Children of Aging Parents, 1609 Woodbourne Rd., Suite 302A, Levittown, PA 19057, (215) 945-6900, also provides referrals to private care coordinators, as well as information on nursing homes, assisted living facilities, and support groups.

24. Arne Querido's famous Amsterdam psychiatric emergency service sent teams to the homes of persons in crises. The San Francisco Geriatrics Screening Project and the Baltimore City Health Department Geriatric Evaluation Service are illustrative of the pioneering screening programs in the United States that stressed home visits.

25. Kane, R., Solomon, D., Beck, J., Keeler, E., & Kane, R. (1980). The future need for geriatric manpower in the United States. *New England Journal of Medicine, 302,*(24), 1327–1332.

26. See Committee on Leadership for Academic Geriatric Medicine. (1987). Report of the Institute of Medicine: Academic geriatrics for the year 2000, *Journal of the American Geriatrics Society, 35,* 773–791.

27. For information on home health-care agencies providing RN, LPN, and home health aide services, contact: The National Association of Home Care, (292) 547-7424, Visiting Nurse Associations of America, (303) 753-0218; Joint Commission on Accreditation of Healthcare Organizations, (708) 916-5600; or the American Association of Retired Persons, (202) 434-2277.

28. Greene, R. (1986). *Social work with the aged and their families.* Hawthorne, NY: Aldine de Gruyter.

29. National Association for Home Care. (1995). *Basic statistics about home care 1995.* Washington, DC: National Association for Home Care.

30. Ayers, R. E. (1990). The physical therapist's role in geriatric care. *Geriatrics, 45*(2), 83–84.

31. Kiemat, J. M. (1979). The use of life review activity with confused nursing home residents. *American Journal of Occupational Therapy, 33,* 306–310. For a general overview of occupational therapy, see Lewis, S. C. (1983). *Providing for the older adult: A gerontological handbook.* Thorofare, NJ: Charles B. Slack.

32. Clark, L. W. (1990, February). Specialists for the communicatively impaired. *Geriatrics, 45*(2), 72–75.

33. Smolkin, S., Stravrianos, M., & Burton, J. (1996, August 29). *Characteristics of food stamp households: Summer 1994.* Alexandria, VA: U.S. Department of Agriculture, Food and Consumer Service, Office of Analysis and Evaluation.

34. Fishman, P. (1990, February). A physician's guide to locating a qualified nutritionist. *Geriatrics, 45*(2), 61–65.

35. For information contact Family Service America, 700 West Lake Park Dr., Milwaukee, WI 53224.

36. Besdine, R. W. (1979). Accidental hypothermia: The body's energy crisis. *Geriatrics, 34,* 51–59; Butler, R. N. (1977, April 5). *Energy and aging: The impact of rising energy costs on older Americans.* Testimony before the U.S. Senate Special Committee on Aging; and U.S. Department of Health, Education and Welfare, National Institute on Aging. (1978). *A winter hazard for the old: Accidental hypothermia.* Pub. No. (NIH) 78–1646.

37. See Bustad, L. R. (1980). *Animals, aging and the aged.* Minneapolis: University of Minnesota Press. See also Schmall, V. L., & Pratt, C. (1985–1986). Elders and pets. *Generations, 10*(4), 44–45.

38. Cusak, O., & Smith, E. (1984). *Pets and the elderly.* Binghamton, NY: The Haworth Press.

39. Order from NCOA Publications, Department 5087, Washington, DC 20061-5087. (202) 479-1200.

40. Hamlet, E., & Read, S. (1990). Caregiver education and support group: A hospital based group experience. *Journal of Gerontological Social Work, 15*(½), 75–88. (Also provides a review of the literature on caregiver support and education.)

41. Light, E., & Lebowitz, B. (1989). *Alzheimer's disease treatment and family stress: Directions for research.* U.S. Department of Health and Human Services, National Institute of Mental Health. DHHS Publication No. (ADM) 89–1564.

42. Personal communication, Kazuo Hasegawa, Chairman, Department of Psychiatry, St. Marianna University, Kowasaki, Japan.

43. Maki, B. E., & Fernie, G. R. (1996). Accidents: falls. In Birren, J. E. (Ed.), *Encyclopedia of gerontology* (vol. 1, pp. 11–18). San Diego, CA: Academic Press.

44. National Center for Health Statistics. (1996). Advance report of final mortality statistics, 1993. *Monthly Vital Statistics Report, 44*(7), supplement. Hyattsville, MD: National Center for Health Statistics.

45. See Tideiksaar, Rein. (1988). *Falling in old age: Its prevention and treatment.* New York: Springer.

46. Stock, R. W. (1996, July 13). Reducing the risks for older drivers. *The New York Times,* C1, C10.

47. Reuben, D. B., Silliman, R. A., & Traines, M. (1988). The aging driver: Medicine, policy, and ethics. *Journal of American Geriatrics Society, 36,* 1135–1142.

48. To be eligible for registration as a therapeutic recreation specialist, it is necessary to be certified by the National Council for Therapeutic Recreation Certification, P.O. Box 479, Thiells, N.Y. 10984, (914) 947-4346.

49. See Flatton, K., Wilhite, B., & Reyes-Watson, E. (1987). *Recreation activities for the elderly.* New York: Springer.

50. Senior centers are sponsored by churches, synagogues, clubs, and nonprofit corporations. Financial support derives from private donations and from local, state, and federal governments.

51. Elderhostel publishes three catalogs: Summer, Fall–Winter, and Spring. Contact Elderhostel, National Office, 75 Federal St., 3rd Fl., Boston, MA 02110-1914. (617) 426-7788.

52. Cross, W., & Florio, C. (1978). *You are never too old to learn.* New York: Academy for Educational Development.

53. For further information on education programs for older persons, contact the AARP, 1909 K St., N.W., Washington, DC 20049, or the Institute of Retired Professionals, The New School, 66 W. 12th St., New York, NY 10011. For a free directory of accredited schools that offer home-study courses, write to the Distance Education and Training Council, 1601 18th St., N.W., Washington, DC 20009.

54. RSVP evolved out of the project SERVE. See Sainer, J. S., & Zander, M. L. (1971). *SERVE: Older volunteers in community service: A new role and a new resource.* New York: Community Service Society.

55. Butler, R. N. (1970). Toward practical ecumenism. *Bulletin of the American Protestant Hospital Association, 34,* 6–12. See also (1970, July). Hospital Progress. *Journal of the Catholic Hospital Association.*

56. An early effort at the coordination of 11 separately sponsored church and community programs serving over 1,300 older recipients is described by McLaughlin, C. B. (1973). Meals on Wheels reach Baltimore's elderly. *Food and Nutrition, 3,* 204.

57. American Association of Homes and Services for the Aging, Public Affairs. (1996). *AAHSA assisted living: Background.* Washington, DC: American Association of Homes and Services for the Aging.

58. Clemmer, E. (1995, February). Assisted living and its implications for long-term care. *AARP Public Policy Institute Issue Brief,* no. 20. Washington DC: American Association of Retired Persons.

59. *Ibid.*

60. Chalfie, D. (1995). *The real Golden Girls: The prevalence and policy treatment of midlife and older people living in nontraditional households.* Washington, DC: American Association of Retired Persons, Women's Initiative.

61. The National Shared Housing Resource Network (NSHRN), 321 East 25th St., Baltimore, MD 21218. For more information contact Alternative Living for Aging (ALA), 937 North Fairfax, West Hollywood, CA 90046, which operates five Cooperative Apartment Communities for older people and offers a free roommate matching service.

62. American Association of Homes and Services for the Aging, Public Affairs. (1996). *Continuing care retirement communities: Background.* Washington, DC: American Association of Homes and Services for the Aging.

63. Somers, A. R. (1995). Continuing care retirement community. In Maddox, G. L. (Ed.), *The Encyclopedia of aging* (pp. 224–227). New York: Springer.

64. American Association of Homes and Services for the Aging, Public Affairs. (1996). *Continuing care retirement communities: Background.* Washington, DC: American Association of Homes and Services for the Aging.

65. Light, E., Lebowitz, B. D., & Bailey, F. (1986). CMHCs and elderly services: An analysis of direct and indirect services and service delivery sites. *Community Mental Health Journal, 22,* 294–302.

66. "The area of mental health services represents one of the most glaring examples of discrimination on the basis of age," according to the U.S. Commission on Civil Rights. (1979). *The age discrimination study.* Washington, DC: U.S. Government Printing Office, p. 6.

67. Matlack, D. R. (1975). The case for geriatric day hospitals. *The Gerontologist, 15,* 109–113.

68. Kubie, S. H., & Landau, G. (1953). *Group work with the aged.* New York: International Universities Press.

69. Also see Helen MacLean, (1987). *Caring for your parents: A source book of options and solutions for both generations.* New York: Doubleday.

70. 1962 Public Welfare Amendment to the Social Security Act. Among pioneering books on protective services is that of Lehmann, V., & Mathiasen, G. (Eds.). (1963). *Guardianship and protective services for older people.* Albany, NY: National Council on Aging Press. More recent references include Regan, J. J. (1990). *The aged client and the law.* New York: Columbia Universities Press; and Strauss, P. J., Wolf, R., & Shilling, D. (1990). *Aging and the law.* Chicago: Commerce Clearing House.

71. In a 1982 national study of protective services, Burr discovered large differences among states in policies, costs, program emphases, methods, procedures, and service standards. See Burr, J. J. (1982). *Protective services for adults.* DHHS Publication No. (OHDS) 82–20505. Washington, DC: U.S. Administration on Aging, Office of Human Development Services.

72. Blenkner, M., Bloom, M., Wasser, E., & Nielsen, M. (1971). Protective services for old people: Findings from the Benjamin Rose Institute study. *Social Casework, 52,* 483–522.

73. Goldfarb, A. I. (1962). Prevalence of psychiatric disorders in metropolitan old age and nursing homes. *Journal American Geriatric Society, 10,* 78–84. See also U.S. Department of Health, Education and Welfare, National Center for Health Statistics. (1965). *Characteristics of residents in institutions for the aged and chronically ill, United States, April-June 1963.* Pub. No. (PHS) 100, Series 12, No. 2. Washington, DC: U.S. Government Printing Office.

74. New York State Department of Mental Hygiene, Mental Health Research Unit. (1960). *A mental health survey of older people.* Albany, NY: New York State Hospital Press.

75. Blenkner et al., pp. 483–522.

76. Zhorowsky, E. (1985). Developments in protective services: A challenge for social workers. *Journal of Gerontological Social Work, 8*(¾), 71–83.

77. Minneapolis Age and Opportunity Center, Inc. (MAO), 1801 Nicollet Ave., Minneapolis, MN 55403. See also One city's controversial plan to give seniors a fair shake on health, *American Medical News,* September 9, 1974.

78. Mercer Meidinger Hansen, W. M. (1989, July). Eldercare. *The Bulletin,* No. 151.

79. Mercer Meidinger Hansen, W. M. *Long term care: The newest employee benefit.* 1211 Avenue of the Americas, New York, NY 10036.

80. New York Business Group on Health. (1989, February). *Assisting employee caregivers: Employers' "eldercare" programs.* 622 Third Avenue, 34th Floor, New York, NY 10017-6763.

81. The U.S. Bipartisan Commission on Comprehensive Health Care (The Pepper Commission). (1990, March 2). *Recommendations to the Congress.* Washington, DC: U.S. Government Printing Office.

CHAPTER 11

PROPER INSTITUTIONAL CARE

We discuss institutional care of all sorts in this chapter, but our discussion is dominated by the overriding issue of nursing home care. Nursing home use has nearly doubled since the introduction of Medicare and Medicaid in 1966. Although only approximately 5% of the older population resides in nursing homes at any given time, the risk of institutionalization increases with age. The percentage of the population who were in nursing homes in 1990 was 6% for those aged 75 to 84 and 24% for those aged 85 and older. The nursing home population, over 1.5 million in 1995, is expected to continue to grow. However, this growth will be less than previously estimated due primarily to the boom in home health care services and utilization.

Our definition of *institutional care* includes any care (medical, nursing, psychiatric, or social) given to older people *not* residing in their own homes or the homes of family and friends. Although efforts should be directed toward helping the mentally or physically ill older person remain independent and in his or her own home, there are many situations in which it is simply not possible or advisable to do so. If active outpatient treatment fails, short- or long-term institutional care is required. Present means of financing care, the inadequacy of many facilities and services, and deficiencies in number and training of personnel

are among the obstacles to the provision of the spectrum of services and facilities needed to dovetail with the wide range of psychiatric, nursing, medical, and social needs of older people. Once again, as in other chapters, we describe what is currently available, balancing this against what would be ideal. Emergency shelter, acute and chronic hospitalization (both medical and psychiatric), nursing homes, homes for the aged, and residential (for example, foster care) homes are the basic forms of institutional care utilized by the older population. We examine what each of these has to offer, both in kind and in quality of service.

THE DECISION TO INSTITUTIONALIZE
AN OLDER PERSON

The unfavorable reputation of U.S. institutions for the elderly combines with the natural reluctance of older people to leave their homes and communities; and the result is active or passive (and often justifiable) resistance to admission. As an extreme example, one older woman came to our attention because she kept an arsenal of guns at home to use on herself or others if someone came to take her to a nursing home or psychiatric hospital. Increased morbidity, disorientation, and mortality have been associated with the movement of people to institutions, since the aged are particularly vulnerable to the stress of sudden change. Thus the decision to institutionalize must be made conservatively and with care to fully prepare and cushion the individual against the inevitable shock.[1]

THE DIFFERENT KINDS OF SHORT- AND LONG-TERM INSTITUTIONAL CARE

Emergency Care and Emergency Shelter

Many older people remain in their homes until an acute psychiatric or medical crisis occurs, necessitating emergency care. Emergency rooms of hospitals have become the primary mode of providing initial care; this means, of course, that the patient must transport him- or herself, be transported by another person, or must obtain the services of an ambulance. Fire departments, police, and rescue squads may provide ambulance services, depending on the particular community, with fire departments the most commonly involved. Psychiatric emergencies are regulated differently from locale to locale, and in a number of communities only the police can legally transport such a patient.

Ambulance service staffs can range from untrained volunteers to paramedics with modern, mobile intensive care units (MICU), which transmit physiological data from the field to the hospital through telemetry. Financing of emergency transport can be a problem; for example, Medicare does not cover ambulance services.

Emergency medicine or "emergentology" is now a medical specialty and is undergoing reform. Improvements in reduction of disabilities in all age groups have resulted. But age prejudice still exists, even in emergency rooms, and private and public hospitals frequently respond less favorably to older persons than they do to younger persons. Medical and psychiatric decisions about older persons are still too often made by avoidance, by taking minimal responsibility, and by failing to consult with the patient, his or her family, and often the family doctor. Some voluntary hospitals continue the ethically dubious practice of dropping the Medicare patient on the doorsteps of the municipal hospital.

Physicians, police, judges, and other community agents as well as families are frequently at a loss to know where to take an older person for emergency care, especially if they need a comprehensive examination or cannot be returned to their homes. Although this does not yet exist in hospitals, emergency shelter admission of the elderly should be made available in all hospitals—to allow, at the very least, for a period of decision making. Not only would the brief admission be useful to effect a proper workup, but also to begin therapy. Changes could be seen that might alter the original diagnostic impression and individual treatment program. For crisis intervention in all age groups, the availability of hospitalization for several days in a unit attached to the emergency room of the hospital would be a step forward in evolving comprehensive social, medical, nursing, and psychiatric care in general hospitals. Complete diagnostic evaluations and a therapeutic trial ideally should precede any admission to long-term mental hospitals or nursing home facilities. This would require a team approach with medical, nursing, mental health, and social evaluations.

The Department of Geriatrics at the Mount Sinai School of Medicine in New York City has developed a 16-bed geriatric evaluation and treatment unit that provides acute geriatric inpatient hospital care. It includes a comprehensive multidisciplinary health care assessment by geriatricians, nurses, psychiatrists, geriatric social workers, and consulting geriatric specialists in neurology, nutrition, pharmacology, psychology, rehabilitation, and ethics. Meetings and case conferences are held with family caregivers. The aim of the geriatric unit is to restore function and preserve a reasonable quality of life whenever possible.

Psychiatric Hospitalization

Acute Psychiatric Hospitalization. The term *acute psychiatric hospitalization* usually applies to hospital stays lasting from a few days to some weeks, during which diagnosis and treatment take place simultaneously. Transient confusional states (reversible brain syndromes) and functional disorders can respond to acute care, sometimes with dramatically positive results.

Psychiatric units in profit-making or in voluntary general hospitals usually provide short-term psychiatric care independent of age; in other words, when an older person is able to pay, he or she is more likely to receive the same degree of care as that given to younger people. If it is believed (either correctly or mistakenly) that the person is suffering from dementia, he or she will at least receive decent care until transfer elsewhere is arranged. Private psychiatric hospitals also do effective work in the acute hospitalization of older persons. In addition, the in-service units of community mental health centers (usually public hospitals), as well as municipal, county, and state hospitals, provide this service with varying degrees of quality. Pre-admission screening units, whether in the community (see Chapter 10) or in general or state psychiatric hospitals, should be alert to the disorders that can respond to acute hospitalization.

During acute hospitalization it is important to maintain orientation—through unrestricted visiting hours, personal belongings, and family liaison. Home pressures, unattended pets and plants, and mail (especially Social Security, pension, and Supplemental Security Income checks) may need attention from hospital social service workers or community agencies that provide home-care services.

Through the Diagnostic Related Groups system (DRGs), created by the 1982 Tax Equity and Fiscal Responsibility Act, a patient's diagnosis determines the fixed number of days a hospital will be reimbursed for the patient's stay. Although DRGs were initially developed for psychiatry, patients admitted to psychiatric hospitals and psychiatric units of general hospitals have been exempt from DRGs. However, any other setting that admits a psychiatric patient for whatever reason (e.g., no psychiatric hospital/unit in the area) must apply for patients to be exempt. If the hos-

pital fails to do so, the patients are then subject to DRG rules.

It is important to note that 50% of patients discharged with a psychiatric diagnosis are affected by DRGs; in other words, these patients were in settings other than psychiatric hospitals or general hospitals with psychiatric units—settings that did not apply for DRG exemption.

Chronic Psychiatric Hospitalization. Schizophrenia and organic brain damage are the major reasons for more permanent psychiatric hospitalization. Persons with chronic physical conditions (for example, stroke victims) may be admitted to nursing homes and, at times, to chronic disease and geriatric hospitals, even though many such persons have accompanying or previously existing mental problems.

Of the 83,502 residents of state and county mental hospitals in 1992, 12,784 (15.3%) were age 65 and over. In addition, 2,832 residents of private mental hospitals and 2,655 residents in psychiatric units of Veterans Administration (VA) hospitals were 65 and over. Males of all ages outnumber females of all ages in mental hospitals overall. The sex ratio is about equal in private mental hospitals and 163 males to 100 females in state and county hospitals. (Sex ratios for those over 65 were not readily available.) The VA hospital population is almost exclusively male.

The Veterans Health Administration (VHA) in the Department of Veterans Affairs provides medical and health services to a predominantly male population that includes the oldest veterans, those who served in World Wars I and II and the Korean Conflict. In recent years special programs have been developed for the increasing female veteran population, including the elderly. There are 173 VA medical centers, 37 VA domiciliaries (31 of which have special programs for homeless veterans), 131 VA nursing homes, and 399 outpatient clinics. Recently, the VHA has been reorganized into 22 Veterans Integrated Service Networks (VISNs). Each VISN includes the full range of inpatient, outpatient, and extended care services. For many years, veterans had de facto unrestricted access to VA medical care. In an effort to contain costs, that access has been curtailed by eligibility requirements such as financial means testing for veterans who do not have service-related disabilities, or are not former POWs (prisoners of war), or World War I pension recipients. In 1996, major eligibility reform for VA services was authorized by Congress.[2]

VA's interest in providing continuous care for older veterans began in the 1970s. Because of the aging of World War II and Korean Conflict veterans, approximately two out of every three males over age 65 in the United States will be veterans by the year 2000. Currently the 65 and older veteran population (8.5 million) comprises over one-third of the total veteran population (26.3 million). Thus, most of the nation's older men will be eligible for various veterans' benefits.[3]

By 1994, the VA was providing comprehensive geriatric and management services in 133 of its facilities. That same year the VA was providing nursing home care for 34,000 veterans on a daily basis; 27% were in over 3,000 community nursing homes under contract with the VA, 38% were in the VA's own nursing homes, and 35% were in state veterans nursing homes. Another 17,000 veterans received services on any given day in VA and State veteran domiciliaries, adult day care centers, hospices, and respite programs, or were provided home-based primary care, and homemaker/home health aide services. An additional 10,000 veterans were in community residential care arranged by the VA. In 1995, the VHA's Under Secretary for Health, Kenneth Kizer, M.D., published the "Vision for Change," which was the blueprint for the major reorganization and culture change occurring in the VA. In restating the mission of the VA, Dr. Kizer identified a number of special emphasis programs that would continue to be supported in the "new" VA. These programs include VA's Geriatric Research, Education, and Clinical Centers (GRECCs), Geriatric Evaluation and Management (GEM) programs, home-based primary care, community-based long-term care, and nursing home care, as well as special mental health and rehabilitation

programs. Thus the VA's commitment to the care of older veterans that started in the 1970s continues as a major strength of the system.[4]

When Is Psychiatric Hospitalization Indicated?
The need for medical care in an institution is fairly apparent and is based on a physician's recommendation. However, it has not been possible to construct strict criteria for voluntary admission and involuntary commitment to state and private psychiatric hospitals; the criteria for nursing homes and homes for the aged are even more nebulous and indefinite.

Earlier, Lowenthal identified five factors that still influence the decision to place older, mentally ill persons in a hospital—some of which are relevant also for other chronic care facilities.[5]

1. Disturbances in thinking and feeling, such as delusions or depressions
2. Physical illness
3. Potentially harmful behavior such as confusion or unmanageability
4. Harmful behavior such as actual violence to others or refusing necessary medical care
5. Environmental factors such as the unavailability or incapacity of a responsible person to care for the patient

It is immediately clear that adequate social supports such as home-care services could prevent the institutionalization of a portion of the older persons described here. Medical hospitalization would be more appropriate for others, and a differentiation should be made between long-term and short-term or intermittent needs for care. The following outline illustrates an effort to build criteria for psychiatric hospitalization of older persons.[6]

1. Clearly appropriate for admission to a psychiatric unit in a general hospital or a psychiatric hospital itself:
   • Those with functional psychoses and without significant physical illness or disability, for whom outpatient treatment is not feasible. For example: patients receiving psy-

chiatric treatment in the community who require brief periods of protection from the consequences of their behavior during episodes of acute disturbance or depression (for example, suicidal or homicidal tendencies, spending sprees, refusal to eat); or chronically mentally ill patients who need protection and management, as well as treatment, during prolonged periods of disruptive or disorganized behavior and who require regular and frequent attendance of a physician

- Alcoholics without significant physical illness or disability who, following detoxification, need a period of inpatient treatment for their alcoholism
- Those with severe organic brain disorders whose usual behavior, intractable to medication, is too disturbing to be managed at home or in a nursing home or home for the aged. For example, the physically aggressive patient, the fire setter, the eloper, or the person otherwise dangerous to himself or others when physically able to carry out his potentially destructive behavior

2. Clearly inappropriate for admission
   - Those with delirium, symptomatic of a grave physical illness, requiring urgent admission to a general hospital
   - Those who are moribund or comatose
   - Those with major medical problems and minor mental symptoms. For example, patients who become mildly confused or disturbed as a result of or in conjunction with recent head injury, cardiovascular disease, diabetes, metabolic disturbance, terminal malignancy, and so on (Psychiatric consultation might be utilized, if required, rather than psychiatric hospital admission.)
   - Those with inconsequential lapses of memory and mild disorientation as a result of organic brain disorders, who are more effectively treated or managed in their own homes or, if necessary, in a foster home, a home for the aged, and so on (A state psychiatric hospital has little to offer and, in

view of the large wards in most state hospitals, may aggravate the patient's confusion.)
   - Those who need only adequate living accommodations, with economic or other social support services

As a footnote to the preceding discussion, it is important to remember that self-destructive or suicidal behavior in older persons may be a slow process associated with prolonged and intense grief, loneliness, and progressive organic disease and may manifest itself in malnutrition, failure to take medicine, and other forms of deteriorating self-care.

Advisability of Voluntary Admission. Wherever possible, the older person—like a person of any age—should participate fully in all decisions regarding him- or herself, including those of institutionalization. The family, of course, should also be closely involved. Making the decision to admit a person to a nursing home, a home for the aged, or a hospital can be extremely difficult, since all these facilities are so often disliked and feared by both older persons and their families.

Moving Trauma. The vulnerability of the aged to death or illness as a result of changing their living arrangements ("transfer mortality") is a serious cause for concern. In a study of 639 elderly, one-half of whom had died, had become physically impaired, or had psychologically deteriorated one year after they had moved, Lieberman and Tobin found that moving is traumatic, regardless of whether the move is to a better or to a worse environment.[7] The older persons in their study who left a rigid, institutionalized setting for a less structured one did not fare substantially better than those who did just the opposite. Shanas's description some 30 years ago of reaction to being moved is still hauntingly true for many:

> Almost all older people view the move to a home for the aged, or to a nursing home with fear and hostility. . . . All old people—without exception—believe that the move to an institution is the prelude to death. . . . [The old person] sees the move to an institution as a decisive change in living

arrangements, the last change he will experience before he dies. . . . Finally, no matter what the extenuating circumstances, the older person who has children interprets the move to an institution as rejection by his children.[8]

Lieberman's early studies showed that a year or more of preparation may be necessary to increase survival during the first six months in an institution, even when the institution is adequate.[9]

Considerable change should be made regarding the concept of institutional care, preparation of older people and their families, and length of stay for residents in such a facility. Many people could be admitted much later if they were given more support at home. In addition, there should always be an expectation and actual possibility of discharge and return home after response to treatment and changes in the person's condition and circumstances.

Involuntary Commitment to State and Private Psychiatric Facilities. Admission to a psychiatric institution should ideally be voluntary, but some circumstances may require commitment against a person's wishes. Extreme civil libertarians urge that legal involuntary commitment to psychiatric hospitals be done away with (but, strangely, have not commented on the de facto assignment of older people into nursing homes and related facilities—with few of the protections afforded in connection with admission to psychiatric hospitals). Others insist that people who are a danger to themselves or a threat to others need the protection of commitment to an appropriate institution. In fact, for a time, a trend arose which made these the only legal grounds for involuntary commitment. Legal procedures are currently not uniform from state to state, but in general the legal justification for action is (1) imminent physical danger to self, (2) imminent physical danger to others, or (3) a clear and present need of immediate care or treatment.

During the 1960s and 1970s, lawyers had been effective in bringing about stringent limitations on involuntary commitment of the mentally ill. This has resulted in unforeseen consequences. For ex-

ample, the homeless mentally ill cannot be treated against their wishes unless they are suicidal or represent a danger to others. Psychiatrists and others have begun to press for legislation to loosen up the commitment criteria. Laws have been passed that aim at preventing a worsening of existent mental illness and reducing the physical harm that mental deterioration might bring. These changes are in keeping with a model law devised by the American Psychiatric Association in 1983, drafted under the strong influence of Allen Stone, a psychiatrist and lawyer at Harvard University.

There has also been an effort to create an "outpatient commitment" procedure whereby persons would be required to seek treatment during the day but could go home at night. Although this may fulfill the concept of the "least restrictive alternative" to psychiatric hospitalization, the outpatient commitment is not commonly used at present.

There are those, including lawyers and psychiatrists, who contend that it is possible to maintain both civil liberties and treatment. A special study group of the American Bar Association issued 50 specific recommendations in 1986 to accomplish both.

Doctors are the only practitioners who are allowed to perform commitment proceedings. Since a large percentage of the U.S. population has no access to a psychiatrist, the family physician is, by default, pressed into service in times of psychiatric emergency. Many doctors fear signing commitment papers because of possible malpractice suits. The following are some safeguards that can protect both the older person and his or her doctor.

1. Know and observe laws regarding involuntary commitment. Get to know the local judge or court clerk available for assistance and advice. Examine the patient within the legal time limit before signing papers.

2. Avoid shortcuts in examination (see discussion of the legal examination in Chapter 9). If the patient is on sedatives, give him or her time to recover from the medication's effects before being examined. If the person is comatose, decide if this is medically or psychiatrically caused. If psychiatric, re-examine at a later time, as the condition may clear up.

3. Remember that taking the word of relatives is always risky.

4. Avoid personal conflict of interest. The physician should have no personal stake in the outcome of a psychiatric examination, especially in the form of obligations, favors, or promises that involve others, including relatives.

5. Avoid use of force (for example, injections, electroconvulsive treatment).

6. Avoid illegal transportation. Most states rule that only a police officer can transport someone against his or her will. In some jurisdictions where liability insurance is lacking or inadequate, the police themselves fear legal action.

7. Avoid institutions that are unfamiliar. Get to know all local facilities.

8. Avoid acting alone when consultation is available.

The informal, nonprotesting admission or emergency admission procedure is helpful when the person is too confused to comprehend what is happening.

Deinstitutionalization. State and county mental hospitals have been the center of long-standing controversy. When the American social reformer Dorothea Lynde Dix (1802–1887) began her efforts, there were practically no hospitals for the mentally ill. The first American asylum for mental patients was established in Williamsburg, Virginia, in 1773, and it was the only facility of its kind for 50 years. Toward the mid-nineteenth century, the belief grew that the mentally and emotionally ill could be helped and that the state owed them help. Dix pressed the idea of hospital care. A state-by-state system of hospitals was established, which now has come increasingly under criticism because of the quality of care and the basic concepts of treatment that it represents. Recent years have seen vigorous efforts to move patients out of these facilities. With cries of "bring the patient

back to the community," states rushed headlong into a course of dismantling the mental hospital system before establishing valid alternatives.

Since 1940, even before the introduction of tranquilizing drugs, mental hospital populations began a downward slope as attempts were made to shorten hospital stays. In the 1950s and 1960s, lower rates of admission began to be encouraged, along with shorter hospitalizations. From the 1960s on, the emphasis was on transferring the older patients out of hospitals wholesale. This was officially called "deinstitutionalization." Unofficially it was known as "dumping." The reason often given was that it was "better" for people; but the real impetus was a fiscal policy in which the states could save money by shifting costs of care to the Federal Supplementary Income (SSI) program and Medicaid. The controversial 1972 legislation regarding "intermediate care facilities" led to further transferring of older mental patients. As the saying goes, "The patient goes where the money flows."

In the meantime, in the 37-year period from 1955 to 1992 the population of state and county mental hospitals dropped from 600,000 to about 80,000 patients. In addition, length of stay became much shorter, usually less than 30 days. As a consequence, an individual is more likely to have a series of short stays rather than one long one. Admission rates for the elderly have a special character. Although the elderly currently make up about 16% of the total mental hospital inpatient population, the rate of new admissions is very low. For example, only 8.7% of all admissions in 1986 were over age 65. And because of these low admissions, the elderly patients are highly selected for exhibiting severe psychiatric symptoms. As a consequence of this selection, few elderly ever leave, largely because their behavior problems are so severe that management outside a hospital would be difficult.

Older patients were increasingly pushed from already inadequate mental institutions into other inadequate custodial facilities, known euphemistically as "the community." The result has been growing numbers of former state and county hospital patients in difficulty in the community, including a proportion who are among the homeless. According to a 1986 review of the literature, the homeless fall into four overlapping categories: (1) street people; (2) people with chronic alcoholism; (3) people with chronic mental illness; and (4) situationally homeless people.[10] The chronically mentally ill are estimated to be 20 to 30% of the homeless in large cities such as New York, Chicago, and others.

Another major effect of deinstitutionalization has been the transfer of many elderly from mental hospitals to nursing homes. Studies indicate that about 40% of the elderly with chronic mental illness who were deinstitutionalized were eventually reinstitutionalized into nursing homes.[11] Of all current nursing home residents, 8 to 10% were previously patients in state mental hospitals or long-term-care hospitals. Consequently, nursing homes have become the major location for the care of the chronically mentally ill elderly, and perhaps up to 88% of nursing home residents have diagnosable mental conditions. Many have serious behavioral problems. The most common conditions are Alzheimer's disease or multi-infarct dementia, and chronic or reactive depressions, with behavioral patterns that include confusion, depression, wandering, disorientation, agitation, withdrawal, lethargy, frustration, stress reaction, dependency, apathy, guilt, irritability, rise and fall of self-esteem, persistent talk of a wish to die, and paranoid delusions.

The 1980 Mental Health Systems Act (see Chapter 10) was one effort to help overcome some of the negative consequences of deinstitutionalization of mental patients and enable more of such persons to live in the community. Unfortunately, it was never funded, and responsibility for care was given over to the states through the mechanism of block grants.

In a new development, a federal law (an amendment to federal budget legislation of 1987) that took effect in January 1989 required that mentally ill and retarded persons in nursing homes who require active treatment be transferred to settings such as community-based centers like halfway houses and group homes. The object of the legislation was to remove mentally ill individuals from nursing homes unless they had Alzheimer's disease or required round-the-clock nonpsychiatric nursing care.

Nursing homes that did not transfer residents into alternative care settings when needed were faced with cutoffs of all payments from Medicare and Medicaid. States were to be forced to provide services in other settings. Critics of the law questioned whether all of the states would be able to afford such facilities and programs. Many worried that the chronically mentally ill would be forced back into state hospitals or into boarding homes. A number of states filed suits to delay or modify implementation of the law and the outcomes are pending.

Foster Care, Personal Care Homes, and Boarding Care

Foster care originated as foster parent programs for children; efforts to encourage families to take in older people who are unrelated to them have never been very successful. Foster care has therefore become a euphemism and really describes, in many areas, an underfinanced, unregulated, unprofessional series of homes operated for profit. Since states have sought to reduce state mental hospital rolls, many older people—usually long-term and predominately schizophrenic patients—have been transferred, often indiscriminately, into foster care, intermediate care, and other so-called nursing homes, as well as boarding homes of various types. Finding locations for community residential facilities is difficult because of state and local zoning legislation and regulations. Often such facilities are forced into high-density, commercial, transient, and low-income areas.

Personal care homes are another variation on the theme of small group homes for the elderly. They are found in different areas of the country and their definitions and regulations differ from area to area.

The passive, non-troublemaking elderly are most likely to be chosen for these residences, since foster care and personal care homes will take only tractable persons who have minimal nursing needs. The approximately 68,000 board-and-care facilities (also called *rest homes, shelter care facilities, domiciliaries,* and *adult congregate care facilities*) in the United States provide over one million elderly, retarded, or mentally handicapped residents with shelter, food, and modest help in day-to-day living.[12] Facilities range in size from two or three residents to several hundred. The average payment through Supplemental Security Income to such homes is hardly enough to provide decent food and the basic amenities, let alone medical, nursing, psychiatric, and social care.

Boarding homes and foster care homes are often not covered by safety codes because they fall into a residential rather than an institutional category. Safety and fire inspections are notoriously negligent. No official government data exist as to how many licensed board-and-care homes are substandard nor how many people live in them. According to a General Accounting Office report, a 1987 industry survey identified about 563,000 board-and-care beds in 41,000 licensed homes serving the elderly, the mentally ill, and the retarded. It is clear that many substandard nursing homes have converted into board-and-care homes, bringing their substandard conditions with them. States regulate these homes, and in many states licensing and regulating are haphazard. Although federal laws have been enacted asking states to certify that those facilities with numerous welfare residents meet certain standards, rigorous state inspections, which would help guarantee the effectiveness of such laws, are lacking.

Nursing Homes

Nursing homes fall into three classes: proprietary or commercial nursing homes, voluntary nonprofit nursing homes (frequently called homes for the aging), and government facilities. Most of the some 16,700 nursing homes, almost 70%, are commercial, while only about 1,400 (8.2%) are government facilities. The remainder are voluntary, nonprofit homes. Because of general confusion over the term *nursing home,* we shall use it here to refer to the commercial homes. The next section, "Voluntary Nonprofit Homes for the Aging," will cover the nonprofit nursing homes.

As of 1995, approximately 1.5 million older people lived in nursing homes in the United States, and these homes have received considerable adverse attention from legislators, the press, and the general public. We wish to emphasize that there are a number of fine commercial or proprietary nursing homes that give good care to older persons, and we would hope to encourage and support their efforts. However, a significant number of homes have major deficiencies, including sanitation and fire safety problems. We will be pointing out a number of such problems in order to present the reader with a picture of what remains to be accomplished in upgrading patient care. We also provide a brief description of some of the reasons why nursing homes are commercial.

Categories of Nursing Homes. Commercial nursing homes are, of course, available to people who can afford to pay for their own care. However, because costs of care have risen so precipitously to over $30,000 per year on the national average, a number of financing mechanisms have been created to assist the majority of people who could not otherwise afford care. Many problems continue to exist;[13] for example, middle-income people may have too much income to be eligible for assistance but not enough to pay for care by themselves.

From 1965 to 1989 there were two major types of long-term care institutions for the aged that were subsidized by the federal government through Medicare and Medicaid (Titles 18 and 19, respectively, of the Social Security Act). These were known as skilled nursing facilities (SNF) and intermediate care facilities (ICF). These categories were often referred to as *levels of care.* Entire sets of standards and reimbursement systems were based on these levels of care. *Skilled nursing care* referred to those services that must be performed under the supervision of professional or registered nurses. *Intermediate care* was "more than room and board, but less than skilled nursing." These terms were very unclear to the public as well as to health professionals, Congress, and the press. There is a tendency to use the term *nursing home* to cover everything described here. The degree of confusion involved in applying the definitions of skilled nursing and intermediate care can be observed in reviewing the percentages of patients classified into the two levels in different states. In New York state, approximately 80% of patients were in skilled nursing, while in New Mexico and Iowa only 15% were classified in this category. Because reimbursement for skilled nursing care was higher than for intermediate care, some states simply transformed (often without much change) ICFs into questionable SNFs. Another problem was the tendency of some nursing home operators to collude with doctors to have most people designated as SNF clients.

Originally SNFs themselves were divided into two categories, (ECFs) extended care facilities (Medicare) and (SNFs) skilled nursing care facilities (Medicaid). The 1972 Social Security Amendments created a single definition and set of standards for ECFs and SNFs; thus the category, skilled nursing facility, was introduced.

A major change in these classifications occurred in amendments to the Social Security Act in 1987 as part of the Omnibus Budget Reconciliation Act (OBRA) of 1987 (Public Law 100–203). The law mandated that the federal nursing home payment/reimbursement programs would offer only one level of facility, titled a nursing facility. Numerous states have obtained waivers from HCFA to support other types of institutional and home-based services for Medicaid recipients.

Number of Nursing Home Beds Available. There were approximately 16,000 nursing homes certified by Medicare and/or Medicaid, with almost 1.8 million beds, in 1995.[14] In addition, there were perhaps one thousand or more uncertified facilities.

Financing of Nursing Homes. In discussing nursing home care, it is important to clarify a few points about the commercial nursing home industry. The United States is one of the few countries in the world where care of sick older persons has become big business, run primarily for commercial gain. The number of nursing homes has proliferated since 1965.

As mentioned earlier, the nursing home industry consists of approximately 16,700 homes with almost 1.8 million beds. (Note: There are differing counts of the number of nursing homes.) About 70% of the homes are profit-making, some owned by large chains with publicly sold stock. Others have nonprofit sponsors such as churches and community organizations. A total of over $72 billion was spent on nursing home care in 1994. Medicaid paid over 47% of all nursing home care; Medicare paid 8.2%; and private funding, mainly out-of-pocket spending, amounted to 42.1% of the total nursing home bill. For 1995 of 13,122 Medicare certified facilities, 27% were nonprofit, 67% were proprietary, and 6% were government controlled.[15]

There are now more than twice the number of nursing homes than existed in 1960. This growth began partly in response to the increasing demand for beds as the aging population increased and was accelerated by the passage of Medicare and Medicaid. Guaranteed payments to nursing homes convinced investors that it was a no-lose proposition. By 1969, Wall Street considered nursing homes a glamour industry. Investments came from real estate developers, the insurance industry, used-car businesses, and others outside the health field. Even physicians, despite obvious conflict of interests, invest in and own nursing homes.

According to the National Center for Health Statistics, slightly over one-half of the United States' nearly 1.8 million nursing home beds are controlled by profit-making corporate chains that operate five or more homes each. The top 20 chains run one-third of the industry and are buying out more and more of the smaller owners. The major reasons for this phenomenon are the following:

1. With inflation and a squeeze in healthcare dollars, chains can outdo small owners by buying in volume, centralizing accounting, and sharing specialists' services. As one executive said, "We can McDonaldize."

2. Chains can buy the sophisticated management necessary to streamline compliance with federal, state, and local standards that often overlap. Small operators are swamped by the paperwork. The chains hire specialists to handle it.

3. Many large firms look at nursing homes as a real estate investment.

4. Corporations can write off a failing or foundering nursing home as a tax loss.

5. There is money to be made (but by 1987 there were less profits and even losses in the industry).

It should also be mentioned that chains own more than half of the nation's private psychiatric hospitals.

Conditions in Nursing Homes.   There are, as we have said, some excellent homes in which emphasis is on meeting patients' needs in every way possible within financial limits. But many homes are cheerless and depressing. Others are stylized, motellike, and antiseptic—patients sit in numb silence with dejected faces or pace endlessly down hallways. According to a 1996 report by the U.S. Department of Health and Human Services, about one quarter of all nursing homes (commercial and noncommercial) that received Medicare and Medicaid funds had deficiencies in storing or serving food under sanitary conditions. About one quarter did not conduct comprehensive assessments of residents or develop comprehensive care plans. Almost one fifth were not free of accident hazards and 15% were deficient in the areas of housekeeping and maintenance.[16] Personal abuse of patients by the staff can easily occur when older people are ill, vulnerable, and unable to defend themselves, and the staff may be untrained, unmotivated, improperly supervised and subject to extremely high job turnover. Many nursing home administrators have had no specific training directly related to their work, although this is changing. There is a shortage of physician services, skilled nursing care, dental care, social services, and psychiatric care. Patients often are overmed-

icated and deprived of any responsibility or decision making on their own behalf.

The Omnibus Budget Reconciliation Act of 1987 (OBRA 1987) and subsequent implementing regulations strengthen requirements to address many of these past problems. All nurses' aides must complete a training program and pass a competency evaluation. Reasonable background checks must be made when hiring nurses' aides and aides who have been convicted of abusing or neglecting a resident must have their name put on a state nurses' aide registry and are not allowed to work in a nursing home. Overmedication with antipsychotics and psychoactive drugs has been addressed by a prohibition of the use of "chemical restraints" except when necessary to treat medical symptoms, and the requirements of physician services, dental care, and social services have been strengthened. A number of nursing homes have opted to reduce or eliminate the use of physical restraints on residents. Several recent research studies have shown that injuries actually decline when physical restraints are removed and that the rate of hip fracture did not change.[17]

Nursing Home Standards.   Individual nursing homes are subject to state and/or federal standards, depending on their financing, but the federal government gives enforcement functions to the states. Yet even those states that have receivership laws, civil financial penalties, and the authority to withhold placements in inadequate facilities have not been altogether effective in providing quality care or in preventing facilities from violating regulations.[18] Homes that do not meet standards are often allowed to remain "temporarily" open, with the explanation given that patients would have no other place to go.

In 1981 the Reagan administration proposed deregulation of the nursing home industry. After pressure from the National Citizens Coalition for Nursing Home Reform (NCCNHR), the public at large, and Congress, the administration backed down. Congress mandated a two-year study by the Institute of Medicine of the National Academy of Sciences, resulting in a 1986 report, *Improving the*

Quality of Care in Nursing Homes. This report urged the federal government to improve the regulation of nursing homes.

Consequently, in 1987, legislation was passed, affecting all aspects of long-term care, from mandating services and standards to deciding payment eligibility. The Health Care Financing Administration (HCFA) promulgated revisions of the Conditions of Participation for skilled nursing facilities and recommended that they also apply to intermediate care facilities, bringing an end to the differences in standards for these two types of facilities. Under provisions of the nursing home reform law of 1987 Congress mandated nursing home reforms that focused not just on health and fire safety, but on the "quality of life." Nursing facilities can no longer employ any nurse's aide for more than three months unless a training and competency evaluation program has been successfully completed. Facilities must provide continuous licensed nursing care seven days a week, with RNs on duty at least 8 hours a day (although the law provides for a waiver system that will allow nursing facilities to operate without professional nursing under certain circumstances). At least one social worker must be available for each facility with more than 120 beds. Physician visits are required every 30 days for the first 90 days of care and every 60 days after that. An independent consultant outside the facility must annually review the appropriateness of the drug program for each resident receiving drugs. Rehabilitative services such as physical therapy and occupational therapy must be provided to every resident when the plan of care requires these services.

In addition, states are responsible for ensuring that applicants seeking admission to a nursing home receive preadmission screening for known or suspected mental illness or retardation and be assessed relative to their needs for active treatment for any mental disability. If such treatment is found to be necessary, referral must be made to a facility which provides such services. Estimates based on the 1987 National Medical Expenditures Survey found 31% of nursing home residents (about 475,000) with a primary or secondary diagnosis of mental illness, excluding those with a primary diagnosis of dementia. When dementia is included in estimates, up to 88% of all nursing home residents exhibit mental health problems.[19]

A nursing home may voluntarily apply for accreditation by the Joint Commission on Accreditation of Healthcare Organizations (JCAHO). Accreditation by JCAHO does not negate the need for federal certification to be eligible to receive Medicare and/or Medicaid funding. According to JCAHO, its certificate of accreditation means that certain basic standards have been met. The Joint Commission has standards for and conducts surveys of long-term care organizations, including subacute programs and dementia special care units. The standards are developed by health professionals and relate to all aspects of a facility's operation, including organization and administration; fire safety and construction; nursing, dietetic, and pharmaceutical services; medical/health records; and social, environmental, and other essential services. Further standards require that a facility continuously evaluate the quality of the care and the services it provides.

Dissatisfaction has long been expressed about the certification process for long-term care facilities. Although regulations had been established for the proper conduct of such facilities for reimbursement purposes, most reimbursements rely on the determination of whether a facility is *capable* of providing the needed service, not on whether it has actually delivered such a service. There had been no systematic way to identify whether the patient was receiving a service or making the progress that he or she should. In other words, survey and certification only evaluated paper compliance, not the quality of care rendered. Deficiencies continued to exist. Many nursing homes continued to operate as usual, ignoring regulations that were designed to implement the nursing home law. The 1987 nursing home reform legislation (OBRA) and the implementing regulations published by HCFA were designed to address these very real problems. The regulations and survey process now focus on individual residents, their quality of life, the care they receive, and the outcomes of that care. In addition, new enforcement regulations provide for a menu of remedies that are alternatives to termination of a nursing home from the Medicare and Medicaid programs. These alternative remedies are designed to encourage nursing homes to quickly correct their deficiencies and to maintain that correction on a continuing basis.

Consumer groups such as the National Citizens Coalition for Nursing Home Reform urge that family members request a copy of their relative's plan of care and monitor its implementation. Complaints should be brought to the attention of nursing home staff and, if necessary, to the office of the long-term-care ombudsman located in every state office on aging. Complaints may also be filed with state nursing home certification agencies.

Patient Characteristics. Nursing home residents tend to be very old (36% are 85 and older), female (72%), and white (88%). The median length of stay is 1.7 years (Table 11.1). However, not everyone who enters a nursing home becomes a "resident," staying for an extended period of time. "Short-stay" patients are admitted for recuperative or terminal care of specific ailments. In 1984–1985 the median length of stay for discharged short-stay patients was 82 days; those discharged alive had a median length stay of 70 days,

compared to those who died, who had a median stay of 163 days. Almost half of all live nursing home discharges went to general or short-stay hospitals; 2.4% went to VA hospitals. See Table 11.2 for the primary medical diagnosis at the time of admission for nursing home residents.

The numbers of people in nursing homes who suffer from psychiatric disorders have been variously estimated. As we have emphasized previously, persons with chronic physical disorders generally have psychiatric symptoms. Added to these patients are the numbers of people who have been transferred from psychiatric hospitals. As described earlier, it is rare for psychiatric care to be available. Nursing homes tend to select persons with the kinds of psychiatric symptoms that cause the least problems. Suicidal, boisterous, or hostile persons are likely to be rejected, along with those who wander off, smoke in bed, or are addicted to drugs or alcohol. The tractable, depressed, withdrawn persons are more acceptable, as well as those with incontinence and definite nursing needs.

The Ongoing Nursing Home Debate. The number of skilled nursing facilities that specialize in providing care for Alzheimer's and Huntington's disease patients is increasing. In addition, a new specialty facility has emerged—the AIDS skilled nursing facility. Much controversy has surrounded this concept and, as a result, few facilities have been designated thus far.

The latest round in the continuing national debate over nursing homes is worth noting. Some insist that too many people are in nursing homes. In 1980, Vladeck's controversial book, *Unloving Care: The Nursing Home Tragedy,* advocated phasing out the worst one-third of the nation's nursing homes and using the savings to expand special housing and home-based services for older people.[20] At that time, Vladeck divided the nursing home population into three categories:

1. Those who are fatally ill or recuperating from acute illnesses who would be better off in a hospital extended care facility where they could

TABLE 11.1 Length of stay of nursing home residents, 1985

DISTRIBUTION OF LENGTH OF STAY	PERCENTAGE OF RESIDENTS
Less than 3 months	13.0
3–6 months	9.5
6–12 months	14.0
1–3 years	31.5
3–plus years	32.0

Median length of stay: 614 days or 1.7 years

Source: U.S. Department of Health and Human Services, National Center for Health Statistics, Washington, DC: Series 13, No. 97, 1989.

TABLE 11.2 Number and percent distribution of nursing home residents by primary diagnosis at admission and at time of survey: United States, 1985

	AT ADMISSION		AT TIME OF SURVEY	
PRIMARY DIAGNOSIS	NUMBER OF RESIDENTS	PERCENT DISTRIBUTION	NUMBER OF RESIDENTS	PERCENT DISTRIBUTION
All categories	1,491,400	100.0	1,491,400	100.0
1. Infectious and parasitic diseases	7,600	.5	5,900	.4
2. Neoplasms	35,000	2.3	35,000	2.3
Malignant neoplasms	30,600	2.1	31,900	2.1
3. Endocrine, nutritional, metabolic, and immunity disorders	83,200	5.6	81,600	5.5
Diabetes mellitus	59,400	4.0	66,000	4.4
4. Diseases of the blood and blood-forming organs	8,500	.6	10,000	.7
Anemias	7,200	.5	8,000	.5
5. Mental disorders	306,800	20.6	330,600	22.2
Senile dementia and other organic psychotic conditions	43,800	2.9	49,300	3.3
Other psychoses	80,400	5.4	81,400	5.5
Neurotic and personality disorders	9,300	.6	10,900	.7
Specific non-psychotic mental disorders due to organic brain damage	111,300	7.5	133,400	8.9
Mental retardation	36,400	2.4	34,900	2.3
Other mental disorders	25,600	1.7	20,700	1.4
6. Diseases of the nervous system and sense organs	142,100	9.5	157,300	10.5
Alzheimer's disease* and other specified and unspecified degeneration of the brain	39,800	2.7	45,800	3.1
Parkinson's disease	31,400	2.1	33,200	2.2
Multiple sclerosis	8,200	.6	9,600	.6
Blindness	*	*	5,900	.4
7. Diseases of the circulatory system	468,600	31.4	486,500	32.6
Essential hypertension	50,900	3.4	49,900	3.3
Heart disease	207,900	13.9	234,100	15.7
Coronary atherosclerosis	80,900	5.4	100,400	6.7
Other ischemic heart disease	19,000	1.3	16,500	1.1
Congestive heart failure	45,000	3.0	46,900	3.1
Other heart disease	63,000	4.2	70,300	4.7
Cerebrovascular disease	165,400	11.1	153,700	10.3
Atherosclerosis	28,500	1.9	33,700	2.3
8. Diseases of the respiratory system	57,300	3.8	51,300	3.4
Pneumonia, all forms	12,400	.8	*	*
Chronic obstructive pulmonary disease and allied conditions	36,000	2.4	39,600	2.7
9. Diseases of the digestive system	35,100	2.4	33,900	2.3

TABLE 11.2 *(Continued)*

	AT ADMISSION		AT TIME OF SURVEY	
PRIMARY DIAGNOSIS	NUMBER OF RESIDENTS	PERCENT DISTRIBUTION	NUMBER OF RESIDENTS	PERCENT DISTRIBUTION
10. Diseases of the genito-urinary system	26,900	1.8	25,800	1.7
Urinary tract infection, N.E.C.	12,300	.8	11,000	.7
12. Diseases of the skin and subcutaneous tissue	13,900	.9	11,300	.8
13. Diseases of the musculo-skeletal system and connective tissue	91,600	6.1	94,700	6.3
Rheumatoid arthritis, osteoarthritis and allied disorders, except spine	33,700	2.3	36,300	2.4
Other arthritis or rheumatism	21,300	1.4	25,500	1.7
Osteoporosis	8,100	.5	8,100	.5
14. Congenital anomalies	5,800	.4	6,400	.4
16. Symptoms, signs and ill-defined conditions	57,100	3.8	59,700	4.0
Senility without psychoses	15,600	1.0	18,100	1.2
17. Injury and poisoning	96,300	6.5	52,400	3.5
Fracture of neck or femur	50,800	3.4	26,600	1.8
Other fractures	30,800	2.1	15,900	1.1
Supplementary classifications	20,000	1.3	16,900	1.1
Persons with potential health hazards related to personal and family history	9,400	.6	9,200	.6
Persons with a condition influencing their health status	8,800	.6	6,700	.5
Unknown	35,600	2.4	31,900	2.1

NOTE: N-E-C. = Not elsewhere classified. Figures may not add to totals because of rounding.

Modified from: U.S. Department of Health and Human Services (1989, Jan.). (Number and percent distribution of nursing home residents by primary diagnosis at admission and at time of survey: United States, 1985). The National Nursing Home Survey: 1985 Summary for the United States. Series 13, No. 97. DHHS Publication No. (PHS) 89-1758. Hyattsville, Md.: National Center for Health Statistics, p. 31.

*AUTHOR'S NOTE: The very low figures for the rate of Alzheimer's disease in nursing homes most probably reflects the fact that Alzheimer's disease is not usually the primary medical diagnosis. However, it is estimated that at least 50% of nursing home residents suffer from some form of dementia.

get the medical attention they need. The majority of these persons die soon after admission to a nursing home (the average stay is six months).

2. Patients with physical disabilities who are in nursing homes because they have no one at home to care for them. Although chronically ill,

these patients could live, with support, outside the nursing home in, for example, congregate housing where housekeeping services, meals, medical services, and so on would be available.

3. Patients who need round-the-clock custodial care. Vladeck believes that nursing homes are necessary for this group, and that only they should be in institutions.

On the other hand, Dunlop and others question whether a significantly reduced rate of institutionalization in nursing homes is feasible.[21] Those older persons with family members who are available to care for them are generally very severely impaired by the time they enter a nursing home. This is because family members tend to help the older person remain at home as long and sometimes much longer than is reasonable. Housekeeping, personal care, and errands are common forms of assistance given by families. When chronic and extensive nursing care becomes necessary, most families turn to nursing homes. In the last stages of illness, it is doubtful whether families could manage home care, even with increased nursing and medical supports. The situation becomes more complicated when we remember what is happening to the family and to American women. (See Chapters 2 and 10 for discussion of caregivers.) More and more middle-aged and even older women, the traditional caregivers to the old, are going to work outside the home. Mobility of family members often produces geographic separations. The size of the family itself is thinning out because of a lowered birth rate. And the increased life expectancy is bringing more four- and five-generation families, with a host of older people for the middle-aged and younger family members to be responsible for. A single-minded focus on increased home care would increase the burden for family members by enabling more of the aged to remain home in a chronically ill condition.

Although generally healthier as a group than patients with families, those nursing home patients with no family on whom to rely would frequently have to have some form of protected living (like congregate housing) as an alternative to a nursing home. This becomes an enormously expensive proposition requiring a whole new set of structures or the remodeling of older structures. Although this might be desirable for older persons, it would not necessarily reduce the cost of long-term care and could conceivably increase it.

Furthermore, unless an entirely new approach were taken, these new "quasi-institutions" might prove to be little improvement over the present facilities where most such older people now live.

All in all, many persons knowledgeable in the field of nursing homes in the United States believe that, at most, 10% of nursing home patients could live on their own in the community with home health or other supports. But this has to be balanced with the thought that perhaps that same number of persons are now existing in the community under unacceptable circumstances and really should be in institutions. Sophisticated epidemiological studies are needed to determine the facts.

By 1989, older persons admitted to nursing homes were considered sicker than in the past. This is because, under the Tax Equity and Fiscal Responsibility Act of 1982, the DRG-driven shortening of hospital stays has led to pressures on the nursing homes (as well as on home care) to meet the needs of frail older persons who are discharged from hospitals before they have fully recovered. Nursing homes have had to become more "medicalized" to care for an increasingly sicker population. They have also begun to transfer patients to acute hospitals more frequently than in the past. An additional issue is that in many parts of the country, there has been a constraint upon the creation or expansion of nursing home beds, while at the same time the older population (especially the 85-plus group) continues to grow.

Selecting a Nursing Home.[22]   Mental health personnel should be thoroughly familiar with any nursing homes to which they refer older people and their families. Initially, personnel should determine whether the home is state-licensed, whether it is certified to participate in government financial assistance programs, whether the administrator is state-licensed, and whether the home provides services such as physical therapy, social work, and specially prescribed diets. Visits to the nursing home in question are useful in order to talk to staff, observe the home and its operations, and view the patients firsthand. Families can contact local agencies (usually local ombudsman programs, public health departments, and voluntary and family agencies) and physicians who may be able to give an idea of the quality of individual homes. Health and welfare councils and mental health associations may provide help in selection. Proper placement must, of course, be based on a comprehensive evaluation of the older person's condition and needs.

Voluntary Nonprofit Homes for the Aging

Homes for the aging are voluntary, nonprofit institutions, usually sponsored by religious organizations, fraternal groups, and other nonprofit agencies. Nonprofit facilities include senior rental apartments, many with supportive services; assisted living facilities; continuing care retirement communities; and nursing homes. Many progressive changes have been made as homes for the aging move away from the limited historic connotation of "old age homes."

While different denominations sponsor their own homes, the people living in them are of varying faiths. Religious, fraternal, and trust homes ordinarily exclude the overtly mentally ill, the severely mentally impaired, and the acutely or notably physically ill. Federal law requires nursing home residents to be given mental health evaluation as well as physical assessments. If an individual's mental health needs cannot be met in the nursing home, the home cannot admit that person.

Since the 1977 Medicare-Medicaid fraud and abuse act, it has been a federal crime to coerce contributions from residents or family members as a condition of admission to or continued stay in a nursing home. Many nonprofit senior housing facilities admit only low-income residents. Assisted living facilities (sometimes called *personal care* or *board and care homes*) serve low-income as well as middle-income elderly. Because most states set their Medicaid payment rates at less than nursing homes' costs, nursing homes often do try to maintain a mix of private pay and Medicaid residents, but this is not a matter of discrimination based on wealth; it is a matter of economic survival. Even nonprofit continuing care retirement communities, whose fees not everyone can afford, subsidize the care of residents who become unable to pay or outlive their resources.

In the past, when illnesses developed after patients were admitted to a home, the patients would probably be transferred to a municipal, county, or state facility because most homes for the aging had insufficient services and personnel to provide the necessary care. Now, due to Medicare policy and the trend toward managed care, hospitals tend to discharge elderly patients home or to long-term care facilities much earlier than they used to. In many cases, today's nonprofit health care facilities can provide more complex nursing and medical care. In addition, nonprofit senior housing facilities increasingly are combining residential services with support services, so residents can get the assistance they need as they "age in place" without having to move prematurely to other care facilities. For example, senior housing may include meals, transportation, social services, counseling, and telephone reassurance. Assisted living, which bridges the gap between independent living and nursing home care, may include assistance with meals, bathing, dressing, eating, medications, housekeeping, and so on. Continuing Care Retirement Communities offer residents long-term care contracts that provide housing, services, nursing, and health care, along with recreational and educational activities.

Many older persons can live in a home for the aging or a nursing home rather than a state hospital if such facilities offer therapeutic programs and can draw on personnel usually found in a hospital. How can all these services be offered? The Philadelphia Geriatric Center has included all the combinations suggested above in one city block: a hospital, the Home for the Jewish Aged (which was the parent institution), two residential apartment buildings, a research institute, and several small-unit, intermediate boarding facilities. A day-care center for older persons exists in another part of the city.

Other homes for the aging have moved beyond their physical structure into the community. Social services, Meals-on-Wheels, and day-care centers are developing in some areas. "Drop-in" centers with recreational services, arts, and crafts may occasionally be found, along with sheltered workshops.

An outstanding long-term care facility is the Jewish Home and Hospital for Aged in New York, founded in 1870. It is the largest nonprofit institution for the care of the aged in New York City, with many programs in teaching (The Frederic D. Zeman Center for Instruction) and research. Over 1,600 individuals are cared for through an integrated group of facilities. The aged in the community are served by a day-care center and geriatric outreach program. Its two main centers provide nursing facilities for all nursing home care needs, depending on patient condition. A middle-income housing project has 320 residents.

Leslie S. Libow, Vice Chairman of the Department of Geriatrics and Adult Development of Mount Sinai Medical Center as well as Chief of Medical Services at the Jewish Home and Hospital for Aged, has continued his pioneering work both in geriatric medical education and in developing the body of knowledge of geriatric medicine at the Jewish Home and Hospital for Aged.

Other institutions of special note, some of which approximate the campus-type of environment, are the Hebrew Home for the Aged (Bronx, New York), the Carmelite Homes (the Mary Manning Walsh Home of New York City and St. Joseph's Manor of Trumbull, Connecticut), the Isabella Home Geriatric Center in New York City, the Avery Convalescent Center in Hartford, Connecticut, the Philadelphia Geriatric Center, Golden Acres (the Jewish Home for the Aged) of Dallas, Texas, the Samarkand of Santa Barbara, California, Lincoln Lutheran of Racine, Wisconsin, Loretto Geriatric Center of Syracuse, New York, Asbury Methodist Village of Gaithersburg, Maryland, the Hebrew Rehabilitation Center for the Aged of Boston, and the Wesley Homes of Atlanta, Georgia.

About 2,500 of the American Association of Homes and Services for the Aging's member or-

ganizations are involved in providing home- and community-based services such as home health care, adult day care, or respite care. Over one hundred of these organizations provide only these services. New York's "Nursing Home Without Walls" was sponsored by State Senator Tarky Lombardi.[23] (See Chapter 10 for a description of the Lombardi program.)

FINANCING INSTITUTIONAL CARE

Personal and economic costs of mental disorders, especially the dementias, are staggering. Patients and their families pay half of the nation's long-term care bill, that is, some 36 billion dollars in 1994. In the same year, Medicare paid for about 8.2% of the total nursing home bill of $72 billion. Medicaid paid for 47%, and 42% was paid for privately, mostly through out-of-pocket spending.[24] Spending per capita for the nation's 1.6 nursing home residents averages over $30,000 a year, and the more expensive homes can cost over $60,000 or more a year. This is a drastic increase from the $8,250 figure in 1955. Some families pay another $1,000 a month to obtain a 24-hour private duty nurse in the nursing home. Private psychiatric hospitals often cost $500 to $1,000 a day, including ancillary expenses.

People past the age of 65 have a 40 to 50% chance of spending some time, however brief, in a nursing home. Nonetheless, by the year 2000, 40% of those needing long-term care in or out of an institution will be under 65, since long-term care is a need throughout the life course. It is now becoming clear that long-term care should be universal and funded on an intergenerational basis.

Historically, the care and treatment of the mentally ill have been left to the individual states. The first federal assistance was offered to the states in the National Mental Health Act of 1946. Part of the Medicaid legislation with significance for mental health was sponsored by Senator Russell Long in 1965. It permits federal financial assistance for persons in the group age 65 and over who are patients in institutions for mental diseases. It is a companion piece to the Title XVIII

(Medicare) legislation, which provides specifically for those older persons with acute brain disorders and other mental illnesses who can be expected to respond to relatively brief but intensive treatment in mental hospitals.[25] The Long Amendment also makes provisions for the very many aged who are suffering from chronic disorders, either organic or functional, and who need long-term continued care in state mental health facilities. In expressing the intent of the amendment, the Senate Committee on Finance stated that it

> wishes to insure that the additional Federal funds to be made available to the States under the provisions of the bill will assist the overall improvement of mental health services in the State. State and local funds now being used for institutional care of the aged will be released as a result of the bill, but there is a great need for increased professional services in hospitals and for development of alternate methods of care outside the hospitals. To accomplish this, States may have to reallocate their expenditures for mental health to promote new methods of treatment and care. The committee bill provides that the States will receive additional federal funds only to the extent that a showing is made to the satisfaction of the Secretary that total expenditures of the States or [their] political subdivisions from their own funds for mental health services are increased.[26]

However, millions of dollars in Medicaid payments have not resulted in better programs or higher medical standards. In most states, monies designated by law for the improvement of the care of older mental patients in state hospitals go into the state general revenue fund and are seldom seen by the hospitals.

About two-thirds of all 244 state hospitals have been certified for the Medicare program. Certification came either from the Joint Commission on Accreditation of Health Care Organization or from the Social Security Administration. Certified hospitals must maintain comprehensive clinical records and must have sufficient staff to carry out "active" and "intensive" psychiatric treatment. The point of these special rules is to avoid custodial care. The Medicare regulations are spelled out in the Social Security Administration booklet

Health Insurance for the Aged: Conditions of Participation for Hospitals.

Private long-term care insurance is limited, covering less than 5% of all home and institutional care. More than 1,000 private long-term care policies were in effect in the United States in 1988, but they were of uncertain value and extremely expensive.[27] A policy's value depends on such factors as (1) the daily benefit provided in dollars; (2) the cost-of-care annual adjustment that is provided; (3) whether the premium remains level or whether it may be increased; (4) whether renewability for life is guaranteed; (5) maximum benefit period offered; (6) waiting period requirement; (7) type of institutional care provided; (8) rules regarding previous hospitalization; and (9) the nature and extent of the homecare benefit.

A current attempt to reduce costs and improve quality of care is the Social Health Maintenance Organization (SHMO), a prepaid, managed approach to acute and long-term care for the elderly population (see Chapter 10). Under this system, one provider takes responsibility for a full range of services under a fixed budget. Once elderly persons voluntarily enroll, they receive all covered services through SHMO providers. The operation is similar to the medical model health maintenance organization (HMO).

FAMILY REACTION
TO INSTITUTIONALIZATION

Families often need help in dealing with their feelings about an older family member's admission to an institution. In one poignant example, we worked with a very conscientious 70-year-old man who was taking care of his 92-year-old mother and his 67-year-old wife, both of whom had severe dementia. He refused institutionalization for either of them and was devoting all of his waking hours to the very difficult task of managing their care by himself in his home. Nursing and social service departments in institutions are especially important in maintaining liaison with relatives. Many family members are extremely ambivalent, both because of the generally negative reputation of institutional care and because of their own feelings of failing or abandoning the person. After placing a relative in a nursing home, some experience a sense of relief about which they later feel guilty. Families who care (as opposed to those who reject the older person—a much less common category) often experience a grief reaction on admission as though the person had already died. This "death" may be more traumatic than the actual death of the older person later on. In some cases family members may actually stop visiting the person because of inability to tolerate their own grief and ambivalence. Some institutional care now has the built-in expectation and real possibility of home visits, which helps prevent families from cutting themselves off emotionally. Families need to be advised that some of the very supportive things they can do for an older person are to visit frequently, take the person on outings and weekend visits home if possible, become involved with the institution by getting to know the staff and administrative personnel, and provide the extra amenities and attention that only a family can give.

The actual day of admission of an older person may be handled insensitively in many institutions. The older person is simply "deposited" without any transition or preparation. This shock approach can result in increased risk of illness and even death; certainly it is questionable psychologically. Flexibility and individualization should be the rule; some persons indeed respond best to a firm, quick (but humane) admission, while many others need to take their time, to absorb things slowly with a good deal of support. The inauguration of day programs, preliminary admissions for weekends, and provisions for family or friends to sleep in the institution (nearby or even in the same room) when the older person is anxious and frightened can soften the suddenness and harshness of admission. Family and friends should be allowed and encouraged to serve as volunteers in institutional activities, from socializing to performing simple services for residents. Children and grandchildren should be given access to older relatives. In general, there should be much more fluidity between the institution and the community.

Group and individual therapy with families can be useful in helping to resolve long-term family conflicts and short-term reactions to institutionalization. See Chapter 12 for further discussion of therapy. For families with Alzheimer's victims who require intense family home care/day care or who will eventually need nursing home care, the Alzheimer's Association has become a major source of information and general support. With its more than 200 affiliated chapters throughout the United States, the Alzheimer's Association can be especially helpful for families scattered across the country. The network of family support groups for caregivers remains the backbone of this organization.[28]

OTHER FACTORS IN INSTITUTIONAL CARE

Right to Treatment

A second legal concept beyond the question of involuntary admission discussed earlier is the "right to treatment."[29] It is difficult to balance the right to freedom with the right to treatment. A federal district court for Alabama ruled in 1972 that patients committed involuntarily to a mental hospital through noncriminal procedures have a constitutional right to "adequate and effective treatment." The court further found that Alabama was failing to provide adequate treatment to the several thousand patients who had been civilly committed to Bryce Hospital in Tuscaloosa. The ruling was made as a result of a class action suit initiated by guardians of patients at Bryce and by certain hospital employees. It was stated that the Constitution requires adequate and effective treatment, because without it the hospital is transformed into a penitentiary where an individual could be held indefinitely without conviction for any offense. The court ordered a report from the hospital within 90 days that was to include a precise definition of the mission and functions of the hospital and a specific plan to deliver adequate treatment to patients.[30]

U.S. District Court Judge Frank M. Johnson, Jr., established three major aspects of an adequate treatment program: (1) a humane physical and psychological environment, (2) staffing adequate in numbers and training to provide treatment, and (3) an individual treatment plan for each patient.

In reviewing Alabama's mental health and retardation facilities in 1979, seven years after the *Wyatt* v. *Stickney* case, Judge Johnson found they still "failed to achieve substantial compliance" with the standards he set down in 1972. He had the institutions placed in receivership and issued two orders aimed at achieving full compliance within 18 months in the class action case, now on its fourth name, *Wyatt v. Ireland.*

In 1986, after 17 years of stalemate and legal proceedings, the state and the original patient complainants finally agreed on a settlement aimed at moving Alabama's mental health bureaucracy from "an almost exclusive reliance on institutions to a balanced system of institutional and community care." The centerpiece of the consent decree was the creation of an unusual five-member committee of independent experts, with each side appointing two members and the fifth member being a director of patient advocacy. The committee has since released its first report (1990) and has shown impressive movement toward its goals of developing community services, successfully convincing the legislature of a need for funds, implementing patient assessment procedures, helping the state achieve accreditation (through the Joint Commission on the Accreditation of Health Organizations) for its hospitals, and establishing quality assurance and patient advocacy programs. However, the committee admits that it is still too early to report on the ultimate success of its efforts to improve treatment and community alternatives for the mentally ill and retarded.[31]

The focus has also turned to other states with conditions as deplorable as in Alabama. Litigation for patients' rights has become more sophisticated and complex; for example, how does a hospital give legally required treatment to patients if they refuse treatment and are supported by law in their refusal?

Individual Treatment Plans

The right to treatment must involve an individual treatment plan for each patient.

> The need for an individual treatment plan cannot be over-emphasized. Without such a plan, there can be no evidence that the hospital has singled out the patient for treatment as an individual with his own unique problems.[32]

Preliminary diagnostic formulation and individualized treatment plans should be accomplished within 12 to 14 hours of admission to any kind of hospital or institution. Reception units or special psychogeriatric units in hospitals should be available for brief hospitalizations, perhaps for three to five days up to three to six weeks, to facilitate proper diagnosis and, in the cases of reversible brain syndromes (like delirium and some dementia) and functional disorders, definitive immediate treatment. The staff should avoid a mental "set" regarding treatability or length of hospitalization. Experience has emphasized that treatment trials constitute a major part of evaluation; for example, considerable time should be given to make certain that a seemingly fixed and permanent organic brain disorder is not a refractory depression or caused by a reversible underlying physical condition.

Periodic and comprehensive reevaluation is important. All residents must be formally assessed concerning their needs on an annual basis. Patients who arrive with one condition may develop others during their stay. Changes in psychiatric symptoms are often caused by physical changes that the patient may be unable to report.

Other Patient Rights and Privileges

The many and pervasive aspects of authoritarianism seen in hospitals and institutions are facets of infantilization and often serve the needs of the providers rather than those served. The goal should be the fewest restrictive conditions necessary to achieve the purposes of institutionalization. Patients' rights must be preserved in very specific ways.

A Hospital Patient's Bill of Rights

The American Hospital Association has devised the following patient's bill of rights:[33]

1. To expect considerate and respectful care
2. To obtain from his or her physician complete current information concerning his or her diagnosis, treatment, and prognosis, in terms he or she can understand
3. To obtain from his or her physician information necessary for informed consent before any procedure or treatment is begun; to obtain information on significant alternatives; and to know the name of the person responsible for the treatment
4. To refuse treatment to the extent permitted by law and to be informed of the medical consequences of refusal
5. To have every consideration of his or her privacy concerning his or her own medical care; persons not directly involved in his or her care must have the patient's permission to be present at case discussion, consultation, examination, and treatment
6. To expect confidentiality of all communications and records pertaining to him or her
7. To expect that within its capacity a hospital make reasonable response to his or her request for service and not transfer him or her to another institution without explanation
8. To obtain information about any relationship of his or her hospital to other health services that concern his or her care and about the existence of any professional relationships among individuals who are treating him or her
9. To be advised if the hospital proposes to engage in human experimentation affecting his or her care and to refuse to participate in such research
10. To expect reasonable continuity of care, including postdischarge follow-up
11. To examine and receive an explanation of his or her bill no matter who pays it
12. To know what hospital rules and regulations apply to his or her conduct as a patient

Resident Rights in Nursing Facilities

The following are requirements that an institution must meet in order to qualify to participate as a nursing facility in the Medicaid and Medicare program.[34] [As mentioned earlier, *nursing facility* in the Medicaid program replaced the terms *skilled nursing facility* (SNF) and *intermediate care facility* (ICF).]

Resident rights include a right to a dignified existence, self-determination, and communication with and access to persons and services inside and outside the facility. A facility must protect and promote the rights of each resident, including each of the following rights:

1. Exercise of rights
   a. The resident has the right to exercise his or her rights as a resident of the facility and as a citizen or resident of the United States.
   b. The resident has the right to be free of interference, coercion, discrimination, or reprisal from the facility in exercising his or her rights.
   c. In the case of a resident adjudged incompetent under the laws of a State by a court of competent jurisdiction, the rights of the resident are exercised by the person appointed under State law to act on the resident's behalf.
2. Notice of rights and services
   a. The facility must inform the resident both orally and in writing in a language that the resident understands of his or her rights and all rules and regulations governing resident conduct and responsibilities during the stay in the facility. Such notification must be made prior to or upon admission and during the resident's stay. Receipt of such information, and any amendments to it, must be acknowledged in writing.
   b. The resident has the right to inspect and purchase photocopies of all records pertaining to the resident, upon written request and 48 hours notice to the facility.
   c. The resident has the right to be fully informed in language that he or she can un-

derstand of his or her total health status, including but not limited to, his or her medical condition.

d. The resident has the right to refuse treatment and to refuse to participate in experimental research; and

e. The facility must:

   i. Inform each resident who is entitled to Medicaid benefits, in writing, at the time of admission to the nursing facility or when the resident becomes eligible for Medicaid, of:

   (a) The items and services that are included in nursing facility services under the State plan and for which the resident may not be charged;

   (b) Those other items and services that the facility offers and for which the resident may be charged, and the amount of charges for those services; and

   ii. Inform each resident when changes are made regarding items and services.

f. The facility must inform each resident before or at the time of admission and periodically during the resident's stay of services available in the facility and of charges for those services, including any charges for services not covered under Medicare or by the facility's per diem rate.

g. The facility must furnish a written description of legal rights which includes a description of the manner of protecting personal funds and a statement that the resident may file a complaint with the State survey and certification agency concerning resident abuse, neglect, and misappropriation of resident property in the facility.

h. The facility must inform each resident of the name, specialty, and way of contacting the physician responsible for his or her care.

i. Effective October 1, 1990, the facility must prominently display written information and provide to residents and potential residents oral and written information about how to apply for and use Medicare and Medicaid benefits and how to receive refunds for previous payments covered by such benefits.

j. Notification of changes

   i. Except in a medical emergency or when a resident is incompetent, a facility must consult with the resident immediately and notify the resident's physician, and, if known, the resident's legal representative or interested family member within 24 hours when there is:

   (a) An accident involving the resident which results in injury;

   (b) A significant change in the resident's physical, mental, or psychosocial status;

   (c) A need to alter treatment significantly; or

   (d) A decision to transfer or discharge the resident from the facility.

   ii. The facility must also promptly notify the resident and, if known, the resident's legal representative or interested family member when there is:

   (a) A change in room or roommate assignment.

   (b) A change in resident rights under Federal or State law or regulations.

   iii. The facility must record and periodically update the address and phone number of the resident's legal representative or interested family member.

3. Protection of resident funds

a. The resident has the right to manage his or her financial affairs and the facility may not require residents to deposit their personal funds with the facility.

In addition to provisions for residents' rights, the 1987 reform law calls for, among other things, unannounced inspection of nursing homes, more and a wider range of penalties and, happily, requirements for training of nurses' aides. In addition, it requires that the home guarantee residents a choice of physicians and that there be a written plan of care for each patient. Specifically, the law states that a nursing facility must provide services and activities to attain or maintain the highest practicable physical, mental, and psychosocial well-being of each resident in accordance with a written plan of cure that is based on the "resident assessment."

The *resident assessment* is a requirement that all nursing facilities, beginning October 1, 1990, must conduct an assessment of the medical, nursing, and psychosocial needs of each resident at least once a year. This assessment is to be based on a "Minimum Data Set" that has been developed by the Secretary of the Department of Health and Human Services, and is to be compiled initially in the first 14 days after admission to a facility. Revisions are to be made quarterly, with a full review annually. The resident assessment is coordinated by a registered nurse with the participation of at least one physician, as well as other health care professionals. The assessment covers a broad spectrum of needs, including assessment of cognitive impairment. It also assesses "customary and daily routines" of each resident, in order to attempt to accommodate individual preferences in food, bedtime, personal hygiene, and so forth.

Each facility must also create a quality assessment and assurance committee consisting of the director of nursing, a physician, and at least three other staff members.

Commitment or voluntary admission to a mental hospital or a move to a nursing home should not per se abrogate the right to manage affairs, to sign contracts, to hold professional, occupational, or vehicle operator's licenses, to marry or obtain a divorce, to register and vote, and to make a will. Direct access to legal counsel is also mandatory.[35] Patients should not be placed incommunicado. Visitation (including small children) and telephone communications should be permitted on a 24-hour basis except when there are clear indications that such communications and visitations promote disturbances in the patient that are untherapeutic and harmful at a *particular* time. Any limit on such contact must be periodically reviewed, and renewal or continuation must not be automatic. This should require a physician's decision, and the physician must not have any ownership ties with the facility, in order not to prejudice his or her judgment.

Patients must have the unrestricted right to receive sealed mail except when responsible staff personnel can clearly defend restriction on the basis of an individualized patient plan. Again, periodic review must occur. The physician must bear ultimate responsibility since only the patient's mental or physical condition could warrant such a restriction on rights and privileges.

Privacy and space to move are other rights. Privacy is obviously qualitative as well as quantitative, and the availability of time alone each day should be made. There must be a minimum of 100 square feet of floor space in one-patient rooms. No multipatient room should exceed four persons. There must be a minimum of 80 square feet of floor space per patient, with soundproofing, screens or curtains, and at least one toilet, lavatory, shower, or tub for each six persons. Each patient bed should have an electronic signal system to call to the staff for help. A comfortable, attractive day room area (40 square feet per patient) with reading lamps, tables, chairs, and recreational facilities is considered necessary, and a dining room should include 10 square feet per patient.

Husbands and wives who both are institutionalized should have the option to live together in an institution if they so desire. If problems arise or separation becomes necessary, skilled counseling should be available to them to avoid estrangement and feelings of desertion. When only one partner is institutionalized, arrangements for conjugal visits should be possible.

Food, abundantly and attractively served, is another patient right, unless medically restricted. The diet must, at minimum, provide the recommended daily dietary allowance developed by the National Academy of Science. Opportunities for snack times (including raiding an icebox), and ordering or even preparing certain favorite foods are psychologically beneficial.

The money available to the older person (including Supplemental Security Income and Social Security checks as well as private funds) must be safeguarded.

Persons should not be stripped of their clothing and made into "patients" with shoddy institutional apparel. Patients have the right to wear their own clothes and have their own possessions with them unless this is legitimately considered dangerous. Personal possessions and clothing help to maintain orientation, self-respect, and identity. Personnel are advised also to avoid calling persons by their first or "pet" names, as this too implies loss of dignity and infantilization. Further, patients should not be on "display" for the amusement of others.

On an institutional visit we were introduced by the chief nurse to an 87-year-old woman. The nurse, who, of course, insisted on being referred to as Mrs. L by the patients, said, "Jane, sing your song for the visitors." "Jane," who had formerly been a teacher of some repute, obediently belted out a popular song. Such callous disregard for patient dignity is perhaps not common, but it does occur all too frequently.

And finally, unless they give permission, patients should not be objects of observation for visiting doctors, students, families, and so forth. Those who are capable of consent should be asked if they would be willing to talk to visitors. All persons should have access to members of the clergy and religious services of their choice.

Community advocates for institutionalized older persons should be given free access to nursing homes, hospitals, and other long-term care facilities. A National Citizens' Coalition for Nursing Home Reform was organized for the following purposes:

1. To operate exclusively for charitable and educational purposes
2. To coordinate the efforts and resources of member organizations and individuals to improve the long-term care system and quality of life for nursing home residents

3. To provide resources and information relative to nursing home reform to members and the general public
4. To solicit sources of funding to finance the Coalition's activities
5. To develop and implement nursing home advocacy training programs
6. To study nursing home issues and report and make recommendations to members and the public at large

As of October, 1990, the Coalition had 315 member organizations in 42 states, a large increase from its 72 groups in 24 states just eight years earlier.

Physical Environment

The environment of hospitals, nursing homes, and other institutions is beginning to change. Efforts are being made to design esthetic and prosthetic environments that help compensate for mental and physical losses. The Retirement Research Foundation, in conjunction with the American Association of Homes for the Aging, has funded a clearing-house on environmental design of nursing homes. In progressive institutions, wandering patients who would have in the past been physically restrained now may have the possibility of orienting themselves through the use of color coding, the buddy system, and adequate staff. Maximum security atmospheres can be reduced by such devices as attractive wooden fences, gates, and even shrubbery rather than iron bars or locked doors. (Few geriatric patients break out of institutions! Most merely need something to discourage confused wandering.)

Protection from accidents and fires needs to be improved, and all institutions should be subject to the Life Safety Code of the National Fire Protection Association. New regulations have improved fire safety in nursing homes, but boarding houses remain hazardous. Air-conditioning in summer and control of temperature and humidity in winter are crucial, since older people cannot withstand extreme atmospheric conditions. In hospitals and nursing homes that are not air-conditioned, excessive numbers of older people die during heat waves.

With the advent of plastic and electronic devices that may be under either direct or remote control, much can be done to make up for deficiencies in ambulation, audition, vision, and general stimulation. Safety devices such as handrails, grab bars, call buttons, and nonslip floors are essential. Calendars, large clocks (set to the *correct* time!), and mirrors are useful orientation devices. The general environment should be reasonably calm but alive with stimuli, lest the capacity to react to the environment atrophy. Good illumination is necessary. Colorful decorations and plants and flowers enhance pleasure. Beauty parlors, barber shops, and canteens add variety. (Easy access to cosmeticians, hairdressers, masseuses, and masseurs does wonders for patient morale.) Music should be available but not, because of the Goldstein catastrophic reaction (Chapter 9), constantly blaring. Outdoor activities such as gardening and perhaps caring for pets in mini-zoos on institutional grounds can be extremely therapeutic.

Physician's Care

Among patients' rights is the right to adequate medical care from a physician. Only 13% of the 20,000 nursing homes surveyed by the National Center for Health Statistics had a full-time equivalent physician on the premises in 1985. Under the 1987 nursing home reform law, each nursing facility must designate a physician to serve as medical director to be responsible for implementing resident care policies and coordinating medical care. All institutions should have physicians with central responsibility and commensurate authority to override private doctors of individual patients if necessary. These physicians should plan the general medical program (routine tests, dental care, immunizations), conduct regular rounds, prescribe medications, respond to emergencies, and be available for consultations with families. Physicians must be clear that they are not there for the convenience of the institution but rather for the

well-being of residents. (For example, prescribing excessive medication may relieve the staff but make "zombies" out of patients.) Physicians themselves should be under the review of all staff members to guard against careless or insensitive treatment.

Teaching/Research Nursing Homes

The National Institute on Aging supports model teaching/research nursing homes at selected academic medical centers to focus on research, education, and service all at once.[36] (Ultimately, of course, it would be ideal if each of the 126 medical schools would have a teaching/research nursing home nearby as part of its program. A number have already developed affiliations.) Teaching/research nursing homes offer the unique opportunity to study disease processes in older people. Because many older people are sent to nursing homes rather than general hospitals or mental hospitals, physicians and other health care personnel in training can observe and study a number of conditions not routinely treated, at least for any great length of time, at hospitals. A major example is senile dementia of the Alzheimer type. Teaching/research nursing homes also encourage study of the effects of nutrition, drugs, exercise, and social interaction on disease; the investigation of better methods of diagnosis and treatment; the analysis of the best methods of delivering services of all kinds to nursing home residents; the training of medical, nursing, social work, psychology, and other health professions' students; and the provision of continuing education for all mental health professionals involved in the care of the aged.

Nursing Care

The role of the registered nurse in administration and in direct care in institutions is absolutely central. A registered nurse's leadership is likely to determine the quality of all aspects of care, including medical care. Supervision and on-the-job teaching of registered and practical nurses and aides are essential.

Nursing of the older patient requires flexibility, good humor without ridicule, and respect without distancing. Wolanin & Phillips (1981) have described nursing staff reactions to incontinence, difficult self-feeding, obscene language, and other unpleasant behaviors. Basic individualized knowledge of the patient is crucial and in keeping with our stress on comprehensive evaluation. The list below notes problems frequently confronted by nursing staffs and presented to medical and psychiatric consultants when they are called in to nursing homes and homes for the aged.

1. Depression among older patients
2. Confusion or other symptoms of delirium or dementia
3. Paranoia
4. Noisiness
5. Restlessness or wandering
6. Combativeness
7. Inappropriate dependency on staff
8. Persistent talk of a wish to die
9. Incontinence
10. Families who are justifiably critical or demanding of the institution

Bed rest can be dangerous, replicating all the untoward effects of chronic, debilitating illnesses: cardiovascular, respiratory, metabolic, and neuromuscular changes. To illustrate, with decreased respiration can come hypostatic pneumonia, and with immobility, a decrease in strength of muscles and weakening of bones (osteoporosis), with the risk of falls and fractures. People should be ambulated quickly, even after surgery.

Bedsores (also called decubiti, trophic ulcers, or pressure sores) can develop quickly, especially in bedridden, debilitated older persons. Such sores occur at pressure points—the bony areas of elbows, hips, and heels, and the buttocks—and are the result of reduced blood supply caused by the body's weight. Persons who are not turned in bed, who are malnourished or anemic (vitamin C deficiency and low protein intake are most dangerous), or who have been allowed to lie in urine until the skin macerates may develop infections in the sores. These infections are indolent, causing little

or no physical pain. Care should include ambulation, rotation of the patient, cleanliness and dryness, avoidance of oversedation, and checking of pressure points for early signs of redness. Physiotherapy through overhead trapeze and activity as well as active and passive exercises, including massage, are indicated. Paraplegic patients may need to be placed in frames that turn (Stryker frames). Indwelling catheters may be necessary to control urinary incontinence. Foam rubber, air mattresses and water beds, pillows, and sheepskin sheets are useful. When an ulcer has developed, it should be cleaned (debridement). Trypsin, an enzymatic digestive agent, along with topical antibiotics (for example, neomycin) is appropriate. Oral zinc therapy is controversial.

Incontinence refers to the inability to control bladder or bowel. Fifteen percent of men over 65 and 35% of women over 65 suffer from urinary incontinence. It has been estimated that one-third to one-half of older nursing home residents have this problem. In fact, it is a major reason for nursing home admission, costing facilities as much as $1 billion a year. The condition may be permanent as a result of severe injury, central nervous system disease, chronic infections, and so on. At other times it is temporary and reversible, related to anxiety, pain, hostility, and inadequate attention. It is important to overcome the idea that urinary incontinence is untreatable and that it is a normal function of aging. To some degree it is a function of bladder shrinkage and weakened muscles. Even persons with organic brain damage may be able to improve control. A careful evaluation and correct assessment as to cause must be made, and a plan for treatment built and kept. Emotional aspects should be dealt with through psychotherapy and staff involvement.

The incontinent patient with no permanent physical damage can often be retrained. In urinary incontinence one begins by giving the patient the bedpan or urinal on a regular schedule to develop a habit (for example, every two hours or on rising, after eating, and before bedtime). Bernard Engel's pioneering work on biofeedback at the National Institute on Aging's Baltimore Longitudinal Study has helped create retraining schedules for strengthening muscles and controlling the bladder and valves that shut off urination. In bowel retraining, proper timing is also of the essence. Timed food intake helps. Passive exercises for the bedridden (bending the knees and pressing the thighs against the abdomen) can sometimes stimulate the urge to defecate. Walking and other efforts to improve muscle tone help. Adult gauze diapers and underpads should be used and frequently changed until control improves.

Sometimes surgery may improve or cure incontinence by repositioning a fallen bladder or removing an obstruction. Surgical implantation of an artificial sphincter muscle to replace the tiny ring-like muscle that closes off the end of the neck of the bladder can also be helpful.[37]

Nursing Staff Problems. Nursing staff morale and dedication are an exceptionally crucial consideration. Decent care for all patients, rich or poor, depends on the goodwill and skill of all levels of staff; yet, much of the time the poor working conditions, low pay, low status, and lack of in-service and outside training for nursing and other personnel have been ignored. Like many other groups providing human services (police, fire fighters, teachers, government workers), nursing personnel are under public pressure not to strike, for the obvious reason—the welfare of patients. Nonetheless, there are three large health care unions: the American Federation of State, County, and Municipal Employees (AFSCME), Service Employees International, and the National Union of Hospital and Health Care Employees (formerly Local 1199). All are affiliates of the AFL-CIO. They organize and undertake collective bargaining efforts in hospitals, nursing homes, and other facilities. The American Nurses' Association and the National Federation of Licensed Practical Nurses are not unions, strictly speaking, but they operate like unions to some degree. There is also the National Conference of Physicians' Unions. (Important to unionization issues, too, are the U.S. Senate Committee on Labor and Public Welfare and, of course, the Federal Mediation and Conciliation Service.)

Some have recommended that the minimum nursing staff-to-patient ratios in long-term care facilities should be 1 registered nurse per 30 residents per shift with an additional 1 nursing staff member per 7 residents per day shift, 1 nursing staff member per 12 residents per evening shift, and 1 nursing staff member per 20 residents per night shift. As a result of the 1987 nursing home reform law, efforts are under way to determine optimal staffing patterns. Obviously, there is a greater need for more staff where there are more total care patients. See Table 11.3 for a description of personnel in various care settings.

Perhaps 80% to 90% of care of institutionalized older persons is provided by nursing aides, assistants, and orderlies. Training for these groups of personnel varied in the past, ranging from no training at all to 160 hours of training in rare cases. The 1987 nursing home reform law requires that nursing homes provide a competency evaluation program for all nurses' aides. All nurses' aides must now receive a minimum of 75 hours of training, including training in caring for the cognitively impaired.

Traditionally, much of the administrative and training responsibility has rested on the registered nurse—who is usually overworked and underrewarded. It is estimated that staff turnover in institutions for the elderly is a fantastic 75% per year! Part of the solution to the problem of high turnover is preservice and in-service training and staff development, including teaching staff to relate to patients, to give psychological counseling, and to learn to do group therapy. All staff should be encouraged and expected to participate in case conferences and decisions about patient or resident care. Technical nursing skills, such as dealing with stroke problems and bowel and bladder retraining, need to be constantly reviewed and updated.

Patient Restraint

It is estimated that over one-half million persons in nursing homes and hospitals have been regularly tied to their beds and chairs. Devices include chest, wrist or ankle ties; belts; mitts; harnesses; sheets; full body suits; side rails; locked doors;

TABLE 11.3 Number and rate per 100 beds of full-time equivalent employees of nursing homes, by facility ownership, certification and bed size

FACILITY CHARACTERISTIC

OCCUPATIONAL CATEGORY		OWNERSHIP				CERTIFICATION				BED SIZE			
		TOTAL	PROPRIETARY	VOLUNTARY NONPROFIT	GOVERNMENT AND OTHER	CERTIFIED BY MEDICARE AND MEDICAID	CERTIFIED BY MEDICARE ONLY	CERTIFIED BY MEDICAID ONLY	NOT CERTIFIED	LESS THAN 50 BEDS	50-99 BEDS	100-199 BEDS	200 BEDS OR MORE
All Full-Time Equivalent Employees	Number	1,333,300	823,000	383,100	127,200	1,055,900	52,800	191,600	33,000	73,000	320,500	674,500	265,300
	Rate per 100 beds	75.3	71.5	81.8	84.2	76.6	88.5	68.4	62.8	83.7	74.5	74.7	75.6
Administrative, Medical and Therapeutic Staff	Number	20,100	13,600	4,900	1,600	15,000	1,900	2,800	400	4,700	5,200	8,400	1,800
	Rate per 100 beds	1.1	1.2	1	1.1	1.1	3.2	1	0.8	5.4	1.2	0.9	0.5
Nursing Total	Number	913,500	574,100	254,300	85,100	727,900	35,800	127,500	22,300	49,600	221,400	468,500	174,000
	Rate per 100 beds	51.6	49.8	54.3	56.3	52.8	60	45.5	42.4	56.8	51.4	51.9	49.6
Registered Nurse	Total	129,700	78,000	38,300	13,300	105,800	7,400	13,600	3,000	10,700	29,200	63,700	26,100
	Rate per 100 beds	7.3	6.8	8.2	9	7.7	12.4	4.8	5.7	12.3	6.8	7.1	7.4
Licensed Practical Nurse	Total	185,700	118,300	51,500	15,900	149,600	7,000	24,300	4,800	11,100	43,000	96,500	35,100
	Rate per 100 beds	10.5	10.3	11	10.5	10.9	11.7	8.7	9.1	12.8	10	10.7	10
Nurses Aide and Orderly	Total	600,500	379,500	164,700	56,300	473,900	21,100	90,400	15,100	29,000	148,800	310,100	112,700
	Rate per 100 beds	33.9	32.9	35.2	37.3	34.4	35.4	32.3	28.7	33.3	34.6	34.4	32.1
All Other Staff	Total	399,700	235,300	123,900	40,500	313,000	15,100	61,300	10,300	18,700	93,900	197,600	89,500
	Rate per 100 beds	22.6	20.4	26.5	26.8	22.7	25.3	21.9	19.6	21.4	21.8	21.9	25.5

Source: National Center for Health Statistics. (1997, January 23). An Overview of Nursing Homes and Their Current Residents: Data From the 1995 National Nursing Home Survey. Advance Data From Vital and Health Statistics, no. 280. Bethesda, MD: National Center for Health Statistics.

and the geriatric chair, which has a lock-tray table. Chemical restraints include sedatives, psychotropic drugs, and antihistamines. Haldol, a psychoactive drug, is the medication most frequently used in nursing homes. Those with dementia and extreme frailty are most likely to be restrained. Such restraint may have continued for months, with both physical and psychological effects. The loss of a sense of autonomy and mastery is perhaps the most disturbing fact of all.

The 1987 nursing home reform law requires facilities to provide as many alternatives to restraint as possible. Each resident is to be free from chemical and physical restraints used for punishment, involuntary seclusion, discipline, or staff convenience. Psycho-pharmacologic drugs can be administered only on order of a physician and as a part of the written plan of care. Such drugs may be used only to eliminate or modify the symptom for which they are prescribed and only if, at least annually, an independent external consultant reviews the appropriateness of the drug plan of each resident. Reducing the present use of drugs and restraints will depend on sensitization and education of nursing home employees to be realized through specific educational programs.[38]

Medical and Psychiatric Experimentation

The Ten Commandments of Medical Research Involving Human Subjects, as employed by the National Institutes of Health, should be in effect. No experimental research on older patients is permissible without express and informed consent, given after consultation with legal counsel. The volunteer should be made fully aware of the risks and benefits of the experiment and his or her right to terminate the experiment at any time. Similarly, any unusual, hazardous, or experimental treatment procedures, such as new drugs or lobotomy, must be introduced only after express and informed consent and consultation on the patient's part with legal counsel. The National Institute on Aging conducted a workshop on human protection in research, which formulated some of the early thinking on this issue.[39]

Institutional Neurosis

Institutional neurosis can occur in hospitals, nursing homes, prisons, or anywhere that persons are removed from society and live in a rigid, isolated community. It can also develop in the person's own home if he or she is isolated. The symptoms are erosion of personality, overdependence, and expressionless face, automatic behavior, and loss of interest in the outside world. Many of the immediate and long-term effects of military or concentration camp imprisonment apply also to isolated institutions for older persons.

Age, Sex, and "Clinical State" Segregation

Federal regulations issued June 1, 1978, require the right to privacy in nursing homes.[40] According to the 1987 reform law, each resident has the right to personal privacy and confidentiality. Gender segregation is a very questionable practice. It is illegal to rule out heterosexual (or homosexual) activities with spouses or other consenting adults, including other patients, as long as no clear physical or psychological danger is present. One of the authors, Dr. Robert N. Butler, established one of the first psychiatric units for older patients, at Chestnut Lodge in 1958–1959, which did not segregate patients by gender and allowed freedom and privacy for sexual activities. The results were a more relaxed patient population and a greater respect for patients' adulthood. Older people should also not be scolded for masturbation. Masturbation is a normal sexual outlet, and staff members in institutions may need help in overcoming their own anxieties about patients' use of this outlet. Conjugal visits with spouses should be encouraged.

There is a question about the wisdom of age-segregated treatment facilities. It is argued that when older persons are placed in age-integrated wards of hospitals, they receive less staff attention and may be injured by young, aggressive patients. (Assaults can be minimized if personnel is adequate.) On the other hand, restriction to an age-segregated unit can result in monotony and difficulties in recruiting and retaining well-trained, dedicated staff. Some studies have indicated that older persons show greater improvement in age-integrated facilities.

Segregation can also occur based on clinical status. Severely impaired older persons often do better in separate facilities that can offer specialized treatment programs not needed by healthier patients. Research can also take place more easily in these circumstances. But the designation of a floor or a section of an institution as the "senile floor" or "senile wing" can lead to much anxiety in healthier patients. ("Will I be moved to the senile wing?" "Does this mean I am losing my mind?") Integration of the severely impaired with the less impaired has some benefits of its own. For example, the healthier patients can benefit from giving help to the more impaired through a "buddy system." As would be expected, for some patients, such integration has a depressing effect. A choice would be ideal, with fluid connections between units to comply with the inclination of patients.

Reality-Orientation, Remotivation, and Rehabilitation Programs

Reality Orientation. *Reality orientation* is a specific set of techniques for helping cognitively impaired or withdrawn older persons remain as oriented and as communicative as their capabilities permit.[41] James C. Folsom first organized a reality orientation program in Winter Veterans Administration Hospital in Topeka, Kansas, in 1958. The bulk of the work was done by the nursing assistants, who spent the most time with the patients.

In a typical reality orientation program, the most severely demented are presented with simple, straightforward information on a regular basis by those who are caring for them. For example, an aide might describe step-by-step exactly what she is doing as she dresses the patient.

Less severely impaired patients have formal classes in which the instructor presents basic personal and current information over and over to each patient, beginning with the patient's name, where he or she is, and the date. Only when he or

she has relearned these basic facts is the patient presented with other facts such as age, home town, and former occupation. Patients are encouraged to verbalize. Caregivers are also trained to use such techniques in the home setting.

Studies of the outcome of such work have been inconclusive. Gains appear to be small and of short duration.[42] There is also a risk of infantilization. Nonetheless, reality orientation offers a method and a philosophy of treatment that makes a sincere and humane attempt to meet the patient at his or her own level and prevent decline resulting from lack of opportunity to learn and to be stimulated by close human contacts. In truth, reality orientation may be of unrecognized value to staff because it offers them hope and a defined approach to patients who might otherwise be experienced as unreachable and hopeless.

Remotivation. Remotivation has been used as a means of reaching the large number of long-term, chronic patients residing in large mental hospitals who do not seem to want to move toward improvement or discharge. It has also been applied in nursing homes.

The remotivation technique consists essentially of the following five steps, which the psychiatric aide uses with small groups of 10 to 15 patients:

1. *The climate of acceptance*—establishing a warm, friendly relationship in the group
2. *A bridge to reality*—reading of simple poetry, current events, and so on
3. *Sharing the world*—development of the topic, introduced above, through planned objective questions, use of props, and so on
4. *An appreciation of work in the world*—designed to stimulate patients to think about work in relation to themselves
5. *The climate of appreciation*—expression of enjoyment at getting together, and so on

Remotivation must be followed by activities leading toward rehabilitation, such as occupational and recreational therapy, and finally, vocational and social rehabilitation.

The Veterans Administration Hospital in St. Cloud, Minnesota, began a program in 1972 in which sixth-grade students served as remotivation therapists for older institutionalized veterans. The students and patients were brought together twice a week for 45-minute periods for 11 weeks at a time. The students were carefully prepared and supervised. Patients were prepared by the staff for separation from the children at the end of the program (although many children kept contact through letters and gifts). Patients demonstrated significant gains in self-awareness and self-esteem during the program but, as with reality orientation, they appeared to lose gains if continued involvement with therapists was not offered.

Rehabilitation. Under federal regulations issued in January 1989, nursing homes must provide rehabilitative services to every resident. Psychiatric hospital and nursing home programs will benefit immeasurably from the routine availability of rehabilitation as a medical specialty (physiatrics), one of the significant developments of twentieth century health care. An important model is the Institute of Rehabilitation Medicine in New York (part of New York University's Medical Center), founded and directed by Dr. Howard Rusk since 1948. The blind, deaf, retarded, hemiplegic, paraplegic, and those suffering from Parkinson's disease—in short, anyone with losses in their neurosensory and physical functions—can benefit from rehabilitative programs. We review physical, occupational and speech therapies in Chapter 10.

The National Institute on Disability and Rehabilitation Research, inspired by former senator Thomas Eagleton, was given the task by Congress to report on research on the handicapped, including the elderly handicapped, being carried out by government agencies. For example, some of the institutes within the National Institutes of Health are developing various prosthetic and rehabilitative devices that may be useful for older people. This is a field where both the development of new technology and the reengineering of devices originally designed for other purposes (as in the NASA space program) are occurring.

Daily exercise should be part of routine physical care in every institution. Each patient should participate, including the bedridden, as long as exercise is geared to physical capacity. Psychological well-being is often improved as an added benefit when exercise is encouraged. Morning exercises to music are becoming a regular part of the treatment programs in some nursing homes, homes for the aged, and other institutions.

The President's Council on Physical Fitness and Sports provides free of charge a number of publications that encourage both younger and older people to exercise. Their fitness book entitled *Pep Up Your Life* is designed for people in senior centers, nursing homes, clubs, and other places where older people are concentrated. Exercises are designed to be done while sitting, standing, or confined to a wheelchair or bed. Individual exercise planning guides in *Pep Up Your Life* help older people keep track of their personal fitness programs.

Dance therapy expands on the idea of exercise by encouraging emotional and psychological expression. Dance is an expressive medium for self-recognition, communication, release of tension, and socialization.

Bibliotherapy is a term used to refer to the healing that lies in the written word. Some institutions are beginning to use circulating libraries as an adjunct to treatment programs rather than simply as a recreational pastime. Audio/video therapy—VCRs, tape recordings, phonographs, and compact discs—provides the elderly with important pleasure and stimulation.

Work Therapy and Sheltered Workshops

"Work therapy" is appropriate only as a truly therapeutic activity and not as compulsory and uncompensated housekeeping and maintenance chores that save the institution money. Patients may volunteer to do work for the institution but should be compensated, at the very least, in accordance with the minimum wage laws. Patients who are physically able should, however, make their own beds, dress themselves, and perform other acts ordinarily encompassed under the rubric of self-care.

The handicapped, including the aged, may participate in *sheltered workshops.* The sheltered workshop is a work-oriented rehabilitation facility with controlled working environment and individualized vocational goals. It utilizes work experiences and related services for assisting handicapped persons to progress toward normal living and productive vocational status.

This kind of shop gives an opportunity to make a modest amount of money, as well as providing activity and promoting pride. Because industries pay on a piece basis, it is economically feasible for them. Packaging, stuffing, stapling, tag stringing, and various types of simple repetitive assembling are examples of activities.

Patient or Resident Government

The 1987 nursing home reform law greatly strengthens the residents' voice in the nursing home. The nursing home survey process under the new law requires direct interviews with nursing home residents concerning their impressions of their care. Survey teams must also meet with residents who are members of resident councils (if they exist) in separate interviews.

There are many legitimate complaints—about food, lack of entertainment, nursing care—legitimate not only because in too many instances the complaints are valid, but also because of the deep frustration and grief associated with institutionalization and the understandable need to ventilate feelings. Therefore, patient government or resident councils, joint patient-staff conferences, and the presence of older people on the boards of trustees of hospitals and homes for the aging should be standard. Older people living in the community would do well to be their own ombudsmen and monitor the conditions and treatment in institutions in which they might some day reside.

Volunteers

With careful selection, a loyal, conscientious group of volunteers can be assembled who are a valuable adjunct to staff and contribute to the quality of the institution. The Red Cross Gray Ladies are an example of a well-trained volunteer group. Some nursing homes are wary of volunteers—fearful perhaps that their weaknesses will be exposed to the public with volunteers moving in and out at will. Others, however, welcome volunteers and use the opportunity to make them an effective component of their programs.

Research

It is imperative that research be built into institutions. Research should be of two kinds: studies concerned with enhancing the understanding of old age and chronic illness (for example, a study of senile dementia) and studies dealing with improvement in services (for example, a study of group therapy). Fortunately, nurses are beginning to be trained in research methods. Rarely is research done in either nonprofit or commercial homes. The Philadelphia Geriatric Center and the Jewish Home and Hospital for Aged (New York) are examples of voluntary institutions that have developed fine research programs.

Major Associations of Nursing Homes and Homes for the Aging

American Association of Homes and Services for the Aging, 901 E St., N.W., Suite 500, Washington, DC 20004-2037.

Membership—represents nonprofit, community-sponsored housing, homes for the aging, and health care and services-providing organizations serving older persons. Homes are sponsored by religious, fraternal, labor, civic, and county organizations.

Size—over one million older persons are served by 5,000 AAHSA member organizations.

American Health Care Association, 1201 L Street, N.W., Washington, DC 20005.

Membership—a federation of state associations of commercial homes in 50 states. 2,023 nonprofit homes also belong, usually small homes with about 60 beds. This is a nonprofit organization.

Size—11,805 facilities, with 1.2 million beds, belong.

National Citizens Coalition for Nursing Home Reform, 1424 16th Street, N.W., Suite L2, Washington, D.C. 20036-2211

Membership—a national nonprofit membership organization to improve the long-term care system and the quality of life for nursing home residents.

Size—296 organizations are members, as well as individuals.

Note: Some 750 homes, like the Mennonite homes, do not belong to any national organization, nor do they participate in Medicaid or Medicare.

SELECTED READINGS

American Nurses' Association. (1970). Standards for geriatric nursing practice. *American Journal of Nursing, 70*(9), 1894–1897.

American Association of Retired Persons. *Pep up your life: A fitness book for seniors.* Washington, DC: Author.

Avorn, J., Dreyer, P., Connelly, K., & Soumerai, S. B. (1989). Use of psychoactive medication and the quality of care in rest homes: Findings and policy implications of a statewide study. *New England Journal of Medicine, 4,* 227–232.

Ball, R. M. (with Bethell, T. N.). (1989). *Because we're all in this together: The case for a national long-term insurance policy.* Washington, DC: Families USA Foundation.

Birkett, P. (1991). *Psychiatry in the nursing home.* Binghamton, NY: The Haworth Press.

Borson, S., Liptzin, B., Nininger, J., & Rabins, P. V. (1989). *Nursing homes and the mentally ill elderly: A report of the task force on nursing homes and the mentally ill elderly.* Washington, DC: The American Psychiatric Association.

Borup, J. H. (1983–84). Transfer trauma. *Generations, 8*(3), 17–22.

Brink, T. L. (Ed.). (1990). *Mental health in the nursing home.* Binghamton, NY: The Haworth Press.

Brody, E. M., Dempsey, N. P., & Pruchno, R. A. (1990, April). Mental health of sons and daughters of the institutionalized aged. *The Gerontologist, 30*(2), 212–219.

Butler, R. N. (1980). Protection of elderly research subjects. *Clinical Research, 28,* 33–35.

Butler, R. N. (1981). The teaching nursing home. *Journal of the American Medical Association, 245*(14), 1435–1437.

Cohn, V. (1990, June 5). Finding the right nursing home. *The Washington Post,* Health Section, 12–15.

The Commonwealth Fund (1996). *Nursing home restraints program review.* New York: The Commonwealth Fund, One East 75th Street, New York, NY 10021-1276.

Consumer Reports. (1995, August). Nursing homes: When a loved one needs care. *Consumer Reports,* 518–28.

Emerson Lombardo, N. B., Fogel, B. S., Robinson, G. K., & Weiss, H. P. (1996, August). *Achieving mental health of nursing home residents: Overcoming barriers to mental health care.* Boston, MA: Hebrew Rehabilitation Center for Aged (1200 Centre St., Boston, MA 02131-1097).

Ennis, B., & Siegel, L. (1973). *The rights of mental patients: The basic ACLU guide to a mental patient's rights.* New York: Richard W. Baron.

Evans, L. R., & Strumph, N. E. (1989). Tying down the elderly: A review of the literature on physical restraint. *Journal of the American Geriatrics Society, 37,* 65–74.

Gleason-Wynn, P. E. (1995) Addressing the educational needs of nursing home social workers. *Gerontology & Geriatrics Education, 16*(2), 31–36.

Greene, R. R., Vourlekis, B. S., Gelfand, D. E., & Lewis, J. S. (1992). Current realities: Practice and education needs of social workers in nursing homes. In Mellor, M. J., & Solomon, R. (Eds.), *Geriatric social work education* (pp. 39–54). Binghamton, NY: The Haworth Press,

Halpern, C. (1969). A practicing lawyer views the right to treatment. *Georgetown Law Journal, 57,* 782–817.

Institute of Medicine. (1982). *Improving the quality in nursing homes.* Washington, DC: National Academy Press.

Kane, R. A., & Kane, R. L. (1987). *Long-term care: Principles, programs, and policies.* New York: Springer.

Katz, P. R., & Calkins, E. (Eds.). (1989). *Principles and practice of nursing home care.* New York: Springer.

Knapp, M., Bahr, Sr., R., & Strumpf, N. (1987). *Standards and scope of gerontologic nursing practice.* Kansas City, MO: American Nurses Association.

Lee, J. L., Cody, M., Cruize, M. J., Munroe, D. J., & Sullivan, T. J. (1990). Career counseling for nurses in skilled nursing facilities. *Gerontology and Geriatric Education, 10*(4), 23–36.

Liu, K. L., Doty, P., & Menton, K. (1990). Medicaid spendown in nursing homes. *The Gerontologist, 30*(1), 7–15.

Lowenthal, M. F. (1964). *Lives in distress.* New York: Basic Books.

Mathew, L., Sloan, P., Kilby, M., & Flood, R. (1988, March–April). What's different about a special care unit for dementia patients? A comparative study. *The American Journal of Alzheimer's Care and Related Disorders and Research,* 16–23.

McCoy, J. L., & Conley, R. W. (1990). Surveying board and care homes: Issues and data collection problems. *The Gerontologist, 30*(2), 147–53.

Mezey, M., Lynaugh, J., & Cartier, M. (1989). *Nursing homes and nursing care: Lessons from the teaching nursing homes.* New York: Springer.

Moss, F., & Halamandaris, V. (1977). *Too old, too sick, too bad: Nursing homes in America.* Germantown, MD: Aspen Systems.

National Association of Social Workers. (1993). *NASW clinical indicators for social work and psychological services in nursing homes.* Washington, DC: National Association of Social Workers.

National Center for Health Statistics. (1997, January 23). An overview of nursing homes and their current residents: Data from the 1995 National Nursing Home Survey. *Advance Data from Vital and Health Statistics,* no. 280. Bethesda, MD: National Center for Health Statistics.

National Center for Health Statistics. (1989). *The National Nursing Home Survey: 1985 summary for the United States.* DHHS Pub. No. PHS 89–1758. Washington, DC: U.S. Government Printing Office.

National Institute on Aging. (1978). *Protection of elderly research subjects.* Pub. no. (NIH) 79–180. Washington, DC: U.S. Government Printing Office.

New York State Senate Health Committee (T. Lombardi, Jr. Chairman). (1988, December). *Nursing home without walls program: A decade of quality care at home for New York's aged and disabled.* Albany, NY: New York State Senate.

Pillemer, K., & Moore, D. W. (1989). Abuse of patients in nursing homes: Findings from a survey of staff. *The Gerontologist, 29*(3), 314–319.

Psychiatric News. (1990, May 4). Alabama's mental health system on the road to recovery 20 years after Wyatt decision. *Psychiatric News,* 4 ff.

Quam, J. K., & Whitford, G. S. (1992). Educational needs of nursing home social workers at the baccalaureate level. In Mellor, M. J., & Solomon, R. (Eds.), *Geriatric social work education* (pp. 143–156). Binghamton, NY: The Haworth Press.

Rivlin, A. M., & Wiener, J. M. (1988). *Caring for the disabled elderly: Who will pay?* Washington, DC: The Brookings Institution.

Rovner, B. W., & Rabins, P. V. (1985). Mental illness among nursing home patients. *Hospital and Community Psychiatry, 36,* 119–20, 128.

Russell, L. B., & Manning, C. L. (1989). The effect of perspective on medicare expenditures. *The New England Journal of Medicine, 7,* 439–444.

Sager, M. A., Easterling, D. V., Kindig, D. A., & Anderson, O. W. (1989). Changes in the location of death after passage of Medicare's prospective payment system: A national study. *The New England Journal of Medicine, 7,* 433–439.

Select Committee on Aging, U.S. House of Representatives. (1989). *Board and care homes in America: A national tragedy.* Comm. pub. no. 101–711. Washington, DC: U.S. Government Printing Office.

Shaughnessy, P. W., & Kramer, A. M. (1990, January 4). The increased needs of patients in nursing homes and patients receiving home health care. *The New England Journal of Medicine, 322*(1), 21–27.

Vladeck, B. C. (1980). *Unloving care: The nursing home tragedy.* New York: The Twentieth Century Fund.

Vourlekis, B. S., Gelfand, D. E., & Green, R. R. (1992). Psychological needs and care in nursing homes: Comparison of views of social workers and administrators. *The Gerontologist, 32*(1), 113–119.

Weber, G. H., & McCall, G. J. (1987). *The nursing assistant's casebook of elder care.* New York: Springer.

ENDNOTES

1. To provide an understanding of the impact of institutional care on people, Erving Goffman's powerful essay, "On the Characteristics of Total Institutions" (1957), should be required reading, along with Stanton and Schwartz's classic study, "The Mental Hospital" (1956).

2. Personal communication, Marsha Goodwin, Director, Geriatrics and Grants Management, Office of Geriatrics and Extended Care, Veterans Health Administration, Department of Veterans Affairs, Washington, DC.

3. *Ibid.*

4. *Ibid.*

5. Lowenthal, M. F. (1964). *Lives in distress.* New York: Basic Books.

6. This outline (somewhat paraphrased) illustrates the effort of one state (Maryland) to establish guidelines (developed when Helen Padula was Coordinator, Services to the Aged, Maryland). Maryland was influenced by a preceding New York state effort. We emphasize that this is merely a guideline and should not be used in a rigid, immutable manner.

7. Lieberman, M. A., & Tobin, S. (1983). *The experience of old age: Stress, coping and survival.* New York: Basic Books. This book explores the psychological life of the elderly. Also see Borup, J. H. (1983–1984). Transfer trauma. *Generations, 8*(3), 17–22.

8. Shanas, E. (1962). *The health of older people: A social survey.* Cambridge, MA: Harvard University Press.

9. Lieberman, M. A. (1968). Psychological effects of institutionalization. *Journal of Gerontology, 23,* 343–353.

10. Fischer, J., & Breakley, W. R. (1986). Homelessness and mental health: An overview. *International Journal of Mental Health, 14,* 6–41.

11. Johnson, C. L., & Grant, L. A. (1985). *The nursing home in American society.* Baltimore, MD: Johns Hopkins University Press.

12. Select Committee on Aging, House of Representatives. (1989). *Board and care homes in America: A national tragedy.* Comm. Pub No. 101–711, Washington, DC: U.S. Government Printing Office; and Stone, R., Newcomber, R. J., & Saunders, M. (1982). *Descriptive analysis of board and care policy trends in 50 states.* San Francisco, CA: University of California, Aging Health Policy Center.

13. For a thorough review of nursing home practices, see *Consumer Reports,* August, 1995, 518–528. "Judging by the dozens of nursing homes we visited . . . and by the results of thousands of inspection reports we reviewed," the magazine says, "facilities range from inadequate to scandalous, and the good ones are hard to find."

14. National Center for Health Statistics. (1997, January 23). An overview of nursing homes and their current residents: Data from the 1995 National Nursing Home Survey. *Advance Data From Vital and Health Statistics,* no. 280. Hyattsville, MD: National Center for Health Statistics.

15. Health Care Financing Administration. (1996, Spring). *Health care financing review, 16*(3). Washington, DC: Health Care Financing Administration.

16. Health Care Financing Administration, U.S. Department of Health and Human Services. (1996, Sept. 5). OSCAR (On-line Survey, Certification, and Reporting system).

17. The Commonwealth Fund. (1996). *Nursing home restraints program review.* New York: The Commonwealth Fund, One East 75th Street, New York, NY 10021-1276.

18. For information on safety in long-term care institutions see *Standards for health care facilities,* National Fire Protection Association, Batterymarch Park, Quincy, MA 02169; and *Managing the environment of care for long-term care,* Joint Commission for Accreditation of Healthcare Organizations, 1 Renaissance Blvd., Oakbrook Terrace, IL 60181

19. Emerson Lombardo, N. B., Fogel, B. S., Robinson, G. K., & Weiss, H. P. (1996, August). Achieving mental health of nursing home residents: Overcoming barriers to mental health care. Boston: Hebrew Rehabilitation Center for Aged (1200 Centre St., Boston, MA 02121-1097)

20. Vladeck, B. C. (1980). *Unloving care: The nursing home tragedy.* New York: The Twentieth Century Fund.

21. Dunlop, B. B. (1980). Expanded home-based care for the impaired elderly: Solution or pipe dream? *American Journal of Public Health, 70*(5), 514–519.

22. Cohn, V. (1990, June 5). Finding the right nursing home. *Washington Post* (Health Section).

23. New York State Senate Health Committee (T. Lombardi, Jr., Chairman) (1988, December). *Nursing home without walls program: A decade of quality care at home for New York's aged and disabled.* Albany, NY: New York State Senate.

24. Health Care Financing Administration. (Spring, 1996). *Health care financing review, 17*(3). Washington, DC: Health Care Financing Administration.

25. Theoretically, the Medicaid legislation is supposed to cover the medically indigent of all ages, not all of whom are on welfare.

26. From U.S. Senate Committee on Finance. (1965). *Social Security Amendments of 1965: Report to accompany H. R. 6675, June 30, 1965.* Washington, DC: U.S. Government Printing Office, p. 149.

27. *Consumer Reports:* Who can afford a nursing home? May 1988.

28. Contact the Alzheimer's Disease and Related Disorders Association, Inc., 919 N. Michigan Ave., Suite 100, Chicago, IL, 60611-1676, (800) 621-0379.

29. We are indebted here to the work of Charles Halpern and his brief in the *Wyatt* v. *Stickney* case in Alabama concerning the right to treatment (Amici's proposed standards for adequate treatment, January 21, 1972).

30. (*Wyatt* v. *Stickney,* U.S. Court for Middle Dist. of Ala., Northern Div., Action No. 3195-N.) The Supreme Court, in handing down its unanimous decision in the landmark case of *Donaldson* v. *O'-Connor* in 1976, avoided the broad issue of "right to treatment" in favor of a more narrow judgment that a state cannot constitutionally confine a non-dangerous mentally ill person who is capable of surviving safely on his or her own.

31. *Psychiatric News:* Alabama's mental health system on road to recovery 20 years after Wyatt Decision. May 4, 1990, 4 ff.

32. Bazelon, Judge D. (1969). Implementing the right to treatment. *University of Chicago Law Review,* 742, 746.

33. Modified from the statement affirmed Nov. 17, 1972 by the Board of Trustees of the American Hospital Association, The Association's most recent "Patient's Bill of Rights" is from 1975. It is expected to be revised in the near future.

34. *Federal Register 54*(21), February 2, 1989.

35. Ennis, B., & Siegel, L. (1973). *The rights of mental patients: The basic ACLU guide to a mental patient's rights.* New York: Richard W. Baron.

36. The concept of academic (teaching/research) nursing is developed in Butler, R. N. (1980). *The impact of Alzheimer's disease on the nation's elderly,* testimony before the U.S. Senate Subcommittee on Aging and the Subcommittee on Labor/HEW Appropriation, July 15, 1980; and in Butler, R. N. (1981). The teaching nursing home.

Journal of the American Medical Association, 245(14), 1435–1437.

37. The DeSimon Foundation of Wilmett, Illinois, advocates research and provides support through patient groups: 1-800-23-SIMON.

38. The October 1985 issue of *Quarterly,* the journal of the Canadian Long-Term Care Association, describes the development of practical and humane alternate solutions to the use of restraints—for example, in cases of "wanderers." Carter and T. Franklin Williams have helped bring national attention to the issue of restraints. The Williamses have reported that, contrary to popular belief, there have been no successful law suits against nursing homes because they failed to use restraints. A current research study, "The Epidemiology and Demonstration Project on Restraint Use," which is funded by the Commonwealth Fund and is being conducted at New York City's Jewish Home and Hospital for the Aged, is a further step toward the achievement of restraint-free environments in U.S. institutions.

39. National Institute on Aging. (1978). *Protection of elderly research subjects.* Pub. No. (NIH) 79–180. Washington, DC: U.S. Government Printing Office. For a summary paper on the subject, see Butler, R. N. (1980). Protection of elderly research subjects. *Clinical Research, 28,* 33–35.

40. See Health Standards and Quality Bureau, Office of Standards and Certification, Health Care Financing Administration, Baltimore, MD.

41. Taulbee, L., & Folsom, J. C. (1966). Reality orientation for geriatric patients. *Hospital and Community Psychiatry, 17,* 133–135.

42. Reisberg, B. (1987). Reality orientation. In Maddox, G. (Ed.), *The encyclopedia of aging* (pp. 558–559). New York: Springer.

CHAPTER 12

PSYCHOTHERAPY
AND ENVIRONMENTAL THERAPY

INDIVIDUAL PSYCHOTHERAPY

GROUP THERAPY

INTERGENERATIONAL FAMILY THERAPY
AND COUPLES THERAPY

BEHAVIORAL THERAPIES

ENVIRONMENTAL THERAPY

In this chapter we discuss the common modalities of psychotherapy—individual, group, family—and consider environmental therapy, under which we include age awareness and acceptance, federal policies to aid older persons, social roles, location and mobilization of resources, registration drives, self-help and self-care, employment and productive aging, advocacy, legal and consultative services, and encouragement of political activity on the part of older people.

We considered the roles of the mental health specialists and the team concept in Chapter 8. All forms of environmental therapy and psychotherapy can be provided by the mental health team as a functioning unit (in varied combinations of mental health specialists, together with the elderly and their family members) or by individual specialists from all of the disciplines.

INDIVIDUAL PSYCHOTHERAPY

Individual psychotherapy is *least* available to older people compared to other age groups, and yet it should be a vital part of the repertoire of treatment in later life. Older persons need the opportunity to talk and to have a listener. They need the therapist's support in their efforts to "seize the day" and build a "life" during the remaining time available.[1]

Therapists in private practice have minimal contact with older persons. Public clinics also report low rates of contact of any kind, but especially little in the way of psychotherapeutic work. Psychiatrists, social workers, psychologists, and other members of mental health teams do not see many older people; when they do, the purposes are usually diagnostic and the effort is "disposition."

Old age is the period in life with the greatest number of profound crises, often occurring in multiples and with high frequency. The critical psychological events in this age group are the familiar human emotional reactions to death and grief, diseases, and disabilities. Depression and anxiety escalate, defensive behavior is seen, earlier personality components may reappear in exaggerated forms, and newly formed functional states are frequently noted. These conditions require psychotherapeutic efforts, in-depth as well as supportive.

The designation of older people as "good" or "poor" candidates for psychotherapy should be questioned, especially the implication that a number of people should not be offered treatment because they cannot "use" it. We wonder how this judgment can be made before treatment has begun. Some older people who meet all the criteria for "good" candidates fail to find therapy helpful, whereas "poor" candidates may show unexpected response and results. The test of objectivity is the willingness to give adequate trials to *all* persons without allowing our theories, prejudices, and fears to interfere. Theories, in any case, can be masterful camouflages. For example, Freud was preoccupied with death and pessimistic about old age. His work reflects his avoidance of the issues of late life and his decision to explain the human personality only in terms of the early years. Ironically, we would barely know of him had he died before the age of 40, since his finest work was done in the latter half of his life.

We submit, on the grounds of clinical experience, that many older persons, if not severely brain-damaged, are very receptive to psychotherapy and can in no way be considered poor candidates. They often exhibit a strong drive to resolve problems, to put their lives in order, and to find satisfactions and the opportunity for a "second chance." Their capacity to change has been demonstrated in many instances; the fact that older people spontaneously begin reviewing their lives in a way similar to psychotherapy (the concept of the "life review") is indicative of the manner in which this process is part of the natural course of late life. Even the brain-damaged elderly can gain from psychotherapy as Goldfarb, among others, demonstrated early on.[2]

Any evidence pointing toward older people as untreatable is usually to be found in the minds of therapists rather than in empirical studies. Powerful forces of countertransference and cultural prejudice are at work, including personal fear and despair over aging and death. Therapeutic pessimism and nihilism are inappropriate, invalid, and inhumane. Older people, like the young, can gain from insight and understanding, from objectivity and empathy. Biology is not destiny in old age any more than in youth. Personal history and cultural influences are of profound importance and form a background against

which change at any age can occur through education and insight.

Theoretical Considerations

Freud and the vast majority of his followers ruled out psychoanalysis for older persons without ever testing its usefulness. Abraham raised some objections to this general negativism, reporting on five persons he called "old" who were in their fifties.[3] He and Jelliffe stated the "age of the neurosis" is more important than the age of the patient.[4] Grotjahn reported on analytic work with a 71-year-old client with "senile brain disease."[5] Wayne, Meerloo, Gitelson, Alexander, Atkin, and Kaufman were among those who first described some limited psychotherapeutic efforts with older people. In spite of early pessimism, psychoanalytic concepts have proved useful in work with the elderly (see Chapter 8).

Jung's concept of stages of development are readily applicable to the elderly condition. It is interesting that two-thirds of Jung's practice was made up of middle-aged and older persons, whereas Freud's private practice was composed of younger patients. These differences may help to account for variations in theoretical emphases, with Freud's therapy concentrating on youth and sex, while Jung emphasized individuation and creativity.

Goldfarb, Busse, Linden, Weinberg, Butler, and others have devoted substantial amounts of their public and private psychiatric clinical work to older people. Goldfarb's "brief therapy" and Linden's work with group therapy became the best known of these early efforts in therapy.[6]

Carl R. Rogers, Abraham Maslow, and Rollo May contributed to the development of the so-called "Third Force" in psychology, distinguishing it from psychoanalysis and behaviorism. (See Chapter 8.) Rogers's client-centered therapy, which referred to adopting an empathic attitude toward patients, emphasized the individual's capacity for life-long growth and development and the importance of an unconditional, positive relationship between client and therapist. In contrast to psychoanalysis, Rogers believed therapy should not dwell on the past, nor should it be built on a medical model of diagnosis and cure. Rather, it should focus on self-actualization as the main motivational force in therapy. Rogers called his perspective "humanistic psychology,"[7] and his emphasis on this approach when working with groups helped develop the "encounter group," the concept of group-centered leadership and a model for the facilitation of learning in educational settings.

Existential therapists have demonstrated little interest in old age. Yet, because of the tendency of older people to review their lives, to seek meaning and to deal with death, there is an obvious existential component to any therapeutic work with them. We have found ideas of Buber[8] (the importance of relationships with others) and Frankl[9] (the possibilities within the confines of the "death camp") to be particularly useful for older people.

Mainstream psychotherapy, in general, has become more eclectic—utilizing the best of varying theories. Especially valuable has been the emergence of cognitive therapy (Aaron Beck) which assumes that depression is based on distorted thinking and unrealistically negative views that patients have about themselves, the world, and the future. The task of the therapy is to reevaluate and correct the thinking.

An allied form of therapy, interpersonal psychotherapy, developed by Gerald Klerman and Myrna Weissman, assumes that depression is something that happens to the individual and requires treatment. Interpersonal psychotherapy focuses on interpersonal and social functioning, and improvement must be made there before the depression will be alleviated. The National Institute of Mental Health study on 250 depressed patients (aged 21 to 60), conducted at the University of Pittsburgh, University of Oklahoma, and George Washington University, found that cognitive behavioral therapy and interpersonal psychotherapy achieved results comparable to a standard antidepressant drug, Imipramine.[10] (Because of its careful and useful design, the study

was described by psychiatrist Jerome Frank, in his introduction to the 1986 annual meeting of the American Psychiatric Association as "the standard against which all other psychotherapy research will be assessed.")

All forms of psychotherapy—from "uncovering" to "supportive" to "reeducative" and from Freudian to Jungian to Rogerian—can contribute to a better understanding of the psychology and psychotherapy of old age. In addition a less "purist" attitude on the part of therapists toward the use of psychoactive medications has led to a more appropriate use of such medications as an adjunct to "talking" therapy. Further integration and eclectic utilization of all contemporary personality theories and practices, including the life-cycle perspective of human life along with the use of medication when appropriate, are needed. The complexities of late life require complex therapy.

> We cannot live the afternoon of life according to the program of life's morning, for what was great in the morning will be little at evening, and what in the morning was true, will at evening have become a lie. I have given psychological treatment to too many people of advancing years, and have looked too often into the secret chambers of their souls, not to be moved by this fundamental truth.[11]

Some Personal Experiences with Older People in Psychotherapy

It is quite amazing that the question most frequently asked by professionals and lay persons alike is whether older people can make use of any psychotherapy that goes beyond support and simple guidance. This implies a quite naive assumption that old age brings an inevitable, implacable, and global loss of mental and emotional faculties. The examples in history, philosophy, literature, music, theology, and every other field of human activity ought to be enough to make us stand in awe of the intellectual, spiritual, emotional, and creative capacities of our elders. They have been and are often our most richly endowed leaders, mentors, and teachers.

Although we have conducted psychotherapy with older persons in a wide assortment of settings and have referred to this work throughout the book, we present here seven brief examples from the recent private practice of author Myrna Lewis to give some of the personal flavor and variety of work with older people:

A married couple in their seventies came for sex counseling. After a number of months of therapy, they wished to work on their sexual concerns more intensively and contacted Masters and Johnson's clinic. They were accepted as patients, flew to St. Louis, and took the intensive 2-week treatment program (paid for with part of their savings). Medical tests also showed the man to have a physical potency problem involving vascular difficulties. They are pursuing treatment for this condition, as well as their relationship problems. Although the final results of all of their efforts are still not clear, they remain determined to try whatever possibly can improve their sex life, since both of them had enjoyed it so much in the past.

A woman in her early sixties, unmarried, with a dependent, childlike demeanor, wished to become more "mature" and less anxious and dependent. During the course of therapy she found a new job where she functioned in a more adult manner, began to move out of her passive habits socially by helping to organize groups for single older persons, and eventually reestablished a former romantic relationship with a man whom she had known for 20 years. She is now involved in developing that relationship with the help of psychotherapy.

A male homosexual couple (one man in his late sixties and one in his late fifties) requested help in resolving problems in their relationship. After having lived together for 15 years, they eventually decided, during the course of therapy, to live in separate homes and have other intimacies but to continue their close friendship and support of one another. The older man, whose health had been deteriorat-

ing, continued to receive help with his disabilities from the younger one.

A middle-aged brother and sister resolved their differences with one another in helping an aged and mentally and physically infirm mother accept a move to a nursing home. The older woman refused to join them in family therapy but was able to communicate her wishes through her children to the therapist so effectively that a solution was found that was acceptable to her as well as to them.

An 80-year-old man was referred by his doctor for depression over his heart problems. However when given the opportunity to talk confidentially, the man revealed the depression centered around his guilt at conducting a long-term affair with a middle-aged housekeeper living in his home while his wife remained unaware of the nature of this relationship. After much soul-searching he concluded that he wished to continue the affair, since his wife, as he put it, was glad to be rid of his requests for sex and affection and seemed totally involved with her many activities. He still phones for an appointment now and then to talk over his concerns about the future of the younger woman when he dies and his own feelings about his eventual death and that of his wife.

A retired married couple in their sixties wished to come to a decision about remaining married. Unable to talk civilly with each other even in the therapist's presence, they are each engaged in writing long essays in between therapy sessions about their anger, hopes, disappointments, and memories of their marriage. These are exchanged with each other and form the basis of a beginning analysis of the problems. Meanwhile, they are being helped by the therapist to learn the elementary tactics of fair fighting and problem solving.

A woman in her middle seventies came, wanting to resolve her lifelong depression and difficulty in relating to people. She felt she was "unable to love."

Through careful and often painful intensive psychotherapy aimed at insight, and after several years of treatment, she began to be able to successfully counter her tendency to avoid intimacy by drawing on her understanding of her childhood relationship with a cold, intellectual mother. In her fascination with this process she also became involved in various church groups aimed at enriching emotional responses, and she eventually moved from participant to training as a group leader, teaching others to lead such support groups. She still uses individual psychotherapy to help recognize when she is starting to withdraw and to deal with her disappointment when she does so.

It seems obvious from our own and others' case examples that we can safely lay to rest the question of the ability of older people to use psychotherapy and concentrate on the more relevant questions about the kind, length, and combinations of therapies that are most useful for the issues of later life.

Common Themes in Psychotherapy with Older Persons

New Starts and Second Chances.   Older people often express a wish to undo some of the patterns of their life, to unritualize behavior and give some newness to their experiences. These people speak of the monotony or dryness of their experiences, a kind of "salt losing its savor" feeling. This should be met not just with feeble efforts to regain what has been lost but with attempts to build new interests and new possibilities.

Death in Disguise.   Some older people have resolved their personal feelings about death. Others manage to deny death without serious emotional consequences. But a number of older people need help, first in recognizing the source of their anxieties and fears (death) and then in reaching some degree of accommodation with the inevitable. Therapists must be able to recognize disguised fears of death in patients (and in themselves—often a reason for avoiding working with the elderly). For example, one man spoke of "running

toward that man and then I saw him and I slowed down to a walk." He was referring to death. In his attempts to revitalize his life, the spectre of death presented him with an ominous impediment that he had to face before therapy (and life) could continue in the direction he wanted to go.

Keen Awareness of Time.   There is an obvious concern with time when it is clear that the remaining days are running short. Younger therapists often have great difficulty understanding what it means *not* to think in terms of a future. We must take our cues from older people who have faced this issue squarely; the development of a sense of immediacy, of the here-and-now, of presentness—all aid in the evolution of a sense of enjoyment and tranquility, which we have called *elementality.*

Grief and Restitution.   Psychotherapy in old age must deal with grief, with losses of loved ones, and with dysfunctioning of one's own body and its parts. It might be said, "Where depression is, let grief be." If grief is denied outlet, it is possible that depression may occur. Insulation or denial of grief is not the sole cause of depression, of course, since ambivalence toward the deceased (that is, anger and conflict) complicates the usual course of grief. A task of therapy is to help open up the grief process. For example, widows or widowers should be encouraged to discuss whether they felt they did all that could be done. Efforts at restitution are crucial. One of the most important goals in therapy is helping the older person find a secure confidant, a person with whom he or she can speak intimately, either in the family or in the person's circle of friends and acquaintances.

Guilt and Atonement.

We have left undone those things which we ought to have done; and we have done those things which we ought not to have done.

The 51st Psalm opens with "Miserere, mei Deus" (Have mercy on me, O God). The cry for mercy, indeed for clemency, in the face of death must be heard. Although the therapist does not often have it within his or her power to "grant" mercy or bring full alleviation of the distress, he or she can listen, really listen, bear witness, be able, as it were, to attest to the realities of the life described, and thus help give meaning and validity to that life. Reality must be central. If there were simple alignments between our drives, our moral strictures, and the workings of the world, if Freud were dead wrong, we could move merrily along. If aging and disability did not exist; if lives were not filled up with malevolence, acts of violence, and real wrongs done to others and oneself, then we could simply reassure the older people who are sick with guilt. But psychotherapy in old age is a therapy of atonement as well as of restitution. One cannot deny cruel and thoughtless acts, falsely reassuring that all is irrational Freudian guilt. Facing genuine guilt as well as the attrition of the person's physical and emotional world is what makes psychotherapy with the aging an intellectually and emotionally powerful experience. The therapist cannot win out against death, but he or she can win out for life, for a sense of the real, for the kind of growth that truly matters, dealing as it does with the evaluation of ways to love—and hate—with the meanings of human conduct, with an appreciation of human nature and the succession of the generations. And after learning to face guilt unflinchingly and honestly, reconciliation may be possible with spouses, siblings, children, and friends.

Autonomy versus Identity. Identity, while an important concept, has been found to be difficult to study in various age groups. In our clinical experience, autonomy should be separated from identity as a concept. The so-called identity crisis of the adolescent is as much a problem of establishing freedom and achieving responsibility and self-sufficiency (autonomy) as it is one of identity ("self-sameness"), if not more so. Erikson deals with only one side of this issue.

> The term identity expresses . . . mutual relation in that it connotes both a persistent sameness within

oneself (self-sameness) and a persistent sharing of some kind of essential character with others.[12]

In old age most healthy people find themselves essentially the same as they have always been (as in data, for instance, from interviews before the mirror, Chapter 9). If significant medical and psychiatric problems emerge, such as major bodily changes and emotional difficulties like depression, the sense of self may go through rapid reevaluation. But again the problem of autonomy, not identity, is the most critical. The older person wonders, "Can I survive independently without being a burden?" It is true, of course, that if one's identity is closely bound to autonomy, the two merge, as it were, together. The person, for instance, whose identity has been that of a dependent person may find it easier to accept illness and institutionalization than the so-called independent, autonomous person whose identity has been structured accordingly. The latter may suffer more in dependent situations despite a "sound" identity by usual standards. Yet it appears to us that, in general, autonomy is a more decisive determinant of human behavior than identity—at all ages.

The eleven-year study at the National Institute of Mental Health from 1955 to 1966 showed that persons with goals and organization in their lives lived longer. The importance of mastery and control over one's life are summarized by Rodin.[13]

With respect to the life review, identity and autonomy are equally important.[14] But here again we find our experiences at variance with Erikson, but for a different reason. We find that older persons often wish to escape their identities and try something new, The fatalistic acceptance proposed by Erikson in his bipolar view of ego identity versus despair is not universal, as seen in those elderly who long for change and renewal—a shedding of their old skins for a new chance at life or a new glimpse of themselves.

Need for Assertion. A sense of helplessness tends to occur especially when one is ill or severely incapacitated in any way. During such bouts of illness, there is seldom adequate opportunity to be assertive in a way that alleviates this feeling. A bedridden person, for example, may finally resort to purposefully urinating in bed to express angry feelings. We have known a number of people who have refused to take baths, sending what seems to be a direct, angry message to their families or caregivers. Others may become dictatorial to nursing staff or family and friends. Persons caring for the ill or handicapped must assist them in finding ways to assert themselves in a positive manner that brings at least a measure of the self-esteem necessary for human dignity.

Self-mastery and control and their relationship to health become more important in old age. Studies such as those conducted by the National Institute of Health show that restrictions in control have detrimental effects on the health of older people. At times, however, greater control over activities and health may produce negative physical and psychological results, such as stress, worry, and self-blame.[15] There may be a point of diminishing returns, beyond which the older person becomes overwhelmed by too much responsibility. This is a psychological "overload," not unlike the Goldstein catastrophic reaction described in Chapter 9.

Therapeutic Issues

Am I a "Patient"? Insight into one's condition—that is, agreement that one has a psychiatric condition—is held by many to be a crucial prognostic indicator. On the other hand, humiliating labeling as a "patient" and all too willing acceptance of the "sick role" are questionable too. We believe it is important that appraisal be flexible and individualized. For some, a useful agreement can be made with the older person to collaborate in an effort to deal with an "illness" or "emotional problem." For other older persons it seems more functionally useful to see that they receive necessary mental health services without having to identify with the patient role.

A Vigilant Search for Signs of Health. Training in the mental health professions tends to emphasize pathology. However, with older people, as with all ages, it is as critical to identify and encourage areas of health as it is to clarify problems. Many beautifully "diagnosed" persons never reach their full potential in treatment because the therapist fails to recognize and utilize their strengths and assets in the therapeutic process. Vigilance in searching out signs of health may be rewarded with faster treatment progress and a more satisfactory outcome.

Significance of Certain Illusions. The therapist must not in any way be destructive of the processes of illusion and denial needed by older people. One must discuss the fact of death, the facts of loss, and the problems of grief, but this must always be in the context of possibilities, restitution, and resolution. The same principle applies in work with persons of all ages; one must work compassionately and carefully to understand and encourage a realistic lowering of defenses rather than attacking them overtly. Too much harsh or painful reality implanted too quickly can lead to overwhelming panic or emotional devastation.

The Question of "Cures." In the strictly biomedical realm, we have come to expect genuine "cures" through the use of such agents as antibiotics and surgical interventions. However, in the emotional or psychological domain, we recognize that "cure" is a continuing and never fully completed process.

Jung wrote,

> The serious problems in life are never fully solved. If ever they should appear to be so, it is a sure sign that something has been lost. The meaning and purpose of a problem seems to lie not in its solution but in our working at it incessantly.[16]

The struggle, the need for change, and the opportunity for change—the really profound problems, the deeper intricacies of human existence—are never completed or cured; yet, they are subject to alteration up to the point of death.

The Value of Listening.   It is imperative to listen attentively, to bear witness, to heed the telltale echoes of the past, to pick up the flatness of speech where distant feelings have died, to observe outbursts of unresolved issues in lives, and to empathize with the irreconcilable, even when the older patient is garrulous, continually reminiscing, importunate, and querulous, the fact is that talk is necessary and listening by another mandatory. One must also listen to and interpret silences.

The American Association of Retired People (AARP) has designed a manual to help train volunteer visitors in the art of listening to and reminiscing with homebound or institutionalized older persons.[17] Such "listeners" are trained to visit the older person and encourage reminiscence for both therapeutic and recreational purposes.

The Possible Worth of Just One Therapeutic Session.   In the best of therapy, each session must involve active work, thinking through, building hypotheses, and persistently searching out ways to assist the person. This is especially true for the older person for whom there may be only one session available (because of impending death, physical weaknesses, or lack of access to the therapist). When this is the case, much can be done in a short time.

Jungian analyst Florida Scott-Maxwell, who herself was in her eighties when she wrote these words, commented:

> A farmer's wife came and told a tragic story where nothing could be done, but her compassion and strength made it possible to continue. As usual with these cases, I asked if she would care to come again; she looked a little surprised, and said, "There is no need, I've told you everything." She had only wanted to confide in someone she respected, in case there was more she could do, and not to be so alone in her hard life. . . . One visit was enough for her.[18]

The brief amount of time must be measured in terms of the quality of the experience rather than the quantity.

Telephone Psychotherapy.   Because of the financial and physical limitations of older people, the therapist should be very flexible about the use of the telephone in conducting psychotherapy.

> *One 75-year-old man, with a history of heart attacks and continuing angina, would talk by phone when he could not travel. Even then he might have to interrupt his sessions to place a nitroglycerin tablet under his tongue. He never took obvious "advantage" of the situation and attended about 90% of his sessions in person.*

Telephone outreach therapy is especially valuable for the homebound older person. (Unfortunately, about one-third of older people do not have telephones, reminding us again of the poverty of old age.) It is also an excellent method for giving support and reassurance to an insecure or unstable person who may need something less than a regularly scheduled office appointment. In addition, volunteers can be used to provide telephone answering services at crisis centers and in telephone reassurance programs. Some elderly (for example, those with chronic schizophrenia) may need the distancing that a telephone provides, while at the same time achieving some degree of verbal closeness. The telephone can also be a substitute for face-to-face sessions during periods of bad weather when many elderly are reluctant to travel. Fees for prearranged phone calls may be charged when such phone sessions serve as alternatives for face-to-face psychotherapy sessions.

Self-Confrontation and the Use of Memory Aids.   Still and motion pictures of the individual as well as audio and video tape recordings have been used in research and in clinical practice for various age groups and diagnostic categories. In our own work, we have used photo albums, the mirror, and the tape recorder in helping older persons come "face to face" with themselves. The need for self-definition in the life review and the problem of memory argue for the value to the patient of being able to take tape recordings and video tapes home, for instance, for further listening and reflection. A major goal of such self-confrontational processes is to encourage an active participation in the therapeutic process, rather than a passive, dependent position.

Memory aids serve a further purpose. Providing direct instructions, for instance, written or taped, for medication schedules and for the statement of general treatment principles or specifics may be useful for the older patient, so long as this is not done in a manner that is disrespectful of the person's own view of his or her capacities for memory.

Life Review Therapy.   Life review therapy is a more structured and purposive concept than simple reminiscence or recalling the past.[19] (See also Chapter 4 for a description of the life review concept.) It includes the taking of an extensive autobiography from the older person and from other family members as indicated. Such memoirs can also be preserved by means of tape recordings or video tapes. The use of family albums, scrapbooks, and other memorabilia, the searching out of genealogies, and pilgrimages back to places of import all evoke crucial memories, responses, and understanding in patients. A summation of one's life work by some means is useful. For those who have children, a summary of feelings about parenting is important. The goals and consequences of these steps include a reexamination of one's life that may result in expiation of guilt, the resolution of intrapsychic conflicts, the reconciliation of family relationships, the transmission of knowledge and values to those who follow, and the renewal of ideals of citizenship and the responsibility for creating a meaningful life. Lieberman and Tobin have confirmed that reminiscence is crucial to the emotional livelihood of an elder person, helping to resolve past conflicts and enabling the development of a coherent life history.[20]

The life review can also be conducted as part of group activity.[21] Groups of all kinds—nursing home residents, senior center participants,[22] social groups, therapy groups—can use the life review to help older persons reconstruct and reevaluate their lives.[23] The concept of life review has been bolstered by an increasing interest in the United States in finding one's ethnic "roots." In fact, a significant part of tourism relates to people tracing their heritage. The United States has people from no fewer than 134 backgrounds. Fifty million, or 22% of the population, claim English lineage, and 49 million trace their lineage to Germany. The next most numerous are, respectively, Irish, African American, French, Italian, Scottish, Polish, Mexican, and American Indian. Handbooks for composing a personal autobiography are being published to aid nonprofessional writers in exploring and describing their history and lives.[24] These accounts form a valuable first-person historical source for use by families, sociologists, cultural historians, and others, in addition to providing therapeutic benefits and satisfaction for the older person.

Attempts are rapidly being made to more clearly conceptualize reminiscence and the life review and test their impact on older persons. A sample list of recent articles that discuss this popular subject appears at the end of this chapter (Selected Readings in Reminiscence).

The Validity of the Life Review.   Although the concept of life review has become entrenched in both the literature and practice of gerontology, nursing, social work, and to some degree psychology and psychiatry, aspects of the life review have been called into question, and many questions remain unanswered. For example, how does one determine whether memories have a factual basis or are defensive distortions? How effective or even possible is external verification of memories? Studies show, for example, that even mothers' memories of the timing of the most simple events in their children's development, such as toilet training, are not always recalled with accuracy. What are the interconnections between emotions and memories? Personal myths emerge from childhood and may be held throughout life, affecting one's self-image and most certainly influencing reminiscences. How do self-representations change over time? What are the connections between memories and identity or self-definition? What is more important, that which we remember or that which we forget, or both? How do we confirm some findings that people regret most the things that they failed to do rather than what they did do?

The life review helps both to uncover and stabilize one's past selfhood. Tolstoy at 81 said, "I remember very vividly that I am conscious of myself in exactly the same way now, at 81, as I was conscious of myself, my 'I,' at five or six years of age. Consciousness is immovable. Due to this alone there is a movement which we call 'time.' If time moves on, then there must be something that stands still, the consciousness of my 'I' stands still."[25] This is a common feeling, substantiated by extensive work at the National Institute on Aging's Baltimore Longitudinal Study of Aging.

There have been some careful studies that demonstrated the effect of life review on some dependent variables, such as depression and life satisfaction. It is true that much work still needs to be done to effectively operationalize outcome measures. But how does one "measure" meaning in life, guilt and expiation, redemption, and reconciliation?

Is the life review a universal occurrence? Studies report that between 49% and 84.1% of older persons have reviewed their lives or are currently reviewing them. Of course, this does not preclude the possibility that all persons might eventually do so. One study showed that those closer to death showed significantly less reminiscence activity and significantly less introspection when compared with matched controls, but this could be consistent with the original theoretical formulation that suggested post-review serenity or ataraxia. Subjects in these studies were not always followed through to the time of death. Some individuals may only review their lives on their death bed. A further complication is the difficulty of determining if the life review has already occurred since the process is not always a conscious one. The life review often occurs over a considerable period of time and only after a significant relationship has been established either with a mental health professional or a trained empathic listener.

One study reported asking questions such as, "Some people review and evaluate their past in order to get an overall picture of their life. This is called a life review. Have you reviewed or are you currently reviewing your life?" This question does not always give access to the life review, and it might not be immediately answerable by all individuals. Such a literal, objective, or conscious approach also contrasts with the context of intensive psychotherapy and intensive research interviews that led to the original formulation. This formulation assumed the existence of the unconscious, the division of the mind in psychoanalytic theory that contains memories or repressed desires, not subject to conscious perception or control but often affecting conscious thought and behavior.

Professionals in nursing, social work, occupational therapy, physical therapy, arts and music therapy, psychology, medicine, and psychiatry have advocated reminiscence and life review as ways to help patients achieve self-esteem. The life review may aid people to resolve conflicts in their lives. Part of the therapeutic value of life review therapy for older persons may be the simple fact that someone is listening to them and that approaching death, affording them little time, is a potent incentive for positive change, such as improvement in mood, increased self-esteem, and so forth.

Life Review and New Directions in Psychiatry. What will happen now that psychiatrists have moved further away from psychodynamics and the inner life to the use of psychoactive medications in their practices? Perhaps more people will feel good and healthier quicker. Painful feelings will be assuaged. But were medications utilized in the context of ongoing psychotherapy, self-understanding might also grow. There need not be a dichotomy here, for both psychoactive medications, such as antidepressants, and psychotherapy should be concurrent and reinforcing.

What about the fact that relatively few gerontologists and psychologists have spent significant amounts of time being with and listening to older people? We will lose opportunities to better understand the inner life if we depend upon drugs alone and if psychologists and gerontologists do not explore human personalities in depth. We do not know how lasting either psychopharmacological or psychotherapeutic approaches are, but it is hard to believe a pill gets to the bottom of genuine guilt due to acts of commission or omission. Is there no place for some measure of human suffering? Is there not also a time for celebration when painful issues are successfully resolved?

The life review concept has contributed to a better understanding of late-life and end-of-life development as well as development across the life span. It has helped demonstrate the therapeutic value of reminiscence for older people and helped eliminate prejudice against those who reminisce. But people and their life stories are more complex than any presently available methods for their study allow. Therefore we must encourage further study of life-span developmental psychology.

It has been suggested that the life review might possibly not be universal or even exclusively precipitated by approaching death. Yet it is remarkably common among older people, and the prospect of death is one of its most common triggers. Only in old age with the proximity of death can one truly experience a personal sense of the entire life cycle. That makes old age a unique state of life and makes the review of life at that time equally unique.

Psychotherapy and the Process of Dying

Psychotherapy.   The fundamental issues in life and, consequently, in psychotherapy—love, guilt and atonement, separation and integration—can be dealt with to the very end of life. It is imperative to encourage the life review and thus aid in the resolution of old as well as recent conflicts.

Each person should have the opportunity to live as fully as possible up to the moment of death. It is unthinking and cruel, as long as they have a "present" existence, to write off as untreatable people who have no dependable "future."

The two major fears of older people with whom we have worked are (1) fear of pain, indignity, loneliness, and depersonalization during dying and the possibility of dying alone; and (2) worry about burdening survivors with the expenses of dying and burial. These fears must be addressed in any work with those who are dying.

In her work Elisabeth Kübler-Ross delineated five psychological stages that occur during the process of dying, as well as providing a therapeutic approach to assist persons with terminal illnesses. As we discussed in Chapter 4, many investigators and clinicians, eventually including Kübler-Ross herself, found the stage theory too rigid and arbitrary in describing what really happens when a person is dying. The reality is more like a jumble of conflicting or alternating reactions running the gamut from denial to acceptance, with a tremendous variation affected by age, sex, race, ethnic group, social setting, and personality. Kübler-Ross's work has brought tremendous attention, sympathy, and interest to the process of dying. Her pioneering work has been expanded on by others in the effort to help the dying in a more humane and psychologically sound manner.

The Hospice Movement.   Dr. Cicely Saunders's innovations in the care of the dying have evoked widespread interest. The modern hospice concept began in 1843 when Catholic widows in Lyons, France, established a hospice for poor women with incurable cancer.[26] In 1967, Saunders opened St. Christopher's Hospice in London for patients in the final stages of fatal disease.

A modern hospice was planned, built, and staffed under the guidance of Dr. Cicely Saunders to enable patients who are in the last stages of their illness to have a peaceful and above all a tranquil closure to life and to be supportive to the patients' relatives and friends in their bereavement. "Contrary to common belief, patients in the proper atmosphere, and helped by modern medicine and nursing, can be maintained in an alert and peaceful frame of mind to the last. . . ."[27]

Family and friends are actively involved in care; a homelike atmosphere is encouraged with flowers, colors, and even visiting pets; and the patient often goes back and forth between hospice and home. Saunders's ideas are now providing a model for a number of hospices and hospice-service programs in the United States. Care is offered on the basis of what is most humane and comforting at each point in the dying person's life.

The National Cancer Institute, the National Institute on Aging, the National Institute on Mental Health, the Administration on Aging, and the Veterans Administration, among other federal agencies, have supported various studies and demonstrations of hospice care.[28]

Hospice concepts ideally should become automatic components of standard health care for the dying in any location, rather than requiring new buildings and new systems of reimbursement. (See Home Hospice Care in Chapter 10.) The concepts and practices central to the care of the dying are:

1. Providing physical care for the dying person, easing pain and other discomforts, giving emotional support, and assisting people to put their lives in order through use of the life review and other psychological therapies.
2. Helping people to die in their home when possible, since this is the preferred location for most people.
3. Helping support the surviving loved ones who are at risk for morbidity and mortality.
4. Educating health and social care providers and the public.

Permitting Death (The "Right to Die").   There are medico-legal considerations that go beyond psychotherapeutic efforts with the dying. Advances in technology through artificial support of circulation, respiration, and nutrition have made it possible to preserve life in persons who in the past would have died earlier.

Euthanasia, a Greek term that means a painless, good death, has become a highly emotional subject. Distinction is usually made between "passive euthanasia" and "active euthanasia" (or "mercy killing"). With passive euthanasia, a physician withdraws or refuses life-support therapy, thereby allowing a terminally-ill patient to die without medical intervention, except for pain medication and other measures solely for provision of comfort. The patient has the right to consent or refuse care. Family involvement occurs with the patient's permission.

In cases of patients too infirm or comatose to express their wishes, documents known as "advance directives" may have been signed in advance. "Living wills" and durable powers of attorney for health care decisions are examples.[29] All states now recognize the right of a patient to provide informed consent via a living will or other document. In some states, oral directives given to relatives or friends may carry legal weight.

When a patient is mentally or physically incompetent and has provided no advance directives, the situation becomes infinitely more complicated. Courts and legislatures are in the process of developing specific legal standards for decision-making. For example, the Supreme Courts of a number of states, along with a number of lower courts, have recently permitted removal of feeding tubes from comatose, severely incapacitated patients. The Council on Judicial and Ethical Affairs of the American Medical Association in 1986 stated that under certain circumstances the withholding of food and fluids from the comatose is not unethical.

On the other hand, "active euthanasia," namely the active intervention of another person to end the life of a terminally-ill person, is illegal in every country of the world, with the exception of certain specific cases in the Netherlands.

It is currently fashionable to regard medical technology as cruel when it is used to keep patients alive who are otherwise near death. At times this argument is valid. But it is extremely easy to go one step further and regard the use of such technology as wasteful when it is used on older people. The powerful devaluation of the old is thereby given new credibility under the guise of "death with dignity." Each patient is different and should receive individual consideration. Medical procedures that may be an unnecessary ordeal for some (for example, major surgery for a close-to-death cancer patient) may be life-prolonging and life-enhancing for others (like surgery to increase mobility for a cancer patient who still has some time to live).

The mental health specialist can help by individual or collective discussions and fact-finding with all the pertinent participants in the decision-making. The true feelings of the patient, if he or she is conscious at all, must be ascertained as clearly as possible. One must check to see if the individual's personal affairs are in order and if appropriate arrangements have been made in the interest of the individual and his or her family. The patient may wish to live only long enough to complete certain personal and tax arrangements. Some persons or their families may want to sustain life, for example, until after a granddaughter is born, or a favored grandson has married. The family should not be put into the difficult position of finally deciding, for the doctor has the ultimate responsibility, with or without legal directives, as deemed appropriate to the case. But the decision must derive from hard data in the context of careful moral and legal considerations. The following example illustrates what can begin to happen if the patient's rights are not carefully monitored:

A 78-year-old man's relative obtained a court order terminating his life-sustaining kidney dialysis treatments, claiming he was "mentally incompetent." The judgment was based on his lack of coherent response to them. Yet the old man was fully conscious and told nurses and a doctor that he did not wish to die. A Massachusetts appeals court judge reversed the lower court decision and ordered the resumption of treatment for the man.

Trepidation still exists around the issue of passive euthanasia. Many fear a "slippery slope" possibly leading to withdrawal of treatment not only from the terminally ill but eventually from the mentally retarded and physically handicapped. Some religious leaders view passive euthanasia as unacceptable tampering with death. Many families are worried that it is at times impossible to predict death, for example for those who may recover from comas. Some see death itself as such an insult and tragedy that any compliance with it is inhumane. Others believe that the medical profession should focus solely on the prolongation of life and should not be allowed to participate in withdrawal of treatment or nutrients. Thus, the debate over the "right to die with dignity" continues, in the attempt to be both humane *and* scrupulous about human rights.

Dr. Jack Kevorkian of Michigan became a major agent provocateur advocating physician-assisted suicide such as occurs in the Netherlands. The state of Oregon passed a law in support of physician-assisted suicide. The Hemlock Society, developed by Derek Humphrey, has also led to increased consideration of end-of-life decisions. One reason for the public attention to Kevorkian and the Hemlock Society is the failure of the medical and nursing professions and American health care institutions to develop effective palliative and end-of-life care. People need not suffer needlessly at the end of life. It is probable that once effective palliative and end-of-life medicine and nursing are developed in the United States, the call for physician-assisted suicide will diminish. The Open Society Institute (supported by financier and philanthropist George Soros) developed the Project on Death in America which is contributing to the transformation of the culture and experience of dying in America.

Helping Survivors with Funeral Arrangements. It is generally accepted that the American funeral system, with the "good funeral" and its obsequies, is outrageously expensive and offers little in the way of meaningful psychological support to mourners. Families are vulnerable to entrenched customs, the dubious approaches of some funeral directors, and the sense that they must "do right by" the deceased. The shock and grief of death are rapidly surcharged with guilt. In 1995, the average American funeral cost about $4,600[30] not including cemetery costs which can be from about $1,500 for a mausoleum to about $3,500 for a plot. Questionable practices of the funeral industry have included:

1. Inadequate presentation of lower cost alternatives, such as cremation and the use of services of memorial societies.

2. Misinformation regarding embalming. (Embalming will not prevent decomposition.) Undertakers embalm without first obtaining survivors' permission. Only some states require embalming and only under certain circumstances, yet the public is led to believe it is required.

3. Lack of availability of price information to the public and consequent reduction in competition within the "funeral industry."

4. Claims of airtight and watertight caskets that lead consumers to believe these features help prevent decomposition of the body.

In 1984, the Federal Trade Commission adopted new regulations, known as "the funeral rule," which was revised in 1994.[31] Under the funeral rule, funeral directors are required to: (1) disclose the costs of all goods and services, either with an itemized price list for in-person inquiries or over the telephone; and (2) make it easier for consumers to purchase individual items rather than predetermined packages of services.

Nonprofit memorial societies offer simple, dignified, and economical funeral arrangements. They tend to make life easier for survivors and give the deceased some control over his or her own demise. These societies are nonprofit organizations, democratically controlled by the members.[32] They are usually initiated by a church or a ministerial association and occasionally are organized by labor, civic, or educational groups. Most have modest lifetime membership fees and a small records charge at the time of death. The first society was created in Seattle, Washington, in 1939; they now exist in many cities in the United States and Canada.

Memorial services can offer valid "psychotherapy" for survivors. "In a funeral the center of attention is the dead body; the emphasis is on death. In a memorial service, the center of concern is the personality of the individual who has died . . . "[33] An honest appraisal of the deceased—with both liabilities and assets—can help the survivors work through their own complicated feelings, sometimes cast in an excessive idealization that may actually prolong grief.

In addition to earth burial and cremation, bequeathal to a medical school provides a valuable service and reduces expense.[34] Only the Orthodox Jewish faith objects to bequeathal of one's body or of organs for transplant. With changing religious attitudes and the desire to spare survivors soaring funeral costs, more bodies are now donated than are needed by medical schools in some parts of the country. Some people—status conscious to the end—want to leave their bodies to prestige schools like Harvard.

Support for the Surviving Spouse or Significant Others. The surviving partner faces practical as well as emotional problems associated with, the loss of a mate: relationships with in-laws and children, financial matters, government benefits, and unwanted callers who read the death announcement in the papers. Some decisions, such as selling one's home and moving to a new location, are best delayed until part of the mourning period is past and the survivor has greater perspective and energy at hand.

The preliminary process of adjusting to the loss of a partner is often an emotional journey of a year or longer. In a sense one never "gets over" a significant loss in one's life. Frequently one year or more of anniversaries—birthdays, Thanksgiving, the Christmas season, the Fourth of July, and all the others—must be experienced nostalgically and sadly before one is ready once again to take up life wholeheartedly. The oldest and youngest survivors may need an even longer period to adjust. Consolation is difficult and, indeed, may not be accepted at all. In therapy the task is to open up grief, uncover any complicating anger, help the person face the loss, develop new relationships, and find activities and meaning.

A comfortable standard of living (so often absent) helps in the struggle against apathy and isolation. Because of social and cultural attitudes that have prevented previous experience with finances, some widowed women may need considerable help, not only in obtaining, but also in managing finances. (See Chapter 7.) The widower may also have special problems. He may be totally unprepared to cook for himself, sew on buttons, and handle other household chores. He will need concrete assistance in learning how to do things for himself.

Socially, surviving spouses (especially women) may have a difficult time of it. They are often left out by old and good friends, since they are now "fifth wheels." If widows are attractive, others' wives may shun them; if they are dreary and mournful, everyone may stay away. Self-pity and outrage at one's fate are futile, and action of a constructive sort must be encouraged to get the person back into contact with understanding, but not patronizing, people.

Post-Cana is a Catholic lay association for widows and widowers set up to assist survivors with not only practical matters, but also with spiritual needs. The Widow-to-Widow program, originally established by Phyllis Silverman in the Boston area as an experimental mental health program of preventive intervention, is directed at new widows and staffed by other widows. It is based on the premise that the best helper of a widow at the time of grief is another widow. Silverman wrote, "Since statistics indicate a higher risk of emotional and psychiatric disturbances among younger widowed women than is to be expected from the population at large, this program was established to find ways of reaching those women (all recently widowed and under the age of 60) to determine what services would ease their distress and grief and, thereby, lessen the possibility of their developing a psychiatric disorder."[35] The idea proved promising and has been set up in various communities, applying the concept to men as well as to women, and to people of all ages.

Silverman makes the point that supportive programs such as the Widow-to-Widow are valuable for preventive purposes. Mental health agencies should offer these services as well because, as Silverman notes:

> Most mental health agencies serve those suffering from a defined psychiatric disorder, such as depression, rather than those in need of preventive services as they pass through a life crisis. This may be because most people suffering from the "hazard of living" that occurs with the death of a spouse do not consult with such agencies unless a prior contact has been established.[36]

Alcoholics Anonymous (for survivors who develop or who have had drinking problems) and Parents Without Partners are also self-help organizations that have been very useful. It is important, however, to have professional skills on hand without at the same time downplaying or interfering with the "natural" talents of the nonprofessionals. Voluntarism, however valuable, must not be used as a substitute for necessary professional services.

Professional concern is also developing for bereaved partners in nontraditional relationships, for example homosexual persons who lose a partner. The AIDS epidemic has heightened awareness of the significance of such loss for both young and older partners.[37]

GROUP THERAPY

Group Experience for Older People

Silver introduced group therapy with dementia patients in 1950.[38] He found a party atmosphere important—with milk, cookies, and music as a focus for patients with severe memory and attention deficits. However, Linden was the first, in 1953, to describe an organized program of group therapy.[39] Goldfarb, also, used the group approach in his work in assisting new residents of nursing homes with orientation.[40] Ebersole found that the use of group reminiscence was helpful to older persons in working through pain and disappointment from the past.[41] Lowy described group work with the frail elderly.[42] Klein et al. reported that community-resident older persons belonging to groups were eager to learn from and share experiences with each other and their group leaders as soon as they had gotten over initial distrust and suspicion.[43] Steuer et al. compared cognitive-behavioral and psychodynamic group psychotherapy in treatment of geriatric depression over a nine-month period.[44]

Group therapy is a very valuable procedure that should be widely used in all institutions (nursing homes, hospitals, etc.) and outpatient services. It utilizes psychotherapeutic principles and techniques from individual psychotherapy as well as techniques directly derived from group process. Yalom describes 10 curative factors potentially present in group therapy: (1) Imparting of information, (2) instillation of hope, (3) universality, (4) altruism, (5) corrective recapitulation of the primary family group, (6) development of socializing techniques, (7) imitative behavior, (8) interpersonal behavior, (9) group cohesiveness, (10) catharsis.[45]

Group therapy has been more widely used in work with older persons in and out of institutions than is generally realized or reflected in professional and scientific literature. This is partly a function of necessity, an outgrowth of the disinterest of many therapists in individual therapy with older people. But group therapy also has its own unique value in providing support, insight, and a variety of other benefits. It is also more economical than one-to-one therapy. Volunteers as well as administrators, aides, social workers, psychologists, and psychiatrists have been trained to varying degrees of competence to conduct group therapy. Nurses probably conduct more group work with older persons than do other professionals because they are already greatly involved in physical care and thus have more direct contact.[46]

Usually sociability, emotional catharsis, and perhaps insight are the main objectives of group therapy. But in institutional settings where the "management" of behavior can become a major consideration, the tendency for providers of services to control rather than help resolve the disturbed and upset feelings and actions of their patients must be questioned. Fortunately, the use of group therapy to achieve understanding and emotional support rather than simply control can result in less temptation to use chemical and physical restraints for difficult behavior.[47] Group therapy can also be useful among staff members of institutions and agencies to help them work through their negative and often unconscious attitudes toward old age.

Social agencies, community and day centers, and "golden age" or senior citizens groups offer group psychotherapy to community-resident elderly. (The overall utilization rate of golden age or senior citizens centers and clubs by the elderly is relatively low, and such activities probably attract the more gregarious older people.) The goal of these groups is usually the personal growth and emotional satisfaction of participating members through positive social experiences. Group workers also develop recreational, cultural, social, and educational group activities in the larger community.

Group therapy has been used to focus on preretirement and retirement problems. However, in general, governmental and private preretirement programs deal less adequately with the psychological and interpersonal aspects of retirement, and more adequately with financial planning and other tangible matters.

As with group therapy in general, the role of the leader in a group of older persons may range from active to passive, and may include questioning, explaining, teaching, protecting, reassuring, and confronting, as well as simply listening. Many consider the central role to be one of serving as a catalyst for emotional interchange while providing protection for individuals and the group from excessively destructive anger and disruptive anxiety among group members.

Not all groups need leaders.

In the city of Washington, one author, Dr. Robert N. Butler, founded a group for older professionals and executives, with two intents: to provide an activist, advocacy group on behalf of older persons and to provide a setting for mutual mental and emotional interchange. In effect, it became a "leaderless" group.

It never had a professional paid leader and, having begun in 1965, it lasted about twenty years, until illness, disability, and death finally decimated its members.

———————————

Groups must have momentum and vitality to maintain continuity and reduce absences and drop-outs. Selection of members is critical. Heterogeneity (aged-integrated groups) has unique advantages, one of which is to help reduce a sense of isolation of the older person from the larger world, Indeed, such group members may forget the factor of age. Groups of one's age peers have virtues of their own, including a sense of sharing a life stage together. Topics in groups composed largely of older people tend to be illness, death, loneliness, and family conflict; age-integrated groups are more likely to deal with the whole range of the life cycle, enabling older members to review and renew their own experiences and values.

Group therapy should be available for the families of older people. Getzel describes the rationale for caregiver groups, along with certain of the major issues that arise as part of the group process.[48] (Family care of the elderly is discussed further in Chapters 2 and 10.) When an older person is admitted to an institution, for example, family members often experience profound conflicts. In one sense, they are already experiencing the death of their older relative and the first grief reaction (the later actual death and subsequent grief reactions may actually have less impact). Work with relatives helps ameliorate guilt and grief and builds liaison for visitation, home stays, and discharge when possible.

Group therapy has a unique applicability and is a powerful instrument in and of itself: it should not be viewed as secondary and less valuable than individual psychotherapy. Individual and group therapy may be usefully combined in work with the same person. The person may need the opportunity for reviewing his or her life on an individual basis and for preparing for the impending encounter with death, while at the same time gaining much from the continuing human inter-

change and the range of emotions—love to hate—that a well-functioning group can provide. Some persons benefit from participating in more than one group. One such man, in his late years, found what he called his "rap sessions" in two separate groups eye-opening because of the differences in the way he was seen by each group.

"Age-Integrated, Life-Crisis" Group Therapy[49]

In the early 1970s, two of the authors, Robert N. Butler and Myrna I. Lewis, conducted and studied four age-integrated life-crisis groups (eight to ten members each) with one contrasting middle-aged group. We experimented with age integration (age range from 15 years to 80 and above), in the belief that age segregation leaves very little opportunity for the rich exchange of feelings, experience, and support possible among generations. "Life crisis" refers to the near-normal to pathological reactions to adolescence, education, married or single life, divorce, parenthood, work and retirement, widowhood, illness, and impending death. Such groups are concerned not only with the intrinsic psychiatric disorders but also with preventive and remedial treatment of people as they pass through the usual vicissitudes of the life cycle. Criteria for membership in our groups included absence of active psychosis and presence of a life crisis (acute, subacute, or chronic). Reactions to life crises followed traditional diagnostic categories, of course, including depression, anxiety states, hysterical reactions, obsessive-compulsive and passive-aggressive reactions, hypochondriasis, alcoholism, and mild drug use. Groups were balanced for age, sex, and personality dynamics. They met once a week for an hour and a half. We found it useful to have a male and a female co-therapist from different disciplines to provide both a psychodynamic and a sociological orientation for each group, as well as opportunities for transference. Individual membership in a group averaged about two years, and new group members were asked to commit themselves to a minimum of three months' participation.

The life-cycle crisis approach to group therapy need be neither strictly encounter nor strictly psychoanalytic. Rather it can be equally concerned with the interaction among and between group members, as determined by reality and the past histories of each member, and with the individual problems of each member. The goals are the amelioration of suffering, the overcoming of disability, and the opportunity for new experiences of intimacy and self-fulfillment. Expression of both anger and positive feelings should be encouraged—not for a mere defusing of feeling but as a step toward constructive resolution of problems and a positive life experience.

Our group patients often continued in individual psychotherapy with their referring therapist. When this was not feasible, individual therapy was encouraged along with group therapy, either with one of the co-therapists or someone else through referral. However, absence of such therapy did not preclude participation in groups.

Regarding older persons, some of the phenomena we observed included (1) pseudo "senility," (2) a "Peter Pan" syndrome (refusal to grow up), and (3) leadership being preempted by the middle-aged, with neglect or "mascoting" of elderly and young (necessitating therapeutic intervention). Unique contributions of older persons included models for growing older, solutions for loss and grief, creative use of reminiscence, historic empathy, and a sense of the entire life cycle. Possibilities for psychological growth continued to the end of life, as illustrated by case notes on a 70-year-old woman in one of our groups:

Repeated hospital admission for psychiatric depression. Living in retirement village. No genuine financial worries but not wealthy. Episodes characterized by increasing depression, hopelessness, remorse, insomnia, and anorexia (no appetite). Attributes her illness to worry over daughter, who is subject to manic-depressive disease and hospitalizations.

Gives impression of quiet older lady who moves and talks little, nearly mute. Face looks grief-stricken and full of worry. Hand-wringing. No signs of organic failure. Slow but appropriate answers.

Denies active suicidal thought but wishes she were dead.

In life-crisis group it emerges that she believes in hereditary and physiological basis for emotional illnesses—and hence blames self for daughter's troubles. Also describes for first time an affair with a married man, conducted at 67 after death of her own husband. She feels unfaithful, disloyal.

During the year, she has become increasingly bright-eyed and alert, listening with interest to the sexual experiences of younger group members and eliciting their views of her own life. Group members focus on helping her deal with guilt over her affair and her notions of total responsibility for her daughter's problems.

INTERGENERATIONAL FAMILY THERAPY AND COUPLES THERAPY

Although family therapy for parents and their dependent or young adult children has become an accepted form of treatment for emotional dysfunction and distress, intergenerational family therapy which includes older persons with their adult children, grandchildren, and even great-grandchildren, is just developing. The lengthening life expectancy that has occurred since the turn of the century has produced many such social lags, as society struggles to catch up with the new longevity. The family should be involved in any work with an older person, unless circumstances dictate otherwise, There are, of course, some older persons who have no living children—but often they have other close relatives or friends who constitute their "family." There should always be clarification as to who constitutes the "patient." Is it an individual or the family as a unit? Sometimes the older person is brought in by a son or daughter, and it is quickly apparent that it is the adult child who needs individual help. But more commonly, the entire family is affected by changes occurring with any one individual member. Issues in family therapy include the need for decisions about the older person, family feelings of guilt and abandonment, ancient but still active family conflicts, and the need to provide continuing care of and involvement with the older member. The therapist may decide to see the entire extended family together—not only those living in the household but also those living separately.

Intergenerational family therapy models began to develop in the 1980s. Greene provides an assessment and treatment framework for work with the elderly and their families and describes an intergenerational approach that integrates a concern with the older person's functioning together with an assessment of the family system in which it takes place.[50] Bumagin and Hirn also approach treatment of the elderly in the context of the multigenerational family.[51] Eyde and Rich describe families as critical partners in both diagnosis and treatment, including their ability to supply information as "silent, unknowing biographers" of family history and to watch for "complex and subtle changes associated with normal or pathological aging" in their older family members.[52] Silverstone and Burack-Weiss focus on work with the frail elderly and their families and emphasize the need to assess the capacity to function rather than looking solely at disease and aging processes per se.[53]

In one of the rare articles on psychotherapy with older people by a private practice psychiatrist, Finkel examines family therapy as well as older forms of treatment.[54] He describes the cycle of trouble that can begin in a family when an older person experiences serious losses of some kind. The cycle can take on much of the predictability of a Rube Goldberg contraption once it gets moving. The parent suffers a loss and turns to his or her family for increased support. Frequently, stirred up feelings of sadness, frustration, and anger are present in the parent, awaiting a sympathetic ear. The family initially offers its help generously but soon begins to feel exhausted by the extra demands. Both parent and adult children struggle with their new roles toward each other. Meanwhile the adult children are carrying additional burdens of their own, specific to middle age—seeing children through college and out into the world, coping with beginning bodily changes and ailments, and carrying major responsibility in

the working world, the family, and community life. The older person begins to feel he or she is a burden. The adult children feel inadequate and ambivalent about the task of doing enough for the older person. Frustrations turn into anger and criticism. The older person may end up feeling rejected, humiliated, and intensely sad. The adult child, seeing this, experiences guilt and remorse. Often there is a brief period of "making up" and reaffirming the old parent–child bond, followed by a repeat of the entire cycle. Family therapy can do much to bring understanding and resolution into this cycle.

Older married couples may also need counseling concerning marital problems, including interpersonal conflicts, confrontations with serious illness and approaching death, and concerns about children and grandchildren. Getzel describes work with the elderly couple in crisis, as well as the changing needs of couples who have remained together for a lifetime.[55] Remarried couples may need help with premarital counseling, marital adjustment, and family reaction to the remarriage.

Systems theory (the concept that a couple or a family interact within a family "system" in which individuals and the larger family group influence each other in a complex and interdependent manner) has provided important techniques for couples and family therapy.[56] A major goal is to analyze and eliminate miscommunications and improve interaction and interdependence.

BEHAVIORAL THERAPIES

Behavioral Modification and Therapy

Lindsley in 1964,[57] developed a theoretical prospectus for the application of operant conditioning (pioneered by B. F. Skinner[58]) to the older institutionalized person. On the whole, older populations, inpatient or outpatient, have not been studied and treated according to either "behavioral modification" or "behavioral therapy."[59] The former is the practical application of operant conditioning and includes, for example, the use of token economy (reinforcing behavior by reward). Behavioral therapy, pioneered by Pavlov, Wolpe, and Skinner, includes aversion techniques (the use of noxious stimuli, desensitization, and reinforcement). Newer techniques include over-correction, habit reversal, anxiety management training, modeling, and social skills training. Many of these could be useful with the elderly. For example, assertiveness training may be valuable for older people having difficulty expressing their needs explicitly.

Biofeedback

Biofeedback, one form of behavioral therapy, refers to techniques that use electronic monitoring devices to teach patients to control selected aspects of their behavior by providing them with continuous biological information about the impact of a variety of their actions. These techniques have been applied therapeutically to a number of conditions that afflict older people, including headaches, backaches, and general anxiety. Work at the National Institute on Aging has resulted in successful application of biofeedback in the reduction of hypertension as well as fecal incontinence with young subjects but not with older subjects. Johnson and Garton have been able to retrain muscles in hemiplegia through the same techniques.[60]

Zeichner and Boczkowski (1986) present a review of recent studies reporting on biofeedback with the elderly as well as an appraisal of its usefulness. They conclude that results are unclear; biofeedback may be effective for only a select group of elderly who are able to master the self-control skills required.

Memory Training

Recent studies indicate that there may be three major kinds of memory: *episodic* for specific events; *semantic* for knowledge and facts; and *implicit* for skills exercised automatically, like speaking grammatically or riding a bike. Seman-

tic and implicit memory have not been shown to decline with age. Declines in episodic memory ("Where did I just put my keys?") show up in most people in their 70s. But researchers are beginning to believe that retirement or changes in use of mental faculties in later life may be a major factor. The mind may be reacting to lack of use and discipline by failing to respond as well as it once did. The aging process no doubt plays a role as well, with studies suggesting a degeneration of the frontal lobes of the brain. But memory strategies may allow people to compensate for memory deterioration, particularly by learning to focus on what is happening without distortions.[61]

Cognitive training for the mildly memory-impaired focuses on training the elderly to use mnemonic (memory) devices in an effort to improve recall of names, faces, lists, and other memory categories. Yesavage finds that the elderly show enormous variability of response and that the old-old subjects have much greater difficulty in learning complex mnemonics than the young-old. He describes the use of pre-training to deal with age-related deficits that appear to be interfering with capacity for both learning and memory. Pilot studies suggest that pre-training as well as lengthened mnemonic training may have a positive effect on old-old learning capacity.[62]

ENVIRONMENTAL THERAPY

We are using the term "environmental therapy" to encompass the development of age awareness, federal policies to aid older persons, social participation,[63] mobilization of community resources, self-care, self-help, and even registration drives, job placement, direct advocacy, legal and consultative services, and political organization, each of which will be discussed later. The courage of many older people in the community is striking, since they must struggle against a system marked by fragmentation, and, frequently, indifference. Self-respect and dignity in old age obviously do not follow from felt and actual powerlessness. Consequently, we regard self-assertion in all the forms just mentioned, including political activism, as supportive of mental health.

Age Awareness and Acceptance

In order to confront the realistic opportunities, challenges, and difficulties of late life, older people must first recognize their age, accept it, and even take pride in it. Second, they must recognize themselves in others of their age, empathize with common experiences, and realize "we are all in this thing together" in spite of economic differences, cultural or social backgrounds, or social status. A significant number of older people refuse to identify with people their own age or with the issues that arise with age. The well-to-do are especially prone to this, thinking of themselves as separate and apart from the poverty-stricken elderly all around them. Yet unless they are extremely wealthy, they too can be devastated financially by just one major illness or period of adversity. And they may be equally susceptible to the emotional devastations of illness and loss. When one is old, there is really no fail-safe way for any social group to escape the effects of a culture that has not yet learned to support and cherish its elderly. The most effective defense is a united challenge that combines practical, direct action with psychological support—both from others and to and from each other.

Federal Policies to Aid Older Persons

Age Discrimination Act.   Age discrimination in programs receiving federal financial support is prohibited by the Age Discrimination Act of 1975. (This act is distinctly different from the Age Discrimination in Employment Act of 1976, which will be discussed later in this chapter.) Yet older people are still often denied access to programs that are not "age-categorical" (that is, programs where age is a specific eligibility criterion). The U.S. Civil Rights Commission, then chaired by activist Arthur S. Flemming, issued a report in 1978 showing age discrimination in 10 of the major social programs of the federal government,

especially in community mental health programs, legal services, and employment training programs. Claims of age discrimination can be brought before the Federal Mediation and Conciliation Service. However the regulations accompanying the Age Discrimination Act have several serious weaknesses: Although the legislative history confirms that Congress was mainly concerned about discrimination against the elderly, the regulations do not specifically emphasize older persons. Federal, state, and local laws have been exempted from the impact of the act.

Older Americans Act.   In 1965 Congress passed the Older Americans Act (OAA), creating the Administration on Aging (AOA). The Administration on Aging, located in the U.S. Department of Health and Human Services, is the only federal agency devoted exclusively to the concerns and potential of all older Americans. AOA's primary goal, as envisioned by the Older Americans Act, are to: (1) support a national network of state and area agencies on aging; (2) develop and oversee a comprehensive and coordinated system of support services and opportunities to meet the social and human service needs of the elderly; and (3) serve as a visible advocate on behalf of older persons.

With further amendments to the act, AOA has grown to become the major federal agency in advocacy and services to the aged. Under Title III State and Community Programs, the AOA works closely with its nationwide network on aging composed of regional offices, state units on aging (also referred to as state agencies on aging) and area agencies on aging to plan, coordinate, and develop community-level systems of services that meet the needs of older persons and their caregivers.

As first enacted, the OAA authorized funding under Title III to support a state agency on aging in each state. AOA awards funds to the 57 state agencies on aging, which are located in every state and territory. Most states are divided into planning and service areas (PSAs) so that programs can be effectively developed and targeted to the needs of the elderly in particular areas. Nationwide some

670 area agencies on aging (AAAs) receive funds from their respective state agencies on aging to plan, develop, coordinate, and arrange for services in each PSA. AAA's in turn contract with public or private groups to provide services, such as home-delivered meals; transportation, home-health and homemaker services, visiting and tele-phone reassurance, legal services, multi-purpose senior centers, outreach, and information and re-ferral services. There are some 27,000 service provider agencies nationwide. In some cases, the AAA may act as the service provider, if no local contractor is available. As an illustration of how this funding process works, state agencies on aging received a total of $800 million Title III funds during fiscal year 1994. These funds were made available to the states on a formula basis upon approval of state plans by the AOA regional offices. States then allocated funds to the area agencies on aging, based on approved area plans, to pay up to 85 percent of the costs of supportive services, senior centers, and nutrition services. The AOA also supports research and training grants to improve quality of life and services for older persons.[64]

The OAA has been amended over the years. The 1987 amendments to the OAA included the establishment within the Administration on Aging of an Office for Native Hawaiian Pro-grams. This office has the responsibility for eval-uating the adequacy of the services provided by Title III to the aforementioned elderly popula-tions and to make recommendations to the Com-missioner on ways the service delivery system can be improved. The 1992 amendments included funds granted to organizations such as commu-nity-based agencies, senior centers, and medical institutions to increase public understanding of how healthy lifestyle choices throughout life re-duce the risk of chronic health conditions in later years. Title VII, the Vulnerable Elder Rights Pro-tection Title, was created by the 1992 amend-ments to OAA. This Title encourages state agencies to concentrate their advocacy efforts on issues affecting those older people who are the most socially and economically vulnerable.

Title VII brings together and strengthens four ex-isting advocacy programs—the Long-Term Care Ombudsman Program; Programs for the Preven-tion of Abuse, Neglect and Exploitation; State Elder Rights and Legal Assistance Development Programs; and Insurance/Benefits Outreach, Coun-seling, and Assistance Programs—and calls for their coordination and linkage within each state. In addition, Title VII calls on state agencies to take a holistic approach to elder rights advocacy by coordinating the four programs and fostering collaboration among programs and other advo-cates in each state to address issues of the high-est priority for the most vulnerable elders.[65]

The OAA is up for reauthorization in 1997. One proposed bill retains all seven titles of the act and reauthorizes it for three years. Another pro-posed bill, however, eliminates some broad social policy objectives that have been the foundation of the act for over 30 years. It also removes priority services, including legal assistance, for low-income, minority, and other vulnerable elders. This represents a serious threat to efforts to pro-tect older Americans.

Mobilization of Community Resources

In previous chapters we stress the role of mental health workers in effectively representing the in-terests of their patients. Older persons should also be encouraged and helped to utilize the social ser-vice system (for example, registration drives). So-cial and family agencies could play leading roles in elder advocacy in helping the elderly deal with other voluntary agencies as well as institutions of government. For instance, family agencies have at times been important community voices in en-couraging community mental health centers (CMHCs) to provide outreach care for older pa-tients.

Community workers can help develop net-works of care within the community. Community support systems are especially valuable for the older person who has no available family. Friends, neighborhood storekeepers, druggists, and others have all been involved by mental health staff in looking out for the older person. This must be done, of course, with two perspectives in mind: the privacy of the person must not be compromised, and the network must be used for strengthening the status of the person rather than undermining it through patronization or infantilization. An analysis of a person's social supports, or "network" is part of a good mental health treatment plan. The availability of support has been found to be more important in adaption to stress than the kind and amount of stress encountered.

Organized sources of information and referral, especially clearinghouses, should be created in district Social Security offices, voluntary agencies, state commissions on aging, and the like.

In the remainder of this chapter, we focus on specific ways to mobilize the community through efforts made by the mental health worker or directly by the older person.

Registration Drives. Registration drives are among important efforts that mental health workers can initiate or support. Cloward and Piven helped generate the idea of registering all eligible recipients for various income and service programs so they could, in fact, benefit from whatever the programs were offering.[66] George Wiley expanded on this thought with the National Welfare Rights Organization, which later became a nationwide movement of welfare recipients. The operations Medicare Alert and FIND (Friendless, Isolated, Needy, Disabled) were outreach programs for older persons. The first registered older people for Medicare Part B (for doctors' coverage); the second resulted in the study "The Golden Years: A Tarnished Myth" done by the National Council on the Aging, demonstrating the enormous needs and poverty of older persons. Workers in specific cities have set up outreach programs designed to put the low-income elderly in touch with the benefits to which they are entitled under existing state and federal legislation.

The Commonwealth Fund Commission on Elderly People Living Alone, composed of national leaders and experts in health policy and aging,

conducted research on the Supplemental Security Income (SSI) Program and demonstrated methods of conducting successful SSI outreach activities on the local level.[67] It concluded that current participation rates in the SSI program are inadequate. Together with the AARP, the Commission has designed, tested, and evaluated effective approaches to increase SSI enrollment. In 1989, the Commissioner of Social Security, Gwendolyn S. King, initiated an effort to enroll many of the estimated one to two million poor people who are eligible for but not on SSI.

Self-Help and Self-Care. The burgeoning self-care, self-help movement in the United States—estimated at 200,000 individual groups belonging to some 400 major groups—promises great, if still not well-defined, potential for older people. *Self-care* refers to actions performed by individuals for their own or their families' health and well-being and the well-being of others; *self-help* is used when groups of people who share a common interest or condition join together to offer one another mutual interchange and support. In essence, the health consumer is taking a more active role in maintaining or improving his or her physical and mental health, sometimes taking over tasks otherwise performed by health care providers and sometimes augmenting such work.

Several social factors have joined to make self-care and self-help popular:

1. A demand for better health care by the consumer movement
2. The rising cost of health care
3. A maldistribution of professional health care
4. The residual from the counterculture movement of the 1960s urging greater self-reliance for individuals

The four steps in self-care are as follows:

1. Self-knowledge (health education)
2. Body monitoring—maintaining healthful habits and detecting health problems in early stages
3. Self-treatment—learning first aid, simple home treatments, and use of a variety of med-

ical tools, such as blood pressure cuffs and simple home treatments

4. Learning when to seek professional help

A few attempts have been made to design self-care programs specifically for older persons. An early example is Sehnert's "Activated Patient" program for Medicare recipients in Reston, Virginia.[68] Many self-care concepts are pertinent to old age, from learning to take one's own blood pressure to improvements in diet and exercise.

Self-help groups usually spring up voluntarily around an issue of shared concern. Examples of self-help groups that are especially relevant for older people are Widow Outreach Programs, the Alzheimer's Association, Emphysema Anonymous, the American Cancer Society, the Arthritis Foundation, Make Today Count (for the terminally ill), the Gray Panthers, Reach to Recovery (for breast cancer patients), Recovery, Inc. (The Association of Nervous and Former Mental Patients), stroke clubs like Opus (Organization of People Undaunted by Stroke, Inc.), the American Diabetes Association, women's consciousness-raising groups, the Parkinson's Disease Foundation, the United Ostomy Association, and the American Heart Association. The National Institute on Aging has prepared a booklet describing and listing major self-help groups of particular value for the elderly.[69]

Many self-help groups and self-care concepts have been enthusiastically supported by health care providers. Other providers have been less positive, fearing encroachment in professional territory, predicting consumers would "go too far" in self-care, or simply doubting the effectiveness of the self-care, self-help movement. Serious studies of the impact of the movement have not yet been done. But the "soft indicators" of client satisfaction show that many find this new health movement satisfying and useful, as judged by their continuing voluntary participation.

Volunteer work is perhaps more highly developed in the United States than anywhere else in the world. The Salvation Army alone depends on the work of 1.2 million volunteers. A 1988 Independent Sector survey by the Gallup Organization found that 45% of all respondents volunteered time and averaged 4.7 hours each per week. Volunteering reached its highest level from ages 65 to 74, with an average of 6.0 hours per week for that age group. (Table 12.1.)

Older persons volunteer for hundreds of organizations, including wide-ranging service organizations like the Red Cross, advocacy groups like the American Association of Retired Persons, and special focus organizations like the Service Corps of Retired Executives Association (SCORE) in which retired men and women counsel people running or starting small businesses.

Those who want help in beginning to volunteer can consult the white pages in the telephone book under Volunteer Center, Voluntary Action Center, or Volunteer Bureau. Specific groups can be found in the yellow pages under "Social Service Organizations."

Employment and Productive Aging. Why do many older people seek or desire employment? Some need money because Social Security or pension checks just will not stretch far enough.[70] Some want to get out of the house to occupy their time. Many want the "meaningfulness" of work. So long as work and money have such profound financial, social, personal, and ethical significance, it is illusory to deny their importance to health, both physical and mental. Some older people are told to do volunteer work—advice that is indeed helpful to some but naive in instances where economic survival or a personal preference for paid employment is at issue.

Job placement for older persons requires vocational evaluation and counseling as critical first steps. The U.S. Employment Service (USES) has been very disappointing in its feeble efforts to place older workers, but pressure should nonetheless be placed on USES and its various offices. There are Federal Job Information Centers in various cities that give advice and information on federal job opportunities. The Women's Bureau in the Department of Labor has taken some interest in the job plight of older women and can offer

TABLE 12.1   Who volunteers

WHO VOLUNTEERS (BY AGE)

	PERCENT WHO VOLUNTEER	AVERAGE VOLUNTEER HOURS PER WEEK
Ages 25–34	44.6%	4.0 hours/week
Ages 35–44	53.9%	5.3 hours
Ages 45–54	47.5%	5.8 hours
Ages 55–64	47.1%	4.7 hours
Ages 65–74	40.0%	6.0 hours
Ages 75 and over	28.6%	4.4 hours

WHO VOLUNTEERS (BY CATEGORY)

Women	46.7%	4.7 hours
Men	43.8%	4.8 hours
Self-employed, full-time	59.1%	4.7 hours
Self-employed, part-time	59.0%	6.4 hours
Other employed, full-time	46.4%	4.4 hours
Other employed, part-time	52.9%	5.7 hours
Not employed	38.0%	4.7 hours

Source: Adapted from Hodgkinson, V. A., Weitzman, M. S., & The Gallup Organization. (1988). *Giving and volunteering in the United States.* Washington, DC: INDEPENDENT SECTOR.

advice. Various communities offer privately sponsored, nonprofit, over-60 employment and counseling services and agencies. In some there are 40-plus clubs for finding employment after age 40. For the handicapped and elderly, sheltered workshops may be available. (See Chapter 11.) In Appendix C we have outlined various governmental employment and volunteer programs to which older people can apply, some of which are specifically designed for the low-income elderly.

The Senior Opportunities Services (SOS) program of the Office of Economic Opportunity is intended to identify and meet the needs of persons over 60 with projects that serve or employ older persons predominately. The various projects include community action programs to provide employment opportunities, home health services, assistance in the Food Stamp plan, and outreach and referral services. As much as possi-

ble, these activities are staffed by older citizens, paid or volunteer. Office of Economic Opportunity Senior Aides and Senior Community Service Aides are engaged in such activities as homemaker and health assistance, nutrition, institutional care, home repair, child care, and social service administration.

Green Thumb, which involves beautification by planting, and Green Light, which employs aides in libraries, schools, and day-care centers, are federal employment programs for older people. Table 12.2 lists other jobs for older persons that could be developed to meet needs that exist in many communities.

Older workers should not feel forced to "think young" or "act young." Their accumulated work skills and experiences have a unique value. Nor should they feel compelled to misrepresent their age for any purpose, including employment. Age

TABLE 12.2 Job options for older people in meeting community needs

Transportation
Station information aides
Bus drivers
Van drivers
Pool arrangers
Improved route sign advisors
Service assistance locators
	Neighborhood
	Guards and monitors
	Clean-up aides
	Repair workers for substandard housing
	Energy conservation advisors and
	    workers
	Mediators, conciliators, and
	    arbitrators
	Fire and safety inspectors
	Pest control workers
	Translators and communicators

Cultural activities Performers and artists Programmers Trainers Sales and promotion workers Facilities maintenance workers Fund raising counselors and assistants Audience development specialists Arts conservators and technicians Resource and information assistants	**Health** Hospital technicians and aides Home health care providers and aides Rehabilitation technicians and aides Medical equipment operators

Employment
Job finders
Trainers
Job developers
Career and job counselors
	Education
	Discipline aides
	Tutors and resource specialists
	Class administration aides
	Library workers
	Career and other counselors
	Special population education
	    programmers and advisors
	Fund raisers
	Special skill enrichment advisors and
	    aides
	Financial aid advisors

Non-profit activities Fund raising/membership counselors Bookkeepers and accountants Government regulations and compliance counselors Coordinators of volunteers Incorporation advisors	
Environment Counselors on pesticide and safety Extended sanitation and special clean-up workers Monitors Materials recycling aides Environmental impact analysts	**Special services to dependent persons** Companions Nutrition advisors Form fillers Eligibility & assistance advisors Readers & communicators Recreation advisors and workers Meal providers and/or feeding helpers Day care providers Home health care aides Rehabilitation technicians & helpers Representative payees & guardians Homemakers Shopping assistance helpers

Employee relations
Mediation, arbitration, and conciliation
    specialists (both employee/management
    and employer/employee relations)	

Source: National Committee on Careers for Older Americans. (1979). *Older Americans: An untapped resource.* New York: Academy for Educational Development. Reprinted by permission.

discrimination in employment is directly related to unemployment in later life. The Age Discrimination in Employment Act of 1976[71] is administered by the Department of Labor, Wage and Hour Administration, in 350 offices throughout the nation. (See listings in the telephone directory.) The act prohibits discrimination on the basis of age in hiring, job retention, compensation, and other terms, conditions, and privileges of employment. it originally applied only to those workers between 40 and 65 years of age; however, amendments in 1978 raised the protected age limit for workers in the private sector to 70 years of age and eliminated the upper age limit entirely for most federal employees. In 1986 mandatory retirement was virtually ended in the United States. Nonetheless, typical ways in which employers avoid hiring the older person are to declare that the person is "overqualified," "unskilled," less needful of a job as compared to the young, and less reliable and flexible.[72]

Advocacy. Advocacy includes use of all means at our disposal, from direct action to moral persuasion, to effectively represent the needs and grievances of older people. The contributions of Saul Alinsky and Ralph Nader should be known to the mental health worker. Class-action cases are essential, for instance, to compel better treatment in state mental hospitals and other governmental facilities.[73] Legal and protective services, private conservatorships, and public guardianships are essential—not only to protect older people but also to advance causes such as better housing and administrative and judicial reviews regarding Social Security and Medicare claims. Contemporary grievance mechanisms are being overhauled and improved following court cases. Contractual and testamentary rights must be protected, especially for the frail elderly. Tenant rights have become increasingly important. Neighborhood legal services, Legal Aid societies, public defenders, and public-interest law firms can be of help to those who cannot afford a private attorney.

Nursing home deficiencies must not be covered up by local, state, or federal governments.

The Freedom of Information Act can be used to compel the Social Security Administration to reveal the names of specific institutions with their particular deficiencies.

There already are existing advocates for older people. Some churches have lay commissions and special ministries to the aging. Cities and states have advisory committees and commissions. Massachusetts created the first cabinet-level Department of Elder Affairs in 1971 to oversee all programs for older persons. The department has authority over such functions as Supplemental Security Income, Disability Assistance, and the provision of a program for income maintenance (formerly functions of the Welfare Department); licensing and inspection of nursing homes, rest homes, and similar facilities for the elderly (formerly the responsibility of the Department of Public Health); and construction and administration of housing and transportation services for older persons (previously vested in the Department of Community Affairs).

The Swedish concept of ombudsman has been adopted in some situations in the United States. An *ombudsman* is a mediator who protects the rights of individual citizens and works with governmental agencies to ensure fair representation. We believe older persons themselves should take ombudsman-type leadership. There are countless ways in which they can counter the myths and prejudices against old age. For example, they should make unannounced visits to nursing homes. When they do not wish to retire, they should be willing to challenge the pressure to leave their jobs.

We have also long urged the formation of a national federation of friends and relatives of nursing home residents rather than depending solely on the establishment of federal, state, and local standards, regulations, and enforcement. The Friends and Relatives of Nursing Home Patients, Inc., a consumer group in Oregon organized principally by Ruth Shepherd in 1972, is an example of a local group whose objective is to have as a member of the organization one family member or friend who is financially or legally responsible for each resident of a nursing home. The development of the National Citizens Coalition for Nursing Home Reform (under the outstanding leadership of Elma Holder) is a move toward monitoring and improving nursing homes on a national basis.[74]

Legal Services. Congress has defined "legal services" in Section 302(4) of the Older American's Act as "legal advice and representation by an attorney (including, to the extent feasible, counseling or other appropriate assistance by a paralegal or law student under the supervision of an attorney) and includes counseling or representation by a non-lawyer where permitted by law, to older individuals with economic or social needs." Amendments to OAA in 1972 specifically included legal services for funding under Title III of the Act through state and area agencies on aging. Over 120 legal services for the elderly projects now exist nationwide, many funded under Title III. Others are financed by Title XX of the Social Security Act, the Housing and Community Development Act, revenue sharing, funds resulting from filing fee legislation, United Way, or private foundations.

The American Bar Association in 1978 created the 15-member interdisciplinary Commission on Legal Problems of the Elderly.[75] Its initial priorities were four: the delivery of legal services to older persons, age discrimination, simplification and coordination of administrative procedures and regulations affecting the elderly, and the rights of persons subject to the process of institutionalization. The 1988 American Civil Liberties Union's guide to older persons' rights is a comprehensive guide for older persons, their families, their lawyers, and members of nonlaw professions, such as social workers and nurses. It incorporates the latest changes in the Social Security Act, the Internal Revenue Code, and the Pension Reform Law.[76]

Consumer Fraud and Quackery. Consumer fraud and quackery are serious legal problems because older people are especially vulnerable.[77] Many have chronic ailments that seem never to get better. Hard-earned savings may be lost to ex-

ploitative medical fakers, land salespeople, hearing aid salespeople, and others.

The human desire for magic cures and salvation runs deep. In late life, additional factors, ranging from brain damage to grief, add to the vulnerability. Public consumer education is not sufficient. Direct advice and discussion by the various service professions and vocations—mental health workers to physicians—carry considerable weight. But legislation, more than we presently have, is necessary, and its strict enforcement is mandatory. An example of such legislation is the Interstate Land Sales Full Disclosure Act.

Credit Discrimination. The Equal Credit Opportunity Act Amendment of 1976 prohibits discrimination in credit transactions, making it unlawful for a creditor to discriminate against any credit applicant on the basis of "race, color, religion, national origin, sex or marital status, or age (provided the applicant has the capacity to contract)."[78]

Consultative Services. Generally speaking, consultants to institutions and agencies provide evaluation and recommendations concerning the institution itself, its staff, or those it serves. The following list further delineates this general observation and offers some models of consultation.

1. *Administrative consultation.* The center consultant meets with the home administrator, usually to discuss staff problems, but sometimes family or financial problems. The focus is on organization and decision-making.

2. *Staff (milieu) consultation.* The center consultant meets with staff groups to discuss and interpret the psychological importance of events in the nursing home that affect staff and patient group behavior.

3. *Client-centered case consultation.* The center consultant discusses a specific case with a staff group or individual. Focus is on the patient.

4. *Consultee-centered consultation.* The focus of discussion is the patient, but the center consultant keeps the staff members' counter-transference in mind during the discussion.

5. *Didactic meetings.* These allow for an organized presentation of basic psychological principles. Many staff have a keen interest in such learning.[79]

Consultative services should be standard to agencies, homes, and religious and other organizations. The following list includes the major users of consultation regarding the problems of older people.

1. Nursing homes
2. Homes for the aged
3. Nonpsychiatrist physicians
4. General hospital inpatient and outpatient sections
5. Boarding homes, public housing for the aged, and similar residential concentrations
6. Public assistance departments, including their sections for protective service for older persons
7. Members of the clergy
8. Senior citizen centers
9. Industry and government
10. Homemaker and home health aide agencies
11. Visiting nurses and public health nurses
12. Planning bodies, such as model cities boards, senior citizen councils, commissions on aging, housing authorities

The Politics of Age. The beginning rumblings of "politics of age" stirred controversy along with some early study and political attention.[80] Binstock (1983) wrote of the weaknesses of using older age as a political rallying point. Others saw an old-age-focused political effort as positive and inevitable. Talk of a "backlash" by the younger generation, begun already in the late 1970s, escalated into public debate in the 1980s.[81]

The severe cutback of services resulting from the $750 billion tax cut initiated by the Reagan Administration has provoked steady criticism that Social Security and Medicare provide entitlements for older people while denying them for the young. Newspapers' distortion of figures concerning a rise in the elderly's median income as

more than that of any other group has led to the emergence of the "new ageism."[82] This dangerous viewpoint envies the elderly for their economic progress, yet resents the poor elderly for being tax burdens and the nonpoor elderly for making Social Security so expensive. As a result, groups, such as the Americans for Generational Equity (AGE), promote Social Security displacement, and former U.S. Secretary of Commerce Peter Peterson strongly opposes Social Security. In 1983, former Colorado Governor Richard Lamm suggested an old-age-based rationing of health care. Daniel Callahan has expounded on this suggestion, seeing the elderly as "a new social threat . . . that could ultimately (and perhaps already) do great harm."[83]

Fortunately, others have counteracted such views. For example, long-term care was an important ingredient on the national agenda in the 1988 presidential campaign, due in large part to the combined successful efforts of AARP, the Villers Foundation, and the Older Women's League. Their "Long-Term-Care '88" Campaign advocated a universal long-term care financing program based on social insurance that would cover all segments of the population, including severely impaired children and all other groups not currently eligible for Medicare/OASDI. The benefit structure was balanced wisely with home care, community care, and nursing home care. Its emphasis on tailoring to individual needs, flexibility, and innovation was particularly congenial to a patient-oriented philosophy.

Several states have an annual governor's conference on aging (for example, Indiana, North Carolina, and Ohio), and others have special days for older people (for example, "Older Vermonters' Day"). Florida, Michigan, Georgia, Missouri, Utah, West Virginia, and other states have what has been called "silver-haired legislatures"— quasi-official groups of older citizens who meet and draft legislation that is then passed on to the state legislators.

Having a sense of power and political participation is therapeutic for the elderly; the active achievement of objectives may not always be successful, but the process itself can be a source of satisfaction and increased self-esteem. Older people are beginning to be more active politically and may soon vote more consistently as a power block (they constitute 17% of the vote). The National Council of Senior Citizens and the American Association of Retired Persons (the two largest organizations for older people) have

lobbied for more favorable Social Security benefits, Medicare, housing, and other areas of concern. The Gray Panthers are a much smaller but more activist group. In addition to their many other advocate activities, the Gray Panthers publish "The Network," an issue-oriented quarterly newspaper covering health care and other age-related topics.[84]

SELECTED READINGS

Aries, P. (1981). *The hour of our death.* New York: Knopf.

Bass, D. M., & Bowman, K. (1990). The transition from caregiving to bereavement: The relationship of care-related strain and adjustment to death. *The Gerontologist, 30*(1), 35–42.

Beck, A. T. (1976). *Cognitive therapy and the emotional disorders.* New York: International Universities Press.

Berezin, M. A., & Cath, S. H. (Eds.) (1965). *Geriatric psychiatry: Grief loss and emotional disorders in the aging process.* New York: International Universities Press.

Berger, R. M. (1995). *Gay and gray: The older homosexual man,* 2nd ed. Binghamton, NY: The Haworth Press.

Binstock, R. H. (1983). The aged and scapegoat. *The Gerontologist, 23,* 136–143.

Birren, J. E., & Hedlund, B. (1987). Contributions of autobiography to developmental psychology. In Eisenberg, N. (Ed.), *Contemporary topics in developmental psychology* (pp. 394–415). New York: John Wiley & Sons.

Brink, T. L. (Ed.). (1990). Mental health in the nursing home. *Clinical Gerontologist, 9*(¾), special issue.

Bumagin, U. E., & Hirn, K. E. (1990). *Helping the aging family: A guide for professionals.* Glenview, IL: Scott, Foresman.

Burnside, I. M. (Ed.). (1986). *Working with the elderly: Group process and techniques,* 2nd ed. Boston, MA: Jones and Bartlett.

Butler, R. N., Burt, R., Foley, K. M., Morris, J., & Morrison, R. S. (1996, June). A peaceful death: How to manage pain and provide quality care. A round-

table discussion: Part 2. *Geriatrics, 51*(6), 32–5, 39–40, 42.

Butler, R. N., Burt, R., Foley, K. M., Morris, J., & Morrison, R. S. (1996, May). Palliative medicine: Providing care when cure is not possible. A roundtable discussion: Part 2. *Geriatrics, 51*(5), 33–6, 42–4.

Butler, R. N., & Gleason, H. P. (Eds.). (1985). *Productive aging: Enhancing vitality in later life.* New York: Springer.

Butler, R. N., Oberlink, M. R., & Schechter, M. (1989). *The promise of productive aging.* New York: Springer.

Byock, I. (1997). *Dying well: The prospect for growth at the end of life.* New York: Riverhead Books.

Cancer Pain Relief and Palliative Care, WHO Expert Committee. (1990). Technical Report, Series 804. Geneva, Switzerland: World Health Organization.

Cantor, M., & Little, V. (1985). Aging and social care. In Binstock, R. H., & Shanas, E. (Eds.), *Handbook of aging and the social sciences* (pp. 745–781). New York: Van Nostrand Reinhold.

Cassell, C., & Omenn, G. S. (Eds.). (1995, September). Caring for patients at the end of life. *Western Journal of Medicine,* no. 163.

Colen, B. D. (1987). *The essential guide to a living will.* New York: Pharos Books.

Collins, C., & Ogle, K. (1994). Patterns of predeath service use by dementia patients with a family caregiver. *Journal of the American Geriatric Society, 42,* 719–722.

Council on Scientific Affairs and Council on Ethical and Judicial Affairs. (1990). Persistent vegetative state and the decision to withdraw or withhold life support. *Journal of the American Medical Association, 263*(3), 426–430.

Daniels, N. (1988). *Am I my parents keeper? An essay on justice between the young and the old.* New York: Oxford University Press.

Dodson, J. E. (Ed.). (1983). *Strengths of black families—An afrocentric educational manual: Toward a non-deficit perspective in services to families and children.* Nashville, TN: University of Tennessee School of Social Work.

Emanuel, E. J., & Emanuel, L. L. (1994). The economics of dying: The illusion of cost savings at the end of life. *The New England Journal of Medicine, 330*(8), 540–544.

Emanuel, E. J., Weinberg, D. S., Gonin, R., et. al. (1993). How well is the Patient Self-Determination Act working? An early assessment. *American Journal of Medicine, 95*(6), 619–628.

Erikson, E. H., Erikson, J. M., & Kivnick, H. Q. (1987). *Vital involvement in old age.* New York: W. W. Norton.

Estes, C. L. (1979). *The aging enterprise: A critical examination of social policies and serviced for the aged.* San Francisco, CA: Jossey-Bass.

Evans, R. L., & Juarequy, B. M. (1982). Phone therapy outreach for blind elderly. *The Gerontologist, 22,* 32–35.

Ferrell, B. A. (1991). Pain management in elderly people. *Journal of the American Geriatric Society, 39,* 64–73.

Finkel, S. I. (1980). Experiences of a private practice psychiatrist working with the elderly in the community. *International Journal of Mental Health, 8,* 147–172.

Finkel, S. I. (1990). Group psychotherapy with older people. *Hospital and Community Psychiatry, 41*(11), 1189–1191.

Finkel, S. I. (1995). Postscript: Research directions for treatment of depression. *International Psychogeriatrics, 7,* 139–140.

Finkel, S. I., & Rogers, S. (1992). The clinical collaboration of a psychiatrist and a geriatric care manager. *Journal of Case Management, 1*(2), 49–52.

Foley, K. M. (1995, September). Pain relief into practice: Rhetoric without reform (editorial). *Journal of Clinical Oncology, 13*(9), 2149–2151.

Foundation for Aging Policy in the 90's. (1990, February). *The 1987 Older Americans Act Amendments. Hearings before the Subcommittee on Human Services of the Select Committee on Aging, House of Representatives.* Washington, DC: U.S. Government Printing Office.

Getzel, G. S. (1983). Group work with kin and friends caring for the elderly. In Saul, S. (Ed.), *Group work with the frail elderly.* Binghamton, NY: The Haworth Press.

Getzel, G. S., & Mellor, J. M. (Eds.). (1985). Gerontological social work practices in the community. *Journal of Gerontological Social Work, 8*(¾), special issue.

Goldfarb, A. (1971). Group therapy with the old and aged. In Kaplan, H., & Saddock, B. (Eds.), *Comprehensive group psychotherapy* (pp. 623–642). Baltimore, MD: Williams and Wilkins.

Goleman, D. (1990, March 27). Studies offer fresh clues to memory. *The New York Times,* 1, 8.

Gorer, G. (1965). *Death, grief and mourning in contemporary Britain.* London: Cresset Press.

Gottlieb, G. L. (1995). Financial issues in geriatric psychiatry. In Kaplan, H. I. & Sadock, B. J. (Eds.), *Comprehensive textbook of psychiatry/IV* (vol. 2, pp. 2656–2661). Baltimore, MD: Williams and Wilkins.

Greene, R. R. (1986). *Social work with the aged and their families.* New York: Aldine de Gruyter.

Greene, R. (1989). A life systems approach to understanding parent–child relationships in aging families. In Hughston, G. A., Christopherson, V. A., & Bonjean, M. J. (Eds.). *Aging and family therapy: Practitioner perspectives on Golden Pond.* Binghamton, NY: The Haworth Press.

Hancock, B. L. (1990). *Social work with older people.* Englewood Cliffs, NJ: Prentice-Hall.

Hughston, G. A., Christopherson, V. A., & Bonjean, M. J. (Eds.). (1989). *Aging and family therapy: Practitioner perspectives on Golden Pond.* Binghamton, NY: The Haworth Press.

Jung, C. G. (1933). The stages of life. In Jung, C. G. *Modern man in search of a soul.* New York: Harcourt, Brace and World.

Kaminsky, M. (Ed.). (1984). *The uses of reminiscence: New ways of working with older adults.* Binghamton, NY: The Haworth Press.

Kaufman, S. R. (1987). *The ageless self: Sources of meaning in late life.* Madison, WI: University of Wisconsin Press.

Klerman, G. L., Weissman, M. W., Rounsaville, B. J., & Chevron, E. S. (1984). *Interpersonal psychotherapy of depression.* New York: Basic Books.

Knight, B. (1996). *Psychotherapy with older adults,* 2nd ed. Thousand Oaks, CA: Sage Publications.

Kübler-Ross, E. (1974). *Questions and answers on death and dying.* New York: Macmillan.

Lawton, M. P. (1983). Environment and other determinants of well-being in older people. *The Gerontologist, 23,* 349–357.

Lerner, M. (1990). *Wrestling with the angel: A memoir of my triumph over illness.* New York: W. W. Norton.

Logan, S. M. L., Freeman, E. M., & McRoy, R. G. (1990). *Social work practice with black families.* New York: Longman.

Lowy, L. (1985). *Social work with the aging.* New York: Longman.

MacLennon, B., Saul, S., & Weiner, M. M. (Eds.). (1988). *Group therapies for the elderly.* Madison, CT: International Universities Press.

Massie, M. J., & Holland, J. C. (1990). Depression and the cancer patient. *Journal of Clinical Psychiatry, 51,* 12–17.

Muller, M. T., van der Wal, G., van Eijk, J. Th. M., et. al. (1994). Voluntary active euthanasia and assisted suicide in Dutch nursing homes: Are the requirements for prudent practice properly met? *Journal of the American Geriatric Society, 42,* 624–629.

Munsterberg, H. (1983). *The crown of life: Artistic creativity in old age.* San Diego, CA: Harcourt Brace Jovanovich.

The National Institute on Community-Based Long-Term Care. (1988). *Care management standards: Guidelines for practice.* Washington, DC: The National Council on Aging.

Nemiroff, R. A., & Colarusso, C. A. (1985). *The race against time: Psychotherapy and psychoanalysis in the second half of life.* New York and London: Plenum Press.

Pinderhughes, E. B. (1982). Family functioning of Afro-Americans. *Social Work, 27,* 91–96.

Quam, J. K. (Ed.). (1996). *Social services for older gay men and lesbians.* Binghamton, NY: The Haworth Press.

Rechtschaffen, A. (1959). Psychotherapy with geriatric patients: A review of the literature. *Journal of Gerontology, 14,* 73–84.

Rodin, J. (1986, September 19) Aging and health: Effects of the sense of control. *Science, 233*(4770), 1271–1276.

Saunders, C. (1959). *Care of the dying.* London: Macmillan.

Schulz, J. H. (1995). *The economics of aging,* 6th ed. Westport, CT: Auburn House.

Sheppard, H. (1989). The new ageism and the "intergenerational tension" issue. *Journal of Foundation Nationale de Gerontologie.* Tampa, FL: International Exchange Center on Gerontology, University of South Florida.

Silverman, P. (1985). *Widow to widow.* New York: Springer.

SUPPORT Principal Investigators. (1995, Nov. 22/29). A controlled trial to improve care for seriously ill hospitalized patients: The Study to Understand Prognoses and Preferences for Outcomes and Risks of Treatments (SUPPORT). *The Journal of the American Medical Association, 274*(20), 1591–1598.

Teno, J., Murphy, D., Lynn, J., et. al. (1994). Prognosis-based futility guidelines: Does anyone win? *Journal of the American Geriatrics Society, 42,* 1–6.

Tolstoy, L. (1969). *The death of Ivan Illych and other stories.* New York: The New American Library of World Literature.

Toseland, R. W. (1990). *Group work with older adults.* New York: New York University Press.

Toseland, R. W., Rossiter, C. M., Peak, T., & Smith, G. C. (1990). Comparative effectiveness of individual and group interventions to support family caregivers. *Social Work, 35*(3), 209–217.

U.S. House of Representatives, Select Committee on Aging. (1988, March 2). Mental health and aging. Hearing before the Select Committee on Aging, U.S. House of Representatives. Washington, DC: U.S. Government Printing Office.

U.S. House of Representatives, Select Committee on Aging and Subcommittee on Human Services. (1989, August 3). Mental health in nursing homes: Barriers and solutions. Joint hearing before the Subcommittee on Human Services and the Select Committee on Aging, U.S. House of Representatives. Washington, DC: U.S. Government Printing Office.

Weinbach, R. W. (1989). Sudden death and the secret survivor: Helping those who grieve alone. *Social Work, 34*(1), 57–60.

Weiner, M. B., Brok, A. J., & Snadowsky, A. M. (1987). *Working with the aged: Practical approaches in the institution and community,* 2nd ed. Norwalk, CT: Appleton-Century-Crofts.

West, R. L. (1985). *Memory fitness over forty.* Gainsville, FL: Triad.

West, R. L. (1989). Planning practical memory training for the aged. In Poon, L. W., Rubin, D. C., & Wilson, B. A. (Eds.), *Everyday cognition in adulthood and later life.* Cambridge: Cambridge University Press.

Wilson, B. A. (1988). *Rehabilitation of memory*. New York: Guilford Publications.

Yalom, I. D. (1985). *The theory and practice of group psychotherapy,* 3rd ed. New York: Basic Books.

Yesavage, J. A. (1990). *Age-associated memory impairment: Conceptual background and treatment approaches*. Presented at the 1990 Sandoz Lectures in Gerontology, March 28–30, 1990.

SELECTED READINGS IN REMINISCENCE AND LIFE REVIEW

American Association of Retired Persons. (1992). *The power of memories: Creative uses of reminiscence*. Washington, DC: Author.

Birren, J. E., & Deutchman, D. E. (1991). *Guiding autobiography groups for older adults: Exploring the fabric of life*. Baltimore, MD: John Hopkins University Press.

Birren, J. E., & Hedlund, B. (1987). Contributions of autobiography to developmental psychology. In Eisenburg, N. (Ed.), *Contemporary topics in developmental psychology* (pp. 394–415). New York: John Wiley & Sons.

Black, G., & Haight, B. K. (1992). Integrality as a holistic framework for the life-review process. *Holistic Nurse Practitioner, 7*(1), 7–15.

Boggs, D, & Leptak, J. (1991). Life review among senior citizens as a product of drama. *Educational Gerontology, 17,* 239–246.

Bruner, J. (1987). Life as narrative. *Social Research, 54,* 11–32.

Burnside, I. (1993). Themes in reminiscence groups with older women. *International Journal of Aging and Human Development, 37,* 177–189.

Burnside, I, & Haight, B. K. (1994). Protocols for reminiscence and life review. *Nurse Practitioner, 19,* 55–61.

Butler, R. N. (1963). The life review: An interpretation of reminiscence in the aged. *Psychiatry, 26,* 65–76.

Chance, S. (1988). The psychological functions of genealogy in the aged. *Journal of Geriatric Psychiatry and Neurology, 1*(4), 113–115.

Colemen. P. (1991). Ageing and life history: The meaning of reminiscence in late life. *Sociological Review (Monograph), 37,* 120–143.

David, D. (1990). Reminiscence, adaptation, and social context in old age. *International Journal of Aging and Human Development, 30,* 175–188.

DeGenova, M. (1991). Elderly life review therapy: A Bowen approach. *American Journal of Family Therapy, 19,* 160–166.

Disch, R. (Ed.). (1988). Twenty-five years of the life review [Special issue]. *Journal of Gerontological Social Work, 12*(¾).

Fishman, S. (1992) Relationships among older adult's life review, ego integrity, and death anxiety. *International Psychogeriatrics, 4,* 267–277.

Freeman, M. (1993). *Rewriting the self: History, memory, narrative*. London: Routledge.

Freud, A. (1936). *Das Ich und die Abwehrmechanismen*. London: Imago.

Galassie, F. (1991). A life-review workshop for gay and lesbian elders. *Journal of Gerontological Social Work, 16,* 75–86.

Haight, B. K., & Webster, J. D. (Eds.). (1995). *The art and science of reminiscing: Theory, research, methods, and applications*. Washington, DC: Taylor and Francis.

Hargave, T. D., & Anderson, W. T. (1992). *Finishing well: Aging and reparation in the intergenerational family*. New York: Brunner/Mazel.

Lewis, M. I., & Butler, R. N. (1974). Life review therapy: Putting memories to work in individual and group psychotherapy. *Geriatrics, 29,* 165–169, 172–172.

Merriam, S. B. (1993). Butler's life review: How universal is it? *International Journal of Aging and Human Development, 37*(3), 163–175.

Rubin, D. C., Wetzler, S. E., & Nebes, R. B. (1989). Autobiographical memory across the life span. In Rubin, D. C. (Ed.), *Autobiographical Memory*. Cambridge: Cambridge University Press.

Ruth, J. E. & Birren, J. E. (1995). Personality and aging: Modes of coping and the meaning of stress. In Kruse, A., & Schmitz-Scherzer (Eds.), *Psychologie des Lebenslaufs*. Festschrift Hans Thomae. Darmstadt: Steinkopf Verlag.

Staudinger, U. M. (1989). *The study of the life review: An approach to the investigation of intellectual development across the life span*. Berlin: Max-Planck-Institut fur Bildungsforschung.

Staudinger, U. M. et al. (1992). Wisdom-related knowledge in a life review task: Age differences and the role of professional specialization. *Psychology and Aging, 7*(2), 271–281.

Webster, J. D. (1993). Construction and validation of the reminiscence functions scale. *Journal of Gerontology, 48,* 256–252.

Wholohan, D. (1992). The value of reminiscence in hospice care. *American Journal of Hospice and Palliative Care, 9,* 272–279.

Zuniga, M. (1989). Mexican-American elderly and reminiscence interventions. *Journal of Gerontological Social Work, 14*(¾), 61–73.

ENDNOTES

1. See "The Shameless Old Lady" (listed in Appendix E), based on a play by Bertolt Brecht in which an elderly widow makes the most of the last 18 months of her life.

2. For example, see Dodgen, J. C., & Ransom, J. A. (1967). Psychotherapy of a sexagenarian. *Diseases of the Nervous System, 28,* 680–683. Also see Goldfarb, A. I. (1971). Group therapy with the old and aged. In Kaplan, H. I., & Saddock, B. J. (Eds.), *Comprehensive group psychotherapy.* Baltimore: Williams & Wilkins; and Goldfarb, A. I. (1955). Psychotherapy of aged persons; IV. One aspect of the therapeutic situation with aged patients. *Psychoanalytic Review, 42,* 100–187.

3. Abraham, K. (1927). The applicability of psychoanalytic treatment to patients at an advanced age. In *Selected papers of Karl Abraham, M. D.* (pp. 312–317). London: Hogarth Press.

4. Jelliffe, S. E. (1925). The old age factor in psychoanalytic therapy. *Medical Journal and Record, 121,* 7–12.

5. Grotjahn, M. (1940). Psychoanalytic investigation of a 71-year-old man with senile dementia. *Psychoanalytic Quarterly, 9,* 80–97.

6. Goldfarb emphasized the dependent relationships of older patients, comparing them with early parent–child relationships. The physician assumes the role of parent figure pressed on him by the patient. Thus sometimes the therapist will be seen as a scapegoat and sometimes as the omnipotent helper. See Goldfarb, A. I. (1971).

7. See Rogers, C. R. (1951). *Client-centered therapy* and (1961). *On becoming a person.* Boston: Houghton-Mifflin.

8. Buber, M. (1957). The William Alanson White memorial lectures, fourth series. *Psychiatry, 20,* 95–129.

9. Frankl, V. (1963). From death camp to existentialism. In *Man's search for meaning.* New York: Washington Square Press.

10. See *Archives of General Psychiatry, 42,* 305–316, March 1985 and *46,* 971–82, November 1989.

11. Jung, C. G. (1933). *Modern man in search of a soul.* New York: Harcourt, Brace and World.

12. Erikson, E. H. (1959). The problem of ego identity. In *Identity and the life cycle, Psychological Issues, 1,* 101–164.

13. Rodin, J. (1986). Aging and health: Effects of the sense of control. *Science, 233,*(4770), 1271–1276.

14. The University of Chicago Committee on Human Development pursued studies of reminiscence. See Gorney, J. E. (1968). *Experiencing and age: Patterns of reminiscence among the elderly,* unpublished Ph.D. dissertation; Falk, J. M. (1969). *The organization of remembered life experience in old age: Its relation to subsequent adaptive capacity and to age,* unpublished Ph.D. dissertation; and Havighurst, R. J., & Glasser, R. (1972). An exploratory study of reminiscence. *Journal of Gerontology, 27,* 245–253.

15. Rodin, J. (1986).

16. Jung, C. G. (1933).

17. For further information on how to obtain the training guide *Reminiscence: Finding Meaning in Memories,* contact the Social Outreach and Support Section, Program Department, AARP, 1909 K St., N.W., Washington, DC 20049.

18. Scott-Maxwell, F. (1968). *The measure of my days.* New York: Alfred A. Knopf.

19. Lewis, M. I., & Butler, R. N. (1974). Life review therapy: Putting memories to work in individual and group psychotherapy. *Geriatrics, 29,* 165–169, 172–173; and Merriam, S. (1980). The concept and function of the reminiscence: A review of the research. *The Gerontologist, 20*(5), 604–609.

20. Lieberman M. A., & Tobin, S. S. (1983). *The experience of old age: Stress, coping and survival.* New York: Basic Books.

21. "Reminiscence group therapy has been found to be most useful in maintaining socialization and establishing group cohesiveness" (p. 965) in Katzman, R. (1986). Alzheimer's disease. *New England Journal of Medicine, 314,* 964–973.

22. For an example of reminiscence in a senior center, see the article "Senior Citizens Produce Book of Remembrances," *The Chronicle* (Milford, Delaware), June 25, 1980. The article describes a book, *The Times We Remember,* produced by residents of the local senior center.

23. Dietsche, L. M. (1979). Facilitating the life review through group reminiscence. *Journal of Gerontological Nursing, 5,* 43–46.

24. Hendricks, L. (1979). *Personal life history. Writing for older adults. A handbook for teaching personal life history classes,* Leon County School Board, Tallahassee, FL; and Daniel, L. (1980). *How to write your own life story: A step by step guide for the non-professional writer.* Chicago: Chicago Review Press.

25. Tolstoy, L. (1960). *Last diaries* (translated by L. Stilman) New York: Putnam-Capricorn, 43.

26. In the Middle Ages, hospices were run by monks for anyone who needed help: the poor, the sick and dying, or travelers and pilgrims going to the Holy Land during the Crusades.

27. From "St. Christopher's Hospice" (editorial), *London Nursing Times,* July 29, 1967. See also Saunders, C. (1959). *Care of the dying.* London: Macmillan.

28. To locate hospice programs contact the Hospice Helpline at (800)658–8898 or the National Hospice Organization, 1901 N. Moore St., Suite 901, Arlington, VA 22209.

29. For a copy of the Living Will or other advance-directive documents, write Choice in Dying, 100 Varick St., New York, New York 10014.

30. Funeral price information from the National Funeral Directors Association (NFDA) *1996 General Price List Survey.* Breakdown available from: National Funeral Directors Association, P. O. Box 27641, Milwaukee, WI 53227–0641.

31. For a copy, contact: Public Reference, Federal Trade Commission, 6th and Pennsylvania Ave. NW, Room 130, Washington, DC 20580.

32. For more information, contact Funeral and Memorial Societies of America, Inc.(FAMSA) P. O. Box 10, Hinesburg, VT 05461.

33. Morgan, E. (1980). *A manual of death education and simple burial,* 9th ed., Washington, DC: Continental Association of Funeral and Memorial Societies. (1828 L St. N.W., Washington, D.C. 20036)

34. Eye and temporal bone banks and the National Kidney Foundation also give the person a sense of valued legacy. Usually only the corneas of older people are acceptable, however. A Uniform Anatomical Gift Act or its equivalent now exists in every state and in most Canadian provinces. A Uniform Donor's Card filled out and signed by the donor and two witnesses (three in Florida) constitutes a legal document. [See Department of Health, Education and Welfare. (1979). *How to donate the body and its organs for transplantation.* Washington, DC: Medical Education and Research, Pub. No (NIH) 77–776.] An individual now has final say over the disposition of his or her body, but if a family strongly objects, most institutions will not go against their wishes. France, England, and West Germany have adopted the "Universal Donor Principle," whereby anyone who dies anywhere in these countries is available as a donor of organs or tissues provided he or she has not previously specified otherwise. When the problem of transplantation rejection is fully solved, the opportunities to help others through donation of body parts will increase significantly.

35. Silverman, P. R. (1970). The widow-to-widow program. *Archives of the Foundation of Thanatology, 2,* 134.

36. *Ibid,* 134.

37. Weinbach, R. W. (1989). Sudden death and secret survivors: Helping those who grieve alone. *Social Work, 34*(l), 57–60.

38. Silver, A. (1950). Group psychotherapy with senile psychiatric patients. *Geriatrics, 5,* 147–150.

39. Linden, M. E. (1953). Group psychotherapy with institutionalized senile women: Study in gerontology in human relations. *International Journal of Group Psychotherapy, 3,* 150–151.

40. Goldfarb, A. I. (1955). Psychotherapy of aged persons, IV. One aspect of the therapeutic situation with aged patients, *Psychoanalytic Review, 42,* 100–187.

41. Ebersole, P. P. (1976). Reminiscing and group psychotherapy with the aging. In Burnside, I. M. (Ed.), *Nursing and the aged* (ch. 12). New York: McGraw-Hill.

42. Lowy, L. (1983). Social group work with vulnerable older persons: A theoretical perspective. *Social Work with Groups, 5*(2), 21–32.

43. Klein, W. H., LeShan, E. J., & Furman, S. S. (1965). *Promoting mental health of older people through group methods.* New York: Mental Health Materials Center.

44. Steuer, J. L., Mintz, J., Hammen, C. L., Hill, M. A., Jarvik, L. F., McCarley, T., Motoike, P., & Rosen, R. (1984). Cognitive–behavioral and psychodynamic group psychotherapy in treatment of geriatric depression. *Journal of Consulting and Clinical Psychology, 52*(2), 180–189.

45. Yalom, I. D. (1985). *The theory and practice of group psychotherapy,* 3rd ed. New York: Basic Books.

46. See Burnside, I. M. (1988). *Nursing and the aged,* 3rd ed. New York: McGraw-Hill; Burnside, I. M. (Ed.), (1986). *Working with the elderly: Group process and techniques,* 2nd ed. Boston: Jones and Bartlett; Blake, D. (1980). Group work with the institutionalized elderly. In Burnside, I. M. (Ed.), *Psychosocial nursing care of the aged,* 2nd ed. New York: McGraw-Hill; Burnside, I. M. (1970). Group work with the aged: Selected literature. *The Gerontologist, 10,* 241–246; and Ebersole, P. (1975). From despair to integrity through reminiscing with the aged. In *A.N.A. clinical sessions.* New York: Appleton-Century-Crofts.

47. Cohen, S. Z., & Hammerman, J. (1974). Social work with groups. In Brody, E., and contributors. *A social work guide for long-term care facilities* (pp. 123–135). Rockville, MD: National Institute of Mental Health.

48. Getzel, G. (1983). Group work with kin and friends caring for the elderly. In Saul, S. (Ed.), *Group work with the frail elderly.* Binghamton, NY: The Haworth Press.

49. Lewis, M. I., & Butler, R. N. (1974). Life review therapy: Putting memories to work in individual and group psychotherapy. *Geriatrics, 29,* 165–169, 172–73. Also in Burnside, I. M. (Ed.). (1986). *Working with the elderly: Group process and techniques,* 2nd ed. (pp. 50–59). Boston: Jones and Bartlett.

50. Greene, R. (1986). *Social work with the aged and their families.* New York: Aldine de Gruyter.

51. Bumagin, V. E., & Hirn, K. F. (1990). *Helping the aging family.* Glenview, IL: Scott, Foresman.

52. Eyde, D. R., & Rich, J. (1983). *Psychological distress in aging: A family management model.* Rockville, MD: Aspen Publications, 45.

53. Silverstone, B., & Burack-Weiss, A. (1983). *Social work practice with the frail elderly and their families.* Springfield, IL: Charles C. Thomas.

54. Finkel, S. I. (1980). Experiences of a private-practice psychiatrist working with the elderly in the community. *International Journal of Mental Health, 8,* 147–172. (Dr. Finkel helped build the American Association for Geriatric Psychiatry.)

55. Getzel, G. (1982). Helping elderly couples in crisis. *Social Casework, 63*(9), 515–521.

56. Greene, R. (1989). A life systems approach to understanding parent–child relationships in aging families. In Hughston, G. A., Christopherson, V. A., & Bonjean, M. J. (Eds.), *Aging and family therapy: Practitioner perspectives on Golden Pond.* Binghamton, NY: The Haworth Press; Freeman, D, S. (1981). *Techniques of family therapy.* New York: Jason Aronson.

57. Lindsley, O. R. (1964). Geriatric behavior prosthetics. In Kastenbaum, R. (Ed.), *New thoughts on old age* (pp. 41–60). New York: Springer.

58. B. F. Skinner's book, *Enjoy old age* (New York: Norton, 1983), provides practical guidance for people growing older. His ideas have been questioned by many, but the approach is interesting to evaluate, given its distinguished author and his life-long interest in adaptation.

59. For illustrative studies, see Hoyer, W. J., Mishara, B. L., & Riekel, R. G. (1975). Problem behaviors as operants: Applications with elderly individuals. *The Gerontologist, 15,* 452–456; Preston, C. E. (1973). Behavior modification: A therapeutic approach to aging and death. *Postgraduate Medicine, 54,* 64–68; and Lisk, N., Howe, M. W., & Pinkstone, E. M. (1975). Behavioral group work in a home for the aged. *Social Work, 20*(6), 454–463.

60. Johnson, H. E., & Garton, W. H. (1973). Muscle reeducation in hemiplegia by use of electromyographic device. *Archives of Physical Medicine and Rehabilitation, 54,* 320–323.

61. Goleman, D. (1990, March 27). Studies offer fresh clues to memory. *The New York Times,* 1, 8.

62. Yesavage, J. A. (1990). *Age-associated memory impairment: Conceptual background and treatment approaches,* presented at the 1990 Sandoz Lectures in Gerontology, March 28–30, 1990.

63. Cavan's early study, now often overlooked, with its sizable sample of 2,988 subjects demonstrated the vast importance of social factors to adjustment. See Cavan, R. S. (1952). Personal adjustment in old age. In Lansing, A. H. (Ed.), *Cowdry's problems of aging,* 3rd ed. Baltimore: Williams & Wilkins.

64. Greenberg, S. (1995, July 30). Title III—State and Community Programs. *The Administration on Aging and the Aging Network.* Administration On Aging Web Site, http://www.aoa.dhhs.gov/aoa.

65. Greenberg, S. (1995, July 30). Title VII—Vulnerable Elder Rights Protection Activities. *The Administration on Aging and the Aging Network.* Administration On Aging Web Site, http://www.aoa.dhhs.gov/aoa.

66. Cloward and Piven argued in 1966 (Cloward, R. A., & Piven, F. F. [1966]. The weight of the poor. . . . a strategy to end poverty, *The Nation, 202,* 510–517) that "adding all eligible persons to the welfare rolls would generate a financial crisis of

such magnitude that the federal government would be pressured to respond with a plan for a guaranteed annual income." An Advisory Council on Public Welfare the same year suggested, as had others, a "national floor under assistance payments" and federal, rather than state, responsibility for public welfare program studies and financing (Advisory Council on Public Welfare. [1966]. *Having the power we have the duty.* Report to the Secretary of Health, Education and Welfare, Washington, DC: U.S. Government Printing Office). This became one of the historical steps in the development of Supplemental Security Income.

67. See The Commonwealth Fund Commission on Elderly People Living Alone. (1988). *Strategies to increase participation in the supplemental security income program: Follow-up study of poor elderly people.* Baltimore, MD: The Commonwealth Fund.

68. Sehnert, K., Awkward, B., & Lesage, D. (1976, March). *The senior citizen as an "activated patient,"* mimeographed book prepared for the Office of Assistant Secretary for Planning and Education, U.S. Public Health Service, Department of Health, Education and Welfare.

69. See also: Wright, B. (1994). *Self help among the elderly: Formal and informal support systems.* New York: Garland Publishers; and Donovan, J. (1994). *The self help directory: A sourcebook for self-help groups in the United States and Canada.* New York: Facts on File. To find out if a self-help organization is operating in a particular area, the following clearinghouses can be contacted: The National Self-Help Clearinghouse, 25 W. 43rd St., Room 620, New York, NY 10036, and The Self-Help Center, Division of MHAI, 150 N. Wacker Dr., Suite 900, Chicago, IL 60606.

70. Self-employment is often "bootleg" work (typing, babysitting, housecleaning, handyman services), which is not reported as income so as to avoid imperiling Social Security pensions.

71. Age Discrimination Act 29 U.S.C. (United States Code) 621 et seq.

72. For the pioneering references, see The National Council on the Aging. (1961, May). *Utilization of older professional and scientific workers;* Shock, N. W. (1947). Older people and their potentialities for gainful employment. *Journal of Gerontology, 2,* 92–102; and McFarland, R. A. (1943, Summer).

The older worker in industry. *Harvard Business Review,* 505–510.

73. See, for example, the classic legal case for better mental hospital care, *Wyatt* v. *Stickney,* Alabama, 1971–1972.

74. See Horn, L., & Griesel, E. (1977). *Nursing homes: A citizen's action guide. How to organize, plan and achieve nursing home reform in your community.* Boston: Beacon Press.

75. Commission on Legal Problems of the Elderly, American Bar Association, 1800 M St., N.W., Washington, DC 20036.

76. Legal Council for the Elderly Staff & Brown, R. N. (1988). *The rights of older persons: The basic ACLU guide to an older person's rights.* Carbondale, IL: Southern Illinois University Press.

77. See Butler, R. N. (1968). Why are older consumers so susceptible? *Geriatrics, 23,* 83–88.

78. P. L. 92–239 amending 15 U.S.C. (United States Code) 1691 et seq.

79. From Group for the Advancement of Psychiatry. (1971, November). *The aged and community mental health: A guide to program development, 8*(81). Formulated by the Committee on Aging.

80. A few studies appeared already in the 1970s. One relates to the question of the alleged development of greater conservatism with age (Rule, W.I.B. [1977]. Political alienation and voting attitudes among the elderly generation. *The Gerontologist, 17*[5], 400–404). Another discusses the question of why minority group elderly have a lower rate of political activity (Torres-Gill, F., & Becerra, F. M. [1977]. The political behavior of the Mexican-American elderly. *The Gerontologist, 17*[51], 392–399).

81. Ragan, P. (1977). Another look at the politicizing of old age: Can we expect a backlash effect? *Urban and Social Change Review, 10*(2), 6–13.

82. Sheppard, H. (1989). The new ageism and the "intergenerational tension" issue. *Journal of Fondation Nationale de Gerontologie.* Tampa, FL: International Exchange Center on Gerontology, University of South Florida.

83. Callahan, D. (1987). *Setting limits: Medical goals in an aging society.* New York: Simon and Schuster.

84. For a subscription to the Gray Panthers' newspaper or information on any of their other printed materials, contact the Gray Panthers, P. O. Box 21477, Washington, DC 20009-9477.

CHAPTER 13

DRUG AND OTHER SOMATIC THERAPIES

Although older people make up 13% of the population, they consume about 35 to 40% of all medications prescribed in the United States, amounting to $12.7 to $14.3 billion of expenditures (approximately $245 to $475 per person).[1] The single largest out-of-pocket health care expense for older persons is the payment for out-of-hospital drugs. Twenty-five percent of those over 65 are discharged from hospitals with prescriptions for six or more drugs, compared to approximately 3% for younger cohorts.[2] Our challenge in this chapter is to better understand what constitutes appropriate treatment for older persons, particularly since they receive such a disproportionately larger share of prescribed medication.

Medical and nursing education does not yet focus adequately on pharmacology and clinical pharmacy as it relates to old age. Research studies too infrequently exclude the old in their observations, and there has been a delay by the U.S. government in issuing guidelines for the pharmaceutical industry on including elderly persons in premarketing clinical tests. We still know precious little about the changes in absorption, distribution, metabolism, and excretion of medications (called *pharmacokinetics*), and the actions and changes in drug sensitivity (*pharmacodynamics*) that occur with aging—an exciting and

important area for research with obviously practical application.[3] And while it has been known for centuries that there are increased drug side effects in the elderly,[4] it is only more recently that adverse reactions have been studied in relation to age. For example, it has been estimated that adverse drug reactions occur in 15 to 25% of elderly patients as compared to 3 to 9% for younger adults.[5]

There is considerable evidence to support the view that we have an "overmedicated society." Much concern, of course, is voiced about use of drugs in the youth culture and about barbiturate, tranquilizer, and alcohol consumption among the middle-aged. But old age has its own drug problems, resulting from high usage of tranquilizers, antidepressants, sedatives, hypnotics, and multiple over-the-counter drugs. To some degree these medications may reflect the greater anxiety, depression, and insomnia perceived in older people. But they also point to the anxiety of doctors and other health personnel, their impatience with older people (to whom they would often rather give a pill than listen), and their own need for instant gratification (treatment results). Unfortunately, drugs reinforce some of the general slowing observed in older people, aggravate a sense of aging and depression, and can contribute to or directly cause acute and chronic brain syndromes. For these reasons, we are once again reminded of the important need to prescribe and supervise these medications carefully.

GENERAL PRINCIPLES IN DRUG TREATMENT WITH THE ELDERLY

The ancient rule of medicine, *primun non nocere* (first do no harm), applies particularly to prescribing medication for older persons. Drugs should be used *only* when necessary and with as few medications used simultaneously as possible. The average older person is already taking several medications (called *polypharmacy*) at any one time, and additional drugs greatly increase the likelihood of drug interactions.[6] Nonetheless, additional medications for behavioral disorders are frequently needed for the elderly, and skills in geriatric psychopharmacology are an essential part of any general practicioner's daily interaction with patients.[7] To help in planning appropriate drug treatment for elderly patients, some guiding principles should be kept in mind.

The Medical Model: Who's the Patient?

It is not uncommon for an older person to be accompanied to a doctor's consulting room by a spouse or younger member of the family. In most circumstances, this situation is perfectly acceptable to both parties, and the diagnostic evaluation and therapy can proceed unencumbered. With the suggestion of a new medication, however, disagreements within the family can occur. Previously unexpressed conflicts and subtle pressures sometimes become manifest at this point, and the clinician is faced with the problem of identifying the most reasonable course of action. A close alliance with the patient, in addition to the "contact" person in the family, can of course be helpful, but the decisions about therapy must remain within the control of the patient him- or herself whenever possible, in order for the proposed treatment to be successfully carried out.

Exceptions might be when mental confusion or physical illness interferes with the patient's judgment.

Diagnostic Accuracy: What's the Problem?

While the insistence on diagnostic accuracy may seem an obvious point, it remains a fact that many more psychiatric medications are prescribed than there are psychiatric conditions. For instance, it is currently believed that about two-thirds of all nursing home patients receive psychotropic drugs, yet only about 20% have psychiatric diagnoses beyond dementia.[8] Insufficient staffing is perhaps the primary reason for overmedicating older persons into more manageable quietude. Other reasons are the possible concealment of a psychiatric diagnosis to get an older person admitted into a nursing home, the failure of the doctors who service nursing homes to keep apprised of the dangers of overmedication, and the fact that some states use Medicaid to pay for drugs but not for careful psychiatric diagnosis and forms of treatment other than drugs.

Drug administration in institutions is marked by special problems of its own.

1. Much medication is prescribed by doctors over the phone, based only on symptoms described by nursing personnel. Errors in diagnosis are therefore common, as well as a tendency to prescribe based on the needs of the institution rather than simply in the patient's best interest.

2. Errors in drug administration occur because medication is often given by untrained or poorly trained aides and orderlies.

3. The possibilities for errors in drug administration are compounded by the number of medications (an average of five to seven) each patient receives at once, often in varying combinations of multiple daily doses.

4. Staff shortages lead to less physical exercise for patients, more use of physical restraints, overuse of catheters, lack of sufficiently individualized diet, less personalized warmth and support, and an unstimulating environment. These problems result in a higher incidence of urinary tract infections, respiratory and circulatory disorders leading to pneumonia and bedsores, and a rise in mental depression and agitation, to name just a few conditions. All of these are eventually treated with drugs when they might have been prevented in the first place. Thus, with the institutionalized and the office-based patients, the physician should carefully reconsider the clinical picture before adding yet another medication (see Chapter 9 for a review of diagnostic evaluations).

Polypharmacy: "Do They Really Need That Extra Medicine?"

With the elderly, multiple medications and general polypharmacy should be considered the rule. It is estimated that Medicare patients receive an *average* of 10 medications in acute care hospitals.[9] The average nursing home patient reportedly receives over nine medications.[10] Furthermore, it is estimated that 70% of the elderly use over-the-counter drugs as opposed to only 10% in the general population.[11]

Older persons experience three times as many adverse reactions as younger persons. The possible adverse interactions of one drug with another should be anticipated and avoided.[12] Before prescribing any drugs for institutionalized or non-institutionalized patients, the physician should ask to see all his or her present medications, including over-the-counter medications and old, empty bottles. The patient should be asked if he or she tends to "self-medicate" and, if so, how much and for what purpose. The physician should also check with the patient's other doctors to learn if previously prescribed drugs should still be taken. Medications should be introduced one at a time when possible in order to monitor their individual effects. The dosage schedule should be kept simple and easily understandable. All medication orders should have automatic discontinuation dates; renewal re-

quires valuable reassessment and averts prolonged, inappropriate, harmful, and useless administration of drugs.

Drug Compliance: "Are They Really Taking Their Medicine?"

Since the prescription medication offered by a physician to a patient is so important, it is short-sighted to limit the prescription process to the exchange of a piece of paper reserved for the closing seconds of an office visit. And yet, that scenario is all too common in busy medical practices. Telephone call-ins of prescriptions to a local pharmacy, hospital ward, or nursing home for the beginning of a new pharmacologic regimen can also be a problem if the doctor has not taken the time to explain the drug and how to take it.

There are many reasons for poor medication compliance: time restrictions, poor instructions, psychological concerns surrounding the question of control and autonomy, or simply forgetfulness and confusion on the part of the older person. Open discussion of these issues are frequently avoided because physicians too often assume compliance will occur automatically.

Mary is an 81-year-old widow who came to the office with her daughter for evaluation of a persistent depression. Her clinical presentation was a classic repeat of an earlier episode which had responded to imipramine, and her physician had appropriately prescribed low doses of the same medication. Three weeks later, the symptoms persisted, and Mary's blood level showed no detectable imipramine. When asked why she was not taking the medication as prescribed, Mary retorted: "Well, since the doctor talked to my daughter the whole time and gave her the slip, I figured she was supposed to take the pills, not me." Somewhat embarrassed, the physician apologized for his mistake. Once he properly addressed his primary patient and reviewed the treatment plan with her directly, she fully complied with the regimen and responded therapeutically as expected.

In addition to the psychological factors involved in taking medications, simply reviewing the details of the drug regimen can be of great value. It is exceedingly valuable for patients when doctors fill out a written sheet on each new drug prescribed so the older person can refer to it later (see Figure 13.1).

Some straightforward aides useful in compliance are the use of pill packs, automatic timers (i.e., digital clocks with buzzers preset for medication times), and clearly labeled signs in the bathroom to function as a reminder. The pharmacist should be instructed to package drugs in easy-to-open containers for older persons. It would also be useful if drug companies routinely used some special device in packaging drugs for older people, as they do with the clever calendar dispensers of the "pill," which aid younger women in remembering to take contraceptives. Such an aid is invaluable in coping with the memory problems of late life. Older patients should be warned not to take medicines in the dark or to keep them on the

Medication: _____

Who prescribed it: _____

Date: _____

For what: _____

Dosage: _____

Schedule: _____

Duration: _____

What to avoid:

  Other drugs: _____

  Alcohol: _____

  Food: _____

Use of machinery: _____

  Driving: _____

  Other: _____

Minor side effects that often occur and what to do about them: _____

_____

_____

_____

_____

Major side effects that can occur and require a call to the doctor: _____

_____

_____

FIGURE 13.1 Sample medication sheet

bedside table (there are exceptions, of course, such as nitroglycerine), since sleepiness can cause errors in judgment.

Older people may have impairments that interfere with hearing and/or understanding the doctor's orders regarding drugs, seeing labels well enough to take the correct medicine and the correct dose, or having a steady enough hand to handle fluids, tiny pills, or "child-proof" (and thus more difficult to open) drug bottles. When specifically requested, it is possible in many pharmacies to get medicine bottles that are not child proof for those elderly who would otherwise have trouble opening the bottles. Impairment of intellect (especially with senile dementia) may cause errors in judgment or lapses in memory with regard to drugs. Consequently the older person's capacity for the self-administration of drugs needs to be evaluated as carefully as his or her medical need for drugs. When forgetfulness or confusion is a frequent issue, supervision of drug taking should be arranged with relatives, friends, or neighbors. It has been estimated that half of all older people who take drugs do not take them as prescribed, and one fourth make errors serious enough to create drug-induced illnesses. It is therefore not surprising that older people comprise about half of all hospital admissions for drug intoxication.

Side Effects: "When Should I Call the Doctor?"

One of the important reasons for informing older people about the drugs they are taking is to help them distinguish side effects from other bodily changes. As we mentioned previously, we have found that older people may misinterpret the retarding effects of the tranquilizers as signs of aging. Doctors remain all too secretive in preparing patients for drug effects, partly because they fear the development of symptoms in suggestible persons. Many also simply do not wish to take the time. It is archaic to assume that "what the patient doesn't know won't hurt him," because often it does. Full disclosure is now imperative for both medical and legal reasons. Patients of

course have the legal right to refuse medications or medical procedures. One must help patients overcome fears of medications while simultaneously encouraging them to respect effects and dangers.

Drug side effects occur in the elderly as often as seven times more frequently than in younger adults.[13] The potential dangers, complications, and side effects should be carefully and fully explained to patients—both the annoying symptoms like dryness of the mouth and the dangerous symptoms such as hypotension (low blood pressure and possible fainting) and extrapyramidal symptoms (parkinsonism). Psychiatric drugs can affect sexuality in varying manner and degree from individual to individual, especially after the age of 50. When sexual problems occur, the doctor may be able to change to another drug. Each medication will have its own "profile" of likely and rare side effects. In addition, each medication will have its own time course of clinical and therapeutic effects. This last point is extremely important because psychiatric medications generally have a delayed onset of therapeutic effects. Unfortunately, the side effects usually occur immediately, so the physician is often in the position of trying to convince the patient to tolerate the side effects long enough to reap the benefits.

The *sedating effects* of a number of medications used in persons over 65 can cause serious problems. Older people who are experiencing a physical slowing of speed and coordination find these features exacerbated by a number of drugs. Some persons react with fear and depression, thinking they are failing fast or even dying. Reassurance is imperative.

The side effects can, of course, outweigh the potential benefits. Educated decision making before the initiation of medication therapy is not the only critical point. It is also important to know when to stop a medication trial (i.e., onset of tardive dyskinesia). If the patient is well informed about the predictable hazards, has easy access to medical backup for information and support from the doctor's office, and has the feeling that the trial can be abandoned if the side effects become too

TABLE 13.1 Selected factors affecting drug response with age

1. Absorption
    Stomach Transit Time
    Hydrochloric acid
2. Distribution
    Proteins in blood
    Body Composition (lean body mass, fat)
    Tissue sensitivity
    Receptors
3. Metabolism
    Liver enzymes
4. Excretion
    Kidney blood flow
    Glomerular filtration rate
5. Multiple drug use (polypharmacy)
6. Overdose (purposive or accidental)
7. Patient Compliance (omission, commission)
8. Physician failure to give complete instructions

difficult, then the "team approach" to medication management has a greater chance of ultimate success. By making side effects more predictable and controllable, one can often minimize the fear surrounding these reactions and thereby avoid the premature cessation of a drug trial.

Drug Metabolism: "Less is Usually Better!"

Older people have qualitative and quantitative differences from younger people in absorption, distribution, metabolism, and excretion of drugs. (See Table 13.1 for factors affecting drug response with age.) In general, drug effects are determined by dosage, absorption (quality and rate), distribution in the body (dependent on factors of body composition such as body fluid, organ blood flow, and cardiac output), hepatic metabolism and renal excretion, nutritional status, and personal habits (for example, smoking and alcohol intake). While the absorption rate in the older person may be slower for some drugs, the total amount of drug absorbed in the bowel by passive diffusion may be the same. Combined with the near universal slowing of liver and kidney clearance of the drugs, the expected time course and duration of drug effects are often altered. This *pharmacokinetic* (excretion of medications) model of altered drug metabolism in the elderly is well outlined in many pharmacologic texts. What is still not well understood is the possible changing of *pharmacodynamics* (the actions and changes in drug sensitivity) in the elderly patient. Drug sensitivity is generally assumed to be increased in the older patient.[14]

Perhaps the simplest principle of pharmacologic management in the elderly is that less drug is usually more effective. In fact, some have suggested that the elderly generally need doses only 30 to 50% as large as those used in younger adults.[15] Drug metabolism in the elderly is a major factor in their drug use, since the liver may have reduced blood flow and thus the rate of drug detoxification may be slowed. Moreover, older people generally have a lower general metabolism rate, causing prolonged drug action or creating exaggerated drug reactions. Kidney impairment can also affect excretion of the drug. The older population also has a relatively greater accumulation of drugs in body fat as compared to younger people; therefore drug effects may be prolonged.

Drug Costs: "How Much Can I Afford?"

One should always think of cost in prescribing drugs for older persons, especially since Medicare does not cover out-of-hospital prescription drug costs. Out-of-pocket health care costs for the elderly have skyrocketed over 90% to $2519 per year since 1987 with prescription drugs making up at least 10% of that burden.[16] It is estimated that the elderly spend $13 to $14 billion per year (an average of $483 per person) on prescription drugs, and the majority of those payments are out-of-pocket. While there has been an increased trend for third-party payers (private insurance and Medicaid) to cover the cost of some drugs, the elderly are less likely to be covered in a voluntary insurance market. Within the elderly population, there is also a huge variance between the young elderly (65 to 69 years) and the oldest elderly (85+ years) who generally spend much more, up to

30% of their family income, in out-of-pocket health care expenses. This is a particularly vexing problem among the poor elderly whose family incomes have grown at only a fraction of the rate of growth for medical expenses, including prescriptions.[17]

Jim B is a 74-year-old retired clerk. He lives on a government pension and has been widowed for six years. After two years of increasing depression, he was referred by his long-time internist to a psychiatrist for evaluation of a major depression. After the initial consultation, the psychiatrist prescribed one of the new serotonergic reuptake inhibitor antidepressants. Mr. B responded partially to a dose of one pill a day, and after two months, the psychiatrist increased the prescription to two pills a day. Three months later, there was no improvement, and the physician called the pharmacy to increase the regimen further to three pills a day as Mr. B was suffering no side effects. To the psychiatrist's surprise, the pharmacist reported that the patient still had two refills left on his prescription, suggesting that he had never increased his dose beyond one pill a day. On further discussion, the patient was embarrassed to admit that he "couldn't afford" the increased expense which would have taken the bill to over $100 per month.

While it is well known that brand name drugs can be four to five times more expensive than their generic counterparts, evidence exists that many older people will not accept a low-priced generic substitute for a brand name just on a pharmacist's advice. Most want their doctor's approval first. Of use are lists of generic drugs such as can be found in the index of Long's *The Essential Guide to Prescription Drugs*. Discount drugs can be obtained by way of the National Council of Senior Citizens,[18] the American Association of Retired Persons,[19] and other organizations. Insurance plans which allow for bulk (i.e., three month) purchase of medications for a one-time reduced fee are also now available.

Unfortunately, not all psychiatric medications are available generically to the elderly. In this situation, the physician and patient must make a cost-benefit decision together. Occasionally, the drug manufacturers offer reduced fee or even free medication for individuals in need (this can be arranged by the physician contacting the manufacturer and filling out the appropriate forms with the patient). More often, the physician must consider other alternatives, including using less expensive generic medications (which may have more side effects) or using a lower dose of the more expensive medication in hopes that it will provide adequate coverage. In any case, the financial impact of psychotropic prescriptions should be considered with all patients, especially those on fixed incomes without medication insurance plans.

SPECIFIC DRUG TREATMENTS

The decision to use a medication in psychiatric treatment is a major therapeutic step with any patient, no matter how compelling the indication. Whereas medical patients often come to their doctors expecting that the prescription of a pill may help them improve, psychiatric patients frequently see the initiation of medication as a failure in their "talking" therapy. Perhaps fostered by years of psychoanalytic resistance to the use of medications in many therapeutic situations, these drugs are too often viewed as "crutches" which may "suppress" the target symptom but not address the underlying psychological mechanism involved. Empirically, however, these medications can work when appropriately prescribed. And while the symptom suppression can be debated endlessly from a psychological perspective, the fact remains that the medications can be an important adjunctive treatment in a therapeutic regimen. What is perhaps more important than any ideological argument between professionals is to understand the patient's life history, psychological defenses, and attitude toward medications before considering their use so as to maximize their utility in the overall treatment scheme. There is no substitute for accurate differential diagnosis and careful preparation of the patient for the potential risks and benefits of medications.

Treatment of Depression in the Elderly

When considering pharmacologic treatments for depressed elderly subjects, several important facts should be recognized immediately. First, there is a general paucity of direct knowledge of these medications in the elderly population; most of the studies with these drugs have been conducted in younger adults. There are only a few dozen placebo-controlled, double-blind antidepressant research trials with the elderly. Second, many of these published "geriatric" studies have focused on the "young-old" subjects with average ages of 60 to 70 years; therefore, the information available about people over the age of 80 is even more scarce. Third, the Food and Drug Administration (FDA) has never required drug companies to compare their products in younger versus older people formally, so we often know very little about how these drugs react in older people until they are released by the FDA and tried by clinicians. What we do know is that drugs generally have longer elimination half-lives as reflected by higher plasma levels in the elderly[20] and that this should always be kept in mind when prescribing for the elderly. Finally, the environments of depressed geriatric patients vary tremendously (i.e., home, hospital, medical clinic, nursing home, etc.), and it is not well known how these different settings might affect the therapeutic response in the elderly or how the medications might interact with other therapies, such as psychotherapy.

With all these limitations in the knowledge base, it is perhaps amazing that antidepressant medications are indeed frequently administered to the elderly. In fact, they are generally used with great success, and the geriatric database is now expanding rapidly as more investigators publish clinical trials. For purposes of review, we will consider three major pharmacologic approaches to the treatment of depression in the elderly: serotonergic reuptake blockers, traditional cyclic antidepressants and monoamine oxidase inhibitors (Table 13.2). In severe cases of depression with psychosis, neuroleptics are frequently employed

as well, and those medications will be discussed in the Psychosis section.

Age itself may be a predictive variable in determining the clinical outcome of patients with antidepressants. In one study, the older patients were found to respond less well to pharmacologic treatment.[21] Other studies have shown that if left untreated for over two years, geriatric depression is more often refractory to any therapy.[22] Thus, it becomes important in the elderly to diagnose depression and initiate antidepressant therapy without undue delays.

Serotonin Reuptake Inhibitors. Since the introduction of fluoxetine (Prozac) to the American market in 1989, there has been a substantial shift in the prescribing practices for the therapy of depression in this country. Additional drugs in this class include sertraline (Zoloft), paroxetine (Paxil), and citalopram (available in Europe). Primarily due to the more limited side effect profile of these drugs compared to previous generations of antidepressants, they are generally more acceptable to patients. However, this class of medications still has many side effects, including anxiety, agitation, insomnia or sedation, nausea and sexual dysfunction.[23] Because of the prolonged elimination half-lives of most of these medications, doses for the elderly are usually reduced from those prescribed for younger subjects. Unfortunately, blood levels of these drugs have not been positively correlated with therapeutic responses, so outpatient monitoring of blood levels is not helpful.[24]

Cyclic Antidepressants. There are a tremendous variety of cyclic compounds available today as clinical antidepressants. The choices are no longer limited to the two original antidepressants, amitriptyline (Elavil) and imipramine (Tofranil). Rather, the selection ranges from the metabolite drugs such as nortriptyline and desipramine to the "second generation" drugs such as trazodone, maprotaline and buproprion. Large-scale reviews have documented the efficacy of these agents, but

TABLE 13.2   Pharmacologic agents frequently used to treat depression
in the elderly

DRUGS AVAILABLE	DOSE (MG/DAY)	COMMENTS
Serotonin Reuptake Inhibitors		
Fluoxetine	10–40	• Not anticholinergic • Long drug half-life • Sexual side effects
Sertraline	50–150	• Not anticholinergic • Shorter drug half-life • Sexual side effects
Paroxetine	10–40	• Fairly anticholinergic • Sexual side effects
Heterocyclic Antidepressants		
Amitriptyline Imipramine Doxepine	25–150	• Highly anticholinergic • Sedating • Can lower blood pressure
Nortriptyline	10–125	• Less anticholinergic • Therapeutic window
Desipramine	25–125	• Less anticholinergic • Can be activating
Trazodone	50–200	• Not anticholinergic • Sedating • Can lower blood pressure
Monoamine Oxidase Inhibitors		
Phenelzine	15–45	• Not anticholinergic • Special diet required • Can lower blood pressure
Tranylcypromine	10–30	• Special diet required • Can be activating • Can lower blood pressure

no single drug has emerged as the "drug of choice" for the treatment of geriatric depression.[25]

Several variables have been suggested that may help predict the response of patients to antidepressants. Jarvik and colleagues originally noted, for instance, that pretreatment orthostatic hypotension (lowering of blood pressure on standing) is associated with improvement following treatment with imipramine or doxepin;[26] unfortunately, imipramine itself may cause undue orthostatic blood pressure changes and be a cause for discontinuing the medication before therapeutic effects are achieved.[27] Nortriptyline, on the other hand, is associated with less orthostatic changes during treatment and furthermore has the advantage of producing dose-related blood levels even in the elderly which may be predictive of therapeutic efficacy, as in younger adults.[28] Because the elderly are generally more sensitive to the cognitive effects of anticholinergic medications,[29] the antidepressant medications can also be differentiated along their anticholinergic potency (see Table 13.2). The clinician is forced to choose amongst the large list of drugs based on the clinical state of the patient and the side effect profile of the individual drug (Table 13.3).

Researchers have reported that from 7 to 35% of older depressives suffer from antidepressant-related confusional episodes as compared to less than 1% in younger adults.[30] While the overall clinical improvement associated with adequate antidepressant treatment often outweighs the deleterious anticholinergic effect on memory, it does seem reasonable to avoid the drugs with the highest anticholinergic potency in the elderly if possible. Other troublesome anticholinergic side effects include dry mouth, constipation (already a problem with many elderly), urinary hesitancy, and tremor. Trazodone, one of the heterocyclic antidepressants, may be a particularly interesting

TABLE 13.3 Relative anticholinergic potency of antidepressant medications

ANTIDEPRESSANT	POTENCY*
Amitriptyline	1
Clomipramine	2.1
Doxepine	4.7
Imipramine	5.1
Paroxetine	6.0
Nortriptyline	8.4
Desipramine	11.2
Maprotiline	31.1
Sertraline	50.9
Amoxapine	56.0
Fluoxetine	112
Buproprion	>1000
Trazodone	>1000
Venlafaxine	>1000

Source: Modified from Richelson, E. (1994): The pharmacology of antidepressants at the synapse: Focus on newer compounds. *Journal of Clinical Psychiatry, 55*(Suppl. A), 34–39. Copyright 1994, Physicians Postgraduate Press. Reprinted by permission.

*Lower number suggests higher potency at muscarinic receptor.

drug in this context. It has the lowest anticholinergic profile of all the cyclic antidepressants and has been shown to have a positive therapeutic effect in agitated aggressive patients. Although there are other side effects associated with trazodone, such as marked sedation, lowering of blood pressure, and priapism (painful sustained penile erections) in young males, it may well have a role in depressed or agitated elderly patients with evidence of cognitive decline.[31]

Monoamine Oxidase Inhibitors. It has been widely recognized for over 30 years that monoamine oxidase inhibitors (MAOIs) are effective antidepressants. Nonetheless, they have seen limited use in the elderly, with less than a dozen careful studies reported in the geriatric literature.[32] The hesitancy to prescribe MAOIs is most likely related to two potential problems with the medications:

1. MAOIs can interact with the naturally-occurring food substance tyramine (found in pickled herring, aged cheddar, Chianti wine, smoked or pickled meats and other foods) and with a large number of drugs to produce malignant hypertension (a life threatening elevation in blood pressure).

2. Postural hypotension is frequently associated with MAOI use and can pose particularly difficult management problems in the elderly who often already have blood pressure difficulties.

With the explosion in use of the serotonic reuptake inhibitors, the MAOIs are now prescribed even less frequently. However, these drugs (i.e., phenelzine 15–90 mg/day, tranylcypromine 10–60 mg/day, and isocarboxazide 20–60 mg/day) have each been shown to produce clinical improvement in older patients with major depression and mixed anxiety-depression syndromes when used carefully.[33] In fact, Georgotas and colleagues have reported that 65% of elderly depressives were responsive to phenelzine, a figure comparable to that with the more commonly prescribed cyclic antidepressants, and the positive outcome was related to the degree of MAO inhibition in the blood.[34] Other reports have suggested that MAOI response is related to pretreatment platelet MAO levels and that baseline MAO levels may indeed increase with age in both brain and platelets.[35]

In all studies of MAOI effectiveness, a positive therapeutic outcome has been contingent on the appropriate education and supervision of patients to insure proper dietary and drug-interaction precautions (see Table 13.4 for details).[36]

With the introduction in Europe of the selective MAOIs, specifically the MAO-B selective inhibitor, selegiline, the dreaded "cheese effect" (so named because of the large tyramine content in many cheeses) was thought to be eliminated. Indeed, at low doses, it appears that selegiline is relatively free of the dangerous hypertensive interaction with tyramine and, presumably, other stimulant agents as well. Unfortunately, at the higher doses probably required for antidepressant therapeutic efficacy, the MAO-B selectivity is ap-

parently less, and the hypertensive reaction is once again present.[37] Since many elderly patients either live in a controlled, supervised setting or are perfectly willing to eliminate Chianti wine, aged cheeses, and the other tyramine-containing foods from their diets, the MAOIs can be an important and effective treatment option for the elderly patient with major depression or atypical anxiety-depression syndromes, particularly those with treatment-resistant depression.[38]

Treatment of Psychosis in the Elderly

The neuroleptics are most commonly prescribed for the treatment of agitated behavior or severely disturbed thinking.[39] However, neuroleptics are not the only medications which can be used for the treatment of agitation and psychosis in the elderly. In recent years, antiseizure medications

TABLE 13.4 Dietary and medication precautions when taking Monoamine Oxidase Inhibitors (MAOIs)

FOODS TO BE AVOIDED	EXAMPLES
Aged, unpasteurized cheeses	Cheddar, Bleu, Camembert, Swiss
Smoked fish, poultry, or meat	Herring, sausage, corned beef
Yeast extracts	Marmite, brewer's yeast
Red wine	Chianti, burgundy, sherry
Bean curd	Soy sauce, fava beans
Cured meat, poultry or fish	Chicken or beef liver, game, pate
Miscellaneous	Shrimp paste, soups, protein extracts, figs, overripe avocados

MEDICATIONS TO BE AVOIDED	EXAMPLES
Stimulants	Amphetamine, cocaine, weight-reducing agents
Decongestants	Cold tablets, nose sprays, asthma or cough medications (Ephedrine, Phenylepherine or Phenylpropanolamine)
Antihypertensives	Reserpine, Methyldopa, Guanethidine
Narcotics	Merperidine (Demerol)
Other antidepressants	Imipramine, Desipramine, Clomipramine
Miscellaneous	L-Dopa, Dopamine, L-Tryptophan

Source: Murphy, D. L., Sunderland, T., Cohen, R. M. (1984). Monoamine oxidase-inhibiting antidepressants: A clinical update. *Psychiatric Clinics of North America, 7,* 549–562. Reprinted by permission.

have been suggested for use in these populations, and preliminary studies are encouraging.[40] Other possible treatments include sedating antidepressant agents such as trazodone. Comparisons are now ongoing in an attempt to offer alternatives to the neuroleptics. The conditions which can produce these disturbances are multiple and include:

1. Chronic Schizophrenia or Late-Onset Delusional Disorder
2. Agitated or Delusional Depression
3. Brief Reactive Psychosis
4. Psychosis associated with a Chronic Organic Syndrome
5. Agitation associated with Intoxication or Delirium

While each condition may benefit from the careful use of medications, the etiologies of these disturbed behaviors are obviously quite different. As a result, side effects and dosing requirements may also vary tremendously across conditions.

Typical Neuroleptics.   The two major classes of typical neuroleptics are the phenothiazines (i.e., chlorpromazine and thioridazine) and the butyrophenones (i.e., haloperidol). An emerging class of neuroleptics with a different profile of side effects is termed the *atypical* neuroleptics (i.e., clozapine). As with the antidepressants, the neuroleptics are often differentiated on the basis of their side effect profile. In general, the phenothiazines tend to be quite sedating and are associated with a lowering of blood pressure.[41] The butyrophenones, on the other hand, cause less sedation and reduction of blood pressure but are more frequently associated with extrapyramidal side effects (i.e., Parkinsonian symptoms of muscular rigidity and mask-like faces). Haloperidol is usually prescribed in much lower doses than the phenothiazines and is therefore called a "high potency" drug.

Over 60 studies of neuroleptic treatment of agitation in the elderly have been reported. In a recent review, Salzman stated that 60 to 70% of the more than 5000 patients with a variety of underlying disorders showed "good to excellent" responses with the neuroleptics. No individual drug demonstrated clear superiority to the others, although as a group, these medications were more effective than other types of medication such as the benzodiazepines.[42] Similar conclusions have also been reached in a recent review of the use of neuroleptics in published studies with over 1200 demented subjects; the symptoms most likely to respond to neuroleptics were agitation, hyperactivity, hallucinations, and hostility.[43] However, it must be emphasized that the neuroleptic side effects can be problematic in the elderly. In some cases, agitated behavior can even be exacerbated with neuroleptic treatment, so the dosing and monitoring of drug treatment must be performed conservatively with specific time-limited goals in mind.[44]

The general rule of thumb for clinical administration of the neuroleptics is the same as with each class of drug in this chapter: "Start low and go slow." For the high potency neuroleptic, haloperidol, a dose of 0.25 mg is often perfectly adequate when given one to three times a day. Higher doses may be necessary but only after failing with a lower dose. Total daily doses above 10 mg are unusual. If chronic doses are needed, they should be reduced once the patient is stabilized so as to minimize the total drug exposure. If the agitation is severe, then a phenothiazine such as chlorpromazine may be indicated. Once again, doses much smaller than those generally used in younger populations (i.e., 10 to 50 mg per day) may be adequate with the older patients. Because a lowering of blood pressure is so common with this agent, vigilance should be maintained to avoid the disastrous effects of serious falls resulting from sudden orthostatic changes. Another likely disadvantage of this class of neuroleptics is the increased anticholinergic potency. A worsening of cognitive functioning is possible, especially in the demented subjects who are known to be more sensitive to anticholinergic drugs.[45] The longer-acting depot neuroleptics (i.e., fluphenazine enanthate, 5 mg/two weeks) have also been tested in older patients with "late paraphrenia" and shown to be superior to oral haloperidol (6 mg/day), perhaps due to the increased compliance with the depot (long-acting, injectable drug dosage) product and the use of a lower dose regimen.[46]

The most worrisome side effect of chronic neuroleptic use is that of tardive dyskinesia (TD), the syndrome of involuntary movements of the tongue, mouth, face, and neck. While TD is usually associated with a long exposure to neuroleptics, it can occur as rapidly as one month after starting a neuroleptic drug. In fact, when elderly psychiatric inpatients of mixed diagnostic backgrounds were carefully evaluated for signs of abnormal movements, 49% showed evidence of TD while 51% revealed some parkinsonism; in this study, the average length of neuroleptic exposure in the TD group was less than 11 months.[47] The incidence of TD in late-onset psychosis is thought to be even higher than that of the early-onset group.[48] The greatest risk appears to be within the first two years of therapy. For bipolar patients treated with neuroleptics, there is increased risk for TD in those patients who show poorer baseline cognitive functioning, fewer depressive episodes, and less overall exposure to lithium.[49] Those with prior organic pathology or evidence of cognitive dysfunction may therefore be at greater risk for the development of TD, so particular caution should be used when prescribing neuroleptics in these populations. There is currently no effective pharmacologic treatment for tardive dyskinesia in the elderly.

Atypical Neuroleptics.   Over the last few years, several "atypical" neuroleptics have been introduced for use in the treatment of psychosis. The major advantage of these agents (i.e., clozapine, resperidol and olanzepine) is that they are generally low risk for extrapyramidal symptoms (EPS) and tardive dyskinesia; however, they do come with their own side effects. Clozapine, for instance, is highly anticholinergic and carries a risk of agranulocytosis. As a result, frequent blood tests are a required part of any clozapine monitoring regimen. Furthermore, clozapine can precipitate seizures or orthostatic hypotension. Resperidone, another new atypical neuroleptic, is

also associated with a lower risk of EPS and TD, at least at doses less than 6 mg a day, but it too can produce orthostatic hypotension. When used at low doses (0.25 mg to 2 mg a day), respiridone is generally safe. Olanzepine appears to be similarly safe from the perspective of EPS risks, but it may be associated with increased risk of weight gain. While these drugs may be more effective with fewer side effects in younger adults, large scale comparison studies in the geriatric population are still needed to assure that this safety profile extends across the age continuum.

Antianxiety Agents in the Elderly

Because the symptoms of anxiety and insomnia are so common in the elderly, the benzodiazepines are frequently prescribed. In the past, up to one third of the elderly patients in medical hospitals were given one of the benzodiazepines,[50] leading to the claim that these drugs were over prescribed in this population. Nonetheless, the benzodiazepines are proven to be effective and relatively safe in the treatment of anxiety, especially when properly fitted to the symptom profile of the individual patient.[51]

There are many age-related changes in response to the benzodiazepines, and these changes are primarily due to the pharmacokinetic alterations in metabolism. Agents which require complicated metabolic transformation to active metabolites (i.e., diazepam, chlordiazepoxide, desmethyldiazepam, florazepam, clorazepate, and prazepam) tend to have an extended duration of action in the elderly and lead to an accumulation of side effects.[52] As much as a ten-fold increase in plasma half-lives has been demonstrated with the benzodiazepines undergoing oxidative metabolism versus those with conjugated metabolism; this effect is more obvious in males than females.[53]

While diazepam and chlordiazepoxide are perhaps the oldest and best known of the benzodiazepines, their relatively long half-lives make them generally less desirable for elderly patients. Oxazepam (10 to 50 mg/day), a short-acting agent with no active metabolites, may be preferable in this population because it does not accumulate in the system. Lorazepam (0.5 to 2 mg/day), a somewhat longer-acting benzodiazepine, is another choice for the elderly because of its uncomplicated metabolic pathway, but it has frequently been associated with specific memory impairments. Flurazepam is one of the longer-acting benzodiazepines with a half-life of up to 72 hours in the elderly. Because of the potential for substantial accumulation and increased side effects, its use should probably be avoided in the aged.[54] Alprazolam is an intermediate-acting drug which has the advantage of having both anxiolytic and antidepressant effects; in the elderly, it has been used safely in divided doses of 0.5 to 4 mg/day with encouraging results.[55] Alprazolam has also been utilized with some benefit in combination with neuroleptics in treatment of young schizophrenics,[56] so there may be additional advantages of this agent with older schizophrenics as well.

Buspirone, a novel anxiolytic with serotonergic agonist activity, has quickly found a place in the treatment of anxiety in the elderly. Generally well tolerated, buspirone has been shown to have similar effectiveness but fewer side effects compared to the benzodiazepines for the treatment of generalized anxiety. Side effects in up to 30% of patients include stomach complaints, dizziness, headache, and occasional sleep disturbance.[57] With the elderly, 20 mg/day in divided doses was associated with decreased anxiety. Of note is that buspirone has had mixed results when studied in patients with cognitive impairments.[58] Other agents which may be considered for the treatment of anxiety in the elderly include beta-blockers, antidepressants, antihistamines and even neuroleptics under certain circumstances.[59]

Lithium

Lithium has been an effective agent in the treatment of patients of all ages with manic-depressive illness. Among older persons, one encounters hypomanic states that often respond to lithium in much smaller doses than would ordinarily be anticipated. Older patients should be kept at somewhat lower maintenance levels (0.6 to 0.7 mEq/L) than younger patients and should be monitored with routine physical examinations, EKGs, blood chemistry tests, and evaluation of kidney and thyroid functions. Older people must be monitored more closely than younger persons. For example, if one doctor prescribes lithium and another diuretics, without collaboration between them, the patient may have dangerous elevation in his or her serum lithium level. Hypomanic states and bipolar depressions are most susceptible to lithium therapy, and improvement can be dramatic. Evidence for the treatment of depressive states is less impressive, except in cases of cyclic depressions treated over time.[60]

Lithium is entirely eliminated from the body by the kidney. Because of the general pharmacokinetic changes with age and the small margin between the therapeutic and toxic doses of lithium, one must be vary careful when prescribing the drug to the elderly. Average doses of approximately 400 mg/day with peak serum levels of 0.8 mmol/liter have been sufficient to achieve good clinical results.[61] With older people on low-sodium diets or diuretics, the need for caution is increased; potentially neurotoxic levels above 1.2 mmol/liter should be avoided in the elderly.[62]

Lithium intoxication can cause permanent neurologic damage; thus, continuous monitoring and patient education (for example, informing patients of early side effects) is critical. This is true even when treatment with lithium salts has previously been well tolerated. Clinical signs of toxicity include diarrhea, vomiting, tremor, mild ataxia, drowsiness, thirst, polyuria (increased urination), muscular weakness, slurred speech, and confusion. The tremor and polyuria may persist for a time after reduction of the dose. It has been suggested that the elderly show earlier evidence of confusion and neuromuscular irritability when becoming lithium toxic and that the course of toxicity can be more severe and unpredictable than with younger patients. Up to 13% of geriatric patients show some toxicity on maintenance lithium therapy during an 18 month follow-up period. As with younger patients, frequent (i.e., every six months) monitoring of the thyroid status should be maintained to avoid the side effect of hypothyroidism. Other regular monitoring should include routine physical examinations, EKGs, blood chemistries, and kidney function tests.

Psychostimulants

The use of central nervous system stimulants with the elderly remains a controversial area. Despite the scarcity of careful, placebo-controlled studies revealing definite improvement in depressed elderly, dextroamphetamine is still frequently used, and many physicians are convinced of anecdotal successes. Side effects include insomnia, poor appetite, weight loss, excitement, paranoia, and palpitations; the drug can also become habit forming. When given to the elderly, doses usually range from 5 to 30 mg/day.[63] Methylphenidate, another mild stimulant, has been used previously in conjunction with psychotherapy[64] and more recently with dementia patients showing varying degrees of depression or apathy.[65] These studies have each claimed modest success with 10 to 30 mg/day of methylphenidate, leading others to call for a reconsideration of the use of psychostimulants, especially in patients with concurrent medical illness.[66] At present, these medications should probably be reserved for those patients who cannot tolerate traditional antidepressant treatment or for whom other approaches have already been exhausted.

Other Medications

In certain psychiatric conditions, combination therapy is indicated and often practiced. Perhaps the best known example is that of co-prescribing neuroleptics with lithium in acute mania. While some problems have been noted with the specific combination of haloperidol and lithium, these combinations are usually quite effective in the most severe psychotic manias. Once the acute mania is under control, however, the neuroleptic can be withdrawn and the patient stabilized on lithium alone. A subsequent combination of lithium with an antidepressant is often required for those bipolar patients with post-manic or post-psychotic depressions. As might be expected, caution must be exercised in each case to monitor blood levels of the respective drugs on a regular basis.

Delusional depression is another well-known condition which often requires combined treatment with an antidepressant plus a neuroleptic or the use of ECT and an antidepressant, at least for the period where the patient is psychotic.[67] Non-delusional but otherwise treatment-resistant depression has also been treated with combination approaches including tricyclic "augmentation" with cytomel (25 to 50 mcg/day) or lithium (300 to 600 mg/day). Interestingly, these combinations are both characterized by a rapid response when the cytomel or lithium is added to a stabilized tricyclic regimen; benefit is often seen within 24 to 48 hours. While these combinations have not been studied extensively in the elderly, there is reason to believe that they might be equally effective if all the usual thyroid and lithium precautions are taken. Another possibility includes the addition of estrogen to ongoing antidepressant therapy, and anecdotal reports of improvement in elderly postmenopausal females suggest that menopause-related mood disorders deserve further investigation.[68]

Medications borrowed from the practice of general internal medicine are sometimes of help in psychiatry and are currently the focus of much research. These drugs include the antiseizure medication, carbamazepine, which has already proven successful in acute and prophylactic treatment of lithium-resistant mania and is now being tested in elderly agitated demented patients.[69] Because of the potential for a hemolytic anemia, however, this drug must be monitored carefully with frequent complete blood counts and carbamezepine blood levels and should only be prescribed by physicians familiar with its use.

Beta-blockers have also been reported to be of help in treating the peripheral manifestations of anxiety. However, the beta-blocker most frequently used, propranolol, has also been shown to induce depressive symptoms, concentration difficulties, and reversible confusional states.[70] Oxprenolol, a beta-blocker which has not been associated with depression, is another alternative which may be safer in the elderly because of its tendency to cause less slowing of the heart. As with all beta-blockers, oxprenolol should not be used with patients with asthma, bronchitis, or diabetes. Finally, while the beta-blockers have been reported to be of value in treating agitated, aggressive behavior in organically impaired patients, there are currently no careful studies of these drugs in demented elderly patients.

Cerebral vasodilators, cerebral stimulants, hormones, and anticoagulants are among other classes of drugs that have been recommended and sold for depressed, "senile," or deteriorated older people. They are of little clinical use and may be dangerous in some instances. Vitamins are useful when there are deficiencies. Hypovitaminosis must be carefully evaluated. Victims of pellagra should receive 500 mg of nicotinic acid orally up to three times daily, as necessary. For older people, a basic vitamin-mineral combination may be given to offset effects of the processing of foods, poor dietary habits, and low appetite related to loneliness and grief.

DRUG TREATMENTS
FOR SLEEP DISORDERS

Five million elderly people in the United States have a severe sleep disorder. About one half of all elderly complain of sleep problems.[71] And although the elderly represent 12% of the population, they consume 40% of the prescribed sedative-hypnotics in the U.S..[72] Since the experience of sleeping is so subjective, the reports of actual sleep time, quality of sleep, and complaints of insomnia are often quite variable in the elderly. Certain sleep changes are common in later life and should not be confused with insomnia. In general, older people sleep less long and less deeply and awaken more easily than earlier in their lives. They have a greater tendency to waken throughout the night and to experience less "dreaming sleep" (stage 4 or rapid eye movement (REM) sleep). Deep sleep (called delta sleep), the period of dreamless oblivion, lessens and may vanish in old age.[73]

The evaluation of sleep in the elderly must be done carefully and systematically because of the variable patterns of sleep in this age group. For the most part, the average amount of bed rest needed by an individual remains from seven to nine hours a day and does not change dramatically over the adult life cycle, as is commonly thought. It is also clear that concurrent medical and psychological problems influence the pattern of sleep in the elderly. For these reasons, the complete 24-hour sleep-wake cycle of the elderly individual must be examined whenever assessing complaints of insomnia. Many older persons retire early because of fatigue, waken at three or four o'clock in the morning, and then fear they have insomnia, when they may, in fact, have had an adequate six to seven hours or more of sleep.

Physiological causes of insomnia include Alzheimer's disease, nocturnal myoclonus (leg twitching), nocturnal cardiac arrhythmias, nocturnal shortness of breath from congestive heart failure, and the discomfort of arthritis. Insomnia can be produced or exacerbated by an institutional environment such as nursing homes or hospitals where the patient has little control over the lights or the timing of medications or meals. Many elderly are awakened at night by the need to go to the bathroom.

Persons with sleep difficulties related to psychological problems may fear sleep itself. In sleep, their defenses against anxiety (including fear of death), anger, and other emotions are more relaxed. The activities that protect them from anxiety during the day are gone. Psychotherapy can help in clarifying and resolving the basis for insomnia.

What may seem like a need for less sleep may therefore be the result of illness, anxiety, depression, or simply the need for more exercise and activity during the day. For example, early morning awakening is more common among the inactive who go to bed early and take catnaps (sometimes leading to serious day-night sleep reversal). This is not to say that a daily nap is not valuable; if not too long or too frequent, naps may relax the person and thus contribute to better sleep at night. Unlike in younger people, early morning awakening in the elderly is not necessarily a sign of depression, especially if there are daytime naps.

Nonpharmacologic treatment approaches for insomnia include the establishment of simple rituals that are followed regularly—perhaps warm baths, a well-made bed, bed boards for support, back massage, eye shields to stop the light, bedtime reading or soft music, or any other comfort mechanisms that suggest protection and relaxation. Patients should be encouraged to avoid excessive daytime napping, particularly the after-dinner snooze, and to have a regular schedule of activities for each day. Daily exercise and avoidance of caffeine-containing beverages like coffee and cola, especially in the afternoon and evening, is also important. There should be no heavy meals after 7:00 P.M., and the emphasis for the evening should be on relaxation when approaching the regular hour of sleep. If insomnia does occur, patients should be encouraged to get out of bed rather than tossing and turning. The psychological association with bed should be sleep, not insomnia. When insomnia becomes a chronic problem, sleep clinics may be useful in evaluating

severe causes of insomnia. A list of members of the American Sleep Disorders Association may be obtained from the national office of the American Sleep Disorders Association, 1610 14th St. N.W., Suite 300, Rochester, Minnesota 55901.

There are many alternative drug treatments for insomnia (Table 13.5). While the benzodiazepines remain by far the most prescribed treatment for insomnia, other medications include chloral hydrate, barbiturates, antihistamines, and propanediols (i.e., meprobamate). Triazolam (Halcion), although a short-acting benzodiazepine, has been criticized as contributing to memory impairment, delirium, and daytime anxiety. Of the alternative treatments, the naturally-occurring amino acid L-tryptophan (500 mg to 2,000 mg at bedtime) was probably considered the safest until the problems with eosinophilic myalgias surfaced.[74]

Antihistamines are frequently suggested but must be used cautiously in the elderly because of their anticholinergic side effects. Barbiturates and meprobamate should probably be avoided altogether in the elderly because of their abuse potential and profound suppressive effects on rapid eye movement (REM) sleep. Chloral hydrate, often overlooked in the age of the benzodiazepines, is still quite effective for occasional use in the elderly at doses of 250 mg to 1000 mg at bedtime, but it can irritate the stomach lining and

TABLE 13.5   Alternative drug treatments for insomnia

MEDICATIONS	DOSE RANGE (MG/DAY)	PROS AND CONS
Serotonin Reuptake Inhibitors		
Chloral Hydrate	250–1000	• Rapidly effective • Stomach irritation possible
Diphendydramine	10–25	• Available without prescription • Relatively mild • Possible confusion
Oxazepam	5–15	• Short-acting for early insomnia • Occassional paradoxical effect • Daytime drowsiness uncommon
Diazepam	0.5–2.0	• Longer-acting for late insomnia • Daytime "hangover" common

has also been associated with confusion in geriatric patients.[75]

Wine has been widely recommended in geriatric medicine and in convalescent care. It is the world's oldest treatment for insomnia. Galen, the great Greek physician, called wine "the nurse of old age." Among the dessert wines, two to three ounces of port is useful for sleep. One must beware, however, of the unfortunate potentiating or synergistic action of alcohol on other sedatives. Many commonly prescribed drugs have altered therapeutic and/or adverse medical effects when taken with alcohol. These drugs include not only benzodiazepines, hypnotics, narcotics, antidepressants, and neuroleptics but also certain antihistamines, analgesics, anticoagulants, and antiinfective agents. In fact, alcohol use in combination with other drugs accounts for approximately 20% of the total number of accidental or suicidal deaths per year that are drug-related. Mental confusion and poor coordination can combine with alcohol to increase the risk of falling, particularly since tolerance for alcohol can decrease with increasing age. In addition, alcohol adversely influences sexual potency. Finally, anyone with alcoholic tendencies should not be encouraged to drink.

Over-the-counter drugs sold as sleep aids or sedatives, like Sominex, Nytal, and Sleep-Eze, are of questionable value, containing unsafe levels of antihistamines developed for the treatment of allergies. They may also contain scopolamine in levels for sleep inducement that can cause outbursts of uncontrolled behavior and a variety of adverse physical effects. Bromides have been used in the past in over-the-counter medications and are considered unsafe.

DRUG TREATMENT OF PAIN

Chronic pain, a physical, psychological, and social state, is conveniently defined as pain that has persisted six months or longer. It is distinguished from acute pain, which is nature's warning system. The discovery of opiate-binding sites (receptors) and endorphins (morphine-like substances) in the brain during the 1970s has moved forward fundamental research in both pain and neurobiology. The emergence of multiple pain clinics throughout the country to help deal with the complex problem of chronic pain has also been welcome. At such clinics, various therapies—acupuncture, transcutaneous electrical stimulation, exercise, psychotherapy, family counseling, and hypnosis—are applied rather than pharmacological approaches alone, which, like surgical interventions, have been disappointing in isolation. Experimental efforts to lessen pain include insertion of electrodes into the patient's brain to stimulate the secretion of enkephalins or endorphins, the brain's own "opiates." Nerve blocks, neurosurgery, and new drugs are other techniques. For older people, and especially those who are in the last days of life, it is important to provide effective, prompt relief of pain and any other discomforts without excessive preoccupation with the potentiality of addiction. Nonetheless, the search for an effective non-addictive analgesic continues.

In addition to suffering, pain brings with it anxiety and, frequently, depression. Chronic malignant pain often requires strong analgesics and certainly consistent emotional and physical support and comfort. Both chronic malignant and benign pain sufferers may also find relief through the use of psychotropic drugs—especially the benzodiazepines and other antianxiety drugs, the phenothiazines, and the antidepressants.

The wise management of chronic pain requires an understanding not only of the effects of pain itself but of the psychological conditioning that can result from the way pain is handled by the patient and by medical personnel. If the patient receives medication only when pain becomes pronounced, he or she begins to learn that only the presence of intense pain will bring relief. If a physician sees the patient only when the pain is prominent, then attention from the doctor becomes a reward for experiencing pain. To avoid such learned behavior, and to "decondition" those who have already learned it, many have recommended the increased availability of pain medication for individual patients.

Patient-controlled analgesia (PCA) has grown in popularity with physicians and patients alike over the past ten years. PCA is a pain relief program in which patients control their own pain by taking medication when they need it. Safeguards such as preset limits or timed intervals are built into PCA programs to avoid accidental or deliberate overdose. However, not all pain killers can be self-administered and not all elderly are able to handle self-medication. The decision to use PCA must be based on the nature of the pain and the needs and abilities of the patient. When used appropriately, PCA can produce a high degree of patient satisfaction and an individually calibrated mechanism for dealing with varying levels of pain.

ELECTROCONVULSIVE THERAPY

Despite being documented as an effective treatment for elderly depressives, electroconvulsive therapy (ECT) is generally underutilized by the elderly.[76] One of the major criticisms and problems with ECT is its well-documented negative effect on memory. Because of the cognitive dysfunction associated with ECT, attempts have been made to reduce the impairments by employing unilateral rather than bilateral convulsive treatment,[77] minimizing the amount of concurrent medications (especially anticholinergic medications such as atropine), and even varying the wave form used in the ECT stimulus.[78] While these efforts have been somewhat successful, there remain quantifiable memory impairments after a course of ECT, especially in geriatric patients.[79] Although some patients, particularly those suffering from "pseudodementia," actually report an improvement in memory,[80] the majority of elderly patients demonstrate cognitive impairments as a side effect of the treatment. Compared to the overall dysfunction associated with severe depression, however, the relative clinical significance of these memory difficulties has been questioned.[81] Nonetheless, the issue of whether and when to use ECT is hotly debated by many, including former patients and professionals within psychiatry itself, such that it is still reserved for

specific situations, often only after multiple pharmacologic treatment failures. Currently, there are three major indications for ECT:

1. Life threatening suicidal depression
2. Antidepressant-resistant depression
3. Medical contraindications to antidepressant medications

Additional indications include delusional depressions, prolonged refusal to eat, and other self-destructive behaviors.

In the presence of truly serious suicidal risk, it may not be advisable to wait out drug trials. After comprehensive evaluation with full patient consent and under careful conditions, including the use of appropriate preshock sedation and muscle relaxants (such as succinylcholine chloride), ECT can be quite effective against the severe depressions of old age that can lead to suicide risk. ECT can often bring about prompt relief with a limited series of four to eight treatments. In these conditions, even a history of cerebrovascular accidents and/or myocardial infarctions is not a contraindication per se. Effects on memory should be assessed at baseline and during treatment, and the number of treatments should be minimal.[82]

Age alone should not be considered a barrier to the use of ECT. In fact, a case report of a 94-year-old woman improving after receiving ECT noted that the patient's daughter "lamented the fact that ECT had been deemed to be contraindicated 15 years earlier on the grounds of advanced age."[83]

Since 1938 when Ugo Cerletti and Lucino Bini first introduced ECT, there has been controversy surrounding its use. Fear and distaste of ECT are commonplace and understandable among patients since it can be an intimidating, if often effective, treatment. Unfortunately, patients who have received ECT often hesitate and resist returning to the doctor even years later if once again they develop serious depression. Some states have passed laws strengthening the patients' right to refuse treatments like ECT; but regardless of law, patients must fully understand the treatment offered and be given the right to accept or refuse it.

Biology of ECT

With the original observation that schizophrenia rarely occurred in epileptics, it was hypothesized that inducing seizures might have an antipsychotic effect. Subsequent experimentation led to the conclusion that either chemically or electrically-induced seizures had an antidepressant effect, but the exact mechanism of that improvement has not yet been discerned. It is clear that the seizure is the key element in the treatment, for simulated ECT is not effective and the presence or absence of anesthesia does not alter outcome. Even the dreaded amnestic effect is not correlated with the antidepressant effect. Current theories about ECT's mechanism of action involve various neurotransmitter systems, especially the serotonergic and noradrenergic systems, neuroendocrine effects on the hypothalamic axis, and the release of peptides (small proteins in the brain which can act as neurotransmitters). Interestingly, ECT produces a biochemical pattern in human spinal fluid and animal experiments which is somewhat different than that found with cyclic antidepressants. Future studies will involve much greater exploration of those biochemical mechanisms, particularly as they effect the cholinergic system. Another intriguing approach will be the study of regional brain changes following ECT with the various neuroimaging techniques.[84]

MENTAL HEALTH THERAPIST'S INVOLVEMENT IN DRUG THERAPY

The mental health therapist's own attitudes toward the use of drugs may influence the effects of drugs on older people. If the therapist is philosophically against drugs (feeling that people should resolve issues for themselves) or is anxious about their side effects and potential complications, he or she is likely to convey these concerns to the older person, even when not stating them explicitly. Ideally, the therapist would be open enough to appreciate the value of drugs that are judiciously employed. There are people who need the *immediate* support of the magical/real expectations of medicine and the "medicine man" (the power of the physician as well as the actual, chemically active drug effects). One rational way of reconciling negative feelings about drugs with occasions when people need them is to note that therapy is a *process,* an experience over time. At various points, drugs might maintain working men or women on their jobs or help parents with their parenthood. But in most therapeutic efforts, drugs should be only part of the total treatment effort, although a very important part in many instances.

However, even if the therapist is totally opposed to drugs, he or she should not deny the patient their usefulness but should collaborate with a physician who will evaluate the usefulness of drugs in situations where they have been found to be helpful for others. Having separate "talking" and "drug" therapists may provoke some divided reactions in the person being treated, with manipulations in some instances, but such behavior can become a part of the treatment process.

Nonphysician mental health personnel should know what drugs an older person is taking, whether for physical or mental conditions. The *Physicians' Desk Reference,* although not ideal, is a source of information about the side effects and complications of all drugs. Long's excellent *The Essential Guide to Prescription Drugs* provides a wealth of information. The *Merck Manual* also may be useful. *The United States Pharmacopoeia* is the Medicare-designated compendium. Psychoactive drugs are classified into five categories (schedules) under the Controlled Substances Act of 1970.

All mental health personnel should be familiar with prescriptions and know how to interpret them for their patients if necessary. Nurses especially may be called on to prepare prescriptions for the signature of the physician in some circumstances.

Some of the common prescription terms are listed below:

Weights (amounts are usually expressed in milligrams, grams, or grains):

milligram   One thousandth of a gram, roughly equivalent to 1/65th grain. It is usually abbreviated mg.

gram   Unit of weight in the metric system. It is usually abbreviated g, gm, or Gm. It is equivalent to about 15.43 gr.

grain   Unit of weight in the avoirdupois system. It is usually abbreviated gr. It is equivalent to 1/480 ounce and to 0.065 gm.

ounce   One twelfth of a pound avoirdupois and equivalent to 31.1 gm. The abbreviation for ounce is oz.

teaspoonful   four to five milliliters (ml).

Note: The metric system is preferred and the old English system is slowly being phased out.

Latin abbreviations:

Rx   "Recipe."

Sig.   To write. It means the directions for taking the drugs.

b.i.d.   *Bis in die,* two times a day.

t.i.d.   *Ter in die,* three times a day.

q.i.d.   *Quater in die,* four times a day.

a.c.   *Antecibum,* before meals.

p.c.   *Post cibum,* after meals.

h.s.   *Hora somni,* before sleep.

p.r.n.   *Pro re nata,* according to circumstances, rather than routine schedule.

s.o.s.   *Si opus sit,* if necessary, if occasion requires.

Rep.   Repeat.

q.h.   *Quaque hora,* every hour.

q.2h.   *Quaque secunda hora,* every second hour, etc.

FUTURE DIRECTIONS IN DRUG AND SOMATIC THERAPIES

The introduction of the serotonin reuptake inhibitors to our treatment arsenal has had a major impact on the field of psychopharmacology over the last few years, but we are a long way from understanding how these drugs and other psychopharmacologic agents really work when given chronically. Despite the massive amount of empiric data that have accumulated over the last 20 years as to the efficacy of the psychotropic medications, our knowledge is still primitive. Labeling drugs as "dopamine blockers"(neuroleptics), "reuptake blockers" (antidepressants), "membrane stabilizers" (lithium), or "anxiolytics" (benzodiazepines) perhaps describes the acute effects of these drugs but gives very little information as to the underlying chronic mechanisms of action. Our knowledge of the workings of ECT is not much further beyond recognizing the importance of generalized seizure activity. In fact, despite similar clinical effects, it appears that ECT and conventional antidepressant drug therapies may have quite different biochemical profiles, further confusing the biology of depression for the moment. In the future, a great deal of work will be focused on the mechanism of action of the various classes of medications, particularly now that more selective and specific agents with different acute biochemical effects are available. Within geriatrics, the comparison of populations with different organic pathologies but similar clinical symptoms (i.e., depression with coexistent cognitive difficulties vs. dementia with depression) may help us better understand the underlying mechanism of depression and test the differential responses to specific medications in these populations.

Another major horizon in drug therapy is the changing responsivity seen with age. While pharmacokinetic changes can explain some of the increased sensitivity generally seen with age, phamacodynamic changes are still poorly understood for the most part and deserve much further study. Finally, the newly emerging field of pharmacogenetics, the study of inherited factors in the interindividual diversity of drug response, may well become increasingly important.[85] Not only could advances in molecular biology and pharmacogenetics help us better understand drug mechanisms at the receptor level, but eventually, the field may lead us to the pharmacologic regulation of phenotypic gene expression. For late-onset conditions, such as delusional syndromes and Alzheimer's disease, a regulatory drug that was effective in altering the phenotypic expression of a gene would have very powerful implications and constitute a major therapeutic advance.

SELECTED READINGS

Ahronheim, J. C. (1992). *Handbook of prescribing medications for geriatric patients.* Boston: Little, Brown and Co.

Alexopoulos, G. S. (1995). Methodology of treatment studies in geriatric depression. *American Journal of Geriatric Psychiatry, 3,* pp. 280–289.

Alexopoulos, G. S., Meyers, B. S., Young, R. C., Chester, J., Feder, M., & Einhorn, A. (1995). Anxiety in geriatric depression: Effects of age and cognitive impairment. *American Journal of Geriatric Psychiatry, 3,* pp. 108–118.

Avorn, J., Soumerai, S. B., Everitt, D. E., Ross-Degnan, D., Beere, M. H., Sherman, D., Salem-Schatz, S. R. & Fields, D. (1992). A randomized trial of a program to reduce the use of psychoactive drugs in nursing homes. *New England Journal of Medicine, 327,* pp. 68–173.

Billig, N., Cohen-Mansfield, J., & Lipson, S. (1991). Pharmacologic treatment of agitation in a nursing home. *Journal of the American Geriatrics Society, 39,* pp. 1002–1005.

Bloom, H. & Shlom, E. A. (1993). *Drug prescribing in the elderly.* New York: Raven Press.

Branconnier, R. J., & Cole, J. O. (1980). The therapeutic role of methylphenidate in senile organic brain syndrome. In Cole, J. O., & Barrett, J. (Eds.), *Psychopathology in the aged.* New York: Raven Press, pp. 183–195.

Bressler, R., & Katz, M. D. (Eds.) (1993). *Geriatric pharmacology.* New York: McGraw-Hill.

Bridge, T. P., Soldo, B. J., Phelps, B. H., Wise, C. D., Francak, M. J., & Wyatt, R. J. (1985). Platelet monoamine oxidase activity: Demographic characteristics contribute to enzyme activity variability. *Journal of Gerontology, 40,* pp. 23–28.

Cadieux, R. J. (1993). Geriatric psychopharmacology: A primary care challenge. *Geriatric Psychopharmocology, 93,* pp. 281–301.

Callahan, C. M., Hendrie, H. C., Dittus, R. S., Brater, D.C., Hui, S. L., & Tierney, W. M. (1994). Improving treatment of late life depression in primary care: A randomized clinical trial. *Journal of the American Geriatrics Society, 42,* pp. 839–846.

Chiarello, R. J., & Cole, J. O. (1987). Psychostimulants: A reconsideration. *Archives of General Psychiatry, 44,* pp. 286–295.

Clauw, D. J., Nashel, D. L., Umhau, A., & Katz, P. (1990). Tryptophan-associated eosinophilic connective tissue disease: A new clinical entity? *Journal of the American Medical Association, 263,* pp. 1502–1506.

Cohen, B. M., & Zubenko, G. S. (1985). Relevance of genetic variability to clinical psychopharmacology. *Psychopharmacology Bulletin, 21,* pp. 641–650.

Colenda, C. C. (1988). Buspirone in the treatment of agitated demented patients. *Lancet, ii,* pp. 411–412.

Cooper, J. W. (1996). Probable adverse drug reaction in a rural geriatric nursing home population: A four-year study. *Journal of the American Geriatrics Society, 44,* pp. 194–197.

Cooper, J. W. (1991). *Drug-related problems in geriatric nursing home patients.* New York: Pharmaceutical Products Press.

Copeland, J. R. M., Davidson, I. A., Dewey, M. E., et al. (1992). Alzheimer's disease, other dementias, depression and pseudodementia: prevalence, incidence and three-year outcome in Liverpool. *British Journal of Psychiatry, 161,* pp. 230–239.

Daly, M. P., Lamy, P. P., & Richardson, J. P. (1994). Avoiding polypharmacy and iatrogenesis in the nursing home. *Maryland Medical Journal, 43,* pp. 1139–1144.

Devanand, D. P., Verma, A. K., Tirumalasetti, F., & Sackeim, H. A. (1991). Absence of cognitive impairment after more than 100 lifetime ECT treatments. *American Journal of Psychiatry, 148,* pp. 929–932.

Dubovsky, S. L. (1994). Geriatric neuropsychopharmacology. In Coffey, C. E., & Cummings, J. L. (Eds.), *Textbook of geriatric psychiatry.* Washington, DC: American Psychiatric Press, pp. 595–631.

Feighner, J. P., Boyer, W. F., Meredith, C. H., & Hendrickson, G. (1988). An overview of fluoxetine in geriatric depression. *British Journal of Psychiatry, 153* (3 Suppl.), pp. 105–108.

Gaspar, D., & Samarasinghe, L. A. (1982). ECT in psychogeriatric practice: A study of risk factors, indications and outcome. *Comprehensive Psychiatry, 23,* pp. 170–175.

Georgotas, A., Friedman, E., McCarthy, M., Mann, J., Krakowski, M., Siegel, R., & Ferris, S. (1983). Resistant geriatric depressions and therapeutic response to monoamine oxidase inhibitors. *Biological Psychiatry, 18,* pp. 195–205.

Georgotas, A., McCue, R. E., Friedman, E., & Cooper, T. (1987). Prediction of response to nortriptyline and phenelzine by platelet MAO activity. *American Journal of Psychiatry, 144,* pp. 338–340.

Gillin, J. C., Duncan, W. C., Murphy, D. L., Post, R. M., Wehr, T. A., Goodwin, F. K., Wyatt, R. J., & Bunney, W. E. (1981). Age-related changes in sleep in depressed and normal subjects. *Psychiatry Research, 4,* pp. 73–78.

Grammans, R. E., Stringfellow, J. C., Hvizdos, A. J., et al. (1992). Use of buspirone in patients with generalized anxiety disorder and coexisting depressive symptoms: a meta-analysis of eight randomized controlled studies. *Neuropsychobiology, 25,* pp. 193–201.

Greenblatt, D. J., Sellers, E. M., & Shader, R. I. (1982). Drug disposition in old age. *New England Journal of Medicine, 306,* pp. 1081–1088.

Hardy, B. G., Shulman, K. I., MacKenzie, S. E., Kutcher, S. P., & Silverberg, J. D. (1987). Pharmacokinetics of lithium in the elderly. *Journal of Clinical Psychopharmacology, 7*(3), pp. 153–158.

Horwitz, G. J., Tariot, P. N., Mead, K., & Cox, C. (1995). Discontinuation of antipsychotics in nursing home patients with dementia. *American Journal of Geriatric Psychiatry, 3,* pp. 290–299.

Jansen, J. H. M., & Andrews, J. S. (1994). The effects of serotonergic drugs on short-term spatial memory in rats. *Journal of Psychopharmacology, 8*(3), pp. 157–163.

Jarvik, L. F., Read, S. L., Mintz, J., Neshkes, R. E., Kane, J. M., Cole, K., Sarantakos, S., Howard, A., & Borenstein, M. (1983). Pretreatment orthostatic hypotension in geriatric depression: Predictor of response to imipramine and doxepin. *Journal of Clinical Psychopharmacology, 3,* pp. 368–372.

Jeste, D. V., Caligiuri, M. P., Paulsen, J. S., Heaton, R. K., Lacro, J. P., Harris, J., Bailey, A., Fell, R. L., & McAdams, L. A. (1995). Risk of tardive dyskinesia in older patients. *Archives of General Psychiatry, 52,* pp. 756–765.

Jeste, D. V., Paulsen, J. S., & Harris, M. J. (1995). Late-onset schizophrenia and other related psychoses. In

Bloom, F. E., & Kupfer, D. J. (Eds.), *Psychopharmacology: The fourth generation of progress.* Raven Press, Ltd., New York, pp. 1437–1446.

Kane, J. M., Cole, K., Sarantakos, S., Howard, A., & Borenstein, M. (1983). Safety and efficacy of bupropion in elderly patients: Preliminary observations. *Journal of Clinical Psychiatry, 44,* pp. 134–136.

Kaufman, M. W., Cassem, N. H., Murray, G. B., & Jenike, M. (1984). Use of psychostimulants in medically ill patients with neurological disease and major depression. *Canadian Journal of Psychiatry, 29,* pp. 46–49.

Kupfer, D. J., & Reynolds III, C. F. (1997). Management of insomnia. *The New England Journal of Medicine, 336,* pp. 341–346.

Lane, R., Baldwin, D., & Preskorn, S. (1995). The SSRI's: Advantages, disadvantages, and differences. *Journal of Psychopharmacology, 9*(2)(Suppl.), pp. 167–178.

Lawlor, B. A., Radcliffe, J., Molchan, S. E., Martinez, R. A., Hill, J. L., & Sunderland, T. (1994). A pilot placebo-controlled study of trazodone and buspirone in Alzheimer's disease. *International Journal of Geriatric Psychiatry, 9,* pp. 55–59.

Lebowitz, B. D., Martinez, R. A., Niederehe, G., Pearson, J. L., et al. (1995). Treatment of depression in late-life. *Psychopharmacology, 31*(1), pp. 185–202, 1995.

Lerer, B. (1986). ECT: Possible mechanisms of action. *Psychopharmacology, 22,* pp. 472–487.

Long, S. H. (1994). *Prescription drug coverage and the elderly: Issues and options.* Washington, DC: Public Policy Institute, AARP, p.2.

Markovitz, P. J. (1993). Treatment of anxiety in the elderly. *Journal of Clinical Psychiatry, 54*(Suppl. 5), pp. 64–68, 1993.

McCall, W. V., Farah, B. A., Reboussin, D., & Colenda, C. (1995). Comparison of the efficacy of titrated, moderate-dose and fixed, high-dose right unilateral ECT in elderly patients. *American Journal of Geriatric Psychiatry, 3,* pp. 317–324.

McKeith, I., Fairbairn, A., Perry R., Thompson, P., & Perry, E. (1992). Neuroleptic sensitivity in patients with senile dementia of Lewy body type. *British Medical Journal, 305,* pp. 673–678.

Molchan, S. E., Martinez, R. A., Hill, J. L., Weingartner, H. J., Thompson, K., Vitiello, B., & Sunderland, T. (1992). Increased cognitive sensitivity to scopolamine with age and a perspective on the scopolamine model. *Brain Research Review, 17,* pp. 215–226.

Moran, M. G., Thompson, T. L., & Nies, A. S. (1988). Sleep disorders in the elderly. *American Journal of Psychiatry, 145,* pp. 1369–1377.

Murphy, D. L., Sunderland, T., & Cohen, R. M. (1984). Monoamine oxidase-inhibiting antidepressants: A clinical update. *Psychiatric Clinics of North America, 7,* pp. 549–562.

Myers-Robfogel, M. W., & Bosmann, H. B. (1984). Clinical pharmacology in the aged: Aspects of pharmacokinetics and drug sensitivity. In Williams, T. F. (Ed.), *Rehabilitation in the aging.* New York: Raven Press, pp. 23–39.

Napoliello, M. J. (1986). An interim multicentre report on 677 anxious geriatric out-patients treated with buspirone. *British Journal of Clinical Practice, 40,* pp. 71–73.

Nelson, J. P., & Rosenberg, D. R. (1991). ECT treatment of demented elderly patients with major depression: a retrospective study of efficacy and safety. *Convulsive Therapy, 7,* pp. 157–165.

Neshkes, R. E., Gerner, R., Jarvik, L. F., Mintz, J., Joseph, J., Linde, S., Aldrich, J., Conolly, M. E., Rosen, R., & Hill, M. (1985). Orthostatic effect of imipramine and doxepin in depressed geriatric out-patients. *Journal of Clinical Psychopharmacology, 5,* pp. 102–106.

O'Connor, C. (1985). Electroshock. *The Washington Post Magazine,* December 1, pp. 12–22.

O'Shea, B., Lynch, T., Falvey, J., & O'Mahoney, G. (1987). Electroconvulsive therapy and cognitive improvement in a very elderly depressed patient. *British Journal of Psychiatry, 150,* pp. 255–257.

Oreland, L., & Gottfries, C.-G. (1986). Brain and brain monoamine oxidase in aging and in dementia of Alzheimer's type. *Progress in Neuro-Psychopharmacology and Biological Psychiatry, 10,* pp. 533–540.

Ouslander, J. (1981). Drug prescribing for the elderly. *Western Journal of Medicine, 135,* pp. 455–462.

Pettinati, H. M., & Bonner, K. M. (1984). Cognitive functioning in depressed geriatric patients with a history of ECT. *American Journal of Psychiatry, 141,* pp. 49–52.

Phanjoo, A. L., & Link, C. (1990). Remoxipride versus thioridazine in elderly psychotic patients. *Acta Psychiatrica Scandinavica, 82*(Suppl. 358), pp. 181–185.

Philpot, M., & Puranik, A. (1994). Psychotropic drugs, aging, and community care. *Drugs and Aging, 5,* pp. 235–241.

Pickett, P., Masand, P., & Murray, G. B. (1990). Psychostimulant treatment of geriatric depressive disorders secondary to medical illness. *Journal of Geriatric Psychiatry and Neurology, 3,* pp. 146–151.

Pitt, B. (1985). The chemotherapy of affective disorders in the elderly. In Dewhurst, W. G., & Baker, G. B. (Eds.), *Pharmacotherapy of affective disorders.* Beckenham: Croon Helm Ltd., pp. 584–616.

Pitts, W. M., Fann, W. E., Sajadi, C., & Snyder, S. (1983). Alprazolam in older depressed inpatients. *Journal of Clinical Psychiatry, 44,* pp. 213–215.

Raskind, M. A. (1993). Geriatric psychopharmacology: Management of late-life depression and the noncognitive behavioral disturbances of Alzheimer's disease. *Psychiatric Clinics of North America, 16,* pp. 815–827.

Ray, W. A., Taylor, J. A., Meador, K. G., Lichtenstein, M. J., Griffin, M. R., et al. (1993). Reducing antipsychotic drug use in nursing homes. *Archives of Internal Medicine, 153,* pp. 713–721.

Reynolds, C. F., Frank, E., Perel, J. M., et al. (1992). Combined pharmacotherapy and psychotherapy in the acute and continuation treatment of elderly patients with recurrent major depression: A preliminary report. *American Journal of Psychiatry, 149*(12), pp. 1687–1692.

Richelson, E. (1994). The pharmacology of antidepressants at the synapse: Focus on newer compounds. *Journal of Clinical Psychiatry, 55*(Suppl. A), pp. 34–39.

Rockwell, E., Lam, R. W., & Zisook, S. (1988). Antidepressant drug studies in the elderly. *Psychiatric Clinics of North America, 11,* pp. 215–233.

Rosenthal, N. E., Sack, D. A., Carpenter, C. J., Parry, B. L., Mendelson, W. B., & Wehr, T. A. (1985). Antidepressant effects of light in seasonal affective disorder. *American Journal of Psychiatry, 142,* pp. 163–170.

Salzman, C., Schneider, L. S., & Alexopoulos, G. S. (1995). Pharmacological treatment of depression in late life. In Bloom, F. E., & Kupfer, D. J. (Eds.), *Psychopharmacology: The fourth generation of progress.* Raven Press, Ltd., New York, pp. 1471–1477.

Salzman, C. (1987). Treatment of the elderly agitated patient. *Journal of Clinical Psychiatry, 48,* pp. S19–S22.

Salzman, C. (Ed.) (1992). *Clinical geriatric psychopharmacology,* 2nd ed. Baltimore, MD: Williams and Wilkins.

Samuels, S. C., & Katz, I. (1994). Neuroleptic medication in elderly people. *Current Opinion in Psychiatry, 7,* pp. 358–363.

Sandborn, W. D., Bendfeldt, F., & Handy, R. (1995). Valproic acid for physically aggressive behavior in geriatric patients. *American Journal of Geriatric Psychiatry, 3,* pp. 239–242.

Schmidt, P. J., & Rubinow, D. R. (1991). Menopause-related affective disorders: A justification for further study. *American Journal of Psychiatry, 148,* pp. 844–852.

Schmucker, D. L. (1985). Aging and drug disposition: An update. *Pharmacological Reviews, 37,* pp. 133–148.

Selma, T. P., Palla, K., Poddig, B., & Brauner, D. J. (1994). Effect of the omnibus reconciliation act of 1987 on antipsychotic prescribing in nursing home residents. *Journal of the American Geriatrics Society, 42,* pp. 648–652.

Shaw, S. M., & Opit, L. J. (1976). Need for supervision in the elderly receiving long-term prescription medications. *British Medical Journal, 1,* pp. 505–507.

Shomoian, C. A. (Ed.) (1992). *Psychopharmacological treatment complications in the elderly.* Washington, DC: American Psychiatric Press.

Shulman, K. I., MacKenzie, S., & Hardy, B. (1987). The clinical use of lithium carbonate in old age: A review. *Progress in Neuro-Psychopharmacology and Biological Psychiatry, 11,* pp. 159–164.

Simpson, P. M., & Foster, D. (1986). Improvement in organically disturbed behavior with trazodone treatment. *Journal of Clinical Psychiatry, 47,* pp. 191–193.

Smith, R. E., & Helms, P. M. (1982). Adverse effects of lithium therapy in the acutely ill elderly patients. *Journal of Clinical Psychiatry, 43,* pp. 94–99.

Solomon, F., White, C. C., Parron, D.C., & Mendelson, W. B. (1979). Sleeping pills, insomnia and medical practice, *New England Journal of Medicine, 300,* pp. 803–808.

Squire, L. R. (1984). ECT and memory dysfunction. In Lerer, B., Weiner, R. D., & Belmacker, R. H. (Eds.), *Basic mechanisms of ECT.* London: John Libby, pp. 156–163.

Squire, L. R., & Zouzounis, J. A. (1986). ECT and memory: Brief pulse versus sine wave. *American Journal of Psychiatry, 143,* pp. 596–601.

Sunderland, T., Lawlor, B. A., Martinez, R. A., & Molchan, S. E. (1991). Anxiety in the elderly: Neurobiological and clinical interface. In Salzman, C., & Lebowitz, B. (Eds.), *Anxiety in the elderly: Treatment and research.* New York, Springer, pp. 105–129.

Sunderland, T., Mueller, E. A., Cohen, R. M., Jimerson, D.C., Pickar, D., & Murphy, D. L. (1985). Tyramine pressor sensitivity changes during deprenyl treatment. *Psychopharmacology, 86,* pp. 432–437.

Sunderland, T., & Silver, M. A. (1988). Neuroleptics in the treatment of dementia. *International Journal of Geriatric Psychiatry, 3,* pp. 79–88.

Sunderland, T., Cohen, R. M., Molchan, S., Lawlor, B. A., Mellow, A. M., Newhouse, P. A., Tariot, P. N., Mueller, E. A., & Murphy, D. L. (1994). High dose selegiline in treatment-resistant older depressives. *Archives of General Psychiatry, 51,* pp. 607–615.

Sunderland, T., Tariot, P. N., Cohen, R. M., Weingartner, H., Mueller, E. A., & Murphy, D. L. (1987). Anticholinergic sensitivity in patients with dementia of the Alzheimer type and age-matched controls: A dose-response study. *Archives of General Psychiatry, 44,* pp. 418–426.

Tariot, P. N., Frederiksen, K., Erb, R., Leibovici, A., Podgorski, C. A., Asnis, J., & Cox, C. (1995). Lack of Carbamazepine toxicity in frail nursing home patients: A controlled study. *Journal of the American Geriatrics Society, 43,* pp. 1026–1929.

Thapa, P. B., Gideon, P., Fought, R. L., & Ray, W. A. (1995). Psychotropic drugs and the risk of recurrent falls in ambulatory nursing home residents. *American Journal of Epidemiology, 142,* pp. 202–211.

Thayssen, P., Bjerre, M., Kragh-Sorensen, P., Moller, M., Petersen, O. L., Kristensen, C. B., Gram, L. F. (1981). Cardiovascular effects of imipramine and nortriptyline in elderly patients. *Psychopharmacology, 74,* pp. 360–364.

Thompson, T. L., Moran, M. G., & Nies, A. S. (1983). Psychotropic drug use in the elderly (Part I). *New England Journal of Medicine, 308,* pp. 134–138.

Thompson, T. L., Moran, M. G., & Nies, A. S. (1983). Psychotropic drug use in the elderly (Part II). *New England Journal of Medicine, 308,* pp. 194–199.

Toenniessen, L. M., Casey, D. E., & McFarland, B. H. (1985). Tardive dyskinesia in the aged: Duration of treatment relationships. *Archives of General Psychiatry, 42,* pp. 278–284.

Veith, R. C., & Raskind, M. A. (1988). The neurobiology of aging: Does it predispose to depression? *Neurobiology of Aging, 9,* pp. 101–117.

Von Moltke, L. L., Greenblatt, D. J., Harmatz, J. S., & Shader, R. I. (1995). Psychotropic drug metabolism in old age. In Bloom, F. E., & Kupfer, D. J. (Eds.), *Psychopharmacology: The fourth generation of progress.* New York: Raven Press, pp. 1461–1469.

Waddington, J. L., & Youssef, H. A. (1988). Tardive dyskinesia in bipolar affective disorder: Aging, cognitive dysfunction, course of illness, and exposure to neuroleptics and lithium. *American Journal of Psychiatry, 145,* pp. 613–616.

Wayne, G. J. (1980). Electroconvulsive treatment in the elderly. *Journal of the National Association of Private Psychiatric Hospitals, 11,* pp. 25–27.

Williamson, J., & Chopin, J. (1980). Adverse reactions to prescribed drugs in the elderly: A multicenter investigation. *Age and Ageing, 9,* pp. 73–80.

Withering, W. (1785). *An account of foxglove, and some of its medical uses: With practical remarks on dropsy, and other diseases.* London: G. G. J. and J. Robinson, 1785.

Wolkowitz, O. M., Breier, A., Doran, A., Kelsoe, J., Lucas, P., Paul, S. M., & Pickar, D. (1988). Alprazolam augmentation of the antipsychotic effects of

fluphenazine in schizophrenic patients. *Archives of General Psychiatry, 45,* pp. 664–671.

Wragg, R. E., & Jeste, D. V. (1988). Neuroleptics and alternative treatments: Management of behavioral symptoms and psychosis in Alzheimer's disease and related conditions. *Psychiatric Clinics of North America, 11,* pp. 195–213.

Yassa, R., Nair, V., & Schwartz, G. (1986). Early versus late onset psychosis and tardive dyskinesia. *Biological Psychiatry, 21,* pp. 1291–1297.

Zohar, J., Shapira, B., Oppenheim, G., Ayd, F. J., & Belmaker, R. H. (1985). Addition of estrogen to imipramine in female-resistant depressives. *Psychopharmacology Bulletin, 21,* pp. 705–710.

ENDNOTES

1. Long, S. H. (1994). *Prescription drug coverage and the elderly: Issues and options.* Washington, DC: Public Policy Institute, AARP, p. 2, April, 1994.

2. Salzman, C., Schneider, L. S., & Alexopoulos, G. S. (1995). Pharmacological treatment of depression in late life. In Bloom, F. E., & Kupfer, D. J. (Eds.), *Psychopharmacology: The fourth generation of progress.* New York: Raven Press, pp. 1471–1477; Myers-Robfogel, M. W., & Bosmann, H. B. (1984). Clinical pharmacology in the aged: Aspects of pharmacokinetics and drug sensitivity. In Williams, T. F. (Ed.), *Rehabilitation in the aging.* New York: Raven Press, pp. 23–39.

3. Von Moltke, L. L., Greenblatt, D. J., Harmatz, J. S., & Shader, R. I. (1995). Psychotropic drug metabolism in old age. In Bloom, F. E., & Kupfer, D. J. (Eds.), *Psychopharmacology: The fourth generation of progress* New York: Raven Press, pp. 1461–1469; and Dubovsky, S. L. (1994). Geriatric neuropsychopharmacology. In Coffey, C. E., & Cummings, J. L. (Eds.), *Textbook of geriatric psychiatry.* Washington, DC: American Psychiatric Press, pp. 595–631.

4. Withering, W. (1785). *An account of foxglove, and some of its medical uses: With practical remarks on dropsy, and other diseases.* London: G. G. J. and J. Robinson.

5. Philpot, M., & Puranik, A. (1994). Psychotropic drugs, aging and community care. *Drugs and Aging, 5,* pp. 235–241; Von Moltke, L. L., Greenblatt, D. J., Harmatz, J. S., & Shader, R. I. (1995). Psychotropic drug metabolism in old age. In

Bloom, F. E., & Kupfer, D. J. (Eds.), *Psychopharmacology: The fourth generation of progress.* New York: Raven Press, pp. 1461–1469; Dubovsky, S. L. (1994). Geriatric neuropsychopharmacology. In Coffey, C. E., & Cummings, J. L. (Eds.), *Textbook of geriatric psychiatry.* Washington, DC: American Psychiatric Press, pp. 595–631.

6. Von Moltke, L. L., Greenblatt, D. J., Harmatz, J. S., & Shader, R. I. (1995). Psychotropic drug metabolism in old age. In Bloom, F. E., & Kupfer, D. J. (Eds.), *Psychopharmacology: The fourth generation of progress.* New York: Raven Press, pp. 1461–1469; Daly, M. P., Lamy, P. P., & Richardson, J. P. (1994). Avoiding polypharmacy and iatrogenesis in the nursing home. *Maryland Medical Journal, 43,* pp. 1139–1144.

7. Cadieux, R. J. (1993). Geriatric psychopharmacology: A primary care challenge. *Geriatric Psychopharmacology, 93,* pp. 281–301.

8. Horwitz, G. J., Tariot, P. N., Mead, K., & Cox, C. (1995). Discontinuation of antipsychotics in nursing home patients with dementia. *American Journal of Geriatric Psychiatry, 3,* pp. 290–299; Selma, T. P., Palla, K., Poddig, B., & Brauner, D. J. (1994). Effect of the omnibus reconciliation act 1987 on antipsychotic prescribing in nursing home residents. *Journal of the American Geriatrics Society, 42,* pp. 648–652; Von Moltke, L. L., Greenblatt, D. J., Harmatz, J. S., Shader, R. I. (1995). Psychotropic drug metabolism in old age. In Bloom, F. E., & Kupfer, D. J. (Eds.), *Psychopharmacology: The fourth generation of progress.* New York: Raven Press, pp. 1461–1469.

9. Dubovsky, S. L. (1994). Geriatric neuropsychopharmacology. In Coffey, C. E., & Cummings, J. L. (Eds.), *Textbook of geriatric psychiatry.* Washington, DC: American Psychiatric Press, pp. 595–631; Ouslander, J. (1981). Drug prescribing for the elderly. *Western Journal of Medicine, 135,* pp. 455–462.

10. Avorn, J., Soumerai, S. B., Everitt, D. E., Ross-Degnan, D., Beere, M. H., Sherman, D., Salem-Schatz, S. R., & Fields, D. (1992). A randomized trial of a program to reduce the use of psychoactive drugs in nursing homes. *New England Journal of Medicine, 327,* pp. 68–173.

11. Philpot, M., & Puranik, A. (1994). Psychotropic drugs, aging and community care. *Drugs and Aging, 5,* pp. 235–241; Thompson, T. L., Moran, M. G., & Nies, A. S. (1983). Psychotropic drug use in the elderly (Part I). *New England Journal of Medicine, 308,* pp. 134–138; Thompson, T. L., Moran, M. G., & Nies, A. S. (1983). Psychotropic drug use in the elderly (Part II). *New England Journal of Medicine, 308,* pp. 194–199.

12. Cooper, J. W. (1996). Probable adverse drug reaction in a rural geriatric nursing home population: A four-year study. *Journal of the American Geriatrics Society, 44,* pp. 194–197; Long, J. W. (1989). *The essential guide to prescription drugs; what you need to know for safe drug use,* 2nd ed. New York: Harper & Row.

13. Dubovsky, S. L. (1994). Geriatric neuropsychopharmacology. In Coffey, C. E., & Cummings, J. L. (Eds.), *Textbook of geriatric psychiatry.* Washington, DC: American Psychiatric Press, pp. 595–631.

14. Salzman, C., Schneider, L. S., & Alexopoulos, G. S. In Bloom, F. E., & Kupfer, D. J. (Eds.), *Psychopharmacology: The fourth generation of progress.* New York: Raven Press, pp. 1471–1477; Molchan, S. E., Martinez, R. A., Hill, J. L., Weingartner, H. J., Thompson, K., Vitiello, B., & Sunderland, T. (1992). Increased cognitive sensitivity to scopolamine with age and a perspective on the scopolamine model. *Brain Research Review, 17,* pp. 215–226; Myers-Robfogel, M. W., Bosmann, H. B. (1984). Clinical pharmacology in the aged: Aspects of pharmacokinetics and drug sensitivity. In Williams, T. F. (Ed.), *Rehabilitation in the aging.* New York: Raven Press, pp. 23–39.

15. Ray, W. A., Taylor, J. A., Meador, K. G., Lichtenstein, M. J., Griffin, M. R., et al. (1993). Reducing antipsychotic drug use in nursing homes. *Archives of Internal Medicine, 153,* pp. 713–721; Salzman, C., Schneider, L. S., & Alexopoulos, G. S. (1995). Pharmacological treatment of depression in late life. *Psychopharmacology: The fourth generation of progress.* New York: Raven Press, pp. 1471–1477; Dubovsky, S. L. (1994). Geriatric neuropsychopharmacology. In Coffey, C. E., & Cummings, J. L. (Eds.), *Textbook of geriatric psychiatry.* Washington, DC: American Psychiatric Press, pp. 595–631.

16. Long, S. H. (1994). *Prescription drug coverage and the elderly: Issues and options.* Washington, DC: Public Policy Institute, AARP, p. 2.

17. AARP Public Policy Institute. (1995). *Coming up short: Increasing out-of-pocket health spending by older Americans.* Report #9507, Washington, DC: Public Policy Institute, AARP.

18. Pastors Pharmacy, 136 S. York Rd., Hatboro, Pa. 19040.

19. 1909 K. St., N. W., Washington, D.C. 20049.

20. Von Moltke, L. L., Greenblatt, D. J., Harmatz, J. S., & Shader, R. I. (1995). Psychotropic drug metabolism in old age. In Bloom, F. E., & Kupfer, D. J. (Eds.), *Psychopharmacology: The fourth generation of progress.* New York: Raven Press, pp. 1461–1469.

21. Rockwell, E., Lam, R. W., & Zisook, S. (1988). Antidepressant drug studies in the elderly. *Psychiatric Clinics of North America, 11,* pp. 215–233.

22. Raskind, M. A. (1993). Geriatric psychopharmacology: Management of late-life depression and the noncognitive behavioral disturbances of Alzheimer's disease. *Psychiatric Clinics of North America, 16,* pp. 815–827.

23. *Ibid.*

24. Lebowitz, B. D., Martinez, R. A., Niederehe, G., Pearson, J. L., et al. (1995). Treatment of depression in late-life. *Psychopharmacology, 31*(1), pp. 185–202; Feighner, J. P., Boyer, W. F., Meredith, C. H., Hendrickson, G. (1988). An overview of fluoxetine in geriatric depression. *British Journal of Psychiatry., 153*(3 Suppl), pp. 105–108; Salzman, C., Schneider, L. S., & Alexopoulos, G. S. (1995). Pharmacological treatment of depression in late life. In Bloom, F. E., & Kupfer, D. J. (Eds.), *Psychopharmacology: The fourth generation of progress.* New York: Raven Press, pp. 1471–1477.

25. For a review, see Raskind, M. A. (1993). Geriatric psychopharmacology: Management of late-life depression and the noncognitive behavioral disturbances of Alzheimer's disease. *Psychiatric Clinics of North America, 16,* pp. 815–827; and Salzman, C., Schneider, L. S., & Alexopoulos, G. S. (1995).

Pharmacological treatment of depression in late life. In Bloom, F. E., & Kupfer, D. J. (Eds.), *Psychopharmacology: The fourth generation of progress.* New York: Raven Press, pp. 1471–1477.

26. Jarvik, L. F., Read, S. L., Mintz, J., Neshkes, R. E., Kane, J. M., Cole, K., Sarantakos, S., Howard, A., & Borenstein, M. (1983). Pretreatment orthostatic hypotension in geriatric depression: Predictor of response to imipramine and doxepin. *Journal of Clinical Psychopharmacology, 3,* pp. 368–372.

27. Neshkes, R. E., Gerner, R., Jarvik, L. F., Mintz, J., Joseph, J., Linde, S., Aldrich, J., Conolly, M. E., Rosen, R., & Hill, M. (1985). Orthostatic effect of imipramine and doxepin in depressed geriatric outpatients. *Journal of Clinical Psychopharmacology, 5,* pp. 102–106; Salzman, C., Schneider, L. S., & Alexopoulos, G. S. (1995). Pharmacological treatment of depression in late life. In Bloom, F. E., & Kupfer, D. J. (Eds.), *Psychopharmacology: The fourth generation of progress.* New York: Raven Press, pp. 1471–1477.

28. Salzman, C., Schneider, L. S., & Alexopoulos, G. S. (1995). Pharmacological treatment of depression in late life. In Bloom, F. E., & Kupfer, D. J. (Eds.), *Psychopharmacology: The fourth generation of progress.* New York: Raven Press, pp. 1471–1477.

29. McKeith, I., Fairbairn, A., Perry R., Thompson, P., & Perry, E. (1992). Neuroleptic sensitivity in patients with senile dementia of Lewy body type. *British Medical Journal, 305,* pp. 673–678; Molchan, S. E., Martinez, R. A., Hill, J. L., Weingartner, H. J., Thompson, K., Vitiello, B., & Sunderland, T. (1992). Increased cognitive sensitivity to scopolamine with age and a perspective on the scopolamine model. *Brain Research Review, 17,* pp. 215–226; Sunderland, T., Tariot, P. N., Cohen, R. M., Weingartner, H., Mueller, E. A., & Murphy, D. L. (1987). Anticholinergic sensitivity in patients with dementia of the Alzheimer type and age-matched controls: A dose-response study. *Archives of General Psychiatry, 44,* pp. 418–426.

30. Meyers, B. S., & Mei-Tal, V. (1983). Psychiatric reactions during tricyclic treatment of the elderly reconsidered. *Journal of Clinical Psychopharmacology, 3,* pp. 2–6.

31. Lawlor, B. A., Radcliffe, J., Molchan, S. E., Martinez, R. A., Hill, J. L., & Sunderland, T. (1994). A pilot placebo-controlled study of trazodone and buspirone in Alzheimer's disease. *International Journal of Geriatric Psychiatry, 9,* pp. 55–59; Simpson, P. M., & Foster, D. (1986). Improvement

in organically disturbed behavior with trazodone treatment. *Journal of Clinical Psychiatry, 47,* pp. 191–193.

32. For review see Sunderland, T., Cohen, R. M., Molchan, S., Lawlor, B. A., Mellow, A. M., Newhouse, P. A., Tariot, P. N., Mueller, E. A., & Murphy, D. L. (1994). High-dose selegiline in treatment-resistant older depressive patients. *Archives of General Psychiatry, 51,* pp. 607–615; Rockwell, E., Lam, R. W., & Zisook, S., op. cit., 1988.

33. Pitts, W. M., Fann, W. E., Sajadi, C., & Snyder, S. (1983). Alprazolam in older depressed inpatients. *Journal of Clinical Psychiatry, 44,* pp. 213–215; and Gerner, R. H., op. cit., 1985.

34. Georgotas, A., Friedman, E., McCarthy, M., Mann, J., Krakowski, M., Siegel, R., & Ferris, S. (1983). Resistant geriatric depressions and therapeutic response to monoamine oxidase inhibitors. *Biological Psychiatry, 18,* pp. 195–205.

35. Oreland, L., & Gottfries, C.-G. (1986). Brain and brain monoamine oxidase in aging and in dementia of Alzheimer's type. *Progress in Neuro-Psychopharmacology and Biological Psychiatry, 10,* pp. 533–540; Bridge, T. P., Soldo, B. J., Phelps, B. H., Wise, C. D., Francak, M. J., & Wyatt, R. J. (1985). Platelet monoamine oxidase activity: Demographic characteristics contribute to enzyme activity variability. *Journal of Gerontology, 40,* pp. 23–28; and Georgotas, A., Friedman, E., McCarthy, M., Mann, J., Krakowski, M., Siegel, R., & Ferris, S. (1983). Resistant geriatric depressions and therapeutic response to monoamine oxidase inhibitors. *Biological Psychiatry, 18,* pp. 195–205.

36. Murphy, D. L., Sunderland, T., & Cohen, R. M. (1984). Monoamine oxidase-inhibiting antidepressants: A clinical update. *Psychiatric Clinics of North America, 7,* pp. 549–562.

37. Sunderland, T., Mueller, E. A., Cohen, R. M., Jimerson, D.C., Pickar, D., & Murphy, D. L. (1985). Tyramine pressor sensitivity changes during deprenyl treatment. *Psychopharmacology, 86,* pp. 432–437.

38. Sunderland, T., Cohen, R. M., Molchan, S., Lawlor, B. A., Mellow, A. M., Newhouse, P. A., Tariot, P. N., Mueller, E. A., & Murphy, D. L. (1994). High dose selegiline in treatment-resistant older depressives. *Archives of General Psychiatry, 51,* pp. 607–615.

39. Avorn, J., Soumerai, S. B., Everitt, D. E., Ross-Degnan, D., Beere, M. H., Sherman, D., Salem-Schatz, S. R., & Fields, D. (1992). A randomized trial of a

program to reduce the use of psychoactive drugs in nursing homes. *New England Journal of Medicine, 327,* pp. 168–173; Billig, N., Cohen-Mansfield, J., & Lipson, S. (1991). Pharmacologic treatment of agitation in a nursing home. *Journal of the American Geriatrics Society, 39,* pp. 1002–1005.

40. Tariot, P. N., Frederiksen, K., Erb, R., Leibovici, A., Podgorski, C. A., Asnis, J., & Cox, C. (1995). Lack of Carbamazepine toxicity in frail nursing home patients: a controlled study. *Journal of the American Geriatrics Society, 43,* pp. 1026–1929.

41. Thapa, P. B., Gideon, P., Fought, R. L., Ray, W. A. (1995). Psychotropic drugs and the risk of recurent falls in ambulatory nursing home residents. *American Journal of Epidemiology, 142,* pp. 202–211. Accidental, spontaneous, or hidden hypothermia is one of the winter hazards of age. Risk factors include the phenothiazines, tricyclic antidepressants, diseases that diminish physical activity and thus decrease heat production such as dementia and Parkinsonism, and increased heat loss such as alcohol-induced vasodilation.

42. Samuels, S. C., & Katz, I. (1994). Neuroleptic medication in elderly people. *Current Opinion in Psychiatry, 7,* pp. 358–363; Raskind, M. A. (1993). Geriatric psychopharmacology: Management of late-life depression and the noncognitive behavioral disturbances of Alzheimer's disease. *Psychiatric Clinics of North America, 16,* pp. 815–827; Salzman, C. (1987). Treatment of the elderly agitated patient. *Journal of Clinical Psychiatry, 48,* pp. S19–S22.

43. Sunderland, T., & Silver, M. A. (1988). Neuroleptics in the treatment of dementia. *International Journal of Geriatric Psychiatry, 3,* pp. 79–88.

44. Jeste, D. V., Paulsen, J. S., & Harris, M. J. (1995). Late-onset schizophrenia and other related psychoses. In Bloom, F. E., & Kupfer, D. J. (Eds.), *Psychopharmacology: The fourth generation of progress.* New York: Raven Press, pp. 1437–1446; Wragg, R. E., & Jeste, D. V. (1988). Neuroleptics and alternative treatments: Management of behavioral symptoms and psychosis in Alzheimer's disease and related conditions. *Psychiatric Clinics of North America, 11,* pp. 195–213.

45. Gerrard, J., Chen, V., & Dowd, B. (1995). The impact of the 1987 Federal guidelines on the use of psychotropic drugs in Minnesota nursing homes. *American Journal of Public Health, 85,* pp. 771–776; McKeith, I., Fairbairn, A., Perry, R., Thompson, P., & Perry, E. (1992). Neuroleptic sensitivity in patients with senile dementia of Lewy

body type. *British Medical Journal, 305,* pp. 673–678; Sunderland, T., et al., 1987, *op. cit.*

46. Raskind, M. A. (1993). Geriatric psychopharmacology: Management of late-life depression and the noncognitive behavioral disturbances of Alzheimer's disease. *Psychiatric Clinics of North America, 16,* pp. 815–827.

47. Toenniessen, L. M., Casey, D. E., & McFarland, B. H. (1985). Tardive dyskinesia in the aged: Duration of treatment relationships. *Archives of General Psychiatry, 42,* pp. 278–284.

48. Jeste, D. V., Caligiuri, M. P., Paulsen, J. S., Heaton, R. K., Lacro, J. P., Harris, J., Bailey, A., Fell, R. L., & McAdams, L. A. (1995). Risk of tardive dyskinesia in older patients. *Archives of General Psychiatry, 52,* pp. 756–765; Yassa, R., Nair, V., & Schwartz, G. (1986). Early versus late onset psychosis and tardive dyskinesia. *Biological Psychiatry, 21,* pp. 1291–1297.

49. Waddington, J. L., & Youssef, H. A. (1988). Tardive dyskinesia in bipolar affective disorder: Aging, cognitive dysfunction, course of illness, and exposure to neuroleptics and lithium. *American Journal of Psychiatry, 145,* pp. 613–616.

50. Shaw, S. M., & Opit, L. J. (1976). Need for supervision in the elderly receiving long-term prescription medications. *British Medical Journal, 1,* pp. 505–507.

51. Grammans, R. E., Stringfellow, J. C., Hvizdos, A. J., et al. (1992). Use of buspirone in patients with generalized anxiety disorder and coexisting depressive symptoms: a meta-analysis of eight randomized controlled studies. *Neuropsychobiology, 25,* pp. 193–201.

52. Von Moltke, L. L., Greenblatt, D. J., Harmatz, J. S., & Shader, R. I. (1995). Psychotropic drug metabolism in old age. In Bloom, F. E., & Kupfer, D. J. (Eds.), *Psychopharmacology: The fourth generation of progress.* New York: Raven Press, pp. 1461–1469.

53. *Ibid.*

54. Greenblatt, D. J., Sellers, E. M., & Shader, R. I. (1982). Drug disposition in old age. *New England Journal of Medicine, 306,* pp. 1081–1088.

55. Pitts, W. M., et al., *op. cit.,* 1983.

56. Wolkowitz, O. M., Breier, A., Doran, A., Kelsoe, J., Lucas, P., Paul, S. M., & Pickar, D. (1988). Alprazolam augmentation of the antipsychotic effects of fluphenazine in schizophrenic patients. *Archives of General Psychiatry, 45,* pp. 664–671.

57. Napoliello, M. J. (1986). An interim multicentre report on 677 anxious geriatric out-patients treated

with buspirone. *British Journal of Clinical Practice, 40,* pp. 71–73.

58. Lawlor, B. A., Radcliffe, J., Molchan, S. E., Martinez, R. A., Hill, J. L., & Sunderland, T. (1994). A pilot placebo-controlled study of trazodone and buspirone in Alzheimer's disease. *International Journal of Geriatric Psychiatry, 9,* pp. 55–59; Colenda, C. C. (1988). Buspirone in the treatment of agitated demented patients. *Lancet, ii,* pp. 411–412.

59. Markovitz, P. J. (1993). Treatment of anxiety in the elderly. *Journal of Clinical Psychiatry, 54*(Suppl.5), pp. 64–68.

60. Shulman, K. I., MacKenzie, S., & Hardy, B. (1987). The clinical use of lithium carbonate in old age: A review. *Progress in Neuro-psychopharmacology and Biological Psychiatry, 11,* pp. 159–164.

61. Dubovsky, S. L. (1994). Geriatric neuropsychopharmacology. In Coffey, C. E., & Cummings, J. L. (Eds.), *Textbook of geriatric psychiatry.* Washington, DC: American Psychiatric Press, pp. 595–631.

62. Smith, R. E., & Helms, P. M. (1982). Adverse effects of lithium therapy in the acutely ill elderly patients. *Journal of Clinical Psychiatry, 43,* pp. 94–99.

63. Kaufman, M. W., Cassem, N. H., Murray, G. B., & Jenike, M. (1984). Use of psychostimulants in medically ill patients with neurological disease and major depression. *Canadian Journal of Psychiatry, 29,* pp. 46–49.

64. Jacobsen, A. (1958). The use of ritalin in psychotherapy of depressions of the aged. *Psychiatry Quarterly, 32,* pp. 474–483.

65. Katan, W., & Raskind, M. (1980). Treatment of depression in the mentally ill elderly with methylplenidate. *American Journal of Psychiatry, 137,* pp. 963–965; Branconnier, R. J., & Cole, J. O. (1980). The therapeutic role of methylphenidate in senile organic brain syndrome. In Cole, J. O., & Barrett, J. (Eds.), *Psychopathology in the aged.* New York: Raven Press, pp. 183–195.

66. Frierson, R. L., Wey, J. J., & Tabler, J. B. (1990). Psychostimulants for depression in the medically ill. Pickett, P., Masand, P., & Murray, G. B. Psychostimulant treatment of geriatric depressive disorders secondary to medical illness. *Journal of Geriatric Psychiatry and Neurology, 3,* pp. 146–151; Chiarello, R. J., & Cole, J. O. (1987). Psychostimulants: A reconsideration. *Archives of General Psychiatry, 44,* pp. 286–295.

67. McCall, W. V., Farah, B. A., Reboussin, D., & Colenda, C. (1995). Comparison of the efficacy of titriated, moderate-dose and fixed, high-dose right unilateral ECT in elderly patients. *American Journal of Geriatric Psychiatry, 3,* pp. 317–324; Dubovsky, S. L. (1994). Geriatric neuropsychopharmacology. In Coffey, C. E., Cummings, J. L. (Eds.), *Textbook of geriatric psychiatry.* Washington, DC: American Psychiatric Press, pp. 595–631.

68. Schmidt, P. J., & Rubinow, D. R. (1991). Menopause-related affective disorders: a justification for further study. *American Journal of Psychiatry, 148,* pp. 844–852; Zohar, J., Shapira, B., Oppenheim, G., Ayd, F. J., & Belmaker, R. H. (1985). Addition of estrogen to imipramine in female-resistant depressives. *Psychopharmacology Bulletin, 21,* pp. 705–710.

69. Tariot, P. N., Frederiksen, K., Erb, R., Leibovici, A., Podgorski, C. A., Asnis, J., & Cox, C. (1995). Lack of Carbamazepine toxicity in frail nursing home patients: A controlled study. *Journal of the American Geriatrics Society, 43,* pp. 1026–1929.

70. Dubovsky, S. L. (1994). Geriatric neuropsychopharmacology. In Coffey, C. E., & Cummings, J. L. (Eds.), *Textbook of geriatric psychiatry.* Washington, DC: American Psychiatric Press, pp. 595–631.

71. For more information, contact: The National Sleep Foundation, 1367 Connecticut Ave. NW, Suite 200, Washington, DC 20036; American Sleep Apnea Association, 2025 Pennsylvania Ave. NW, Suite 905, Washington, DC 20006; or Restless Legs Syndrome Foundation, Dept. A., P. O. Box 7050, Rochester, MN 55903–7050. Also see: Klinkenborg, V. (1997, January 5). Awakening to Sleep. *The New York Times Magazine,* pp. 26–31, 41, 48, 51, 55–56.

72. Moran, M. G., Thompson, T. L., & Nies, A. S. (1988). Sleep disorders in the elderly. *American Journal of Psychiatry, 145,* pp. 1369–1377.

73. Reynolds, C. F., Dew, M. A., Monk, T. H. & Hoch, C. C. (1994). Sleep disorders in late life: A biopsychosocial model for understanding pathogenesis and intervention. In Coffey, C. E., Cummings, J. L. (Eds.), *Textbook of geriatric psychiatry.* Washington, DC: American Psychiatric Press, pp. 325–331; Gillin, J. C., Duncan, W. C., Murphy, D. L., Post, R. M., Wehr, T. A., Goodwin, F. K., Wyatt, R. J., & Bunney, W. E. (1981). Age-related changes in sleep in depressed and normal subjects. *Psychiatry Research, 4,* pp. 73–78.

74. Clauw, D. J., Nashel, D. L., Umhau, A., & Katz, P. (1990). Tryptophan-associated eosinophilic connective tissue disease: a new clinical entity? *Jour-*

nal of the American Medical Association, 263, pp. 1502–1506.

75. Shader, R. I., & Greenblatt, D. J. (1982). Management of anxiety in the elderly: The balance between therapeutic and adverse effects. *Journal of Clinical Psychiatry, 43,* pp. 8–18.

76. McCall, W. V., Farah, B. A., Reboussin, D., & Colenda, C. (1995). Comparison of the efficacy of titriated, moderate-dose and fixed, high-dose right unilateral ECT in elderly patients. *American Journal of Geriatric Psychiatry, 3,* pp. 317–324.

77. McCall, W. V., Farah, B. A., Reboussin, D., & Colenda, C. (1995). Comparison of the efficacy of titriated, moderate-dose and fixed, high-dose right unilateral ECT in elderly patients. *American Journal of Geriatric Psychiatry, 3,* pp. 317–324.

78. Squire, L. R. (1984). ECT and memory dysfunction. In Lerer, B., Weiner, R. D., & Belmacker, R. H. (Eds.), *Basic mechanisms of ECT.* London: John Libby, pp. 156–163; Squire, L. R., & Zouzounis, J. A. (1986). ECT and memory: Brief pulse versus sine wave. *American Journal of Psychiatry, 143,* pp. 596–601.

79. Nelson, J. P., & Rosenberg, D. R. (1991). ECT treatment of demented elderly patients with major depression: a retrospective study of efficacy and safety. *Convulsive Therapy, 7,* pp. 157–165; Pettinati, H. M., & Bonner, K. M. (1984). Cognitive functioning in depressed geriatric patients with a history of ECT. *American Journal of Psychiatry, 141,* pp. 49–52.

80. O'Shea, B., Lynch, T., Falvey, J., & O'Mahoney, G. (1987). Electroconvulsive therapy and cognitive improvement in a very elderly depressed patient. *British Journal of Psychiatry, 150,* pp. 255–257.

81. McCall, W. V., Farah, B. A., Reboussin, D., & Colenda, C. (1995). Comparison of the efficacy of titriated, moderate-dose and fixed, high-dose right unilateral ECT in elderly patients. *American Journal of Geriatric Psychiatry, 3,* pp. 317–324; Gaspar, D., & Samarasinghe, L. A. (1982). ECT in psychogeriatric practice: A study of risk factors, indications, and outcome. *Comprehensive Psychiatry, 23,* pp. 170–175.

82. The possible persistence of memory loss after ECT remains controversial. See Devanand, D. P., Verma, A. K., Tirumalasetti, F. & Sackeim, H. A. (1991). Absence of cognitive impairment after more than 100 lifetime ECT treatments. *American Journal of Psychiatry, 148,* pp. 929–932.

83. O'Shea, et. al., *op. cit.,* 1987.

84. Lerer, B. (1986). ECT: Possible mechanisms of action. *Psychopharmacology, 22,* pp. 472–487.

85. Dubovsky, S. L. (1994). Geriatric neuropsychopharmacology. In Coffey, C. E., & Cummings, J. L. (Eds.), *Textbook of geriatric psychiatry.* Washington, DC: American Psychiatric Press, pp. 595–631; Cohen, B. M., & Zubenko, G. S. (1985). Relevance of genetic variability to clinical psychopharmacology. *Psychopharmacology Bulletin, 21,* pp. 641–650.

APPENDIXES

SOURCES OF GERONTOLOGICAL LITERATURE

GENERAL BOOKS
MEDICAL, PSYCHOLOGY, SOCIAL WORK, AND NURSING BOOKS

PERIODICALS
PAMPHLETS, BULLETINS, AND REPORTS

GENERAL BOOKS

Annual review of gerontology and geriatrics. (1980, and all subsequent years). New York: Springer.

Binstock, R. H., & George, L. K. (Eds.) (1995). *Handbook of aging and the social sciences,* 4th ed. Orlando, FL: Academic Press.

Birren, J. E. (Ed.). (1996). *Encyclopedia of gerontology.* San Diego, CA: Academic Press.

Birren, J. E. (Ed.) (1985). *Handbook of aging,* three vols., 2nd ed. New York: Van Nostrand Reinhold

Birren, J. E., Sloane, R. B., & Cohen, G. D. (Eds.). (1992). *Handbook of mental health and aging,* 2nd ed. San Diego, CA: Academic Press.

Birren, J. E., & Schaie, K. W. (Eds.) (1996). *Handbook of the psychology of aging,* 4th ed. Orlando, FL: Academic Press.

Busse, E. W., & Blazer, D. G. (Eds.) (1995). *The American psychiatric press textbook of geriatric psychiatry.* Washington, DC: American Psychiatric Association.

Ferraro, K. F. (1990). *Gerontology: Perspectives and issues.* New York: Springer.

Harris, D. K. (1988). *Dictionary of gerontology.* New York: Greenwood Press.

Hayflick, L. (1994). *How and why we age.* New York: Ballantine Books.

Kastenbaum, R. (Ed.) (1993). *The encyclopedia of adult development.* Phoenix, AZ: Oryx Press.

Maddox, G. L. (Ed.) (1995). *The encyclopedia of aging,* 2nd ed. New York: Springer.

Magai, C., & McFadden, S. H. (Eds.). (1996). *Handbook of emotion, adult development and aging.* Orlando, FL: Academic Press.

McKee, P. (Ed.) (1982). *Philosophical foundations of gerontology.* New York: Human Sciences Press.

McKee, P., & Kauppinen, H. (1987). *The art of aging.* New York: Insight Books.

National Institutes of Health. (1986). *Established populations for epidemiologic studies of the elderly: Research data book.* Baltimore, MD: National Institute on Aging.

Ricklefs, R. E., & Finch, C. E. (1996). *Aging: A natural history.* New York: W. H. Freeman.

Riley, M. W., & Foner, A. (Eds.) (1968, 1969, 1972). *Aging and society: Vol. 1, An inventory of research findings; Vol. 2, Aging and the professions; Vol. 3, A sociology of age stratification.* New York: Russell Sage Foundation.

Schneider, E. L., & Rowe, J. L. (Eds.) (1996). *Handbook of the biology of aging,* 4th ed. Orlando, FL: Academic Press.

Shock, N. W. (1951, 1957, 1963). *A classified bibliography of gerontology and geriatrics: Vol. 1, 1900–1948; Vol. 2, 1948–1955; Vol. 3, 1956–1961.* Stanford, CA: Stanford University Press. [Also see: Shock, N. W. (Published quarterly through 1980). Index to current periodical literature. *Journal of Gerontology.*]

Turner, J. S. (Ed.). (1996). *Encyclopedia of relationships across the lifespan.* Westport, CT: Greenwood Press.

MEDICAL, PSYCHOLOGY, SOCIAL WORK, AND NURSING BOOKS

Abrams, W. B., Beers, M. H., & Berkow, R. (Eds.) (1995). *The Merck manual of geriatrics,* 2nd ed.. Whitehouse Station, NJ: Merck.

Albert, M. S., & Moss, M. B. (Eds.) (1988). *Geriatric neuropsychology.* New York: Guilford Press.

American Psychiatric Association. (1994). *Diagnostic and statistical manual of mental disorders: DSM-IV,* 4th Ed. Washington, DC: American Psychiatric Association.

American Psychiatric Association. (1994). *Diagnostic criteria from DSM-IV.* Washington, DC: American Psychiatric Association.

Bienefeld, D. (1990). *Verwoerdt's clinical geropsychiatry,* 3rd. ed. Baltimore, MD: Williams & Wilkins.

Blazer, D. (1993). *Depression in late life,* 2nd. ed. St. Louis, MO: Mosby Year-Book.

Breckman, R., & Adelman, R. (1988). *Strategies for helping victims of elder mistreatment.* Thousand Oaks, CA: Sage.

Brocklehurst, J. C. (Ed.) (1992). *Textbook of geriatric medicine and gerontology,* 4th ed. New York: Churchill Livingstone.

Burnside, I. M. (1988). *Nursing and the aged: A self care approach,* 3rd ed. New York: McGraw Hill.

Burnside, I., & Schmidt, M. G. (1994). *Working with older adults: Group process.* Boston: Jones & Bartlett.

Calkins, E., Ford, A. B., & Katz, P. R. (Eds.) (1992). *Practice of geriatrics,* 2nd ed. Philadelphia: Saunders.

Cassel, C. K., et. al. (Eds.) (1996). *Geriatric medicine,* 3rd. ed. New York: Springer-Verlag.

Coffey, C. E., & Cummings, J. L. (Eds.) (1994). *Textbook of geriatric psychiatry.* Washington, DC: American Psychiatric Press.

Hazzard, W. R., Andres, R., Bierman, E. L., & Blass, J. P. (Eds.) (1994). *Principles of geriatric medicine and gerontology,* 3rd ed. New York: McGraw Hill.

Institute of Medicine, Committee for a National Research Agenda on Aging Staff. (1991). *Extending life, enhancing life: A national research agenda on aging.* Washington, DC: National Academy Press.

Jenike, M. A. (1989). *Geriatric Psychiatry and Psychopharmacology.* Chicago, IL: Mosby Year-Book.

Kane, R. L., Ouslander, J. G., & Abrass, I. B. (1994). *Essentials of clinical geriatrics.* New York: McGraw Hill.

Kent, B., & Butler, R. N. (Eds.) (1987). *Human aging research: Concepts and techniques.* New York: Lippincott-Raven.

Lazarus, L. W., Jarvik, L. F., Foster, J. R., Lieff, J. D., & Mershon, S. R. (Eds.) (1988). *Essentials of geriatric psychiatry: A guide for health professionals.* New York: Springer.

National Council on the Aging. (1990). *Caregiver support groups in America.* Washington, DC: National Council on the Aging, Department 5087.

Perlmutter, M., & Hall, E. (1992). *Adult development and aging,* 2nd ed.. New York: John Wiley & Sons.

Rowe, J. W., & Besdine, R. W. (1988). *Geriatric medicine,* 2nd ed. Boston: Little, Brown.

Salzman, C. (1992). Clinical Geriatric Psychopharmacology, 2nd ed. Baltimore, MD: Williams & Wilkins.

Shock, N. W., Greulick, R. C., Andres, R., Arenberg, D., Costa, Jr., P. T., Lakatta, E. G., & Tobin, J. D. (1984). *Normal human aging: The Baltimore longitudinal study of aging.* Washington, DC: U.S. Government Printing Office.

Turner, F. J. (Ed.) (1992). *Mental health and the elderly: A social work perspective.* New York: The Free Press.

Warner, H. R., Butler, R. N., Sprott, R. L., & Schneider, E. L. (Eds.) (1987). *Modern biological theories of aging.* New York: Raven Press.

PERIODICALS

AFAR Newsletter. New York: American Federation for Aging Research.

Age and Ageing. British Geriatrics Society and British Society for Research on Ageing. Oxford, England: Oxford University Press.

Ageing International. Montreal, Canada: International Federation on Ageing.

Aging and Mental Health. Oxfordshire, UK, Cambridge, MA, and Cammeray, Australia: Carfax Publishing Company.

Aging Network News. McLean, VA: Hansan Group, Inc.

Aging and Work: A Journal on Age, Work and Retirement, 1978–1984 (formerly *Industrial Gerontology,* 1973–1977). Washington, DC: National Council on Aging.

Alzheimer's Disease and Associated Disorders. Philadelphia: Lippincott-Raven Press.

American Journal of Nursing. (American Nurses' Association) New York: American Journal of Nursing, Co.

American Journal of Public Health. Washington, DC: American Public Health Association.

Behavior, Health and Aging. New York: Springer.

Clinical Gerontologist: The Journal of Aging and Mental Health. Binghamton, NY: The Haworth Press.

Comprehensive Gerontology. Copenhagen: Munksgaard International Publishers. (ceased publication in 1989)

Currents. Washington, DC: American Association of Homes and Services for the Aging.

Contemporary Long Term Care. New York: Bill Communications.

Dementia. Basil, Switzerland: S. Karger AG.

Developmental Psychology. Washington, DC: American Psychological Association.

Educational Gerontology. Bristol, PA: Taylor & Francis.

Generations. San Francisco, CA: The American Society on Aging.

Geriatric Nursing: American Journal of Care for the Aging. St. Louis, MO: Mosby Year-Book.

Geriatrics. Cleveland, OH: Advanstar.

The Gerontologist. Washington, DC: Gerontological Society of America.

Gerontology and Geriatrics Education. Binghamton, NY: The Haworth Press.

Home Health Aide Digest. Kalamazoo, MI: Stonerock & Associates.

Home Health Care Services Quarterly. New York: The Haworth Press.

Human Development (formerly *Vita Humana*). Basel, Switzerland: S. Karger AG.

International Journal of Aging and Human Development. Amityville, NY: Baywood Journals.

International Journal of Geriatric Psychiatry. New York and W. Sussex, England: John Wiley & Sons.

International Journal of Geriatric Psychopharmacology. Hants, UK: Stockton Press.

International Psychogeriatrics. New York: Springer.

The Journal of Aging and Ethnicity. New York: Springer.

Journal of Aging Studies. Greenwich, CT and London, England: JAI Press Inc.

Journal of the American Geriatrics Society. Baltimore, MD: Williams & Wilkins.

Journal of Applied Gerontology. Thousand Oaks, CA: Sage.

Journal of Chronic Diseases. Oxford, England: Pergamon Press.

Journal of Elder Abuse and Neglect. Binghamton, NY: The Haworth Press.

Journal of Geriatric Psychiatry. Madison, CT: International Universities Press.

Journal of Gerontological Nursing. Thorofare, NJ: Slack.

Journal of Gerontological Social Work. Binghamton, NY: The Haworth Press.

Journal of Long-Term Care Administration. Alexandria, VA: American College of Nursing Home Administrators.

Journal of Nutrition for the Elderly. Binghamton, NY: The Haworth Press.

Journal of Women & Aging. Binghamton, NY: The Haworth Press.

Journals of Gerontology (Series A: Biological Sciences and Medical Sciences; Series B: Psychological Sciences and Social Sciences). Washington, DC: Gerontological Society.

Life-Span Development and Behavior. Mahwah, NJ: Lawrence Erlbaum Associates.

Loss, Grief & Care. Binghamton, NY: The Haworth Press.

Maturitas. New York: Elsevier Science.

McKnight's Long Term Care News. (formerly *Today's Nursing Home*) Northfield, IL: McKnight Medical Communications.

Modern Health Care. Chicago, IL: Crain Communications.

Modern Maturity. New York: American Association of Retired Persons.

NCEA Exchange (National Center on Elder Abuse). Newark, DE: College of Human Resources, University of Delaware.

NRTA (National Retired Teachers Association) Bulletin. Washington, DC: American Association of Retired Persons.

The Network. Washington, DC: The Gray Panthers.

Neurobiology of Aging. New York: Elsevier Science.

NSCL Washington Weekly. Washington, DC: National Senior Citizens Law Center.

Nursing Home Medicine. Plainsboro, NJ: MultiMedia HealthCare/Freedom, LLC.

Nursing Homes; Long Term Care Management. Cleveland, OH: Medquest Communications.

Nursing Outlook. (American Academy of Nursing). St. Louis, MO: Mosby Year-Book.

Omega: Journal of Death and Dying. Amityville, New York: Baywood Journals.

Perspective on Aging. Washington, DC: National Council on Aging.

Physical & Occupational Therapy in Geriatrics. Binghamton, NY: The Haworth Press.

Research on Aging: A Quarterly of Social Gerontology and Adult Development. Thousand Oaks, CA: Sage.

Retirement Life. Washington, DC: National Association of Retired Federal Employees.

Senior Citizens News. Silver Spring, MD: National Council of Senior Citizens.

Provider. Washington, DC: American Health Care Association.

Social Work. Washington, DC: National Association of Social Workers.

Women and Aging Letter. Waltham, MA: National Policy and Resource Center on Women and Aging, Brandeis University.

PAMPHLETS, BULLETINS, AND REPORTS

American Association of Retired Persons. *Age Line—* an on-line bibliographic data base available for a small fee.

National Center for Health Statistics. Reports.

National Institute on Aging. *Age Pages.*

Social Security Administration Bulletin.

U.S. Bureau of the Census. Reports.

U.S. Senate Special Committee on Aging. Hearings and Task Force reports.

ORGANIZATIONS PERTAINING TO THE ELDERLY

GENERAL ORGANIZATIONS

ORGANIZATIONS CONCERNED
WITH OLDER WOMEN

LEGAL RESOURCES FOR THE ELDERLY

GENERAL ORGANIZATIONS

AFL-CIO Department of Employee Benefits*
815 16th St. NW
Washington, DC 20006

AFSCME Retiree Program*
1625 L St. NW
Washington, DC 20036

Aging Network Services
Suite 907
4400 East-West Highway
Bethesda, MD 20814
Nationwide for-profit network of private-
practice geriatric social workers who serve as
care managers for older parents who live at a
distance.

Alliance for Aging Research*
2021 K St. NW
Suite 305
Washington, DC 20006

Alzheimer's Association*
919 N. Michigan Ave.
Suite 1000
Chicago, IL 60611-1676
Internet: http://www.alz.org
Information and Chapter Referral:
(800) 272-3900

Alzheimer's Disease Education and Referral
Center
P.O. Box 8250
Silver Spring, MD 20907-8250
Internet:
http://www.alzheimers.org/adear/adcdir.html
Information: (800) 438-4380

American Aging Association (AGE)
2129 Providence Ave.
Chester, PA 19013-5506
Made up of scientists and others, mostly in
the biomedical field, it promotes research in
aging.

American Art Therapy Association
1202 Allanson Rd.
Mundelein, IL 60060
Internet:
http://www.louisville.edu/groups/aata-www/w/

American Academy of Physical Medicine and
Rehabilitation
Suite 2500
One IBM Plaza
Chicago, IL 60611

American Association for Geriatric Psychiatry
7910 Woodmont Ave.
Suite 1350

Bethesda, MD 20814-3004
Internet: http://www.aagpgpa.org/

American Association for Marriage and Family
Therapy
1133 15th St. NW
Suite 300
Washington, DC 20005-2710
Internet: http://www.aamft.org

American Association for International Aging*
1900 L St. NW
Suite 510
Washington, DC 20036-5002

American Association of Homes and Services
for the Aging (AAHSA)*
901 E St. NW
Suite 500
Washington, DC 20004-2037
Internet: http://www.aahsa.org
AAHSA represents nonprofit homes and other
service providers for the aging—religious,
municipal, trust, fraternal.

American Association of Retired Persons
(AARP)*
601 E St. NW
Washington, DC 20049
Internet: http:www.aarp.org

American Association of Senior Physicians
(AASP)
American Medical Association (AMA)
515 North State St.
Chicago, IL 60610
Retired and non-retired physicians and
spouses aged 55 and older whose primary aim
is to advance the rights and benefits of senior
physicians.

American Cancer Society
1599 Clifton Rd. NE
Atlanta, GA 30329
Internet: http://www.cancer.org/
Cancer Response System: (800) ACS-2345

American College of Health Care Administrators
325 S. Patrick St.
Alexandria, VA 22314

American Counseling Association
Association for Adult Development and
Aging
5999 Stevenson Ave.
Alexandria, VA 22304
Internet: http://www.counseling.org/
Information: (800) 347-6647

American Dance Therapy Association (ADTA)
2000 Century Plaza
Suite 108
Columbia, MD 21044

American Diabetes Association
1660 Duke St.
Alexandria, VA 22314
Internet: http://www.diabetes.org

American Federation for Aging Research
(AFAR)
18th Floor
1414 Avenue of the Americas
New York, NY 10019
Internet: http://www.afar.org/

American Foundation for the Blind*
11 Pennsylvania Plaza
Suite 300
New York, NY 10001
Internet: http://www.afb.org/afb
Information: (800) AFB-LINE [232-5463]

American Geriatrics Society*
770 Lexington Ave.
Suite 300
New York, NY 10021
Internet: http://www.americangeriatrics.org
Made up of physicians and other health care
professionals.

American Health Care Association
1201 L St. NW
Washington, DC 20005
Represents nursing home, assisted living, and
subacute care facilities. Provides information
on long-term care.

American Heart Association
7272 Greenville Ave.
Dallas, TX 75231

Internet: http://www.amhrt.org
To find affiliate office:
(800) AHA-USA1 [242-8721]
Stroke Connection:
(800) 553-6321

American Horticultural Therapy Association
362 A Christopher Ave.
Gaithersburg, MD 20879-3660
Internet:
http://www.hort.vt.edu/human/ahta.html
Information: (800) 634-1603

American Legion
700 N. Pennsylvania St.
P.O. Box 1055
Indianapolis, IN 46206
Internet: http://www.legion.org/

American Nurses Association
Council for Community Primary and
Long-Term Care Nursing Practice
Suite 100 W
600 Maryland Ave. SW
Washington, DC 20024-2571
Internet: http://www.nursingworld.org/about.
Information: (800) 274-4262

American Occupational Therapy Association, Inc.
4720 Montgomery Lane
P.O. Box 31220
Bethesda, MD 20824-1220

American Optometric Association
243 N. Lindbergh Blvd.
St. Louis, MO 63141
Internet: http://www.webcom.com/aoanet/
welcome.html

American Osteopathic Association
142 E. Ontario St.
Chicago, IL 60611
Internet: http://www.am-osteo-assn.org/
Information: (800) 621-1773

American Parkinson's Disease Association
Suite 4B
1250 Hylan Blvd.
Staten Island, NY 10305
Information: (800) 223-2732

American Physical Therapy Association
Section on Geriatrics
1111 N. Fairfax St.
Alexandria, VA 22314
http:/www.geriatricpt.org/

American Podiatric Medical Association
9312 Old Georgetown Rd.
Bethesda, MD 20814
Internet: http://www.apma.org/
Foot Care Information Center: (800) FOOT-
CARE [366-8227]

American Psychiatric Association
1400 K St. NW
Washington, DC 20005
Internet: http://www.psych.org/

American Psychological Association
750 First St. NE
Washington, DC 20002
Internet: http:/www.apa.org
Information: (800) 336-5500

American Psychological Association
Division 20: Adult Development and Aging
Lisa C. McGuire Ph.D.
Allegheny College
Department of Psychology
Meadville, PA 16335
Internet:
http://www.iog.wayne.edu/apadiv20/apadiv20.
htm

American Public Health Association
Section of Gerontological Health
1015 15th St. NW
Suite 300
Washington, DC 20005
Internet: http://apha.org/

American Public Welfare Association
810 First St. NE
Suite 500
Washington, DC 20002-4267
Internet: http://apwa.org/

American Red Cross
430 17th St. NW
Washington, DC 20006

Internet: http://www.redcross.org
Local chapters' services are available to older persons without charge. Interesting volunteer opportunities.

American Society for Geriatric Dentistry
211 E. Chicago Ave.
Suite 948
Chicago, IL 60611

American Society on Aging*
833 Market St.
Suite 511
San Francisco, CA 94103
Internet:
http://www.housecall.com/sponsors/asa/asa/index.html

Arthritis Foundation
1314 Spring St. NW
Atlanta, GA 30309
Information: (800) 283-7800
Internet: http://www.arthritis.org

Asian and Pacific Coalition on Aging, Inc.
3100 W. Jefferson Blvd.
Los Angeles, CA 90018

Asociacion Nacional por Personas Mayores—National Association for Hispanic Elderly
3325 Wilshire Blvd.
Suite 800
Los Angeles, CA 90010-1724
Project MAS (More Access to Services): (800) 953-8553

Assisted Living Facilities Association of America
10300 Eaton Pl.
Suite 400
Fairfax, VA 22031

Association for Gerontology Education in Social Work (AGE-SW)
School of Social Work
University of Maryland at Baltimore
525 W. Redwood St.
Baltimore, MD 21201-1777
Internet: http://www.cs.umd.edu/users/conn

Association for Gerontology in Higher Education*
1001 Connecticut Ave NW
Suite 410
Washington, DC 20036-5504
Internet: http://www.aghe.org/

Association for Gerontology and Human Development in Historically Black Colleges and Universities*
1424 K. St. NW
Suite 601
Washington, DC 20005

B'nai B'rith Center for Senior Housing and Services*
1640 Rhode Island Ave, NW
Washington, DC 20036
Internet: http://www.bnaibrith.org/

Brookdale Center on Aging
425 E. 25th St.
New York, NY 10010
Internet: http://www.hunter.cuny.edu/health/htmls/bcoahp.html.
Information:
(800) 64-STAFF [647-8233]

Catholic Golden Age*
430 Penn Ave.
Scranton, PA 18503
Information: (800) 836-5699

Children of Aging Parents
Suite 302-A
1609 Woodbourne Rd.
Levittown, PA 19057
Information and Referral Service: (800) 227-7294

Clearinghouse on Abuse and Neglect of the Elderly (CANE)
College of Human Resources
University of Delaware
Newark, DE 19716

Council of Better Business Bureaus
4200 Wilson Blvd.
Suite 800

Arlington, VA 22203-1804
Internet: http:www.bbb.org

Disabled American Veterans
807 Maine Ave. SW
Washington, DC 20024
Internet: http://www.dav.org

Elder Craftsmen
921 Madison Ave.
New York, NY 10020

Eldercare America, Inc.*
1141 Loxford Terrace
Silver Spring, MD 20901

Elderhostel
80 Boylston St.
Suite 400
Boston, MA 02116
Internet: http://www.elderhostel.org/
This organization provides an international
educational program for people over 60 and a
unique vacation opportunity. Participants live
and eat on campus, and take advantage of
sports, social activities, and choose from
numerous interesting courses.

Episcopal Society for Ministry on Aging
323 Wyandotte St.
Bethlehem, PA 18015

Families USA Foundation (formerly Villers
Foundation)*
1334 G St. NW
Washington, DC 20005
Internet: http://epn.org/families.html

Family Caregiver Alliance
425 Bush St.
Suite 500
San Francisco, CA 94108
Internet: http://www.caregiver.org
Information, education, and services for adults
with cognitive disorders such as Alzheimer's,
stroke, head injury, Parkinson's, and
Huntington's diseases.

Family Services America
11700 W. Lake Park Dr.

Milwaukee, WI 53224
Agencies are located in nearly every state
and in most medium to large cities.
Programs include homemaker services
adapted to meet the needs of older people
and confidential casework to help solve
personal problems.

Foundation for Hospice and Home Care
513 C St. NE
Washington, DC 20002

French Foundation for Alzheimer Research
Suite 820
11620 Wilshire Blvd.
Los Angeles, CA 90025
Information: (800) 477-2243

Generations United
c/o CWLA
440 First St. NW
Suite 310
Washington, DC 20001-2086
Internet: http://www.gu.org

The Gerontological Society of America*
1275 K. St. NW
Suite 350
Washington, DC 20005-4006
Internet: http://www.geron.org
Professional society that promotes the
scientific study of aging in the biological,
medical, and social sciences.

Gray Panthers*
2025 Pennsylvania Ave. NW
Suite 821
Washington, DC 20006
Information: (800) 280-5462
Activist group of older people working for
social change.

Green Thumb, Inc.*
2000 N. 14th St.
Suite 800
Arlington, VA 22201
Promotes employment and training
opportunities for older people, particularly
providing essential community services.

Group for the Advancement of Psychiatry
P.O. Box 28218
Dallas, TX 75228

Homedco
3800 Annapolis Lane
Suite 195
Minneapolis, MN 55447
Provides respiratory and infusion therapy, and
rents and sells medical equipment.

Huntington's Disease Society of America
140 W. 22nd St.
6th Floor
New York, NY 10011-2420
Information: (800) 345-4372

Impotence World Association
Impotence Institute of America
Impotence World Services
(includes Impotents Anonymous and I-Anon)
10400 Little Patuxent Parkway
Suite 485
Columbia, MD 21044-3502
Information: (800) 660-1603

The Institute for Retired Professionals
The New School for Social Research
60 W. 12th St.
New York, NY 10011
This pioneering school led the way in
providing intellectual activities for retired
professional people.

The International Federation on Aging
380 St. Antoine St. SW
Suite 3200
Montreal, PQ, Canada H2Y 3X7
Confederation of aging organizations of
various nations.

International Institute on Ageing
(United Nations—Malta)
117 St. Paul St.
Valletta, Malta
Internet: http://www.inia.org.mt

International Hearing Society
20361 Middlebelt Rd.
Livonia, MI 48152

Information: (800) 521-5247
Society of hearing aid specialists.

International Longevity Center—U.S.
1216 Fifth Ave.
Room 552
New York, NY 10029

International Psychogeriatric Association
5700 Old Orchard Rd.
Skokie, IL 60077

International Senior Citizens Organization
255 S. Hill St.
Suite 409
Los Angeles, CA 90012

Mature Outlook
P.O. Box 10448
Des Moines, IA 50306
Information: (800) 336-6330
This for-profit organization for individuals
over 50 provides benefits, services, discounts
and information to members.

Medic Alert Foundation International
1735 N. Lynn St.
Suite 950
Arlington, VA 22209-2022

National Alliance of Senior Citizens
1700 18th St. NW
Suite 401
Washington, DC 20002
Lobbies state and federal legislatures.

National Asian Pacific Center on Aging*
Melbourne Tower, Suite 914
1511 3rd Ave.
Seattle, WA 98101

National Association for Continence (NAFC)
P.O. Box 8310
Spartanburg, SC 29305-8310
Information:
(800) BLADDER [252-3337]

National Association for Home Care*
228 7th St. SE
Washington, DC 20003
Internet: http://www.nahc.org/

National Association for Human Development
  1424 16th St. NW
  Suite 102
  Washington, DC 20036
  Information: (800) 424-5153

National Association for Independent Living
  Independent Association
  55 City Hall Plaza
  Brockton, MA 12401

National Association for Music Therapy
  1 Station Plaza
  Ossining, NY 10562

National Association for Senior Living
Industries
  184 Duke of Gloucester St.
  Annapolis, MD 21404-2523
  NASLI is a nonprofit association of
  companies and organizations who provide
  services to older persons. Its aim is to
  improve the quality of living environments
  available to older Americans through applied
  research, counseling, training, and education
  of the industry and the general public.

National Association of Activity Professionals
  1401 I St. NW
  Suite 900
  Washington, DC 20005

National Association of Area Agencies on
Aging*
  1112 16th St. NW
  Suite 100
  Washington, DC 20036-4823

National Association of Black Social
Workers, Inc.
  8436 West McNichols
  Detroit, MI 48221

National Association of Community
Health Centers
  1330 New Hampshire Ave NW
  Suite 122
  Washington, DC 20036

National Association of Counties
Aging Program

  440 1st St. NW
  8th Floor
  Washington, DC 20001
  Internet: http://www.naco.org

National Association of Foster Grandparent
Program Directors*
  Union/Snyder FGP
  Laurelton Center
  Box 300
  Laurelton, PA 17835

National Association of Meal Programs*
  1414 Prince St.
  Suite 202
  Alexandria, VA 22314

National Association of Nutrition and Aging
Services Programs*
  2675 44th St. SW
  Suite 305
  Grand Rapids, MI 49509

The National Association of Professional
Geriatric Care Managers
  1604 North Country Club Rd.
  Tucson, AZ 85716

National Association of Retired Federal
Employees*
  1533 New Hampshire Ave. NW
  Washington, DC 20036
  Internet: http://www.narfe.org/

National Association of Retired Senior Volunteer
Program Directors, Inc.*
  Audobon Area RSVP
  1650 W. 2nd St.
  Owensboro, KY 42301

National Association of Senior Companion
Project Directors*
  Senior Companion Program
  Lutheran Social Service of Minnesota
  2414 Park Ave.
  Minneapolis, MN 55404

National Association of Social Workers
  750 1st St. NE
  Suite 700
  Washington, DC 20002

National Association of State Units on Aging*
  1225 I St. NW
  Suite 725
  Washington, DC 20005
  Information: (800) 989-6537
  Eldercare Locator: (800) 677-1116
  Information resources on state policies on aging. Represents and lobbies for state agencies at the federal level.

National Association of the Deaf
  814 Thayer Ave.
  Silver Springs, MD 20910

National Caucus and Center on Black Aged, Inc.*
  1424 K. St. NW
  Suite 500
  Washington, DC 20005
  Provides comprehensive program of coordination, information, and consultative services to meet the needs of older African Americans to improve their quality of life.

National Center for Vision and Aging
  The Lighthouse, Inc.
  111 E. 59th St.
  New York, NY 10022
  Information and Resource Service:
  (800) 334-5497

National Center on Elder Abuse
  810 1st St. NE
  Suite 500
  Washington, DC 20002-1267
  Internet: http://www.interinc.com/NCEA

National Citizens' Coalition for Nursing Home Reform
  1424 16th St. NW
  Suite 202
  Washington, DC 20036-2211

National Committee for the Prevention of Elder Abuse, Inc.
  Medical Center of Central Massachusetts
  Institute on Aging
  119 Belmont St.
  Worcester, MA 01605

National Committee to Preserve Social Security and Medicare*
  2000 K St. NW
  Suite 800
  Washington, DC 20006
  Internet: http://ncpssm.org
  Senior Flash Hotline (800) 998-0180

National Conference of State Legislatures
  1560 Broadway
  Suite 700
  Denver, CO 80202
  Internet: http://www.ncsl.org

National Consumers League
  1701 K St. NW
  Suite 1200
  Washington, DC 20006
  National Fraud Information Center: (800) 876-7060
  Internet://www.fraud.org

National Council of Senior Citizens*
  1331 F St. NW
  Washington, DC 20009
  Internet: http://www.ncscinc.org
  Represents and lobbies for the needs of older persons. Membership at any age.

The National Council on Aging, Inc.*
  409 3rd St. SW
  Second Floor
  Washington, DC 20024
  Research and service regarding older persons.

National Family Caregivers Association
  9621 E. Bexhill Dr.
  Kensington, MD 20895-3104
  Internet: http://www.nfcacares.org
  Information: (800) 896-3650

National Federation of Licensed Practical Nurses
  1418 Aversboro Rd.
  Garner, NC 27529-4547

National Gerontological Nursing Association
  7250 Parkway Dr.

Suite 510
Hanover, MD 21076
Information: (800) 723-0560

National Hispanic Council on Aging*
2713 Ontario Rd. NW
Suite 200
Washington, DC 20009

National Hospice Organization
1901 N. Moore St.
Suite 901
Arlington, VA 22209
Internet: http://www.nho.org
Hospice Referral Line: (800) 658-8898

National Indian Council on Aging
City Centre
6400 Uptown Blvd. NE
Suite 510W
Albuquerque, NM 87110

National Institute of Senior Centers
c/o National Council on the Aging
409 3rd St. SW
2nd Floor
Washington, DC 20024

National Institute on Adult Daycare
c/o National Council on the Aging
409 3rd St. SW
2nd Floor
Washington, DC 20024

National Interfaith Coalition on Aging
National Council on the Aging
409 3rd St. SW
Suite 200
Washington, DC 20024
Coordinates the involvement of religious
groups in meeting the needs of the elderly.

National League for Nursing
350 Hudson St.
New York, NY 10014
Internet: http://www.nln.org
Information: (800) 669-1659

National Long Term Care Ombudsman
Resource Center

National Citizens' Coalition for Nursing
Home Reform
1424 16th St. NW
Suite 202
Washington, DC 20036-2211

National Mental Health Association
1021 Prince St.
Alexandria, VA 22314-2971
Internet: http://www.nmha.org
Information:
(800) 969-NMHA [969-6642]

National Osteoporosis Foundation*
1150 17th St. NW
Suite 500
Washington, DC 20036-4603
Internet: http://www.nof.org

National Policy Resource Center on Nutrition
and Aging
Florida International University
Department of Dietetics and Nutrition, OE200
Miami, FL 33199

National Resource Center on Long Term Care
National Association of State Units on Aging
1225 I St. NW
Suite 725
Washington, DC 20005

National Retired Teachers Association
Division of AARP
601 E St. NW
Washington, DC 20042
Members once active in an educational
system, public or private.

National Self-Help Clearinghouse
25 W. 43rd St.
Rm. 620
New York, NY 10036

National Senior Service Corps Directors
Associations*
4958 Butterworth Place NW
Washington, DC 20016

National Society to Prevent Blindness
500 E. Remington Rd.

Schaumberg, IL 60173
Center for Sight: (800) 331-2020
Through local societies in many states, it
promotes and supports local glaucoma
screening programs and provides consultation
and information to individuals with eye
problems.

National Stroke Association
8480 East Orchard Rd.
Suite 1000
Englewood, CO 80111-5015
Internet: http://www.stroke.org

National Therapeutic Recreation Society
2775 S. Quincy St.
Suite 300
Arlington, VA 22206

National Voluntary Organizations for
Independent Living for the Aging (NVOILA)
National Council on Aging
409 3rd St. SW
Suite 200
Washington, DC 20024

North American Association of Jewish Homes
and Housing for the Aging*
316 Pennsylvania Ave SE
Suite 402
Washington, DC 20003-1175

Retired Officers Association
201 N. Washington St.
Alexandria, VA 22314-2529
Internet: http://www.troa.org
Represents the needs of retired U.S. military
officers.

The Salvation Army
National Headquarters
615 Slaters Ln.
Alexandria, VA 22313
Its services for older people include
educational, cultural, recreational, and
religious activities, in addition to camping and
limited residence facilities.

Senior Action in a Gay Environment (SAGE)
208 W. 13th St.

New York, NY 10011
Serves the older gay community.

SeniorNet
One Kearney St.
3rd Floor
San Francisco, CA 94108
Internet: http://www.seniornet.org
Information: (800)747-6848
National nonprofit organization teaches older
people computer skills, and maintains on-line
network.

Sexuality Information and Education Council of
the United States
130 W. 42nd St.
Suite 350
New York, NY 10036-7802
Internet://www.siecus.org
Part of its program is to provide sex
information to older people.

Society for Neuroscience
11 Dupont Circle NW
Suite 500
Washington, DC 20036
Internet: http://www.sfa.org

United Auto Workers Retired Members
Department*
8731 E. Jefferson Ave.
Detroit, MI 48214

United Seniors Health Cooperative
1331 H St. NW
Suite 500
Washington, DC 20005-4706
Internet: http://www.mgt.com/ushc

U.S. Conference of Mayors
1620 Eye St. NW
Washington, DC 20006
Internet: http://www.usmayors.org/uscm

* Denotes membership in the Leadership Council of
Aging Organizations, 1997. The LCAO is a voluntary
coalition of national organizations concerned with the
well-being of the elderly and committed to representing
the elderly and the elderly's interests in the federal policy arena. The coalition is chaired on a rotating basis by
a different member organization each year.

ORGANIZATIONS CONCERNED
WITH OLDER WOMEN

AARP Women's Initiative
  American Association of Retired Persons
  1909 K. St. NW
  Washington, DC 20049

American College of Obstetricians and
Gynecologists
  409 12th St. SW
  Washington, DC 20024-2188
  Internet: http://www.acog.com

International Menopause Society
  Avenue de Broqueville 116
  Boîte 9
  B-1200 Brussels, Belgium

National Action Forum for Midlife and Older
Women
  Box 816
  Stony Brook, NY 11790-0609

National Black Women's Health Project
  1237 Abernathy Blvd. SW
  Atlanta, GA 30310

National Organization for Women
  1000 16th St. NW
  Suite 700
  Washington, DC 20006
  Internet: http://www.now.org

National Policy and Resource Center on Women
and Aging
  Heller School MS 035
  Brandeis University
  P.O. Box 9110
  Waltham, MA 02254-9110

National Women's Health Network
  514 10th St. NW
  Suite 400
  Washington, DC 20004

National Women's Health Resource Center
  2425 L. St. NW
  Washington, DC 20037

The National Women's Political Caucus
  1211 Connecticut Ave. NW

  Suite 425
  Washington, DC 20036
  Internet: http://www.feminist.com/nwpc.html

North American Menopause Society
  P.O. Box 94527
  Cleveland, OH 44101
  Internet: http://www.menopause.org

Older Women's League*
  666 11th St. NW
  Suite 700
  Washington, DC 20001
  Chapter Information:
  (800) TAKE-OWL [825-3695]

Wider Opportunities for Women and the
National Commission on Working Women
  815 15th St. NW
  Suite 916
  Washington, DC 20005

Women's Bureau
  U.S. Dept. of Labor
  200 Constitution Ave. NW
  Room S-3002
  Washington, DC 20210-0002
  Internet: http://www.dol.gov/dol/wb
  Information: (800) 827-5335

Women Work!
  National Network for Women's Employment
  1625 K. St. NW
  Suite 300
  Washington, DC 20006

LEGAL RESOURCES FOR THE ELDERLY

Black Elderly Legal Assistance Support Project
  National Bar Association
  1225 11th St. NW
  Washington, DC 20001

The Center for Social Gerontology
  2307 Shelby Ave.
  Ann Arbor, MI 48103
  Focus is on legal rights, guardianship and
  alternative protective services, and delivery of
  legal services.

Commission on the Legal Problems of the
Elderly
American Bar Association
740 15th St. NW
Washington, DC 20005-1009
Internet:
http://www.abnet.org/elderly/home.html
A 15 member interdisciplinary commission
which focuses on Social Security, housing,
long-term care, age discrimination, and
improving the availability of legal
services.

Eldercare Initiative in Consumer Law
National Consumer Law Center, Inc.
18 Tremont St.
Suite 400
Boston, MA 02108

Legal Counsel for the Elderly, Inc.
American Association for Retired Persons
601 E St. NW
Washington, DC 20049

Legal Services for the Elderly
130 W. 42nd St.
17th Floor
New York, NY 10036

The National Academy of Elder Law
Attorneys, Inc.
1604 N. Country Club Rd.
Tucson, AZ 85716
Internet:
http://www.primenet.com/~rbf/naela.html
Provides information, education, networking,
and assistance to attorneys, bar organizations,
and other individuals or groups advising
elderly clients and their families.

National Clearinghouse for Legal Services, Inc.
205 W. Monroe St.
2nd Floor

Chicago, IL 60606-5013
Internet: http://nclsplp.com

National Eldercare Legal Assistance Project
National Senior Citizens Law Center
1815 H St. NW
Suite 700
Washington, DC 20006

National Senior Citizens Law Center*
1815 H St. NW
Suite 700
Washington, DC 20006
Internet: http://www.nsclc.org
A national support center, specializing in the
legal problems of the older poor, funded by
the Legal Services Corporation, the Administration on Aging, and the Community
Services Administration. Its principal function
is to provide support services to legal service
attorneys and other publicly funded programs
providing legal assistance to older persons.

Pension Rights Center
918 16th St. NW
Suite 704
Washington, DC 20006
Offers pension attorney referral service.

Selected Legal Reference Books

Arnason, S., Rosenzweig, E., & Koski, A.
(1995). *The legal rights of the elderly.* New
York: Practicing Law Institute.

Frolik, L. A., & Brown, M. C. (1992,
supplemented semi-annually). *Advising the
elderly client.* Boston: Warren, Gorham &
Lamont.

Strauss, P. J., & Lederman, N. M. (1996). *The
elder law handbook.* New York: Facts on File,
Inc.

APPENDIX C

GOVERNMENT PROGRAMS
FOR THE ELDERLY

VOLUNTEER AND EMPLOYMENT
PROGRAMS FOR OLDER PEOPLE

FEDERAL, CONGRESSIONAL, AND
EXECUTIVE OFFICES CONCERNED
WITH OLDER PEOPLE

STATE AND LOCAL GOVERNMENT OFFICES
CONCERNED WITH OLDER PEOPLE

VOLUNTEER AND EMPLOYMENT PROGRAMS FOR OLDER PEOPLE

VOLUNTEER EMPLOYMENT PROGRAM	SPONSOR	PURPOSE	ADDRESS
RSVP (Retired Senior Volunteer Program)	Corporation for National Service—National Senior Service Corps	Funds for volunteer programs in public and nonprofit institutions; volunteers reimbursed for expenses	RSVP, Corporation for National Service, 1201 New York Ave. NW, Washington, DC 20525; Internet: http://www.cns.gov; Information: (800) 424-8867
Foster Grandparent Program	Corporation for National Service—National Senior Service Corps	Foster grandparents serve 20 hours a week caring for mentally disabled, physically disabled, or troubled children and young people.	Foster Grandparent Program, Corporation for National Service, 1201 New York Ave. NW, Washington, DC 20525; Internet: http://www.cns.gov; Information: (800) 424-8867
Senior Companions Program	Corporation for National Service—National Senior Service Corps	Senior Companions serve 20 hours a week assisting seniors who have difficulty with daily living tasks.	Senior Companions Program, Corporation for National Service, 1201 New York Ave. NW, Washington, DC 20525;

(Continued)

VOLUNTEER EMPLOYMENT PROGRAM	SPONSOR	PURPOSE	ADDRESS
			Internet: http://www.cns.gov; Information: (800) 424-8867
AmeriCorps*VISTA (Volunteers in Service to America)	Corporation for National Service	Adult volunteers of all ages serve in disadvantaged communities in the United States.	AmeriCorps*VISTA, Corporation for National Service, 1201 New York Ave. NW, Washington, DC 20525; Internet: http://www.cns.gov; Information: (800) 942-2677
Peace Corps	Independent federal agency	Overseas service	Peace Corps, 1990 K St. NW, Washington, DC 10526; Internet: http://www. peacecorps.gov; Information (800) 424-8580.
Older American Act Programs	Administration on Aging	Volunteers augment paid staff at local aging agencies, help with senior meal programs, and/or deliver meals to homebound elderly.	Contact local Area Agency on Aging or call AoA's Eldercare Locator: (800) 677-1116.
SCORE (Service Corps of Retired Executives) Association	U.S. Department of Commerce, Small Business Administration	Retired businesspersons advise novices in business.	SCORE, 409 3rd St. SW, 4th Floor, Washington, DC 20024; Internet: http://www.sbaonline. sba.gov/SCORE/
Senior Community Service Employment Program (SCSEP)	U.S. Department of Labor (state and territorial governments and 10 national sponsors that administer this program, see below)	Part-time employment opportunities for low-income persons aged 55 and older, also promotes transition to unsubsidized employment.	Senior Community Service Employment Program, 200 Constitution Ave. NW, Room C4524, Washington, DC 20210
Senior Environmental Employment Program	Environmental Protection Agency and Administration on Aging	Provides funding for people aged 55 and older to work with EPA Pollution abatement and control programs.	Senior Environmental Employment Program, 401 M St. SW, 3711 Mall, Washington DC 20460.

VOLUNTEER EMPLOYMENT PROGRAM	SPONSOR	PURPOSE	ADDRESS
Volunteers in Parks	National Park Service	Volunteers in national parks	Volunteers in Parks, National Park Service, P.O. Box 37127, Washington, DC 20013-7127.
International Executive Service Corps (IESC)	Independent organization supported by government and nongovernment funds	Overseas service by executives	International Executive Service Corps (IESC), 333 Ludlow St., Stamford, CT 06902

SENIOR COMMUNITY SERVICE EMPLOYMENT PROGRAM (SCSEP) NATIONAL SPONSORS

1. Green Thumb, Inc., Senior Community Service Employment Program, 2000 North 14th St., Suite 800, Arlington, VA 22201
2. National Senior Citizen's Education and Research Center, Senior AIDES, 8403 Colesville Rd., Suite 1200, Silver Spring, MD 20910
3. National Council on the Aging, Inc., Senior Community Service Employment Program, 409 3rd St. SW, Suite 200, Washington, DC 20024
4. American Association of Retired Persons, Senior Community Service Employment Program, 601 E. St. NW, Washington, DC 20049
5. Asociacion Nacional por Personas Mayores, Senior Community Service Employment Program, 3325 Wilshire Blvd., Suite 800, Los Angeles, CA 90010
6. National Caucus/Center on Black Aged, Inc., Senior Community Service Employment Program, 1424 K. St. NW, Suite 500, Washington, DC 90010
7. National Indian Council on Aging, Inc., Senior Community Service Employment Program, 6400 Uptown Blvd. NE, City Center, Suite 510 West, Albuquerque, NM 87100
8. National Asian Pacific Center on Aging, Senior Community Service Employment Program, Melbourne Tower, 1511 3rd Ave., Suite 914, Seattle, WA 98101
9. National Urban League, Inc., Seniors in Community Service Program, 500 E. 82nd St., 11th Floor, New York, NY 10021
10. USDA—Forest Service, Senior Community Service Employment Program, Human Resource Programs, 1621 N. Kent St., Room 1010, RP-E, Rosslyn, VA 22209

FEDERAL, CONGRESSIONAL, AND EXECUTIVE OFFICES CONCERNED WITH OLDER PEOPLE

The following is a selected list of the many federal offices that deal with older people. For more information contact the Administration on Aging, or see the *Directory of Aging Resources,* published yearly by Business Publishers, Inc. in Silver Spring, MD. Information can also be obtained by contacting Federal Information Centers (FICs), part of the General Service Administration. If your local phone directory does not list a Federal Information Center, call (301) 722-9000, or reach their home page (http://www.gsa.gov/et/fic-firs/fichome.htm) for a list of local phone numbers. Several areas have toll-free numbers available.

Legislative Branch

1. U.S. Senate (http://www.senate.gov)
   a. U.S. Senate Special Committee on Aging
      G31 Dirksen Senate Office Building
      Washington, DC 20510
      Internet: http://www.senate.gov/~aging/
   b. U.S. Senate Committee of Labor and Human Resources Special Subcommittee on Aging
      615 Hart Senate Office Building
      Washington, DC 20510
   c. U.S. Senate Finance Committee Health Subcommittee
      219 Dirksen Senate Office Building
      Washington, DC 20510
   d. U.S. Senate Finance Committee Social Security and Family Policy Subcommittee
      219 Dirksen Senate Office Building
      Washington, DC 20510
   e. U.S. Senate Veterans' Affairs Committee
      412 Russell Senate Office Building
      Washington, DC 20510
   f. U.S. Senate Appropriations Committee Subcommittee on Labor, Health, Human Services, and Education
      184 Dirksen Senate Office Building
      Washington, DC 20510

2. U.S. House of Representatives (http://www.house.gov)
   a. Education and the Workforce Committee Early Childhood, Youth and Families Subcommittee (has jurisdiction over Older Americans Act programs)
      2181 Rayburn House Office Building
      Washington, DC 20515
   b. Appropriations Committee Subcommittee on Labor, Health, Human Services and Education
      2358 Rayburn House Office Building
      Washington, DC 20515
   c. Veteran's Affairs Committee
      335 Cannon House Office Building
      Washington, DC 20515-6335
   d. Ways and Means Committee
      I. Health Subcommittee
         1136 Longworth House Office Building
         Washington, DC 20515
      II. Human Resources Subcommittee
         B317 Rayburn House Office Building
         Washington, DC 20515
      III. Social Security Subcommittee
         B317 Rayburn House Office Building
         Washington, DC 20515
   e. House Older Americans Caucus
   f. House Congressional Social Security Caucus
      2407 Rayburn House Office Building
      Washington, DC 20515

Executive Branch

1. U.S. Department of Health and Human Services
   200 Independence Ave. SW

Washington, DC 20201
Internet: http://www.dhhs.gov

a. Administration on Aging
Department of Health and Human
Services
330 Independence Ave. SW
Washington, DC 20201
Internet: http://www.aoa.dhhs.gov
Eldercare Locator: (800) 677-1116

  I.   10 AoA Regional Offices

  II. 57 State Agencies (or Units) on
       Aging (see below)

  III. 660 Area Agencies on Aging

  IV. Title VI Programs for Older
       Indians, Alaska Natives, and Native
       Hawaiians

  V.   AoA Supported Resource Centers

   (1) National Resource Centers for
       Long-Term Care
       National Resource Center on
       Long Term Care
       National Association of State
       Units on Aging
       1225 I St. NW
       Suite 725
       Washington, DC 20005

   (2) National Long-Term Care
       Omsbudman Resource Center
       National Citizens' Coalition for
       Nursing Home Reform
       1424 16th St. NW
       Suite 202
       Washington, DC 20036-2211

   (3) National Center on Elder Abuse
       810 1st St. NE
       Suite 500
       Washington, DC 20002-1267
       Internet:
       http://www.interinc.com/NCEA

   (4) National Policy and Resource
       Center on Nutrition and Aging
       Florida International University
       Department of Dietetics and

Nutrition, OE200
Miami, FL 33199

   (5) National Policy and Resource
       Center on Women and Aging
       Heller School MS 035
       Brandeis University
       P.O. Box 9110
       Waltham, MA 02254-9110

   (6) National Minority Aging
       Organizations

   (7) National Resource Centers for
       Older Indians, Alaska Natives,
       and Native Hawaiians

  VI. Legal Assistance for the Elderly
       Support Centers

  VII. National Aging Information Center
       (NAIC)
       Administration on Aging
       330 Independence Ave. SW
       Room 4656
       Washington, DC 20201
       Internet: http://www.ageinfo.org

b. Agency for Health Care Policy and
   Research (AHCPR)
   Department of Health and Human
   Services
   2101 E. Jefferson St.
   Suite 600
   Rockville, MD 20852
   Internet: http://www.ahcpr.gov

c. Health Care Financing Administration
   (HCFA) (Administers Medicare and
   Medicaid)
   P.O. Box 340
   Columbia, MD 21045
   Medicare Hotline: (800) 638-6833
   Internet: http://www.hcfa.gov

d. National Institutes of Health
   Division of Public Information
   9000 Rockville Pike
   Bethesda, MD 20892
   Internet: http://www.nih.gov

  I.   National Institute on Aging (NIA)
       Public Information Office

National Institutes of Health
9000 Rockville Pike
Building 31, Room 5C27
Bethesda, MD 20892-2292
Internet: http:www.nih.gov/nia
Information Clearinghouse: (800)
222-2225, TTY (800) 222-4225

II.   National Institute of Mental Health
(NIMH)
Public Affairs
National Institutes of Health
5600 Fishers Lane
Room 7C-99
Rockville, MD 20857
Internet: http://www.nimh.nih.gov

III. National Cancer Institute
Office of Cancer Communications
Building 31, Room 10A07
31 Center Dr. MSC 2580
Bethesda, MD 20892-2580
Internet: http://www.nci.nih.gov
Cancer Information Service:
(800) 4-CANCER [422-6237]

IV.   National Eye Institute
Information Office
900 Rockville Pike
Building 31, Room 6A32
Bethesda, MD 20892-2510
Internet: http://www.nei.nih.org

V.   National Institute of Arthritis and
Musculoskeletal and Skin Diseases
31 Center Dr., MSC 2350
Building 31, Rm. 4C32
Bethesda, MD 20892-2350
Internet: http://www.nih.gov/niams

VI.   National Institute on Deafness and
Other Communication Disorders
National Institutes of Health
31 Center Dr., MSC 2320
Bethesda, MD 20892
Internet: http://www.nih.gov/nidcd

e. Federal Council on Aging (Advises the
President, the Secretary of Health and
Human Services, the Assistant Secretary
on Aging, and Congress on matters

relating to the needs of older
Americans.)
Wilbur J. Cohen Building
330 Independence Ave., SW
Room 4661
Washington, DC 20210

f. Substance Abuse and Mental Health
Services Administration (SAMHSA)
Public Health Service
Parklawn Building
5600 Fishers Ln.
Room 12-105
Rockville, MD 20857
Internet: http://www.samhsa.gov

I.   Center for Mental Health Services
Internet: http://www.samhsa.gov/
cmhs/cmhs.htm
National Mental Health Services
Knowledge Exchange Program
(KEN)
P.O. Box 424901
Washington, DC 20015
Information: (800) 789-2647
Internet: http://www.mentalhealth.org

II.   Center for Substance Abuse
Prevention (CSAP)
Internet: http://www.samhsa.gov/
csap/csap.htm

III. Center for Substance Abuse
Treatment (CSAT)
Internet: http://www.samhsa.gov/
csat/csat.htm
National Drug and Alcohol
Treatment Routing Service:
(800) 662-HELP (4357)

IV.   National Clearinghouse for Alcohol
and Drug Information (NCADI)
P.O. Box 2345
Rockville, MD 20847-2345
Internet: http://www.health.org
Information and Publications:
(800) 729-6686

V.   National Resource Center for the
Prevention of Alcohol, Tobacco,
Other Drug Abuse and Mental

Illness in Women
Information: (800) 354-8824

g. Health Resources and Services
Administration
Public Health Service
Parklawn Building
5600 Fishers Ln.
Room 14-05
Rockville, MD 20857
Internet: http://www.hrsa.dhhs.gov

I. The Interdisciplinary, Geriatrics, and
Allied Health Branch (Supports
Geriatric Education Centers)
Division of Associated, Dental, and
Public Health Professions
Bureau of Health Professions
Health Resources and Services
Administration
5600 Fishers Lane—Room 8-103
Rockville, MD 20857

2. Department of Veterans Affairs
Internet: http://www.va.gov
Benefits Information: (800) 827-1000

a. Veterans Health Administration
810 Vermont Ave., NW
Washington, DC 20420

I. Office of Geriatrics and Extended
Care
Department of Veterans Affairs
810 Vermont Ave. NW
Mail Code 114
Washington, DC 20420

3. Social Security Administration
Office of Public Inquiries
6401 Security Blvd.
Room 4-C-5 Annex
Baltimore, MD 21235
Internet: http://www.ssa.gov
Information: (800) 772-1213

4. Pension Benefit Guaranty Corporation
1200 K St. NW
Washington, DC 20005
Internet: http://www.pbgc.gov
Information: (800) 400-7242
If a pension plan is terminated or about to

be terminated, information about payment
of benefits can be obtained here.

5. U.S. Department of Agriculture
14th St. and Independence Ave. SW
Washington, DC 20250
Internet: http://www.usda.gov

a. Nutrition Program for the Elderly
Food Distribution Division
Food and Consumer Services
Park Office Center
3101 Park Center Dr.
Room 503
Alexandria, VA 22302

b. Human Nutrition Research Center
on Aging
711 Washington St.
Room 911
Boston, MA 02111

c. Food Stamp Program
Food and Consumer Services
Park Office Center
3101 Park Center Dr.
Room 710
Alexandria, VA 22302

d. Child and Adult Care Food Program
Child Nutrition Division
Park Office Center
3101 Park Center Dr.
Room 1017
Alexandria, VA 22302

6. U.S. Department of Housing and Urban
Development
451 7th St. SW
Washington, DC 20401
Information: (800) 669-9777
Internet: http://www.hud.gov

a. Housing for the Elderly Program
(Section 202)
Housing for the Elderly and
Handicapped People Division
Elderly and Assisted Housing Office
Federal Housing Administration
451 7th St. SW
Room 6120
Washington, DC 20401

b. Section 8 Housing for Very Low-Income Families
Moderate Rehabilitation Division
Elderly and Assisted Housing Office
Federal Housing Administration
470 L'Enfant Plaza East SW
Room 3201
Washington, DC 20024

7. Department of Commerce
14th St. and Constitution Ave. NW
Washington, DC 20230
Information: (800) 424-5197
Internet: http://www.doc.gov

a. U.S. Bureau of the Census
U.S. Department of Commerce
Washington, DC 20233
Internet: http://www.census.gov

8. Department of Education
440 Maryland Ave. SW
Washington, DC 20202
Internet: http://www.ed.gov

a. Adult Education and Literacy Division

9. Equal Employment Opportunity Commission
1801 L St. NW
Washington, DC 20507

a. Age Discrimination in Employment Act (ADEA) Division
1801 L St. NW
Suite 6017
Washington, DC 20507

10. U.S. Department of Justice
10th St. and Constitution Ave. NW
Washington, DC 20530
Information: (800) 546-3224
Internet: http://www.usdoj.gov

a. Civil Rights of Institutionalized Persons
Special Litigation Section
Civil Rights Division
P.O. Box 66400
Washington, DC 20035-6400

b. Protection of Voting Rights
Voting Section
Civil Rights Division

P.O. Box 66128
Washington, DC 20038-6128

11. U.S. Department of Labor
200 Constitution Ave. NW
Washington, DC 20210
Internet: http://www.dol.gov

a. Pension and Welfare Benefits Administration (PWBA)
U.S. Dept. of Labor
200 Constitution Ave. NW
Room S-2524
Washington, DC 20210
Internet: http://www.dol.gov/dol/pwba

b. Senior Community Service Employment Program
U.S. Dept. of Labor
200 Constitution Ave. NW
Room C-4524
Washington, DC 20210

c. Job Training Partnership Act Programs
U.S. Dept. of Labor
200 Constitution Ave. NW
Room N-4459
Washington, DC 20210

d. Women's Bureau
U.S. Dept. of Labor
200 Constitution Ave. NW
Room S-3002
Washington, DC 20210-0002
Internet: http://www.dol.gov/dol/wb
Information: (800) 827-5335

12. U.S. Department of the Treasury

a. Internal Revenue Service
Office of Public Affairs
1111 Constitution Ave. NW
Washington, DC 20224
Internet: www.irs.ustreas.gov

I. Tax Counseling for the Elderly
Taxpayer Services Branch
Internal Revenue Service
1111 Constitution Ave. NW
Washington, DC 20224
Free tax counseling and filing is available for people aged 60 and older.

Contact local IRS office or call AARP toll-free at (888) 227-7669.

13. General Service Administration (GSA)

a. Consumer Information Center
P.O. Box 100
Pueblo, CO 81009
Internet: http://www.pueblo.gsa.gov/

14. Railroad Retirement Board
844 N. Rush St.
Chicago, IL 60611-2092
Information: (800) 772-4258

15. Office of Personnel Management
Retirement Operations Center
Boyers, PA 16017
Internet: http://www.opm.gov/retire

STATE AND LOCAL GOVERNMENT OFFICES CONCERNED WITH OLDER PEOPLE

1. National Association of Counties, Aging Program
440 1st St. NW
8th Floor
Washington, DC 20001
Internet: http://www.naco.org

2. U.S. Conference of Mayors
1620 Eye St. NW
Washington, DC 20006
Internet: http://www.usmayors.org/uscm

3. National Association of State Units on Aging
1225 I St. NW
Suite 725
Washington, DC 20005
Information: (800) 989-6537

4. National Conference of State Legislatures
1560 Broadway
Suite 700
Denver, CO 80202
Internet: http://www.ncsl.org

5. State Agencies (or Units) on Aging
All states have offices on aging that help coordinate services for older persons. The following is a list of the names and addresses of state agencies that should help in locating local Area Agencies on Aging.

Alabama
Alabama Commission on Aging
RSA Plaza, Suite 470
770 Washington Avenue
Montgomery, Al, 36130

Alaska
Alaska Commission on Aging
Division of Senior Services
Department of Administration
P.O. Box 110209
Juneau, AK 99811-0209

Arizona
Aging and Adult Administration
Department of Economic Security
1789 West Jefferson—950A Street
Phoenix, AZ 85007

Arkansas
Division of Aging and Adult Services
Arkansas Department of Human Services
P.O. Box 1437, Slot 1412
1417 Donaghey Plaza South
Little Rock, AR 72203-1437

California
California Department of Aging
1600 K Street
Sacramento, CA 95814

Colorado
Aging and Adult Services
Department of Social Services
110 16th St., Suite 200
Denver, CO 80202-4147

Connecticut
Community Services
Division of Elderly Services
25 Sigourney Street
Hartford, CT 06106-5033

Delaware
Delaware Department of Health
and Social Services
Division of Services for Aging and Adults
with Physical Disabilities
1901 North DuPont Highway
New Castle, DE 19720

District of Columbia
District of Columbia Office on Aging
441 4th St. NW, Suite 900 South
Washington DC 20001
(202) 724-5622

Florida
Department of Elder Affairs
4040 Esplanade Way
Tallahassee, FL 32399-7000

Georgia
Division of Aging Services
Department of Human Resources
2 Peachtree St. NE, 18th Floor
Atlanta, GA 30303

Guam
Division of Senior Citizens
Department of Public Health
& Social Services
P.O. Box 2816
Agana, Guam 96932

Hawaii
Hawaii Executive Office on Aging
335 Merchant Street, Room 241
Honolulu, HI 96813

Idaho
Idaho Commission on Aging
Room 108—Statehouse
Boise, ID 83720

Illinois
Illinois Department on Aging
421 East Capitol Ave., Suite 100
Springfield, IL
62701-1789

Indiana
Division of Disability, Aging and Rehabili-
tative Services
Family and Social Services Administration
Bureau of Aging and In-Home Services
402 W. Washington St.
Indianapolis, IN 46027-7083

Iowa
Department of Elder Affairs
Jewett Building—Suite 236
914 Grand Ave.
Des Moines, IA 50319

Kansas
Department on Aging
Docking State Office Building, Room 150
915 SW Harrison
Topeka, KS 66612-1505

Kentucky
Kentucky Division of Aging Services
Department of Social Services
275 East Main Street, 6 West
Frankfort, KY 40621

Louisiana
Governor's Office of Elderly Affairs
P.O. Box 80374
Baton Rouge, LA 70898-0374

Maine
Bureau of Elder and Adult Services
Department of Human Services
35 Anthony Ave.
State House—Station #11
Augusta, ME 04333

Maryland
Maryland Office on Aging
State Office Building, Room 1004
301 West Preston St.
Baltimore, MD 21201-2374

Massachusetts
Massachusetts Executive Office of Elder
Affairs

One Ashburton Place, 5th Floor
Boston, MA 02108

Michigan
Office of Services to the Aging
P.O. Box 30026
Lansing, MI 48909

Minnesota
Minnesota Board on Aging
444 Lafayette Road
St. Paul, MN 55155-3843

Mississippi
Division of Aging and Adult Services
750 State Street
Jackson, MS 39202

Missouri
Division on Aging
Department of Social Services
P.O. Box 1337
615 Howerton Court
Jefferson City, MO 65102-1337

Montana
Senior and Long Term Care Division
Department of Public Health and Human
Services
P.O. Box 4210
Helena, MT 59604

Nebraska
Office on Aging
P.O. Box 95044
301 Centennial Mall South
Lincoln, NE 68509-5044

Nevada
Nevada Division for Aging Services
Department of Human Resources
340 North 11th St., Suite 203
Las Vegas, NV 89101

New Hampshire
Division of Elderly and Adult Services
State Office Park South

115 Pleasant St., Annex Bldg. #1
Concord, NH 03301-6501

New Jersey
New Jersey Division on Aging
Department of Community Affairs
101 South Broad Street—CN 807
Trenton, New Jersey 08625-0807
1(800) 792-8820

New Mexico
State Agency on Aging
La Villa Rivera Building, Ground Floor
228 East Palace Avenue
Santa Fe, NM 87501

New York
New York State Office for the Aging
2 Empire State Plaza
Albany, NY 12223-1251
1(800) 342-9871

North Carolina
Division of Aging
CB 29531
693 Palmer Dr.
Raleigh, NC 27626-0531

North Dakota
Department of Human Services
Aging Services Division
600 South 2nd Street, Suite IC
Bismarck, ND 58504

North Mariana Islands
Office on Aging
Department of Community & Cultural
Affairs
Civic Center
Commonwealth of the Northern Mariana
Islands
Saipan, MP 96950

Ohio
Ohio Department of Aging
50 W. Broad St., 8th Floor
Columbus, OH 43266-0501

Oklahoma
Services for the Aging
Department of Human Services
P.O. Box 25352
Oklahoma City, OK 73125

Oregon
Senior and Disabled Services Division
500 Summer Street NE, 2nd Floor
Salem, OR 97310-1015

Palau
State Agency on Aging
Republic of Palau
Koror, PW 96940

Pennsylvania
Pennsylvania Department of Aging
Commonwealth of Pennsylvania
400 Market St., 6th Floor
Harrisburg, PA 17101-2301

Puerto Rico
Commonwealth of Puerto Rico
Governor's Office of Elderly Affairs
Call Box 50063
Old San Juan Station, PR 00902

Rhode Island
Department of Elderly Affairs
160 Pine Street
Providence, RI 02903-3708

American Samoa
Agency on Aging and Food and Nutrition
Services (AAFNS)
Government of American Samoa
Pago Pago, American Samoa 96799

South Carolina
South Carolina Division on Aging
202 Arbor Lake Drive, Suite 301
Columbia, SC 29223-4535

South Dakota
Office of Adult Services and Aging
Richard F. Kneip Building

700 Governors Drive
Pierre, SD 57501-2291

Tennessee
Commission on Aging
706 Church Street—Suite 201
Nashville, TN 37243-0860

Texas
Texas Department on Aging
P.O. Box 12786 Capitol Station
Austin, TX 78711

Utah
Division of Aging & Adult Services
Box 45500
120 North 200 West
Salt Lake City, UT 84145-0500

Vermont
Vermont Department of Aging
and Disabilities
Waterbury Complex
103 South Main St.
Waterbury, VT 05676

Virginia
Virginia Department for the Aging
700 East Franklin Street, 10th Floor
Richmond, VA 23219-2327

Virgin Islands
Virgin Islands Department of Human
Services
Knud Hansen Complex, Building A
1303 Hospital Ground
Charlotte Amalie, VI 00840

Washington
Aging and Adult Services Administration
Department of Social & Health Services
P.O. Box 45050
Olympia, WA 98504-5050

West Virginia
West Virginia Commission on Aging
Holly Grove—State Capitol

1900 Kanawha Boulevard East
Charleston, WV 25305-0160

Wisconsin
Bureau on Aging
Department of Health and Social Services
P.O. Box 7851
Madison, WI 53707

Wyoming
Department of Health
Division on Aging
117 Hathaway Building—Room 139
Cheyenne, WY 82002-0480

TRAINING AND EDUCATION IN GERONTOLOGY AND GERIATRICS

EDUCATIONAL ASSOCIATIONS

SOURCES OF INFORMATION ON CLINICAL GERIATRIC PSYCHIATRY TRAINING OPPORTUNITIES

ACCREDITED PROGRAMS IN GERIATRIC PSYCHIATRY

GERIATRIC EDUCATION CENTERS

ALZHEIMER'S DISEASE RESEARCH CENTERS

GERIATRIC RESEARCH, EDUCATION, AND CLINICAL CENTERS (GRECC)

EDUCATIONAL ASSOCIATIONS

Association for Gerontology Education in Social Work (AGE-SW)
School of Social Work
University of Maryland at Baltimore
525 W. Redwood St.
Baltimore, MD 21201-1777
Internet:
http://www.cs.umd.edu/users/conn

Association for Gerontology in Higher Education (AGHE)
1001 Connecticut Ave. NW
Suite 410
Washington, DC 20036-5504

For information on schools offering course work in gerontology, see *The National Directory of Educational Programs in Gerontology and Geriatrics* (contact AGHE for latest edition), or for a small fee they will conduct a search of their National Database on Gerontology in Higher Education.

SOURCES OF INFORMATION ON CLINICAL GERIATRIC PSYCHIATRY TRAINING OPPORTUNITIES

American Board of Psychiatry and Neurology, Inc.
Committee on Certification in Added Qualification in Geriatric Psychiatry
500 Lake Cook Rd.
Suite 335
Deerfield, IL 60015

American Medical Students Association
Geriatric Health Task Force
1902 Association Drive
Reston, VA 22091
Internet: http://www.amsa.org

National Institute of Mental Health
Mental Disorders of the Aging Research Branch
5600 Fishers Lane
Rockville, MD 20857

Department of Veterans Affairs
Office of Geriatrics and Extended Care
810 Vermont Ave. NW

Mail Code 114
Washington, DC 20420

ACCREDITED PROGRAMS
IN GERIATRIC PSYCHIATRY

Alabama
University of Alabama Medical Center Geriatric
Psychiatry Program
University of Alabama at Birmingham
1713 6th Ave. South
CPM 253
Birmingham, AL 35233-0018
Participating Institutions:
University of Alabama School of Medicine
University of Alabama Hospital
Veterans Affairs Medical Center (Birmingham)

California
Stanford University Geriatric Psychiatry Program
Stanford University
101 Quarry Rd.
Stanford, CA 94305
Participating Institutions:
Stanford University School of Medicine
Stanford University Hospital

UCLA Medical Center Geriatric Psychiatry
Program
UCLA Neuropsychiatry Institute
760 Westwood Plaza
Los Angeles, CA 90024-1759
Participating Institutions:
UCLA School of Medicine
Veterans Affairs Medical Center
(West Los Angeles)
Veterans Affairs Medical Center (Sepulveda)
UCLA Neuropsychiatric Hospital

University of California (San Diego) Geriatric
Psychiatry Program
University of California, San Diego, School of
Medicine
9500 Gilman Drive, 9116A
La Jolla, CA 92093-9116

Participating Institutions:
University of California, San Diego, School of
Medicine
University of California, San Diego, Medical
Center
Veterans Affairs Medical Center (San Diego)

Florida
University of Florida Geriatric Psychiatry
Program
University of Florida Health Science Center
P.O. Box 100256
Gainesville, FL 32610
Participating Institutions:
University of Florida College of Medicine
Shands Hospital at the University of Florida
Veterans Affairs Medical Center (Gainesville)
University of Florida College of Medicine

University of Miami—Jackson Memorial
Medical Center Geriatric Psychiatry Program
University of Miami School of Medicine
1400 NW 10th Ave.
Suite 702
Miami, FL 33136
Participating Institutions:
University of Miami School of Medicine
Mount Sinai Medical Center of Greater Miami
University of Miami—Jackson Memorial
Medical Center
Miami Jewish Home and Hospital for the Aged

University of South Florida Geriatric Psychiatry
Program
TGH University Psychiatry Center
3515 E. Fletcher Ave.
Tampa, FL 33613
Participating Institutions:
University of South Florida College of Medicine
James A. Haley Veterans Hospital
TGH University Psychiatry Center

Georgia
Emory University Geriatric Psychiatry Program
The Emory Clinic at Wesley Woods

1841 Clifton Rd.
Atlanta, GA 30329
Participating Institutions:
Emory University School of Medicine
Emory University Hospital
Wesley Woods Geriatric Hospital

Hawaii
University of Hawaii Geriatric Psychiatry
Program
University of Hawaii
1356 Lusitana St.
4th Floor
Honolulu, HI 96813
Participating Institutions:
University of Hawaii at Manoa
Hawaii State Hospital
University of Hawaii John A. Burns School of
Medicine
VA Regional Office—Outpatient Clinic
(Honolulu)

Illinois
McGaw Medical Center of Northwestern
University Geriatric Psychiatry Program
McGaw Medical Center of Northwestern
University
446 E. Ontario
Suite 840
Chicago, IL 60611
Participating Institutions:
Northwestern University Medical School
Northwestern Memorial Hospital

Indiana
Indiana University School of Medicine Geriatric
Psychiatry Program
Indiana University School of Medicine
541 Clinical Dr.
Room 289
Indianapolis, IN 46202-5111
Participating Institutions:
Indiana University School of Medicine
William N. Wishard Memorial Hospital
Richard L. Boudebush Veterans Affairs Medical
Center
Clarian Indiana University Hospital

Kansas
University of Kansas (Wichita) Geriatric
Psychiatry Program
University of Kansas School of Medicine—
Wichita
1010 N. Kansas
Wichita, KS 67214-3199
Participating Institutions:
University of Kansas School of Medicine—
Wichita
Via Christi Regional Medical Center—St.
Francis
Via Christi Regional Medical Center—St. Joseph

Louisiana
Louisiana State University Geriatric Psychiatry
Program
Louisiana State University Medical Center
1542 Tulane Ave.
New Orleans, LA 70112
Participating Institutions:
LSU School of Medicine in New Orleans
Touro Infirmary
Louisiana State University School of Medicine

Maryland
Johns Hopkins University Geriatric Psychiatry
Program
John Hopkins Hospital
Meyer 279
600 N. Wolfe St.
Baltimore, MD 21287-7279
Participating Institutions:
John Hopkins University School of Medicine
John Hopkins Bayview Medical Center
John Hopkins Hospital

University of Maryland Geriatric Psychiatry
Program
Baltimore Veterans Administration
10 N. Greene St., 116A
Baltimore, MD 21201
Participating Institutions:
University of Maryland School of Medicine
University of Maryland Medical System
Veterans Affairs Medical Center
(Baltimore)

Massachusetts
McLean Hospital Geriatric Psychiatry Program
McLean Hospital
115 Mill St.
Belmont, MA 02178
Participating Institutions:
Harvard Medical School
McLean Hospital
Deaconess Hospital

Michigan
University of Michigan Geriatric Psychiatry
Program
University of Michigan
900 Wall St.
Ann Arbor, MI 48105
Participating Institutions:
University of Michigan Medical School
University Of Michigan Hospitals
Veterans Affairs Medical Center (Ann Arbor)

Wayne State University/LaFayette Clinic
Geriatric Psychiatry Program
Wayne State University
Walter P. Reuther Psychiatric Hospital
30901 Palmer
Westland, MI 48185
Participating Institutions:
Wayne State University School of Medicine
Walter P. Reuther Psychiatric Hospital

Minnesota
University of Minnesota Geriatric Psychiatry
Program
University of Minnesota
VA Medical Center
One Veterans Drive
Minneapolis, MN 55417
Participating Institutions:
University of Minnesota Medical School
Veterans Affairs Medical Center (Minneapolis)

Missouri
St. Louis University Group of Hospitals
Geriatric Psychiatry Program
St. Louis University Health Sciences Center
David P. Wohl Sr. Memorial Institute

1221 S. Grand Blvd.
St. Louis, MO 63104
Participating Institutions:
St. Louis University School of Medicine
St. Louis University Hospital

Nebraska
Creighton University/University of Nebraska
Geriatric Psychiatry Program
University of Nebraska Medical Center
600 S. 42nd St.
P.O. Box 98-5575
Omaha, NE 88198-5575
Participating Institutions:
University of Nebraska College of Medicine
University of Nebraska Medical Center

New Hampshire
Dartmouth Hitchcock Medical Center Geriatric
Psychiatry Program
Dartmouth Hitchcock Medical Center
1 Medical Center Drive
Lebanon, NH 03756-0001
Participating Institutions:
Dartmouth Medical School
New Hampshire Hospital
Mary Hitchcock Memorial Hospital

New Jersey
UMDNJ-Robert Wood Johnson Medical School
Geriatric Psychiatry Program
UMDNJ-CMHC at Piscataway
COPSA Institute for Alzheimer's Disease
667 Hoes Lane
P.O. Box 1392
Piscataway, NJ 08855-1392
Participating Institutions:
UMDNJ—Robert Wood Johnson Medical
School
Robert Wood Johnson University Hospital
Medical Center at Princeton

New York
Albert Einstein College of Medicine at Beth
Israel Medical Center Geriatric Psychiatry
Program
Beth Israel Medical Center

1st Ave. at 16th St.
New York, NY 10003
Participating Institutions:
Albert Einstein College of Medicine
Beth Israel Medical Center

Albert Einstein College of Medicine Geriatric
Psychiatry Program
Montefiore Medical Center
111 E. 210th St.
Bronx, NY 10457
Participating Institutions:
Albert Einstein College of Medicine
Bronx Psychiatric Center
Albert Einstein College of Medicine at Yeshiva
University

Albert Einstein College of Medicine at Long
Island Jewish Medical Center Geriatric
Psychiatry Program
Long Island Jewish Medical Center
Hillside Hospital Research Building
P.O. Box 38
Glen Oaks, NY 11004
Participating Institutions:
Albert Einstein College of Medicine
Long Island Jewish Medical Center
Central Islip Psychiatric Center
St. John's Episcopal Hospital—South Shore
Hillside Hospital (Long Island Jewish Medical
Center)

Columbia University (Binghampton) Geriatric
Psychiatry Program
Center for Geriatrics and Gerontology
100 Haven Ave.
#3-30F
New York, NY 10032
Participating Institutions:
Binghampton Psychiatric Center
Presbyterian Hospital in the City of New York
Tompkins Community Hospital
United Health Services Hospitals—
Binghampton

Mount Sinai School of Medicine Geriatric
Psychiatry Program
Mount Sinai Hospital
One Gustave L. Levy Place

Box 1230
New York, NY 10029
Participating Institutions:
Mount Sinai School of Medicine
Veterans Affairs Medical Center (Bronx)
Elmhurst Hospital Center—Mount Sinai Services

New York Hospital—Westchester
Division/Cornell Medical Center Geriatric
Psychiatry Program
Cornell University College of Medicine
21 Bloomingdale Rd.
White Plains, NY 10605
Participating Institutions:
Cornell University Medical College
New York Hospital
New York Hospital—Westchester Division

New York Medical Center at St. Vincent's
Hospital and Medical Center of New York
Geriatric Psychiatry Program
New York Medical College
153 W. 11th St.
New York, NY 10011
Participating Institutions:
New York Medical College
St. Vincent's Hospital and Medical Center of
New York

New York University Medical Center Geriatric
Psychiatry Program
New York University Medical Center
550 1st Ave.
New York, NY 10015
Participating Institutions:
New York University School of Medicine
Goldwater Memorial Hospital
Bellevue Hospital Center
Manhattan Psychiatric Center
New York University Medical Center

SUNY Health Science Center at Brooklyn
Geriatric Psychiatry Program
SUNY Health Science Center at Brooklyn
450 Clarkson Ave.
Brooklyn, NY 11203
Participating Institutions:
SUNY Health Science Center at Brooklyn
Kingsboro Psychiatric Center

St. John's Episcopal Hospital—South Shore University Hospital—SUNY Health Science Center at Brooklyn

University of Rochester Geriatric Psychiatry Program
University of Rochester Medical Center
300 Crittenden Blvd.
Rochester, NY 14642-8409
Participating Institutions:
University of Rochester School of Medicine
Rochester Psychiatric Center
Strong Medical Hospital of The University of Rochester

Ohio
University of Cincinnati Hospital Group Geriatric Psychiatry Program
University of Cincinnati College of Medicine
231 Bethesda Ave.
P.O. Box 670559
Cincinnati, OH 45267-0559
Participating Institutions:
University of Cincinnati College of Medicine
University of Cincinnati Hospital

Oregon
Oregon Health Sciences University Geriatric Psychiatry Program
Oregon Health Sciences University
Psychiatry Service (116A-P)
P.O. Box 1034
Portland, OR 97207-9823
Participating Institutions:
Oregon Health Sciences University School of Medicine
Oregon Health Sciences University Hospital
Oregon State Hospital
Veterans Affairs Medical Center (Portland)

Pennsylvania
Albert Einstein Medical Center Geriatric Psychiatry Program
Belmont Center for Comprehensive Treatment
4200 Monument Rd.
Philadelphia, PA 19131

Participating Institutions:
Temple University School of Medicine
Belmont Center for Comprehensive Treatment
Albert Einstein Medical Center

Milton S. Hershey Medical Center of Pennsylvania State University Geriatric Psychiatry Program
Milton S. Hershey Medical Center
PA State University
500 University Dr.
Hershey, PA 17033
Participating Institutions:
Pennsylvania State University College of Medicine
Penn State University Hospital—Milton S. Hershey Medical Center

University Health Center of Pittsburgh Program
University of Pittsburgh Medical Center
3811 O'Hara St.
Room 827
Pittsburgh, PA 15213-2593
Participating Institutions:
University of Pittsburgh School of Medicine
Western Psychiatric Institute and Clinic/UPMC
University Health Center of Pittsburgh

University of Pennsylvania Geriatric Psychiatry Program
Ralston-Penn Center
3615 Chestnut St.
Philadelphia, PA 19104-2676
Participating Institutions:
University of Pennsylvania School of Medicine
Hospital of the University of Pennsylvania

South Carolina
Medical University of South Carolina Geriatric Psychiatry Program
Medical University of South Carolina
Institute of Psychiatry PH141
171 Ashley Ave.
Charleston, SC 29425
Participating Institutions:
Medical University of South Carolina College of Medicine

Texas
University of Texas Southwestern Medical
School Geriatric Psychiatry Program
University of Texas Southwestern Medical
School at Dallas
5323 Harry Hines Blvd.
Dallas, TX 75235-9070
Participating Institutions:
University of Texas Southwestern Medical
School
Presbyterian Hospital of Dallas
Dallas County Mental Health and Mental
Retardation Center

Virginia
University of Virginia Geriatric Psychiatry
Program
Blue Ridge Hospital
Charlottesville, VA 22901
Participating Institutions:
University of Virginia School of Medicine
University of Virginia Medical Center
Western State Hospital

Washington
University of Washington Geriatric Psychiatry
Program
VA Medical Center
GREEC (182B)
1660 South Columbian Way
Seattle, WA 98108
Participating Institutions:
University of Washington School of Medicine
University of Washington Medical Center
Harborview Medical Center

Wisconsin
University of Wisconsin Geriatric Psychiatry
Program
William S. Middleton Memorial Hospital
Department of Psychiatry and Medicine
2500 Overlook Terrace
Madison, WI 53705
Participating Institutions:
University of Wisconsin Medical School

University of Wisconsin Hospital and Clinics
William S. Middleton Veterans Hospital
Mendota Mental Health Institute

GERIATRIC EDUCATION CENTERS

Geriatric Education Centers (GECs), funded by
U.S. Department of Health and Human Services
grants administered by the Bureau of Health Professions of the Health Resources and Services Administration, offer intensive geriatric education to
professionals in various health care disciplines
to enhance to quality and quantity of geriatric care.
Education functions include faculty and curriculum development, consultation and technical assistance, information collection and dissemination,
and continuing education.

The grants for Geriatric Education Centers are
currently under review. For an updated list of centers contact:

The Interdisciplinary, Geriatrics, and Allied
Health Branch
Division of Associated, Dental, and Public
Health Professions
Bureau of Health Professions
Health Resources and Services
Administration
5600 Fishers Lane—Room 8-103
Rockville, MD 20857

**ALZHEIMER'S DISEASE
RESEARCH CENTERS**

These centers are funded by the National Institute
on Aging in an effort to increase understanding
of the causes of the disease and what can be done
for its treatment. Research projects vary at individual institutions, with each center having its
own focus.

Alabama
Department of Neurology
University of Alabama at Birmingham
1720 7th Ave. South

Sparks Center 454
Birmingham, AL 35294-0017

California
Alzheimer's Disease Center
Alta Bates Medical Center
University of California, Davis
2001 Dwight Way
Berkeley, CA 94704

Department of Neurology and Psychiatry
University of California, Los Angeles
710 Westwood Plaza
Los Angeles, CA 90095-1769

Department of Neuroscience (0624)
University of California, San Diego School of
Medicine
9500 Gilman Dr.
La Jolla, CA 92093-0624

Division of Neurogerontology
Ethel Percy Andrus Gerontology Center
University Park, MC-0191
University of Southern California
3715 McClintock Ave.
Los Angeles, CA 90089-0191

Georgia
Department of Pathology and Laboratory
Medicine
Emory University School of Medicine
VA Medical Center (151)
1670 Clairmont Rd.
Decatur, GA 30033

Illinois
Cognitive Neurology and Alzheimer's Disease
Research Center
Northwestern University Medical School
320 E. Superior St.
Searle 11-450
Chicago, IL 60611

Rush Alzheimer's Disease Center
Rush-Presbyterian—St. Lukes Medical Center
1645 W. Jackson Blvd.

Suite 675
Chicago, IL 60612

Indiana
Indiana Alzheimer's Disease Center
Indiana University School of Medicine
635 Barnhill Dr.
Indianapolis, IN 46202-5120

Kansas
Department of Neurology
University of Kansas Medical Center
3901 Rainbow Blvd.
Kansas City, KS 66160-7314

Kentucky
Sanders-Brown Research Center on Aging
University of Kentucky
101 Sanders-Brown Building
800 South Lime
Lexington, KY 40536-0230

Maryland
The John Hopkins Medical Institutions
Department of Pathology
The John Hopkins University School of
Medicine
558 Ross Research Building
720 Rutland Ave.
Baltimore, MD 21205-2196

Massachusetts
Boston University Alzheimer's Disease Center
Geriatric Research, Education and Clinical
Center (182B)
Bedford VA Medical Center
200 Springs Rd.
Bedford, MA 10730

Massachusetts Alzheimer's Disease Research
Center
Department of Neurology
Massachusetts General Hospital
WAC 830
15 Parkman St.
Boston, MA 02114

Michigan
Michigan Alzheimer's Disease Research
Center
Department of Neurology
University of Michigan
1914 Taubman St.
Ann Arbor, MI 48109-0316

Minnesota
Department of Neurology
Mayo Clinic
200 1st St. SW
Rochester, MN 55905

Missouri
Alzheimer's Disease Research Center
Washington University Medical Center
4488 Forest Park Ave.
St. Louis, MO 63108-2881

New York
Alzheimer's Disease Research Center
Department of Pathology
Columbia University
630 W. 168th St.
New York, NY 10032

Department of Psychiatry
Mount Sinai School of Medicine
Mount Sinai Medical Center
1 Gustave Levy Place
Box #1230
New York, NY 10029-6574

Aging and Dementia Research Center
Department of Psychiatry (THN314)
New York University Medical Center
550 1st Ave.
New York, NY 10016

Alzheimer's Disease Center
Department of Neurobiology and Anatomy,
Box 603
University of Rochester Medical Center
601 Elmwood Ave.
Rochester, NY 14642

North Carolina
Joseph and Kathleen Bryan Alzheimer's Disease
Research Center (Duke University)
2200 Main St.
Suite A-230
Durham, NC 27705

Ohio
Alzheimer's Disease Research Center (Case
Western Reserve University)
University Hospitals of Cleveland
11100 Euclid Ave.
Cleveland, OH 44106

Oregon
Oregon Alzheimer's Disease Center (L226)
Oregon Health Sciences University
3181 SW Sam Jackson Park Rd.
Portland, OR 97201-3098

Pennsylvania
Pathology and Laboratory Medicine
University of Pennsylvania School of
Medicine
Room A009, Basement Maloney/HUP
36th and Spruce Streets
Philadelphia, PA 19104-4283

Alzheimer's Disease Research Center
University of Pittsburgh Medical Center
Montefiore University Hospital, 4 West
200 Lothrop St.
Pittsburgh, PA 15213

Texas
Alzheimer's Disease Research Center
Department of Neurology
Baylor College of Medicine
6501 Fannin, NB302
Houston, TX 77030-3498

Alzheimer's Disease Research Center
University of Texas
Southwestern Medical Center at Dallas
5323 Harry Hines Blvd.
Dallas, TX 75235-9036

Washington
Alzheimer's Disease Research Center
Department of Pathology
Box 357470, HSB K-543
University of Washington
1959 Pacific Ave.
Seattle, WA 98195-7470

**GERIATRIC RESEARCH, EDUCATION,
AND CLINICAL CENTERS (GRECC)**

Geriatric research, education and clinical centers
are located in VA medical centers throughout the
United States. Their role is to develop the capabil-
ity of the VA health care system to provide care to
older veterans. GRECCs develop new knowledge
regarding aging and geriatrics, disseminate information through education and training to health
care professionals and students, and develop and
evaluate alternative models of geriatric care.

Arkansas
John L. McClellan Memorial Hospital
4300 W. 7th St.
Little Rock, AR 72205-5484

California
VA Medical Center*
3801 Miranda Ave.
Palo Alto, CA 94304
Research Areas: Cognitive Function/Chronic
Disease, Affective Disorders

VA Medical Center*
16111 Plummer St.
Sepulveda, CA 91343
Research Areas: Alzheimer's Disease

VA Medical Center
Wilshire & Sawtelle Blvds.
West Los Angeles, CA 90073

Florida
VA Medical Center*
1601 SW Archer Rd.

Gainesville, FL 32608-1197
Research Areas: Dementia

VA Medical Center
1201 NW 16th St.
Miami, FL 33125

Maryland
VA Medical Center
10 N. Green St.
Baltimore, MD 21201

Massachusetts
Boston GRECC—Bedford Division*
Edith Nourse Rogers Memorial Hospital
200 Springs Rd.
Bedford, MA 01730
Research Areas: Neuroscience/Cognitive
Disorders, Management of Advanced
Alzheimer's Disease and Other Dementias

Boston GRECC
VA Medical Center
1400 VFW Parkway
West Roxbury, MA 02132

Michigan
VA Medical Center
2215 Fuller Rd.
Ann Arbor, MI 48105

Minnesota
VA Medical Center*
One Veterans Dr.
Minneapolis, MN 55417
Research Areas: Aging Nervous System:
Neurobiology, Neurology and Psychiatry,
Behavioral Neurobiology, Alzheimer's Disease,
Epedemiology of Dementia (has dementia
department headed by a psychiatrist), Delirium,
Psychopharmacology

Missouri
VA Medical Center
Jefferson Barracks Division

#1 Jefferson Barracks Dr.
St. Louis, MO 63125-4199

North Carolina
VA Medical Center
508 Fulton St.
Durham, NC 27705

Texas
Audie L. Murphy Memorial
VA Medical Center
7400 Merton Minter Blvd.
San Antonio, TX 78484

Utah
VA Medical Center
500 Foothill Dr.
Salt Lake City, UT 84148

Washington
VA Medical Center*
1660 Colombian Way
Seattle, WA 98108

American Lake VA Medical Center*
Tacoma, WA 98493
Research Area (Seattle and American Lakes
Divisions): Alzheimer's Disease, Dementia (has
dementia department headed by a psychiatrist),
Depression

Wisconsin
William S. Middleton Memorial Hospital
2500 Overlook Terrace
Madison, WI 33125

* These GRECC's conduct research related to mental
health. Other GRECC's, however, provide psychiatric
services.

STAFF INSERVICE EDUCATIONAL
MATERIAL FOR WORK
WITH OLDER PEOPLE

RECOMMENDED FICTION
LITERARY ANTHOLOGIES
PULITZER PRIZE–WINNING PLAYS
FEATURE FILMS
AUDIOVISUAL REVIEW SOURCES
AUDIOVISUAL RESOURCE GUIDES

SELECTED HISTORICAL REFERENCES
LIFE REVIEWS: ORAL HISTORY
PHOTOGRAPHY AND DRAWINGS OF
OLD AGE
PHILOSOPHY

RECOMMENDED FICTION (CONCERNING LATER LIFE, MEMORY, TIME, AGING, DISEASE, AND DEATH)

In James Hilton's *Goodbye, Mr. Chips* (1934), the elderly protagonist reminisces in his room across from the school where he taught three generations of English boys.

Aldous Huxley's *After Many a Summer Dies the Swan* (1939) is a satirical novel. The hero is a California multimillionaire terrified of death. His physician is working on a theory of longevity. The novel ends in horror.

Georges Simenon's *The Bells of Bicetre* (English title: *The Patient*) portrays a powerful French newspaper owner who has a stroke that leaves him speechless and paralyzed. At first he is passive, with no wish to recover. His mind is clear; he views his wife, his doctor, and his own life with detachment. As his memories flow through his mind and he begins to recover his speech and movement, his mental attitude changes favorably.

In Muriel Spark's *Momento Mori* (1959), a woman's death and an anonymous phone caller who says "remember you must die" provoke a series of humorous adventures for a group of elderly English aristocrats.

Leo Tolstoy, in *The Death of Ivan Ilych* (1884), describes a Russian judge who learns that his wealth, status, and power are useless to him when he becomes ill. His painful disease and his death are merely inconveniences to his family and life-long friends. A young peasant servant is his only comfort.

In John Updike's *The Poorhouse Fair* (1959), residents of an old folks' home put on their annual fair despite the well-intentioned mistakes of the new administrators and poor weather.

Adams, S. H. (1947). *Grandfather stories.* New York: Random House.

Albee, Edward. (1961). *The American dream.* New York: Coward, McCann and Geoghegan.

Ashton-Warner, S. (1961). *Spinster (1959).* New York: Bantam Books.

Balzac, Honore de. (1950). *Pere goriot.* New York: Modern Library.

Beckett, S. (1958). *Krapp's last tape* (1957). New York: Grove Press.

Bromfield, L. (1949). *Mrs. Parkington.* New York: Harper & Brothers.

Cary, J. (1942). *To be a pilgrim.* London: Michael Joseph.

Cervantes, M. (1957). *Don Quixote* (part 1, 1605; part II, 1615). New York: New American Library.

Chekov, A. (1958). *Uncle Vanya* in *Four great plays.* New York: Bantam Books.

Garcia Marquez, G. (1988). *Love in the time of cholera.* New York: Alfred A. Knopf.

Gardner, H. (1988). *I'm not Rappaport.* New York: Grove Press.

Hansberry, L. (1961). *A raisin in the sun.* New York: Random House.

Heinlein, Robert A. (1973). *Time enough for love.* New York: G. P. Putnam & Sons.

Hemingway, E. (1952). *The old man and the sea.* New York: Charles Scribner's Sons.

Ibsen, H. (1935). *The master builders.* In *Eleven plays of Henrik Ibsen,* New York: Random House.

James, H. (1945). "The beast in the jungle" (1903). In Fadiman, C., ed. *The short stories of Henry James.* New York: Random House, pp. 548–602.

Kaufman, G., & Hart, M. (1937). *You can't take it with you.* New York: Simon & Schuster.

Lampedusa, C. di. (1960). *The leopard.* New York: Pantheon Books.

Lessing, D. (1983). *The summer before dark.* New York: Random House.

Mann, Thomas. (1924). *Buddenbrooks.* New York: Random House.

Mann, T. (1954). *The black swan.* New York: Alfred A. Knopf.

Miller, A. (1949). *Death of a salesman.* New York: Viking Press.

Moliere, Jean. *The miser.* Available in various collections (in paperback and on record).

Paton, Alan. *Cry the beloved country.* Available in many editions.

Porter, K. A. (1930). "The jilting of Granny Weatherall." In *Flowering Judas.* New York: Harcourt, Brace & World.

Proust, M. (1934). *Remembrance of things past* (1913–1922). New York: Random House (two volumes).

Richter, C. (1960). *The waters of Kronos.* New York: Alfred A. Knopf.

Romains, J. (1961). *The death of a nobody* (1911). New York: Signet Book.

Shakespeare, W. (1960). *King Lear* (1608). Cambridge, England: Cambridge University Press.

Shaw, G. B. (1947). *Back to Methuselah.* Collection of five linked plays: *In the beginning; The gospel of the brothers Barnabas; The thing happens; The tragedy of an elderly gentleman;* and *As far as thought can reach.* New York: Oxford University Press.

Sophocles. *Oedipus at Colonus.* Available in various collections and in paperback.

Stegner, W. E. (1976). *The spectator bird.* Garden City, NJ: Doubleday.

Strindberg, J. August. (1964). *Storm.* In *Plays of Strindberg, Vol.1,* New York: Random House.

Trollope, A. (1882). *The fixed period.* Tauchnitz editions of English authors, Leipzig.

Turgenev, I. (1959). "A nest of gentlefolk." In *A nest of gentlefolk and other stories.* New York: Oxford University Press.

Uhry, A. (1988). *Driving Miss Daisy.* New York: Publishing Center for Cultural Resources.

Van Velde, J. (1960). *The big ward.* New York: Simon & Schuster.

Waugh, E. (1948). *The loved one.* Boston: Little, Brown & Co.

Wilde, O. (1956). *Picture of Dorian Gray* (1906). New York: Dell Books.

Williams, Tennessee. (1959). *Sweet bird of youth.* In *Three Plays.* New York: New Directions (paperback).

Yeats, W. B. (1957). "Underlying Love for Maud Sonne." In *The collected poems of William Butler Yeats.* New York: Macmillan.

LITERARY ANTHOLOGIES

Borenstein, Audrey. (1983). *Chimes of change and hours: Views of older women in twentieth century America.* London and Toronto: Associated University Presses.

Cole, T. R., & Winkler, M. G. (1994). *The Oxford book of aging.* New York: Oxford University Press.

Fowler, M., & McCutcheon, P. (1991). *Songs of experience: An anthology of literature and growing old.* New York: Ballantine Books.

Lyell, R. G. (Ed.) (1980). *Middle age, old age: Short stories, poems, plays and essays.* New York: Harcourt Brace Jovanovich.

Yahnke, R., & Eastman, R. M. (1996). *Literature and gerontology: A research guide.* Westport, CT: Greenwood Press.

PULITZER PRIZE–WINNING PLAYS

Coburn, D. L. *The gin game.*
Cristofer, M. *The shadow box.*
Uhry, A. *Driving Miss Daisy.*

FEATURE FILMS

The last laugh (1924), directed by F. W. Murnau. The story of an old doorman demoted to washroom attendant. 60 minutes.

Make way for tomorrow (1937), directed by Leo McCarey. An elderly couple are in financial difficulty and have to be parted because their children will not help. 92 minutes.

Goodbye, Mr. Chips (1939), directed by Sam Wood. Shy schoolmaster devotes his life to his students until a woman brings him out of his shell. 114 minutes.

Sunset boulevard (1950), directed by Billy Wilder. Faded silent-film star lives in the past. 110 minutes.

Ikiru (To live) (1952), directed by Akira Kurosawa. A bureaucrat discovers he has only six months to live and desperately struggles to accomplish something worthwhile. 143 minutes.

Umberto D. (1952), directed by Vittorio de Sica. Concerns an aging impoverished pensioner who considers suicide as he tries to keep his dignity while growing old in the squalor of postwar Italy. 89 minutes.

Tokyo story (1953), directed by Yasujiro Ozu. The story of an elderly couple's last visit to their children, its disappointments, its sadness. 134 minutes.

Wild strawberries (1957), directed by Ingmar Bergman. Concerns a 76-year-old physician who learns to love on the brink of eternity. 80 minutes.

The leopard (1965), directed by Luchino Visconti. Story of an aging Sicilian prince who realizes, "If one wants things to stay as they are, things have to change." 205 minutes.

The two of us (1968), directed by Claude Berri. About a 75-year-old man and a 9-year-old boy. 86 minutes.

The shameless old lady (1969), directed by Rene Allio. Story of a 70-year-old French widow who, having spent her life serving others, serves herself in the last 18 months of her life. 94 minutes.

I never sang for my father (1970), directed by Gilbert Cates. A sensitive son begins to lose patience with his cantankerous elderly father. 92 minutes.

Harold and Maude (1971), directed by Hal Ashby. A 19-year-old falls in love with a free-spirited septuagenarian. 92 minutes.

The autobiography of Miss Jane Pittman (1974), directed by John Forty. A 110-year-old slave remembers her life experiences, spanning the Civil War to the start of the civil rights movement. 110 minutes.

Harry and Tonto (1974), directed by Paul Mazursky. A retired schoolteacher travels cross-country with his faithful cat. 115 minutes.

Sendakan 8 (1975), directed by Kei Kumai. The offbeat story of an aging gangster. 104 minutes.

Atlantic City (1981), directed by Louis Malle. The offbeat story of an aging gangster. 104 minutes.

On Golden Pond (1981), directed by Mark Rydell. A man struggles with the ravages of age. 109 minutes.

The twilight years (Kookotsu No Hito) (1984), directed by Sawako Ariyoshi.

Cocoon (1985), directed by Ron Howard. A fun piece of science fiction, where retirement villagers feel young again, thanks to visitors from another planet. 117 minutes.

Ran (1985), directed by Akira Kurosawa. Masterful Japanese adaptation of Shakespeare's *King Lear.* 161 minutes.

Whales of August (1988), directed by Lindsay Anderson. Story about the fates of two sisters who have spent over 60 summers together on a Maine island as they face the challenges of growing old. 90 minutes.

Driving Miss Daisy (1989), directed by Bruce Beresford. Chronicles the social changes occurring in the South between 1948 and 1973, while embracing the 25-year friendship between an elderly Jewish woman and her black chauffeur. 1989 Academy Award Winner. 99 minutes.

Near death (1989), directed by Frederick Wiseman. 350 minutes.

Avalon (1990), directed by Barry Levinson. Story of the transitions experienced by families over time. 126 minutes.

Dreams (1990), directed by Akira Kurosawa.

Strangers in good company (1991), directed by Cynthia Scott. Seven women ages 68–92, and one 31, (played by non-actors) get to know each other when their bus breaks down and strands them in the Canadian wilderness for three nights. 100 minutes.

Toto le heros (1991), directed by Jaco Van Dormeal. This Belgian film about an old man's life review revolves around the man's conviction that he was switched at birth with his neighbor. 90 minutes.

Fried green tomatoes (1991), directed by John Avnet. A younger woman befriends an older woman living in a nursing home and, through their relationship, both find meaning in their lives. 130 minutes.

Tatie Danielle (1991), directed by Etienne Chatilez. French black comedy about a mourning widow who wreaks havoc on people around her. 110 minutes.

I can't sleep (1995), directed by Claire Denis. Based on an actual serial murder case of old women in France. 110 minutes.

The line king (1996), directed by Susan Dryfoos. Biographical film about the artist Al Hirschfeld.

AUDIOVISUAL REVIEW SOURCES

National Institute on Human Resources and Aging
c/o Brookdale Center on Aging
425 E. 25th St.
New York, NY 10010-2590
Information: (800) 64-STAFF
Extensive filmographies and AV reviews are organized by topics and updated bi-monthly.

The Gerontologist (Washington, DC:
Gerontological Society of America)
Seven to ten audiovisuals produced within the last three years are reviewed in each bi-monthly issue.

AUDIOVISUAL RESOURCE GUIDES

Association of Gerontology in Higher Education. (1993). *Audiovisuals on aging.* Washington, DC: Association of Gerontology in Higher Education. A selective annotated bibliography of recommended AVs on a variety of topics.

Los Angeles Caregiver Resource Center. (1992). *Audiovisual guide: Resources in gerontology and geriatrics.* Los Angeles Caregiver Resource Center. USC Gerontology Center. 3715 McClintock Ave., Los Angeles, CA 90089-3191. A comprehensive, annotated bibliography of over 800 AV's under 75 subject headings.

National Council on the Aging. (1986). *An arts and aging media sourcebook.* Washington, DC: National Council on the Aging. AVs on the creative arts.

Yahnke, R. (1988). *The great circle of life: A resource guide to film on aging.* Baltimore, MD: Williams & Wilkins. Films, with synopses, previewing notes, group activities, scene summaries, discussion questions and worksheets, are categorized under 6 headings: Portraits of Aging, Documentaries, Symbolic Statements, Intergenerational Relationships, Relationships in Old Age, and Loss.

SELECTED HISTORICAL REFERENCES

Achenbaum, W. A. (1978). *Old age in the new land: The American experience since 1790.* Baltimore: The Johns Hopkins University Press.

Altmeyer, A. J. (1966). *The formative years of social security.* Madison, WI: University of Wisconsin Press.

Aries, P. (1962). *Centuries of childhood.* New York: Random House.

Charcot, J. M. (1881). *Clinical lectures on the diseases of old age (Lecons cliniques sur les maladies des vieillards et les maladies chroniques* [1867]). Hunt, L., translator. New York: William Wood.

Cicero, M. T. (1967). *De Senectute,* Copley, F. D., translator. Ann Arbor, MI: The University of Michigan Press.

Elder, G. (1975). *Children of the depression.* Chicago: The University of Chicago Press.

Emerson, R. W. (1862). Old age. *Atlantic Monthly.* 9:134–138.

Fischer, D. H. (1977). *Growing old in America.* New York: Oxford University Press.

Gruman, G. J. (1966). *A history of ideas about the prolongation of life: The evolution of prolongevity hypotheses to 1800.* Philadelphia: The American Philosophical Society.

Hall, G. S. (1922). *Senescence: The last half of life.* New York: D. Appleton.

Hareven, T. K. (1976). The last stage: Historical adulthood and old age. *Daedalus* 105: 20.

Metchnikoff, E. (1908). *The prolongation of life.* New York: G. P. Putnam's Sons.

Minot, C. S. (1885). Senility. In Buck, A. H., (Ed.), *Reference handbook of medical science,* vol. 6. New York: William Wood, p. 388.

Nascher, I. L. (1914). *Geriatrics.* Philadelphia: P. Blakiston's Son.

Rush, B. (1793). An account of the state of the mind and body in old age. In *Medical inquiries and observations,* 4 vol., (reprinted Philadelphia: Thomas Dobson, 1797).

Steams, P. N. (1976). *Old age in European society: The case in France.* New York: Holmes and Meier Publishers.

Stone, L. (1977, May 12). Walking over grandma. *New York Review of Books.*

Zeman, F. D. (1944–1947). Life's later years: Studies in the medical history of old age (series). *Journal of Mt. Sinai Hospital.*

LIFE REVIEWS: ORAL HISTORY

Blythe, R. (1979). *Akenfield: Portrait of an English village.* New York: Pantheon Books.

Hareven, T. K., & Langenbach, R. (1978). *Amoskeag: Life and work in an American factory city.* New York: Pantheon Books.

PHOTOGRAPHY AND DRAWINGS OF OLD AGE

Jacques, M. (1980). *Images of age.* Cambridge, MA: ABT Books.

Martine, F. (1980). *Le temps de vieillir.* Paris, France: Editions Filipacchi.

Miller, P. R., & Tupin, J. P. (1972). Multimedia teaching of introductory psychiatry. *American Journal of Psychiatry,* 128, 1219–1222.

PHILOSOPHY

McKee, P. L. (1982). *Philosophical foundations of gerontology.* New York: Human Sciences Press.

APPENDIX F

U.S. POLICY ON AGING: A HISTORICAL SUMMARY

1920: *The Civil Service Retirement Act* was enacted to provide a retirement system for many government employees, including members of the U. S. Congress and those in the uniformed and civil services.

1935: *The Social Security Act* was passed and signed into law by President Roosevelt "to provide protection as a matter of right for the American worker in retirement." Major provisions included "Old Age Assistance" and "Old Age Survivors Insurance."

1937: *The Railroad Retirement Act* was enacted to provide annuities (pensions) for retired railroad employees and their spouses.

1939: Benefits for dependents and survivors added to the Social Security Act.

1945: The State of Connecticut was among the first to establish a state agency on aging through its designation of a "State Commission on the Care and Treatment of the Chronically Ill, Aged and Infirm."

1950: The first national conference on aging convened in Washington, DC, sponsored by the Federal Security Agency.

1953: The Department of Health, Education, and Welfare (DHEW) was established in April to replace the former Federal Security Agency.

1956: A special staff on aging was assigned coordinative responsibilities for aging within the Office of the Secretary of DHEW.

1958: Representative John E. Fogarty introduced bill in Congress calling for a White House Conference on Aging.

1959: *The Housing Act* was enacted, authorizing a direct loan program of nonprofit rental projects for the elderly at low interest rates. Provisions also reduced the eligible age for public low-rent housing for low-income older persons to age 62 for women and age 50 for disabled individuals.

Creation of the U.S. Senate Special Committee on Aging.

1960: Social Security amendments made a number of changes in the law, including: (a) eliminating "age 50" as a minimum to qualify for disability benefits, and (b) liberalizing the retirement test and the requirement for fully insured status.

1961: First White House Conference on Aging convened in Washington, DC.

Social Security amendments lowered retirement age for men from age 65 to 62; increased minimum benefits paid; broadened program to include additional categories of retired persons; increased benefits to aged widows; and liberalized the retirement test.

1962: Legislation proposed by Senator McNamara and Representative Fogarty calling for the establishment of a permanent and independent three-member Commission on Aging attached to the presidency to serve as the focal point within federal government for developing national aging policy. More than 160 bills introduced in Congress related to the aged and aging— eight were enacted.

1965: Medicare health insurance program for the elderly was legislated. Financed through the Social Security system, the enactment culminated years of "extensive and comprehensive efforts at the Congressional level."

The Older Americans Act was passed and signed into law by President Johnson on July 14. Major provisions included establishment of the Administration on Aging within DHEW and grants to states for community planning, services and training. The Act also stipulated that state agencies on aging be established to administer the programs.

"Community Service and Continuing Education Programs" were authorized under the Higher Education Act of 1965. Emphasis was directed to solving community problems in urban and suburban areas and to expanding available learning opportunities for adults not adequately served by educational offerings in their communities.

Social Security amendments established Title XIX, "Grants to States for Medical Assistance."

1967: Amendments to the Older Americans Act extended its provisions for two years and directed the Administration on Aging to undertake a study of personnel needs in the aging field.

Age Discrimination Act of 1967 was passed and signed into law by President Johnson.

The Administration on Aging was removed from the Office of the Secretary of DHEW and placed in a newly created Social and Rehabilitative Service Agency (SRS) within the Department.

1969: Amendments to the Older Americans Act extended its provisions for three years and authorized the use of Title III funds to support area-wide model projects.

1971: Second White House Conference on Aging convened in Washington, DC.

1972: Supplemental Security Income program (SSI) created.

Automatic annual cost-of-living allowances were established for Social Security benefits.

The Nutrition Program for the Elderly Act was passed and signed into law by President Nixon (redesignated Title VII of the Older Americans Act, as amended in 1973).

The Federal Council on Aging and the House Select Committee on Aging were created.

1973: The Older Americans Comprehensive Service Amendments established area agencies on aging under an expanded Title III authority. Amendments also authorized the use of Title III grants for model projects, senior centers and multidisciplinary centers of gerontology, added a new Title IX, "Older Americans Community Service Employment Act," authorized funding for Title VII nutrition projects, and extended the Act's provisions for two years.

The Domestic Volunteer Service Act was passed and signed into law by President Nixon on October 1. Major provisions included the RSVP and Foster Grandparent programs. Title VI of the Older Americans Act, as a result, was later repealed.

The Comprehensive Employment and Training Act (CETA) was enacted "to provide job training and employment opportunities for economically disadvantaged, unemployed or underemployed persons, including those facing barriers to employment commonly experienced by older workers."

1974: Amendments to the Older Americans Act added a special transportation program under Title III "model projects."

The Housing and Community Development Act became law on August 22.

Major provisions included a directive to the Secretary of Housing and Urban Development (HUD) to consult with the Secretary of HEW to ensure the acceptable provision of low-income housing for the elderly or handicapped, pursuant to the U. S. Housing Act of 1937.

Social Security Amendments authorized Title XX, "Grants to States for Social Services." Among the programs which could be supported under this provision were: protective services; homemaker services; adult day care services; transportation services; training; employment opportunities; information and referral; nutrition assistance; and health support.

Congress authorized the establishment of the National Institute on Aging (NIA) on May 31 "to conduct and support biomedical, social and behavioral research and training related to the aging process and the diseases and other special problems and needs of the aging."

Title V, "Farm and Rural Housing" program of the National Housing Act of 1949 was expanded to include the rural elderly as a special target group.

1975: Amendments to the Older Americans Act added new language authorizing the Commissioner on Aging to make grants under Title III to Indian tribal organizations. For the first time, Priority Services were mandated (transportation, home care, legal services and home renovation/repair). Amendments also made minor changes in Title IX, "Community Service Employment for Older Americans."

The Age Discrimination Act of 1975 was passed and signed into law by President Nixon. It specifically excluded from its purview age discrimination in employment except as it related to participation in government-funded employment programs.

1977: Amendments to the Older Americans Act authorized changes in the Title VII nutrition services program, primarily related to the availability of surplus commodities through the U.S. Department of Agriculture.

1978: Comprehensive amendments to the Older Americans Act consolidated Titles III, V and VII (social services, multipurpose centers and nutrition services, respectively) into one Title III: redesignated the previous Title IX (Community Service Employment Act) as Title V; and added a new Title VI, "Grants for Indian Tribes."

The Congregate Housing Services Act was passed and signed into law on October 31. Major provisions authorized the Secretary of Housing and Urban Development (HUD) to enter into contracts with local public housing agencies and with nonprofit corporations to provide congregate services programs for the purpose of promoting and encouraging maximum independence within a home environment for individuals capable of self-care.

Amendments to the Age Discrimination in Employment Act were passed containing provisions reflective of the recommendations of the U. S. Civil Rights Commission which showed that the Age Discrimination Act of 1975 had been interpreted to allow discrimination in employment, which was clearly not the intent of Congress.

1980: The Department of Health and Human Services (DHHS) was created, replacing DHEW.

1981: Amendments to the Older Americans Act extended its program for three years through September 30, 1984.

The Third White House Conference on Aging convened in Washington, DC.

1984: Amendments to the Older Americans Act clarified the roles of state and area agencies on aging in coordinating community-based services and in maintaining accountability for the funding of national priority services (legal, access and in-home services); increased the flexibility in administering programs by providing for increased transfer authority between Parts B and C of Title III; a new Title VII was added providing for an Older Americans Personal Health Education and Training Program for funding grants to institutions of higher education and to develop standardized programs of health education and training for older persons to be operated in multipurpose senior center facilities; and the program was extended for three years, through September 30, 1987.

1985:   *A Compendium of Papers Honoring the Twentieth Anniversary of the Older Americans Act* was compiled by the U.S. House of Representatives Select Committee on Aging, Subcommittee on Human Services, and published by the U. S. Government Printing Office, Washington, DC.

1987:   Amendments to the Older Americans Act included the establishment of the Office for Native Hawaiian Programs within the Administration on Aging. It also authorized new initiatives on mental health, elder abuse, home health care for the frail elderly, and outreach to eligible SSI recipients.

1992:   Amendments to the Older Americans Act included the addition of Title VII, the Vulnerable Elders Rights Protection Title, and funded efforts to increase education on how healthy lifestyles reduce the risk of chronic health problems in later life.

1995:   The fourth White House Conference on Aging convened in Washington, DC.

1997:   The Older Americans Act is up for reauthorization.

PERSONAL MENTAL HEALTH DATA FORM FOR OLDER PERSONS

PERSONAL MENTAL HEALTH DATA FORM FOR OLDER PERSONS

Note to patients   Confidential

This Personal Data Form is an inventory, an overview of your past and present situation. For our purposes, it provides basic background data. For you, it is a way to begin reviewing your life, finding themes, in terms of both strengths and difficulties.

The material is confidential and will be treated with care. We do not share this material with **anyone** outside our office, unless specifically given permission by you. Thus candor and comprehensiveness, which add to the value, are encouraged. Some of the questions will be irrelevant, in which case simply leave blanks. If more writing space is needed, add an extra sheet.

You may be asked to write to other psychotherapists, doctors, and hospitals who have knowledge of you, giving them permission to send us extended summaries of their contacts with you. If you wish, we will furnish you with a copy of this form for your own use or for use with other health personnel such as your internist.

Thank you very much,

(signed by chief administrator)

This form was created by Myrna I. Lewis and Robert N. Butler, Mt. Sinai School of Medicine, New York. Revised 1997.

INFORMATION FOR OUR USE IN YOUR INSURANCE FORMS

TO BE COMPLETED BY PATIENT Date: _____

Patient's name: _____

Social Security no.: _____ Medicare no.: _____

Medicaid no.: _____ Supplemental Security Income (SSI): _____

Date first seen at our office: _____

Approximate date symptoms appeared: _____

Health coverage *(indicate by a check mark)*

☐ None
☐ Blue Cross-Blue Shield:
☐ Aetna
☐ Kaiser Permanente
☐ Other Private Insurance (name): _____
☐ Champus
☐ Medicare: ☐ Part A   ☐ Part B
☐ Medicare Supplement
☐ Medicaid
☐ HMO/Managed Care (name): _____
☐ Veterans Administration
☐ Long Term Care Insurance Coverage
☐ Other *(name):* _____

Disability payments *(indicate by a check mark)*

☐ Private
☐ Social Security
☐ Veterans
☐ State

TO BE COMPLETED BY THERAPIST

Psychiatric diagnosis (NOTE TO PATIENTS: *We shall discuss any diagnosis with you before submitting it to your insurance company.*)

_____

_____

Nature of treatment *(indicate date treatment began)*

Consultation alone (diagnosis and evaluation): _____

Individual psychotherapy: _____

Group psychotherapy: _____

Couples (conjoint) therapy: _____

Family therapy: _____

Reminiscence or life review therapy: _____

Cognitive therapy: _____

Behavioral therapy: _____

Activities therapy (art, music, dance): _____

Drug therapy (specify drugs): _____

Referral for ECT: _____

Referral for hospitalization: _____

Case management/care coordination: _____

Emergency referral: _____

Other *(specify)*: _____

PERSONAL DATA FORM (LIFE REVIEW FORM)

I. BASIC BACKGROUND INFORMATION   Date: _____

A. Patient's full name: _____

Nickname(s): _____   Preferred first name: _____

Age: _____   Complete birth date: _____

Birthplace: _____

Present addresses: Residence: _____
                                        (Street)

_____
                    (City)   (State)   (Zip)

_____
                    (E-mail)

         Work: _____
                                        (Street)

_____
                    (City)   (State)   (Zip)

_____
                    (E-mail)

Telephone numbers: Residence: _____   Fax: _____

                         Work: _____   Fax: _____

NOTE: *If you do not wish to be called at work except for emergencies, check here ☐.*
           If you cannot be called at work at all, check here ☐.

REFERRAL SOURCE

Patient referred by: _____

IN CASE OF MEDICAL EMERGENCY: *Current doctor(s)*

1. Name: _____

Address: _____

Phone: _____   Specialty: _____

2. Name: _____

Address: _____

Phone: _____   Specialty: _____

3. Name: _____

Address: _____

Phone: _____   Specialty: _____

IN CASE OF EMERGENCY: *Nearest relatives and/or friends*

Name: _____

Address: _____   Phone: _____

Name: _____

Address: _____   Phone: _____

I. BASIC BACKGROUND INFORMATION—cont.

If you live alone, please give the name and phone number of a nearby neighbor or friend.

Name: _____   Phone: _____

B. Religion

Of family of origin: _____

Present religious affiliation, if any: _____

Are you active religiously? _____

Any religious conflict? _____

No religion: _____

C. Ethnic, racial, or cultural background: _____

Year of immigration to U.S.: _____

From where: _____

First language spoken: _____

Second language spoken: _____

D. Family status

Present marital status: ☐ Single

☐ Separated

☐ Widowed

☐ Married

☐ Divorced

☐ Living with someone

Most current marriage or living partner *(circle which)*

Full name of spouse or living partner: _____

Age difference: _____ (years older than you)

_____ (years younger than you)

Religion of spouse or living partner: _____

Place of birth of spouse or living partner: _____

Your courtship duration: _____

Date of marriage or when you began living together (month, day, year): _____

Closest anniversary attained: _____

Date of separation: _____

Date of divorce or widowhood (month, day, year): _____

Previous marriage or living partner *(circle which)*

Full name of spouse or living partner: _____

Age difference: _____ (years older than you)

_____ (years younger than you)

Religion of spouse or living partner: _____

PERSONAL DATA FORM—Page 3

Place of birth of spouse or living partner: _____

Your courtship duration: _____

Date of marriage or when you began living together (month, day, year): _____

Closest anniversary attained: _____

Date of separation: _____

Date of divorce or widowhood (month, day, year): _____

Other marriages or partnerships (describe): _____

_____

_____

Children:	Name	Sex	Age	City and state of residence	If deceased, date and cause of death
1.					
2.					
3.					
4.					
5.					
6.					

(Add an extra page for children if needed; include miscarriages, stillbirths, etc.)

Note: If any children are adopted, place an "A" after their name.
If any children are stepchildren, place an "S" after their name.

Your age when last child left home: _____

What are your feelings about being a parent? _____

_____

_____

Grandchildren:	Name	Sex	Age	City and state of residence	If deceased, date and cause of death
1.					
2.					
3.					
4.					
5.					
6.					

(Add an extra page for grandchildren if needed)

Note: If any grandchildren are adopted, place an "A" after their name.
If any grandchildren are step-grandchildren, place an "S" after their name.

Your age at birth of first grandchild: _____

What are your feelings about being a grandparent? _____

_____

_____

I. BASIC BACKGROUND INFORMATION—cont.

Great-Grandchildren:	Name	Sex	Age	City and state of residence	If deceased, date and cause of death
1.					
2.					
3.					
4.					
5.					
6.					

(Add an extra page for great-grandchildren if needed.)

Note: If any great-grandchildren are adopted, place an "A" after their name.
If any great-grandchildren are step-great-grandchildren, place an "S" after their name.

Your age at birth of first great-grandchild: _____

What are your feelings about being a great-grandparent? _____

_____

_____

Members of current household (include everyone who lives with you):

Name	Sex	Age	Relationship to you
1.			
2.			
3.			
4.			
5.			
6.			

E. Family history

Parents

Father's full name: _____

Occupation: _____

Year of birth: _____ Birthplace: _____

If dead: Year of death: _____ His age at death: _____

Cause of death: _____

Your age at his death: _____

Educational level he attained: _____

Brief description of his personality: _____

_____

_____

Mother's full name: _____

Occupation: _____

Year of birth: _____ Birthplace: _____

If dead: Year of death: _____ Her age at death: _____

Cause of death: _____

Your age at her death: _____

Educational level she attained: _____

Brief description of her personality: _____

_____

_____

With whom did you live up to age 21?: _____

Were you raised in a rural, small town, urban, or suburban setting? *(describe):* _____

_____

During childhood, who lived in your home other than immediate family? *(include relatives, nurses, maids, boarders, etc.):* _____

_____

Did anyone other than your parents help care for you? *(describe):* _____

_____

Siblings:	Name	Age	City and state of residence	If deceased, date and cause of death
1.				
2.				
3.				
4.				
5.				
6.				

(Add an extra page for siblings if needed.)

Note: If any siblings are step-siblings, place an "S" after their name.
If any siblings are half-siblings, place an "H" after their name.

Grandparents (amount and quality of contact with them)

Paternal: _____

_____

Maternal: _____

_____

Your socioeconomic conditions during childhood:

    Poor _____

    Average _____

    Wealthy _____

I. BASIC BACKGROUND INFORMATION—cont.

F. **Education (your years of schooling):** _____

Description of schools:	Name of school	Year of graduation	Degree
Grammar school:			
High school:			
Trade, technical, or vocational school:			
College:			
Graduate or professional school:			
Later courses; other education:			
Elderhostel:			

Self-rating, as a student (check): ☐ Above average   ☐ Average   ☐ Below average

Any honors, awards, scholarships: _____

_____

Who was the first person in your immediate or extended family to have a college education? ____

_____

Would you like to obtain further education? *(describe):* _____

_____

G. Work

Your occupation or profession: _____

Government Service (G.S.) level *(if applicable):* _____

Your second occupation or profession *(describe):* _____

Last three jobs and the durations of employment:

1. _____

2. _____

3. _____

How physically demanding has your work been (including physical labor, housework, etc.)?

☐ Mildly demanding: _____

☐ Moderately demanding: _____

☐ Severely demanding *(describe):* _____

_____

Average number of hours a day that you work: _____

Occupation of spouse: _____

What are your major work interests? _____

_____

Were you in military service? _____ Which branch? _____

Did you experience age, sex, racial, ethnic, or other discrimination at work? *(describe):* _____

_____

_____

How physically active was your work? _____

_____

Postretirement

Did you work after retirement? _____

If so, describe employment: _____

How many hours per week? _____

Employed or self-employed? _____

Did you experience any form of discrimination at work? *(describe:)* _____

_____

Are you currently employed? _____ If not, would you like to be? _____

H. Retirement

Your age at retirement: _____ Date of retirement: _____

Was it voluntary? _____ Welcomed? _____

Was it compulsory through company or union? _____

Was it forced because of illness? _____

Did you have preretirement preparation (seminars, etc.)? _____

Did you have postretirement counseling? _____

I. Economic status *(check all sources of income, not amount [s])*

☐ Employment   ☐ Public pension plan

☐ Social Security   ☐ Public assistance

☐ Veterans benefits   ☐ Insurance payments

☐ Disability benefits   ☐ Annuities

☐ Teachers' Insurance and Annuity Association   ☐ Savings

☐ College Retirement Equities Fund   ☐ IRA

☐ Railroad Retirement   ☐ Investments

☐ Private pension plan   ☐ Assistance from family

☐ Other: _____

Do you pay or receive alimony? _____

Do you pay child support? _____

Your annual family income:

☐ over $150,000   ☐ $90,000–$150,000   ☐ $60,000–$90,000

☐ $30,000–$60,000   ☐ $15,000–$30,000   ☐ $10,000–$15,000

☐ $5,000–$10,000   ☐ $3,000–$5,000   ☐ Less than $3,000

Do you have serious financial problems? *(describe):* _____

_____

_____

Has there been a recent income drop? _____

If so, what is the reason? _____

I. BASIC BACKGROUND INFORMATION—cont.

Have you given over power of attorney? _____

Durable? _____ To whom? _____

Have you established a guardianship? _____

Have you established a conservatorship? _____

Have you established any advance directives? (Check)

☐ Right to die with dignity card

☐ Instructions regarding "Do Not Resuscitate"

☐ Donation of body organs

☐ Other instructions (describe): _____

J. Residence (check)

☐ House (☐ Owned   ☐ Rented)   ☐ Mental hospital

☐ Condominium (☐ Owned   ☐ Rented)   ☐ Chronic disease hospital

☐ Apartment (☐ Owned   ☐ Rented)   ☐ Personal care home

☐ Hotel   ☐ Foster care

☐ Rooming house   ☐ Public housing

☐ Boarding house   ☐ Mobile home, trailer

☐ "Assisted living"   ☐ "202"

☐ Nursing home   ☐ No regular residence

☐ Home for aged

☐ Other (describe): _____

Total monthly cost of housing: _____

Any problems with living situation? *(describe):* _____

Is there an elevator? _____

If no elevator, how many flights of stairs? _____

Any problems in neighborhood? (describe): _____

If you are temporarily not in your own home, is someone caring for your

☐ Possessions?   ☐ Plants?   ☐ Pets?

Have you moved since retirement? _____ From what kind of housing? _____

K. Transportation and mobility

Do you have a driver's license? _____

Do you own a car? _____

Do you have access to a car? _____

Do you regularly wear a seatbelt in cars? _____

How do you usually travel around? _____

Is public transportation available? _____

Do you use it? _____

Any physical disabilities that affect your mobility *(describe):* _____

_____

_____

Do you feel safe going out during the day? _____

Do you feel safe going out during the night? _____

Do you have a telephone? _____

L. Interests and pleasures *(describe)*

Avocations or hobbies: _____

_____

Sports: _____

Commercial recreation (movies, nightclubs, etc.): _____

Music: _____

Languages: _____

Travel (places and years): _____

_____

Vacation habits (what do you do and how often?): _____

_____

Gardening: _____

Collect anything: _____

Pet(s): _____

Use of community centers, senior centers, etc.: _____

_____

What is the *most* characteristic thing you do to relax and unwind? _____

_____

How many hours a day do you watch T.V.? _____

How many hours a day do you engage in your other interests and pleasures (excluding T.V.)? ____

_____

Are you satisfied with the balance between work and play in your life? _____

_____

M. Active community involvements *(describe)*

Memberships—organizations, clubs, etc.: _____

_____

Retiree or "senior citizens" groups: _____

_____

Political activity: _____

_____

I. BASIC BACKGROUND INFORMATION—cont.

Veterans organization: _____

_____

Voluntary work: _____

_____

Church work: _____

_____

Other: _____

N. Friendship patterns

Do you have someone to depend on in an emergency? _____

If so, who? _____

Are you lonely? _____

Is there someone you can talk to whenever you feel like it? _____

If so, who? _____

Who are the three closest living persons in your life?

Name	**How are they important?**
1. _____	
2. _____	
3. _____	

Describe contacts (list names, frequency of contact, and nature of contact; is the relationship a good one for you?)

1. Children: _____

_____

2. Grandchildren: _____

_____

3. Great-grandchildren: _____

_____

4. Siblings: _____

_____

5. Other relations: _____

_____

6. Friends: _____

_____

7. Neighbors: _____

_____

(Add an extra page for these descriptions if needed.)

O. Caregiving Responsibilities *(describe):*

  1. Are you caring for any children? *(describe):* _____

_____

  2. Are you caring for any disabled person age 18–64? *(describe):* _____

_____

  3. Are you caring for any elders? *(describe):* _____

_____

P. Prejudice (directed against you) *(describe)*

  Age: _____

  Sex (male or female): _____

  Race: _____

  Ethnic origin: _____

  Religion: _____

  Sexual preference: _____

II. MEDICAL INFORMATION

List significant doctors or medical specialists you see now or saw in the recent past:

Name	Address	Phone	Problem
1.			
2.			
3.			
4.			
5.			

Date of your last medical checkup: _____

How do you rate your general medical health? (check)

  ☐ Excellent   ☐ Good   ☐ Fair   ☐ Poor

History (any health problems)

  When born: _____

  When growing up: _____

Are there any physical or mental health conditions that seem to run in your family? *(describe):*

_____

_____

_____

_____

_____

Any heart disease? _____

Any cancer? _____

Any senile dementia? _____

II. MEDICAL INFORMATION—cont.

Blood type: _____

Transfusion: ☐ Yes   When? _____
                 ☐ No

Have you ever had the following? *(list dates)*

1. Accidents, injuries, and falls

    Concussion or other head injury: _____

    Fracture: _____

    Hip injury: _____

    Other: _____

    Any operation as a result: _____

2. Operations:

Date	Type of operation	Name of hospital	City
1. _____			
2. _____			
3. _____			

3. Circulatory disorders

    Heart disease: _____

    History of rheumatic fever: _____

    High blood pressure: _____

    Transient ischemic attack (TIA): _____

    Stroke: _____

       Any residual: _____

    Leg cramps: _____

    Cholesterol levels: _____

    HDL level (high-density lipoprotein): _____

    LDL level (low-density lipoprotein): _____

    Triglycerides level: _____

4. Angina: _____

5. Heart attack: _____

6. Arthritis: _____

    Rheumatoid arthritis: _____

    Osteoarthritis: _____

    Gout: _____

7. Lung conditions (bronchitis, emphysema, tuberculosis): _____
_____

8. Osteoporosis: _____

    Bone pain? _____

Loss of height? _____

Fracture history (describe): _____

_____

9. Diabetes: _____

10. Cancer: _____

11. Thyroid problems (hyper- or hypo-): _____

12. Anemia: _____

13. Gastrointestinal problems: _____

Diverticulitis: _____

Constipation: _____

Diarrhea: _____

14. Bladder problems: _____

Decline in continence: _____

Nocturia (need for night time urination): _____

15. Kidney problems: _____

16. Prostate problems: _____

17. "Change of life" or menopausal problems: _____

18. Allergies (hay fever, drugs, etc.): _____

19. Foot problems: _____

20. Other symptoms

Malaise and fatigue: Nervousness, tension: _____

Frequent, severe headaches: _____

Other pain: _____

Difficulty in breathing (dyspnea): _____

Dizziness: _____

Fainting spells: _____

Fever: _____

Ringing or buzzing in ears: _____

Bleeding: _____

21. Psychosomatic disorders

Asthma: _____

Peptic ulcer: _____

Essential hypertension: _____

Ulcerative colitis: _____

Ileitis: _____

Other: _____

22. Epilepsy or seizures: _____

23. Parkinsonism: _____

Flu from the epidemic of 1918–1919: _____

II. MEDICAL INFORMATION—cont.

24. Venereal diseases: _____

25. AIDS: _____

26. Herpes Zoster (Shingles): _____

27. Other: _____
_____
_____

Do you have anything that you consider to be a significant handicap? *(describe)*: _____
_____
_____

Do you have any chronic health problems? *(describe)*: _____
_____
_____

Occupational Safety and Health:

Air pollution? *(describe)*: _____

Significant asbestos exposure? _____

Vinyl chloride? _____

Benzene? _____

Cotton dust? _____

Coal dust? _____

Accidents? _____

Noise? _____

Other? *(describe)*: _____

Do you have any of the following physical limitations?

☐ Hearing loss

Do you wear a hearing aid? _____

Do you have any problems with your hearing aid? _____

Did you have occupational or other prolonged exposure to noise during your life? _____
_____

☐ Vision loss

Do you wear glasses? _____

Macular Retinal Degeneration: _____

Cataracts: _____

Glaucoma: _____

Diabetic Retinopathy: _____

Other: _____

☐ Memory loss

Mild? _____

Moderate? _____

Severe? _____

Do you wear dentures?   ☐ Partial   ☐ Complete

    Do you have any problems with your dentures? _____

Do you have any problems with manual dexterity (describe)? _____

_____

Do you use a cane? _____

    Wheelchair? _____

    Walker? _____

    Crutches? _____

Do you have a need for any other medical equipment or prosthetic devices? _____

_____

_____

Are you receiving any of the following therapies?

    ☐ Physical   ☐ Occupational   ☐ Speech   ☐ Inhalation   ☐ Recreational

    ☐ Other (specify): _____

Do you like physical massage? _____

Do you receive regular massage? How often? _____

Daily living habits

    Do you consider any of the following to be a serious personal problem?

        ☐ Overeating   ☐ Overdrinking   ☐ Smoking   ☐ Underactivity

    Alcohol consumption

    How many cocktails, highballs, etc. a day? _____

    How many glasses of beer a day? _____

    How many glasses of wine a day? _____

    Do you drink in the morning? _____

    How much before dinner? _____

    How much before bed? _____

    Water consumption: _____ (glasses a day)

    Caffeine consumption a day: Coffee _____   Tea _____   Cola _____

    Carbonated drink consumption a day: _____

    Do you smoke cigarettes, cigars, or a pipe? _____

      How much do you smoke a day? _____

      How long have you smoked? _____

      Have you had a heavy exposure to others smoking? (passive smoking) _____

_____

      Do you chew tobacco?_____

    Are you on a special diet? *(describe):* _____

_____

_____

Type of diet:

    ☐ Diabetic   ☐ Low-salt   ☐ Low-fat   ☐ Low-cholesterol   ☐ Other: _____

II. MEDICAL INFORMATION—cont.

Is diet medically prescribed or self-prescribed? _____

How many meals a day do you eat? _____

Are you a vegetarian? _____

Do you take vitamin or mineral supplements? _____

    What kind?

        ☐ Vitamin B   ☐ Vitamin C   ☐ Vitamin D   ☐ Vitamin E

        ☐ Other *(specify):* _____

Do you drink milk? _____   How many glasses a day? _____

    Is it skim, low-fat, or regular? _____

Do you have lactose intolerance? _____

Do you take calcium supplements? *(describe):* _____

Do you have frequent sunlight exposure for Vitamin D? _____

Do you take iron? *(describe dosage):* _____

Current weight: _____

    Has there been recent loss or gain and how much? _____

    What has been your maximum and minimum weight? Maximum: _____ Minimum: _____

Current height: _____ Any shrinkage in your original height? _____

Exercise

    Do you exercise regularly? _____

    What kind of exercise? (check)

        ☐ Aerobic (for the heart)

        ☐ Muscle strengthening

        ☐ Stretching (for flexibility)

        ☐ Other *(describe):* _____

How often each week? _____

How long each time? _____

Sleep

    Any difficulty falling asleep? _____

    Any difficulty staying asleep (sleep fragmentation)? _____

    Early awakening? _____

    Do you take naps? _____

    Average number hours of sleep a day: _____

    Have your sleeping patterns changed recently? _____

    Any sleep reversal with wakefulness at night and sleepiness in day? _____

    Do you take sleeping pills? _____ What kind? _____

    Do you snore? _____

Describe recurrent dreams (e.g., examination dreams, flight, falling, or chase dreams): _____

_____

_____

_____

_____

Is there any dream that seems highly significant to you? _____

_____

_____

_____

_____

Drug usage (dates drugs recently were or are now taken as well as schedule and amount of dosage)

Prescription drugs (describe)

Sedatives: _____

Tranquilizers: _____

Antidepressants: _____

Lithium: _____

Stimulants: _____

Diuretics: _____

Digitalis: _____

Reserpine: _____

Antihypertensives other than reserpine: _____

Hormones: _____

   Estrogen (specific type and dosage): _____

   Progestin (specific type and dosage): _____

Thyroid replacements: _____

Nitroglycerin: _____

Other: _____

Over-the-counter drugs taken regularly:

Laxatives: _____

Aspirin (for headache, pain, etc.): _____

Baby aspirin (for stroke prevention): _____

Others: _____

_____

_____

Immunizations (dates)

Pneumonia vaccine: _____

Tetanus vaccine: _____

Annual flu shot: _____

Hepatitis A: _____

Hepatitis B: _____

II. MEDICAL INFORMATION—cont.

Sexual activity and concerns

Do you experience a desire for sexual activity? _____

Has there been a recent change in your sexual desire? *(describe):* _____

_____

Do you currently have sexual outlets? *(describe):* _____

_____

How frequently? _____

Are there any problems—emotional, physical, social—as far as you are concerned regarding sex? (describe): _____

_____

_____

Males: Any problems with potency? _____

Females: Any vaginal pain or irritation? _____

                Any urine leakage problems? _____

                Any uterine prolapse? _____

                Do you do special (Kegel) exercises? _____

How important is sexual activity in your life?

☐ Very important   ☐ Moderately important   ☐ Unimportant

Are you satisfied with your current sex life? *(describe):* _____

_____

_____

III. PSYCHIATRIC INFORMATION

A. General

What brought you here (complaints, concerns, symptoms)? _____

_____

_____

_____

_____

_____

_____

_____

_____

_____

How long have you had the above problems? _____

_____

Have you recently felt

☐ Depressed   ☐ Anxious   ☐ Lonely   ☐ Guilty   ☐ Angry

☐ Resentful   ☐ Fearful *(describe specific fears):* _____

Have you had recent losses of any kind (health, loved ones, job, etc.)? _____

_____

Previous psychiatric contact

Name(s) of therapist(s): _____

_____

Discipline (psychiatrist, psychologist, social worker, nurse, other): _____

_____

City where therapy was received: _____

When: _____

Describe general form of treatment (individual or group therapy, family therapy, couples therapy, parent and child therapy, sex counseling, other): _____

_____

_____

Have you had a specialized form of therapy or experience such as cognitive, Gestalt, encounter, EST, biofeedback, behavior modification, hypnosis, primal therapy, psychodrama, reevaluation counseling, feminist consciousness-raising, or other (identify)? _____

_____

_____

How long were you in treatment? _____

Were drugs given? _____ Which ones? _____

_____

Did you receive electroconvulsive (ECT) treatments? _____

Were you hospitalized and for how long? _____

_____

Outcome of treatment in your opinion: _____

_____

_____

_____

_____

Have you belonged to any self-help organizations such as Weight Watchers, Alcoholics Anonymous, Recovery, Inc., Parents without Partners, or others? _____

_____

_____

_____

When? _____

What was the outcome? _____

III. PSYCHIATRIC INFORMATION—cont.

Has your spouse or partner had psychiatric problems? _____

_____

Is there anyone in your current or previous family with psychiatric problems? _____

_____

Have you ever taken psychological tests? _____

Which ones? _____

Done by whom? _____

For what purpose? _____

Briefly, what is your own theory as to why you are currently having difficulties? _____

_____

_____

_____

What "first-aid" techniques or home remedies have you found that make you feel or function better (e.g., "keeping busy," going to sleep, prayer, shopping, talking, sports)? _____

_____

_____

_____

How long does improvement last? _____

_____

Therapy goals

What are the goals you wish to achieve in treatment?_____

_____

_____

_____

_____

If married or living with someone, do you feel your partner would benefit from the following?
☐ Individual psychotherapy   ☐ Group psychotherapy   ☐ Couples therapy
☐ Brief consultation about your problem   ☐ Family therapy

B. Your attitudes toward aging and death

First experience with death *(describe):* _____

_____

Losses of loved ones (include relatives, friends; describe person and date)

When you were a child (up to 10 years of age): _____

_____

From 10 to 21 years: _____

_____

From 21 to 60 years: _____

_____

After age 60: _____
_____

What are your feelings about old age? _____
_____

What are your feelings about death? _____
_____

Do you worry much about illness? _____
_____

Do you worry much about your own death? _____
_____

Do you worry much about death of others? _____
_____

Describe any arrangements you have already made concerning your death (funeral arrangements, a "living will," donation of your body for science and medicine, donation of various organs for transplant, etc.): _____
_____
_____

Are you a member of a memorial society? _____
Have you made a will? _____
Are there any further arrangements you still wish to make? _____
Describe the old age of your parents: _____
_____
_____
_____

Describe the old age of your grandparents: _____
_____
_____
_____

Have you modeled your own later life after that of anyone else? _____
If so, who? _____
_____

C. **Self-view** (use extra space as needed)
Describe yourself (appearance, personality, personal assets, and liabilities): _____
_____
_____
_____
_____
_____

III. PSYCHIATRIC INFORMATION—cont.

_____

_____

_____

_____

How do you feel about your present status in life? _____

Do you feel you have much control over your own life? _____

Are you positive and optimistic? _____

Do you plan your days? _____

Do you have substantial goals or purpose in your life? _____

Do you feel you have much influence on others? _____

Have you been an independent person in the past? _____

Are you now an independent person? _____

Do you live alone? _____

Have you lived alone in the past and for how long? _____

What are your feelings about living alone? _____

Describe persons or things that have most influenced your life (friends, family, teachers, books, etc.): _____

_____

_____

_____

Do you tend to reminisce? _____

  What is the most frequent subject matter? _____

_____

What are your earliest memories? _____

_____

_____

Who loved you most as a child? _____

Who disliked you most? _____

Who hurt you most? _____

Who disappointed you most? _____

Have you composed a diary? _____

    kept a photograph album? _____

    written an autobiography? _____

    saved letters, mementoes, souvenirs? _____

What are the two or three most traumatic events (and your approximate age at the time) in your life that specifically stand out in your memory (e.g., accidents, deaths, fires, moves, divorces, personal failures of any kind, illnesses, etc.)? _____

_____

_____

_____

_____

_____

What are the two or three happiest and most satisfying events that specifically stand out in your memory (and your approximate age at the time)? _____

_____

_____

_____

_____

_____

CONCLUSION

What have been your reactions to this review of your life? _____

_____

_____

_____

_____

_____

_____

_____

_____

_____

_____

GLOSSARY

age cohort Groups of similar age moving through time; or all those who grew up in the same time period.

age grading Age used for the assignment of roles and opportunities for people in the society.

age norms Role expectations at various age levels.

ageism Aversion, hatred, and prejudice toward the aged and their manifestation in the form of discrimination on the basis of age.

androgen Any one of a number of male sex hormones.

arteriosclerosis The loss of elasticity or the hardening of the walls of the arteries.

atheroma A fatty plaque or deposit on the inner wall surface (intima) of blood vessels (usually arteries).

atherosclerosis A fibrous thickening of the inner walls (intima) of blood vessels, accompanied by the accumulation of soft, pasty, acellular fatty material.

autoimmunity Attack response by the immune system of the body to its own tissues as a result of the production of antibodies against such antigens.

cross-sectional study Research focusing on many different persons at the same period of time.

demography The statistical study of the incidence or distribution within populations of births, deaths, marriages, diseases, and so on.

dependency ratio The number of old (65 and over) plus the number of young (under 18) divided into the total working generation (those aged 18 to 65).

estrogen The generic term for the hormonal substance involved in the female monthly cycle or estrus; the female sex hormone.

geriatrics The practice of medicine concerned with the diseases associated with old age.

gerontocracy Governmental rule by older persons.

gerontology The branch of science concerned with aging.

gerontophilia Exalting and/or venerating the aged.

gerontophobia Fear and aversion of aging.

involution The return to a former, more primitive condition or previous form (for example, the involution of the uterus after giving birth); also, a degenerative change.

life expectancy The statistical prediction of how long an organism will live beyond a given initial age.

life span The maximum span of life of a specific species.

lipofuscin Brown pigment granules representing lipid-containing residues of lysosomal digestion, usually occurring with increased incidence with advancing age in certain tissues.

longitudinal study Research that focuses on the same persons over many years of time.

neuroplasticity The reestablishment of nerve connections in the central nervous system. Nerve receptors denervated because of death of neurons or brain cells may be reinervated by unaffected neurons. The terms "recircuitry" and "reactive symptogenesis" have been used.

osteoarthritis Inflammation of the articular extremities of bone resulting from structural changes in the cartilage and degeneration of the bones with osteophytic growths (bony outgrowths).

osteoporosis A gradual resorption of bone such that the tissue becomes unusually porous and fragile.

prolongevity Defined by Gruman in 1955 as "the belief that it is possible and desirable to extend significantly the length of life by human action." Another definition is "the significant extension of the length of life by human action."

social network Structural characteristics of a social group, such as the number of social ties, types of family members, and frequency of contact, which form the basis of a person's social support.

social support Social others who provide information, psychological and emotional support, material and economic aid, and assistance with activities and tasks. In terms of supporting the frail elderly, the term "care-giving" is often used.

AUTHOR INDEX

Note: Page numbers in italics locate entries in Endnotes or Suggested Readings.

SUBJECT INDEX